UNEQUAL DEMOCRACY

UNEQUAL DEMOCRACY

THE POLITICAL ECONOMY OF THE NEW GILDED AGE

SECOND EDITION

Larry M. Bartels

RUSSELL SAGE FOUNDATION • NEW YORK

PRINCETON UNIVERSITY PRESS • PRINCETON AND OXFORD

Published by Princeton University Press, 41 William Street,
Princeton, New Jersey 08540

In the United Kingdom: Princeton University Press, 6 Oxford Street,
Woodstock, Oxfordshire OX20 1TW

press.princeton.edu

Russell Sage Foundation, 112 East 64th Street,
New York, New York 10065

russellsage.org

Jacket design by Carmina Alvarez

The cartoon that opens chapter 5 is a Nick Anderson editorial cartoon
© Nick Anderson. All rights reserved. Used with the permission of
Nick Anderson and the Washington Post Writers Group
in conjunction with the Cartoonist Group.

The cartoon that opens chapter 7 is by Jim Borgman © Cincinnati
Enquirer. Reprinted with permission of UNIVERSAL UCLICK.
All rights reserved.

The photo of that opens chapter 11 is of New Orleans residents
waiting to be rescued from the floodwaters of Hurricane Katrina
on September 1, 2005 (AP Photo / David J. Phillip, Pool).

Library of Congress Cataloging-in-Publication Data

Names: Bartels, Larry M., 1956– author.
Title: Unequal democracy : the political economy of the new
Gilded Age / Larry M. Bartels.
Description: Second edition. | New York : Russell Sage Foundation,
[2016] | Includes bibliographical references and index.
Identifiers: LCCN 2016013822 | ISBN 9780691172842
(hardcover : acid-free paper)
Subjects: LCSH: United States—Economic conditions—1945– |
Equality—Economic aspects—United States. | Political culture—
United States—History. | Social classes—Political aspects—United
States. | Power (Social sciences)—Economic aspects—United States. |
Democracy—Economic aspects—United States.
Classification: LCC HC106.5 .B347 2016 | DDC 330.973–dc23
LC record available at https://lccn.loc.gov/2016013822

British Library Cataloging-in-Publication Data is available

This book has been composed in Sabon and Gill Sans

Printed on acid-free paper. ∞

Printed in the United States of America

10 9 8 7 6 5 4 3 2 1

For my brother, Thomas Raymond Bartels,
who lived poor and died young

Contents

Preface to the Second Edition   xi

Preface to the First Edition   xv

1. The New Gilded Age   1
   Escalating Economic Inequality   7
   Interpreting Inequality   16
   Economic Inequality as a Political Issue   23
   Inequality and American Democracy   28

2. The Partisan Political Economy   33
   Partisan Patterns of Income Growth   35
   A Partisan Coincidence?   38
   Partisan Differences in Macroeconomic Policy   48
   Macroeconomic Performance and Income Growth   52
   Do Presidents Still Matter?   57
   Partisan Redistribution   62
   Democrats, Republicans, and the Rise of Inequality   69

3. Partisan Biases in Economic Accountability   74
   Myopic Voters   76
   The Electoral Timing of Income Growth   82
   Class Biases in Economic Voting   87
   The Wealthy Give Something Back: Partisan Biases
      in Campaign Spending   93
   The Political Consequences of Biased Accountability   98

4. Do Americans Care about Inequality?   105
   Egalitarian Values   108
   Rich and Poor   113
   Perceptions of Inequality   118
   Facts and Values in the Realm of Inequality   124

5. Homer Gets a Tax Cut   136
   The Bush Tax Cuts   138

Public Support for the Tax Cuts   144
Unenlightened Self-Interest   150
The Impact of Political Information   155
The Long Sunset   163

6. The Strange Appeal of Estate Tax Repeal   170
Public Support for Estate Tax Repeal   173
Is Public Support for Repeal a Product of Misinformation?   181
Did Interest Groups Manufacture Public Antipathy
    to the Estate Tax?   189
Elite Ideology and the Politics of Estate Tax Repeal   193

7. The Eroding Minimum Wage   198
The Economic Effects of the Minimum Wage   202
Public Support for the Minimum Wage   205
The Politics of Congressional Inaction   209
Democrats, Unions, and the Eroding Minimum Wage   217
Local Action   223
The Earned Income Tax Credit   228

8. Economic Inequality and Political Representation   233
Congressional Representation   235
Unequal Responsiveness   239
Partisan Differences in Responsiveness   248
Systemic Responsiveness   249
Plutocracy?   254
Why the Poor Are Unrepresented   257

9. Stress Test: The Political Economy of the Great Recession   269
The 2008 Election and "the New New Deal"   274
Reaction and Gridlock   281
The Political Impact of the Recession   286
But Did It Work?   295
Geithner's World   301
Not the New New Deal   305

10. The Defining Challenge of Our Time?   309
A "National Conversation"?   311
The Class War Gets Personal: Inequality as an
    Issue in the 2012 Campaign   315
Obama and Inequality   329
The Political Challenge   334

11. Unequal Democracy   342
   Who Governs?   344
   Partisan Politics and the "Have-nots"   347
   Political Obstacles to Economic Equality   352
   The City of Utmost Necessity   358

   Postscript   365

   References   367

   Index   385

Preface to the Second Edition

In the eight years since the original publication of *Unequal Democracy*, the issue of inequality has moved to the forefront of American politics. When I wrote the book, I certainly did not foresee the epic financial crisis of 2008, the dramatic election of Barack Obama in the midst of that crisis, the extraordinary measures taken to rescue Wall Street and stem the Great Recession that followed, the political reactions on the left (with the rise and fall of the Occupy Wall Street movement) and right (with the rise of the Tea Party and the Republican takeovers of the House and Senate), or a close-fought presidential election pitting a polarizing incumbent who identified inequality as "the defining issue of our time" against a fabulously wealthy businessman with a controversial career in leveraged buyouts. My primary aim in revising the book has been to take due account of these momentous events, all of which seem to me to be highly relevant to the economic and political issues it addressed.

The past eight years have also seen a flourishing of research and writing on these issues. I have been informed and inspired by Jacob Hacker and Paul Pierson's *Winner-Take-All Politics*, Timothy Noah's *The Great Divergence*, Kay Schlozman, Sidney Verba, and Henry Brady's *The Unheavenly Chorus*, Joseph Stiglitz's *The Price of Inequality*, Martin Gilens's *Affluence and Influence*, Hedrick Smith's *Who Stole the American Dream?*, Nicholas Carnes's *White-Collar Government*, Lane Kenworthy's *Social Democratic America*, and Thomas Piketty's *Capital in the Twenty-First Century*, among many other works. While I have not attempted to provide a comprehensive review of relevant literature, I have done my best to integrate what I have learned from the very welcome outpouring of books, articles, and working papers on the political economy of inequality.

It is common for revised editions of scholarly books to add a new chapter or "afterword" to an otherwise unaltered text. That is convenient for authors and publishers, but sometimes less helpful for readers. Given the profusion of political events, new scholarship, and new data relevant to the issues addressed here, I have felt it necessary to provide a much more extensive revision. As well as adding two entirely new chapters, I have made substantial changes in most of the existing chapters, incorporating new developments, revising tabulations and statistical analyses using the most recent available data, rethinking a few conclusions, and rephrasing many more. In order to prevent the book from becoming too unwieldy, I have also excised one whole chapter and many shorter passages that seemed tangential to the main lines of analysis. I thank Chuck Myers and Eric Crahan, my past and present editors at Princeton University Press, and Suzanne Nichols, director of publications at the Russell Sage Foundation, for being splendidly supportive of this effort.

Portions of the new material are based on articles, essays, and blog posts in which I have attempted to make sense of ongoing political developments. I am indebted to John Sides for providing me with a comfortable perch at *The Monkey Cage* blog, to Harvard University's Center for American Political Studies for recruiting me as a commentator on Theda Skocpol's 2011 Alexis de Tocqueville Lecture (subsequently published as *Obama and America's Political Future*), and to Sheldon Danziger for involving me in a conference and symposium on the Great Recession for *The ANNALS of the American Academy of Political and Social Science*.[1] I am also grateful for opportunities to present the evolving argument of the book in lectures and keynote addresses at the University of Georgia, the Institute for Policy Research at Northwestern University, Lafayette College, Loyola University, Southern Illinois University, the Society for the Advancement of Socio-Economics, the American Sociological Association, San Diego State University, American University, Diego Portales University, and the Southern Political Science Association.

In addition to expressing my continuing gratitude to all of the institutions and individuals who contributed to the making of the original book, I thank Vanderbilt University, Chancellor Nicholas Zeppos, John Geer, and my colleagues and students in Vanderbilt's Department of Political Science for providing a stimulating and extremely supportive scholarly environment in which to revise it. The resources associated with the May Werthan Shayne Chair of Public Policy and Social Science have been instrumental in facilitating my research. The staff of the Department of Political Science and the Center for the Study of Democratic Institutions—Tina Bembry, Jayne Cornwell, Darlene Davidson, Natasha Duncan, and Shannon Meldon-Corney—have been unfailingly gracious and helpful.

Even by the saintly standards of spouses in prefaces, my wife Denise deserves extraordinary gratitude—not only for her unfailing daily love and support, but also for uprooting her life for the sake of my personal and professional well-being.

Connie Mercer and her colleagues at Homefront (http://www.homefrontnj .org) have provided an inspiring example of effective social action and a good home for the proceeds.

---

[1] Bartels (2012; 2013b).

I have benefited from a great deal of constructive feedback on the original edition of *Unequal Democracy* from colleagues, students, and reviewers. Chris Achen, Kathy Cramer, Marty Gilens, Marc Hetherington, Ben Page, Wendy Rahn, Lynn Vavreck, and John Zaller have been compatriots, friendly critics, and critical friends. I am especially grateful to a distinguished group of colleagues who traveled to Nashville for a workshop critiquing the original edition and providing advice for revision: Cramer, Page, Zaller, Jared Bernstein, Hank Farber, Jennifer Hochschild, Gary Jacobson, Lane Kenworthy, Don Kinder, and Tim Smeeding. Although I have not adopted all of their good advice, I have adopted enough of it to make the book substantially better.

Finally, I am indebted both intellectually and personally to readers from beyond the walls of academia for their thoughts, questions, and encouragement. One of them, Daniel Wasik, has kindly consented to let me appropriate his words, providing a more eloquent conclusion to the book than any I could have written myself.

Nashville, Tennessee
February 2016

Preface to the First Edition

THIS BOOK REPORTS the results of a six-year exploration of the political causes and consequences of economic inequality in America. It is inspired, in significant part, by a major change in American society over the past three decades—the substantial escalation of economic inequality that I refer to as the "New Gilded Age." That economic transformation has attracted considerable attention from economists but much less attention from political scientists. It seemed to me, as a student of American politics, that careful attention to public opinion, partisan politics, and public policy might shed valuable new light on how and why the economic fortunes of affluent, middle-class, and poor people have diverged so dramatically in the contemporary United States.

As a student of democracy, it also seemed important to me to explore the ramifications of escalating economic inequality for the American political system. Probably most sentient observers of American politics suspect that the concentration of vast additional wealth in the hands of affluent people has augmented their influence in the political arena, while the stagnating economic fortunes of middle-class and poor people have diminished their influence. However, systematic measurement of political influence is at a very rudimentary stage, leaving political scientists remarkably ill-equipped to confirm, refute, or qualify that suspicion. I have attempted here, through a combination of systematic statistical analysis and case studies, to assess the extent to which economic inequality in contemporary America gets translated into political inequality.

Some readers are likely to see the product of my efforts as a rather partisan book, at least by academic standards. For what it is worth, I can report that it did not start out that way. I began the project as an unusually apolitical political scientist. (The last time I voted was in 1984, and that was for Ronald Reagan.) While I was prepared to find that parties and partisanship play an important role in the politics of economic inequality, as they do in many domains of American politics, I was quite surprised to discover how often and how profoundly partisan differences in ideologies and values have shaped key policy decisions and economic outcomes. I have done my best to follow my evidence where it led me.

In telling this story I have attempted to balance the demands of scholarship and accessibility. My aim has been to make the text and figures comprehensible to general readers—at least to general readers who have some patience for the twists and turns of serious arguments and systematic evidence. Tables and notes provide additional scholarly detail, some of which will only be intelligible or interesting to people with some background in social science or statistics or both. I recognize that any compromise of this sort is bound to leave readers in both camps less than fully satisfied; however, I view it as a necessary accommodation to the prevalence of social-scientific illiteracy among Americans who read (and write) about politics and public affairs.

I suspect that the prevalence of social-scientific illiteracy in American public discourse is both a cause and an effect of the fact that social-scientific research is woefully undersupported in American society. However, I have been unusually fortunate in finding generous financial, institutional, and personal support for my work, and it is a great pleasure to acknowledge that support here.

Princeton University and its Woodrow Wilson School have provided time and facilities for research, as well as regular access to stimulating students and colleagues. I am grateful to the past and present deans of the Woodrow Wilson School, Michael Rothschild and Anne-Marie Slaughter, for building and maintaining a vibrant intellectual community in which to pursue serious analysis of significant public issues. I am also grateful to students in my Wilson School seminar on Inequality and American Democracy for serving as an invaluable test-audience for the first complete draft of the book, and to my colleagues Roland Bénabou, Angus Deaton, Alan Krueger, Jonathan Parker, and Mark Watson for providing generous advice about economic issues and literature.

Within the Woodrow Wilson School, my primary home for the past eight years has been the Center for the Study of Democratic Politics. The faculty, visitors, students, and staff there have provided abundant intellectual and moral support, including appropriate mixtures of criticism and encouragement in response to half-baked arguments presented in lunch seminars, conferences, and common room chats. I am especially grateful to Doug Arnold, Brandice Canes-Wrone, Michele Epstein, Marty Gilens, Dave Lewis, Nolan McCarty, and Markus Prior for helpful reactions and suggestions. As I have come to expect over the years, Chris Achen provided especially cogent advice and especially generous encouragement. He also graciously tolerated the constraints imposed by this project on the progress of our long-running collaborative work on democratic accountability. Next!

I have also benefited greatly, and repeatedly, from the generous support of the Russell Sage Foundation and its president, Eric Wanner. The first stages of my research were conducted as part of the Princeton Working Group on Inequality, one of several interdisciplinary research teams supported by the Russell Sage Foundation through its Social Dimensions of Inequality project. I thank Bruce Western, the ringleader of the Princeton Working Group, for involving me in the project, and Bruce, Paul DiMaggio, Leslie McCall, Nolan McCarty, and Howard Rosenthal for providing a supportive collaborative setting in which to tackle issues well outside the range of my previous scholarly expertise. Annual meetings of the various Russell Sage Foundation working groups at Harvard (2001), Wisconsin (2002), Maryland (2003), Princeton (2004), Berkeley (2005), and UCLA (2007) served as a floating boot camp introducing me to many of the toughest issues and much of the best current research in the field.

The Russell Sage Foundation provided a separate grant to support the collection of new survey data on inequality and public policy as part of the 2002 American National Election Study (ANES). Those data figure prominently in chapters 4, 5, and 6 of this book—and in related work by many other scholars. It was a pleasure to collaborate with Nancy Burns and Don Kinder, the principal investigators of the 2002 ANES project, in designing the inequality module. I am grateful to them and to their colleagues at ANES for implementing the survey and sharing the data. More generally, I am indebted to the long succession of principal investigators, staff, and overseers who have contributed to the invaluable accumulation and dissemination of ANES data over more than half a century. Much of the analysis presented here would not have been possible without their efforts.

A third (and, so far, final) grant from the Russell Sage Foundation provided the concentrated time required to pull the various strands of my research together, fill in some important missing pieces, and turn it all into a book. Significant additional support for this phase of my work came from the Carnegie Corporation of New York in the form of a Carnegie Scholars Grant and from Princeton University in the form of a quota leave.

Along the way, Theda Skocpol invited me to participate in the American Political Science Association's Task Force on Inequality and American Democracy. I learned a great deal about inequality and how to study it from the distinguished group assembled by Theda, and especially from our able task force chair, Larry Jacobs. The Task Force's report and the volume of supporting material edited by Jacobs and Skocpol, *Inequality and American Democracy: What We Know and What We Need to Learn*, provide an authoritative introduction to many aspects of the politics of inequality that I have ignored or underemphasized here.

Over the past five years I have presented various versions of various portions of the book in lectures, colloquia, and conferences at UCLA, the University of Chicago, Columbia, Duke, Fordham, Harvard, Illinois, Michigan, Minnesota, Notre Dame, Oxford, the University of Pennsylvania, Penn State, Princeton, Syracuse, Wisconsin, Yale, the Brookings Institution, the Public Policy Institute of California, and the Juan March Institute in Madrid, and at annual meetings of the American Political Science Association

(2002, 2003, 2005, and 2006), the American Economic Association (2003), the Midwest Political Science Association (2005), the European Consortium for Political Research (2005), and the National Tax Association (2006). Each of these presentations generated stimulating questions and comments, helping me to hone my analyses and arguments.

Through these avenues and others, I have been fortunate to benefit from helpful reactions and suggestions from Kathy Bawn, Robert Bernstein, Benjamin Bishin, Phil Converse, David Ellwood, John Griffin, Jennifer Hochschild, Sandy Jencks, Jacob Hacker, Douglas Hibbs, Skip Lupia, Paul Pierson, John Roemer, Thomas Schwartz, Jeff Stonecash, Rick Valelly, Lynn Vavreck, Ronald Weber, and Robert Weissberg, among others. As always, John Zaller has been an especially perceptive and supportive critic.

Jonathan Ladd, Gabriel Lenz, and Jeff Tessin provided able research assistance, producing very helpful literature reviews and carefully collecting and organizing data for my analyses. Helene Wood solved myriad logistical problems with skill and good cheer. Karen Pulliam and Shirley Smith of the U.S. Census Bureau provided assistance in interpreting the bureau's historical income data.

A much-abbreviated version of chapter 2 appeared in "Economic Behavior in Political Context" (*American Economic Review*, with Henry E. Brady). Portions of chapters 4, 5, and 6 are based on "Homer Gets a Tax Cut" (*Perspectives on Politics*) and "Unenlightened Self-Interest: The Strange Appeal of Estate Tax Repeal" (*The American Prospect*). Portions of chapters 5, 6, and 7 were published in "A Tale of Two Tax Cuts, a Wage Squeeze, and a Tax Credit" (*National Tax Journal*). Portions of chapter 11 are based on "Is the Water Rising? Reflections on Inequality and American Democracy" (*PS: Political Science & Politics*).[1] I am grateful to the publishers of these pieces for permission to draw upon them here.

Suzanne Nichols at the Russell Sage Foundation and Chuck Myers and his colleagues at Princeton University Press have ably shepherded the manuscript to publication. Suzanne commissioned anonymous reviews that provided very helpful feedback on an earlier draft of the book; I am especially grateful to one grumpy reviewer who went far beyond the call of duty in providing impetus and guidance for my efforts to clarify and tighten my argument. Chuck's own reading helped me excise much, though alas not all, of the jargon and academic indirection.

My daughters, Elizabeth and Meghan, somehow grew into unusually charming young adults during the years in which this book took shape. They have been a source of great pleasure, pride, and inspiration. Moreover, unlike most children in prefaces, they provided invaluable critical feedback, including detailed comments on the text.

---

[1] Bartels and Brady (2003); Bartels (2005; 2004; 2006c; 2006a).

Finally, my greatest and most heartfelt debt is to my wife, Denise, who has contributed so much to the rest of my life while I have been working. This book would not have been nearly as good, or nearly as much fun to write, without her.

Princeton, New Jersey
September 2007

UNEQUAL DEMOCRACY

CHAPTER 1

The New Gilded Age

IN THE FIRST sentence of one of the greatest works of modern political science, Robert Dahl posed a question of profound importance for democratic theory and practice: "In a political system where nearly every adult may vote but where knowledge, wealth, social position, access to officials, and other resources are unequally distributed, who actually governs?"[1]

Dahl's answer to this question, for one American city in the late 1950s, was that political power was surprisingly widely dispersed. Examining politics and policy-making in New Haven, Connecticut, he concluded that shifting, largely distinct coalitions of elected and unelected leaders influenced key decisions in different issue areas. This pluralistic pattern was facilitated by the fact that many individuals and groups with substantial resources at their disposal chose not to devote those resources to political activity. Even "economic notables"—the wealthy property owners, businessmen, and bank directors constituting the top tier of New Haven's economic elite—were "simply one of the many groups out of which individuals sporadically emerge to influence the policies and acts of city officials."[2]

The significance of Dahl's question has been magnified, and the pertinence of his answer has been cast in doubt, by dramatic economic and political changes in the United States over the past half-century. Economically, America has become vastly richer and vastly more unequal. Perhaps most strikingly, the share of total income going to people at the level of Dahl's "economic notables"—the top 0.1% of income-earners—has tripled, from 3.3% in the late 1950s to 10.3% in 2014. The share going to the top 1% of income-earners—a much broader but still very affluent group—doubled over the same period, from 10.4% to 21.2%.[3] The nation's wealth

---

[1] Dahl (1961, 1).

[2] Of the 238 people in this group, only three were among the 23 most influential participants in the city's politics and policy-making. Nine more were "minor leaders"—all in the field of urban redevelopment, a policy area of distinctive relevance for their economic interests (Dahl 1961, 72, and chap. 6).

[3] These figures are from tabulations in the World Top Incomes Database constructed by Facundo Alvaredo, Tony Atkinson, Thomas Piketty, and Emmanuel Saez (http://topincomes .parisschoolofeconomics.eu/#Database:) and include capital gains. In both cases, the share of

is even more concentrated, with the wealthiest 1% of households holding 41.8% and the wealthiest 0.1% holding 22.0%.[4] It seems natural to wonder whether the pluralistic democracy Dahl found in the 1950s has survived this rapidly escalating concentration of economic resources in the hands of America's most affluent citizens.[5]

Meanwhile, the political process has evolved in ways that seem likely to reinforce the advantages of wealth. Political campaigns have become dramatically more expensive since the 1950s, increasing the reliance of elected officials on people who can afford to help finance their bids for reelection. Major campaign finance regulations imposed in response to the Watergate scandal of the early 1970s have been significantly weakened by a series of Supreme Court decisions—most notably in *Citizens United v. FEC* in 2010—chipping away at contribution limits and allowing unlimited contributions to "super PACs" engaged in putatively independent campaign expenditures. Even more importantly, lobbying activities by corporations and business and professional organizations have accelerated greatly, outpacing the growth of public interest groups. Meanwhile, membership in labor unions has declined substantially, eroding the primary mechanism for organized representation of working people in the governmental process.

How have these economic and political developments affected "who actually governs"? Political scientists since Aristotle have wrestled with the question of whether substantial economic inequality is compatible with democracy, but until recently that question was far from the forefront of contemporary empirical research. In 2004, a task force on inequality and American democracy convened by the American Political Science Association concluded that political scientists knew "astonishingly little" about the "cumulative effects on American democracy" of recent economic and political changes. However, the task force members worried "that rising economic inequality will solidify longstanding disparities in political voice and influence, and perhaps exacerbate such disparities."[6]

---

income going to top earners was even higher in 2007, but declined in the Great Recession and by 2014 had not (yet) fully recovered.

[4] These figures are from 2012, the most recent year available as of this writing. The corresponding wealth shares in the late 1950s were 29% and 10%. Saez and Zucman (forthcoming), online appendix (http://gabriel-zucman.eu/files/SaezZucman2016QJEAppendix.pdf), "Table B1: Top Wealth Shares, Individual-Level Unit of Observation."

[5] Dahl himself continued to revise and elaborate his account of the workings of American democracy. His *Dilemmas of Pluralist Democracy* (1982) was especially pertinent in this respect: chapter 8 addressed the ramifications of economic inequality for the American political system and the potential significance of economic inequality as a political issue. His 2006 book *On Political Equality* examined more broadly whether the ideal of political equality is compatible with fundamental aspects of human nature.

[6] Task Force on Inequality and American Democracy (2004, 662); Jacobs and Skocpol (2005).

The work of the APSA task force helped to stimulate a substantial body of new research focusing on economic inequality and American democracy.[7] While that work is far from complete, and much of it remains controversial, political scientists have made real progress in tracing the political consequences of economic inequality. Their findings suggest that elected officials and public policy are largely unresponsive to the policy preferences of millions of low-income citizens, leaving their political interests to be served or ignored as the ideological whims of incumbent elites may dictate. Dahl suggested that democracy entails "continued responsiveness of the government to the preferences of its citizens, considered as political equals."[8] The contemporary United States is a very long way from meeting that standard.

While it has become increasingly clear that economic inequality has profound ramifications for democratic politics, that is only half the story of this book. The other half of the story is that politics also profoundly shapes economics. While technological change, globalization, demographic shifts, and other economic and social forces have produced powerful pressures toward greater inequality in recent decades, politics and public policy can and do significantly reinforce or mitigate those pressures, depending on the political aims and priorities of elected officials. I trace the impact of public policies on changes in the U.S. income distribution over almost seven decades, from the tripled income share of Dahl's "economic notables" at the top to the plight of minimum wage workers at the bottom. I find that partisan politics and the ideological convictions of political elites have had a substantial impact on the American economy, especially on the economic fortunes of middle-class and poor people. Economic inequality is, in substantial part, a *political* phenomenon.

In theory, public opinion constrains the ideological convictions of political elites in democratic political systems. In practice, however, elected officials have a great deal of political leeway. This fact is strikingly illustrated by the behavior of Democratic and Republican senators from the same state, who routinely pursue vastly different policies while "representing" precisely the same constituents. On a broader historical scale, political latitude is also demonstrated by consistent, marked shifts in economic priorities and performance when Democrats replace Republicans, or when Republicans replace Democrats, in the White House. In these respects, among others, conventional democratic theory misses much of what is most interesting and important about the actual workings of the American political system.

---

[7] For example, Bartels (2008); Page and Jacobs (2009); Hacker and Pierson (2010); Gilens (2012); Schlozman, Verba, and Brady (2012); Carnes (2013); Page, Bartels, and Seawright (2013); Gilens and Page (2014).

[8] Dahl (1971, 1).

My examination of the partisan politics of economic inequality, in chapter 2, reveals that Democratic and Republican presidents since the late 1940s have presided over dramatically different patterns of income growth. On average, the real incomes of middle-class families have grown more than twice as fast under Democrats as they have under Republicans, while the real incomes of working poor families have grown *ten times* as fast under Democrats as they have under Republicans. These substantial partisan differences persist even after allowing for differences in economic circumstances and historical trends beyond the control of individual presidents. They demonstrate that escalating inequality is *not* simply an inevitable economic trend—and that a great deal of economic inequality in the contemporary United States is specifically attributable to the policies and priorities of Republican presidents.

Any satisfactory account of the American political economy must therefore explain how and why Republicans have had so much success in the American electoral arena despite their startlingly negative impact on the economic fortunes of middle-class and poor people. My analysis in chapter 3 identifies three distinct biases in political accountability that explain much of their success. One is a myopic focus of voters on very recent economic performance, which rewards Republicans' surprising success in concentrating income growth in election years. Another is the peculiar sensitivity of voters at all income levels to high-income growth rates, which rewards Republicans' success in generating election-year income growth among affluent families specifically. Finally, the responsiveness of voters to campaign spending rewards Republicans' frequent advantage in fund-raising. Together, these biases probably account three times over for the Republican Party's net advantage in popular votes cast in presidential elections since the end of World War II—and for four of the nine instances in which Republicans won the White House. Voters' seemingly straightforward tendency to reward or punish the incumbent government at the polls for good or bad economic performance turns out to be warped in ways that are both fascinating and politically crucial.

In chapter 4, I turn to citizens' views about equality; their attitudes toward salient economic groups such as rich people, poor people, big business, and labor unions; and their perceptions of the extent, causes, and consequences of economic inequality in contemporary America. My analysis reveals considerable concern about inequality among ordinary Americans and considerable sympathy for working-class and poor people. However, it also reveals a good deal of ignorance and misconnection between values, beliefs, and policy preferences among people who pay relatively little attention to politics and public affairs, and a good deal of politically motivated misperception among better-informed people. As a result, political elites retain considerable latitude to pursue their own policy ends.

Chapters 5, 6, and 7 provide a series of case studies of politics and policy-making in issue areas with important ramifications for economic inequality. Chapter 5 focuses on the Bush tax cuts of 2001 and 2003, which dramatically reduced the federal tax burdens of wealthy Americans. I find that public opinion regarding the Bush tax cuts was remarkably shallow and confused considering the multi-*trillion*-dollar stakes. A year after the 2001 tax cut took effect, 40% of the public said they had not thought about whether they favored or opposed it, and those who did take a position did so largely on the basis of how they felt about their own tax burden. Views about the tax burden of the rich had no apparent impact on public opinion, despite the fact that most of the benefits went to affluent taxpayers; egalitarian values reduced support for the tax cut, but only among strong egalitarians who were also politically well informed.

Chapter 6 focuses on the campaign to repeal the federal estate tax. As with the Bush tax cuts more generally, I find that repeal of the estate tax has been remarkably popular among ordinary Americans, regardless of their political views and economic circumstances, and despite the fact that the vast majority of them never have been or would be subject to estate taxation. Moreover, the strange appeal of estate tax repeal long predates the efforts of conservative interest groups in the 1990s to manufacture public opposition to the estate tax. Thus, the real political mystery is not why the estate tax was temporarily phased out in 2001, but why it has survived for nearly a century despite the public's antipathy. The simple answer is that the views of liberal elites determined to prevent repeal have been more consequential than the views of ordinary citizens.

In chapter 7, I turn from wealthy heirs to working poor people and the eroding minimum wage. Here, too, the views of ordinary citizens seem to have had remarkably little impact on public policy. The real value of the federal minimum wage has declined by one-third since the late 1960s, despite remarkably strong and consistent public support for minimum wage increases. My analysis attributes this erosion to the declining political clout of labor unions and to shifts in partisan control of Congress and the White House. As with the estate tax, the politics of the minimum wage underscores the ability of determined elites in the American political system to postpone or prevent policy shifts. However, in this case the determined elites have not been liberal Democrats intent on taxing the bequests of millionaires, but conservative Republicans intent on protecting the free market (and low-wage employers) from the predations of people earning $7.25 per hour. Conversely, the adoption of higher state-specific minimum wage rates has mostly hinged upon the political strength of unions and Democratic politicians rather than mass opinion, even in states with initiative and referendum procedures.

My case studies of the Bush tax cuts, estate tax repeal, and the eroding minimum wage shed light on both the political causes and the political consequences of escalating economic inequality in contemporary America. In chapter 8, I attempt to provide a more general answer to Dahl's fundamental question: who governs? I examine broad patterns of policy-making across a wide range of issues, focusing on disparities in the responsiveness of elected officials to the views of their constituents. I find that the roll call votes cast by members of the U.S. Senate and House of Representatives are much better accounted for by their own partisanship than by the preferences of their constituents. Moreover, insofar as constituents' views do matter, political influence seems to be limited mostly to affluent and middle-class people. In the case of senators, the opinions of millions of ordinary citizens in the bottom one-third of the income distribution have *no* discernible impact on the behavior of their elected representatives.

Chapters 9 and 10 carry the analysis through the Obama era. In chapter 9, I examine the responses of policy-makers and citizens to the greatest economic calamity of our time, the Great Recession. Many observers expected the economic crisis to shift American politics significantly to the left. It did contribute to the dramatic election of Barack Obama, whose response to the recession underlined once again the significance of partisan ideologies in shaping public policy. However, voters' predictable impatience with a slow economic recovery and their predictable resistance to ideological overreach combined with the intransigence of Republicans in Congress to constrain and then stifle Obama's "New New Deal." Meanwhile, the persistent tendency of policy-makers to see the world through privileged eyes—personified by Treasury Secretary Timothy Geithner's perceptions and judgments during and after the tumultuous Wall Street meltdown—arguably tilted economic policy in favor of wealthy interests at the expense of ordinary Americans.

In chapter 10, I assess the politics of inequality in the wake of the Great Recession, the rise and fall of the Occupy Wall Street movement, and President Obama's high-profile rhetoric identifying inequality as "the defining challenge of our time." My analysis suggests that these developments have had remarkably little impact on Americans' perceptions and values regarding inequality, on their policy preferences, and on their voting behavior. Even a presidential election in which "the chasm between the rich and ordinary workers" became "a crucial talking point in the Democratic Party's arsenal" turned much less on voters' views about taxing the wealthy than on their perceptions of the Republican nominee as an out-of-touch plutocrat.[9]

Writing in the 1980s, at an early stage in the most recent wave of escalating inequality, political scientists Sidney Verba and Gary Orren depicted an ongoing back-and-forth between the powerful forces of economic inequality and political equality: "Political equality . . . poses a constant challenge to economic inequality as disadvantaged groups petition the state for redress.

---

[9] Eduardo Porter, "Inequality Undermines Democracy," *New York Times*, March 20, 2012.

Egalitarian demands lead to equalizing legislation, such as the progressive income tax. But the continuing disparities in the economic sphere work to limit the effectiveness of such laws, as the economically advantaged groups unleash their greater resources in the political sphere. These groups lobby for tax loopholes, hire lawyers and accountants to maximize their benefit from tax laws, and then deduct the costs."[10]

In the long run of American political history, Verba and Orren's depiction seems apt. However, in the current economic and political environment it is easy to wonder whether the "constant challenge to economic inequality" posed by the ideal of political equality is really so constant or, in the end, so effective. This book provides strong evidence that economic inequality impinges powerfully on the political process, frustrating the egalitarian ideals of American democracy. The countervailing impact of egalitarian ideals in constraining disparities in the economic sphere seems to be considerably more tenuous, notwithstanding the comfortable notion among many liberals that the public has been or soon will be mobilized in support of "equalizing legislation."

Escalating Economic Inequality

Most Americans have only a vague sense of the contours of the nation's income distribution—especially for parts of the income distribution that extend beyond their personal experience. Annual tabulations published by the U.S. Census Bureau provide a useful summary of the incomes of families at different points in the distribution. For example, in 2014 the typical American family had a total pre-tax income of $66,632. More than 16 million families—one out of every five—earned less than $29,100. A similar number earned more than $129,000. Even higher in the distribution, the richest 5% of American families had incomes of more than $230,000.[11]

The Census Bureau provides similar annual tabulations of income going back to 1947 for families at the 20th, 40th, 60th, 80th, and 95th percentiles of the income distribution. These tabulations constitute the longest

---

[10] Verba and Orren (1985, 19).

[11] U.S. Census Bureau, Current Population Survey (CPS), Annual Social and Economic Supplements, "Table F-1: Income Limits for Each Fifth and Top 5 Percent of Families (All Races): 1947 to 2014." These data are derived from the Census Bureau's March CPS and are intended to reflect total pre-tax income for families consisting of two or more people. Pre-tax income includes wages, interest and dividends, and cash transfers such as Social Security payments, but does not include the value of government services such as Medicare and food stamps. The data and additional information are available from the Census Bureau website (http://www.census .gov/hhes/www/income/data/historical/families/).

consistent data series included in the Census Bureau's Historical Income Tables.[12] Although they do not reflect the economic fortunes of very poor families at one extreme or very wealthy families at the other extreme, they do represent a broad range of economic circumstances, encompassing working poor families at the 20th percentile, middle-class families at the 40th and 60th percentiles, affluent families at the 80th percentile, and even more affluent families at the 95th percentile. Thus, they provide an invaluable record of the changing economic fortunes of American families over a period of almost seven decades.[13]

The distribution of income in American society has shifted markedly in that time. The broad outlines of this transformation are evident in figure 1.1, which shows how the real pre-tax incomes (in 2014 dollars) of families at various points in the income distribution have changed since 1947. It is clear from figure 1.1 that the period since World War II has seen substantial gains in real income for families throughout the income distribution, but especially for those who were already well off. The average rate of real income growth over the entire period covered by the figure increased uniformly with each step up the income distribution, from 1.0% per year for families at the 20th percentile to 1.7% per year for families at the 95th percentile.

The difference between 1.0% and 1.7% may sound small, but it has compounded into a dramatic difference in *cumulative* real income growth over the past 67 years: 98% for families at the 20th percentile versus 207% for families at the 95th percentile. Of course, the contrast in economic gains between poor families and rich families is even starker in absolute terms than it is in percentage terms. The real incomes of families at the 20th percentile increased by less than $15,000 (2014 dollars) over this period, while the real incomes of families at the 95th percentile increased by more than ten times that much.

These figures convey a striking disparity in the economic fortunes of rich and poor American families since the late 1940s. However, they fail to capture another important difference in the experience of families near the bottom of the income distribution and those near the top: poor families

[12] The Census Bureau's definition of families excludes a growing proportion of households consisting of single or unrelated people. (In 2014, 34% of households were not families by the Census Bureau's definition, up from 18% in 1967, and the median income of all households was $53,657, almost 20% less than the median income of families.) However, a parallel series of income tabulations for the larger universe of households displays generally similar income trends over the period for which the two series overlap, 1967–2014.

[13] Obviously, specific families do not remain at exactly the same point in the income distribution from year to year. Indeed, the specific families included in the Current Population Survey, from which these tabulations are derived, change from year to year. Nevertheless, the data reflect the aggregate economic fortunes of poor, middle-class, and rich families and how they have changed.

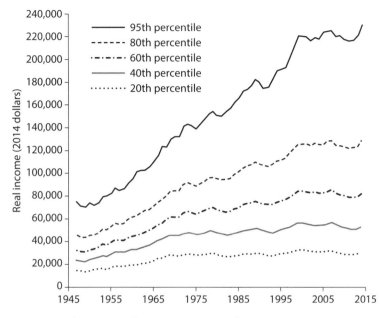

FIGURE 1.1 Family Incomes by Income Percentile, 1947–2014

have been subject to considerably larger fluctuations in income growth rates. For example, families at the 20th percentile experienced declining real incomes in 25 of the 67 years represented in figure 1.1, including six declines of 3% or more since the mid-1970s; by comparison, families at the 95th percentile have experienced only one decline of 3% or more in their real incomes since 1951.

Although it may not be immediately apparent in figure 1.1, the pattern of income growth in the past 40 years has differed sharply from the pattern in the first half of the postwar era. In the 1950s and 1960s, families in every part of the income distribution experienced robust income growth. Since the mid-1970s, income growth has been a good deal slower and a good deal less evenly distributed. These differences are evident in figure 1.2, which compares cumulative rates of real income growth for families in various parts of the income distribution from 1947 to 1974 and from 1974 to 2014.[14]

From the late 1940s through the early 1970s, American income growth was rapid and remarkably egalitarian, at least in percentage terms. Indeed, the real incomes of working poor families (at the 20th percentile of the income distribution) and affluent families (at the 80th percentile) both grew

[14] This figure is modeled on a similar presentation of the same data by Mishel, Bernstein, and Boushey (2003, 57).

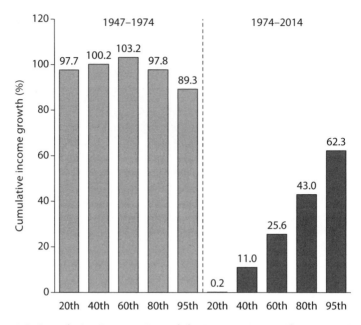

Figure 1.2 Cumulative Income Growth by Income Percentile, 1947–1974 and 1974–2014

by the same 98% over this period. Income growth was slightly higher for middle-class families and slightly lower for families at the 95th percentile, but every income group experienced real income growth between 2.4% and 2.6% per year.

Over the past four decades, income growth has been much slower and much less evenly distributed. Even for families near the top of the income distribution, the average rate of real income growth has been cut in half, from 2.4% per year to 1.2% for families at the 95th percentile. For less affluent families, real income growth has slowed to a crawl. Families at the 60th percentile experienced real income growth of 0.6% per year—less than one-fourth as fast as in the earlier period. The real incomes of families at the 20th percentile barely grew at all over these four decades, increasing by just 0.004% per year. Much of the income growth that did occur was attributable to increases in working hours, especially from the increasing participation of women in the workforce.

Even the disparities in income growth for affluent, middle-class, and working poor American families charted in figures 1.1 and 1.2 under-state the extent of escalating inequality since the 1970s in two important ways. First, they miss a noteworthy deterioration of economic circum-stances at the very bottom of the income distribution. Shifts in public policy, including welfare reform and the expansion of the Earned Income Tax Credit, have increasingly focused government aid on the "deserving poor"—people with jobs and families—rather than the poorest of the poor. Thus, while assistance for single parents with incomes just above the poverty line increased by 74 percent from 1983 to 2004, assistance for those with the lowest incomes fell by more than one-third. About 5% of Americans live in "deep poverty" (with household incomes below *half* the poverty line, even after taking account of food stamps, housing assistance, and other government aid), and that proportion has remained virtually unchanged since the early 1970s.[15]

Kathryn Edin and Luke Shaefer have focused attention on an even poorer stratum of low-income households—those with cash incomes of less than $2 per person per day. They estimated that 0.5% of U.S. children lived in such households on a "chronic" basis (for at least seven months of the year) in 1996. But in that year a Republican Congress and a Democratic president who had pledged to "end welfare as we know it" joined forces to scrap the 60-year-old Aid to Families with Dependent Children program, replacing it with the more restrictive Temporary Assistance for Needy Families. Welfare rolls shrank precipitously, but not all of those who lost their welfare entitlements found work. By 2005, the proportion of children living in chronic $2-a-day poverty had more than doubled, to 1.2%. By 2012, that proportion had more than *tripled*, to 1.7%, and many more households were experiencing "episodic" $2-a-day poverty (for three to six months of the year). Edin and Shaefer characterized these changes as "a fundamental shift in the circumstances of households with children at the very bottom of the bottom in the United States."[16]

At the other end of the income distribution, the growing affluence of families at the 95th percentile (the highest stratum represented in the Census Bureau figures in figure 1.1) is dwarfed by the even more dramatic gains made by people at the very top of the top. Economists Thomas Piketty and Emmanuel Saez have used information collected by the Internal Revenue Service (IRS) to track the economic fortunes of people much higher up the economic ladder than the Census Bureau tabulations reach. Figure 1.3 presents their tabulations of the real incomes (in 2014 dollars) of taxpayers at

[15] Eduardo Porter, "Electing to Ignore the Poorest of the Poor," *New York Times*, November 17, 2015; Fox et al. (2015); Kathleen Short, "The Supplemental Poverty Measure: 2014," Current Population Reports P60-254, U.S. Census Bureau, September 2015.

[16] Edin and Shaefer (2015); Shaefer, Edin, and Talbert (2015, 127–129, 136). The $2-a-day threshold is a poverty standard commonly employed by the World Bank in less developed countries. The proportions of children living in $2-a-day poverty are lower if food stamps are counted as cash, but Edin and Shaefer argued that, for very poor families, food stamps are neither fully fungible nor culturally equivalent to cash.

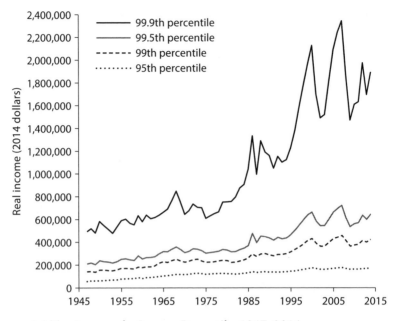

FIGURE 1.3 Top Incomes by Income Percentile, 1947–2014

the 95th, 99th, 99.5th, and 99.9th percentiles of the income distribution since 1947.[17]

What is most striking in figure 1.3 is that, even within this affluent sub-group, income growth over the past four decades has accelerated with every additional step up the economic ladder. The impressive growth of real incomes at the 95th percentile, which looms so large in figure 1.1, is virtually invisible in figure 1.3. The real incomes of taxpayers at the 99th percentile—the threshold for entry into "the 1%"—*doubled* between 1981 and the pre-recession income peak in 2007. The threshold for entry into the top one-tenth of the 1% more than *tripled* over the same period, from about $760,000 to $2.3 million in annual income, before falling to "just" $1.9 million in the depths of the Great Recession.

---

[17] Piketty and Saez (2003, table A6). Updated data are available from the World Top In-comes Database (http://topincomes.parisschoolofeconomics.eu/#Database:). These figures de-rived from IRS data are not directly comparable with the Census Bureau figures charted in figure 1.1. For example, the Census Bureau's income figure for families at the 95th percentile in 2014 is $230,030; the corresponding IRS figure for the 95th percentile of tax filers is $174,240. The latter figure represents annual gross income (including capital gains) reported on individ-ual tax returns. Comparisons are complicated by the fact that some families do not file tax returns, while others file more than one return. For recent years, Piketty and Saez assumed that non-filers had incomes equal to 20% of the average income of filers.

Even higher up in the distribution (and literally off the chart in figure 1.3), the real incomes of taxpayers at the 99.99th percentile more than *quadrupled* between 1981 and 2007. The real income *threshold*—not the *average* income—for this hyper-rich stratum (comprising about 16,500 taxpayers in 2014) was more or less constant for three decades following the end of World War II, but it escalated rapidly from about $2 million (2014 dollars) in the mid-1970s to about $5 million in the early 1990s, $12 million at the height of the tech bubble in 2000, and $13.1 million on the eve of the Great Recession. Although this hyper-rich income threshold fell by 45% between 2007 and 2009, it soon began to rebound, as it has from every previous setback, reaching $9.7 million in 2014.

Another illuminating way to look at Piketty and Saez's tabulations is in terms of the *shares* of total income going to people in different economic strata. Figure 1.4 shows these income shares for the top 5% of taxpayers (the solid line) and the top 1% (the dotted line) over the past century. For the period since World War II, the picture here is quite consistent with the picture presented in figures 1.1 and 1.3. The share of income going to the rich remained remarkably constant from the mid-1940s through the 1970s and then began to escalate rapidly. For example, the top 5% of taxpayers accounted for 23% of total income in 1981, but almost 38% in 2014. The top 1% accounted for 10% of total income in 1981, but more than 21% in 2014; after declining gradually over most of the 20th century, their share of the pie doubled in the course of a single generation.[18]

Two other features of the historical trends in income shares stand out in figure 1.4. One is that the increasing share of income going to people in the top 5% of the distribution is entirely accounted for by the increasing share going to the top 1%; the distance between the solid and dotted lines, which represents the share going to people between the 95th and 99th percentiles, remained virtually constant. As in figure 1.3, it is clear here that the really dramatic economic gains over the past 40 years have been concentrated among the extremely rich, largely bypassing even the vast majority of ordinary rich people in the top 5% of the income distribution.

---

[18] Piketty and Saez (2003, table A3); World Top Incomes Database (http://topincomes .parisschoolofeconomics.eu/#Database:). The income shares reported in figure 1.4 include capital gains as well as other sources of income. Piketty and Saez noted that capital gains are "a volatile component" of income and "tend to be realized in a lumpy way." Some of this lumpiness is real (as with the spikes in top income shares coinciding with the peaks of the tech bubble in 2000 and the real estate bubble in 2007), while some reflects artifacts of tax accounting (as with the spike corresponding to the tax reform of 1986). Nevertheless, the historical trends in income shares are generally similar whether capital gains are included or excluded (compare Piketty and Saez 2003, table A1). However, ignoring capital gains understates the income share of the richest taxpayers. For example, the average income share of the top 1% of taxpayers in 2005–2014 was 17.8% excluding capital gains but 21.1% including capital gains.

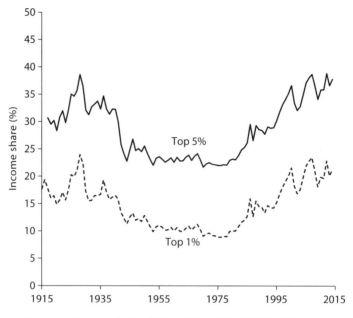

Figure 1.4 Income Shares of Top 5% and Top 1%, 1915–2014

Indeed, economists Frank Levy and Peter Temin used Piketty and Saez's data to show that more than four-fifths of the total increase in Americans' real pre-tax income between 1980 and 2005 went to the top 1% of taxpayers. Around the same time, a front-page story in the *New York Times* declared that "the hyper-rich have emerged in the last three decades as the biggest winners in a remarkable transformation of the American economy." Of course, several years later "the 1%" became the bête noire of the Occupy Wall Street movement.[19]

Because Piketty and Saez's tabulations go back to the advent of the federal income tax system, they also provide important historical perspective on the absolute magnitude of inequality in the contemporary American income distribution. Although it is impossible to reliably compare current levels of inequality with those prevailing in the original Gilded Age in the late 19th century, it *is* possible to compare the position of today's economic elite with their counterparts in what most economic historians consider the other notable highpoint of economic inequality in American history—the 1920s. Whether we focus on the share of income going to the top 5% of taxpayers or the share going to the even richer top 1%, figure 1.4 suggests

[19] Levy and Temin (2007, 49–50); David Cay Johnston, "Richest Are Leaving Even the Rich Far Behind," *New York Times*, June 5, 2005; Gitlin (2012).

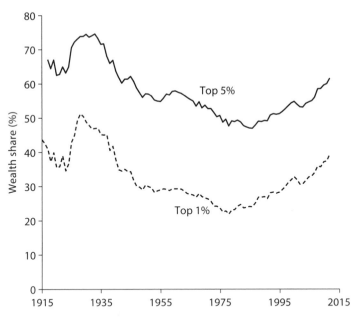

FIGURE 1.5 Wealth Shares of Top 5% and Top 1%, 1915–2012

that current levels of inequality rival those of the Roaring Twenties, before the Great Depression wiped out much of the financial wealth of the nation's reigning upper class. By this metric, America's New Gilded Age is a retrogression of historic scope.[20]

Finally, it is worth noting that wealth in the contemporary United States (as in virtually all capitalist societies) is even more concentrated than income.[21] Piketty's *Capital in the Twenty-First Century*, a scholarly tome on the dynamics of wealth accumulation, became an unlikely worldwide bestseller in 2014. For the United States, Saez and Gabriel Zucman have used the same income tax data underlying figures 1.3 and 1.4 to impute the distribution of wealth over the past century. Their estimates of the shares of wealth held by the richest 5% and the richest 1% of households are presented in figure 1.5. The pattern of wealth concentration generally mirrors the trend

[20] I do not know who first referred to the contemporary era as a "New Gilded Age." The term served as the title of a collection of pieces from the *New Yorker* magazine on "the culture of affluence" (Remnick 2000). It subsequently appeared in an influential essay by Paul Krugman in the *New York Times Magazine* ("For Richer: How the Permissive Capitalism of the Boom Destroyed American Equality") on October 20, 2002, and in the headline of a front-page article by Louis Uchitelle in the *New York Times* ("Age of Riches: The Richest of the Rich, Proud of a New Gilded Age") on July 15, 2007.

[21] Wolff (2002).

in top income shares in figure 1.4, but with two important distinctions. First, changes in the concentration of wealth have generally been slower and smoother than changes in the concentration of income. For example, whereas the decline in top income shares in the wake of the Wall Street crash of 1929 was mostly over by 1944, the decline in top wealth shares continued for another 35 years. On the other hand, top wealth shares had a good deal further to fall, since the top 1% of wealth-holders accounted for more than half of America's net worth on the eve of the crash and the top 5% accounted for almost three-quarters. The corresponding wealth shares in 2014 were 42% for the top 1% and 65% for the top 5%, reflecting a 35-year rebound largely uninterrupted by the fluctuations in top income shares produced by the bursting of the tech bubble at the turn of the century and the housing bubble in 2008. [22]

INTERPRETING INEQUALITY

What are we to make of these economic trends? To some people, they reflect an era of economic dynamism and expanding opportunity. Others are made uneasy by the sheer magnitude of the gulf between the rich and the poor in contemporary America, even if they cannot quite pinpoint why. Still others are less concerned about inequality per se than about the absolute living standards of the poor or about the extent of their opportunity to work their way up the economic ladder. For the most part, discussions of escalating inequality have focused on four related issues: economic growth, economic mobility, fairness, and inevitability.

One crucial—and highly contentious—question is whether dramatic income gains among the hyper-rich "trickle down" to middle-class and poor people, increasing the size of everyone's piece of the pie. After all, even the influential liberal political theorist John Rawls argued that inequality is just insofar as it contributes to the well-being of the least well-off members of society.[23] Many ordinary Americans believe that "large differences in income are necessary for America's prosperity," as one standard survey question puts it.[24] However, economists who have studied the relationship

[22] Piketty (2014); Saez and Zucman (forthcoming, online appendix, Table B1). Imputing wealth from income tax returns sounds like a hazardous undertaking, and it is. However, Saez and Zucman's imputations closely match more direct evidence of the distribution of wealth from other, more fragmentary sources, such as the Survey of Consumer Finances and estate tax returns. Additional evidence regarding trends in wealth-holding in recent decades appears in chapter 9.

[23] Rawls (1971, chap. 2).

[24] This question has been included in several General Social Surveys conducted as part of the International Social Survey Programme (http://www.issp.org/). In four surveys conducted

between inequality and economic growth have found little evidence that large disparities in income and wealth promote growth.[25] There is not even much hard evidence in support of the commonsense notion that progressive tax rates retard growth by discouraging economic effort. Indeed, one liberal economist, Robert Frank, has written that "the lessons of experience are downright brutal" to the notion that higher taxes stifle economic growth by causing wealthy people to work less or take fewer risks.[26]

In recent years, some economists have gone beyond the observation that inequality does not seem to be "necessary for America's prosperity" to argue that high levels of inequality actually inhibit economic growth. In a much-discussed 2012 speech, Alan Krueger, the chairman of President Obama's Council of Economic Advisers, noted that he "used to have an aversion to using the term inequality," but had come to the conclusion that "the rise in inequality in the United States over the last three decades has reached the point that inequality in incomes is causing an unhealthy division in opportunities, and is a threat to our economic growth." Nobel laureate Joseph Stiglitz published not one but two books arguing that economic inequality is inimical to growth. And a large cross-national study released by the International Monetary Fund in 2014 concluded that "*lower net inequality is robustly correlated with faster and more durable growth*" and that "*redistribution appears generally benign in terms of its impact on growth; only in extreme cases is there some evidence that it may have direct negative effects on growth*. Thus the combined direct and indirect effects of redistribution—including the growth effects of the resulting lower inequality—are on average pro-growth."[27]

Much of the economic argument in favor of economic inequality hinges on the assumption that large fortunes will be invested in productive economic activities. In fact, however, there is some reason to worry that the new hyper-rich are less likely to invest their wealth than to fritter it away on jewelry, yachts, and caviar. According to one press report, the after-tax savings rate of households in the top 5% of the income distribution fell by more than half from 1990 through 2006 (from 13.6% to 6.2%), while real sales growth in the luxury retail industry averaged more than 10% per year.[28]

---

between 1987 and 2000, the proportion of the U.S. public agreeing that large differences in income are necessary for prosperity ranged from 26% to 32%, while the proportion disagreeing ranged from 38% to 58% (McCall 2005, appendix table 1).

[25] Alesina and Rodrik (1994); Persson and Tabellini (1994); Bénabou (1996); Perotti (1996).

[26] Robert H. Frank, "In the Real World of Work and Wages, Trickle-Down Theories Don't Hold Up," *New York Times*, April 12, 2007.

[27] Alan B. Krueger, "The Rise and Consequences of Inequality in the United States," remarks as prepared for delivery to the Center for American Progress, January 12, 2012; Stiglitz (2012; 2015); Ostry, Berg, and Tsangarides (2014, 4, emphasis in original).

[28] Anna Bernasek, "The Rich Spend Just Like You and Me," *New York Times*, August 6, 2006. Bernasek drew upon detailed data on growth in the luxury retail sector through 2001

Even if inequality did promote overall economic growth, that would not necessarily imply that it contributed to the well-being of the least well-off members of society. The benefits of economic growth may or may not "trickle down" to the poor. Although it is common for Americans to suppose that the nation's collective wealth makes even poor people better off than they otherwise would be, the reality is that poor people in America seem to be distinctly *less* well off than poor people in countries that are less wealthy but less unequal. A careful comparison of the living standards of poor children in 13 rich democracies in the 1990s found the United States ranking next to last, 20% below Canada and France and 35% below Norway, despite its greater overall wealth.[29] Moreover, even holding constant the absolute economic status of the least well-off, there is good reason to worry that inequality itself may have deleterious social implications—not only for the poor, but for all Americans—in the realms of family and community life, health, and education.[30]

An even more dramatic indication of the momentous consequences of economic inequality is the increasing disparity in life expectancy between affluent and poor Americans. According to a tabulation by the Social Security Administration, the difference in life expectancy between 60-year-old men in the top and bottom halves of the earnings distribution increased from 1.2 years in the early 1970s to 5.8 years in 2001. A Brookings Institution study found that the difference in life expectancy between men in the top and bottom deciles of the earnings distribution increased from six years for those born in 1920 to 14 years for those born in 1950, while the corresponding gap for women increased from less than five years to 13 years. The differences in life expectancy between earnings groups are partly attributable to differential risks of smoking and prescription drug abuse, but one public health expert noted that these and other specific risk factors are manifestations of broader economic and social inequities "that high-tech medicine cannot fix."[31]

---

compiled by Jonathan Parker, Yacine Ait-Sahalia, and Motohiro Yogo (2004) and supplemented with bits of subsequent data from individual high-end retailers such as Tiffany.

[29] The comparison was for children at the 10th percentile of the income distribution in each country, based on data from the Luxembourg Income Study. The authors suggest that this difference would be reduced (though not eliminated) by counting non-cash benefits such as schooling—but only by assuming, rather implausibly, that American children regardless of family income levels benefit equally from public spending on education. See Osberg, Smeeding, and Schwabish (2004, 826–834).

[30] Neckerman (2004) and Wilkinson and Pickett (2009) provided comprehensive reviews of research in these domains. For recent additions to the literature, see Marmot (2015) on health, Bradbury et al. (2015) on education, and Putnam (2015) on social life.

[31] Bosworth, Burtless, and Zhang (2016); Sabrina Tavernise, "Disparity in Life Spans of the Rich and the Poor Is Growing," *New York Times*, February 12, 2016.

Another important strand of debate focuses on the extent of economic mobility and the relationship between inequality and mobility. As one journalistic account put it, "Mobility is the promise that lies at the heart of the American dream. It is supposed to take the sting out of the widening gulf between the have-mores and the have-nots. There are poor and rich in the United States, of course, the argument goes; but as long as one can become the other, as long as there is something close to equality of opportunity, the differences between them do not add up to class barriers."[32]

For some observers, the dynamism of the modern economy is vividly reflected in the extent of turnover at the pinnacle of the income distribution. For example, *Forbes* classified 69% of the people on its 2014 list of the 400 richest Americans as "self-made," compared to fewer than half in 1984. It is worth noting, however, that capitalists interpret the "self-made" designation pretty broadly, including not only genuine rags-to-riches billionaires like George Soros and Oprah Winfrey but also people like Rupert Murdoch, who "inherited two newspapers when his father died." Donald Trump, whose modest origins famously included "a small loan of a million dollars" from his father, barely missed *Forbes*'s "self-made" cut-off.[33]

While the composition of the *Forbes* 400 list has symbolic significance, there is little reason to believe that it reflects patterns of economic mobility in American society as a whole. Leaving aside this handful of billionaires, to what extent are the economic fortunes of ordinary Americans determined by their starting positions in the economic hierarchy? One commentator, Michael Kinsley, warned that "immobility over generations is what congeals financial differences into old-fashioned, European-style social class."[34] However, a recent large-scale analysis of matched tax records demonstrated that the correlation between contemporary Americans' income ranks and those of their parents was twice as strong as in Canada or Denmark. Broader studies showed that the United States has "significantly less economic mobility than Canada, Finland, Sweden, Norway, and possibly Germany; and the United States may be a less economically mobile society than Britain."[35]

[32] Janny Scott and David Leonhardt, "Class in America: Shadowy Lines That Still Divide," *New York Times*, May 15, 2005.

[33] Nina Munk, "Don't Blink. You'll Miss the 258th-Richest American," *New York Times*, September 25, 2005; Agustino Fontevecchia, "The New Forbes 400 Self-Made Score: From Silver Spooners to Bootstrappers," *Forbes*, October 2, 2014; "Verbatim: Donald Trump on the Rough Life, and Getting $1 Million from His Father," *New York Times*, October 26, 2015. If Trump had simply invested his $40 million share of his father's real estate company in a stock index fund in 1974, his fortune in 2015 would have been nearly $3 billion; *Forbes* estimated his net worth in that year at $4.5 billion, perhaps owing in part to vigorous lobbying on Trump's part for a higher valuation. Randall Lane, "Inside the Epic Fantasy That's Driven Donald Trump for 33 Years," *Forbes*, September 29, 2015.

[34] Michael Kinsley, "Mobility vs. Nobility," *Washington Post*, June 5, 2005.

[35] Chetty et al. (2014a, 15–16); Beller and Hout (2006, 30).

These comparisons suggest—contrary to the fervent beliefs of many Americans—that the contemporary United States outclasses Europe in the rigidity of its hidebound European-style class structure.

Comparisons of intergenerational mobility over time within the United States also suggest that the impact of parents' fortunes on their children's fortunes has increased, at least for men. One large recent study found that "rank-based measures of mobility remained stable" among children born between 1971 and 1993, but that "the consequences of the 'birth lottery'" have increased because the "rungs of the ladder have grown further apart," owing to increasing inequality. A broader study measuring the impact of a wide range of family background factors (including family structure, race and ethnicity, parental education and income, and region) similarly found that "the economic gap between advantaged and disadvantaged men increased because economic inequality increased" during the 1970s, 1980s, and 1990s, while "the gaps in women's outcomes remained constant." Another study found that the effect of parental income on men's economic fortunes "declined between 1940 and 1980 but increased during the 1980s and 1990s."[36]

Generally similar trends seem to have affected income mobility measured across decades rather than generations. While the probability of any given family rising from the bottom quintile of the income distribution into the top quintile over the course of a decade increased slightly (from 3.3% in the 1970s to 4.3% in the 1990s), the proportion of families in the top quintile of the income distribution who remained there a decade later also increased; at the same time, the proportion of families falling from the top quintile into the bottom quintile, or from the top two quintiles into the bottom two quintiles, declined. The long-term economic mobility of individual earners (measured by decade-average earnings at 10-year intervals) seems to have increased in the 1960s and early 1970s but stagnated thereafter, with declines in mobility among men balanced by increases among women.[37]

Some observers have downplayed the significance of snapshots of economic inequality at a given point in time on the grounds that individual economic fortunes fluctuate from year to year, making earnings over the course of a lifetime much less unequal than earnings in any given year. However, a detailed study of individual earnings trajectories based on Social Security records going back to the late 1930s found that "increases in annual earnings inequality are driven almost entirely by increases in permanent earnings inequality, with much more modest changes in the variability of transitory earnings." Thus, "annual snapshots of the distribution provide a good

---

[36] Chetty et al. (2014b); Beller and Hout (2006, 30), summarizing studies by Harding et al. (2005) and Aaronson and Mazumder (2005). See also Solon (2002) and Hout (2004).

[37] Bradbury and Katz (2002, 66); Kopczuk, Saez, and Song (2010, 119).

approximation of the evolution of the longer-term measures of inequality."
If anything, the year-to-year correlation in income ranks may have increased
slightly, from .855 in 1960 to .869 in 1980 and .898 in 2002.[38]

Another key point of contention is the extent to which escalating inequality reflects the "just" rewards accruing to education and skills in the
modern economy. According to one conservative observer, *New York Times*
columnist David Brooks,

> the market isn't broken; the meritocracy is working almost too well. It's
> rewarding people based on individual talents. Higher education pays
> off because it provides technical knowledge and because it screens out
> people who are not organized, self-motivated and socially adept. But
> even among people with identical education levels, inequality is wid-
> ening as the economy favors certain abilities. . . . What's needed is not
> a populist revolt, which would make everything worse, but a second
> generation of human capital policies, designed for people as they actu-
> ally are, to help them get the intangible skills the economy rewards.[39]

On the other hand, Brooks's liberal counterpart on the *Times* op-ed page,
Paul Krugman, attacked "the notion that the winners in our increasingly
unequal society are a fairly large group—that the 20 percent or so of American workers who have the skills to take advantage of new technology and
globalization are pulling away from the 80 percent who don't have these
skills." Noting that the real incomes of college graduates had risen by less
than 1% per year over the preceding three decades, Krugman argued that
"the big gains have gone to a much smaller, much richer group than that."
Nevertheless, the "80-20 fallacy," as he called it, "tends to dominate po-
lite discussion about income trends, not because it's true, but because it's
comforting. The notion that it's all about returns to education suggests that
nobody is to blame for rising inequality, that it's just a case of supply and
demand at work. . . . The idea that we have a rising oligarchy is much more
disturbing. It suggests that the growth of inequality may have as much to do
with power relations as it does with market forces."[40]

Krugman cited economists Ian Dew-Becker and Robert J. Gordon's detailed analysis of productivity and income growth over four decades. According to Dew-Becker and Gordon, "most of the shift in the income distribution has been from the bottom 90 percent to the top 5 percent. This is
much too narrow a group to be consistent with a widespread benefit from

---

[38] Kopczuk, Saez, and Song (2010, 125, 116). The Gini coefficient for 11-year average earnings increased from .437 in 1950–1960 to .477 in 1973–1983 to .508 in 1994–2004.

[39] David Brooks, "The Populist Myths on Income Inequality," *New York Times*, September 7, 2006.

[40] Paul Krugman, "Graduates Versus Oligarchs," *New York Times*, February 27, 2006.

SBTC [skill-biased technical change]." They found that some of the occupations that should have flourished if the dynamic economy of the 1990s was simply rewarding technical skills actually saw very modest income growth. For example, the earnings of mathematicians and computer scientists increased by only 4.8% between 1989 and 1997, while the earnings of engineers actually declined by 1.4%. In contrast, the earnings of CEOs increased by 100%.[41]

Evidence of a serious mismatch between skills and economic rewards seems likely to fan concerns about the "fairness" of recent changes in the U.S. income distribution. So, too, does the juxtaposition of rapid productivity growth with stagnant middle-class wages. Dew-Becker and Gordon found that economic productivity had increased substantially over the period covered by their analysis, but that "the broad middle of working America has reaped little of the gains in productivity over the past 35 years. . . . The micro data tell a shocking story of gains accruing disproportionately to the top one percent and 0.1 percent of the income distribution." They characterized the first five years of the 21st century as "an unprecedented dichotomy of macroeconomic glow and gloom." On one hand, labor productivity and output growth exploded; on the other hand, median family income fell by 3.8 percent from 1999 to 2004.[42]

The "unprecedented dichotomy" noted by Dew-Becker and Gordon between booming output and stagnant or declining incomes for ordinary workers was a recurrent political problem for the Bush administration. The "strange and unlikely combination" of "strong and healthy aggregate macroeconomic indicators and a grumpy populace," one report said, was "a source of befuddlement to the administration and its allies." Treasury Secretary Henry Paulson acknowledged that "amid this country's strong economic expansion, many Americans simply aren't feeling the benefits." Paulson blamed that fact on "market forces" that "work to provide the greatest rewards to those with the needed skills in the growth areas."[43]

Paulson's predecessor as treasury secretary, John Snow, spoke in similar terms about the "long-term trend to differentiate compensation." According to one observer, "'Long-term,' when used this way by this sort of official, tends to mean 'fundamentally unstoppable.' And, in this case, inexplicable, like a sort of financial global-warming process that may be man-made or (who knows?) a natural cycle that we would welcome if only we knew its function. Snow, a trained economist and former corporate CEO, doesn't

[41] Dew-Becker and Gordon (2005, 73, 74).

[42] Ibid., 60, 3, 1.

[43] Daniel Gross, "When Sweet Statistics Clash with a Sour Mood," *New York Times*, June 4, 2006; remarks prepared for delivery by Treasury Secretary Henry H. Paulson at Columbia University, August 1, 2006.

pretend to be able to explain what's causing this whole compensation differential. Nor does he seem tortured by his ignorance. 'We've moved into a star system for some reason,' he said, 'which is not fully understood.'"[44]

The notion that economic inequality is an inevitable, purely natural phenomenon has been given a pseudo-scientific patina by a self-proclaimed "econophysicist" at the University of Maryland, Victor Yakovenko. Yakovenko noted that, aside from a long upper tail, the dispersion of U.S. incomes closely approximates an exponential distribution—the same kind of distribution characteristic of many natural phenomena. According to an account of Yakovenko's work published in the *New York Times Magazine*'s 2005 survey of "The Year in Ideas," "To an econophysicist, the exponential distribution of incomes is no coincidence: it suggests that the wealth of most Americans is itself in a kind of thermal equilibrium. . . . Yakovenko told *New Scientist* that 'short of getting Stalin,' efforts to make more than superficial dents in inequality would fail."[45]

ECONOMIC INEQUALITY AS A POLITICAL ISSUE

Interpretations of economic inequality are politically consequential because they shape political responses to inequality. If the differences between rich and poor in contemporary America "do not add up to class barriers," if "the market isn't broken" and "meritocracy is working," or if "efforts to make more than superficial dents in inequality" are doomed to failure, then inequality is unlikely to rise to the top of the political agenda. Many observers have been perplexed by the modest salience of inequality as a political issue in America. For example, Dahl wrote that, "for all the emphasis on equality in the American public ideology, the United States lags well behind a number of other democratic countries in reducing economic inequality. It is a striking fact that the presence of vast disparities in wealth and income, and so in political resources, has never become a highly salient issue in American politics or, certainly, a persistent one."[46] Is that because Americans assume that "efforts to make more than superficial dents in inequality" would fail?

The fact that most other rich democracies are considerably less unequal than the United States provides some reason to think that political arrangements short of Stalinism might not be entirely futile in mitigating economic inequality. For that matter, even the limited range of policies implemented in the United States in the postwar era has had substantial effects on prevailing levels of economic inequality. In short, politics matters.

[44] Walter Kim, "Way Upstairs, Downstairs," *New York Times Magazine*, April 16, 2006, 11.
[45] Christopher Shea, "Econophysics," *New York Times Magazine*, December 11, 2005, 67.
[46] Dahl (1982, 175).

If this claim seems controversial, that is probably because so much public discussion of economic inequality in the New Gilded Age ignores its political dimension. Journalists and commentators may not dwell on the "econophysics" of thermal equilibrium as reflected in the exponential distribution, but they often frame discussions of inequality in a curiously passive, technical, and distinctly apolitical way. The standard perspective is typified by a cover story in *The Economist* on "Inequality in America." The report summarized trends in the American economy in the 1990s and early 2000s:

> Thanks to a jump in productivity growth after 1995, America's economy has outpaced other rich countries' for a decade. Its workers now produce over 30% more each hour they work than ten years ago. In the late 1990s everybody shared in this boom. Though incomes were rising fastest at the top, all workers' wages far outpaced inflation.
>
> But after 2000 something changed. The pace of productivity growth has been rising again, but now it seems to be lifting fewer boats. . . . The fruits of productivity gains have been skewed towards the highest earners, and towards companies, whose profits have reached record levels as a share of GDP.[47]

The report provided no hint of what "something" might have changed after 2000. Nor did it offer any explanation for why "America's income disparities suddenly widened after 1980," nor why "during the 1990s, particularly towards the end of the decade, that gap stabilized and, by some measures, even narrowed."

Hello? George W. Bush? Ronald Reagan? Bill Clinton? In 3,000 words, the report offered no suggestion that any policy choice by these or other elected officials might have contributed to the economic trends it summarized. Rather, "the main cause was technology, which increased the demand for skilled workers relative to their supply, with freer trade reinforcing the effect." The report also suggested that "institutional changes, particularly the weakening of unions," might have "made the going harder for people at the bottom" and that "greedy businessmen" might be "sanction[ing] huge salaries for each other at the expense of shareholders."

Reports of this sort obviously do little to make "the presence of vast disparities in wealth and income" noted by Dahl "a highly salient issue in American politics." Indeed, the authors of the *Economist*'s cover story began by assuring their readers that "Americans do not go in for envy. The gap between rich and poor is bigger than in any other advanced country, but most people are unconcerned. Whereas Europeans fret about the way the economic pie is divided, Americans want to join the rich, not soak them.

[47] "The Rich, the Poor and the Growing Gap Between Them," *The Economist*, June 17, 2006, 28.

Eight out of ten, more than anywhere else, believe that though you may start out poor, if you work hard, you can make pots of money. It is a central part of the American Dream."[48]

The political economy of inequality might be very different if, contrary to Dahl's observation, the presence of vast disparities in wealth and income *was* a highly salient issue in American politics. How likely is that, and how might it happen?

One admittedly unsystematic barometer of the popular zeitgeist is the annual "What People Earn" issue of *Parade* magazine, a popular Sunday newspaper supplement claiming more than 50 million readers. For more than 30 years, *Parade* has published annual "Special Reports" including dozens of Americans' names, photos, occupations, and salaries. Most are ordinary people with five-figure incomes; some are immensely wealthy celebrities like Michael Jordan, Donald Trump, and SpongeBob Squarepants. The stories accompanying these "salary surveys" address the current economic climate and job prospects, shedding light on the shifting resonance of economic inequality in contemporary American culture.

In 2002, for example, financial writer Andrew Tobias put the gulf between the incomes of the rich and famous, on one hand, and ordinary people, on the other, in reassuring perspective, noting that in "Uganda or Peru . . . plumbers and librarians earn a whole lot less" than in the United States. "Yes. Life *is* unfair," Tobias wrote. "But for most of us, it could be a lot worse. And in America there's at least a fighting chance that, if you work at it, you—or your kids anyway—can close the gap."[49]

The following year Tobias revisited the issue of economic inequality, but in a rather different tone. While remaining sanguine about the millions earned by Ben Affleck, Madonna, and Stephen King ("I don't mind a bit. This is America! More power to them!"), he was more skeptical about the earnings of CEOs, suggesting that in some cases "the market isn't really free and the CEO largely sets his own pay." Noting that one modestly paid CEO earned more than "the Joint Chiefs of Staff and the presidents of Harvard, Yale and Princeton—combined!" Tobias concluded, somewhat defensively, that "it is not class warfare to face these facts, observe these trends and raise these questions. Many will conclude that all is as it should be. Others will say things have gotten out of whack. The ability to confront, debate and occasionally course-correct is one of our nation's greatest strengths."[50]

In 2005, the *Parade* report noted that productivity "has risen steadily; but economists say that, so far, the resulting benefits have gone into corporate

[48] Ibid.

[49] Lynn Brenner, "How Did *You* Do?" *Parade*, March 3, 2002, 4–5; Andrew Tobias, "Are They Worth It?" *Parade*, March 3, 2002, 8.

[50] Andrew Tobias, "How Much Is Fair?" *Parade*, March 2, 2003, 10–11.

profits." By 2007, the disparity between "government statistics" and the "daily experience" of workers had become a major theme of *Parade*'s annual report. Prominent subheads announced that "most Americans didn't see the long economic boom reflected in their paychecks" and that "the salary gains of the last five years have gone to the highest-paid workers." The body of the story reported that "many Americans are troubled by the income gap between the nation's highest earners and everyone else—a gap that has grown dramatically in recent decades." By 2010, *Parade* was profiling people forced by the Great Recession to "hunker down," work part-time, or change jobs. "Across America," readers were told, "workers' resilience is being tested." But the piece left little doubt that resilience would win out: "Frustrating? Yes. Discouraging? No way."[51]

Meanwhile, in a very different segment of the Sunday magazine market, the *New York Times Magazine* in 2007 published a special "Money Issue" titled "Inside the Income Gap." Lengthy articles focused on class disparities in schooling, John Edwards's "poverty platform" in the 2008 presidential race, and the implications of an increasingly global labor market. However, the impact of these weighty examinations of the sociology and politics of economic inequality was diminished by the distracting interspersion of colorful advertisements for investment companies, exotic consumer goods, and high-end real estate. One three-page article on "The Inequality Conundrum" ("How can you promote equality without killing off the genie of American prosperity?") was woven around advertisements for a private bank and financial planning company ("an entire team of wealth experts"), high-definition flatscreen televisions ("the ultimate TV experience"), the national airline of the Cayman Islands ("Endless beauty. Non-stop flights"), and luxury apartments on New York's Fifth Avenue ("From $10.25 million").[52]

The lifestyles of *New York Times Magazine* readers are emblematic of a striking social gulf between the people who are most likely to read lengthy articles (or books!) on the subject of inequality and the people who have themselves been on the losing end of escalating inequality in the past 40 years. That social gulf has been exacerbated by the economic trends of the New Gilded Age, and it constitutes a significant obstacle to political progress in responding to those trends. One can only wonder how many affluent readers will get around to pondering "The Inequality Conundrum" as soon as they return from the Cayman Islands.

Occasionally the luxury-porn gets seamlessly integrated with social commentary in the magazine's editorial content. In 2015 *T: The New York*

[51] Lynn Brenner, "How Did *You* Do?" *Parade*, March 13, 2005, 4–10; Lynn Brenner, "How Did *You* Do?" *Parade*, April 15, 2007, 4–8; George Anders, "How We're Making It Work," *Parade*, April 11, 2010.

[52] "Inside the Income Gap," *New York Times Magazine*, June 10, 2007.

Times Style Magazine dispatched op-ed luminary David Brooks to check in on "The Ultimate Vacation," a 24-day round-the-world tour organized by Four Seasons hotels at a cost of "roughly" $120,000 per person. "I tried but failed to ward off the second bottle of champagne," Brooks's report began. He detailed the charms of the group's private jet, Russian caviar, and "squad of local greeters" and functionaries at each stop on the whirlwind global jaunt. "Sometimes it is the structure of things that you shall be pampered," he philosophized, "and you have no choice but to sit back and accept that fact." Yet he went on to assure readers that his fellow travelers were "rich but not fancy," that they "spent their lives busy with work and family," and that "very few of these people were born to money." (Did he ask, or could he just tell?) "Of course, we all have a responsibility to reduce inequality in our society," Brooks concluded. "But maybe not every day."[53]

As one perceptive commentator noted, "countless Americans don't even have time to worry about reducing societal inequality, because they're at work every day."[54] And since the Four Seasons tour would have cost a typical American couple two and a half years of vacation time and about four years of income, *they* probably won't have to sit back and accept the "fact" that "the structure of things" sometimes (somehow) results in lavish intercontinental pampering. Yet Brooks's only real misgiving seems to have been that this sliver of what he called "the lower end of the upper class" did not spend enough time on a day trip to Ephesus to read St. Paul and "talk about how to reconcile material happiness with spiritual joy."[55]

If the juxtaposition of social concern and conspicuous consumption in the *New York Times Magazine* symbolizes the ambivalent resonance of the New Gilded Age among its winners, the various conflicting themes in the *Parade* reports on "What People Earn" underscore the complexity of the cultural norms and values that shape thinking about economic inequality among the people whose economic fortunes have stagnated. American workers are suffering from wage freezes, benefit reductions, and shrinking job security, but they are better off than their counterparts in Uganda or Peru. Celebrities are entitled to their millions, but perhaps there *is* something troubling about CEOs earning more than the combined salaries of the Joint Chiefs of Staff and the presidents of Harvard, Yale, and Princeton. The income gap between the rich and the rest has grown dramatically, but in America, you—or your kids anyway—can close the gap. Or maybe not.

[53] David Brooks, "The Ultimate Vacation," *T: The New York Times Style Magazine*, November 15, 2015, 118–122.

[54] Max Ehrenfreund, "What David Brooks Discovered About the Rich on a $120,000 Vacation," *Washington Post*, *Wonkblog*, November 16, 2015.

[55] Brooks, "The Ultimate Vacation."

Inequality and American Democracy

To a famously perceptive foreign observer of 19th-century America, Alexis de Tocqueville, the spirit of equality was the hallmark of American culture: "Any man and any power which would contest the irresistible force of equality will be overturned and destroyed by it." However, Tocqueville recognized that equality in the social and political realms could coexist with a great deal of economic inequality. "There are just as many wealthy people in the United States as elsewhere," he observed. "I am not even aware of a country where the love of money has a larger place in men's hearts or where they express a deeper scorn for the theory of a permanent equality of possessions."[56]

Tocqueville's juxtaposition of social equality and economic inequality has been a recurrent theme in commentary on the place of equality in American political culture. According to Verba and Orren, for example, ordinary Americans have complex views about the value of equality:

> Their sentiments are far more egalitarian in some areas than in others. They assign different goods to different spheres of justice. There are spheres for money, political power, welfare, leisure time, and love. . . . The aim of egalitarianism is not the elimination of all differences, which would be impossible, nor even the elimination of differences within any one of these spheres, which might also be impossible unless the state continually intervened. Rather, the goal is to keep the spheres autonomous and their boundaries intact. Success in one sphere should not be convertible into success in another sphere. Political power, which is the most dangerous social good because it is the easiest to convert, must be constrained against transmutation into economic power, and vice versa.[57]

One of the most important questions explored in this book is whether political equality can be achieved, or even approximated, in a society marked by glaring economic inequalities. When push comes to shove, how impermeable are the boundaries separating the economic and political spheres of American life?

At some points in American history, at least, those boundaries have been remarkably permeable. The original Gilded Age in the late 19th century is a dramatic case in point. Rapid economic expansion and transformation coexisted with intense partisan conflict and political corruption. Social Darwinism provided a powerful ideological rationale for letting the devil take the hindmost. The mordant novel by Mark Twain and Charles Warner that

---

[56] Tocqueville (1835/1840, 587, 64).
[57] Verba and Orren (1985, 7–8).

gave the era its name portrayed a political process in which the greedy and cynical preyed on the greedy and gullible.[58]

In *Wealth and Democracy: A Political History of the American Rich*, political analyst Kevin Phillips called attention to a variety of striking economic and political parallels between the "capitalist heydays" of the Gilded Age, the Roaring Twenties, and the contemporary era. Economically, he argued, all three periods were marked by "major economic and corporate restructuring," "bull markets and rising, increasingly precarious levels of speculation, leverage, and debt," "exaltation of business, entrepreneurialism, and the achievements of free enterprise," and "concentration of wealth, economic polarization, and rising levels of inequality." Politically, all three periods featured "conservative politics and ideology," "skepticism of government," "reduction or elimination of taxes, especially on corporations, personal income, or inheritance," and "high levels of corruption," among other factors.[59]

Having surveyed the rise and fall of great economic fortunes through more than two centuries of American history, Phillips emphasized the regularity with which concentrations of wealth in new industries, regions, and families have been spurred, subsidized, and supported by government policies. "From the nursery years of the Republic," he wrote, "U.S. government economic decisions in matters of taxation, central bank operations, debt management, banking, trade and tariffs, and financial rescues or bailouts have been keys to expanding, shrinking, or realigning the nation's privately held assets. . . . Occasionally public policy tilted toward the lower and middle classes, as under Jefferson, Jackson, and Franklin D. Roosevelt. Most often, in the United States and elsewhere, these avenues and alleyways have been explored, every nook and cranny, for the benefit of the financial and business classes."[60]

In the same vein, Paul Krugman has emphasized the importance of social and political forces in shaping the economic trends of the past 75 years:

> Middle-class America didn't emerge by accident. It was created by what has been called the Great Compression of incomes that took place during World War II, and sustained for a generation by social norms that favored equality, strong labor unions and progressive taxation. Since the 1970's, all of those sustaining forces have lost their power.
>
> Since 1980 in particular, U.S. government policies have consistently favored the wealthy at the expense of working families—and

---

[58] Twain and Warner (1873).

[59] Phillips (2002, 297). For an earlier exploration of similar themes, see Phillips (1990).

[60] Phillips (2002, 214).

under the current [George W. Bush] administration, that favoritism has become extreme and relentless. From tax cuts that favor the rich to bankruptcy "reform" that punishes the unlucky, almost every domestic policy seems intended to accelerate our march back to the robber baron era.[61]

While economists have spent a good deal of scholarly energy describing and attempting to explain the striking escalation of economic inequality in the United States over the past 40 years, they have paid remarkably little attention to social and political factors of the sort cited by Krugman. For example, one comprehensive summary of the complex literature on earnings inequality attempted to ascertain "what shifts in demand, shifts in supply, and/or changes in wage setting institutions are responsible for the observed trend?" The authors pointed to "the entry into the labor market of the well educated baby boom generation" and "a long-term trend toward increasing relative demand for highly skilled workers" as important causal factors. Their closest approach to a political explanation was a passing reference to a finding that "the 25 percent decline in the value of the minimum wage between 1980 and 1988 accounts for a small part of the drop in the relative wages of dropouts during the 1980s."[62]

It probably should not be surprising, in light of their scholarly expertise and interests, that economists have tended to focus much less attention on potential *political* explanations for escalating economic inequality than on potential *economic* explanations. In a presidential address to the Royal Economic Society, British economist Anthony Atkinson criticized his colleagues' tendency to ignore or downplay the impact on the income distribution of social and political factors, arguing that "we need to go beyond purely economic explanations and to look for an explanation in the theory of public choice, or 'political economy.' We have to study the behaviour of the government, or its agencies, in determining the level and coverage of state benefits."

Atkinson went on to criticize economists who *have* considered political factors for their uncritical reliance on the rather mechanical assumption that government policy responds directly to the economic interests of the so-called median voter—the ideological centrist whose vote should be pivotal in any collective decision arrived at, directly or indirectly, by majority rule. He urged them to go beyond this simple framework to gauge the extent to

---

[61] Paul Krugman, "Losing Our Country," *New York Times*, June 10, 2005.

[62] Levy and Murnane (1992, 1335, 1336, 1363–1364). Other prominent examples of economic analyses of wage inequality include Blank and Blinder (1986); Cutler and Katz (1991); and Hines, Hoynes, and Krueger (2001). A 2007 paper by Frank Levy and Peter Temin provided a richer institutional account, concluding that "only a reorientation of government policy can restore the general prosperity of the postwar boom, can recreate a more equitable distribution of productivity gains where a rising tide lifts all boats" (41).

which redistributive policies are shaped "by the ideology or preferences of political parties, or by political pressure from different interest groups, or by bureaucratic control of civil servants or agencies."[63]

Atkinson's criticism seems apt, since political economists wedded to the familiar majoritarian model have remarkable difficulty even in explaining why the numerous poor in democratic political systems do not expropriate the much less numerous wealthy. If taxes are proportional to income and government benefits are distributed equally, for example, everyone with below-average income—a clear majority of the electorate in any democratic political system with enough capitalism to generate a wealthy class—has an economic incentive to favor a tax rate of 100%.[64] Even if redistribution entails some waste, most people should favor some redistribution, and poorer people should prefer more. Furthermore, increases in economic inequality should result in higher taxes and more redistribution.[65]

Of course, the reality is that very few people—even very few poor people—favor aggressive redistribution of the sort implied by these simple economic models. Nor is aggressive redistribution anywhere in sight. Writing more than three decades ago, before most of the substantial increase in economic inequality documented in figures 1.1 and 1.3, Dahl noted that, "after half a century of the American welfare state . . . the after-tax distribution of wealth and income remains highly unequal."[66] Now, after more than 80 years of an expanding American welfare state, the distributions of wealth and income are even more unequal than they were when Dahl wrote. Moreover, systematic analyses suggest that the extent of economic inequality has little impact on the extent of redistribution, either across nations or within the United States.[67] Certainly, recent American experience amply demonstrates that escalating economic inequality need not prevent the adoption of major policy initiatives further advantaging the wealthy over the middle class and poor. The massive tax cuts of the Bush era, whose gains went mostly to people near the top of the income distribution, are a dramatic case in point.[68]

---

[63] Atkinson (1997, 315, 316). On the theoretical importance of the "median voter" in competitive elections, see Downs (1957).

[64] McCarty, Poole, and Rosenthal (2006, 124) calculated that the *average* income of American families in 2000 exceeded the *median* income (excluding non-citizens) by about 40%. Even if non-voters are excluded from the calculation of the median, the average income of all families exceeded the median income *of voters* by more than 20%.

[65] Meltzer and Richard (1981) provided an influential formalization of the political economy of redistribution. Recent applications and extensions include Roemer (1999) and McCarty, Poole, and Rosenthal (2006, chaps. 3 and 4).

[66] Dahl (1982, 172).

[67] Bénabou (1996); Perotti (1996); Rodriguez (1999; 2004).

[68] On the Bush tax cuts as a test of the responsiveness of the American political system to the policy preferences of the median voter, see Hacker and Pierson (2005a).

In the following pages, I explore these glaring disjunctions between the predictions of simple majoritarian models and actual patterns of policy-making in the United States over the past half-century. As Atkinson surmised, the gulf between theoretical expectations and reality turns out to have a great deal to do with "the ideology or preferences of political parties" and with "political pressure from different interest groups." For example, I find, in chapter 7, that although Americans have strongly and consistently favored raising the federal minimum wage, their elected representatives have allowed the real value of the minimum wage to decline by one-third since the late 1960s. Moreover, my analysis in chapter 8 shows that elected officials voting on a minimum wage increase paid no attention at all to the views of people poor enough to be directly affected by that policy change. My broader analysis indicates that this sort of unresponsiveness is no anomaly, but a very common pattern in American policy-making.

The gap between the predictions of conventional political-economic models and the actual workings of American democracy also reflects the profound difficulties faced by ordinary citizens in connecting specific policy proposals to their own values and interests. Economic analyses often take such connections for granted, but for many people in many policy domains they are misconstrued or simply missing. Egalitarian impulses often fail to get translated into policy because ordinary citizens do not grasp the policy implications of their egalitarian values. For example, I show in chapter 6 that almost two-thirds of the people who said the rich pay less than they should in taxes nevertheless favored repealing the federal estate tax—a tax that affected only the richest 1–2% of taxpayers at the time and affects many fewer now. Any serious attempt to understand the political economy of the New Gilded Age requires grappling with the political psychology of American voters and with the real limitations of public opinion as a basis for democratic policy-making.

Escalating economic inequality poses a crucial challenge to America's democratic ideals. The nature of that challenge has been nicely captured by Michael Kinsley: "According to our founding document and our national myth, we are all created equal and then it's up to us. Inequality in material things is mitigated in two ways: first, by equal opportunity at the start, and, second, by full civic equality despite material differences. We don't claim to have achieved all this, but these are our national goals and we are always moving toward them."[69]

It is a nice sentiment—but is it true? As we will see in the following pages, the evidence is far from reassuring.

---

[69] Michael Kinsley, "Mobility vs. Nobility," *Washington Post*, June 5, 2005.

CHAPTER 2

The Partisan Political Economy

> . . . as our economy grows, market forces work to provide
> the greatest rewards to those with the needed skills in the
> growth areas. . . . This trend . . . is simply an economic re-
> ality, and it is neither fair nor useful to blame any political
> party.
>
> —*Treasury Secretary Henry Paulson, 2006*[1]

SECRETARY PAULSON'S ATTRIBUTION of increasing economic inequality to impersonal "market forces" was politically convenient in light of his prominent position in the Bush administration, which presided over booming corporate profits but stagnant wages for most working people. Nonetheless, his perspective is symptomatic of a much broader tendency to think of the economy as a natural system existing prior to, and largely separate from, the political sphere.

In the run-up to the 2004 presidential election, for example, the Associated Press (AP) reported that, "over two decades, the income gap has steadily increased between the richest Americans, who own homes and stocks and got big tax breaks, and those at the middle and bottom of the pay scale, whose paychecks buy less." While the AP story noted that Democratic presidential candidate John Kerry was attempting to make the economy a campaign issue, the last word went to the chief economist for Wells Fargo: "This really has nothing to do with Bush or Kerry, but more to do with the longer-term shift in the structure of the economy." Similarly, in the run-up to the 2006 midterm election business columnist Ben Stein noted that "there is extreme income inequality in this country. It is hard to say whether it's the fault of President Bush, since there was also extreme income inequality

---

[1] Remarks prepared for delivery by Treasury Secretary Henry H. Paulson at Columbia University, August 1, 2006.

under former President Bill Clinton, and in fact there has always been extreme income inequality."[2]

The tendency to think of economic outcomes as natural and inevitable is politically significant because it discourages critical scrutiny of their causes and consequences. If escalating inequality is "simply an economic reality," it may seem pointless to spend too much energy worrying about how and why it arises. Moreover, if "there has always been extreme income inequality" under Republicans and Democrats alike, it may seem pointless to hope that public policies might mitigate that inequality. As prominent policy analyst Lawrence Mead rather breezily put it, in a response to the report of the American Political Science Association's Task Force on Inequality and American Democracy cited in chapter 1, "The causes [of growing economic inequality] are not well understood and have little tie to government."[3]

My aim in this chapter is to refute the notion that the causes of economic inequality in contemporary America "have little tie to government." Indeed, I suggest that the narrowly economic focus of most previous studies of inequality has caused them to miss what may be the most important single influence on the changing U.S. income distribution in the postwar era—the contrasting policy choices of Democratic and Republican presidents. Under Republican administrations, real income growth for lower- and middle-income families has consistently lagged well behind the income growth rate for the rich—and well behind the income growth rate for the lower and middle classes themselves under Democratic administrations.

In addition to documenting these substantial partisan disparities in income growth, the analyses presented in this chapter address a variety of potential explanations for them. I show that the dramatic differences in patterns of income growth under Democratic and Republican presidents are quite unlikely to have occurred by chance; nor can they be attributed to oil price shocks or changes in the structure of the labor force or other purely economic factors, or to cyclical corrections by each party of the other party's policy excesses. Rather, they seem to reflect consistent differences in policies and priorities between Democratic and Republican administrations. The cumulative effect of these partisan differences has been enormous. My projections based on the historical performance of Democratic and Republican presidents suggest that income inequality would have been no greater in 2014 than it was in the late 1940s had the patterns of income growth characteristic of Democratic administrations operated throughout that period. Conversely, continuous application of the patterns of income growth

---

[2] Associated Press, "Gap Between the Rich, Others Grows," *Trenton Times*, August 17, 2004; Ben Stein, "You Can Complain, or You Can Make Money," *New York Times*, October 15, 2006.

[3] Mead (2004, 671).

observed during periods of Republican control would have produced a much greater divergence in the economic fortunes of rich and poor people than we have actually experienced—a Platinum-Gilded Age.

PARTISAN PATTERNS OF INCOME GROWTH

As suggested in chapter 1, economists have generally paid only perfunctory attention to potential *political* explanations for increasing economic inequality in contemporary America. They have paid even less attention to *partisan* political explanations—perhaps because marked partisan differences in economic outcomes are difficult to account for within the framework of standard economic models. While political economists have documented consistent partisan differences in economic policy, they have seldom focused on the implications of those differences for income inequality or for the specific economic fortunes of people in different parts of the income distribution.[4]

The most notable exception to this pattern of neglect is the work of Douglas Hibbs, who produced pioneering studies of the impact of partisan politics on a variety of macroeconomic outcomes, including the money supply, unemployment, real output, and income inequality. Using data from 1948 through 1978 (before most of the substantial increase in income inequality documented in chapter 1), Hibbs found that the ratio of the share of post-tax income received by the top 20% of the income distribution to the share received by the bottom 40% declined during periods of Democratic control but increased during periods of Republican control. Applying these estimates to his entire period, Hibbs concluded that inequality declined markedly (by a total of about 25%) during the 14 years of Democratic control covered by his analysis, while remaining essentially unchanged during the 17 years of Republican control. Hibbs and Christopher Dennis extended this analysis through the early 1980s and embedded it in a somewhat broader analysis of partisan differences in macroeconomic policy.[5]

The analysis presented in this chapter extends Hibbs and Dennis's analyses in a variety of ways—most notably by incorporating decades of additional historical experience, including most of the period of escalating inequality described in chapter 1. My focus is on partisan patterns of real income growth for affluent, middle-class, and working poor families. I employ the tabulations from the U.S. Census Bureau's Historical Income Tables introduced in chapter 1 to examine year-to-year changes in real pre-tax

---

[4] Hibbs (1977; 1987); Keech (1980); Beck (1982); Alesina and Sachs (1988).
[5] Hibbs (1987, 232–243); Hibbs and Dennis (1988).

TABLE 2.1

Real Income Growth Rates by Income Level
and Presidential Partisanship, 1948–2014

Average annual real pre-tax income growth (%) for families at various points in
the income distribution (with standard errors in parentheses). Partisan control
measured from one year following inauguration to one year following subsequent
inauguration.

	All presidents	*Democratic presidents*	*Republican presidents*	*Partisan difference*
20th percentile	1.02 (.44)	1.98 (.68)	.20 (.56)	+1.78 (.87)
40th percentile	1.19 (.35)	1.91 (.51)	.57 (.46)	+1.34 (.68)
60th percentile	1.40 (.31)	1.98 (.46)	.90 (.41)	+1.08 (.62)
80th percentile	1.55 (.29)	1.99 (.44)	1.17 (.39)	+.82 (.59)
95th percentile	1.68 (.34)	1.77 (.55)	1.60 (.42)	+.17 (.68)
N	67	31	36	67

Source: Census Bureau, Historical Income Tables.

income for families at the 20th, 40th, 60th, 80th, and 95th percentiles of the
income distribution from 1948 through 2014.[6]

It will not be surprising, in light of the discussion in chapter 1, that the
average rate of real income growth during this period was higher for affluent families than for those lower in the income distribution. These average growth rates, which appear in the first column of table 2.1, range
from 1.7% for families at the 95th percentile down to 1.0% for families at
the 20th percentile. What may be surprising is that this pattern of differential growth is entirely limited to periods in which Republicans controlled
the White House. The second and third columns of table 2.1 present separate tabulations of real income growth during Democratic and Republican administrations, respectively. Under Democratic presidents, poor and

---

[6] Here and elsewhere, I compute percentage changes as $100 \times ln(Y_t/Y_{t-1})$. The natural log-
arithm converts income gains and losses to an equivalent scale and allows for additive accumulation over multiple time periods. The log of the ratio of this year's income to last year's
income is approximately equal to the fractional change (when the change is not too large), and
multiplying it by 100 translates it into more intuitive percentage points.

middle-class families did slightly better than richer families (at least in proportional terms), producing a slight net decrease in income inequality. Under Republican presidents, however, rich families did vastly better than poorer families, producing a considerable net increase in income inequality.

Since it seems unreasonable to expect a new president to have an immediate impact on income growth in his first year in office, my measure of partisan control of the White House is lagged by one year. Thus, for example, income changes in 2009 are attributed to Republican George W. Bush, despite the fact that Democrat Barack Obama took office in January of that year. The assumption of a one-year lag in partisan policy effects is consistent with macroeconomic evidence regarding the timing of economic responses to monetary and fiscal policy changes; it also fits the observed data better than an assumption of no lag or of a two-, three-, four-, or five-year lag.[7]

Figure 2.1 provides a graphical representation of the patterns documented in the second and third columns of table 2.1. The starkly different patterns of income growth under Democratic and Republican administrations are very clear in the figure, and essentially linear over the entire range of family incomes represented in the figure (that is, for incomes ranging from about $30,000 to $230,000 in 2014). Affluent families have generally fared well regardless of which party controls the White House. However, the real incomes of middle-class families have increased more than twice as fast under Democratic presidents, while for working poor families, real income growth has been *ten times* as fast under Democrats as under Republicans.

If patterns of income growth have differed so dramatically under Democratic and Republican presidents, it seems natural to wonder whether similar differences might be attributable to Democratic and Republican members of Congress. Unfortunately, the historical pattern of change in the partisan composition of Congress in the postwar era makes it very hard to tell. With Democrats holding an uninterrupted majority in the House of Representatives from 1955 through 1994 and Republicans in control through most of the period since 1995, any effect of variation in the partisan composition of Congress is likely to be confounded with the effects of broader economic trends. Thus, although simple tabulations of income growth levels suggest that they have generally been higher when Congress has been more Democratic, those differences cannot be considered dispositive.[8]

---

[7] Christiano, Eichenbaum, and Evans (1999); Blanchard and Perotti (2002). I have investigated the statistical fit of alternative lags by replicating the analysis presented in table 2.2 using current (unlagged) presidential partisanship, as well as presidential partisanship lagged by two, three, four, or five years. In every case the resulting regression model fits the data less well (by 2.2% to 3.9%) than the model with presidential partisanship lagged by one year.

[8] Adding a measure of the average proportion of Democrats in the House and Senate to the statistical analyses reported in table 2.1 suggests that real income growth at all income levels was probably higher at times when there were more Democrats in Congress. The difference in

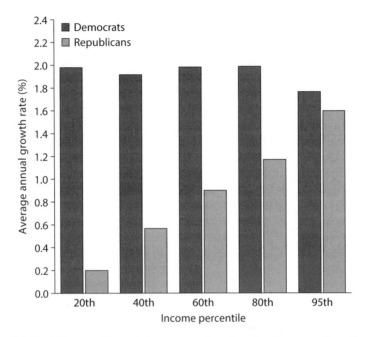

FIGURE 2.1 Real Income Growth by Income Level under Democratic and Republican Presidents, 1948–2014

A PARTISAN COINCIDENCE?

The partisan differences in characteristic rates of income growth documented in figure 2.1 would seem to be of immense economic and political significance—if they are real. They suggest that middle-class and working poor families in the postwar era have routinely fared much worse under Republican presidents than they have under Democratic presidents. By this accounting, economic inequality in contemporary America is profoundly shaped by partisan politics.

But to what extent are these patterns really attributable to partisan politics rather than to accidental historical factors? One way to address this question is to examine their consistency across a range of presidents and

expected income growth for working poor families between the largest Democratic and Republican congressional majorities on record amounts to 2.5 percentage points (with a t-statistic of 1.6), while the apparent effect of Democratic presidents is reduced by about 9%. However, unlike the differences in growth patterns under Democratic and Republican presidents, these differences in growth patterns under Democratic and Republican Congresses disappear in a more elaborate statistical analysis paralleling the one reported in table 2.2.

circumstances. Additional analyses focusing on various subsets of the 67-year period only reinforce the conclusion that partisan politics plays an important role in modern economic inequality. For example, substantial partisan differences appear even if any one or two administrations are omitted from the comparison,[9] if years with unusually high or low growth are ignored,[10] or if presidential election years or partisan transition years are excluded.[11] In each of these analyses, the overall pattern of partisan differences in income growth is qualitatively similar to the pattern shown in figure 2.1.

The notion that these partisan differences in income growth reflect conscious policy choices on the part of Republican and Democratic presidents is reinforced by a more detailed analysis of their political timing. Alberto Alesina has noted that Democratic and Republican administrations are characterized by distinct cycles of economic growth, with expansion in the second year of a Democratic president's term typically followed by slower growth in the third and fourth years, and contraction in the second year of a Republican president's term typically followed by more robust growth in the third and fourth years.[12] These cycles are unsurprising in light of the fact that presidents tend to be most popular and have their greatest influence over policy in the first year of each administration—the "honeymoon" period immediately following election or reelection.[13] The effects of that influence are felt one year later, in the second year of each four-year term.

The political economic cycle identified by Alesina appears conspicuously in data on growth rates in real GDP per capita over the entire postwar era. In the second year of each four-year cycle, Democrats presided over average GDP growth of 3.7%, while Republicans presided over average growth of –0.5%.[14] By contrast, average GDP growth rates in the third and fourth years of each president's term and the first year of the subsequent term were virtually identical: 2.2% for Democrats versus 2.1% for Republicans.

---

[9] Omitting each of the 12 postwar presidents in turn from the comparison reported in table 2.1 produces estimates of the partisan difference in income growth at the 20th percentile ranging from 1.10 (with a t-statistic of 1.2), omitting Lyndon Johnson, to 2.28 (with a t-statistic of 2.8), omitting Dwight Eisenhower.

[10] Excluding 24 years in which real income growth at the 20th percentile was greater than 5% or less than –2% produces a partisan difference of 1.28 (with a t-statistic of 2.5).

[11] The partisan difference in income growth at the 20th percentile excluding presidential election years is 2.46 (with a t-statistic of 2.5). The corresponding estimate in a model excluding partisan transition years (1953, 1961, 1969, 1977, 1981, 1993, 2001, and 2009) is 1.83 (with a t-statistic of 1.9).

[12] Alesina (1988); Alesina and Rosenthal (1989); Alesina, Londregan, and Rosenthal (1993).

[13] Mueller (1973); Light (1999).

[14] The t-statistic for this difference is 4.6, indicating that it is extremely unlikely to be due to chance. The t-statistics for the partisan differences in income growth in honeymoon years in figure 2.2 are 2.6, 3.6, 3.6, 3.5, and 2.4, respectively, for families at the 20th, 40th, 60th, 80th, and 95th percentiles of the income distribution.

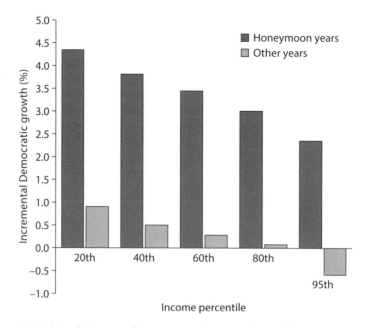

Figure 2.2 Political Timing of Democratic Income Growth Premium, 1948–2014

Alesina's political economic cycle also appears clearly in income growth rates for families in every part of the income distribution. Figure 2.2 compares the differences in average income growth rates at each income level under Democratic and Republican presidents in their second ("honeymoon") years and in the following three years. The largest partisan differences by far appear in the second year of each administration—the first year in which a new or newly reelected president's policies could be expected to have a significant economic effect. Democratic presidents in those years presided over average real income growth for working poor families of 3.3%, while the corresponding average growth rate under Republican presidents was –1.0%—a remarkable partisan difference of 4.3 percentage points. The corresponding partisan differences in income growth for middle-class and affluent families were also substantial, ranging from 3.8 percentage points at the 40th percentile down to 2.4 percentage points at the 95th percentile.

By comparison, partisan differences in income growth in other years were much more muted, ranging from an additional 0.9 percentage points under Democratic presidents for families at the 20th percentile of the income distribution to an additional 0.6 percentage points under Republican presidents for families at the 95th percentile. (None of these differences in non-honeymoon years is large enough to be statistically reliable.)

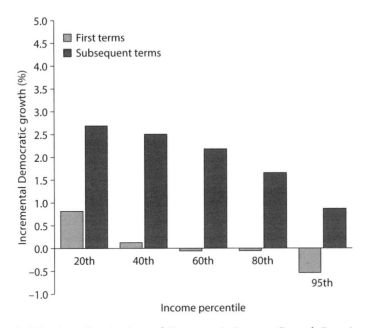

FIGURE 2.3 Partisan Continuity and Democratic Income Growth Premium, 1948–2014

The dramatic differences in output and income growth associated with Democratic and Republican "honeymoon" periods strongly suggest that presidents in the post-Keynesian era have had a significant impact on the economy. At the point in the electoral cycle when presidents are most politically influential, Democratic presidents have generally presided over vibrant economic expansions producing income growth for families in every part of the income distribution; in contrast, Republicans have generally presided over economic contractions and declining incomes for middle-class and working poor families. The surprisingly consistent political timing of these partisan differences in output and income growth seems very hard to square with the notion that they simply reflect the working of apolitical market forces.

It may be tempting to suppose that these very different patterns of income growth under Democratic and Republican presidents reflect a cycle of partisan equilibration in which Democrats pursue expansionary policies in reaction to Republican contractions and Republicans produce contractions as an antidote to Democratic expansions. However, the timing of partisan differences in income growth strongly contradicts that notion. Figure 2.3 shows the magnitude of the Democratic growth premium at each income level separately for terms in which the president was of the opposite party as his predecessor (denoted by lighter bars) and those in which the president succeeded himself or a member of his own party (denoted by darker bars).

If slow growth for middle-class and poor families under Republican presidents represented a hangover from unsustainable expansion under Democratic presidents, and vice versa, we would expect to see the greatest partisan differences in administrations where Republicans succeeded Democrats or Democrats succeeded Republicans. However, the actual pattern is exactly the opposite: the partisan differences in average growth rates at every income level are much larger in terms with no partisan turnover than they are in the first terms of new partisan regimes. Democratic presidents have generally presided over similar income growth rates for families in every part of the income distribution, regardless of whether they were in their first or subsequent terms, but average income growth has been consistently higher (by from 1.1 to 1.7 percentage points) when Democrats succeeded Democrats than when Democrats replaced Republicans. Conversely, average income growth has been consistently *lower* (by 0.3 to 0.8 percentage points) when Republicans succeeded Republicans than when Republicans replaced Democrats.[15]

James Campbell has argued that partisan differences in income growth are "artifacts of the conditions under which the two parties have assumed the presidency." However, it is hard to see how that could be the case when the differences are concentrated in terms in which the president's party has already been in office for at least four years. Real GDP growth in second and subsequent terms averaged 2.8% under Democratic presidents but only 1.0% under Republican presidents. Real income growth for working poor families averaged 2.6% under Democrats but –0.1% under Republicans. In both cases these partisan differences were largest in honeymoon years, suggesting once again that they reflect systematic differences in the policies pursued by newly reelected Democratic and Republican presidents rather than "legacies" or sheer luck.[16]

---

[15] The *t*-statistics for the partisan differences in income growth in second and subsequent terms in figure 2.3 are 2.3, 2.6, 2.5, 1.9, and 0.8.

[16] Campbell (2011, 23). The legacy effects identified by Campbell hinge on the assumption that changes in economic output in the third and fourth quarters of a new president's term are attributable to the policies of the outgoing president. Thus, for example, George W. Bush gets credit for the fact that output grew in 2010 on the grounds that it began to grow in the second half of 2009 (after falling by more than 5% over the preceding year). Even on that assumption, only one of the recessions "inherited" by a Republican president from a Democratic predecessor (Eisenhower's in 1953) reduced real output by as much as 1%—much too small a "legacy" to matter for the broad comparisons presented here. Campbell's conclusion that "there are no significant differences between the presidential parties" rests on the further odd assumption that only growth in the second half of each year affects subsequent economic outcomes, as well as on a failure to account for the fact that growth in the second half of each year is itself, in part, a result of partisan policies. A properly specified model of quarterly

Income growth was also more unequal in Republican administrations with no partisan turnover than it was under first-term Republican presidents. For affluent families, average income growth under Republican presidents fell from 1.8% in first terms to 1.5% in subsequent terms. For working poor families, the corresponding decline was from 0.6% to –0.1%. Thus, the gap in economic fortunes between the affluent and the poor widened faster the longer Republicans held the White House. Here, too, it seems very hard to interpret the Republican record as somehow reflecting the legacy effects of misguided policies inherited from Democratic predecessors.

Another way to gauge the robustness of the partisan differences in income growth presented in figure 2.1 is to consider a variety of potential non-political explanations for those differences. Perhaps Republican presidents have just been unlucky in occupying the White House at times when powerful external forces depressed income growth for middle-class and poor families. In order to explore this possibility, table 2.2 presents the results of a series of parallel statistical analyses relating each year's real income growth at each income level to a variety of potentially relevant economic and social conditions. The estimated effects of partisan control in these analyses represent the difference in average income growth under Democratic and Republican presidents for families at each income level, net of any differences attributable to historical trends or current economic circumstances.[17]

One economic circumstance of particular significance for income growth rates is the real price of oil—perhaps the most volatile and economically important commodity in modern industrial economies. Since major oil price shocks are largely outside the control of presidents, it would be misleading to attribute income changes associated with those shocks to partisan politics. As it turns out, however, fluctuations in oil prices have had little impact on income *inequality*; the statistical results presented in table 2.2 suggest

---

economic growth produces little evidence of "legacy" effects and suggests that average annual growth rates have been more than half a percentage point higher under Democratic presidents than under Republicans (Achen and Bartels 2016, chap. 6). Alternatively, simply focusing on second and subsequent terms (to avoid any possible bias due to "legacy" effects) shows that average GDP growth was 1.8 percentage points higher under Democratic presidents (with a *t*-statistic of 2.3) and 4.0 percentage points higher under Democratic presidents in honeymoon years (with a *t*-statistic of 2.8).

[17] The seemingly unrelated regression (SUR) estimator (Zellner 1962) exploits cross-equation correlations of the regression disturbances to produce more efficient parameter estimates than with ordinary least squares (OLS) regression. Not surprisingly, the residuals from the parallel regression models considered here are strongly correlated, reflecting the extent to which economic shocks affect families at all income levels in similar ways. The ten cross-equation correlations range from .30 to .91, with an average value of .69. As a result, some of the SUR parameter estimates reported in table 2.2 are a good deal more precise than the corresponding OLS parameter estimates.

TABLE 2.2

Statistical Analysis of Income Growth, 1949–2014

Annual real pre-tax income growth (%) for families at various points in the income distribution. Parameter estimates from seemingly unrelated regression models (with standard errors in parentheses). Partisan control measured from one year following inauguration to one year following subsequent inauguration. "Linear trend" and "quadratic trend" reflect cumulative change from 1948 through 2014.

	20th percentile	40th percentile	60th percentile	80th percentile	95th percentile
Democratic president	2.08 (.72)	1.37 (.51)	1.29 (.48)	1.07 (.47)	.49 (.57)
Oil prices (lagged %Δ)	−.0275 (.0175)	−.0311 (.0125)	−.0353 (.0119)	−.0274 (.0115)	−.0317 (.0140)
Labor force participation (Δ%)	4.47 (1.29)	4.32 (.93)	2.97 (.88)	2.73 (.85)	3.24 (1.03)
Lagged growth	−.226 (.082)	−.268 (.069)	−.304 (.071)	−.374 (.084)	−.007 (.110)
Lagged 95th percentile	.455 (.146)	.305 (.108)	.263 (.102)	.298 (.105)	—
Linear trend	−15.10 (5.71)	−16.69 (4.12)	−12.15 (3.88)	−9.35 (3.73)	−6.54 (4.55)
Quadratic trend	12.68 (5.77)	13.87 (4.15)	8.97 (3.91)	6.80 (3.77)	5.42 (4.60)
Intercept	2.76 (1.22)	3.97 (.88)	3.87 (.84)	3.56 (.80)	2.92 (.97)
Standard error of regression	2.82	1.99	1.89	1.85	2.23
Adjusted R²	.39	.51	.44	.35	.28
N	66	66	66	66	66

Source: Census Bureau, Historical Income Tables.

that a 50% increase in the real price of oil would reduce the real incomes of families at every income level by about 1.5 percentage points.[18]

Income growth rates are also sensitive to changes in labor force participation, since adding another family member to the workforce is likely to

[18] Annual percentage changes in the real price of oil are derived from monthly spot prices (for West Texas Intermediate) compiled by Dow Jones & Company and published by the Federal Reserve Bank of St. Louis (http://research.stlouisfed.org/fred2/series/OILPRICE/).

produce a significant increase in family income. The proportion of adults in the labor force increased from 59% in the early 1960s to 67% at the turn of the 21st century, largely owing to an increase in the number of working women. The statistical results presented in table 2.2 indicate that this increase significantly bolstered the incomes of American families, especially those in the bottom half of the income distribution. The subsequent ebbing of labor force participation (to 63% of the working-age population in 2014) erased about half of those gains.[19]

The price of oil and the increasing participation of women in the labor force are just two of a great many economic and social forces beyond the control of presidents that might be expected to affect the American economy and, perhaps, patterns of income inequality. For example, college education is much more common today than it was at the end of World War II, immigrants and the elderly make up larger shares of the population, the average size of families has become smaller, and imports constitute a larger share of the economy than they once did. Any or all of these changes may have contributed to changing patterns of income growth over the past sixty-six years. However, because these long-term trends have been so glacial, and so intertwined, it is very difficult to discern their distinct effects on the shape of the income distribution.[20]

Fortunately, from the standpoint of *political* analysis, the very fact that these social and economic trends have been gradual and fairly steady implies that their effects are unlikely to be confounded with the effects of alterations in control of the White House, which occur episodically and have produced only a very slight increase over time in the frequency of Republican governance.[21] Thus, rather than attempting to pinpoint specifically how these and other long-term trends have affected patterns of income growth, I simply allow for the possibility that expected income growth rates have gradually changed over the period covered by my analysis. Given the crudeness of this strategy for capturing long-term trends in income growth, it is important to note that the apparent effects of presidential partisanship are insensitive to a variety of alternative strategies for taking account of secular changes in the structure of the American

---

[19] My measure of labor force participation is the annual change in the percentage of non-institutionalized civilians over the age of 15 who are employed or seeking work, as tabulated by the Bureau of Labor Statistics (http://data.bls.gov/timeseries/LNS11300000).

[20] Annual levels of labor force participation, college education, immigration, elderly population, family size, and imports as a share of GDP are all highly correlated with each other and with my simple linear trend variable.

[21] The correlation between time and partisan control of the White House over the period covered by my analysis is only .06. The correlations between partisan control of the White House and the various social and economic indicators mentioned in the text range from weak to non-existent.

economy and society. The statistical evidence for a partisan political effect turns out to be surprisingly robust in this respect.[22]

The estimated effects associated with the linear and quadratic trend terms in table 2.2 imply that the average rate of real income growth for families below the 95th percentile has declined by almost half a percentage point per decade over the postwar era. However, the negative trend in income growth was much milder for families near the top of the income distribution—less than one-fourth of a percentage point per decade.[23] In this respect, among others, there is a fairly striking disconnection between the pattern of income growth for families at the 95th percentile and the pattern for less affluent families. Income growth at the 95th percentile was also virtually unrelated to growth in the previous year and was relatively unaffected by presidential partisanship. Thus, the most affluent families represented in the Census Bureau's tabulations have been surprisingly insulated from the structural shifts in the U.S. economy that have eroded income growth among less affluent families over the past 65 years, and they have fared very well regardless of which party controls the White House.

Income growth among these affluent families does seem to have spurred significant subsequent income growth among middle-class and, especially, working poor families. This "trickle-down" phenomenon is reflected in the positive effects of the previous year's growth rate for families at the 95th percentile on current growth for families at lower income levels in table 2.2. Conversely, current growth for families at each income level was negatively related to the previous year's growth rate at the same income level, suggesting some tendency toward equilibration (with growth spurts in one year leading to slumps the following year, and vice versa), or perhaps some measurement error in the year-by-year growth rates derived from the Census Bureau's Current Population Surveys.

Despite the constellation of alternative explanatory factors represented in table 2.2, the impact of presidential partisanship emerges clearly in

---

[22] The regression models presented in table 2.2 include linear and quadratic trend terms intended to capture change in expected growth rates over time. Adding a cubic trend term reduces the estimated impact of presidential partisanship by less than 1%. Replacing the linear and quadratic trend terms with an indicator variable for the period after 1973 or after 1981 increases the apparent impact of presidential partisanship on income growth rates by 9–10%. Including additional social and economic trend variables, singly or in combination, also produces generally similar patterns of estimated partisan effects.

[23] My time trend variable runs from zero in 1948 to one in 2014. Thus, the total decline in annual income growth rates at each income level over the entire period covered by my analysis is captured by the sum of the "linear trend" and "quadratic trend" coefficients in the corresponding column of table 2.2. The implied cumulative declines in average income growth rates over 66 years, holding other factors constant, are 2.4, 2.8, 3.2, 2.6, and 1.1 percentage points, respectively, for families at the 20th, 40th, 60th, 80th, and 95th percentiles of the income distribution.

these analyses. Indeed, the partisan differences in growth rates reported in table 2.2 are, if anything, somewhat larger in magnitude than those reported in table 2.1, ranging from 2.1 percentage points at the 20th percentile down to 0.5 percentage points at the 95th percentile of the family income distribution. They are also more precisely estimated than in table 2.1, making it even more unlikely that they are due simply to chance (except for the most affluent families, who may plausibly have fared as well under Republican presidents as they did under Democrats, other things being equal).[24] These statistical results provide strong evidence that the striking differences in the economic fortunes of middle-class and working poor families under Democratic and Republican administrations are not an artifact of the different conditions under which Democrats and Republicans have happened to hold the reins of government, but a reflection of the fundamental significance of partisan politics in the political economy of the postwar United States.

Finally, it is worth noting that the partisan pattern of postwar income growth is not limited to the United States. Stuart Soroka and Christopher Wlezien calculated that over a 50-year period, income inequality in the United Kingdom (as measured by the Gini coefficient) increased substantially (by an average of .05 per decade) under Conservative governments but remained essentially constant (increasing by just .0004 per decade) under Labour governments. According to a report by the Institute for Fiscal Studies, "income inequality rose substantially during the 1980s" under Conservative Margaret Thatcher (as it did under Republican Ronald Reagan). However, inequality continued to increase under Thatcher's Conservative successor, John Major, (while the real incomes of working poor families in the United States increased by more than 15% under Democratic president Bill Clinton). Conversely, the increase in inequality in Britain was slowed substantially and poverty declined under the Labour government of Tony Blair (while the real incomes of working poor families in the United States fell by more than 7% under Republican George W. Bush). The report noted that the Labour government instituted a variety of major policy initiatives aimed at mitigating inequality, including a national minimum wage (1999), an education maintenance allowance (2004), increased maternity and paternity leave for working families (2006), and a new employment support allowance (2008). It concluded that these changes "have benefitted the poor more than the rich," whereas the "direct tax and benefit changes made by the previous Conservative governments acted to increase income inequality."[25]

[24] The *t*-statistics for partisan differences in income growth range from 2.9 at the 20th percentile down to 2.3 at the 80th percentile.

[25] Soroka and Wlezien (2014, 110); Brewer et al. (2009).

Partisan Differences in Macroeconomic Policy

Probing the remarkable partisan differences in patterns of income growth in the postwar era provides good reasons to think that these differences are real, not a historical coincidence or a statistical illusion. But how do Democratic and Republican presidents actually *produce* such strikingly different patterns of income growth?

One important source of partisan differences in income growth is that Democratic and Republican presidents have consistently pursued rather different economic policies. That claim would hardly be surprising to students of comparative politics. As Edward Tufte wrote, summarizing cross-national research through the mid-1970s, "Party platforms and political ideology set priorities and help decide policy. The consequence is that the governing political party is very much responsible for major macroeconomic outcomes—unemployment rates, inflation rates, income equalization, and the size and rate of expansion of the government budget."[26] In the United States, however, at least until recently, many observers have described the Democratic and Republican Parties as more similar than distinct, implicitly accepting George Wallace's claim that there is "not a dime's worth of difference" between them.

In this section I sketch some consistent partisan differences in key policy areas in the postwar era and provide some examples of contrasting Democratic and Republican policies that seem likely to have mitigated or exacerbated economic inequality. The case studies presented in chapters 5 through 9, though still far from comprehensive, are intended to supplement this brief overview with more detailed examinations of partisan politics in some especially important domains—tax policy, minimum wage policy, and responses to the Great Recession.

In the United States, as in many other industrial democracies, differences in the class composition of the parties' respective supporting coalitions have encouraged them to adopt distinctive macroeconomic priorities. Douglas Hibbs, writing in the mid-1980s, summarized these distinctive priorities simply and forcefully: "Democratic administrations are more likely than Republican ones to run the risk of higher inflation rates in order to pursue expansive policies designed to yield lower unemployment and extra growth." Hibbs added that "six of the seven recessions experienced since the Treasury–Federal Reserve Accord of 1951, which made possible activist monetary policies coordinated with fiscal policies, occurred during Republican administrations. Every one of these contractions was either intentionally created or passively accepted, at least for a while, in order to fight inflation."[27]

---

[26] Tufte (1978, 104). Carles Boix (1998) and Evelyne Huber and John Stephens (2001) have provided more recent and detailed analyses of partisan differences in economic and social welfare policies in affluent democracies.

[27] Hibbs (1987, 218).

The testimony of policy-makers, both contemporary and retrospective, provides ample evidence of important differences in economic philosophies and priorities between Republican and Democratic administrations. For example, Tufte noted that "the Eisenhower administration memoirs, fiscal histories, and diaries . . . bristle with determined statements on the need to avoid inflation and reduce the federal budget. Stimulative interventionist policies by the government were to be avoided because they ultimately stifled creative business initiative and because they served little purpose, since economic downturns and unemployment were seen as self-curing."[28]

In stark contrast, within weeks of John Kennedy's inauguration, the new Democratic administration was being bombarded with pleas from a future Nobel laureate, Paul Samuelson, for stimulative interventionist policies: "WHAT THIS COUNTRY NEEDS IS AN ACROSS THE BOARD RISE IN DISPOSABLE INCOME TO LOWER THE LEVEL OF UNEMPLOYMENT, SPEED UP THE RECOVERY AND THE RETURN TO HEALTHY GROWTH, PROMOTE CAPITAL FORMATION AND THE GENERAL WELFARE, INSURE DOMESTIC TRANQUILITY AND THE TRIUMPH OF THE DEMOCRATIC PARTY AT THE POLLS."[29]

Two more future Nobel laureates, James Tobin and Robert Solow, were among the key members of Kennedy's economic policy-making team who drafted the administration's blueprint for economic recovery, a report by the Council of Economic Advisers entitled "The American Economy in 1961: Problems and Policies." In their diagnosis, "the real challenge of economic policy in the months ahead" was to absorb some $50 billion in slack economic capacity. To that end, Kennedy had already "proposed programs in education, health, natural resources and highways, which, while fully justified on their own merits, promise additional benefit in the form of speedier recovery." If more stimulation proved necessary, "a further program for economic recovery might consider a speed-up in Government construction and related projects, an expansion of housing programs, and tax reduction."[30]

Income growth under Kennedy was substantially stronger than it had been under Eisenhower for middle-class and working poor families, although affluent families fared less well.[31] Kennedy's successor, Lyndon Johnson, presided over five years of extraordinarily rapid, broad-based income growth. From 1964 through 1969, the real incomes of families from the 40th percentile to the 95th percentile of the income distribution grew by

---

[28] Tufte (1978, 17).

[29] Paul Samuelson, "Memorandum for the President and the Council of Economic Advisers: That 'April Second Look' at the Economy," March 21, 1961, John F. Kennedy Presidential Library, quoted in Tufte (1978, 7).

[30] Tobin and Weidenbaum (1988, 54, 46, 48–49).

[31] The average real income growth rate for families at the 20th percentile of the income distribution increased from 1.9% under Eisenhower to 3.7% under Kennedy. Middle-class incomes grew by 2.2% under Eisenhower and 3.2% under Kennedy, while the growth rate for families at the 95th percentile declined from 3.1% to 1.4%.

more than 4% per year. The real incomes of working poor families grew
even more rapidly, by 5.5% per year. That fact was at least partly attributable to a variety of new anti-poverty policies and programs implemented as
part of Johnson's "Great Society" initiative, including Medicare and Medicaid, Job Corps, food stamps, and the Community Action Program.

Johnson's successor, Richard Nixon, is sometimes viewed as a rather un-
conventional, non-ideological Republican president, at least in the realm of
domestic policy. However, the first few years of Nixon's presidency "fit the
stylized pattern of Republican economic priorities well: An orthodox policy of fiscal and monetary restraint was pursued to raise the rate of unemployment and contain the inflationary pressures inherited from the Johnson
administration." The result of these policies was also consistent with the
typical Republican pattern: the robust egalitarian income growth that had
persisted for five years under Johnson screeched to a halt in 1970, replaced
by slow growth for the affluent and sharp declines in income for the working
poor. Only in August 1971, with a reelection campaign on the horizon, did
Nixon launch a "New Economic Policy," which included "fiscal stimulation,
monetary expansion, a wage-price freeze, and a devaluation of the dollar."[32]

Nixon's New Economic Policy produced a booming economy in 1972,
with real income growth ranging from 4.5% for working poor families to
6.6% for families at the 95th percentile of the income distribution. This robust growth contributed significantly to Nixon's landslide reelection. However, income growth slowed considerably in 1973 and disappeared in 1974.
By the time Nixon resigned in disgrace in the wake of the Watergate scandal,
in August 1974, the country was sliding into a severe recession.

The recession of 1974–1975 was triggered by a massive oil price shock
engineered by the Organization of Petroleum Exporting Countries (OPEC).
The real price of oil increased by 140% in 1974, throwing the industrial
sector of the United States and other advanced economies into a tailspin.
Accidental president Gerald Ford entered the White House in the midst of a
major economic crisis not of his own making.

Although every president's economic performance is shaped by unpredictable and uncontrollable events, presidents' *responses* to those events
are often strongly colored by their partisan priorities and predispositions.
Given President Ford's conventional Main Street Republican background, it
is perhaps unsurprising that he "initially refused to respond" to the OPEC
price shock "with policies to restore aggregate demand," as most Democrats
would have done. Instead, he "launched the 'Whip Inflation Now' program
of fiscal and monetary restraint, which helped prolong the deep post-OPEC

---

[32] Hibbs (1987, 271). Real income growth rates in 1969 had ranged from 3.7% to 5.4%; in
1970 they declined monotonically from 1.8% for families at the 95th percentile of the income
distribution to –2.8% for families at the 20th percentile.

slump in employment and output through 1974 and into 1975. . . . Only after a long and sharp decline in real output did President Ford finally propose a one-year tax rebate in January 1975. The Democratic-dominated Congress passed the bill two and a half months later, after increasing the amount of the rebate substantially and redistributing it in favor of low-income and middle-income individuals."[33] Real incomes, which had declined significantly in 1975, rebounded in 1976—almost, but not quite, enough to get Ford reelected.

The economic recovery that had begun in President Ford's final year in office accelerated under his Democratic successor, Jimmy Carter. However, as incomes grew and unemployment fell, the nature of the recovery also shifted markedly. Under Ford, both the recession and the recovery were marked by the class bias characteristic of Republican administrations: low-income families lost much more real income than affluent families in 1975 and regained much less in 1976 and 1977. In marked contrast, real income growth in 1978 was robust across the board, with families at the 20th and 40th percentiles gaining 3% and 3.3%, respectively.

President Carter's economic policies were surprisingly consistent with traditional Democratic tendencies and priorities given his own ideological moderation, his often-rocky relations with the Democratic leadership in Congress, and the difficult economic times in which he governed—"An Age of Limits," as one scholarly account put it. Carter and Congress negotiated a stimulus package including tax cuts and increased government spending, as well as an increase in the minimum wage and an expansion of federal employment programs. The administration refused to tolerate higher unemployment in order to check inflation, reckoning that "the human and social costs of this approach are prohibitive," according to one White House policy memorandum.[34]

Within months of taking office, Carter obtained congressional support for almost $10 billion in new funding for employment programs, much of it through the Comprehensive Employment and Training Act (CETA). The new money, channeled through local governments, paid for training grants, full-time public service jobs for up to two years, and summer jobs for low-income high school students. Four years later, Carter's secretary of labor announced proudly that he had presided over "more than a two and a half fold increase" in funds for employment and training, and that "about 4 million economically disadvantaged persons received training and job opportunities" under CETA in each year of the Carter administration.[35]

---

[33] Hibbs (1987, 272).

[34] Biven (2002, 198, 71, 128).

[35] Ray Marshall, "The Labor Department in the Carter Administration: A Summary Report—January 14, 1981," U.S. Department of Labor (http://www.dol.gov/oasam/programs/history/carter-eta.htm).

The unemployment rate declined through most of Carter's term but spiked back up in the wake of a second major oil price shock in 1979–1980. Slow growth was coupled with double-digit price inflation—an unprecedented combination of economic ills dubbed "stagflation." Running for reelection in the midst of recession as well as foreign crises in Iran and Afghanistan, Carter was defeated by a popular vote margin of almost 10 percentage points.

When Carter's Republican successor, Ronald Reagan, assumed office in 1981, the unemployment rate stood at 7.5%—exactly the same level as four years earlier. However, Reagan's response to the unemployment problem stemming from an oil price shock was dramatically different from Carter's. Reagan's first budget gutted the controversial public service employment component of CETA and significantly reduced funding for job training programs. When CETA expired in 1982, the Reagan administration reluctantly agreed to support a much smaller successor program, the Job Training and Partnership Act (JTPA), with no public service employment and primary reliance on the private sector rather than local governments. "At its peak," one summary of domestic policy in the Reagan years noted, "CETA had funded more than three-quarters of a million full-time public service jobs. JTPA funds training, but not wages, for a smaller number of participants, who are enrolled, on average, for less than half the year. Spending on employment and training programs fell from about $22 billion to about $8 billion (in 1992 dollars) between 1979 and 1982. . . . Spending was also reduced for Food Stamps, school lunches, legal services, and social services."[36]

President Reagan's broader macroeconomic policies reflected a decisive choice between the horns of the "stagflation" dilemma. As Hibbs put it, "Monetary policy during the Reagan years leaned harder and longer against inflation than at any time since the Eisenhower administrations. The monetary restraint succeeded in breaking the inflationary legacy of the 1970s, but at the cost of the highest unemployment rates since the last years of the Great Depression."[37]

Macroeconomic Performance and Income Growth

The contrasting responses of Jimmy Carter and Ronald Reagan to the economic ills of "stagflation" are emblematic of surprisingly consistent partisan differences in the macroeconomic policies and priorities of Democratic and Republican presidents in the postwar era. Rather than multiplying examples, I turn in this section to the question of how those contrasting policies have affected the economic fortunes of American families. As it turns out,

[36] Danziger and Gottschalk (1995, 25).
[37] Hibbs (1987, 281).

they have resulted in striking differences in macroeconomic performance between Democratic and Republican presidents, and those differences account for much of the partisan difference in income growth patterns evident in figure 2.1.

Here, too, my analysis builds on pioneering work by Douglas Hibbs. His empirical analyses, based on data from 1953 through 1983, documented significant partisan differences in macroeconomic performance between Democratic and Republican administrations. In particular, Hibbs found that "after adjustment lags the unemployment rate tends to be about 2 percentage points lower under the Democrats than under the Republicans" and that "real output tends to be about 6 percent higher."[38]

Figure 2.4 presents comparisons of overall macroeconomic performance between Democratic and Republican administrations over the longer (67-year) period covered by my analysis. Unlike Hibbs's non-linear regression estimates, these are simple average values of unemployment, per capita GDP growth, and inflation under each party's presidents, again assuming a one-year lag in presidential influence.[39] Despite these differences in time frames and approaches, the comparisons of unemployment and GDP growth rates are quite consistent with Hibbs's: the average rate of unemployment over the entire postwar era has been almost a full percentage point lower under Democratic presidents than under Republicans, while the average rate of real per capita GDP growth has been more than a full percentage point higher.[40] However, despite Republicans' traditional emphasis on curbing inflation, the average inflation rate has been virtually identical under Republican and Democratic presidents over this period.[41] While differential sensitivity to inflation may have contributed to partisan differences in unemployment and economic growth, as Hibbs suggested, it is less obvious that Republican presidents have actually been more successful than Democrats in containing inflation.

---

[38] Ibid., 226. For an earlier version of these analyses, see Hibbs (1977).

[39] The annual unemployment rate for the civilian labor force (over the age of 15) is reported by the Bureau of Labor Statistics, "Household Data: Annual Averages: Table 1: Employment Status of the Civilian Noninstitutional Population, 1945 to Date" (http://www.bls.gov/cps/cpsaat01 .pdf). The GDP growth rate is calculated from annual data on real GDP per capita (chained dollars) reported by the Bureau of Economic Analysis (BEA), National Income and Product Accounts (NIPA), table 7.1 (http://www.bea.gov). The inflation rate is calculated from the Census Bureau's consumer price index; see "Table 24: Historical Consumer Price Index for All Urban Consumers (CPI-U): U.S. City Average, All Items" (http://www.bls.gov/cpi/cpid1411.pdf).

[40] The *t*-statistics for the partisan differences in GDP growth and unemployment are 2.1 and −2.3.

[41] The average annual *change* in the inflation rate, not shown in figure 2.4, is also virtually identical under Republican and Democratic presidents (−0.24 versus −0.10; the *t*-statistic for the difference is 0.3).

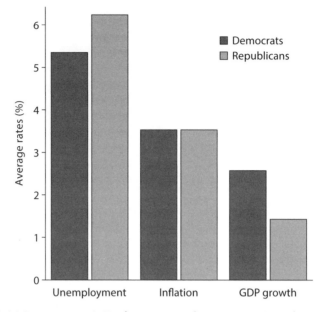

FIGURE 2.4 Macroeconomic Performance under Democratic and Republican Presidents, 1948–2014

As with the partisan differences in income growth documented in figure 2.1, the partisan differences in macroeconomic outcomes documented in figure 2.4 cannot plausibly be attributed to differences in the circumstances in which Republican and Democratic presidents have occupied the White House. In table 2.3, these partisan comparisons are embedded in a statistical analysis paralleling the analysis of income growth presented in table 2.2. The results provide strong evidence of significant partisan differences in unemployment and GDP growth between Republican and Democratic administrations, even after allowing for differences in specific economic circumstances and general historical trends.[42]

The partisan differences in macroeconomic performance documented in table 2.3 account for the lion's share of the partisan differences in income growth evident in table 2.2. Once differences in GDP growth, unemployment, and inflation are taken into account, the additional real income

[42] There is also some suggestive evidence in table 2.3 of higher inflation rates under Democratic presidents once linear and quadratic trends in inflation are taken into account. However, the relevant parameter estimate is quite imprecise (with a t-statistic of 1.2), making it very hard to tell how much, if any, of the apparent Republican advantage in constraining inflation reflects systematic partisan differences in economic policies.

TABLE 2.3

Statistical Analysis of Macroeconomic Performance, 1949–2014

Parameter estimates from seemingly unrelated regression models (with standard errors in parentheses). Partisan control measured from one year following inauguration to one year following subsequent inauguration. "Linear trend" and "quadratic trend" reflect cumulative change from 1948 through 2014.

	Real per capita GDP growth (%)	Unemployment (%)	Inflation (%)
Democratic president	1.65 (.50)	–.66 (.21)	.55 (.45)
Lagged level	–.272 (.073)	.863 (.044)	.499 (.102)
Oil prices (lagged %Δ)	–.0315 (.0118)	.0150 (.0051)	.0107 (.0122)
Labor force participation (Δ%)	2.71 (.93)	–1.27 (.39)	1.31 (.82)
Linear trend	–.03 (3.93)	2.26 (1.72)	10.14 (4.09)
Quadratic trend	–.61 (3.95)	–2.60 (1.72)	–9.41 (4.12)
Intercept	1.87 (.85)	.91 (.41)	–.61 (.77)
Standard error of regression	1.97	.86	1.78
Adjusted R^2	.27	.72	.57
N	66	66	66

Sources: Bureau of Labor Statistics; Bureau of Economic Analysis.

growth associated with Democratic administrations (in the first row of table 2.4) is only about two-thirds of a percentage point—and that additional growth is virtually constant across the income spectrum.

The rest of the statistical results presented in table 2.4 provide a clearer sense of how partisan differences in macroeconomic performance get translated into partisan patterns of income inequality. GDP growth and unemployment have substantial effects on income growth rates for working poor and middle-class families but very little impact on the incomes of affluent families. Thus, the higher GDP growth rates and lower unemployment rates that have generally prevailed during Democratic administrations have been much more beneficial to families near the bottom of the income distribution

TABLE 2.4
Statistical Analysis of Income Growth Including
Macroeconomic Conditions, 1949–2014

Annual real pre-tax income growth (%) for families at various points in the income distribution. Parameter estimates from seemingly unrelated regression models (with standard errors in parentheses). Partisan control measured from one year following inauguration to one year following subsequent inauguration. "Linear trend" and "quadratic trend" reflect cumulative change from 1948 through 2014.

	20th percentile	40th percentile	60th percentile	80th percentile	95th percentile
Democratic president	.73 (.59)	.57 (.38)	.58 (.36)	.77 (.40)	.69 (.53)
GDP growth (%)	.769 (.145)	.520 (.093)	.476 (.084)	.293 (.093)	.138 (.125)
Unemployment (%)	−.526 (.232)	−.462 (.146)	−.409 (.135)	−.243 (.146)	.068 (.193)
Inflation (%)	−.133 (.130)	−.254 (.085)	−.283 (.079)	−.373 (.088)	−.534 (.119)
Oil prices (lagged %Δ)	−.0052 (.0145)	−.0099 (.0094)	−.0134 (.0089)	−.0061 (.0099)	−.0064 (.0132)
Labor force participation (Δ%)	2.25 (1.06)	2.87 (.70)	1.72 (.65)	2.24 (.72)	3.70 (.97)
Lagged growth	−.136 (.088)	−.227 (.069)	−.264 (.070)	−.371 (.087)	.003 (.103)
Lagged 95th percentile	.195 (.119)	.120 (.083)	.099 (.077)	.215 (.092)	—
Linear trend	−7.20 (5.11)	−7.22 (3.37)	−2.71 (3.12)	.11 (3.48)	3.38 (4.69)
Quadratic trend	5.98 (5.06)	5.43 (3.32)	.48 (3.08)	−1.99 (3.44)	−4.18 (4.64)
Intercept	4.10 (1.53)	5.28 (1.00)	4.98 (.92)	4.14 (.99)	2.14 (1.27)
Standard error of regression	2.12	1.36	1.28	1.45	1.90
Adjusted R²	.65	.77	.74	.60	.47
N	66	66	66	66	66

Source: Census Bureau, Historical Income Tables.

than to those near the top. Conversely, the impact of inflation is negligible near the bottom of the income distribution but substantial at higher income levels. It is clear from these analyses that partisan differences in macroeconomic performance in the postwar era have translated into substantial differences in family incomes and in patterns of income inequality.

Of course, noting that partisan differences in income growth patterns seem to stem in significant part from partisan differences in macroeconomic performance begs the question of how and why Democratic presidents have produced lower unemployment and higher GDP growth. In the first edition of this book, I suggested that understanding the economic bases of partisan growth patterns "would constitute a fruitful research agenda for a small army of economists." While no army has been forthcoming, two prominent economists, Alan Blinder and Mark Watson, have provided "an econometric exploration" of the gap in overall GDP growth between Democratic and Republican presidencies in the postwar era. They reported that real annual GDP growth was "1.8 percentage points higher under Democrats—a stunningly large partisan gap." They noted that the gap was associated with Democratic control of the White House rather than Congress, and that a similar partisan gap appeared in Canada but not in the United Kingdom, France, or Germany.

Blinder and Watson's attempt to account for the partisan difference in GDP growth attributed about half of the gap to oil shocks, productivity shocks, international conditions, and more optimistic consumer expectations under Democratic presidents—factors they described as "mostly 'good luck,' with perhaps a touch of 'good policy.'" On the other hand, partisan differences in taxes, government spending, and monetary policy seem to have had little discernible effect on overall GDP growth. The remaining half of the Democratic advantage was unaccounted for in their analysis, leading them to "invite other researchers" to the "still mostly-unexplored continent" of partisan economic performance.[43]

Do Presidents Still Matter?

So far, the analyses presented in this chapter have sought to identify consistent partisan patterns in income growth over the entire postwar era. However, there are good reasons to think that these patterns may have changed significantly over time. For one thing, the economic trends stressed in conventional accounts of growing inequality—most notably, globalization and technological change—may have reduced the ability of political leaders to

---

[43] Blinder and Watson (2014, 35–36).

make a difference. For another thing, changes in the parties' ideologies and economic policies may have blunted traditional partisan patterns of income growth. Thus, economist Robert Pollin argued that "important differences between Democrats and Republicans on economic policy did continue after the 1970s. But the terms of the debate had shifted decisively away from New Deal/Great Society–type commitments to egalitarianism," and "differences between Democrats and Republicans had diminished on central matters relating to economic equality."[44]

As Pollin noted, inequality barely declined during Bill Clinton's eight years in the White House, despite strong overall economic growth. The ratio of income at the 80th percentile of the income distribution to income at the 20th percentile declined by just 0.3% under Clinton. That ratio *increased* by a similar (tiny) amount during Barack Obama's first term. Thus, one might conclude that recent Democratic presidents have made no progress at all in reducing economic inequality. But if we contrast their record with that of recent Republican presidents, no progress looks rather impressive. The 80/20 ratio increased by 8.4% under Ronald Reagan, by 5.8% under George H. W. Bush, and by 6.5% under George W. Bush, for a cumulative increase of 20% in 20 years of Republican government.

Figure 2.5 presents a tabulation of partisan patterns of income growth limited to the second half of the postwar era—beginning with Reagan and ending with Obama (through 2014, the most recent data available as of this writing). As with the tabulation for the entire postwar era in figure 2.1, figure 2.5 reveals substantial differences in income growth under Democratic and Republican presidents. However, comparing the two figures clearly suggests that the nature of those differences has shifted over time. Republicans beginning with Reagan presided over much lower growth across the income spectrum, with declines in average income growth rates of 1.3 or 1.4 percentage points at every income level compared to earlier postwar Republican presidents. Clinton and Obama, on the other hand, presided over significantly less income growth than their Democratic predecessors among low- and middle-income families (by 1.4 to 1.6 percentage points) but virtually identical growth rates among affluent families (with an average growth rate less than 0.1 percentage points lower than in the earlier period). Thus, the changing partisan pattern of income growth reflects a substantial overall decline in income growth across the board, with the sole exception being the essentially unchanged growth rate among affluent families under Democratic presidents.

The implication of the average income growth rates in figure 2.5 is that Republican presidents since the 1980s have contributed about as much to income inequality as their predecessors did. (Overall growth was much

---

[44] Pollin (2010, 153); Kenworthy (2010).

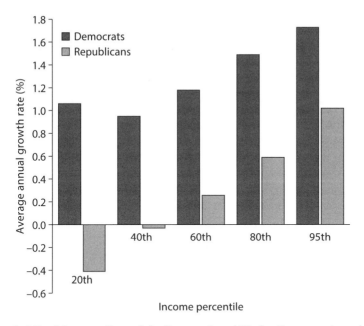

FIGURE 2.5 Real Income Growth by Income Level Under Democratic and Republican Presidents, 1982–2014

slower in the later period, but average income growth among families at the 20th percentile of the income distribution lagged a full percentage point behind the rate for families at the 80th percentile—and 1.4 percentage points behind families at the 95th percentile—under Republican presidents in both halves of the postwar era.) On the other hand, recent Democratic presidents have not managed to *decrease* income inequality—as their Democratic predecessors did—but have merely stemmed the rate of increase. (Income growth at the 95th percentile of the income distribution exceeded growth at the 20th percentile by 0.7 percentage points per year under Clinton and Obama, a difference about half as large as under Reagan, Bush, and Bush.)

Of course, partisan comparisons of this sort over a relatively short period of time—33 years spanning five Republican and three Democratic terms—are especially subject to potential biases stemming from differences in the circumstances under which each party held the White House. We can take systematic account of such circumstances, allowing for a more reliable analysis of changes in partisan income growth patterns using the same statistical framework set out in table 2.2. Table 2.5 reports statistical results paralleling those in table 2.2, but with separate estimates of partisan differences in income growth in the first and second halves of the postwar era, 1948–1981 and 1982–2014. These separate estimates are obviously less precise than

TABLE 2.5
Statistical Analysis of Income Growth, 1948–2013

Annual real pre-tax income growth (%) for families at various points in the income distribution. Parameter estimates from seemingly unrelated regression models (with standard errors in parentheses). Partisan control measured from one year following inauguration to one year following subsequent inauguration. "Linear trend" and "quadratic trend" reflect cumulative change from 1948 through 2014.

	20th percentile	40th percentile	60th percentile	80th percentile	95th percentile
Democratic president (1949–1981)	2.37 (.98)	1.48 (.70)	1.24 (.66)	.78 (.64)	−.23 (.77)
Democratic president (1982–2014)	2.00 (1.12)	1.40 (.80)	1.42 (.76)	1.51 (.73)	1.49 (.89)
Oil prices (lagged %Δ)	−.023 (.019)	−.028 (.013)	−.034 (.013)	−.026 (.012)	−.031 (.015)
Labor force participation (Δ%)	4.49 (1.29)	4.34 (.93)	2.99 (.88)	2.76 (.84)	3.29 (1.01)
Lagged growth	−.230 (.082)	−.273 (.069)	−.309 (.072)	−.378 (.085)	−.044 (.111)
Lagged 95th percentile	.473 (.150)	.314 (.110)	.265 (.105)	.286 (.107)	—
Linear trend	−16.55 (6.02)	−17.57 (4.35)	−12.50 (4.10)	−9.53 (3.93)	−6.42 (4.74)
Quadratic trend	12.74 (5.83)	13.84 (4.21)	8.83 (3.97)	6.30 (3.81)	4.27 (4.60)
Post-1981	1.13 (1.54)	.64 (1.10)	.22 (1.05)	.07 (1.01)	−.24 (1.22)
Intercept	2.82 (1.30)	4.05 (.94)	3.97 (.89)	3.80 (.86)	3.42 (1.03)
Standard error of regression	2.81	1.99	1.89	1.84	2.19
Adjusted R^2	.40	.51	.44	.36	.30
N	66	66	66	66	66

Source: Census Bureau, Historical Income Tables.

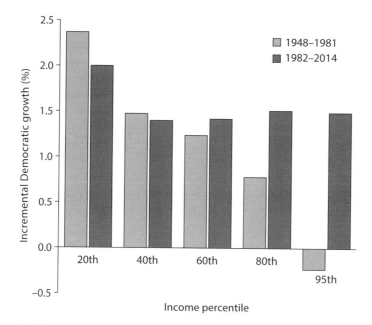

FIGURE 2.6 Democratic Income Growth Premium in First and Second Halves of the Postwar Era

those reported in table 2.2, since they are each based on only half as much historical experience. Nonetheless, there is a good deal of statistical evidence of higher income growth rates under Democratic presidents in both halves of the postwar era.[45]

The magnitudes of the estimated partisan differences in income growth for these two distinct periods are presented graphically in figure 2.6. In the immediate postwar period the Democratic advantage in income growth declined more or less linearly across the income spectrum, from about 2.4 percentage points per year among working poor families to –0.2 percentage points per year among affluent families. In the later period the Democratic income growth premium was more evenly distributed across the income spectrum, with differences ranging from 2 percentage points per year among working poor families to 1.4 percentage points per year among middle-class families. While it would be hazardous to make too much of these differences between periods, given the limitations of the data on which they are based, they suggest that the Democratic income growth premium has persisted and

[45] The *t*-statistics for partisan differences in income growth in the period after 1981 range from 1.7 to 2.1.

perhaps even increased in recent decades, but that its implications for *inequality* have probably declined.[46]

PARTISAN REDISTRIBUTION

The partisan differences in income growth documented in figures 2.1 and 2.5 are especially striking in light of the fact that the tabulations reported there focus entirely on pre-tax income figures. Those figures include cash benefits from the government such as Social Security and unemployment benefits, but they do not reflect any partisan differences in the distribution of non-cash government benefits (such as food stamps or health care) or in effective tax rates. Since taxes and transfers are the most obvious policy levers available to presidents with partisan distributional goals, the pre-tax income tabulations may miss much of what is distinctive about Democratic and Republican policies.[47]

In the original edition of this book, I used additional Census Bureau data on the distribution of post-tax incomes to examine partisan differences in taxes and transfers. Those "experimental measures" were (and still are) available only for households up to the 80th percentile of the income distribution for the period 1979–2003. My analysis identified partisan differences in post-tax income growth qualitatively similar to the pre-tax differences for the whole postwar era shown in figure 2.1, leading me to suggest that recent presidents "have been quite successful in using taxes and transfers to shape the post-tax income distribution along familiar partisan lines." However, as Lane Kenworthy pointed out, those partisan differences in post-tax income growth owed less to taxes and transfers than to another component of the Census Bureau's "experimental measures": imputed returns on home equity. In effect, the Census Bureau's methodology credited Democrats for high interest rates (which increased the imputed value of home equity) under Jimmy Carter following the oil price shock of 1979–1980 rather than for more progressive taxes or spending.[48]

Nathan Kelly provided a more cogent analysis of partisan patterns of redistribution in the postwar era. He constructed estimates of both pre-tax and post-tax income inequality from 1947 through 2000 and used them to assess partisan dynamics in both "pre-redistribution" inequality and the

---

[46] The largest difference between time periods in figure 2.6, for families at the 95th percentile of the income distribution, has a *t*-statistic of 1.5; none of the others exceeds 0.7.

[47] Slemrod (1994).

[48] "Table RDI-6: Income Limits for Each Fifth of Households, by Selected Definition of Income: 1979 to 2003" (https://www.census.gov/hhes/www/income/data/historical/measures/rdi6.html); Bartels (2008, 54–60); Kenworthy (2010, 93–97, 110–112).

reduction in that inequality due to redistribution through government taxes and transfers. He found that the extent of redistribution was significantly greater when Democrats held the White House, when there were more elderly and unemployed people, and when inequality in market incomes was increasing.[49]

While Kelly's analysis provided significant evidence of partisan differences in redistribution over a span of more than five decades, it left open the question of how Democratic and Republican presidents produced those differences. However, additional data compiled by the Congressional Budget Office (CBO) can shed some light on that question. Like the Census Bureau's "experimental measures" of income, these data cover a much shorter period (currently 1979 through 2011). However, because they include separate tabulations of "market income" (including wages and salaries, business income, and capital gains), government transfers (including both cash payments and in-kind benefits from federal, state, and local governments), and taxes (including federal income taxes, payroll taxes, and imputed corporate taxes and excise taxes, but not state or local taxes), they make it possible to analyze separately partisan patterns of redistribution through taxes and through transfers. While these data provide much less scope for historical comparison than Kelly's estimates or the family income tabulations summarized in table 2.1, they include 13 years under three different Democratic presidents (Carter, Clinton, and Obama) and 20 years under three different Republican presidents (Reagan, George H. W. Bush, and George W. Bush).[50]

Partisan differences in economic philosophy and distributional priorities are especially striking in the realm of tax policy. Presidents of both parties have implemented significant tax cuts, but they have done so in very different ways and for very different reasons. For example, when President Kennedy's economic team argued for a tax cut in the early 1960s, they reasoned that "the beneficiaries of a personal income tax cut, especially in the lower brackets, would promptly spend a large part of the proceeds on goods and services, thereby stimulating production, employment, and income." In contrast, the supply-side theory adopted in the Reagan administration suggested that tax cuts "could not be given to the middle class or even the poor. In order to be successful, tax cuts had to be directed primarily toward the

[49] Kelly (2009, chap. 4 and appendix B). Though official tabulations of post-tax income only begin in 1979, Kelly estimated the ratio of post-tax income in the top quintile of the income distribution to the bottom two quintiles using published summaries of family and individual income for earlier years. His measure of redistribution was the percentage reduction in inequality comparing the post-tax ratio to the pre-tax ratio. (Thus, the same *absolute* reduction in inequality counts for less when the pre-tax ratio is higher.)

[50] Congressional Budget Office, "The Distribution of Household Income and Federal Taxes, 2011," table 1 (http://www.cbo.gov/publication/49440).

wealthy because of their larger role in saving and investing. . . . Tax cuts for everyone else might stimulate additional consumption, but that was not what supply-side economics was all about."[51]

In the early 1980s President Reagan's tax-cutting philosophy strongly reinforced pre-existing trends contributing to increasing economic inequality. Between 1980 and 1982 the average total federal tax on the top 1% of income-earners fell by 6.4 percentage points, with successively smaller percentage decreases at each step down the income ladder (and a slight *increase* for the bottom quintile of income-earners). Later in Reagan's term some of these cuts were rolled back in response to a ballooning federal budget deficit, but the top 1% of income-earners were still paying 4.1% less of their income in taxes in 1988 than they had been in 1980 (while those in the bottom quintile were paying 0.5% *more* than they had been).[52]

When Bill Clinton entered the White House in 1993, he apparently felt a good deal more constrained by the Federal Reserve Board and the bond markets than previous Democratic presidents had been. Rather than relying on macroeconomic stimulation or across-the-board tax cuts to complete the economy's recovery from the recession of 1991, Clinton focused on reducing the deficit. Nevertheless, in his first year in office he proposed, and Congress passed, a major expansion of the Earned Income Tax Credit for working poor people. Higher up the income ladder, tax brackets were revised to make them somewhat more progressive while increasing total revenue. Overall, federal taxes on the bottom quintile fell by 1.2 percentage points over Clinton's eight years in office, while taxes on the top quintile increased by 2.3 percentage points.[53]

Clinton succeeded so well at reining in the budget deficit that his Republican successor, George W. Bush, inherited a substantial budget surplus. Bush took advantage of the opportunity to engineer a series of major tax cuts. However, in marked contrast to Clinton's strategy of targeting tax cuts to mitigate the effects on the income distribution of technological changes, globalization, and shifting labor markets, Bush exacerbated those effects by reverting to President Reagan's emphasis on reducing the tax burden of wealthy individuals and corporations. I examine the politics

---

[51] Tobin and Weidenbaum (1988, 49); Karier (1997, 76). Owen Zidar (2015, 39) examined the impact on employment growth of state-by-state tax changes affecting people in different parts of the income distribution since 1980. He estimated that an exogenous tax increase amounting to 1% of GDP imposed on taxpayers in the bottom half of the income distribution reduced state employment growth by 7–8%, while the same tax increase imposed on taxpayers in the top half of the income distribution reduced employment growth by only 0.3%.

[52] CBO, "The Distribution of Household Income and Federal Taxes, 2011," table 1.

[53] As one sympathetic account had it (Page and Simmons 2000, 158), "Taxes were raised a bit and made more progressive (helping to balance the budget). What followed, contrary to alarmist predictions, was not an economic crash, but rather a sustained economic boom."

and ramifications of the Bush tax cuts in much more detail in chapter 5. For now, it is sufficient to note that by 2008 the average federal tax rate had declined by 4.3 percentage points for the top 1% of income-earners and by 4.1 percentage points for the top quintile; in both cases these rates were back to their 1986 levels.

Under President Obama, taxes on top income-earners went up substantially once again owing to new Medicare taxes imposed to help fund the Affordable Care Act of 2010, a reversion of the top income tax rate from 35% to 39.6%, and higher tax rates on capital gains and dividends. In his second term Obama proposed further upward shifts in the tax burden but met with staunch resistance from Republican majorities in Congress.[54]

The cumulative effect of these tax policy initiatives has been to produce noticeably different patterns of taxation under Democratic and Republican presidents, especially for people near the top of the income distribution. In assessing partisan patterns of taxation, I count each president's control as beginning in the year he was inaugurated rather than one year later. Whereas partisan shifts in macroeconomic policy are likely to take some time to affect family incomes, changes in tax policy are generally implemented immediately. Thus, for example, the effective tax rate on top-percentile income-earners declined by 2.7% in Ronald Reagan's first year in office, increased by 3.5% in Bill Clinton's first year, fell again in George W. Bush's first year, and increased again in Barack Obama's first year. All of these changes were substantially due to the new presidents' policy initiatives.

Table 2.6 shows average federal tax rates for households in various income strata over this period. The average rates range from 6.5% of pre-tax income (including both market income and cash transfers) in the lowest income group to 30.4% in the top income percentile. (Middle-income households paid about 16% of their pre-tax income in federal taxes.) The second and third columns of the table show separate tabulations for Democratic and Republican presidencies, while the fourth column shows the partisan difference in average tax rates for each income group.

The most striking partisan differences in tax burdens in table 2.6 appear at the top of the income distribution. Overall, taxpayers in the top income decile paid an additional 1.6% of their income in taxes under Democratic presidents over this period, while those in the top percentile—"the 1%"—paid almost 4% more of their income in taxes under Democrats. (This substantial partisan difference will become even wider as the effects of President Obama's tax policy changes are fully reflected in the CBO data.) On the other hand, low-income households paid less of their income in federal taxes under Democratic presidents—a difference

[54] Jeanne Sahadi, "Taxing the Rich: The Record Under Obama," *CNN Money*, January 30, 2015 (http://money.cnn.com/2015/01/30/pf/taxes/obama-taxes-rich/).

TABLE 2.6
Partisan Differences in Federal Tax Rates, 1979–2011

Average federal tax rate (%) for households, by pre-tax income group (with standard errors in parentheses). Taxes include individual income taxes, payroll taxes, and imputed corporate income taxes and excise taxes. Incomes are adjusted for household size. Partisan control includes inauguration year.

Income percentile	All presidents	Democratic presidents	Republican presidents	Partisan difference
1–20	6.46	5.68	6.96	–1.28
	(.39)	(.68)	(.44)	(.77)
21–40	11.94	11.55	12.19	–.64
	(.42)	(.75)	(.49)	(.86)
41–60	16.07	15.92	16.16	–.25
	(.41)	(.77)	(.48)	(.85)
61–80	19.42	19.50	19.38	+.13
	(.35)	(.68)	(.38)	(.72)
81–90	22.10	22.27	21.99	+.28
	(.27)	(.55)	(.286)	(.56)
91–95	23.77	24.18	23.51	+.67
	(.23)	(.47)	(.20)	(.45)
96–99	25.77	26.64	25.21	+1.43
	(.23)	(.37)	(.23)	(.41)
Top percentile	30.42	32.78	28.88	+3.90
	(.50)	(.65)	(.44)	(.75)
N	33	13	20	33

Source: Congressional Budget Office.

of 1.3% in the bottom income quintile and about half that in the second income quintile. Between these two extremes, the tax burdens of middle- and upper-middle-income taxpayers (those in the 40th to 90th percentiles of the income distribution) were essentially similar under Democratic and Republican presidents.

The partisan differences in average tax burdens at the top and bottom of the income distribution shed important light on the politics of redistribution. However, they only reflect how the federal government has *raised* money, not how it has *spent* that money. Redistribution through government transfers may have as much or more impact on the income distribution as redistribution through progressive taxation. The CBO calculated Gini coefficients—a standard measure of inequality—for "market income" (before taxes and transfers), "before-tax income" (after government transfers but before taxes), and "after-tax income."[55] The differences between these three measures reflect the separate impacts on income inequality of government transfers (including both cash transfers such as Social Security payments and the value of other government benefits such as Medicare and food stamps) and federal taxes.

Over the period from 1979 to 2011, the CBO's average Gini coefficient for market income was .541. The average Gini coefficient for before-tax post-transfer income was .452, indicating that government transfers reduced inequality by an average of almost 9 percentage points. The progressivity of federal taxes reduced inequality by an additional 3.5 percentage points by this measure, to .417. Thus, both government transfers and taxes have contributed to mitigating income inequality in the contemporary United States—but the overall impact of transfers has been much larger than the overall impact of progressive taxation.[56]

A simple comparison of the average reductions in Gini coefficients under Democratic and Republican presidents suggests that there has generally been more income redistribution under Democrats than under Republicans over the 33 years covered by the CBO tabulations. Government transfers reduced the Gini coefficient by an average of 9.3 percentage points under Democrats and 8.7 percentage points under Republicans. Redistribution through the tax system averaged an additional 3.9 percentage points under Democrats and 3.2 percentage points under Republicans. These comparisons suggest that partisan differences in taxes and in transfers have contributed roughly equally to the greater overall level of redistribution under Democratic presidents.[57]

However, these raw partisan differences take no account of the economic and social conditions under which Democratic and Republican presidents have adopted tax and transfer policies. The statistical analyses presented in table 2.7 embed partisan effects within a model allowing for shifts in market income inequality and redistribution over time and in response to changing economic conditions. (These analyses are directly analogous to the statistical analyses of income growth presented in tables 2.2 and 2.5.)

Allowing for these differences in context does little to alter the raw partisan difference in redistribution through taxation. Although the direct impact of Democratic presidents on redistributive taxation in table 2.7 (.228) is

---

[55] The Gini coefficient is interpretable as the share of income that would have to be redistributed in order to produce a completely equal distribution. It ranges from zero (if every household's income is the same) to one (if one household has all the income).

[56] Cross-national comparisons show that income redistribution generally depends more on government spending than on tax progressivity. That fact helps to explain why the United States achieves less redistribution than other affluent democracies do, despite having a much more progressive tax system. Lucy Barnes, "The Facts About Tax Progressivity," *The Monkey Cage*, February 16, 2012.

[57] The *t*-statistics for these partisan differences are 1.6 and 4.4, respectively.

TABLE 2.7

Statistical Analysis of Income Inequality and Redistribution, 1979–2011

Inequality measured by Gini coefficient (× 100); redistribution measured by reduction in Gini coefficient (× 100). Parameter estimates from seemingly unrelated regression models (with standard errors in parentheses). Partisan control includes inauguration year for redistribution only. "Linear trend" and "quadratic trend" reflect cumulative change from 1948 through 2014.

	Market income inequality	Redistribution via transfers	Redistribution via taxation
Democratic president	−.460 (.195)	.051 (.152)	.228 (.079)
Lagged value	.424 (.115)	.700 (.120)	.703 (.091)
Lagged market income inequality (Gini)	—	−.163 (.087)	−.091 (.038)
Oil prices (lagged %Δ)	−.0002 (.0040)	.0021 (.0030)	−.0018 (.0015)
Labor force participation (Δ%)	1.97 (.45)	−.80 (.33)	.01 (.15)
Linear trend	19.80 (8.46)	−7.44 (6.25)	5.81 (2.75)
Quadratic trend	2.86 (6.03)	5.49 (4.52)	−3.50 (1.95)
Intercept	38.54 (2.89)	5.22 (2.51)	−1.33 (.95)
Standard error of regression	.54	.38	.17
Adjusted R²	.97	.85	.90
N	32	32	32

Source: Congressional Budget Office.

much smaller than the raw difference of 0.7 percentage points, the long-run impact (allowing for the substantial stability of shifts in taxation from one year to the next) is .77, slightly larger than the raw difference.[58] While this

[58] The statistical analyses presented in table 2.7 include lagged values of the dependent variables among the explanatory factors. In dynamic models of this sort, the estimated long-run effect of each explanatory factor depends on both its short-run effect on the current Gini coefficient and the persistence of that effect implied by the coefficient on the lagged Gini coefficient.

difference is of modest magnitude relative to the overall increase in inequality observed over this period, it is fairly substantial relative to the average reduction in inequality produced by progressive taxation (3.5 percentage points).

On the other hand, there is little apparent partisan difference in redistribution via (cash and non-cash) federal transfers once differences in context are taken into account. While transfer programs contributed substantially to reducing inequality, they seem to have done so similarly under Democratic and Republican presidents. Perhaps that should not be surprising. Most redistribution occurs through transfer programs that are relatively broad and formulaic. Presidents and Congress may adjust the indexing of Social Security or extend eligibility for unemployment benefits, but most of the year-to-year fluctuation in spending on these programs occurs automatically when more people reach retirement age or become unemployed.[59] By comparison, the programs that are most likely to generate significant partisan disagreement are relatively small in magnitude.

Thus, for example, Douglas Hibbs noted that President Reagan "succeeded in reversing the trend of increasing federal commitments to the poor and near-poor." However, most government transfers do not go to the poor and near-poor. Moreover, those that do increased automatically during the recession of 1980–1982. Thus, redistribution through transfers *increased* from 8.4 percentage points in 1980 to 8.6 percentage points in 1982 before falling to about 8 percentage points in Reagan's second term. On the other hand, redistribution through the tax system fell from 3.8 percentage points in 1980 to a low of 2.3 percentage points in 1986 before rebounding to about 3 percentage points by the time Reagan left office. Thus, as Hibbs noted, "most important of all, Reagan achieved a dramatic redistribution of the federal tax burden from corporations and high-income classes to moderate- and low-income groups."[60] Here, too, the partisan political economy seems to be of considerable importance for the economic fortunes of ordinary Americans.

DEMOCRATS, REPUBLICANS, AND THE RISE OF INEQUALITY

Economists have generally associated the escalation of inequality over the past 40 years with important structural changes in the American economy, including demographic shifts, globalization, and technological change.

The long-run effects implied by the statistical analyses in the three columns of table 2.7 are $1/(1 - .424) = 1.74$, $1/(1 - .700) = 3.33$, and $1/(1 - .703) = 3.37$ times as large as the corresponding short-run effects. On the algebra of partial adjustment in dynamic models, see, for example, Gujarati (1995, 599–601), or Kennedy (1998, 156).

[59] This fact presumably accounts for Kelly's (2009, 107) finding that the two main factors associated with long-run changes in redistribution (aside from presidential partisanship) were changes in the elderly share of the population and in the unemployment rate.

[60] Hibbs (1987, 281).

While there is no reason to doubt that these factors have played an important role in increasing the income gap between rich and poor people in the contemporary United States, it does not follow that escalating inequality is "simply an economic reality," as Treasury Secretary Paulson asserted. Indeed, in recent years some economists have begun to emphasize the potential significance of political factors exacerbating these economic trends. If "market forces are shaped by politics," as economist Joseph Stiglitz wrote, then "another world is possible." Despite Ben Stein's observation that "there has always been extreme income inequality," presidents and their policy choices can have a significant effect on the extent of inequality at any given time.[61]

The cumulative impact of these partisan policy choices is illustrated in figure 2.7. The line in the center of the figure represents the actual course of inequality since the late 1940s, as measured by the ratio of family incomes at the 80th and 20th percentiles of the income distribution. The upper line represents the projected course of the 80/20 income ratio over the same period given the pattern of income growth that prevailed under Republican presidents during this period, while the lower line represents the projected course of the 80/20 income ratio under Democratic presidents.[62]

The projections in figure 2.7 imply that continuous Democratic control would have produced little or no net increase in economic inequality since the late 1940s. While the technological, demographic, and global competitive forces emphasized in economists' accounts of escalating inequality would have produced some increase in inequality since the late 1970s even under Democratic presidents, that increase would have been modest in magnitude and would barely have offset a significant *decline* in inequality over the preceding three decades. In contrast, the projections imply that continuous Republican control would have produced a significant increase in inequality even before the mid-1970s and a much sharper polarization between affluent and poor than has actually occurred over the past 40 years. The projected 80/20 income ratio in 2014, given a steady diet of Republican policies, is 6.1—far higher than the actual ratio of 4.4, and almost twice the projected Democratic ratio of 3.1.[63]

---

[61] Stiglitz (2012, 265–66). Other prominent examples include Krugman (2007) and Atkinson (2015).

[62] These projections are constructed on the basis of the statistical analysis reported in table 2.5, allowing for distinct partisan differences in the two halves of the postwar era. The upper line assumes continuous Republican control throughout the period, while the lower line assumes continuous Democratic control.

[63] The 80/20 income ratio increased by 32% between 1979 and 2014. The projections in figure 2.7 suggest that it would have increased by 45% under continuous Republican control but by only 17% under continuous Democratic control (offsetting a 17% decline between 1948 and 1979).

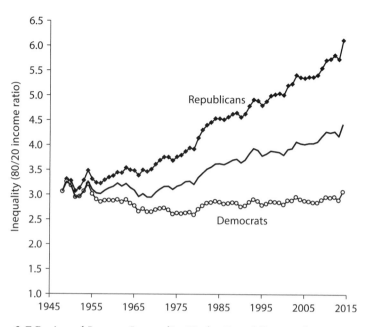

FIGURE 2.7 Projected Income Inequality Under Republican and Democratic Presidents, 1948–2014

The projections presented in figure 2.7 are based on an arguably unrealistic assumption: that if either party had uninterrupted control of the White House, it would do all the time what it in fact does only half the time. It is impossible to know whether either party would actually have the political will or the power to produce economic redistribution of the cumulative magnitude suggested by these projections. Nevertheless, the cumulative differences portrayed in figure 2.7 convey the fundamental significance of partisan politics in ameliorating or exacerbating economic inequality in the postwar era.

In the first half of that period, the partisan differences in income growth documented in this chapter implied robust growth for middle-class and poor families under Democratic presidents and more modest growth under Republicans. In the less propitious economic circumstances prevailing in the early 21st century, not even a steady succession of Democratic presidents and policies would be likely to reproduce the robust, broad-based income growth of the 1960s. However, that does not make the choice between Democrats and Republicans any less consequential.

The magnitude of what is at stake in partisan control of economic policy may be demonstrated by considering the ramifications of a few hundred votes in Florida in the presidential election of 2000. In his eight years in office, President George W. Bush presided over a 0.6% cumulative increase in the real incomes of families at the 95th percentile of the income distribution, but a 3–4% *decline* in the real incomes of middle-class families and a 7.7% decline in the real incomes of working poor families. (Of course, these figures are skewed by the onset of the Great Recession at the end of Bush's second term, but even at the peak of the business cycle in 2007 the real incomes of working poor families were lower than they had been when Bush entered the White House.) However, the statistical analyses presented in table 2.5 imply that, had President Al Gore governed during those eight years, the real incomes of middle-class and working poor families would probably have *grown* by 8–10%, despite the onset of recession, while the real incomes of affluent families would probably have grown by about 12%.[64] For most American families, this alternative economic universe would have been dramatically better than the one they actually experienced.

Finally, it is worth noting that these partisan differences in income growth are not just a matter of incremental economic gains. They may also have important social ramifications that are only beginning to attract scholarly attention. For example, psychiatrist James Gilligan documented a striking statistical connection between changing rates of violent death in the United States throughout the 20th century and the party of the president. He concluded that Republican administrations are "risk factors for lethal violence." According to Gilligan, recessions, unemployment, and economic inequality have been "more frequent and prolonged" under Republicans, producing substantial negative effects on "individual emotional and psychological health and welfare." On the other hand, "compensatory measures" to mitigate these stressors "have been more extensive and effective under Democratic than under Republican presidents." As a result, from 1900 through 2007 the age-adjusted suicide rate increased by an average of 2.4 per million per year under Republican presidents but decreased by an average of 2.8 per million per year under Democratic presidents. The age-adjusted homicide rate increased by an average of 0.9 per million per year under Republicans but decreased by an average of 1.0 per million per year under Democrats. These differences may sound small, but they add up to tens of thousands of lives over a four-year term.[65]

---

[64] Taking into account the indirect effects of lagged growth, the parameter estimates reported in table 2.5 imply additional real growth under Democratic presidents of about 2.2% per year at the 20th percentile, 1.5% per year at the 40th percentile, and 1.4% per year at the 60th, 80th, and 95th percentiles during this period.

[65] Gilligan (2011); Larry Bartels, "Politics Is a Matter of Life and Death (Times 23,000)," *The Monkey Cage*, January 30, 2012.

In the same vein, an interdisciplinary team of social scientists has found "a robust, quantitatively important association" between infant mortality rates and the party of the president from 1965 through 2010. While overall infant mortality rates declined significantly over this period, deviations around that trend were strongly partisan, with about 3% higher infant mortality rates under Republicans presidents than under Democrats. This difference appeared consistently among whites and blacks for both neonatal and post-neonatal mortality rates, with or without a variety of statistical controls. Here, too, it appears that partisan politics is a matter of life and death.[66]

As Edward Tufte insisted almost 40 years ago, "economic life vibrates with the rhythms of politics."[67] Thus, while it may be "neither fair nor useful to blame any political party" for the structural changes in the economy that make income growth and income inequality much more pressing issues now than they were in the postwar boom years of the 1950s and 1960s, it certainly seems fair—and perhaps even useful—to hold political parties accountable for the profound impact of their policies on the economic and social well-being of affluent, middle-class, and poor American families.

Of course, whether voters *do* hold political parties accountable for the profound impact of their policies is another question. I address that question in chapter 3, which turns Tufte's maxim on its head by exploring the ways in which American political life vibrates with the rhythm of economics.

---

[66] Rodriguez, Bound, and Geronimus (2013).
[67] Tufte (1978, 137).

CHAPTER 3

Partisan Biases in Economic Accountability

> Of all races in an advanced stage of civilization, the
> American is the least accessible to long views. . . . Always
> and everywhere in a hurry to get rich, he does not give a
> thought to remote consequences; he sees only present ad-
> vantages. . . . He does not remember, he does not feel, he
> lives in a materialist dream.
> —*Moiseide Ostrogorski, 1902*[1]

THE PARTISAN PATTERN of economic performance documented in chapter 2 raises a perplexing political question. Real income growth has historically been much stronger under Democratic presidents than under Republican presidents, especially for middle-class and poor people. So why do so many people—including middle-class and poor people—persist in voting for Republicans? Even allowing for some class bias in turnout, it is clear that most voters have been substantially worse off in economic terms under Republican presidents than under Democrats. Yet Republicans have won most of the presidential elections of the postwar era and received 50.7% of all the votes cast for major-party candidates from 1948 through 2012.[2] If we suppose that voters want, or should want, to use their power at the ballot box to advance their own economic fortunes or those of their fellow citizens, the fact that Republicans have won even a bare plurality of votes seems baffling.

The implication of this anomaly for economic inequality should be clear from figure 2.7, which suggests that the marked escalation of inequality over the course of the postwar era would simply not have occurred under a steady diet of Democratic presidents and policies. Thus, the ability of

---

[1] Ostrogorski (1902, 302–303).

[2] Republican presidential candidates won a total of 730 million popular votes over this period, Democratic candidates 709 million. All of the election results cited in this chapter are based on the tabulations reported in *Dave Leip's Atlas of U.S. Presidential Elections* (http://uselectionatlas.org/).

Republicans to thrive in the electoral arena despite the negative impact of their policies on the economic fortunes of middle-class and poor people must loom large in any convincing account of the political economy of the New Gilded Age.

Many observers have attributed Republican electoral successes to the false consciousness of white working-class voters seduced by the "hallucinatory appeal" of conservative Republican stances on "cultural wedge issues like guns and abortion"; but that account turns out to be vastly exaggerated.[3] A less familiar but much more convincing resolution of this political puzzle hinges on three notable biases in the workings of economic accountability in contemporary American electoral politics.

First, voters are myopic, responding strongly to income growth in presidential election years but ignoring or forgetting most of the rest of the incumbent administration's record of economic performance. As Ostrogorski surmised more than a century ago, the American voter "sees only present advantages." It is by no means obvious that this quirk of voter psychology should have had significant implications for the balance of power between Democrats and Republicans over the past several decades, but it has. That is the result of a striking disparity in the timing of income growth under Democratic and Republican presidents in the postwar era. The tabulations presented in figure 2.1 show that Democrats have generally presided over more robust income growth, especially for families of modest means. However, that partisan pattern of income growth has disappeared in presidential election years, with most families experiencing faster growth—and affluent families experiencing much faster growth—under Republican presidents than they have under Democratic presidents.

Second, election-year income growth for affluent families turns out to be much more consequential at the polls than income growth for middle-class and poor families. Voters—even middle- and low-income voters—seem to be much more sensitive to the economic fortunes of the affluent than to the fortunes of their own income class or, for that matter, the nation as a whole. Again, it is not obvious that this odd sensitivity should have had significant partisan implications, but it has. As we saw in figure 2.1, Republican presidents in the postwar era have presided over much more income growth for affluent families than for middle-class and poor families. Democrats, on the other hand, have presided over slightly *less* income growth for affluent families than for middle-class and poor families—and much less in presidential election years, when income growth translates most powerfully into electoral support. Thus, the fact that voters tend to respond much more strongly to the economic fortunes of affluent families than of middle-class

---

[3] Frank (2004, 45). For a detailed critique of this thesis, see Bartels (2006b; 2008, chap. 3).

and poor families has provided a substantial electoral boost to Republican incumbents and their successors.

Third, voters are swayed by the balance of campaign spending between incumbents and challengers. Here, too, the general effect has been to bolster Republican electoral prospects, since Republicans have outspent Democrats in 13 of the past 16 presidential races (and in seven of the nine contests in which spending disparities were substantial). Since most campaign contributions come from relatively wealthy people, and since most wealthy people are conservatives, this Republican spending advantage is presumably due in part to ideological affinity. However, the partisan disparity is magnified by a strong tendency for campaign donors to reward incumbents for election-year income growth, especially election-year income growth for affluent families. Thus, the fact that Republicans have generally presided over much more election-year income growth for affluent families than Democrats have turns out to skew voting behavior indirectly—through the effect of differential campaign spending—as well as directly.

Over the past several decades, each of these three biases has produced an electoral advantage for Republican candidates amounting to one or two percentage points—more than enough to account for the net Republican plurality of presidential votes in the postwar era. Together, they have probably added almost four percentage points to the average Republican popular vote and altered the outcomes of five of the past 16 presidential elections. Four of those elections were won by Republicans—including every instance in the past half-century in which a Republican challenger ousted the Democrats from the White House. Thus, biases in economic accountability go a long way toward accounting for the otherwise puzzling disconnect between partisan economic performance and partisan electoral fortunes in the political economy of America's New Gilded Age.

Myopic Voters

The political puzzle of Republican electoral success is predicated on the notion that voters assess which party has produced a better record of income growth, either for themselves or for the country as a whole, and vote accordingly. That notion seems to be supported by a great deal of evidence linking the state of the economy and the political fortunes of the incumbent party in both presidential and congressional elections.[4] It also seems

---

[4] This literature is too vast to cite in detail. Kramer (1971) and Tufte (1978) made important early contributions. Erikson (1989; 1990) analyzed presidential and midterm congressional results, respectively. For presidential elections, Bartels and Zaller (2001) compared a variety of alternative measures of economic performance and probed the robustness of the statistical

eminently sensible, since competent governments in the post-Keynesian era are thought to exert real influence over the course of the national economy. Indeed, the strong tendency of voters to reward incumbents for good economic times and punish them for bad times has often been viewed as a mark of the rationality of democratic electorates. One of the earliest academic analysts of economic voting, Gerald Kramer, characterized his results as demonstrating "that election outcomes are in substantial part responsive to objective changes occurring under the incumbent party; they are not 'irrational,' or random, or solely the product of past loyalties and habits, or of campaign rhetoric and merchandising." Another prominent political scientist, V. O. Key Jr., interpreted evidence of retrospective voting as support for the "perverse and unorthodox argument" that "voters are not fools."[5]

One of the primary attractions of this perspective on electoral accountability is that it does not seem to require too much from ordinary citizens. According to another influential theorist of retrospective voting, Morris Fiorina, voters "typically have one comparatively hard bit of data: they know what life has been like during the incumbent's administration. They need *not* know the precise economic or foreign policies of the incumbent administration in order to see or feel the *results* of those policies. . . . In order to ascertain whether the incumbents have performed poorly or well, citizens need only calculate the changes in their own welfare."[6]

Analysts have routinely treated this feature of the retrospective theory of political accountability as unproblematic. Individual voters' economic perceptions may reflect substantial partisan biases, rationalization, and sheer randomness, but the electorate as a whole is assumed to respond systematically and sensibly to actual economic experience under the incumbent administration.[7]

Here I examine one important respect in which the rationality of the American electorate falls short of this standard: the time horizon over which voters assess changes in the state of the economy.[8] If voters want to reward incumbents for contributing to their own incomes or to the economic well-being of the nation as a whole—or to punish incumbents for failing to provide prosperity—they should be sensitive to economic conditions "over the incumbent's entire term of office, with little or no backward time

---

results to variations in model specification. Achen and Bartels (2016, chap. 4) reviewed the logic of retrospective political accountability and the empirical evidence for retrospective voting on the basis of economic conditions.

[5] Kramer (1971, 140); Key (1966, 7).

[6] Fiorina (1981, 5).

[7] On idiosyncratic economic experience, rationalization, and partisan bias, see Kramer (1983); Conover, Feldman, and Knight (1987); Bartels (2002a); Erikson (2004).

[8] My analysis here builds upon joint work with Christopher Achen (Achen and Bartels 2004; Achen and Bartels 2016, chap. 6).

discounting of performance outcomes," as Douglas Hibbs put it. However, the striking fact is that most analyses of retrospective economic voting focus on economic conditions during the election year, or even some fraction of the election year, rather than over the longer haul of an entire term.[9] In effect, they assume that voters attempt "to ascertain whether the incumbents have performed poorly or well" on the basis of a very limited—and potentially misleading—assessment of "changes in their own welfare."

Is that assumption warranted? Figure 3.1 summarizes the relationship between cumulative income growth and the incumbent party's electoral fortunes in the 16 presidential elections from 1952 through 2012. Election years are arrayed along the horizontal axis based on the total growth in real disposable personal income per capita in the second, third, and fourth years of each administration—the years in which the incumbent president's policies would most plausibly have some impact on the state of the economy.[10] The vertical axis shows the popular vote margin (in percentage points) for the incumbent party's presidential candidate.

Figure 3.1 displays a strong, though not overwhelming, connection between cumulative income growth and presidential election outcomes. On one hand, the incumbent party lost five of the six elections (1960, 1976, 1980, 1992, 2008, and 2012) in which cumulative income growth was less than 5%. On the other hand, the incumbent party's average vote margin was about 7 percentage points in the five elections in which cumulative income growth exceeded 10%. However, the range of outcomes in those elections reflects the imprecision of the overall relationship between cumulative income growth and voting behavior. Incumbent presidents won reelection by landslides in two of those cases (1964 and 1972), but incumbent vice presidents were narrowly defeated in two others (1968 and 2000, albeit with a slim popular vote plurality in the latter case), and in 1952 the incumbent party's candidate was trounced despite much-higher-than-average cumulative income growth.

---

[9] Hibbs (2006, 7). Hibbs's own analysis is rare in focusing on the extent of temporal discounting in voters' reactions to economic conditions. He found relatively modest discounting of past economic performance; however, other analysts employing similar models have found that recent economic performance is much more relevant than previous performance (Bartels and Zaller 2001; Erikson, Bafumi, and Wilson 2002; Achen and Bartels 2004).

[10] Real disposable personal income (BEA, NIPA, table 7.1, line 12) includes wages and salaries, investment income, and government transfers (including, for example, Social Security and unemployment benefits but not in-kind government services such as public education) minus taxes paid. Thus, it arguably provides a better gauge of economic well-being than the pre-tax income figures for households or families reported by the Census Bureau. It may also better capture the direct impact of government policies intended to bolster incomes in the short run, such as tax cuts or benefit increases. Of course, per capita income is an average value, and changes in the average may not reflect the economic fortunes of most individuals when income is distributed unequally, as it increasingly has been over the decades analyzed here.

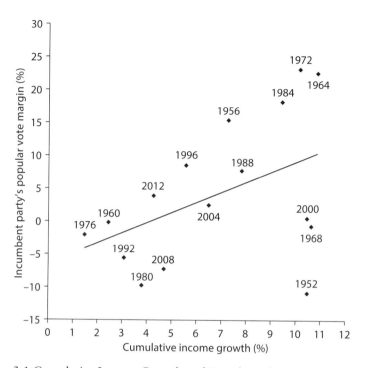

FIGURE 3.1 Cumulative Income Growth and Presidential Election Outcomes, 1952–2012

By comparison, the relationship depicted in figure 3.2 is a good deal stronger and more consistent. The difference here is that elections are arrayed along the horizontal axis not on the basis of cumulative income growth over the president's second, third, and fourth years in office but rather on the basis of income growth in the presidential election year only. Knowing how the economy fared during the election year turns out to be much more helpful in accounting for the incumbent party's fortunes than knowing how it fared over the entire three years leading up to the election. There are still substantial deviations from the overall pattern in specific elections. For example, incumbent presidents (or their successors) did much better than election-year income growth alone would have suggested in 1956, 1964, 1972, and 1996, and significantly worse in 1952, 1968, 1992, and 2000. However, the average deviation is almost 25% smaller than in figure 3.1.

The relationships depicted in figures 3.1 and 3.2 are elaborated in the statistical analyses reported in table 3.1. The first two columns of the table simply document the contrasting relevance of long-term and short-term income growth visible in the figures. While cumulative income growth is clearly

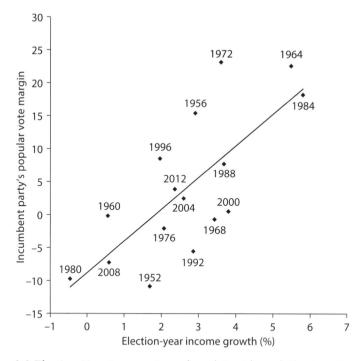

FIGURE 3.2 Election-Year Income Growth and Presidential Election Outcomes, 1952–2012

related to election outcomes, it accounts for only 16% of the variance in incumbent vote margins, leaving an average discrepancy of 10 percentage points between expected and actual outcomes. However, election-year income growth alone accounts for 51% of the variance in election outcomes, reducing the average discrepancy between expected and actual vote margins to less than 8 percentage points.

The analyses reported in the third and fourth columns of table 3.1 include an additional explanatory factor—the incumbent party's tenure in office. There is a fairly strong tendency for the incumbent party's electoral fortunes to decline with each additional year that it has held the White House. Presumably this pattern reflects the cumulative effect of exhausted policy agendas, personnel turnover, and accumulating scandals on voters' desire for a change in leadership. Over the course of a typical four-year term, these forces reduced the incumbent party's popular vote margin by about six percentage points. However, allowing for this negative effect of tenure on the incumbent party's electoral fortunes leaves the comparison of long-term and short-term economic factors essentially unchanged. The results presented in the third column of

TABLE 3.1

Myopic Economic Voting in Presidential Elections, 1952–2012

Ordinary least squares regression parameter estimates (with standard errors in parentheses) for incumbent party's popular vote margin (%).

	(1)	(2)	(3)	(4)	(5)
Cumulative disposable income growth (%)	1.55 (.80)	—	1.71 (.57)	—	.49 (.66)
Election-year disposable income growth (%)	—	4.81 (1.19)	—	4.16 (.92)	3.49 (1.30)
Incumbent party tenure (years)	—	—	−1.66 (.44)	−1.22 (.36)	−1.30 (.38)
Intercept	−6.38 (5.97)	−8.79 (3.72)	4.12 (5.08)	1.47 (4.14)	.56 (4.39)
Standard error of regression	10.05	7.68	7.19	5.82	5.92
Adjusted R^2	.16	.51	.57	.72	.71
N	16	16	16	16	16

Sources: Dave Leip's Atlas of U.S. Presidential Elections; Bureau of Economic Analysis.

table 3.1 suggest that each additional percentage point of cumulative income growth translated into a gain of about 1.7 percentage points in the incumbent party's expected vote margin, whereas those in the fourth column suggest that each additional percentage point of election-year income growth boosted the incumbent party's vote margin by more than four percentage points. Again, the analysis focusing on election-year income growth does a significantly better job of accounting for actual election outcomes, with an average error of less than six percentage points. The most notable outliers in figure 3.2 are all much better accounted for in this version of the analysis (since 1956, 1964, 1972, and 1996 were all elections in which the incumbent party had held office for just four years, while 1952, 1968, 1992, and 2000 were all cases in which the incumbent party had held office for eight years or more).

Taking simultaneous account of both long-term and short-term income growth (in the fifth column of table 3.1) does little to improve upon the simpler analysis in the fourth column employing election-year income growth alone. While it is impossible to rule out the possibility that income growth in the first two years of each president's term had some modest effect on his electoral fortunes, that effect pales by comparison with the impact of election-year income growth. What happened earlier seems to be mostly irrelevant, if not utterly forgotten, by the time of the next election.[11]

These results shed important light on the nature of the economic accountability provided by presidential elections. Election outcomes are sensitive to real changes in the nation's economic fortunes under the incumbent party—but only if those changes occur in close proximity to Election Day. Voters reward their elected leaders for *some* good times and punish them for *some* bad times. Does this myopic focus on "present advantages" have significant political consequences?

The Electoral Timing of Income Growth

More than a quarter-century ago, political scientist Edward Tufte noted that the electorate's short time horizon with respect to economic evaluations could produce "a bias toward policies with immediate, highly visible benefits and deferred, hidden costs—myopic policies for myopic voters." Tufte worried that political manipulation of economic policy could generate significant social costs due to wasteful government spending and other forms of "economic instability and inefficiency" aimed at making the economy flourish around election time. He provided statistical evidence of electoral cycles in transfer payments, income growth, unemployment, and inflation, as well as considerable qualitative evidence of specific efforts by incumbents to produce those cycles. Richard Nixon in 1972 was a particularly energetic manipulator of everything from the money supply (through his erstwhile political ally Arthur Burns, the chairman of the Federal Reserve Board) to effective dates of increases in Social Security benefits and payroll taxes; as Tufte delicately put it, "The extremes of 1972 were special because Richard Nixon was special."[12]

Subsequent research on political business cycles has produced less clear results. According to one observer, "while the general logic behind the theory is quite persuasive, the empirical evidence for electoral-economic cycles is spotty at best."[13] Figure 3.3 redeploys the Census Bureau's figures on in-

---

[11] Indeed, even the "short-term" measure of election-year income growth employed here may exaggerate voters' attention spans. Using quarterly rather than annual data, Achen and Bartels (2016, chap. 6) showed that income growth in just the middle two quarters of each election year accounted for election outcomes even better than income growth over the entire election year.

[12] Tufte (1978, 143, 63). Tufte argued that Nixon's enthusiasm for political manipulation of the economy arose in significant part from his unhappy experience with an *un*manipulated economy in his first presidential campaign in 1960. According to Nixon (quoted by Tufte 1978, 6): "In October, usually a month of rising employment, the jobless rolls increased by 452,000. All the speeches, television broadcasts, and precinct work in the world could not counteract that one hard fact." Nixon lost the election by fewer than 120,000 votes.

[13] Schultz (1995, 79).

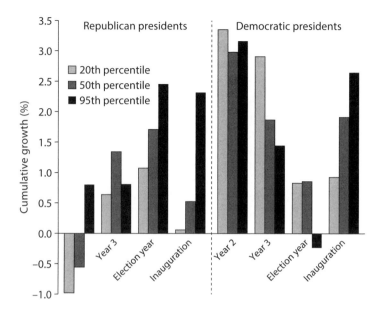

FIGURE 3.3 Electoral Cycles in Income Growth Under Republican and Democratic Presidents, 1948–2014

come growth from chapters 1 and 2 to explore whether presidents have produced unusual income growth in election years. Separately for families at the 20th, 50th, and 95th percentiles of the income distribution, the figure shows average levels of real income growth in each year of the election cycle, beginning with the year after a new (or reelected) president is inaugurated and continuing through the subsequent inauguration year.[14]

The pattern of income growth under Republican presidents (in the left panel of the figure) is generally consistent with Tufte's account of a political business cycle. Whether we focus on the working poor, the middle class, or affluent families, the average rate of real income growth clearly peaked in presidential election years. The election-year boosts in average income growth by comparison with non-election years exceed a full percentage point. But if Tufte's concerns about the possibility of a political business cycle seem to be confirmed by the economic record of Republican administrations, Democratic presidents have quite remarkably produced an *anti–political business cycle*. The right panel of figure 3.3 shows that Democratic presidents have produced substantially *less* income growth in presidential

---

[14] Here, as in chapter 2, I lag partisan control by one year to allow time for a president's policies to affect income growth. Thus, each president's influence is assumed to run from the year after his inauguration through the year after his election (the following inauguration year).

election years than at other times. Under Democrats, average income growth reached an early peak in the second year of each four-year term, then declined markedly in the third and fourth (election) years. Thus, the "spotty" evidence of an electoral cycle in income growth reflects two very different partisan regimes—one highly cyclical and the other counter-cyclical.

The reason for this remarkable pattern is by no means obvious. One possible explanation is a partisan bias in the Federal Reserve's monetary policy. Economists James Galbraith, Olivier Giovannoni, and Ann Russo found that monetary policy in the period from 1970 to 2006 was "more permissive" in the run-ups to presidential elections when Republicans held the White House and "more restrictive" when Democrats were in office. William Clark and Vincent Arel-Bundock likewise found "systematic differences in Fed behavior under Republican and Democratic presidents since the Fed became operationally independent in the middle of the twentieth century. These differences are most acute in pre-electoral periods and, so, could plausibly affect electoral outcomes."[15]

Another possible explanation for the partisan difference in electoral cycles is that the characteristic economic strategies of Democratic and Republican presidents in the "honeymoon" periods at the *beginning* of each four-year term have predictable spillover effects at the time of the next election. The tabulations presented in figure 2.2 show that the largest partisan differences in income growth, by far, were concentrated in the second year of each four-year presidential term—the first year in which new post-election policies would be likely to influence income growth. Democratic presidents have routinely produced extremely strong income growth in these "honeymoon" years; real disposable income per capita grew by an average of 3.2%, while family incomes in every part of the income distribution grew by an average of 2.9% to 3.4%. However, it seems that these expansionary bursts cannot be sustained indefinitely; by the time of the next presidential election, income growth under Democratic presidents typically slowed to a crawl, especially for families near the top of the income distribution. In stark contrast, the second years of Republican terms have often seen significant economic contractions; in fact, middle-class and working poor families experienced *negative* income growth in seven of the nine postwar Republican "honeymoon" years.[16] But contractions, like expansions, have a finite duration, and

---

[15] Galbraith, Giovannoni, and Russo (2007, 22); Clark and Arel-Bundock (2013, 1).

[16] The real incomes of middle- and low-income families fell in 1954, 1958, 1970, 1974, 1982, 1990, and 2002. In two of those cases—1982 and 2002—incomes had already begun to fall in the first year of the new Republican president's term, before his policies were likely to have had much effect. However, even leaving aside first terms, the onset of recessions within 20 months following three of the five postwar Republican reelections (August 1957, November 1973, and July 1990) contrasts with the record of spectacular income growth in the corresponding portions of Democratic administrations.

TABLE 3.2
The Presidential Election Cycle and Partisan Income Growth, 1948–2014

Annual real pre-tax income growth (%) for families at various points in the income distribution (with standard errors in parentheses). Partisan control measured from one year following inauguration to one year following subsequent inauguration.

	Democratic presidents	Republican presidents	Partisan difference
Presidential election years			
20th percentile	.83	1.08	−.25
	(1.32)	(1.27)	(1.83)
40th percentile	1.02	1.87	−.85
	(.89)	(1.07)	(1.41)
60th percentile	1.21	1.67	−.46
	(1.17)	(1.02)	(1.55)
80th percentile	.66	1.91	−1.25
	(.97)	(1.04)	(1.43)
95th percentile	−.24	2.46	−2.69
	(.98)	(.97)	(1.39)
N	8	9	17
Non-election years			
20th percentile	2.37	−.09	+2.47
	(.79)	(.61)	(.98)
40th percentile	2.22	.14	+2.08
	(.61)	(.47)	(.76)
60th percentile	2.24	.64	+1.60
	(.48)	(.43)	(.65)
80th percentile	2.45	.93	+1.52
	(.46)	(.39)	(.60)
95th percentile	2.46	1.31	+1.15
	(.60)	(.45)	(.74)
N	23	27	50

Source: Census Bureau, Historical Income Tables.

by the time of the next presidential election income growth had typically rebounded significantly.

Table 3.2 provides a detailed comparison of income growth rates under each party in presidential election years and non-election years. Under Republican presidents, average growth at every income level has been from 1.0 to 1.7 percentage points higher in presidential election years than in

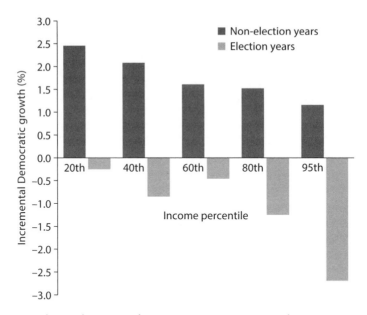

FIGURE 3.4 Electoral Timing of Democratic Income Growth Premium, 1948–2014

non-election years. In stark contrast, Democrats have presided over much *less* income growth in election years than in non-election years; these differences range from 1.0 to 2.7 percentage points. The largest falloff in election-year income growth has been among affluent families (at the 95th percentile of the income distribution), whose real incomes declined in four of the eight election years in which Democrats held the White House.[17]

The striking difference in the relative economic performance of Democratic and Republican presidents in table 3.2 is illustrated in figure 3.4, which compares the Democratic advantage in income growth at each income level in election years and non-election years. In non-election years, families at every income level experienced much faster income growth under Democratic presidents than under Republican presidents; the differences range from almost 2.5 percentage points among working poor families down to 1.2 percentage points among affluent families. However, when the partisan comparison is limited to presidential election years, families at every income level turn out to have fared better under *Republican* presidents than under

[17] The largest one-year decline in the real incomes of affluent families, 5.5%, occurred in 1948. The average income growth rate in the other seven election years with Democratic incumbents was positive (.51), but still far below the average growth rate in non-election years (2.46).

Democrats; these differences are small for working poor families, but very large—2.7 percentage points—for affluent families. Whether through political skill or pure good luck, Republican presidents have been remarkably successful in targeting income growth to coincide with presidential elections, while Democratic presidents have been remarkably *un*successful in producing election-year prosperity.

If voters judiciously weighed the entire record of income growth over each incumbent's term, this striking disparity between Democratic and Republican administrations in the timing of income growth would be politically inconsequential. Good and bad times would be factored into voters' assessments of incumbent performance regardless of when they occurred. Conversely, if partisan patterns of income growth were identical in election years and non-election years, economic myopia would be a mere psychological curiosity of little political relevance—simply one more entry in an extensive catalog of heuristics and biases that shape human decision-making. In tandem, however, the myopia of voters and the peculiar success of postwar Republican presidents in producing robust income growth in the run-up to presidential elections have significantly bolstered electoral support for Republican candidates.

Democratic presidents, in contrast, have routinely been punished by myopic voters for slow election-year growth but given little credit for robust income growth in non-election years. The statistical analysis presented in the fifth column of table 3.1 suggests that voters probably gave Democratic presidents little or no electoral credit for producing very strong across-the-board income growth in the second years of their four-year terms (with average real growth rates ranging from 2.9% to 3.4%), while Republican presidents have paid little or no electoral cost for presiding over frequent declines in real income for middle-class and working poor families in the second years of their four-year terms.

CLASS BIASES IN ECONOMIC VOTING

Since partisan differences in average income growth are greatest for middle-class and working poor families, those families are the most obvious economic losers from the partisan bias in accountability produced by voters' short time horizons. The result, obviously, is to exacerbate economic inequality. As if that were not enough, middle-class and poor families are also distinctly disadvantaged by a different kind of bias in economic voting—a significant class bias in sensitivity to income growth. American voters, regardless of their own place in the income distribution, seem to be quite sensitive to the economic fortunes of high-income families but much less sensitive to income growth among middle-class and poor families. Here, too, the political result is to bolster the Republican Party, and the economic result is to further exacerbate income inequality.

In exploring the possibility of class bias in economic voting, it may be helpful to begin by assessing the contributions of voters at different income levels to the overall relationship between economic conditions and presidential election outcomes documented in figure 3.2 and table 3.1. The American National Election Studies (ANES) project has conducted high-quality surveys in connection with every presidential election since 1952.[18] The data from these surveys make it possible to examine the distinctive responsiveness of various subgroups of the electorate, including high-, middle-, and low-income voters, to national economic conditions.[19] The survey data also make it possible to take account of other potentially relevant characteristics of individual voters—most importantly, the long-standing psychological attachments of most American voters to one or the other of the major political parties.[20]

The statistical analyses of presidential election outcomes reported in table 3.1 show that the incumbent party's electoral fortunes are strongly affected by election-year income growth and by how long the incumbent party has held office. The first column of table 3.3 presents the results of a parallel analysis employing ANES survey data from the same 16 elections, relating the presidential vote choices of almost 19,000 voters to these same factors, plus the voters' own partisan attachments. The results are quite consistent with those presented in table 3.1. They imply that each additional percentage point of median income growth during the election year increased an otherwise undecided voter's probability of supporting the incumbent party by almost five percentage points, while each additional term in office reduced her probability of supporting the incumbent party by almost six percentage points.[21]

---

[18] Data and documentation are publicly available from the ANES website (http://www .electionstudies.org/). In presidential election years, the ANES surveys have included pre-election interviews conducted between Labor Day and Election Day and post-election reinterviews with 85–90% of the pre-election respondents. Most of the surveys were conducted in respondents' homes by interviewers employed by the University of Michigan's Survey Research Center. The survey samples are intended to be representative of citizens of voting age living in households in the continental United States (excluding Alaska and Hawaii). My analyses employ the survey weights provided in the ANES Cumulative Data File (VCF0009x) but are additionally weighted by the ratio of national turnout to surveyed voters in each election year (in order to avoid over-weighting or under-weighting years with unusually large or small survey sample sizes).

[19] I use survey respondents' self-reports of family income to create three income groups of roughly equal size in each election year, excluding those (about 7%) who declined to report their families' incomes. The differences in reported sample sizes for the three groups reflect differences in election turnout rates across income groups.

[20] The classic scholarly explication of party identification and its effects is by Campbell et al. (1960). Bartels (2000) tracked the relationship between party identification and voting behavior in presidential and congressional elections over the second half of the 20th century.

[21] The statistical results presented in table 3.3 are not directly comparable with those presented in table 3.1, since they are based on probit analyses of the *probability* of voting for the

TABLE 3.3

Economic Voting by Income Group, 1952–2012

Probit parameter estimates (with standard errors in parentheses) for probability of incumbent party vote. Weighted data clustered by election year; major-party voters only.

	All income groups	High income	Middle income	Low income
Cumulative disposable income growth (%)	–.026 (.027)	–.034 (.029)	–.022 (.032)	–.023 (.026)
Election-year disposable income growth (%)	.124 (.049)	.132 (.062)	.146 (.042)	.080 (.057)
Incumbent party tenure (years)	–.037 (.013)	–.039 (.015)	–.033 (.014)	–.051 (.015)
Incumbent party identification (–1 to +1)	1.600 (.076)	1.678 (.085)	1.589 (.084)	1.531 (.083)
Intercept	.161 (.183)	.259 (.219)	.013 (.169)	.334 (.223)
Log likelihood	–7,582.9	–2,567.7	–2,409.9	–2,090.7
Pseudo-R²	.42	.43	.42	.42
N	18,975	6,580	5,947	5,244

Source: 1952–2012 ANES surveys.

Repeating the same analysis separately for high-, middle-, and low-income voters produces generally similar results (presented in the second, third, and fourth columns of table 3.3), with one notable exception: voters in the bottom third of the income distribution appear to have been somewhat less sensitive than affluent and middle-class voters to election-year income growth. One possible explanation for this difference is that *average*

---

incumbent party's presidential candidate rather than ordinary regression analyses of the incumbent party's aggregate vote *margin*. One implication of the probit model is that the implied effects of the explanatory factors are non-linear, reaching their maximum levels among voters who are otherwise equally likely to support either party. (For example, the impact of economic conditions is assumed to be greater among political independents than among strong partisans, since the latter are likely to vote for their party's candidate regardless of whether the economy is booming or slumping.) That the estimated effects reported in the text, for an otherwise undecided voter, are almost twice as large as the *average* effects for the electorate as a whole implies that an additional percentage point of election-year income growth would increase the incumbent party's vote *margin* by about 5.5 points and that an additional term in office would decrease the incumbent party's vote margin by about 6.6 points. The corresponding estimates derived from the fifth column of table 3.1 are 3.5 points and 5.2 points, respectively.

TABLE 3.4
The Electoral Impact of High- and Low-Income
Growth by Income Group, 1952–2012

Probit parameter estimates (with standard errors in parentheses) for probability of incumbent party vote. Weighted data clustered by election year; major-party voters only.

	All income groups	High income	Middle income	Low income
Election-year high-income (95th percentile) growth	.126 (.013)	.128 (.017)	.139 (.015)	.115 (.018)
Election-year low-income (20th percentile) growth	−.026 (.015)	−.031 (.016)	−.030 (.015)	−.021 (.017)
Incumbent party tenure (years)	−.049 (.011)	−.054 (.014)	−.041 (.011)	−.058 (.010)
Incumbent party identification (−1 to +1)	1.649 (.065)	1.721 (.083)	1.647 (.070)	1.586 (.067)
Intercept	.252 (.102)	.337 (.136)	.155 (.098)	.321 (.104)
Log likelihood	−7,414.3	−2,516.0	−2,354.2	−2,038.2
Pseudo-R²	.44	.45	.43	.44
N	18,975	6,580	5,947	5,244

Source: 1952–2012 ANES surveys.

disposable income growth may not really reflect the economic experiences of low-income families, even over the limited time horizon of an election year. Perhaps employing a more class-specific measure of income growth would produce more robust evidence of economic voting. With that possibility in mind, the statistical analyses reported in table 3.4 repeat those in table 3.3, but with separate measures of election-year income growth for affluent and working-poor families (at the 95th and 20th percentiles of the income distribution, respectively). If voters are specifically sensitive to their own economic fortunes or those of their own income class, we should expect to see high-income growth mattering more for high-income voters and low-income growth mattering more for low-income voters.

Surprisingly, the results presented in table 3.4 provide no indication of class-specific economic voting patterns. Rather, the clear pattern for high-, middle-, and low-income voters alike is that high-income growth mattered a great deal at the polls, while low-income growth conveyed no electoral

TABLE 3.5

The Electoral Impact of High-Income Growth by Income Group, 1952–2012

Probit parameter estimates (with standard errors in parentheses) for probability of incumbent party vote. Weighted data clustered by election year; major-party voters only.

	All income groups	High income	Middle income	Low income
Election-year high-income (95th percentile) growth (%)	.096 (.016)	.093 (.021)	.097 (.018)	.100 (.014)
Election year disposable income growth (%)	.018 (.028)	.023 (.039)	.038 (.027)	−.022 (.035)
Incumbent party tenure (years)	−.046 (.012)	−.050 (.015)	−.037 (.011)	−.059 (.011)
Incumbent party identification (−1 to +1)	1.640 (.064)	1.716 (.082)	1.634 (.068)	1.577 (.065)
Intercept	.203 (.151)	.273 (.195)	.057 (.127)	.382 (.170)
Log likelihood	−7,425.5	−2,521.6	−2,356.8	−2,039.8
Pseudo-R^2	.43	.45	.43	.44
N	18,975	6,580	5,947	5,244

Source: 1952–2012 ANES surveys.

advantage at all to the incumbent party, even among low-income voters. The analyses reported in table 3.5 provide even more remarkable evidence of class biases by comparing the effects of high-income growth and overall income growth (as measured by election-year changes in real disposable personal income per capita). Again, the results indicate that voters in every income group were highly sensitive to high-income growth, but much less sensitive to overall income growth. For the electorate as a whole, each percentage point of income growth for affluent families seems to have produced as much additional support for the incumbent party as *five* points of growth in overall real disposable income per capita. If anything, this bias was strongest among low-income voters, who were highly responsive to income growth among the affluent but attached no apparent weight at all to overall income growth.

Although the statistical results presented in tables 3.3, 3.4, and 3.5 are based on nearly 19,000 individual vote choices, they represent only 16 distinct configurations of election-year contexts. Thus, it is not impossible that the markedly disproportional electoral significance of high-income growth in tables 3.4 and 3.5 is merely a statistical fluke. However, if it *is* a fluke, it is a very persistent one. It certainly is not attributable to any one anomalous election, since the effect holds up strongly when each election is dropped from the analysis in turn.[22] Nor is it limited to years in which Republicans, or Democrats, held the White House, or to the first half or the last half of the postwar era.[23]

Moreover, class-biased economic voting does not seem to be limited to the United States. Timothy Hicks, Alan Jacobs, and J. Scott Matthews have used the framework outlined here to examine the electoral significance of high-income growth in a variety of affluent democracies. Their comparative study included detailed analyses of survey data from the United States (replicating and extending the analyses presented in the original edition of this book), the United Kingdom, Sweden, and Canada, as well as broader cross-national evidence from over 200 elections in 15 countries from 1945 to 2010. They concluded that low- and middle-income voters "seem remarkably poor at defending—and, indeed, seem to systematically undermine—their own distributive interests. We see widespread demand for inequality across the advanced democracies—an electoral bonus to governments that preside over a concentration of gains at the top. And we find no evidence whatsoever that governments pay a penalty among any income group or in the electorate as a whole for upwardly biased distributions of growth."[24]

In the case of the United States, as we saw in chapter 2, "upwardly biased distributions of growth" have occurred rarely under Democratic presidents but routinely under Republicans. The stark implication of the analyses presented here is that the dramatic shortfalls in income growth for middle-class and working poor families under Republican presidents evident in figure 2.1 have had little or no electoral impact. If economic voting is viewed as a mechanism by which middle- and low-income voters might "defend . . . their own distributive interests"—or, for that matter, the economic interests of the American public as a whole—then the class biases documented here have rendered that mechanism utterly ineffectual.

[22] The estimated effects of high-income growth for the full sample range from .088 (omitting the 1968 election) to .113 (omitting the 2008 election). The estimated effects of overall disposable income growth range from –.016 (omitting the 1980 election) to .037 (omitting the 2008 election). The analysis omitting 2008 is the only one in which the estimated effect of high-income growth is less than four times as large as the estimated effect of overall disposable income growth.

[23] In the nine elections with Republican incumbents, the estimated effects of high-income growth and overall growth were .082 and .003; in the seven elections with Democratic incumbents, the estimated effects were .141 and .028. In the eight elections from 1952 through 1980, the estimated effects were .123 and .010; in the eight elections from 1984 through 2012, the estimated effects were .106 and –.022.

[24] Hicks, Jacobs, and Matthews (2015, 31).

THE WEALTHY GIVE SOMETHING BACK: PARTISAN BIASES IN CAMPAIGN SPENDING

Why do affluent, middle-class, and poor voters all seem so exquisitely sensitive to election-year income growth for affluent families? One plausible possibility is that their subjective impressions of how the national economy is faring are themselves subject to a class bias—perhaps because the mass media pay more attention to the economic fortunes of affluent people than to the economic fortunes of middle-class and poor people. This does appear to be part of the explanation: perceptions of national economic conditions seem to be disproportionately sensitive to income growth for families at the top of the income distribution. However, this class bias in voters' perceptions of national economic conditions is not strong enough to account for most of the apparent class bias in economic voting shown in table 3.5.[25]

If biased perceptions of economic conditions are not the answer, what else might account for the odd sensitivity of voters at every income level to election-year income gains among affluent families? Perhaps income gains for affluent families get translated into campaign contributions to the incumbent party, which in turn influence the behavior of other voters in ways that are not directly captured in the statistical analyses presented here. Certainly, most campaign contributions come from relatively wealthy people.[26] If they are inspired to show their gratitude to the incumbent party by giving a bit more generously when their election-year pocketbooks are flush, that would produce an indirect but potentially potent connection between high-income growth and presidential voting behavior.

---

[25] ANES surveys since 1980 have regularly included a question asking whether "over the past year the nation's economy has gotten better, stayed the same, or gotten worse." A statistical analysis of responses to that question indicates that they are sensitive to overall election-year income growth, as one might expect, but also to the specific income growth rate for families at the 95th percentile of the income distribution. The latter effect is about half as large as the former effect, suggesting that the specific economic fortunes of affluent families had a significant impact on perceptions of the state of the national economy, over and above the impact of general income growth, even among people who were themselves far from affluent. However, much of the statistical impact of high-income growth rates on electoral support for the incumbent party documented in table 3.5 seems to persist even when voters' perceptions of the national economy are included in the analyses as a separate explanatory factor. Thus, the electoral significance of high-income growth does not appear to be entirely, or even primarily, mediated by biased perceptions of national economic conditions.

[26] For example, Verba, Schlozman, and Brady (1995, 194, 565) found that people in the top quartile of the income distribution accounted for almost three-quarters of the total campaign contributions in their 1989 Citizen Participation Study. The broad middle class accounted for almost all the rest; people in the bottom quintile of the income distribution accounted for only 2% of total contributions.

The statistical analysis reported in the first column of table 3.6 relates the incumbent party's spending advantage in each election to real election-year income growth for families at the 95th percentile of the income distribution—the sorts of people who are most likely to be contributors to political campaigns. My measure of each presidential candidate's campaign spending is scaled in (inflation-adjusted 2015) dollars per voter. By that measure, spending has increased substantially over the period covered by my analysis, from about $1.75 per voter (for both parties combined) in the 1950s to almost $9.40 per voter in 2012. The spending differential between the two candidates in each election ranged from a few cents (in 1960 and 1976) to more than two dollars (in 1972, 1980, and 1984).[27]

There is indeed a substantial relationship between the incumbent party's spending advantage and income growth at the top of the income distribution, as the results presented in the first column of table 3.6 show. However, this analysis makes no allowance for the fact that election-year income growth rates, especially at the top of the income distribution, have generally been higher under Republican presidents than under Democratic presidents. And since campaign contributors are likely to have other, ideological reasons to prefer Republican candidates to Democrats, the relationship between incumbent partisanship and high-income growth may produce a spurious statistical association between high-income growth and the incumbent candidate's campaign spending advantage.

In order to allow for this possibility, the analysis presented in the second column of table 3.6 includes the party of the incumbent president as an additional explanatory factor. As expected, Republican incumbents have generally enjoyed much larger spending advantages than Democratic incumbents in election years with similar economic conditions; the partisan difference amounts to $1.28 per voter. Taking account of this Republican

[27] The system of financing presidential election campaigns has changed markedly over the past half-century, most notably with the institution of public funding following the Watergate scandal in the early 1970s. In principle, public funding equalized spending by the two major-party candidates in general election campaigns from 1976 through 2004. (Barack Obama in 2008 was the first general election candidate to decline public funding in order to avoid associated spending limits.) However, a rising tide of spending by parties and other groups during this period undoubtedly had important spillover effects on voters in presidential elections. I attempt to allow for these changes by measuring campaign spending somewhat differently in the pre- and post-Watergate eras. For 1952 through 1976, I use estimates of general election spending compiled by Herbert Alexander (1980, 5). For 1980 through 2000, I count the public funds allocated to each presidential candidate for the general election campaign (ignoring spending during the primary season) plus half the total spending by their parties reported by the Federal Election Commission. For 2004 through 2012, I use the detailed estimates of total general election spending compiled by Candice Nelson (2014, 125), which include spending by the presidential candidates, coordinated expenditures by the parties, and independent expenditures by parties and other groups in support of each presidential candidate (or against his opponent).

TABLE 3.6

Sources of the Incumbent Party's Campaign Spending Advantage, 1952–2012

Ordinary least squares regression parameter estimates (with standard errors in parentheses) for the incumbent party's spending advantage (in 2015 dollars per voter).

	(1)	(2)	(3)	(4)
Election-year high-income (95th percentile) growth (%)	.385 (.097)	.303 (.090)	.223 (.085)	.145 (.091)
Election-year disposable income growth (%)	—	—	.291 (.125)	.307 (.116)
Republican incumbent	—	1.28 (.47)	1.25 (.41)	1.55 (.42)
Incumbent party extremity (difference in absolute DW-NOMINATE scores)	—	—	—	−3.33 (1.91)
Intercept	−.81 (.29)	−1.31 (.33)	−2.03 (.42)	−2.16 (.40)
Standard error of regression	1.00	.86	.74	.69
Adjusted R²	.50	.63	.72	.76
N	16	16	16	16

Sources: Alexander (1980); Federal Election Commission; Nelson (2014).

advantage reduces the apparent effect of high-income growth on campaign contributions, although the effect still appears to be substantial.

The apparent effect of high-income growth on campaign contributions is further reduced by allowing for the possibility that campaign contributors may also be sensitive to *overall* income growth in the election year. The results presented in the third column of table 3.6 suggest that both over-all election-year income growth and high-income growth had significant positive effects on the incumbent party's spending advantage. The analysis reported in the fourth column of the table includes one more potential explanatory factor: the relative ideological extremism of the incumbent party. Although the effect of extremism is not very precisely estimated, these results suggest that campaign contributors may shy away from supporting parties that are too ideological.[28] Allowing for that effect further reduces the apparent impact of high-income growth on campaign spending.

---

[28] This result may help to account for the fact that Democratic presidential candidates significantly outspent their Republican opponents in 2004 and 2008—something that had not happened previously in the postwar era. However, it would be a mistake to attach too much

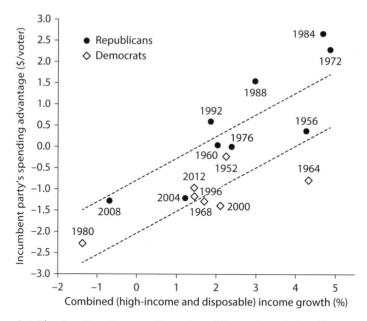

FIGURE 3.5 Election-Year Income Growth and Incumbents' Spending Advantage, 1952–2012

Figure 3.5 provides a graphical summary of the relationship between election-year income growth, incumbent partisanship, and presidential campaign spending.[29] Clearly, there was a strong tendency for incumbent candidates of both parties to spend more, relative to their opponents, in years with robust election-year income growth. The difference in the incumbent candidate's expected spending advantage between the best and worst election-year economies of the postwar era amounts to $3.20 per voter, a substantial fraction of the difference between the largest incumbent

weight to the result given the crudeness of the measurement on which it is based. I compared the absolute values of Poole and Rosenthal's (2007) DW-NOMINATE scores for each party's congressional delegation (averaging the median scores for party caucuses in the House and Senate). The scores generally range from –1 (for the most liberal members) to +1 (for the most conservative members) in each Congress, although additional restrictions intended to harmonize the scores across Congresses sometimes produce values outside that range. By this measure, the relative extremism of the Republican Party has increased steadily since the 1980s; thus, any other factor that eroded the Republican fund-raising advantage over time would contribute to the apparent effect of extremity in table 3.6.

[29] The measure of election-year income growth in figure 3.5 combines the figures for real disposable income per capita and 95th-percentile income growth, each weighted by its estimated effect on relative spending from the third column of table 3.6.

spending advantage on record ($2.67 in 1984) and the largest disadvantage (–$2.28 in 1980). However, even after taking account of election-year income growth, there is a substantial gap between the spending advantages typically enjoyed by Republican incumbents (represented by black dots in figure 3.5) and Democratic incumbents (represented by white diamonds). The average Republican advantage, reflected in the distance between the two dotted lines in the figure, is $1.25 per voter.

Table 3.7 elaborates the statistical analyses of presidential voting behavior presented in table 3.5 to allow for the impact of differential campaign spending on voters' choices. The results for the entire electorate suggest that campaign spending did have a substantial effect on voters' choices. For a voter who was otherwise equally well disposed toward both candidates, they imply that each additional dollar of campaign spending increased the probability of supporting the candidate who spent the money by about three percentage points. The implied effect is, of course, much smaller for voters who were strongly predisposed on other grounds to favor one candidate or the other. Nevertheless, this effect is large enough to suggest that differential campaign spending has probably had a significant electoral impact in presidential elections over the past half-century.[30]

Surprisingly, campaign spending seems to have had a considerably stronger effect among affluent voters than among voters of modest means. The separate analyses for high-, middle-, and low-income voters in table 3.7 suggest that campaign spending was about twice as effective among high-income voters as among middle-income voters—but utterly ineffective among voters in the bottom one-third of the income distribution. And since the incumbent party's edge in campaign spending has been strongly correlated with election-year income growth for affluent families ($r = .73$), the variation across income groups in the apparent effect of campaign spending produces offsetting variation in the apparent effect of high-income growth on support for the incumbent party's presidential candidate. For the electorate as a whole, the estimated effect of high-income growth is about 25% smaller in table 3.7 than in table 3.5. For high-income voters, it is about 55% smaller, while for low-income voters it is slightly *larger*.

---

[30] There is reason to worry that the estimated effects of campaign spending in table 3.7 might be exaggerated owing to unobserved features of the election context that influence both the incumbent party's spending advantage and the incumbent party's electoral success. Replacing the observed spending advantage in each election year with predicted values (instrumental variables) derived from the statistical analyses in table 3.6 produces even larger estimated effects than those reported in table 3.7. Nevertheless, the estimated effects of campaign spending in table 3.7—and their inferred impact on the outcomes of specific elections in table 3.8—must be considered no more than rough estimates.

The Political Consequences of Biased Accountability

The statistical analyses presented in table 3.7 suggest that presidential campaign spending has had a significant impact on voting behavior over the past half-century. However, they do not speak directly to the political *consequences* of that fact. Those consequences are spelled out more clearly in the first column of table 3.8, which reports the estimated impact of differential campaign spending on the outcome of each of the past 16 presidential elections.[31] Since Republican candidates outspent their Democratic opponents in 13 of those elections, it is not surprising to find that they would generally have done less well if campaign spending had been equal. The estimated impact of differential campaign spending on the average Republican vote share over all 16 elections amounts to 1.5 percentage points, more than enough to account for the entire net popular vote margin for Republican presidential candidates over the past several decades. In three cases—1972, 1980, and 1984—their share of the two-party vote was more than three points larger than it probably would have been with equal spending, and in two cases—1968 and 2000—Republican candidates won close elections that they very probably would have lost had they been unable to outspend their Democratic opponents.

The second column of table 3.8 reports parallel estimates of the impact of class biases in economic voting on the Republican vote share in each election.[32] Even after allowing for the effect of differential campaign spending, the statistical analyses reported in table 3.7 indicate that incumbent party candidates did markedly better in election years when high-income growth was especially robust. This effect is substantial in magnitude, especially for low-income voters. However, as we saw in the top panel of table 3.2,

[31] My projections are based on the separate results for high-, middle-, and low-income voters presented in the second, third, and fourth columns of table 3.7. Thus, they allow for greater sensitivity to campaign spending on the part of high-income voters. They also allow for greater sensitivity on the part of voters who were otherwise equally likely to support either candidate (most notably, those who claimed that they did not identify with, or lean toward, either party). Having estimated the impact of unequal campaign spending on the probability of supporting the incumbent party's candidate for each major-party voter in the ANES surveys, I aggregated these estimated effects in each election year to produce the projected impact of unequal spending on the Republican share of the two-party vote.

[32] The projections are constructed along the same lines as those reported in the first column of table 3.7. Voters are allowed to be myopic (responding only to election-year income growth), and they are allowed to be responsive to campaign spending and other factors to the extent implied by the statistical results reported in table 3.7. Differences between actual and projected voting behavior are computed by comparing each voter's probability of casting a Republican vote based on the parameter estimates and data in table 3.7 with the corresponding probability calculated by substituting the growth rate of median family income in each election year for the observed growth rate among families at the 95th percentile of the income distribution.

TABLE 3.7

The Electoral Impact of Campaign Spending by Income Group, 1952–2012

Probit parameter estimates (with standard errors in parentheses) for probability of incumbent party vote. Weighted data clustered by election year; major-party voters only.

	All income groups	High income	Middle income	Low income
Incumbent spending advantage ($ per voter)	.078 (.038)	.157 (.037)	.082 (.051)	−.023 (.040)
Election-year high-income (95th percentile) growth (%)	.071 (.021)	.042 (.026)	.072 (.023)	.108 (.020)
Election-year disposable income growth (%)	−.003 (.035)	−.019 (.037)	.013 (.039)	−.017 (.036)
Incumbent party tenure (years)	−.049 (.010)	−.055 (.011)	−.040 (.009)	−.058 (.012)
Incumbent party identification (−1 to +1)	1.650 (.064)	1.722 (.082)	1.647 (.071)	1.572 (.065)
Intercept	.330 (.183)	.526 (.214)	.197 (.177)	.347 (.181)
Log likelihood	−7,410.4	−2,500.6	−2,351.8	−2,039.5
Pseudo-R²	.44	.45	.43	.44
N	18,975	6,580	5,947	5,244

Source: 1952–2012 ANES surveys.

Republicans have presided over considerably more election-year income growth for affluent families than for middle-class and poor families, while Democrats have presided over considerably less election-year growth for affluent families than for middle-class and poor families. (The partisan difference in average election-year income growth for families at the 95th percentile is 1.9 percentage points.) Thus, the peculiar sensitivity of voters across the income spectrum to high-income growth has contributed powerfully to Republican successes in postwar presidential elections.

The estimated effects of class-biased economic voting suggest that Republican candidates garnered an additional 1.2% of the two-party vote, on average, owing to voters' sensitivity to high-income growth. In most cases the bias was too small to be decisive, but in 1968 and 2000 Republicans won elections they would have lost if voters had responded to median-income growth rather than high-income growth. The discrepancy in 1968 is

TABLE 3.8

The Effects of Unequal Campaign Spending, Class Bias, and Economic
Myopia on Presidential Election Outcomes, 1952–2012

Projected impact on Republican share of two-party popular vote. Italic entries
represent years in which actual and projected election winners differ.

Election year (Republican vote %)	Estimated effect of unequal campaign spending (%)	Estimated effect of differential sensitivity to high-income growth (%)	Estimated effect of differential sensitivity to election-year growth (%)	Combined effect of myopia, class bias, and unequal spending (%)
1952 (55.5)	+0.4	–0.0	–2.4	+1.6
1956 (57.8)	+0.6	–0.5	+4.5	+4.9
1960 (49.9)	+0.1	+2.7	+0.4	+2.4
1964 (38.7)	+1.2	+1.1	–1.6	+2.1
1968 (50.4)	**+2.2**	**+7.8**	**+6.5**	**+9.0**
1972 (61.8)	+4.3	+2.8	+6.1	**+12.6**
1976 (48.9)	–0.0	–0.4	+4.3	+4.9
1980 (55.3)	+3.9	–1.6	+5.0	**+8.3**
1984 (59.2)	+4.7	+0.0	+0.6	+8.0
1988 (53.9)	+2.9	+2.6	–0.4	+2.7
1992 (46.5)	+1.0	+1.9	+2.4	+3.5
1996 (45.3)	+2.1	+0.9	+1.3	+3.9
2000 (49.7)	**+2.2**	**+0.9**	**+4.9**	**+5.8**
2004 (51.2)	–2.0	–0.8	–0.6	–2.3
2008 (46.3)	–2.1	+1.7	–2.6	**–5.2**
2012 (48.0)	+1.8	–0.4	–1.2	–0.1
Average (51.2)	+1.5	+1.2	+1.7	+3.9

Source: Calculations based on parameter estimates in table 3.7.

especially large—almost eight percentage points—because of a striking disparity between booming income growth for most families and an election-year slump for affluent families.[33]

The estimated effects of economic myopia are reported in the third column of table 3.8, which compares the actual Republican popular vote in

[33] The median family's real income grew by 4.6% in 1968, with working poor families gaining 6.2% and even those at the 80th percentile gaining 3.9%, but affluent families' real incomes *declined* by 0.6%.

each election with the projected outcome based on cumulative economic growth rather than election-year growth.[34] The projections suggest that economic myopia inflated the average Republican vote by about 1.7 percentage points, benefiting Republican candidates substantially in six of the past 16 elections and marginally in four more. Richard Nixon in 1968 and George W. Bush in 2000 probably owed their accessions to the White House to the fact that voters forgot (or simply ignored) strong periods of income growth early in the terms of their Democratic predecessors.

Finally, the fourth column of table 3.8 addresses the combined effects of the three distinct partisan biases examined in this chapter—economic myopia, class biases in sensitivity to election-year income growth, and differential campaign spending.[35] The results suggest that, in combination, these three distinct partisan biases increased the average postwar vote for Republican candidates by almost four percentage points. Since the actual average Republican vote share over this period was 51.2%, the combined estimated effect of these partisan biases in economic accountability is large enough to account for the average Republican plurality three times over. In four instances—1968, 1972, 1980, and 2000—partisan biases were very probably essential to Republican presidential victories. These elections include every case in the past half-century in which Republican challengers have managed to defeat Democratic incumbents or their successors. Dwight Eisenhower in 1952 was probably the only Republican in the postwar era who would have won the job in his own right, without the benefit of incumbency, myopic voters, and differential campaign spending.

---

[34] The estimated effects of myopia are based on the assumption that non-myopic voters in each election year would have weighed income growth in the second, third, and fourth years of the incumbent president's term equally. This assumption implies that each additional percentage point of income growth would have increased the incumbent party's popular vote by one-third of the amount implied by the corresponding election-year estimate in table 3.7, regardless of whether that growth occurred in the election year or in either of the two preceding years.

[35] The relevant counterfactual for these calculations is how each election would have turned out if the two major-party candidates had spent the same amount of money on their campaigns and if economic voting had been based on cumulative growth in median family income and real disposable income per capita over the second, third, and fourth years of each president's term. The projections are based on the income-specific probit parameter estimates reported in table 3.7. The estimated combined effects of the three biases reported in the fourth column of table 3.8 are not equal to the sums of the separate estimated effects in the preceding columns because the adjustments for class bias and myopia in the fourth column are applied simultaneously (replacing election-year high-income growth rates with cumulative median-income growth rates) rather than separately (replacing election-year high-income growth rates with election-year median-income growth rates to estimate the impact of class bias and with cumulative high-income growth rates to estimate the impact of myopia).

On the other hand, Barack Obama in 2008 turned the usual partisan pattern of biased accountability on its head by winning an election that he might well have lost had voters been more "accessible to long views," as Ostrogorski put it.[36] In one sense, Obama's election was unsurprising given the economic and political conditions at the time of the election. The economy was already plunging into recession as the election year began, and by Election Day it was in a full-scale meltdown. Real disposable income per capita grew by about half a percentage point in 2008, thanks in part to a spring tax cut aimed at bolstering the slumping economy. However, annual median pre-tax income plunged by 3.5%, and even the incomes of affluent families fell by 2.4%. Moreover, George W. Bush had clearly worn out his welcome after eight years in the White House; his Gallup job approval rating did not reach 35% at any point in the election year and often fell below 30%. The 2008 result was quite consistent with projections taking account of these economic and political circumstances.[37]

In another sense, however, Obama's victory was remarkable. Only once in the postwar era—at the end of Dwight Eisenhower's second term—had election-year income growth under a Republican president been as anemic as it was in 2008. The substantial declines in pre-tax income at every income level contrasted dramatically with the usual pattern of robust income growth at the end of Republican terms. In 2004, George W. Bush had been the first Republican president in more than 70 years to preside over an election-year dip in the incomes of affluent families, but that 0.6% drop was dwarfed by the 2.4% decline in 2008. In part for that reason, John McCain was even more soundly outspent by Obama than Bush had been by John Kerry in 2004.

The projections presented in table 3.8 suggest that biases in economic accountability contributed both directly and indirectly to Obama's election. On one hand, voters' myopia expunged the political credit that McCain might otherwise have received for income growth over the first three years of Bush's second term, probably costing McCain 2–3% of the popular vote. On the other hand, Obama's dominance in fund-raising as the election-year

---

[36] Ostrogorski (1902, 302).

[37] Obama's popular vote margin in 2008 was 7.3 percentage points. The analysis presented graphically in figure 3.2 suggests that he "should" have won by about six percentage points solely on the basis of low election-year disposable income growth. The analysis reported in the second column of table 3.1 incorporating incumbent party tenure suggests that he "should" have won by about 5.8 percentage points. An analysis incorporating both election-year disposable income growth and high-income growth (along with incumbent party tenure) suggests that he "should" have won by about eight percentage points. An analysis based on incumbent party tenure and disposable income growth in the middle two quarters of the election year suggests that he "should" have won by about 9.3 percentage points. By any of these benchmarks, the 2008 outcome was well within the range of expected outcomes based on postwar electoral history.

economy tanked produced a rare Democratic edge in campaign spending, costing McCain another 2% or so of the popular vote. Even with some allowance for voters' sensitivity to high-income growth—which bolstered support for McCain, since less affluent families were faring even worse—the combined effect of these biases was probably sufficient to account for Obama's victory.

There is an obvious irony in the fact that Obama owed his election to the Great Recession that he would spend most of his presidency struggling to overcome. But there is also a less obvious irony in the fact that even the onset of the Great Recession would probably not have gotten Obama elected if it had not happened in an election year. Through the entire postwar era, Republican electoral fortunes had frequently been significantly boosted by voters' myopia. In 2008 the shoe was on the other foot.

The analyses presented in this chapter have only begun to unravel the ways in which contemporary American electoral politics is shaped by partisan biases in economic accountability. More data and more detailed analysis will be necessary to confirm the patterns established here and to clear up significant remaining puzzles—perhaps most importantly, providing a clearer account of the peculiar sensitivity of voters to the economic fortunes of families at the top of the income distribution. In the meantime, however, it seems clear that voters' inaccessibility to long views, their tendency to see only present advantages, and their "materialist dream" of economic solidarity with the upper class all create important failures of economic accountability in the American electoral process.

These biases cast a less-than-optimistic light on the mechanisms of retrospective evaluation that contemporary political scientists have placed at the heart of democratic accountability. If "voters are not fools," as V. O. Key Jr. insisted, neither are they the "rational god of vengeance and of reward" that many scholars have counted upon to ensure the responsiveness of elected officials to the interests of their constituents.[38] From a political standpoint, the most important consequence of the resulting failures of accountability has been to greatly bolster the electoral fortunes of the Republican Party. Absent the partisan biases documented here, my analysis suggests that Republican presidential candidates probably would have won only about half as many elections as they actually did win over the past half-century. In light of the substantial cumulative impact of Republican policies on the economic

---

[38] Key (1966, 7; 1964, 568). Although the colorful phrase "rational god of vengeance and reward" is frequently (mis)quoted in connection with the optimistic view of retrospective accountability that Key set out in *The Responsible Electorate*, its actual use in his earlier textbook, *Politics, Parties, and Pressure Groups*, is more specific and negatory: "The Founding Fathers, by the provision for midterm elections, built into the constitutional system a procedure whose strange consequences lack explanation in any theory that personifies the electorate as a rational god of vengeance and of reward."

fortunes of middle-class and poor families documented in chapter 2, that political consequence has momentous implications for the workings of the American political economy. A great deal of economic inequality in contemporary America is a curious by-product of peculiarities in voting behavior utterly unrelated to voters' taste or tolerance for inequality.

CHAPTER 4

Do Americans Care about Inequality?

THE ANALYSIS PRESENTED in chapter 3 suggests that much of the Republican Party's electoral success in the postwar era—and thus, much of the escalation in economic inequality associated with Republican administrations and policies—is a by-product of partisan biases in economic accountability. From the standpoint of democratic theory, that is a peculiarly unsatisfying conclusion. Good democrats like to think that government policy stems, directly or indirectly, from the will of the people. If it stems instead from such irrelevant quirks of voter psychology as myopia, misperceptions, and responsiveness to campaign spending, the warm glow seems distinctly diminished.

Democratic optimists, however, will note that elections are by no means the only possible avenue by which the will of the people may shape public policy. Political science provides many examples of analyses suggesting that public opinion may have significant direct effects on public policy regardless of whether Republicans or Democrats happen to be in charge.[1] Thus, my accounts of policy-making in chapters 5 through 9 will involve careful weighing of the apparent influence of public sentiment, on one hand, and partisan elite ideology, on the other.

Assessing and interpreting the role of public opinion in the policy-making process requires, first, some clear understanding of what that public opinion *is*. Citizens may have crystallized views regarding specific matters of public policy, or they may not.[2] Insofar as citizens do have meaningful policy pref-

---

[1] Perhaps the most ambitious work along these lines is by Erikson, MacKuen, and Stimson (2002), though, as I note in chapter 11, their statistical analyses seem to imply smaller direct effects of public opinion on policy and larger electoral effects than one might suppose from their prose.

[2] Writing in response to the first wave of enthusiasm for plebiscitary democracy at the turn of the 20th century, A. Lawrence Lowell (1913, 45–46) noted that "no people, however civilized, are capable of forming real opinions on all subjects," and that "no real public opinion is possible" unless "the essential facts are matters of common knowledge from everyday experience, or where they have been so much discussed that familiarity with them has been generally diffused."

erences, those preferences may be internally consistent and sensibly related to their broader political values, or they may not.[3] Public opinion touching on issues related to inequality is likely to be especially complex given the deep and multifaceted resonance of the value of equality in American political culture.

Much popular commentary suggests that ordinary Americans find inequality both natural and unobjectionable—that the ideal of equality, despite its prominence in our official ideology, has little real resonance in American political culture. According to sociologist Nathan Glazer, for example, "Americans, unlike the citizens of other prosperous democracies, not to mention those of poor countries, do not seem to care much about inequality. . . . [E]ven after the Enron and other scandals, most Americans remain apathetic about inequality: What we have today is outrage against those who do not play fair—not outrage over inequality as such." In a similar vein, business writer Robert Samuelson argued that, "on the whole, Americans care less about inequality—the precise gap between the rich and the poor—than about opportunity and achievement: are people getting ahead?"[4]

Analysts of American ideology have often emphasized the potential for conflict and contradiction between the core values of economic opportunity and political equality. For example, Jennifer Hochschild found that people have quite distinct normative intuitions about economic, social, and political inequality. In the economic domain, her rich and poor respondents tended to "agree on a principle of differentiation, not of equality. . . . They define political freedom as strict equality, but economic freedom as an equal chance to become unequal." Similarly, Herbert McClosky and John Zaller wrote that vast differences in wealth and life chances result "partly from the play of economic interests and the desire of those who have prospered to retain their advantages, and partly from the widespread acceptance of a powerful set of values associated with the private enterprise system that conflicts with egalitarianism." Stanley Feldman provided evidence that people use distinct, often conflicting principles to assess "micro-justice" (individual rewards) and "macro-justice" (the social distribution of rewards).[5]

In light of these conflicts and complexities, it should not be surprising that analysts have also noted important exceptions to the general pattern of

---

[3] Philip Converse's (1964) essay on "The Nature of Belief Systems in Mass Publics" is the single most influential assessment of the coherence and consistency of political opinions. Achen and Bartels (2016, especially chap. 2) summarized the relevant scholarly literature and its implications for democratic responsiveness.

[4] Glazer (2003, 111); Robert J. Samuelson, "Indifferent to Inequality?" *Newsweek*, May 7, 2001, 45.

[5] Hochschild (1981, 111, 278); McClosky and Zaller (1984, 63); Feldman (2003).

acceptance of economic inequality. For example, Hochschild found that "almost everyone, rich and poor, is incensed that the very wealthy do not pay their fair share of taxes. They argue that loopholes are too large and that the tax structure itself is insufficiently progressive." McClosky and Zaller noted "signs of resentment toward the advantages enjoyed by corporations and the wealthy. A sizable majority of the mass public believes that corporations and the rich 'really run the country,' that they do not pay their fair shares of taxes, and that they receive better treatment in the courts than poor people do. A fair number of respondents (though not a majority) also believe that the laws mostly favor the rich."[6]

In this chapter I explore three important facets of Americans' views about equality. First, I examine public support for broad egalitarian values and the political consequences of that support. Second, I examine public attitudes toward salient economic groups, including rich people, poor people, big business, and labor unions, among others. Third, I examine public perceptions of inequality and opportunity, including perceptions of growing economic inequality, normative assessments of that trend, and explanations for disparities in economic status—and how these views are shaped by the interaction of political information and political ideology.

The first half of the chapter provides strong evidence of the importance of egalitarian values in American political culture. The vast majority of Americans express support for equality in the abstract, and perhaps more surprisingly, those egalitarian values are translated into support for a variety of concrete social welfare policies, including government services, employment programs, health insurance, and aid to African-Americans. At a more visceral level, survey respondents say that they feel much warmer toward "working-class people" and "poor people" than toward "business people" and "rich people"—and those class feelings, too, bolster support for egalitarian policies. Most people also believe that the rich pay less than they should in taxes.

All of this sounds like fertile ground for a populist backlash against the escalating inequality of the New Gilded Age. Perhaps it is. However, the second half of this chapter provides some significant grounds for doubt. Three-fourths of Americans said that "the difference in incomes between rich people and poor people in the United States today" was larger than it was 20 years ago, but those responses appear to reflect cynical folk wisdom more than close attention to actual economic trends. The proportion of the public agreeing with the sardonic adage that "the rich get richer and the poor get poorer" increased markedly in the 1960s and early 1970s—a period in which the poor became rather *less* poor, though poverty became more salient. However, the substantial increase in economic inequality over

[6] Hochschild (1981, 280); McClosky and Zaller (1984, 177–178).

the following three decades had virtually no effect on perceptions of inequality. Meanwhile, among people who did recognize that income differences had increased, more than one-third said that they had not thought about whether that was a good thing or a bad thing.

Public ignorance and inattention have important implications for the politics of inequality—implications I shall explore in more detail in chapters 5 and 6. However, my consideration of public opinion in the realm of inequality also highlights a very different limitation on the translation of egalitarian values into populist politics. Whereas uninformed people may often fail to grasp the political relevance of their beliefs and values, well-informed people may often deny or distort inconvenient facts, preserving a false consistency between their beliefs about the causes, extent, and meaning of inequality in contemporary American society, on one hand, and their ideological or partisan predilections, on the other. In this way, too, genuine allegiance to the ideal of equality may comfortably coexist with fervent support for policies that exacerbate inequality.

EGALITARIAN VALUES

Sure, we hold this truth to be self-evident, that all men are created equal. But it is far from self-evident what that means. Is it inconsistent with American ideals for corporate CEOs to earn 300 times as much as their workers? Are ordinary Americans offended by the fact that the top 1% of income-earners have hauled in more than half of the nation's total gains in real income over the past two decades? Is it wrong for millions of children to grow up without access to decent schools and routine health care? If not, then escalating economic inequality may, after all, be a perfectly understandable and unobjectionable outcome of (small "d") democratic politics.

One useful starting point in examining public thinking about economic inequality in the New Gilded Age is to assess people's allegiance to equality as a general value, sidestepping for the moment the complexities that may arise in *applying* that value to specific cases. While it would be foolhardy to confuse pronouncements of support for equality in the abstract with support for specific policies promoting specific kinds of equality in specific circumstances, it would be equally foolhardy to deny that people's allegiance to abstract values may have important practical political consequences.

As it happens, American National Election Studies surveys over the past three decades have regularly asked random samples of Americans a detailed battery of questions about egalitarian values, as well as questions about a wide variety of concrete political issues in which equality might figure as an important consideration. Responses to these questions make it possible to

TABLE 4.1
Public Support for Egalitarian Values

	Agree strongly	Agree somewhat	Neither; DK	Disagree somewhat	Disagree strongly
Our society should do whatever is necessary to make sure that everyone has an equal opportunity to succeed	60.9%	26.8%	5.4%	4.8%	2.0%
If people were treated more equally in this country, we would have many fewer problems	32.4%	33.7%	14.2%	14.2%	5.4%
One of the big problems in this country is that we don't give everyone an equal chance	22.6%	29.9%	13.6%	23.0%	10.8%
It is not really that big a problem if some people have more of a chance in life than others	7.7%	23.9%	19.2%	28.2%	20.9%
We have gone too far in pushing equal rights in this country	15.9%	28.1%	16.0%	20.6%	19.3%
The country would be better off if we worried less about how equal people are	18.6%	28.8%	16.0%	20.7%	15.9%

Source: 1984–2012 ANES surveys. N = 19,357–20,652.

gauge the extent and bases of public support for equality in the abstract—and to assess the impact of egalitarian values on specific policy preferences. Table 4.1 provides a summary of the responses.[7]

[7] Feldman (1988) provided a detailed discussion of the theoretical pedigree and measurement properties of these items.

The first question in table 4.1 has consistently elicited the most enthusiastically egalitarian opinion. In periodic surveys going back to the early 1980s, more than 85% of Americans have agreed that "our society should do whatever is necessary to make sure that everyone has an equal opportunity to succeed," and more than 60% have agreed strongly with that statement. Interpreted literally, these responses imply an astounding level of public support for what would have to be a very radical program of social transformation. Inherited wealth would have to be outlawed; local funding of public schools would have to cease; every child would have to be assigned competent and loving parents; and prejudices based on race, ethnicity, religion, and sex would have to be eradicated, along with social and economic advantages derived from intelligence, physical attractiveness, and freakish athletic skills. Of course, this is not really what people mean when they agree that we "should do whatever is necessary to make sure that everyone has an equal opportunity to succeed." Nevertheless, their willingness to endorse such a statement, even as a matter of verbal ritual, provides a striking testament to the force of "equal opportunity" in American culture.

More generally, the questions in table 4.1 referring to "an equal chance" or equal treatment generated favorable responses from half to two-thirds of the respondents, while those referring to "how equal people are" and "pushing equal rights" were rather less popular.[8] These differences suggest a consequential distinction in public thinking between equality of opportunity and equality of results. Nevertheless, more detailed analysis of individual response patterns suggests that there is a fair degree of consistency in people's responses to all six questions, regardless of their precise wording. Thus, it is convenient to combine responses to all six questions in a summary scale measuring general support for egalitarian values.[9] The summary scale values range from –1 to +1, with an average value of +.21. Twenty percent of the ANES respondents had very egalitarian scale scores (in excess of +.5), while fewer than 3% had very inegalitarian scores (below –.5).

Of course, given the high level of generality of the survey items comprising the egalitarian values scale, it is possible that the responses to these

[8] The three items in table 4.1 inviting respondents to *agree* with egalitarian sentiments all elicit more egalitarian responses than the three inviting them to *disagree* with egalitarian sentiments. Are people simply prone to agree with such statements regardless of their content? A comparison of responses to the third and fourth questions, which seem closest to being mirror images of each other, is fairly reassuring on this score: the two questions generated similar distributions of responses, with pluralities of 52–34 and 49–32, respectively, for the egalitarian position.

[9] A factor analysis of responses to all six questions produces a strong first factor reflecting support for egalitarian values and a much weaker second factor reflecting a response tendency to agree with all six items regardless of whether they measure agreement or disagreement with the egalitarian position. Since all six items load fairly similarly on the first (substantive) factor (and since the items are balanced between agreement and disagreement), I combine them into a summary scale by simply averaging each respondent's answers to the six questions.

TABLE 4.2: Egalitarian Values and Policy Preferences

Ordinary least squares regression parameter estimates (with standard errors in parentheses). Policy preferences range from 1 (for the most conservative position) to 7 (for the most liberal position). Observations clustered by year; year-specific intercepts not shown.

	Government jobs	Government services	Aid to blacks	Health insurance
Egalitarian values only				
Egalitarian values (−1 to +1)	1.69 (.10)	1.40 (.06)	1.68 (.03)	1.39 (.12)
Standard error of regression	1.69	1.49	1.60	1.86
Adjusted R²	.14	.14	.16	.09
N	14,625	14,883	16,456	11,674
Egalitarian values, ideology, and party identification				
Egalitarian values (−1 to +1)	1.23 (.10)	.89 (.06)	1.35 (.05)	.72 (.08)
Liberal ideology (−1 to +1)	.49 (.05)	.53 (.06)	.41 (.02)	.75 (.08)
Democratic party identification (−1 to +1)	.49 (.03)	.50 (.04)	.31 (.05)	.61 (.05)
Standard error of regression	1.63	1.42	1.57	1.77
Adjusted R²	.20	.22	.19	.18
N	14,183	14,472	16,009	11,220

Source: 1984–2012 ANES surveys.

items represent little more than lip service to the ideal of equality. Do they have any real, concrete political impact? The analyses presented in table 4.2 suggest that they do. These analyses show that people who were more egalitarian took much more liberal positions on each of the major social welfare policy issues that have appeared consistently in ANES surveys over the past three decades—support for government jobs and income maintenance,[10] for

---

[10] "Some people feel the government in Washington should see to it that every person has a job and a good standard of living. Suppose these people are at one end of a scale, at point 1. Others think the government should just let each person get ahead on their own. Suppose

government spending and services,[11] for government aid to blacks,[12] and for government health insurance.[13]

The analyses reported in the top panel of the table show how positions on each of these issues varied with attachment to egalitarian values. For government jobs and aid to blacks, the most egalitarian people were, on average, more than three points to the left of the most inegalitarian people on the seven-point policy scale—a difference between moderately liberal positions, on one hand, and solidly conservative positions, on the other. For views about government spending and services and health insurance, the average differences were almost as large, about 2.8 points.

Of course, people's views about equality are strongly correlated with their broader political ideology and partisanship. Thus, one may wonder whether the strong relationships documented in the top panel of table 4.2 are simply reflections of these more concrete political allegiances. However, that does not turn out to be the case. Not surprisingly, liberals and Democrats were significantly more supportive of government action in each of these issue areas than conservatives and Republicans were.[14] Nevertheless, even after taking account of differences in policy preferences attributable to ideology and partisanship, the analyses presented in the bottom panel of table 4.2 suggest that egalitarian values had a substantial independent impact. For two of the four issues (government jobs and aid to blacks), the estimated effects of egalitarian values on policy preferences exceeded the *combined* effects of ideology and partisanship.

The fact that social welfare policy preferences seem to be strongly shaped by broader views about equality is especially important in light of the overall level of support for egalitarian values in the American public. If opponents

---

these people are at the other end, at point 7. And, of course, some other people have opinions somewhere in between, at points 2, 3, 4, 5, or 6. Where would you place yourself on this scale, or haven't you thought much about this?"

[11] "Some people think the government should provide fewer services even in areas such as health and education in order to reduce spending. . . . Other people feel it is important for the government to provide many more services even if it means an increase in spending. . . ."

[12] "Some people feel that the government in Washington should make every effort to improve the social and economic position of blacks. . . . Others feel that the government should not make any special effort to help blacks because they should help themselves. . . ."

[13] "There is much concern about the rapid rise in medical and hospital costs. Some people feel there should be a government insurance plan which would cover all medical and hospital expenses for everyone. . . . Others feel that all medical expenses should be paid by individuals through private insurance plans like Blue Cross or other company paid plans. . . ."

[14] Partisanship is measured using the standard ANES seven-point party identification scale. Ideology is measured by self-placement on a seven-point liberal-conservative scale, with respondents who said that they didn't know or "haven't thought much about" their position (about 28% of the sample) reclassified as moderates. For comparability with the egalitarian values scale, both measures are recoded to range from −1 to +1.

of equality were just as numerous as proponents of equality, even the strong effects of egalitarian values on policy preferences reported in table 4.2 would not alter the average levels of public support for government action in these policy areas. However, the combination of net support for egalitarian values in table 4.1 and strong effects of egalitarian values on policy preferences in table 4.2 translates into significant additional net public support for liberal policies. For the issues of government jobs and aid to blacks, the overall distributions of public opinion are a good deal less conservative than they would otherwise be; for the issues of government services and health insurance, distributions of opinion that would otherwise be precisely balanced between liberal and conservative extremes instead lean in a liberal direction.[15] In this respect, at least, Americans' support for egalitarian values is much more than just lip service—it has significant political consequences. As Sidney Verba and Gary Orren put it, "values are instrumental in shaping the public policies that give practical effect to political belief."[16]

RICH AND POOR

Ordinary people's responses to such abstract questions as whether we should "make sure that everyone has an equal opportunity to succeed" or whether we have "gone too far in pushing equal rights in this country" turn out to be strongly related to their views about important issues of public policy. However, it seems unlikely that most public thinking about inequality occurs at such a high level of abstraction. Indeed, political scientists have amassed a good deal of evidence suggesting that ordinary citizens engage in rather little abstract reasoning in most realms of politics, relying instead on positive or negative attitudes toward salient social groups to shape their reactions to specific public policies, political candidates, and social conditions.[17]

In the realm of economic inequality, such salient groups might include rich people, poor people, big business, and the working class, among others. ANES surveys over the years have measured public attitudes toward these and a variety of other social groups using a "feeling thermometer." Survey respondents are invited to rate each group on a scale ranging from 0 to 100,

---

[15] The average values on the 1 (conservative) to 7 (liberal) policy scales are 3.51 for aid to blacks, 3.66 for government jobs, 4.15 for government services, and 4.17 for health insurance. The corresponding averages setting the effects of egalitarian values in the bottom panel of table 4.2 to zero would be 3.22 for aid to blacks, 3.40 for government jobs, 3.96 for government services, and 4.02 for health insurance.

[16] Verba and Orren (1985, 2).

[17] The classic statement of this point is by Converse (1964). Nelson and Kinder (1996) examined how the "group-centrism" of issue preferences can be promoted or inhibited by variations in how issues are framed.

TABLE 4.3
Average "Feeling Thermometer" Ratings for Social Groups
Ratings range from zero (least favorable) to 100 (most favorable).

	2004	2008	2012	Average
Working-class people	82.6	82.7	83.9	83.1
The military	79.8	79.6	83.2	80.9
Middle-class people	76.8	76.4	77.3	76.8
Poor people	73.4	72.0	71.0	72.1
Business people	69.3	NA	NA	69.3
Catholics	69.0	67.3	66.3	67.5
Conservatives	60.9	60.3	57.6	59.6
The Democratic Party	58.7	57.2	55.3	57.1
Rich people	59.5	57.3	54.2	57.0
Christian fundamentalists	58.8	56.3	53.4	56.2
Feminists	56.2	56.6	54.2	55.7
Labor unions	58.2	55.6	52.5	55.4
Big business	56.1	53.2	53.4	54.2
People on welfare	55.9	54.4	52.3	54.2
Liberals	54.9	54.7	52.1	53.9
Muslims	53.6	50.3	47.9	50.6
Gay men and lesbians	47.5	49.4	53.7	50.2
The Republican Party	53.9	47.7	47.2	49.6
N	1,003–1,178	1,886–2,259	1,777–2,012	—

Source: 2004–2012 ANES surveys.

with 50 meaning "you don't feel particularly warm or cold" toward the group, ratings above 50 representing "favorable and warm" feelings, and ratings below 50 representing "unfavorable and cool" feelings. Table 4.3 reports the average thermometer ratings for various groups in the 2004–2012 ANES surveys. The groups are listed in order of popularity: at one extreme, "working-class people" received an average rating of 83 out of 100; at the other extreme, the Republican Party received an average rating of 50—just below Muslims and gay men and lesbians.

What, if anything, do these feeling thermometer ratings suggest about the politics of inequality? To the extent that people's political views are colored by their sympathy for economic classes, they are, perhaps surprisingly, quite likely to side with poor people (with an average rating of 72) over rich people (with an average rating of 57). If anything, that gap has increased in recent years, from 14 points in 2004 to 15 points in 2008 and 17 points in 2012. While ordinary Americans may hope, and perhaps even expect, to become rich someday, in the meantime they express rather little warmth for those who have already made it. Big business fared even worse than rich people, with an average rating of 54—the same average rating as for people on welfare. The less pejorative phrase "business people" elicited much warmer feelings (with an average rating of 69); however, even business people were rated less favorably than poor people.

Labor unions (with an average rating of 55) fared slightly better than big business, but much worse than (presumably unorganized) working-class people. Indeed, working-class people (with an average rating of 83) were held in even higher esteem than middle-class people (with an average rating of 77). Given the frequent characterization of America as a society that exalts the middle class, it seems remarkable that most Americans express even more positive feelings about working-class people than about middle-class people.

If people understand and assess public policies, in part, on the basis of their implications for salient social groups, we might expect that the feelings toward the working class, the rich, and other economic groups summarized in table 4.3 would color views about issues like government spending and services and health insurance. The analyses in table 4.4 test this expectation by adding a summary measure of class sympathies to the analyses of policy preferences in table 4.2. The summary measure of class sympathies compares the warmth of people's feelings toward the poor, the working class, and labor unions, on one hand, and the rich, the middle class, and big business, on the other hand.

The results presented in table 4.4 suggest that class sympathies do have significant effects on policy preferences, over and above the effects of egalitarian values, political ideology, and party identification. Most people's class sympathies did not push them strongly in either direction (because they reported fairly warm feelings about *all* of the groups included in the summary measure). Nonetheless, those with moderately egalitarian class sympathies (one standard deviation above the mean) took positions that were about half a point more liberal than those with moderately inegalitarian class sympathies (one standard deviation below the mean) on three of the four seven-point scales. For these three policies—government jobs, government services, and health insurance—the estimated effects of class sympathies rival in importance the estimated effects of egalitarian values and ideology. (For aid to blacks, a policy domain in which class sympathies are presumably less relevant, the estimated effect was much smaller, about one-fifth of a point.)

TABLE 4.4

Class Sympathies and Policy Preferences

Ordinary least squares regression parameter estimates (with standard errors in parentheses). Policy preferences range from 1 (for the most conservative position) to 7 (for the most liberal position). Observations clustered by year; year-specific intercepts not shown.

	Government jobs	Government services	Aid to blacks	Health insurance
Class sympathies (−1 to +1)	1.69 (.14)	1.39 (.34)	.56 (.26)	1.51 (.19)
Egalitarian values (−1 to +1)	.92 (.04)	.66 (.10)	1.07 (.05)	.56 (.04)
Liberal ideology (−1 to +1)	.56 (.05)	.56 (.07)	.34 (.03)	.93 (.06)
Democratic Party identification (−1 to +1)	.55 (.04)	.59 (.10)	.54 (.03)	.57 (.17)
Standard error of regression	1.55	1.35	1.57	1.67
Adjusted R^2	.28	.32	.22	.26
N	3,426	3,241	4,076	3,487

Source: 2004–2012 ANES surveys.

The 2002 and 2004 ANES surveys included another set of questions tapping attitudes toward rich people and poor people in the specific context of a policy issue where class sympathies are presumably even more relevant. These questions asked whether rich people, poor people, and the respondents themselves are asked to pay too much, too little, or about the right amount in federal income taxes. The distributions of responses to these questions are presented in table 4.5.[18]

As with the feeling thermometer ratings of rich people and poor people, these responses demonstrate a rather striking skew in favor of the poor over the rich. For example, 45% of the ANES respondents said that poor people are asked to pay more than they should in federal income taxes, while only 13% said that rich people are asked to pay more than they should. More

---

[18] The tax burden questions were each asked twice in the 2002 ANES survey, before and after the election. The pre-election responses are reported in table 4.5, since they seem less likely to be affected by sensitization stemming from the extensive battery of questions focusing on inequality and tax policy in the 2002 ANES survey.

TABLE 4.5

Perceived Tax Burdens

"Do you feel you are asked to pay more than you should in federal income taxes, about the right amount, or less than you should? What about rich people? What about poor people?"

	2002	2004	Average
Own tax burden			
Pay more than I should	48.3%	39.6%	44.0%
Pay about the right amount	46.2%	51.2%	48.7%
Pay less than I should	3.8%	4.8%	4.3%
Rich people			
Pay more than they should	15.3%	10.3%	12.8%
Pay about the right amount	29.9%	24.9%	27.4%
Pay less than they should	53.2%	60.4%	56.8%
Poor people			
Pay more than they should	45.8%	46.3%	46.1%
Pay about the right amount	43.7%	42.1%	42.9%
Pay less than they should	8.7%	7.0%	7.8%
N	1,495–1,504	1,210–1,211	—

Source: 2002 and 2004 ANES surveys.

than half the respondents said that rich people are asked to pay *less* than they should, while only 8% said that poor people are asked to pay less than they should. Of course, these responses may be based on very inaccurate perceptions of how much rich people and poor people actually pay in federal income taxes. Still, if taken at face value, they seem to demonstrate substantial public support for increasing, rather than decreasing, the progressivity of the tax system.

Respondents' perceptions regarding their *own* tax burdens were not too different from their perceptions regarding the tax burdens borne by poor people. Fewer than 5% said that they are asked to pay *less* than they should, but almost half said that they are asked to pay "about the right amount." The proportion who said that they are asked to pay too much was almost identical to the proportion who said that poor people are asked to pay too much (43% versus 45%). Insofar as these results imply any sort of class solidarity on the part of ordinary Americans, it is class solidarity with the poor rather than with the rich.

People's attitudes about the tax burdens of the rich and the poor—like their attitudes about these groups more generally—reveal a good deal less sympathy for the rich, and a good deal more sympathy for the poor, than one might expect. While it may be true that "Americans do not go in for envy," as a report in *The Economist* put it, neither do they seem especially solicitous of rich people or their problems.[19] Nor do they seem to be punitive in their attitudes toward poor people, except when the focus is shifted to "people on welfare," and even *they* are viewed about as warmly as big business, and more warmly than the Republican Party. Insofar as the policy preferences of ordinary citizens are colored by their class sympathies, those sympathies are more likely to reinforce broadly egalitarian values than to negate them.

Perceptions of Inequality

Ordinary citizens' values and sympathies are likely to be politically significant only when they are connected to consequential political actors or issues. But the political activation of values and sympathies is far from automatic. For example, egalitarian impulses are likely to gain real political traction only when citizens perceive contradictions between egalitarian ideals and social realities.[20] Given the enormous complexity of politics and public affairs, connections of that sort may require a good deal of political information and attention. As the acute political observer Walter Lippmann noted almost a century ago, the fact that much everyday political thinking occurs in a "pseudo-environment" only loosely connected to social reality often postpones or prevents "the murder of a Beautiful Theory by a Gang of Brutal Facts."[21]

In the present context, it seems well worth exploring how much ordinary Americans know about the Brutal Facts of escalating inequality sketched in chapter 1. Recent ANES surveys have included a variety of questions probing respondents' perceptions of economic inequality, its causes, and its consequences. Table 4.6 presents the distribution of responses to a question in the 2002–2012 surveys assessing people's recognition of growing income inequality. The question asked whether "the difference in incomes between rich people and poor people in the United States today is larger, smaller, or about the same as it was 20 years ago." Those who said "larger" or "smaller" were asked whether the difference was *much* larger or smaller or only *somewhat* larger or smaller.

The distribution of responses in table 4.6 seems to demonstrate widespread public recognition of the sheer fact of growing economic inequality

---

[19] "The Rich, the Poor and the Growing Gap Between Them," *The Economist*, June 17, 2006, 28.

[20] Kluegel and Smith (1986); McCall (2013).

[21] Lippmann (1922, 10).

TABLE 4.6
Perceptions of Economic Inequality

"Do you think the difference in incomes between rich people and poor people in the United States today is larger, smaller, or about the same as it was 20 years ago?"

	2002	2004	2008	2012	*Average*
Much larger	42.2%	47.9%	54.9%	52.5%	49.4%
Somewhat larger	32.3%	31.1%	23.7%	26.8%	28.5%
About the same	16.3%	15.9%	13.9%	10.4%	14.1%
Somewhat smaller	6.0%	2.5%	4.2%	3.6%	4.1%
Much smaller	1.8%	0.3%	1.3%	1.7%	1.3%
Don't know	1.5%	2.2%	2.0%	5.1%	2.7%
N	1,508	1,065	2,099	2,051	—

Source: 2002–2012 ANES surveys.

in contemporary America. Overall, almost 80% of the ANES respondents said that the difference in incomes between rich people and poor people was larger than it was 20 years ago, and almost half said it was *much* larger. Only about 5% said it was smaller.

However, the reality of this apparent recognition is called into question by the stability of Americans' perceptions of inequality over the past half-century. As it turns out, survey respondents have consistently been quite likely to endorse the notion that inequality is increasing, regardless of actual economic trends. In a detailed survey of Americans' awareness of rising inequality, Leslie McCall presented a time series dating back to the mid-1970s of responses to a Harris poll question asking, "Do you tend to feel or not feel that . . . the rich get richer and the poor get poorer?" As McCall summarized her results, "this question does not appear to be tapping perceptions of high *levels* of inequality, or at least not perceptions that are accurate. Nor is it necessarily tapping a more general sense that inequality is rising in one period (the 1990s) as compared to an earlier period (the 1970s). Moreover, the vast majority of Americans agree throughout the 1970s, 1980s, and 1990s, that American society is structured in a way that benefits the rich and penalizes the poor, or more loosely that rising inequality is a natural state of affairs."[22]

Figure 4.1 presents an even longer tracking of responses to the Harris question, derived from 51 surveys conducted between April 1966 and May 2011. The responses to the Harris question over this longer period do show a significant increase in public perceptions of economic inequality. However,

[22] McCall (2005, 8).

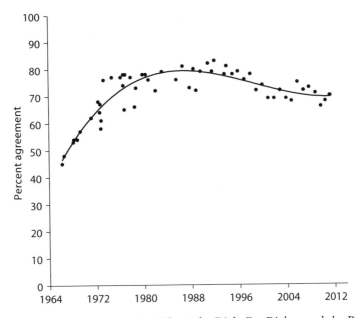

FIGURE 4.1 Americans' Perceptions That "the Rich Get Richer and the Poor Get Poorer," 1966–2011

that increase was concentrated in the late 1960s and early 1970s—a period in which actual economic inequality was modest by today's standards and probably not yet increasing.

By 1973, about three-quarters of the Harris respondents agreed that "the rich get richer and the poor get poorer." That percentage fluctuated in a fairly narrow band (from a low of 65% to a high of 83%) for the next four decades. There is some evidence of an increase in the late 1980s and early 1990s, with a corresponding decline in the mid to late 1990s, but these shifts were quite modest. The remarkable fact is that, by this measure, perceptions of economic inequality were *less* prevalent under George W. Bush and Barack Obama than they had been under Gerald Ford and Jimmy Carter.

The fact that public perceptions of economic inequality bear so little relationship to actual trends in inequality must temper any overly optimistic assessment of the extent to which ordinary people are aware of changes in the relative fortunes of the rich and the poor. However, it does not follow that perceptions of economic inequality are meaningless or politically inconsequential. Even a ritualistic endorsement of the folk wisdom that "the rich get richer and the poor get poorer" may signal unhappiness with this apparently self-reinforcing reality. But then again, it may not.

TABLE 4.7
Assessments of Economic Inequality

"Do you think the difference in incomes between rich people and poor people in the United States today is larger, smaller, or about the same as it was 20 years ago? [If larger or smaller,] do you think this is a good thing, a bad thing, or haven't you thought about it?"

	A good thing	A bad thing	Haven't thought about it; DK	Total
Much larger	2.4%	31.6%	10.6%	44.6%
Somewhat larger	2.1%	12.4%	17.3%	31.9%
About the same	—	—	—	16.1%
Somewhat smaller	1.5%	0.5%	2.5%	4.6%
Much smaller	0.3%	0.6%	0.2%	1.1%
Don't know	—	—	—	1.7%
Total	6.3%	45.2%	30.6%	100%

Source: 2002 and 2004 ANES surveys. N = 2,573.

In the 2002 and 2004 ANES surveys, people who said that differences in income had gotten larger (or smaller) were also asked whether that change was "a good thing" or "a bad thing." The distribution of responses to that question is shown in table 4.7. Among those who said that inequality had increased, most thought that was "a bad thing," but a substantial minority said that they hadn't thought about whether it was a good thing or a bad thing. (Fewer than 6% said that increasing inequality was a good thing.)

If we ask where there is potential political support for egalitarian redistribution in these responses, the obvious place to begin is with the 32% of the public who said that the difference in incomes between rich and poor was much larger than it had been *and* that that was a bad thing. Those people were at the core of a somewhat larger group—44% of the public—who both recognized and regretted the fact that economic inequality had increased. In contrast, outright supporters of economic inequality—those who applauded the fact that inequality had increased or believed with regret that inequality had declined—constituted less than 6% of the public.

The remainder of the public was divided into two broad groups. The first of these, consisting of about 24% of the total population, did not recognize that economic inequality had increased. (Most of these people said that the difference in incomes between rich people and poor people was "about the same" as 20 years ago; the rest thought that it had decreased or said that they didn't know.) People in this group lacked, but could conceivably acquire, a *factual* basis for seeing growing economic inequality as a social problem. The second group, even more numerous (about 28% of the total population), recognized that inequality had increased, but had not thought about whether that was good or bad. What these people seem to have lacked was a *moral* basis for seeing growing economic inequality as a social problem.

Perhaps, like a few of the people in Jennifer Hochschild's much more detailed conversations about distributive justice, people in this second group "do not seek redistribution because they do not care one way or the other about it." But if her respondents are indicative, it is more likely that they "are not forced to face the question of redistribution" in their day-to-day lives and thus "fail to support any system of distributive justice very fully. They sometimes seek equality; at other times, they seek differentiation; too often, they do not know what they want or even how to decide what the possibilities are."[23]

In addition to asking respondents about their perceptions and evaluations of economic inequality, the 2002 ANES survey included a battery of questions inviting respondents to explain why, "in America today, some people have better jobs and higher incomes than others do."[24] The survey offered a variety of potential explanations ranging from "some people just don't work as hard" to "discrimination holds some people back" to "God made people different from one another." Respondents were asked to indicate whether each potential explanation was "very important," "somewhat important," or "not important." Their answers are summarized in table 4.8, which lists the seven potential explanations in order of popularity.

The quintessential American belief that economic success is a matter of hard work fares well in table 4.8, with 45% of the public saying that unequal effort is a "very important" cause of economic inequality. However, there is even more support (about 55%) for the notion that unequal access to a good education is very important. Two other social factors, discrimination and government policies, also loom fairly large as explanations for economic inequality. And while one-third of the respondents said that differences in "inborn ability to learn" are very important, almost half rejected the idea that income differences exist because "God made people different from one another." These responses certainly do not suggest that most Americans

---

[23] Hochschild (1981, 279, 278, 283).

[24] Respondents were also asked an open-ended version of the same question. Half were asked the fixed-choice questions in the pre-election survey and the open-ended version in the post-election survey; the other half got the open-ended version first and the fixed-choice questions in the post-election survey. The responses to the fixed-choice questions from the two random half-samples were generally similar, except that those who responded in the post-election survey attached somewhat less importance to "government policies"—despite the fact that the intervening survey content called attention to a variety of relevant government tax and spending policies.

TABLE 4.8

Explanations for Economic Inequality

"Next, we'd like to know why you think it is, that in America today, some people have better [worse] jobs and higher [lower] incomes than others do. I'm going to read you some possible explanations, and I want you to tell me how important you think each is—very important, somewhat important, or not important at all."

	Very important	Somewhat important	Not important
Some people don't get a chance to get a good education	54.5%	35.1%	9.1%
Some people just don't work as hard	44.7%	41.4%	12.9%
Some people have more inborn ability to learn	33.8%	42.1%	23.4%
Discrimination holds some people back	26.4%	50.2%	22.5%
Government policies have helped high-income workers more	26.0%	38.2%	33.6%
Some people just choose low-paying jobs	19.4%	38.8%	39.6%
God made people different from one another	22.2%	26.5%	48.5%

Source: 2002 ANES survey. *N* = 1,427.

view economic inequality as a merely natural phenomenon, even if they do think it is attributable in part to differences in character and ability.

Some evidence also suggests that Americans' attitudes about economic inequality may have shifted in recent years. In a 1987 survey conducted as part of the International Social Survey Programme, Americans were evenly split on the question of whether "large income differences are necessary for a country's prosperity." But support for that proposition had declined noticeably in a follow-up survey conducted in 1992 and declined still further by 1999, to a level almost identical to those prevailing in the United Kingdom, Germany, Spain, Sweden, and Norway. Over the same 12-year period, the differences in salaries that respondents considered appropriate for people in a variety of specific jobs declined by almost 25%. These results suggest that Americans probably have less tolerance for economic inequality than they used to, and even that their views about its necessity are not much different from those prevailing in other, more egalitarian democracies.[25]

[25] Osberg and Smeeding (2003, tables 2.1 and 4.2-1).

Facts and Values in the Realm of Inequality

So, do Americans care about inequality? Here, as so often, it is easy to disagree about whether the glass is half full or half empty. Almost 45% of Americans say that the difference in incomes between rich people and poor people has increased over the past 20 years and that that is a bad thing—but an even larger proportion either do not acknowledge the fact or have not thought about whether it is good or bad. More than 60% agree that government policies have exacerbated economic inequality by helping high-income workers more, but more than one-third disagree, and more than 85% say that "some people just don't work as hard." Half the public thinks that rich people are asked to pay less than they should in federal income taxes—but almost half does not think so.

What accounts for these differences in perceptions of inequality and its causes and implications? In particular, why is there so much apparent resistance to acknowledging the extent of inequality in a society where more than 85% of the public agrees that we "should do whatever is necessary to make sure that everyone has an equal opportunity to succeed"?

Psychologists have spent considerable scholarly energy elaborating "just world" or "system justification" theories. Their basic idea is that "living in an unpredictable, uncontrollable, and capriciously unjust world would be unbearably threatening, and so we cling defensively to the illusion that the world is a just place." In the economic realm, one result is a widespread belief in the basic fairness of capitalism, even among people who seem to be on the losing end of the free-market system. At the individual level, similar psychological pressures produce unrealistic optimism about one's own economic prospects and an illusion of control over uncontrollable events, both "adaptive forms of self-deception that facilitate coping with environmental stress and uncertainty."[26]

Although the psychological urge to deny injustice and economic vulnerability is presumably universal, some scholars have maintained that political conservatives are, as a matter of personality, especially sensitive to the stresses of an unpredictable, uncontrollable environment—and thus especially strongly motivated to deny its threatening features. On the other hand, conservatives may be especially likely to downplay the potentially troubling features of the prevailing economic system, not because they have fundamentally different personalities but simply because they are psychologically committed to a belief in the justice and efficiency of that system. As

---

[26] For example, in a 1998 Gallup poll focusing on "Perceptions of Fairness and Opportunity," 52% of the respondents with household incomes below $15,000 and 51% of those who described themselves as "have-nots" nevertheless said that "the economic situation in the United States is basically fair." Jost et al. (2003, 55–56, 58, 60). See also Lerner (1980); Jost and Banaji (1994).

TABLE 4.9

Political Ideology and Perceptions of Inequality

Ordered probit parameter estimates (with standard errors in parentheses).
Additional response thresholds not shown.

	The income gap has increased	The larger gap is a bad thing[a]	The poor don't get a fair trial	Hard work is very important
Conservative ideology (–1 to +1)	–.298 (.049)	–.560 (.062)	–.418 (.077)	.408 (.066)
Family income (0 to 1)	.091 (.081)	.509 (.101)	.240 (.128)	–.201 (.110)
2004 survey	.229 (.044)	.121 (.054)	—	—
Intercept	.639 (.053)	–.066 (.063)	.670 (.072)	–.058 (.064)
Log likelihood	–3,040.4	–1,644.5	–1,010.6	–1,378.8
Pseudo-R²	.01	.03	.02	.01
N	2,525	1,976	1,499	1,414

Source: 2002 and 2004 ANES surveys.

[a] Includes only those respondents who said that the difference in incomes between rich people and poor people has increased.

one study put it, "conservatism is a prototypical system-justifying ideology, in that it preserves the status quo and provides intellectual and moral justification for maintaining inequality in society." Either way, we might expect ideological rationalization to produce considerable consistency between perceptions of fact and assessments of value in the realm of inequality.[27]

The statistical analyses reported in table 4.9 shed further light on the ideological bases of differences in perceptions of the extent and implications of economic inequality in American society. The questions on which these analyses are based range from purely factual—whether "the difference in incomes between rich people and poor people in the United States today is larger, smaller, or about the same as it was 20 years ago"—to purely normative—whether increasing income differences are "a good thing" or "a bad thing." The analyses also include two questions from the 2002 ANES survey that are factual in nature but less straightforward than the question about the difference in incomes between rich people and poor people. One

[27] Jost et al. (2003, 63). On personality and political ideology more generally, see McClosky (1958) and Stenner (2005).

of these questions asked whether "a poor person has the same chance of getting a fair trial as a wealthy person does"; the other asked whether the fact that "some people just don't work as hard" is a "very important" explanation for economic inequality. For each of these questions, the table shows how responses varied with political ideology. (The analyses also allow for differences due to family income levels, as well as for differences in responses between 2002 and 2004 for questions asked in both years.)

Perhaps unsurprisingly, the largest effect of political ideology was on responses to the purely normative question—whether the increasing difference in incomes between rich people and poor people is a good thing or a bad thing. (People who said that the difference in incomes had not increased or that they did not know—about 24% of the ANES respondents—are excluded from this analysis.) Extreme conservatives were only half as likely as extreme liberals to say that growing inequality is a bad thing (38% versus 79%) and almost three times as likely to say that it is a good thing or (more commonly) that they had not thought about whether it was good or bad (62% versus 21%).[28] This difference underlines the extent to which "conservatism . . . provides intellectual and moral justification for maintaining inequality in society."[29]

It should not be surprising that conservatism provides moral justification for inequality. However, it *should* be surprising that ideological commitments also had substantial effects on responses to the factual questions included in the table. Extreme conservatives were twice as likely as extreme liberals to say that hard work is a very important explanation for income differences (60% versus 28%). They were also more than three times as likely as extreme liberals to insist that poor people have the same access to justice that rich people do (36% versus 11%), though even most extreme conservatives disagreed with this proposition. Given the complexity of these questions and the paucity of hard evidence available to adjudicate them, liberals and conservatives managed to construct very different, ideologically congenial pictures of the social reality of inequality.

Even in the case of the most straightforwardly factual question included in the table—whether the income gap between rich and poor had increased—the responses of conservatives and liberals were strongly colored by their ideological perspectives. Almost 90% of extreme liberals, but only 73% of extreme conservatives, thought that income differences had increased. Put the other way, conservatives were more than twice as likely as liberals to deny that the difference in incomes between rich people and poor people

---

[28] These probabilities represent response tendencies for extreme conservatives and extreme liberals with median incomes, and they split the difference in responses between people interviewed in 2002 and 2004.

[29] Jost et al. (2003, 63).

had grown larger. In light of the magnitude of the economic trends described in chapter 1, it is striking that more than one in four extreme conservatives persisted in believing that income differences between rich people and poor people have not, in fact, increased over the past two decades.

The statistical results presented in table 4.9 are derived from the responses of a representative national sample of the adult population. Such a sample includes many people who pay little attention to news and have only the vaguest grasp of public affairs. If these inattentive citizens relied on ideological surmise because they lacked solid information about actual trends in economic inequality, the ideological disparities in perceptions evident in the table might simply reflect the (potentially remediable) limits of civic education in this domain.

In order to address that possibility, the statistical analyses presented in table 4.9 must be elaborated to allow for the (potentially distinct) effects of political information within each ideological group. I do that using general measures of political information in the ANES surveys. The 2004 ANES survey included questions asking: (1) which party had more members in the House of Representatives prior to the election; (2) which party had more members in the Senate prior to the election; (3) which party was more conservative at the national level; (4) what job or political office Dennis Hastert held; (5) what job or office Dick Cheney held; (6) what job or office Tony Blair held; and (7) what job or office William Rehnquist held. I constructed a political information scale based on correct answers to these seven questions. (Two of the 1,066 respondents answered all seven questions correctly; 22% gave five or more correct answers, while 42% gave two or fewer correct answers.) The 2002 ANES survey did not include an analogous battery of factual questions about politics; instead, I employed a subjective rating of respondents' "general level of information about politics and public affairs" (on a five-point scale ranging from "very low" to "very high") provided by the interviewer at the end of each interview.[30]

When the ANES survey respondents are differentiated on the basis of political information, it appears that general political awareness makes people markedly more pessimistic on a variety of scores about the extent and implications of inequality in contemporary America. The statistical results presented in table 4.10 imply that people at the top of the information scale

[30] For evidence regarding the validity of the interviewers' assessments of respondents' political information, see Zaller (1985). For respondents interviewed both before and after the 2002 election, I averaged the ratings provided (almost always by different interviewers) at the end of the pre-election and post-election interviews. For respondents who were not reinterviewed after the election (11% of the sample in 2002 and 12% in 2004), I used the pre-election interviewers' ratings only. In every case, I calibrated the resulting information scale to reflect each respondent's position in the overall distribution of political information, from zero (for the least informed) to one (for the most informed). The actual range is from .014 to .999.

were more likely than those at the bottom to say that income differences had increased (84% versus 74%) and much more likely to see that as a bad thing (73% versus 46%). They were also more likely to deny that "a poor person has the same chance of getting a fair trial as a wealthy person does" (85% versus 71%).[31] These differences and others suggest that better-informed people have distinctive views about the nature, sources, and consequences of economic inequality.[32]

Most of the differences between better-informed and less-informed people in table 4.10 parallel those between liberals and conservatives in table 4.9. Better-informed people were more likely to say that income inequality had increased and more likely to say that was a bad thing. They were also more likely to say that poor people were disadvantaged in the legal system and (slightly) less likely to say that differences in hard work were a very important cause of inequality. In each of these respects, political information shifted people's views in the same direction as liberal political ideology.

Although the primary effects of political information and liberal ideology were generally reinforcing, table 4.10 also presents strong evidence of *interactions* between information and ideology: increasing political awareness seems to have had very different effects on liberals and conservatives. Indeed, for each of the four questions included in the table, greater political awareness shifted the views of liberals and conservatives in opposite directions.

This pattern is evident even for the most straightforwardly objective question analyzed in the table—whether differences in income between rich people and poor people had increased or decreased. The solid and dotted lines in figure 4.2 reflect the response tendencies of extreme liberals and extreme conservatives, respectively, based on the statistical results presented in table 4.10. At low levels of political information, the figure shows that conservatives and liberals were about equally likely to recognize that income

[31] These percentage differences are calculated for ideological moderates with average incomes. Since the statistical results presented in table 4.10 provide strong evidence of *interactions* between political information and ideology, the effects of information among liberals and conservatives are quite different from those reported here. These differences are highlighted in figures 4.2, 4.3, and 4.4.

[32] Better-informed people also provided systematically different *explanations* for economic inequality, stressing social causes (inequality in educational opportunities, discrimination, and government policies) more heavily than less-informed people did. They were also somewhat less likely to say that rich people are asked to pay too much in taxes—but no more or less likely to say that poor people are asked to pay too much or that *they* are asked to pay too much. Nor were they more or less likely to think that corporate accounting scandals are widespread. As for perceptions of the partisan politics of inequality, they were much more likely to recognize the differences in positions of the Democratic and Republican Parties on specific tax policies and much more likely to say that the Republicans are "generally better for rich people" and that the Democrats are "generally better for poor people."

TABLE 4.10

Political Information, Ideology, and Perceptions of Inequality

Ordered probit parameter estimates (with standard errors in parentheses).
Additional response thresholds not shown.

	The income gap has increased	The larger gap is a bad thing[a]	The poor don't get a fair trial	Hard work is very important
Political information (0 to 1)	.365 (.093)	.728 (.117)	.470 (.165)	−.150 (.138)
Conservative ideology (−1 to +1)	.210 (.113)	.094 (.141)	−.111 (.191)	−.037 (.170)
Political information × ideology	−.971 (.193)	−1.294 (.251)	−.618 (.348)	.843 (.298)
Family income (0 to 1)	.015 (.086)	.347 (.106)	.144 (.135)	−.194 (.116)
2004 survey	.240 (.045)	.142 (.055)	—	—
Intercept	.502 (.062)	−.352 (.077)	.491 (.094)	.014 (.083)
Log likelihood	−3,024.0	−1,618.0	−1,005.8	−1,374.5
Pseudo-R²	.02	.05	.02	.02
N	2,525	1,976	1,499	1,414

Source: 2002 and 2004 ANES surveys.

[a] Includes only those respondents who said that the difference in incomes between rich people and poor people has increased.

differences had increased over the past 20 years. However, the perceptions of better-informed conservatives and liberals diverged significantly. Among liberals, recognition of increasing income inequality rose markedly with general political awareness, to 86% for people of average political awareness (corresponding to the open circle halfway along the solid line) and a near-unanimous 96% at the highest information level.[33] However, the proportion of extreme conservatives who were willing to admit that economic inequality had increased actually decreased with political information, from

[33] Among ideological moderates, recognition of the growing income gap increased less dramatically than among liberals, but still significantly: from 74% at the lowest information level to 84% at the highest information level.

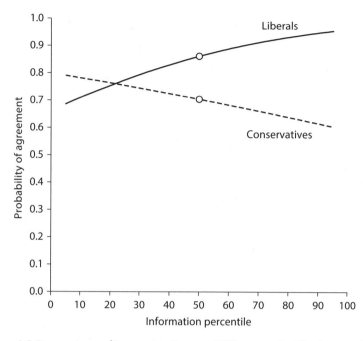

FIGURE 4.2 Perceptions of Increasing Income Differences by Ideology and Information Level

80% among those who were generally least informed about politics to 70% for people of average political awareness to a little less than 60% among those at the top of the distribution of political information.[34] Conservatives who were generally better informed about politics were *less* likely to get this salient fact straight.

The pattern of ideological polarization in figure 4.2 will appear familiar to readers of John Zaller's influential book *The Nature and Origins of Mass Opinion*. Zaller's model of opinion formation encompasses situations in which a "mainstream message" produces uniform shifts in opinion among politically aware conservatives and liberals. However, in situations where political elites are ideologically polarized, Zaller's model implies a very different pattern, with politically aware conservatives and liberals pulled in opposite directions by the contrasting arguments of their respective elites. The result is a characteristic diverging pattern, with undifferentiated (and

[34] For extreme conservatives, the information effect implied by the probit analysis is −.606 (with a standard error of .192); for extreme liberals, the effect is +1.336 (with a standard error of .235).

generally moderate) policy preferences among less-aware conservatives and liberals, but increasing ideological disparity among those who are more attentive to elite rhetoric.[35]

The significance of political awareness in Zaller's model stems from the fact that logical (or merely conventional) connections between broad ideologies and specific policies are not likely to be automatically and identically evident to all conservatives and liberals. Rather, their apprehension requires careful thought—or, more likely, secondhand exposure to careful thought—about specific facts and values in the light of broad ideological commitments. People who are unusually attentive to political discourse and sophisticated in their political thinking are especially likely to grasp those connections.

The difference here is that political awareness produced sharp ideological polarization not just in policy preferences but also in perceptions of a seemingly straightforward, objective fact. Rather than contributing to accurate apprehension of that fact by conservative and liberal observers alike, political awareness seems mostly to have taught people how the political elites who share their ideological commitments would *like* them to see the world. In particular, what is most significant in figure 4.2 is that the conservatives who were most politically aware were most likely to *deny* that income differences had increased. In this instance, political awareness did more to facilitate ideological consistency than it did to promote an accurate perception of real social conditions.[36]

While perceptions of increasing income differences provide a striking example of ideological disparity in the effect of political information, the example is by no means an isolated one. The statistical analysis presented in table 4.10 reveals an even larger ideological disparity in the impact of political information on people's *moral assessments* of increasing inequality than on their *factual perceptions* of increasing inequality. Among ideological moderates, the probability of saying that increasing inequality was a bad thing (among those who recognized that inequality had, in fact, increased) ranged from 46% among the least informed to 73% among the

---

[35] Zaller (1992, chaps. 6 and 9).

[36] Christopher Achen and I have developed a mathematical model of political inference in which political awareness increases the weight attached to both partisan predispositions and reality in the construction of political judgments (Achen and Bartels 2006). Insofar as the former effect dominates the latter effect, this model implies not only that partisan disparities in political judgment will be concentrated among people who are high in political awareness, as in Zaller's model, but also that people who are generally better informed about politics may be most inaccurate in their political perceptions. Danielle Shani (2006) has presented a good deal of empirical evidence suggesting that partisan biases in perceptions of political conditions are exacerbated by political information. On partisan biases in perceptions more generally, see Bartels (2002a).

best informed. The impact of information among liberals was even greater, with the best informed virtually unanimous in saying that increasing inequality was a bad thing. Among conservatives, however, the impact of political awareness was reversed: the best-informed conservatives were significantly *less* likely than those who were relatively uninformed to say that an increasing income gap between rich people and poor people was a bad thing.[37] Thus, for moral assessments as well as factual perceptions of inequality, the impact of information was strongly conditioned by ideological predispositions.

Figure 4.3 shows how ideology and political information combined to influence the probability that respondents in the ANES surveys would both recognize *and* regret the growth of economic inequality. Among extreme liberals (represented by the solid line in the figure), that probability increased dramatically with increases in general political awareness. At the bottom of the distribution of information, only about two-thirds of extreme liberals recognized that inequality had increased, and fewer than half of those who recognized an increase said that was a bad thing. (Most of the rest said that they had not thought about whether increasing inequality was good or bad.) However, among the best-informed liberals, more than 95% recognized that inequality had increased, and more than 95% of that 95% said that was a bad thing. In contrast, among extreme conservatives (represented by the dotted line in figure 4.3) the effect of political information was to depress both recognition of growing inequality and opposition to growing inequality. Thus, while the least-informed conservatives were about as likely as the least-informed liberals to recognize and regret growing inequality, only about one in six of the best-informed conservatives did so.

Qualitatively similar interactions between political information and ideology also appear in responses to the other questions included in table 4.10. For example, highly informed liberals were much more likely than uninformed liberals to deny that a poor person has the same chance as a wealthy person of getting a fair trial (96% versus 75%), but highly informed conservatives were slightly *less* likely than uninformed conservatives to perceive economic bias in the legal system (62% versus 67%).[38] An even starker ideological gap appears in assessments of the importance of hard work as an explanation for income differences, which are presented graphically in figure 4.4. At the bottom of the information scale, conservatives and liberals were equally likely to see differences in hard work as a very important source of

---

[37] For extreme conservatives, the information effect implied by the probit analysis is −.566 (with a standard error of .245); for extreme liberals, the effect is +2.022 (with a standard error of .306).

[38] The implied information effects in the probit analysis are +1.088 (with a standard error of .421) for extreme liberals and −.149 (with a standard error of .344) for extreme conservatives.

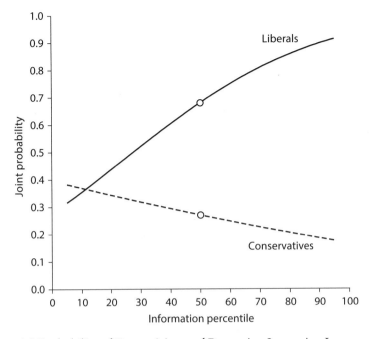

FIGURE 4.3 Probability of Recognizing *and* Regretting Increasing Income Differences

economic inequality. However, conservatives and liberals at the top of the information scale had vastly different views on this issue: more than 70% of highly informed conservatives, but only 15% of highly informed liberals, considered it very important that "some people just don't work as hard."[39]

The patterns of ideological polarization evident in figures 4.2, 4.3, and 4.4 suggest that American beliefs about inequality are profoundly political in their origins and implications. Well-informed conservatives and liberals differ markedly, not only in their normative assessments of increasing inequality, as one might expect, but also in their perceptions of the causes, extent, and consequences of inequality. This is not simply a matter of people with different values drawing different conclusions from a set of agreed-upon facts. Analysts of public opinion in the realm of inequality—as in many other realms—would do well to recognize that the facts themselves are very much subject to ideological dispute. For their part, political actors in the realm of inequality—as in many other realms—would do well to recognize that careful logical arguments running from factual premises

---

[39] The implied information effects in the probit analysis are +.693 (with a standard error of .309) for extreme conservatives and −.993 (with a standard error of .347) for extreme liberals.

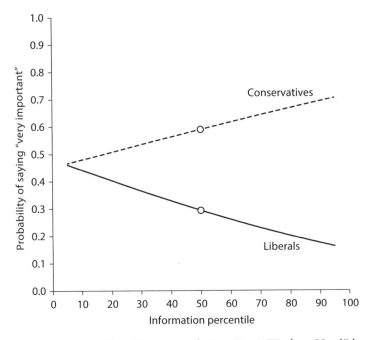

FIGURE 4.4 Perceptions That "Some People Just Don't Work as Hard" by Ideology and Information Level

to policy conclusions are unlikely to persuade people who are ideologically motivated to distort or deny the facts. While it is certainly true, as Jennifer Hochschild has argued, that "Where You Stand Depends on What You See," it is equally true that what you are willing to see depends in significant part on where you stand.[40]

At the same time, it is important to bear in mind that cleavages in beliefs and values are much more muted among relatively uninformed people than among those who pay close attention to politics. In fact, liberals and conservatives in the least-informed stratum of the public are virtually indistinguishable in the analyses reported in table 4.10.[41] In the context of factual

[40] Hochschild (2001); Hochschild and Einstein (2015).

[41] The one instance in table 4.10 in which the main effect of ideology (that is, the effect of ideology among people at the bottom of the distribution of political information) is large enough to be reliably distinguishable from zero is for the factual question about increasing differences in incomes—and that effect suggests, quite implausibly, that uninformed conservatives were more likely than uninformed liberals to recognize that incomes had become more unequal. I suspect that this anomalous result reflects some non-linearity in the effect of political information that is not adequately captured by the simple statistical specification reported in the table.

questions, this apparent consensus across ideological lines may seem reassuring. When it comes to policy preferences, however, agreement between uninformed liberals and conservatives may suggest that people on one side or the other—or both—are failing to recognize the implications of their own values for their views about crucial public issues.

The analyses presented in the next five chapters turn from facts and values to public policies. My aim is to account for how policies are formulated in the American political system of unequal democracy. Chapters 5, 6, and 7 provide detailed case studies of key policies with major ramifications for the economic fortunes of rich, middle-class, and working poor Americans—the Bush tax cuts of 2001 and 2003, the campaign to repeal the estate tax, and the long-term erosion of the federal minimum wage. Chapter 8 provides a much more general analysis of policy-making across a broad range of issues, while chapter 9 focuses on the response of the American political system to the Great Recession following the Wall Street meltdown of 2008.

In examining the role of public opinion in the policy-making process, it will be crucial to consider the ways in which citizens' policy preferences reflect political values and sympathies of the sort examined in this chapter. However, it will be equally important to bear in mind the extent to which many ordinary citizens fail to translate their broad values and sympathies into consistent views about specific policy issues. As we saw in tables 4.2 and 4.4, egalitarian values and sympathies do seem to undergird liberal positions on a variety of important policy issues. But the analyses presented in chapters 5 and 6 will suggest that the political significance of economic inequality is mostly lost on many Americans. Although they may express genuine allegiance to egalitarian values, they are not sufficiently attuned to the political debate to apply their values sensibly and consistently in formulating responses to some of the most important issues in contemporary American politics.

CHAPTER 5

Homer Gets a Tax Cut

THE PORTRAIT OF public opinion presented in chapter 4 provides several impressive-looking grounds for optimism regarding the politics of inequality. Most Americans express strong support for egalitarian values; they feel warmer toward working-class and poor people than toward rich people and business people; and they think the rich should bear a larger share of the tax burden. In light of these views, a naive observer might expect the growing economic inequality documented in chapter 1 to provoke a substantial popular backlash, impelling elected officials to engage in aggressive redistribution, raising taxes on the wealthy and investing heavily in programs enhancing human capital and bolstering economic opportunity for working-class and poor people.

Far from it. Indeed, quite to the contrary, one of the most significant domestic policy initiatives of the new millennium was a massive, government-engineered transfer of wealth from ordinary Americans to the rich in the form of substantial reductions in federal income taxes. Congress passed, and President Bush signed, two of the largest tax cuts in history in 2001 and 2003. A calculation by the Congressional Budget Office put the direct cost to the federal treasury through 2011 (not including additional interest payments stemming from the resulting increase in the budget deficit) at $1.63 *trillion*—almost three times the total federal surplus accumulated during Bill Clinton's last four years in office.[1] Some independent estimates of the cost of the tax cuts were substantially higher. For example, a 2013 estimate by the Center on Budget and Policy Priorities put the total cost of the Bush-era tax cuts (including debt-service costs) at $1.96 trillion from 2001 through 2008 and an additional $4.15 trillion—a sum equal to about half the total projected federal budget deficit—from 2009 through 2019.[2]

Many of the specific provisions of the Bush tax cuts disproportionately benefited wealthy taxpayers, including cuts in the top rate, reductions in taxes on dividends and capital gains, and a gradual elimination of the estate tax. As a result, according to projections by the Institute on Taxation and Economic Policy, the total federal tax burden in 2010 declined by 25% for the richest 1% of taxpayers and by 21% for the next richest 4%, but by only 10% for taxpayers in the bottom 95% of the income distribution.[3] A subsequent calculation by the Tax Policy Center estimated that the tax cuts were worth $56,000, on average, to households in the top 1% in 2010 (raising after-tax income by 6.4%), but only $700 to a typical middle-class household (raising after-tax income by 2.1%).[4]

[1] Congressional Budget Office, "Changes in CBO's Baseline Projections Since January 2001," June 7, 2012 (https://www.cbo.gov/sites/default/files/112th-congress-2011-2012/reports/06-07 -ChangesSince2001Baseline.pdf). According to the CBO report, this figure represents "CBO's estimates of costs or savings associated with new laws" on a year-by-year basis relative to baseline projections of revenues and outlays; however, "effects of legislation may have turned out to be different from the original estimates either because those baseline projections were off-target or because the results of the legislation deviated from what CBO anticipated."

[2] Kathy Ruffing and Joel Friedman, "Economic Downturn and Legacy of Bush Policies Continue to Drive Large Deficits," table 1, Center on Budget and Policy Priorities (http://www .cbpp.org/research/economic-downturn-and-legacy-of-bush-policies-continue-to-drive-large -deficits, updated February 28, 2013).

[3] Citizens for Tax Justice, "Effects of First Three Bush Tax Cuts Charted," June 4, 2003 (http://www.ctj.org/pdf/allbushcut.pdf). This calculation was based on the assumption that major provisions scheduled to expire by 2010 would, in fact, be extended. Absent that assumption, the total tax cut for the richest 1% would be reduced by about one-third and the total tax cut for the bottom 95% would be reduced by about one-half, making the disparity in benefits even greater.

[4] William Gale and Benjamin Harris, "The Bush Tax Cuts," Tax Policy Center, January 23, 2008 (http://tpcprod.urban.org/briefing-book/background/bush-tax-cuts/2003.cfm, last updated January 23, 2008). An additional calculation allocating the cost of the tax cuts (future tax increases or spending cuts) in proportion to household income implied that middle-income households would actually be worse off, with a net liability in 2010 of $1,200 (reducing

What is most remarkable is that this massive upward transfer of wealth attracted a good deal of support and surprisingly little opposition from ordinary Americans, despite their egalitarian-sounding views. My primary aim in this chapter is to explore and explain that public reaction. One striking finding is that public opinion about the Bush tax cuts was extremely tenuous. Notwithstanding the multi-*trillion*-dollar stakes, surveys conducted in 2002 and 2004 found 40% of the public saying that they had not thought about whether they favored or opposed the 2001 tax cut. That in itself points to severe limits on the force of public opinion in the policy-making process.

Among those who did form opinions, supporters of the tax cut outnumbered opponents by a substantial margin. My analysis suggests that most of these people supported President Bush's plan not because they were indifferent to economic inequality, but because they failed to bring relevant values to bear in formulating their policy preferences. Most of the people who recognized and regretted the fact that economic inequality had been increasing nevertheless supported the tax cuts. People who wanted to spend more money on a variety of government programs were *more* likely to support the tax cuts than those who did not, other things being equal. And people's opinions about the tax cuts were strongly shaped by their attitudes about their *own* tax burdens, but virtually unaffected by their attitudes about the tax burden of the rich—even in the case of the estate tax, which only affected the wealthiest 1% or 2% of taxpayers.

The response of the American public to the Bush tax cuts provides a dramatic case study of apparent misconnection between egalitarian sentiments and concrete policy preferences. More broadly, the success of President Bush and his allies in crafting and implementing such an ambitious policy shift with so little political fallout provides a dramatic case study of the considerable latitude provided by the American political system to policy-makers pursuing their own ideological goals.

The Bush Tax Cuts

Tax-cutting was a centerpiece of George W. Bush's 2000 presidential campaign platform. Less than five months after President Bush took office, and at his urging, Congress passed the Economic Growth and Tax Relief Reconciliation Act (EGTRRA), a major package of tax cuts including phased reductions in federal income tax rates, increased child credits, higher limits on contributions to tax-free retirement and educational savings accounts, and a gradual elimination of the federal estate tax. The Joint Committee on

---

after-tax income by 3.5%), while households in the top 1% would save $54,200 (increasing after-tax income by 6.2%).

Taxation estimated that the total EGTRRA package would cost the federal treasury more than $1.3 trillion through 2011.[5]

The key legislative vehicle for the 2001 tax cut was the annual congressional budget resolution. Although the budget reconciliation process was constructed in the 1970s to facilitate budget-balancing, two decades of parliamentary maneuvering had provided precedents for extending its application from deficit-cutting to tax-cutting. As a report in the legislative newsmagazine *CQ Weekly* explained in the midst of the process,

> Such bills are given special procedural protections: a shield from a filibuster, a 20-hour limit on debate and restrictions on amendments. In the evenly split senate, these advantages will be essential to enact anything like the tax package that Bush ceremonially presented to Congress on Feb. 8. Without an adopted budget resolution, the chances for the broadest and deepest tax cut in 20 years all but disappear.[6]

The budget resolution provided crucial procedural leverage for President Bush and the Republican congressional leadership. However, that leverage came with a substantial cost: because the congressional budget process operates within a 10-year time frame, only policy changes within that time frame would be considered germane for consideration within the context of the annual budget resolution. Thus, implementing tax cuts through the budget reconciliation process necessitated "sunsetting" provisions that would cause them to expire at the end of a decade, returning the whole tax system to the *status quo ante*. The president and his allies could hope and expect that future Congresses would feel compelled to make the cuts permanent—at an additional cost to the treasury of more than $200 billion per year—but that outcome was by no means guaranteed.

For that matter, during President Bush's first 100 days in office some political observers thought it was politically unrealistic to suppose that his ambitious tax-cutting agenda could achieve even a bare majority in the evenly divided Senate. In early February, a congressional journalist questioned "whether the final product will look anything like the proposal Bush transmitted to Capitol Hill." With the shadow of recession lengthening, a bipartisan group of Senate moderates began to lobby for a "trigger mechanism" that would condition the implementation of tax cuts on the realization of projected budget surpluses. Polling data signaled a public preference for bolstering Social Security and Medicare over tax cuts, suggesting "that

[5] Joint Committee on Taxation, "Estimated Budget Effects of the Conference Agreement for H.R. 1836," May 26, 2001.

[6] Andrew Taylor, "Law Designed for Curbing Deficits Becomes GOP Tool for Cutting Taxes," *CQ Weekly*, April 7, 2001, 770; Daniel J. Parks, with Andrew Taylor, "The Republican Challenge: Roping the Fiscal Strays," *CQ Weekly*, February 10, 2001, 314.

the American people believe the Democrats are right," according to Senate Minority Leader Tom Daschle. Charles Grassley, the chairman of the Senate Finance Committee and a Bush ally, acknowledged that "we have some nervous Nellies in both parties."[7]

By early May, Grassley and his Democratic counterpart, Max Baucus, were "tweaking" Bush's proposal in the Senate Finance Committee. Grassley and Baucus "followed the outlines of Bush's plan," but "rewrote the pieces, often in ways designed to keep the package's scope and cost within the confines of the budget. In addition, they crammed in several more provisions, principally to secure the support of four pivotal fiscal moderates on the panel"—Republicans James Jeffords and Olympia Snowe and Democrats Robert Torricelli and Blanche Lincoln. Grassley and Baucus fended off dozens of amendments and motions to recommit, eventually crafting a bill that cleared their committee with the support of all ten Republicans and four of ten Democrats.[8]

A week later, when the bill reached the Senate floor, it survived another cavalcade of amendments. A bid by Republican John McCain to trim the top rate reduction and expand the 15% tax bracket failed on a tie vote, with five Democrats joining 45 Republicans in opposition. A miscellaneous collection of minor amendments cobbled together by Grassley and Baucus was adopted by voice vote, and the bill was passed by a 62–38 margin, with a dozen Democrats voting in favor. According to one account, that was "a sign that it had captured the middle ground." Perhaps; however, it is striking that 11 of those 12 Democrats had helped to craft the Finance Committee's bill (Baucus, John Breaux, Lincoln, and Torricelli) or faced very tough reelection fights in 2002 (Jean Carnahan, Max Cleland, Tim Johnson, and Mary Landrieu) or were themselves multimillionaires (Diane Feinstein, Herbert Kohl, and Ben Nelson).[9]

---

[7] Lori Nitschke, "Tax Plan Destined for Revision," *CQ Weekly*, February 10, 2001, 318; Lori Nitschke, "Proposals to Alter Bush's Tax Plan Multiply Despite White House Appeals for Unity," *CQ Weekly*, February 17, 2001, 377; Andrew Taylor, "Tax Fight Energizes Democrats," *CQ Weekly*, March 3, 2001, 465; Lori Nitschke, "Tax-Cut Bipartisanship Down to One Chamber," *CQ Weekly*, March 10, 2001, 529.

[8] Lori Nitschke, "Scaled-Down Version of Bush Tax Plan Taking Bipartisan Form at Senate Finance," *CQ Weekly*, May 5, 2001, 1003; Lori Nitschke, "Senate Tax Bill Trade-offs Leave a Fragile Coalition," *CQ Weekly*, May 19, 2001, 1145.

[9] Lori Nitschke, "Tax Cut Deal Reached Quickly as Appetite for Battle Fades," *CQ Weekly*, May 26, 2001, 1251. As it turned out, Carnahan and Cleland were defeated in 2002, Johnson was reelected by a 50–49 margin, and Landrieu won by a 52–48 margin in a runoff election. Kohl, Feinstein, and Nelson reported net worth in excess of $5 million in 2002, according to a CNN tally; see Sean Loughlin and Robert Yoon, "Millionaires Populate U.S. Senate," *CNN.com*, June 13, 2003 (http://www.cnn.com/2003/ALLPOLITICS/06/13/senators.finances/). The 12th Democratic vote in favor of the tax cut was cast by Zell Miller of Georgia, who subsequently endorsed President Bush at the 2004 Republican National Convention.

Agreement was facilitated by the imminent defection of pivotal senator James Jeffords from the Republican ranks and by the shadow of new, more pessimistic budget surplus projections. "White House officials abandoned the administration's previous resistance to compromise and urged their Republican allies to quickly embrace any version of a tax cut deal that could become law." Just two days later, "the weary Republican leadership in the House and Senate agreed to a deal with the ever-more-powerful centrist Senate Democrats," and both chambers adopted a conference report representing a "slightly altered version" of the Senate bill.[10]

The final product was widely criticized for providing too much tax relief to the wealthy and too little to the middle class and the working poor. McCain, one of two Senate Republicans who voted against the conference report, announced, "I cannot in good conscience support a tax cut in which so many of the benefits go to the most fortunate among us at the expense of middle-class Americans who most need tax relief." A study released by the research and advocacy group Citizens for Tax Justice estimated that the top 1% of households would receive a total of $477 billion in tax breaks over the 10-year period covered by the bill (an average of $34,247 per household per year), while the bottom 60% would receive a total of $268 billion (an average of $325 per household per year). Moreover, because most of the broad-based tax cuts in the law took effect immediately while most of the benefits for very wealthy taxpayers were back-loaded, "the distribution of the tax cuts changes remarkably over time," with the estimated share of benefits going to the top 1% of households increasing gradually from 7.3% in 2001 to 51.8% in 2010.[11]

Even aside from its distributional implications, the back-loading of benefits raised alarms on fiscal grounds. Facing the necessity of keeping the putative 10-year cost of the tax cut within the cap imposed by the congressional budget resolution, "in crafting the final compromise, conferees followed the Senate model of postponing some effective dates and lengthening some phase-ins to make room for some priorities of both conservatives and moderates." Kent Conrad, the ranking Democrat on the Senate Budget Committee, called the result "'a monument to fiscal irresponsibility' because so many of its provisions would take effect in the second part of the decade, when the Baby Boomers neared retirement and the surplus projections on which the tax cut depends are the least reliable." Charles Rangel, the ranking Democrat on the House Ways and Means Committee, warned that "the

---

[10] Nitschke, "Senate Tax Bill Trade-offs Leave a Fragile Coalition"; Nitschke, "Tax Cut Deal Reached Quickly as Appetite for Battle Fades."

[11] Daniel J. Parks, with Bill Swindell, "Tax Debate Assured a Long Life as Bush, GOP Press for New Cuts," *CQ Weekly*, June 2, 2001, 1304; Citizens for Tax Justice, "Year-by-Year Analysis of the Bush Tax Cuts Shows Growing Tilt to the Very Rich," June 12, 2002 (http://ctj.org /ctjreports/2002/06/year-by-year_analysis_of_the_bush_tax_cuts_shows_growing_tilt_to_the _very_rich.php#.Vv6a7KQrLIU).

Republicans have lit the fuse on a time bomb. . . . Our kids and grandkids are the real losers today, because they will have to dig out of the hole that this tax bill causes."[12]

Meanwhile, conservatives began to prepare the ground for additional rounds of tax-cutting. Rangel's Republican counterpart, House Ways and Means Chairman Bill Thomas, complained that "$1.35 trillion stretched out over 10 years just doesn't get you what it used to." A representative of the U.S. Chamber of Commerce acknowledged that "we have a long list" of proposals for business tax breaks omitted from the EGTRRA package. Charles Schwab proposed a dividend tax cut to bolster the stock market, and, "conveniently, the White House's top economist, R. Glenn Hubbard, had an elegant proposal on just that subject for the president."[13]

Sure enough, in January 2003 President Bush proposed a further "economic growth" package including more than $700 billion in additional tax cuts—and, in a modest concession to the lingering effects of the 2001 recession, $4 billion for personal reemployment accounts.[14] The centerpiece of the new package was a proposal to exempt corporate dividends from taxation as personal income and reduce capital gains taxes on sales of corporate stock. Bush also proposed accelerating major elements of the 2001 tax cut scheduled to take effect between 2006 and 2010, including reductions in the top four tax rates, making them effective immediately.

Bush's plan "drew a cautious response from many in his own party. . . . Grassley called Bush's proposal 'good policy,' but said it will not win Senate passage without changes to draw the votes of GOP moderates and some Democrats."[15] Critics called attention to the apparent mismatch between the putative goal of short-term economic stimulus and the upper-class tilt of the new round of proposed tax cuts.[16] (Almost half of all capital gains

---

[12] Nitschke, "Tax Cut Deal Reached Quickly as Appetite for Battle Fades"; Nitschke, "Senate Tax Bill Trade-offs Leave a Fragile Coalition"; Parks, with Swindell, "Tax Debate Assured a Long Life as Bush, GOP Press for New Cuts."

[13] Parks, with Swindell, "Tax Debate Assured a Long Life as Bush, GOP Press for New Cuts"; Jill Barshay, "White House Bonds with Moderates for Victory on Dividend Cuts," CQ Weekly, May 17, 2003, 1173.

[14] The Joint Committee on Taxation put the 11-year price tag at $726 billion, including $396 billion for the dividend tax repeal. Joint Committee on Taxation, "Estimated Budget Effects of the Revenue Provisions Contained in the President's Fiscal Year 2004 Budget Proposal," March 4, 2003.

[15] Jill Barshay and Alan K. Ota, "White House Tax Cut Package Gets a Wary Hill Reception," CQ Weekly, January 11, 2003, 68.

[16] Critics were not alone in noting this apparent mismatch. According to one political columnist sympathetic to the proposal, "When critics say the plan the president proposed Tuesday will have negligible short-term stimulative effects, the right responses are: Of course. And: good." George F. Will, "The Long and Short of the 'Stimulus Package'," Washington Post, January 8, 2003.

income goes to households with incomes over $1 million.) They also raised alarms about the budgetary consequences of major additional tax cuts in the altered climate of economic stagnation, increasingly pessimistic deficit forecasts, and an expanding global war on terror. As one business reporter observed, Bush "proposed massive tax cuts during the 2000 campaign, when things were booming, and proposed the same cuts when things tanked. Now he wants more cuts." The *New York Times* claimed that "Bush's Multitude of Tax-Cut Ideas Leaves Even Supply-Siders Dizzy."[17]

In March, pivotal moderate Republican senators concerned about the budget deficit and the cost of the war in Iraq sided with Democrats in moving to limit the new tax cut to $350 billion—less than half of what President Bush had proposed. Grassley acceded to their demand, precipitating a feud with the rather more conservative House leadership. Republicans in the House and Senate bargained, postured, and traded accusations of "arrogance and broken promises" for two more months before settling on a compromise bill brokered by Vice President Richard Cheney, the Jobs and Growth Tax Relief Reconciliation Act (JGTRRA).[18]

Despite adhering to the moderates' $350 billion ceiling, JGTRRA succeeded in accommodating much of what Bush had asked for by making the most popular elements—tax breaks for married couples and an increased child credit—expire in two years and the more expensive cuts in taxes on dividends and capital gains expire in five years. The prevailing assumption was that they would be renewed in due course. The revised package was passed by the House (231–200) and by the Senate (51–50, with Cheney casting the tie-breaking vote). Of 532 votes cast, only 13 (eight in the House and five in the Senate) crossed party lines.

This new round of tax cuts was subjected to even more scathing criticism than the 2001 law. According to political columnist David Broder, "The Republicans in Congress cobbled together one of the strangest, least plausible tax bills in history and sent it off to President Bush, who discovered hidden virtues in a measure whose provisions he had repeatedly called woefully inadequate for the task of stimulating a sickly economy." A former Republican cabinet official complained in equally strong terms about "Republicans' irresponsible obsession with tax cutting."[19]

Criticism of JGTRRA was heightened when it became clear that a "last-minute revision by House and Senate leaders" would prevent millions of

[17] Allan Sloan, "The Tax Cut: Whose Is Bigger?" *Newsweek*, May 5, 2003, 53; Edmund L. Andrews, "Too Many Pennies from Heaven?" *New York Times*, February 16, 2003.

[18] David E. Rosenbaum and David Firestone, "$318 Billion Deal Is Set in Congress for Cutting Taxes," *New York Times*, May 22, 2003; John Cochran, "GOP Turns to Cheney to Get the Job Done," *CQ Weekly*, May 31, 2003, 1306.

[19] David Broder, "The Tax-Cut Skeptics Back Home," *Washington Post*, May 28, 2003; Peter G. Peterson, "Deficits and Dysfunction," *New York Times Magazine*, June 8, 2003, 18.

families with incomes between $10,500 and $26,625 from receiving $400 checks reflecting the increased child credit in the new bill. In the face of that criticism, the Senate Republican leadership and the Bush White House signaled their willingness to extend the child credit, at a cost of $3.5 billion. An amendment to that effect passed the Senate by a margin of 94–2. (One supporter, Republican Trent Lott, "voted for it while mimicking a person gagging by poking a finger toward his open mouth.") The House, however, was less amenable. "At a House GOP Conference meeting . . . members were urged to seek to reframe the debate as being about a 'welfare' provision, not a 'child tax credit,' because the proposed tax break would go to those who pay no federal income taxes." House leaders refused to consider the measure except as part of a broader package including $78 billion in additional tax cuts for middle- and upper-income taxpayers. Charles Rangel called that "'one of the most cynical and hypocritical moves' he had ever seen." Democrats described it as "an indirect attempt by the House to kill the tax credits." If they were right, it worked. A few weeks later, child credit checks began to go out to more than 25 million middle-class families, but the "firestorm" of criticism regarding the exclusion of working poor families had quickly burned itself out, and their checks never arrived.[20]

Meanwhile, despite having seen President Bush's 2003 proposal cut in half, conservatives expressed optimism regarding prospects for further tax cuts. As one observer put it, "to conservative groups, who have every intention of pushing for an annual tax cut, arguments over the size of each one are hardly worth worrying about in the long run. 'We're going to be negotiating over the size of the tax cut every year for 10 years,' said Grover Norquist, president of Americans for Tax Reform. 'At the end of 10 years, you're going to see how much progress "not getting everything you want" gets you.'"[21]

PUBLIC SUPPORT FOR THE TAX CUTS

The policy priorities reflected in the 2001 and 2003 tax cuts—reductions in the top marginal tax rates, more favorable treatment of business and investment income, and a phaseout of the estate tax—were all long-standing priorities of conservative Republicans. To varying degrees, each provided much more substantial benefits to wealthy taxpayers than to people of modest means. Anyone looking at the evidence presented in table 4.5 on

[20] David Firestone, "Tax Law Omits $400 Child Credit for Millions," *New York Times*, May 29, 2003; Jill Barshay and Alan K. Ota, "GOP Scrambles to Limit Damage of Child Tax Credit Controversy," *CQ Weekly*, June 7, 2003, 1371; David Firestone, "House Expands Child Credit as Part of a Larger Tax Cut," *New York Times*, June 13, 2003.

[21] Alan K. Ota, "Tax Cut Package Clears Amid Bicameral Rancor," *CQ Weekly*, May 24, 2003, 1245; David Nather, "GOP Infighting: Not Fatal," *CQ Weekly*, May 31, 2003, 1309.

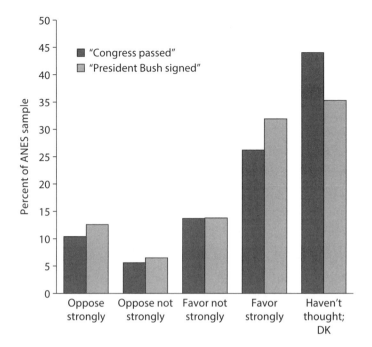

FIGURE 5.1 Public Support for the 2001 Tax Cut

public attitudes about the tax burden borne by rich people would have good grounds for imagining that tax cuts aimed so disproportionately at the very wealthy would have generated substantial public opposition. In fact, however, the public was generally quite supportive of the Bush tax cuts. The same American National Election Studies surveys that showed majority support for the proposition that rich people pay less than they should in federal income taxes also demonstrated a remarkable degree of public support for the "big tax cut" passed in 2001—a policy designed in large part to ensure that rich people would pay much less in federal income taxes in the coming decade.

Respondents in the 2002 ANES survey were asked two different versions of the "big tax cut" question: half the respondents were asked whether they favored or opposed the tax cut "Congress passed," while the other half were asked about the tax cut "President Bush signed."[22] The distributions of opinion for both versions of the question are shown in figure 5.1. A comparison of the results suggests that associating the tax cut explicitly with President Bush had

[22] "As you may recall, [Congress passed/President Bush signed] a big tax cut last year. Did you FAVOR or OPPOSE the tax cut, or is this something you haven't thought about? Did you [favor/oppose] the tax cut STRONGLY or NOT STRONGLY?"

a polarizing effect, increasing strong support by almost six percentage points but also increasing opposition by a few percentage points. However, the more surprising fact is that, regardless of how the question was posed, supporters of the tax cut outnumbered opponents by more than two to one, with most of those supporters saying that they favored the tax cut "strongly."[23]

The extent of public support for the Bush tax cuts was especially impressive in light of widespread public suspicion, even before they were passed, that the benefits would go mostly to the rich. For example, an NBC News/ *Wall Street Journal* poll in March 2001 asked respondents about "things that might happen if a tax cut were passed." The results, presented in table 5.1, suggest the public had significant concerns about the likely distribution of benefits from the Bush plan. Almost three-fourths of the respondents said that they expected the wealthy to benefit more than the middle class. Two-thirds doubted that they personally would get "substantial tax relief." A smaller majority doubted that the "average taxpayer" would get substantial relief, and most people also said they expected that the tax cut would not "give enough help to those with lower incomes."

Similar concerns appeared in a variety of other surveys. A CBS News poll the following month found 55% of the respondents saying that "rich people" would "benefit most" from Bush's 2001 tax cut plan; only 26% said that "middle-income people" would benefit most.[24] A Harris poll in June 2003 found 42% saying that the 2003 tax cut would help "the rich" a lot, and only 11% said that it would help "the middle class" a lot.[25] What is striking, though, is that in each of these cases a clear plurality of the respondents said that they favored the tax cuts despite their skepticism regarding the likely distribution of benefits.[26]

---

[23] These results echoed the results of an earlier ANES survey, conducted during the 2000 presidential campaign, in which people agreed by a two-to-one margin "that most of the expected federal budget surplus should be used to cut taxes." On the other hand, an even larger proportion of the 2000 ANES respondents (81%) agreed that "most of the expected federal budget surplus should go to protecting social security and Medicare," while only 16% disagreed with that proposition.

[24] "From what you've heard so far, who do you think would benefit most from George W. Bush's tax cut plan: rich people, poor people, or middle-income people?" Rich people, 55%; poor people, 4%; middle-income people, 26%; other/don't know, 13%.

[25] "Do you think that the tax cut will help the rich a lot, some, only a little, or not at all?" A lot, 42%; some, 30%; only a little, 12%; not at all, 6%; not sure, 10%. "Do you think that the tax cut will help the middle class a lot, some, only a little, or not at all?" A lot, 11%; some, 39%; only a little, 31%; not at all, 11%; not sure, 8%.

[26] A March 2001 NBC News/*Wall Street Journal* poll asked: "As you may know, George W. Bush has proposed a $1.6 trillion tax cut over ten years. Do you favor or oppose this proposal?" Favor, 57%; oppose, 32%; not sure, 11%. April 2001 CBS News poll: "Do you favor or oppose George W. Bush's $1.6 trillion tax cut for the country over the next 10 years?" Favor, 51%; oppose, 37%; don't know, 12%. June 2003 Harris poll: "The Congress passed and the President has signed a new tax cut. Overall do you think this tax cut was a good or bad thing?" Good thing, 50%; bad thing, 35%; not sure, 15%.

TABLE 5.1

Public Expectations for the 2001 Tax Cut

"As you may know, George W. Bush has proposed a $1.6 trillion tax cut over ten years. . . . I am going to read you a list of things that might happen if a tax cut were passed. For each item that I read, please tell me whether you think it is something that you expect to happen or whether it is something that you do not expect to happen."

	Expect	Do not expect	Depends; not sure
The wealthy will benefit more from the tax cut than the middle class	74%	21%	5%
The tax cut won't give enough help to those with lower incomes	57%	38%	5%
It will help prevent an economic recession	50%	40%	10%
Special-interest groups will benefit the most from a tax cut	50%	40%	10%
The tax cut will leave too little money for social programs	42%	50%	8%
The average taxpayer will get substantial tax relief	38%	57%	5%
You personally will get substantial tax relief	28%	67%	5%

Source: NBC News/*Wall Street Journal* poll, March 2001. N = 2,024.

Political scientists Jacob Hacker and Paul Pierson provided a more comprehensive compilation of results from 25 separate opinion surveys conducted in the early months of 2001 on the topic of President Bush's proposed tax cut. On average, they found 56% of the respondents supporting the president's plan and only 33% opposing it. However, Hacker and Pierson argued that "for determining voter preferences, these results are close to meaningless" because they "say almost nothing about what kind of tax cuts the public wanted and how much priority they gave them."[27]

In an effort to shed light on the latter questions, Hacker and Pierson compiled ten surveys from 1999, 2000, and early 2001 in which respondents were offered choices between tax cuts and other potential uses of the federal budget surplus. Depending upon the menu of alternatives offered, support for tax cuts ranged from 14% to 36% in these surveys. When tax cuts were pitted against funding Social Security, Medicare, or both, sizable

[27] Hacker and Pierson (2005a, 37).

majorities preferred the latter options. When funding "domestic programs" and Social Security (or Social Security and Medicare) were included as separate choices, debt reduction and tax cuts together commanded support from only about one-third of the public. Hacker and Pierson concluded from this evidence that "voters consistently saw tax cuts as a lower priority than plausible alternative uses of the forecasted surpluses."[28] However, these results may mostly reflect the remarkably high levels of public support for Social Security and Medicare. When tax cuts and debt reduction were pitted against "improving funding for needed government programs," with no specific mention of Social Security or Medicare, only 16% to 22% of the survey respondents chose government programs while 32% to 41% chose debt reduction and 34% to 42% chose "an across-the-board tax cut."[29]

Hacker and Pierson might have added that when survey respondents were offered a choice between President Bush's plan and alternative tax-cutting proposals actually circulating in Washington in the spring of 2001, they mostly preferred the alternatives. In the March NBC News/*Wall Street Journal* poll, respondents agreed by a margin of 52% to 41% that "we should only allow cuts in the income tax rates for middle- and low-income taxpayers, so the government has enough money for debt reduction and specific spending increases in priority areas such as education."[30] In a *Los Angeles Times* poll conducted a few days later, respondents favored a Democratic proposal for a tax cut "about half as big with more money devoted to spending on domestic programs such as Medicare and education and

[28] Ibid., 38–39.

[29] "The federal government will have a surplus of funds in the next few years. For which one of the following would you like to see the surplus funds used—reducing the national debt, improving funding for needed government programs, or providing an across-the-board tax cut?" Across four months in 2000, the responses to a monthly NBC News/*Wall Street Journal* poll were: reducing the national debt, 32% (June), 32% (July), and 41% (September); improving funding for needed government programs, 22% (June), 20% (July), and 16% (September); providing an across-the-board tax cut, 38% (June), 42% (July), and 34% (September); all/none/other (volunteered), 7% (June), 4% (July), and 7% (September); and not sure, 4% (June), 2% (July), and 2% (September). None of these figures, from the Roper Center's iPOLL archive, match those reported by Hacker and Pierson for the only NBC News/*Wall Street Journal* poll in their table; I have been unable to determine the source of this discrepancy.

[30] "I am going to read you two positions on taxes and spending and then ask which comes closer to your view. Statement A: President Bush says that the budget surplus is large enough to cut income tax rates for all taxpayers, while still leaving room for debt reduction and some spending increases in priority areas such as education. Statement B: Democrats say that the budget surplus is not that large and we should only allow cuts in the income tax rates for middle- and low-income taxpayers, so the government has enough money for debt reduction and specific spending increases in priority areas such as education." Statement A (agree with President Bush), 41%; statement B (agree with Democrats), 52%; neither/depends (volunteered), 4%; not sure, 3%.

reducing the debt" by a margin of 55% to 30%.[31] A CBS News/*New York Times* poll conducted the same month found respondents favoring President Bush's plan to divide the surplus equally between tax cuts, debt reduction, and "other purposes including government spending" over a Democratic proposal to "use more than half of the budget surplus to reduce the debt" by a margin of 49% to 41%, but it is hard to know how much of that plurality was attracted by the prospect of bigger tax cuts and how much by the prospect of more government spending.[32] As for the overall magnitude of the tax cut, another NBC News/*Wall Street Journal* poll the following month found respondents favoring "the Senate's $1.2-trillion tax cut" to "the President's $1.6-trillion tax cut" by a margin of 57% to 32%.[33]

Based on their detailed examination of public opinion data like these, Hacker and Pierson concluded that, "far from representing popular wishes, the size, structure, and distribution of the tax cuts passed in 2001 were directly at odds with majority views. . . . The most striking characteristic of the tax cuts . . . is how far a policy produced by elected officials diverged from the preferences of most voters." While I do not doubt that most voters would have preferred alternative packages of tax cuts, spending increases, and deficit reduction to the package that actually emerged from the legislative process in 2001, I believe it is a mistake to suppose that *any* specific package could be said to represent "popular wishes" or "majority views" regarding such a complex matter of public policy. For one thing, detailed probing would almost certainly reveal a good deal of ambivalence, uncertainty, and outright contradiction in the views of individual citizens regarding the various provisions of any specific plan.[34] What is more, even

[31] The March 2001 *Los Angeles Times* poll asked: "George W. Bush has proposed a tax cut of $1.6 trillion and eliminating about two-thirds of the national debt over the next 10 years, which is about $2 trillion. Democrats say the tax cut should be about half as big with more money devoted to spending on domestic programs such as Medicare and education and reducing the debt. Which comes closer to your view?" Bush's proposal, 30%; Democrats' proposal, 55%; neither (volunteered), 4%; don't know, 11%.

[32] "Which approach for using the budget surplus do you prefer—George W. Bush's (use about a third of the budget surplus to cut taxes, about a third to reduce the debt, and about a third for other purposes including government spending and a reserve fund), or the Democrats' in Congress (use more than half of the budget surplus to reduce the debt and divide the rest equally among a tax cut, other government spending, and a reserve fund)?" Bush's, 49%; congressional Democrats', 41%; neither (volunteered), 3%; both (volunteered), 1%; don't know, 6%.

[33] "As you may know, President Bush proposed a $1.6-trillion tax cut to return more of the surplus to the taxpayers and to encourage long-term economic growth. The Senate proposed reducing the President's tax cut to $1.2 trillion to leave more money for domestic policy priorities and for reducing the national debt. Which proposal do you favor—the President's $1.6-trillion tax cut or the Senate's $1.2-trillion tax cut?" President Bush's $1.6 trillion tax cut, 32%; Senate's $1.2 trillion tax cut, 57%; neither/depends (volunteered), 5%; not sure, 6%.

[34] On these aspects of public opinion, see, for example, Hochschild (1981, chap. 8); Zaller (1992, chaps. 4–5); Bartels (2003).

if individual citizens were splendidly clear and consistent, "majority views" would not be; political theorists have demonstrated that for policy issues of any real complexity, there is generally *no* specific policy outcome that could not be defeated by some other proposal in a majority vote.[35] Thus, the appealing-seeming notion of popular sovereignty is both psychologically unrealistic and logically incoherent.

In any case, democracies do not make public policy on the basis of "popular wishes," at least not in any straightforward sense. Democratic policy agendas are set by elected leaders, not by voters. As political scientist E. E. Schattschneider aptly put it 75 years ago, "The people are a sovereign whose vocabulary is limited to two words, 'Yes' and 'No'."[36] In the case of the tax cuts, President Bush posed the question and the people's response, insofar as they responded at all, was a vigorous "Yes."

Unenlightened Self-Interest

Taken at face value, the results of opinion surveys provide considerable evidence of strong public support for tax cuts along the lines pursued by President Bush—at least if the alternative was no tax cut. However, there are good reasons to suspect that public opinion in this domain should *not* be taken entirely at face value. Notwithstanding the vastness of the stakes, public thinking about the Bush tax cuts seems to have been remarkably superficial. Perhaps the strongest evidence of this fact is hiding in plain sight in figure 5.1. Unlike most commercial opinion surveys, the 2002 ANES survey invited respondents to say that they "haven't thought about" whether they favored or opposed the 2001 tax cut. Remarkably, in view of the fiscal and political significance of the tax cut, 40% of the respondents availed themselves of that opportunity.[37] Even associating the tax cut with President Bush reduced the proportion who said that they "haven't thought about it" only modestly, to about 35%, while asking about the tax cut "Congress passed" left almost 45% of the respondents unable to say whether they favored or opposed it.

---

[35] The classic formal demonstration of the logical limitations of collective choice procedures is Kenneth Arrow's (1951) theorem. William Riker (1982) provided a less technical explication of these limitations and a discussion of their implications for democratic theory.

[36] Schattschneider (1942, 52).

[37] Figure 5.1 does not differentiate between people who said that they "haven't thought about" whether they favored or opposed the tax cut and those who volunteered that they didn't know whether they favored or opposed it. Since the former group outnumbered the latter group by 504 to 11, I simply refer to both groups as not having thought about whether they favored or opposed the tax cut.

A good deal of additional evidence of public inattention and uncertainty in the general domain of tax policy appeared in an extensive 2003 survey of Americans' views on taxes sponsored by National Public Radio, the Kaiser Family Foundation, and Harvard University's John F. Kennedy School of Government. Asked whether they pay more in federal income tax or Social Security and Medicare tax, 34% of respondents said they didn't know (and most of the rest were probably wrong).[38] Asked whether they were eligible for the Earned Income Tax Credit, 28% said they did not know.[39] Asked whether Americans pay more or less of their income in taxes than Western Europeans, 42% said they did not know.[40] Asked whether they had heard about a proposal in Washington to do away with taxes on corporate dividends—the centerpiece of President Bush's new tax proposal and a prominent feature of political debate in the month before the survey—61% said no.[41] Asked whether the 2001 tax cuts should be speeded up, 48% said they did not know.[42] Asked whether the cuts should be made permanent rather than being allowed to expire in 2011, 60% said they did not know.[43] Asked whether speeding up the cuts and making them permanent would mainly help high-income, middle-income, or lower-income people, 41% said they did not know.[44]

[38] "Over the course of a year, do you pay more federal income tax, or more Social Security and Medicare tax, or don't you know?" More federal income tax, 52%; more Social Security and Medicare tax, 14%; don't know, 34%; refused, 1%. (In fact, a substantial majority of taxpayers pay more in payroll taxes than in federal income tax.)

[39] "The last time you filed your taxes, were you eligible for the Earned Income Tax Credit, or not, or don't you know?" Yes, 21%; no, 50%; don't know, 28%.

[40] "Compared with the citizens of Western European countries, do you think Americans pay a higher percentage of their income in taxes, a smaller percentage of their income in taxes, about the same percentage of their income in taxes, or don't you know enough to say?" A higher percentage, 21%; a smaller percentage, 30%; about the same percentage, 6%; don't know enough, 42%.

[41] "There is a proposal in Washington now to do away with personal income taxes on corporate dividends. Dividends are what many companies pay to owners of their stock. Have you heard about this proposal, or not?" Yes, 38%; no, 61%; don't know, 1%.

[42] "As you may know, in 2001 Congress passed President Bush's proposals for tax cuts that are to be phased in over the next few years. Do you favor or oppose speeding up those tax cuts so they go into effect sooner, or don't you know enough to say?" Favor, 31%; oppose, 21%; don't know enough to say, 48%.

[43] "As you may know, the 2001 tax cuts are set to expire in 2011. Do you support or oppose making those tax cuts permanent, or don't you know enough to say?" Support, 23%; oppose, 17%; don't know enough to say, 60%.

[44] "In his State of the Union address President Bush proposed speeding up the tax cuts and making them permanent. Do you think this mainly would help high-income people, middle-income people, or lower-income people, or would it treat everyone equally, or don't you know enough to say?" High-income people, 29%; middle-income people, 7%; lower-income people, 6%; treat everyone equally, 18%; don't know enough to say, 41%.

In short, while public opinion was generally supportive of the Bush tax cuts, there is also plenty of evidence of ignorance and uncertainty about the workings of the tax system and the policy options under consideration—or actually adopted—in Washington. Much of the public was unclear about basic facts in the realm of tax policy; some of what the public did "know" was patently false; and a remarkable number of people, when offered the chance, said that they had not thought about a policy innovation whose consequences were reckoned by experts in *trillions* of dollars.

How did ordinary people, ignorant and uncertain as they were in this domain, formulate any views at all about such a complex matter of public policy? If they happened to know that the tax cut was proposed and pushed by President Bush, they may have relied on partisan sentiment to favor or oppose it. If they associated tax-cutting with small government, they may have been swayed by opinions about government programs or general ideological predispositions. The statistical analyses reported in table 5.2 indicate that party identification and political ideology did have significant effects on people's views about the tax cut: as expected, Republicans and conservatives were much more likely to support the tax cut than Democrats and liberals were.[45] However, the apparent effects of government spending preferences, perceptions of government waste, and people's own income levels are less readily explicable. People with higher incomes and those who thought that the government wastes a lot of money were generally *less* supportive of the tax cut, other things being equal, while those who said that they supported more spending on a variety of government programs were *more* likely to favor the tax cut. These results suggest a good deal of confusion in the connections between people's political values and their policy preferences—even leaving aside the 40% of ANES respondents who said that they had not thought about whether they favored or opposed the tax cut.[46]

The impression of confusion is reinforced when we turn to the apparent impact of people's views about tax burdens on their support for the 2001

[45] The statistical results presented in table 5.2 are derived from an instrumental variables estimator, which produces less efficient parameter estimates than ordinary regression analysis but avoids substantial biases due to measurement error in the survey responses employed as explanatory variables. I use the difference in feeling thermometer ratings assigned to conservatives and liberals as an instrument for *conservative ideology*, respondents' 2000 presidential votes as an instrument for *Republican Party identification*, an index derived from eight government spending items in the post-election wave of the 2002 ANES survey as an instrument for the corresponding index of *government spending preferences* in the pre-election wave of the survey, and perceptions of trust in government (whether government can be trusted to do what is right, whether government is run for the benefit of all, and whether government officials are crooked) as instruments for *perceived government waste*. More detailed discussion of the statistical analyses appears in Bartels (2005).

[46] A more complex estimation strategy designed to guard against potential selection bias due to this censoring of the sample (Heckman 1979) produced generally similar parameter estimates.

TABLE 5.2

Self-Interest, Political Values, and Support for the 2001 Tax Cut

Parameter estimates from instrumental variables regression analyses (with standard errors in parentheses). Support for the tax cut ranges from −1 (oppose strongly) to +1 (favor strongly). Respondents who said that they "haven't thought about" the tax cut are excluded from the analysis.

	(1)	(2)	(3)
Own tax burden (−1 to +1)	.370 (.094)	.251 (.092)	.477 (.107)
Rich tax burden (−1 to +1)	.354 (.070)	−.067 (.081)	−.058 (.082)
Poor tax burden (−1 to +1)	.049 (.119)	.137 (.113)	−.046 (.126)
Republican Party identification (−1 to +1)	—	.607 (.134)	.495 (.138)
Conservative ideology (−1 to +1)	—	.248 (.209)	.479 (.216)
Government spending preferences (−1 to +1)	—	—	.282 (.194)
Perceived government waste (0 to 1)	—	—	−.901 (.271)
Family income (0 to 1)	−.001 (.094)	−.242 (.096)	−.266 (.100)
"President Bush" wording	−.030 (.051)	−.140 (.049)	−.082 (.052)
Intercept	.305 (.074)	.341 (.080)	.809 (.229)
Standard error of regression	.745	.711	.710
Adjusted R^2	.11	.19	.20
N	889	889	889

Source: 2002 ANES survey.

tax cut. The most salient feature of the tax cut was, obviously, that taxes would be cut. Thus, it is hardly surprising that ordinary people reasoning about the tax cut drew heavily upon their views about taxes. What may be surprising, however, is that they seem to have done so in ways that mostly reflected rather simple-minded—and sometimes misguided—considerations of self-interest stemming from their views about their own tax burdens.

Respondents in the ANES surveys were not asked directly whether they thought they would benefit personally from the Bush tax cut. However, the question about respondents' own tax burdens sheds significant indirect light on the impact of perceived self-interest among other potential influences on their views about tax policy. To the extent that people who thought that they paid more than they should in taxes were more likely to support the tax cut, even after allowing for the effects of partisanship, political ideology, and other characteristics, it seems plausible to infer that the additional support had something to do with their subjective sense of their own tax burden. The parallel questions in the ANES survey about the tax burdens of rich people and poor people provide a valuable check on reasoning of this sort, since more general antipathy to taxes would presumably be reflected in one or both of those questions as well as in the question about respondents' *own* tax burdens.

Since the 2001 tax cut included some direct benefits for most taxpayers, there was some reason for respondents who thought they were asked to pay too much to support it. However, since most of the benefits were targeted to wealthy taxpayers—according to one estimate, 63% to the top one-fifth of households and 36% to the top one-hundredth, but only 20% to the bottom three-fifths—most respondents had even better reason to oppose the tax cuts if they felt that rich people were asked to pay too little, and perhaps some additional reason to oppose the cuts if they felt that they were asked to pay too much—since tax cuts for the rich would be likely, one way or another, to increase their own future taxes through burden-shifting.

Considering the apparent effects of tax burdens alone, the statistical results in the first column of table 5.2 suggest that respondents who wanted rich people to bear a larger share of the tax burden *were* significantly more likely to oppose the tax cut than those who said that the rich pay too much or about the right amount.[47] However, the additional analyses reported in the second and third columns of the table suggest that this apparent effect mostly reflects the correlation of perceptions of rich people's tax burdens with respondents' more general political values. Once differences in

---

[47] The parameter estimates are from instrumental variables regression analyses with perceived tax burdens in the 2002 post-election ANES survey used as instruments for the corresponding perceived tax burdens in the pre-election survey. (Since the tax cut questions appeared in the pre-election wave of the survey, using perceived tax burdens in the post-election wave as instruments for perceived tax burdens in the pre-election wave guards against the possibility that survey context or question ordering effects inflate the relationship between perceived tax burdens and views about the tax cut.) The correlations between perceived tax burdens in the pre-election and post-election surveys are .55 for respondents' own taxes, .55 for the rich, and .44 for the poor. Even with some allowance for genuine change in respondents' views between the two surveys, correlations of this magnitude suggest that the responses are subject to substantial measurement error.

partisanship and ideology are taken into account, views about whether rich people should pay more or less in taxes—a consideration that seems on its face to be of considerable relevance in evaluating a policy whose benefits were targeted mostly to people in the upper reaches of the income distribution—had no apparent effect on views about the tax cut.

In marked contrast, respondents' views about their *own* tax burdens had a strong independent impact on support for the tax cut, even after allowing for the effects of broader partisan and ideological predispositions. Indeed, in the analysis presented in the third column of table 5.2, respondents' perceptions of their own tax burdens rivaled partisanship and ideology as predictors of support for the tax cut. Moreover, because the distribution of responses to the question about respondents' own tax burdens was highly skewed (with 51% of the respondents saying that they were asked to pay too much and only 4% saying that they were asked to pay too little), this effect turns out to account for most of the net support for the tax cut in the ANES sample.[48]

Additional analysis suggests that this impact was even greater for respondents who were asked about the tax cut "Congress passed" rather than the tax cut "President Bush signed." In the absence of any clear cues about where the tax cut came from or whose interests it served, people seem mostly to have fallen back on simple-minded self-interest in deciding what (if anything) they thought about it.[49]

THE IMPACT OF POLITICAL INFORMATION

I have argued that public support for the Bush tax cuts derived in considerable part from unenlightened considerations of self-interest among people who did not recognize the implications of President Bush's policies for their own economic well-being or their broader political values. Millions of citizens believed that the federal government should spend more money on a

[48] The sample mean value for the (–1 to +1) tax cut variable (excluding respondents who said that they "haven't thought about" whether they favored or opposed it) was .354. Multiplying the sample mean perceived *own tax burden* among these same respondents, .478, by the corresponding parameter estimate in the third column of table 5.2, .477, accounts for 64% of this net support for the tax cut.

[49] The results reported in table 5.2 are from analyses combining responses to both versions of the question. Results for the two half-samples considered separately (not shown) suggest that the impact of respondents' own perceived tax burdens was substantially greater for the tax cut that "Congress passed" than for the tax cut that "President Bush signed." For example, in analyses paralleling those reported in the third column of table 5.2, the estimated effect of respondents' own perceived tax burden was .670 (with a standard error of .153) on their views about the tax cut that "Congress passed," but .299 (with a standard error of .151) on their views about the tax cut that "President Bush signed."

wide variety of programs, that the rich were asked to pay too little in taxes, and that growing economic inequality was a bad thing—but they simultaneously supported a package of policies whose main effect was to reduce the tax burden of the rich, constrain funding for government programs, and exacerbate growing economic inequality. One is left to wonder how these people might resolve the contradictions implied by their simultaneous antipathies toward inequality and taxation—if they recognized those contradictions.

Elsewhere, I have proposed a way to explore admittedly hypothetical questions of this sort by observing how the political preferences of well-informed citizens differ from those of less-informed citizens who are similar in politically relevant ways.[50] If well-informed citizens have systematically different perceptions and preferences, the logic goes, might not additional information move less-informed citizens in the same directions? In the present context, if well-informed citizens seem to reason differently, draw on different premises, and reach different conclusions about tax policy, might not additional information move less-informed citizens to do likewise?

Obviously, empirical analyses along these lines require some reliable way to distinguish well-informed citizens from less-informed citizens. To that end, I rely here on the same general measures of political information employed in chapter 4.[51] I use those measures to investigate the extent to which better-informed people had different views about the 2001 tax cut than those who were otherwise similar but less well informed.

I begin by considering the impact of political information on attention to and knowledge about the tax cut. Perhaps unsurprisingly, better-informed people were much more likely to express an opinion for or against the tax cut, much more likely to consider the issue important, and much more likely to recognize the respective positions of the Republican and Democratic Parties. For example, the statistical results presented in table 5.3 imply that someone at the bottom of the distribution of political information had only a 29% chance of having "thought about" the 2001 tax cut, but that probability increased to 87% at the top of the distribution.[52] Conservatives, more affluent people, and those who were asked about the tax cut "President

---

[50] For a variety of empirical analyses along similar lines, see Althaus (1998); Bartels (1990; 1996); Delli Carpini and Keeter (1996); Fishkin (1997); and Gilens (2001).

[51] In the 2004 ANES survey, the information scale is based on respondents' answers to a series of factual questions about politics; in the 2002 survey, the information scale is based on subjective ratings of general political knowledge supplied by the ANES interviewers at the end of the pre- and post-election interviews. More detailed descriptions of the scales appear in chapter 4.

[52] These calculations are for an ideological moderate with average family income. They split the difference between the statistical results reported in the table for the tax cut that "President Bush signed" and the tax cut that "Congress passed." Similarly, in the case of having "thought

TABLE 5.3

Political Information, Ideology, and Attention to the 2001 Tax Cut

Ordered probit parameter estimates (with standard errors in parentheses).
Additional response thresholds not shown.

	Have "thought about" tax cut	Say tax cut is "very important"	Republicans support tax cut	Democrats oppose tax cut
Political information (0 to 1)	1.686 (.109)	.712 (.133)	1.716 (.143)	1.133 (.136)
Conservative ideology (–1 to +1)	.232 (.129)	.782 (.165)	.696 (.168)	.100 (.162)
Political information × ideology	–.021 (.232)	–1.061 (.287)	–.682 (.311)	.290 (.292)
Family income (0 to 1)	.584 (.099)	–.141 (.111)	.587 (.118)	.273 (.113)
"President Bush" wording	.223 (.072)	.019 (.059)	.146 (.062)	.258 (.060)
2004 survey	.016 (.064)	—	—	—
Intercept	–.953 (.080)	–.898 (.088)	–1.157 (.091)	–1.052 (.087)
Log likelihood	–1,593.8	–1,400.7	–1,241.7	–1,350.6
Pseudo-R^2	.12	.02	.09	.05
N	2,723	1,503	1,511	1,511

Source: 2002 and 2004 ANES surveys.

Bush signed" (rather than the tax cut "Congress passed") were also more likely to express an opinion for or against the 2001 tax cut, but all those differences were modest by comparison with the difference due to general political information.

Better-informed people also attached a good deal more importance to the 2001 tax cut; someone at the highest information level was about twice as likely as someone at the lowest information level to say that the issue was "very important" (40% versus 17%). However, in this case there was a strong interaction evident between information and ideology: well-informed

about" the tax cut—where the analysis includes responses from both the 2002 and 2004 ANES surveys—the calculations split the difference between the two years.

conservatives were actually *less* likely than uninformed conservatives to say that the tax cut was "very important" (30% versus 43%), while well-informed liberals were vastly *more* likely than uninformed liberals to say so (51% versus 4%).

Better-informed people were also much more likely to recognize the parties' positions on the tax-cutting issue; the probability of recognizing that the Democratic Party opposed the tax cut increased from 21% at the lowest information level to 64% at the highest information level, while the probability of recognizing that the Republican Party favored the tax cut increased from 21% to 82%. (In addition, people who were asked about the tax cut "President Bush signed" were significantly more likely to be able to characterize the parties' positions correctly than people who were asked about the tax cut "Congress passed," with no cues provided by the question wording about who was on which side of the issue.)

It should not be surprising that better-informed people were more attentive to the tax-cutting issue. What is more consequential is that they developed markedly different opinions about the issue than those who were less well informed. That fact is evident from the statistical results presented in table 5.4, which focus on the relationship between political information and support for the 2001 tax cut. For a person with average income, the estimated probability of supporting the tax cut declined markedly with increasing information, from 75% at the bottom of the information scale to 66% in the middle of the information scale to 57% at the top of the information scale.[53]

Arthur Lupia and his colleagues have pointed out that this impact of political information on support for the 2001 tax cut differed dramatically between conservatives and liberals and between Republicans and Democrats.[54] Their finding is echoed in the second, third, and fourth columns of table 5.4, which provide separate estimates of the impact of political information on support for the tax cut among Republicans, independents, and Democrats, respectively.[55] These results suggest that information had *some*

[53] These estimated information effects are smaller than those reported in my previously published analysis of support for the Bush tax cuts (Bartels 2005). The difference primarily reflects the inclusion here of additional data from the 2004 ANES survey, which were unavailable when that piece was written. The estimated information effects corresponding to the estimate of –.510 in the first column of table 5.4 are –.849 (with a standard error of .166) for the 2002 data alone and –.299 (with a standard error of .157) for the 2004 data alone. The decline is concentrated among Republicans (from –1.01 in 2002 to –.00 in 2004); the estimated information effect among Democrats actually increased in magnitude, from –1.48 in 2002 to –1.72 in 2004.

[54] Lupia et al. (2007).

[55] The separate analyses for the three partisan groups capture some other interesting differences in patterns of support for the tax cut. First, family income—insofar as it mattered at all—probably only mattered among Republicans. Second, the question wording associating the tax cut with President Bush produced a noticeable decline in support among Democrats, but

TABLE 5.4

Partisanship, Political Information, and Support for the 2001 Tax Cut

Ordered probit parameter estimates (with standard errors in parentheses) for probability of (strongly or not strongly) favoring the 2001 tax cut. Additional response thresholds not shown.

	All	Republicans	Independents	Democrats
Political information (0 to 1)	−.510 (.112)	−.384 (.230)	−.359 (.182)	−1.572 (.207)
Family income (0 to 1)	.268 (.105)	.221 (.205)	−.019 (.177)	.018 (.186)
"President Bush" wording	.030 (.078)	.008 (.149)	.017 (.135)	−.216 (.134)
2004 survey	−.192 (.065)	.148 (.119)	−.346 (.109)	−.317 (.124)
Intercept	.624 (.093)	1.507 (.208)	.601 (.155)	.969 (.158)
Log likelihood	−2,216.7	−487.0	−812.0	−665.8
Pseudo-R²	.01	.01	.01	.06
N	1,767	599	621	547

Source: 2002 and 2004 ANES surveys.

negative effect on support for the tax cut even among Republicans and independents, but that the effect was much more powerful among Democrats. Even among the best-informed Republicans, 90% supported the tax cut. So did a bare majority (53%) of the best-informed independents. However, among Democrats, support for the tax cut declined from 76% at the bottom of the information distribution to only 19% at the top of the information distribution.

Figure 5.2 provides a graphical representation of the distinct information effects for Republicans and Democrats implied by the statistical results in table 5.4. The general pattern here is reminiscent of the pattern of ideological polarization evident in figures 4.2, 4.3, and 4.4, but with two notable differences. First, there is a sizable partisan difference in support for the tax cut even among people at the bottom of the information distribution. Thus,

no corresponding increase in support among Republicans or Independents. And third, both Independents and Democrats showed a significant decline in support for the tax cut between 2002 and 2004; however, Republicans became, if anything, more likely to support the tax cut in 2004 than they had been in 2002.

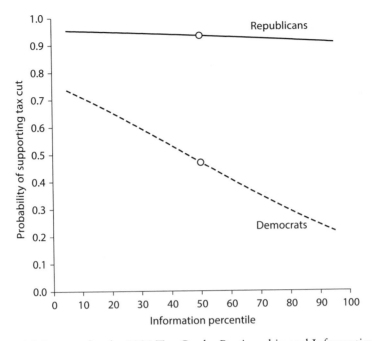

FIGURE 5.2 Support for the 2001 Tax Cut by Partisanship and Information Level

whereas the implications of political ideology for views about inequality seem to have been entirely opaque to the least-informed citizens, even they seem to have recognized that their partisan loyalties were of some relevance in thinking about whether they favored or opposed the tax cut—especially when the wording of the question associated the tax cut with President Bush.

Second, and more importantly, whereas the patterns of polarization in figures 4.2, 4.3, and 4.4 were roughly symmetrical, the pattern in figure 5.2 is highly asymmetrical. While increasing information produced a steep decline in support for the tax cut among Democrats, it produced no corresponding increase in support for the tax cut among Republicans—because even very uninformed Republicans were already virtually certain to say that they supported the tax cut, if they expressed any view at all. Rather than simply blurring the partisan differences evident among better-informed people, political ignorance had a marked effect on the overall level of public support for the tax cut.

A rather similar pattern appears with respect to egalitarian values (which were measured in the 2004 ANES survey, though not in the 2002 survey). Not surprisingly, opposition to the tax cut was concentrated among people

TABLE 5.5

Egalitarian Values, Political Information, and Support for the 2001 Tax Cut

Ordered probit parameter estimates (with standard errors in parentheses) for probability of (strongly or not strongly) favoring the 2001 tax cut. Additional response thresholds not shown.

	All	*Non-egalitarian*	*Moderately egalitarian*	*Strongly egalitarian*
Political information	–.367	.398	–.219	–1.314
(0 to 1)	(.167)	(.315)	(.263)	(.328)
Family income	.337	.889	.402	–.250
(0 to 1)	(.170)	(.321)	(.265)	(.337)
Intercept	.319	.003	.358	.390
	(.120)	(.251)	(.182)	(.222)
Log likelihood	–896.3	–254.0	–350.4	–221.0
Pseudo-R^2	.00	.02	.00	.05
N	705	229	282	194

Source: 2004 ANES survey.

who expressed strong support for egalitarian values. However, that opposition only appeared among egalitarians who were generally well informed about politics. The statistical analyses presented in table 5.5 summarize the relationship between egalitarian values, political information, and support for the tax cut among the 63% of respondents in the 2004 ANES survey who favored or opposed the tax cut. The results indicate that political information had a significant negative effect on support for the tax cut, just as in table 5.4. However, the subgroup analyses presented in the second, third, and fourth columns of the table show that the impact of information on support for the tax cut was almost entirely limited to the most egalitarian segment of the public—the minority of people (fewer than 30%) with scores above +.5 on the –1 to +1 scale of egalitarian values introduced in chapter 4.

The patterns of support and opposition implied by these results are presented graphically in figure 5.3. Among strong egalitarians, the average level of support for the tax cut declined sharply with political information, from almost 60% among the least-informed to less than 20% among the best-informed. Conversely, among the roughly similar-sized group of people with scores less than or equal to zero on the egalitarian values scale, support for the tax cut *increased* modestly with political information, from a bit less than 70% among the least-informed to about 80% among the best-informed.

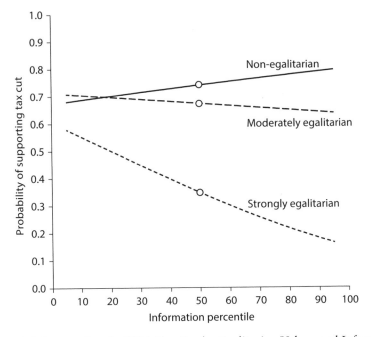

FIGURE 5.3 Support for the 2001 Tax Cut by Egalitarian Values and Information Level

What is most striking in figure 5.3, however, is the pattern of support for the 2001 tax cut among the 40% of ANES respondents who expressed moderate support for egalitarian values (scale scores between zero and +.5). Their views differed only modestly from those of outright opponents of egalitarian values; even when they were highly informed about politics, almost two-thirds favored the tax cut, if they took any position at all. Thus, consistent opposition to the tax cut was concentrated among the relatively small minority of people who were politically well informed *and* strongly committed to egalitarian values.

The results presented in tables 5.3, 5.4, and 5.5 suggest that, had the public as a whole been better informed, support for the tax cut would have been significantly lower than it actually was. Indeed, projections based on the statistical results in tables 5.3 and 5.4 imply that more than 80% of the *net* majority in favor of the tax cut in 2002 and 2004 (among people who took a position one way or the other) would have disappeared had the entire public been "fully" informed (at the top of the ANES distribution), reducing the actual 32-point margin of support to a six-point margin.[56] Thus, to a

[56] These figures are derived from the separate parameter estimates for Republicans, independents, and Democrats reported in table 5.4. Actual values of the explanatory variables (for

remarkable degree, popular support for the 2001 tax cut seems to have been grounded in the political ignorance of ordinary citizens.

THE LONG SUNSET

In his first three years as president, George W. Bush presided over two of the biggest tax cuts in American history. In both cases the benefits went disproportionately to the wealthy while the costs were put off to the future, presumably to be borne a good deal more equally in the form of eventual tax increases, cuts in government programs, and deficit economics. And in both cases the views of ordinary Americans, insofar as those views could be said to exist, were largely supportive of Bush's policy initiatives.

Some observers inferred from these facts that ordinary people were simply confused about what was in their own interests. For example, in the course of describing 2004 Democratic presidential candidate Richard Gephardt's proposal to repeal President Bush's tax cuts and spend the money on universal health care, *New York Times* columnist Paul Krugman wrote that, "if American families knew what was good for them, then most of them—all but a small, affluent minority—would cheerfully give up their tax cuts in return for a guarantee that health care would be there when needed."[57]

Other observers, while a bit more circumspect about stipulating what people would do if they knew what was good for them, raised similar doubts about the capacity of the American public to reason effectively about tax policy. For example, in a reflection on the Bush era of "'Let Them Eat Cake' Economics," *Newsweek* columnist Jonathan Alter worried that "even if the tax cuts help stimulate a modest recovery, we have dug ourselves a deep hole." He added that

> explaining all this politically is a "bank shot," to use a billiards term. It requires trusting the voters with complexity. Will they see that their new $400 child credits are chump change compared with all the new fee hikes and service cuts? Will they understand that they're paying

---

each respondent in the 2002 and 2004 ANES surveys who expressed a view for or against the tax cut) imply a 66–34 margin of support. Substituting a "perfect" information score of 1.0 for each respondent's actual information score produces a 55–45 margin of support. However, that calculation takes no account of the fact that many of the people who said that they "haven't thought about" the tax cut would have done so had they been better informed. Using the parameter estimates reported in the first column of table 5.3 to capture this effect reduces the margin of support for the tax cut from 55–45 to 53–47 (since the people who *would have* taken a position had they been better informed would have been somewhat less likely than those who *did* take a position to support the tax cut). In terms of the total population, the actual margin of support to opposition was 41% to 22% (with 37% taking no position), while the fully-informed margin of support to opposition would have been 47% to 41% (with 12% taking no position).

[57] Paul Krugman, "Roads Not Taken," *New York Times*, April 25, 2003.

more in state and local taxes so that a guy with a Jaguar putting up a McMansion down the block can pay less in federal taxes? Will they connect those 30 kids cramming their child's classroom to decisions in far-away Washington?[58]

One way to answer Alter's questions is to see how well public support for the Bush tax cuts held up as their implementation proceeded and their effects were—or were not—felt by ordinary people. The 2004 ANES survey showed some evidence of a decline in public support for the tax cut over the course of President Bush's first term. Only 27% of the respondents said that they strongly favored the tax cut, down from 32% in 2002; 17% strongly opposed the tax cut, up from 13% in 2002.[59] Perhaps relatedly, the public perceptions of tax burdens documented in table 4.6 also shifted perceptibly between 2002 and 2004. By 2004, people were less likely to say that they were asked to pay more than they should (by 8.5 percentage points) and more likely to say that rich people were asked to pay less than they should (by 6.6 percentage points). These changes may reflect some recognition of the fact that the 2001 and 2003 Bush tax cuts significantly reduced overall federal tax rates, especially for the wealthiest taxpayers.

Despite these shifts, however, supporters of the 2001 tax cut continued to outnumber opponents by 38% to 25% in the 2004 ANES survey—a 3–2 margin among those who expressed a view one way or the other. Another 37% of the public still had not thought about whether they favored or opposed the tax cut. More than three years after the tax cut began to take effect, Alter's "bank shot" seemed to have missed the pocket.

Meanwhile, having relied on aggressive "sunsetting" provisions to fit the tax cuts within the parameters of the congressional budget reconciliation process, Republican leaders and conservative interest groups began a decade-long effort to get them extended indefinitely. Unsurprisingly, they attempted to frame the debate by portraying resistance to extending the Bush tax cuts as support for tax *increases*. Within a week of the passage of EGTRRA in 2001, a White House spokesman told reporters that President Bush expected the tax cuts to be extended and that "to do anything other than that is to raise taxes on the American people." Later, that viewpoint was even inserted into official budget calculations by simply assuming that the tax cuts would be made permanent—a bit of creative bookkeeping justified on the grounds that "the 2001 Act and 2003 Act provisions were not intended to be temporary, and not extending them

---

[58] Jonathan Alter, "'Let Them Eat Cake' Economics," *Newsweek*, July 28, 2003, 36.

[59] Since respondents in 2004 were asked about the tax cut "President Bush signed," their responses are compared with responses from the random half of the 2002 sample that answered the same version of the question.

in the baseline raises inappropriate procedural roadblocks to extending them at current rates."[60]

In 2006 the Senate voted, largely along party lines, to extend some elements of the Bush tax cuts at a cost of nearly $70 billion. However, as one reporter noted, even this limited extension "could set the stage for budgetary heartburn in the years ahead," while full-scale extension "would cost hundreds of billions of dollars a year, posing excruciating budget choices for the next president." Meanwhile, economic conservatives were becoming increasingly disgruntled as the Bush administration's fiscal policies showed no evidence that huge tax cuts would spur spending discipline. Bruce Bartlett, a prominent supply-sider who helped shape economic policy under President Reagan and the first President Bush, advocated a substantial new value-added tax to cope with inevitable increases in the cost of federal entitlement programs. "Whose beast was being starved?" Bartlett asked. "There's no evidence that it was working. We need to deal with reality."[61]

When Democrats won majorities in both chambers of Congress in the 2006 election, the prospects for further changes in tax policy became even more circumscribed. The new Democratic chairmen of the House and Senate tax-writing committees ruled out any attempt to rescind the tax cuts due to expire in 2010. However, it was clear that they had little interest in extending those cuts. Instead, they "hoped to forge an agreement with the Republicans in limiting the growing reach of the alternative minimum tax, which has started to hit many middle-class Americans who claim deductions for state taxes and other expenses"—many of whom lived in wealthy, high-tax Democratic states.[62] Senate Democrats proposed a five-year budget extending the tax cuts through 2011 and 2012—but only if $400 billion could be found to pay for them. Unsurprisingly, that plan went nowhere.

During the 2008 presidential campaign, Barack Obama pledged not to raise taxes on families earning less than $250,000 per year—the vast majority of American taxpayers. In keeping with that pledge, he proposed to keep

---

[60] Parks, with Swindell, "Tax Debate Assured a Long Life as Bush, GOP Press for New Cuts," 1304; David Broder, "Trillion-Dollar Gimmick: Extending Bush's Tax Cuts Through Sleight of Hand," *Washington Post*, February 19, 2006. Broder added a "Translation: If you tell Congress the cost of making those tax cuts permanent, lawmakers might have second thoughts about doing it." He also noted that "Bush tried to get Congress to go along with this bookkeeping switch back in 2004, actually submitting legislation to authorize the change. The House refused to accept it. He put it back in his budget last year, with the same result. But this year he's back again, with more urgency, as he presses the case to make these tax cuts permanent."

[61] Edmund L. Andrews, "Senate Approves 2-Year Extension of Bush Tax Cuts," *New York Times*, May 12, 2006; Eduardo Porter, "When Even Supply-Siders Say Taxes Must Rise, an Unpopular Policy Looks Inevitable," *New York Times*, December 5, 2005.

[62] Stephen Labaton and Steven R. Weisman, "Talking About Common Ground: Victorious Democrats Vow Cooperative Approach on Taxes and Economy," *New York Times*, November 9, 2006.

most of the Bush tax cuts intact but to let the top tax rate revert to its 2000 level.[63] In effect, his aim was to blunt the impact of what I have called "un-enlightened self-interest" by driving a wedge between people's views about their own tax burdens and their views about the tax burdens of the rich.

From a political standpoint, Obama's pledge seems to have been fairly effective. In a YouGov survey conducted shortly before the 2008 election, 38% of respondents said that they favored the two-tier plan, while another 14% wanted to let all the tax cuts expire as scheduled; only 30% preferred the Republican proposal to make all the tax cuts permanent.[64] Perhaps even more surprisingly, Obama's pledge seemed to defuse the Republican Party's long-standing political advantage on the issue of taxes. The YouGov survey respondents were roughly evenly split on the question of whether their own taxes would be lower under Obama (34%) or Republican candidate John McCain (31%).[65] The political ramifications of that balance of opinion are underlined by the fact that an astounding 98% of those who thought that their taxes would be lower under Obama reported supporting him, while 95% of those who thought that their taxes would be lower under McCain reported voting for him.

As president, Obama continued to support letting the Bush tax cuts for top income-earners expire as scheduled at the end of 2010, despite a concerted effort by conservatives to insist that none of the tax cuts should be allowed to expire in the midst of a recession. The results of an October 2010 YouGov survey, presented in the first column of table 5.6, indicate that a plurality of Americans continued to support Obama's position. The survey found that 42% of the public favored letting the high-end tax cuts expire (a four-point increase from 2008), while another 11% wanted to let all the tax cuts expire. Only 28% (slightly fewer than in 2008) favored retaining all the tax cuts, including those for the richest taxpayers.

---

[63] Obama's main competitor for the Democratic nomination, Hillary Clinton, advocated letting all the Bush tax cuts expire in 2010; Edmund L. Andrews, "2008 Democratic Hopefuls Propose a Ceiling on the President's Tax Cuts," *New York Times*, April 21, 2007. In contrast, all of the major Republican candidates—including John McCain, one of only two Republican senators who opposed the 2001 EGTRRA tax cut and one of only three who opposed the 2003 JGTRRA tax cut—pledged to preserve the cuts if elected; James Pethokoukis, "Democrats Spoil GOP Strategy," *U.S. News & World Report*, Capital Commerce Blog, May 10, 2007.

[64] "As you probably know, many of the major tax cuts passed by Congress during the Bush administration are due to expire at the end of next year. Would you favor . . . ?" Making these tax cuts permanent, 30%; extending the tax cuts for households earning less than $250,000 per year but letting the tax cuts expire for households earning more than $250,000, 38%; letting all the tax cuts expire as scheduled, 14%; don't know, 16%.

[65] About one-third of the respondents said that there would not be much difference (23%) or that they didn't know (11%). Among those who said they would vote in the presidential election, the plurality shifted back to McCain, but by a fairly narrow (38–33%) margin.

TABLE 5.6

Tax-Cutting Preferences in the 2010 Midterm Campaign

"As you probably know, many of the major tax cuts passed by Congress during the Bush administration are due to expire at the end of this year. Would you favor . . . ?"

	All	Congressional voters	Democratic congressional vote intention	Obama approval
Making these tax cuts permanent	28.5%	38.7%	−.219 (.042)	−.184 (.027)
Extending the tax cuts for households earning less than $250,000 per year (only)	41.6%	40.5%	.057 (.040)	.029 (.024)
Letting all the tax cuts expire as scheduled	11.2%	12.2%	.091 (.048)	.043 (.033)
Democratic Party identification (−1 to +1)	—	—	.442 (.018)	.327 (.015)
Don't know	18.7%	8.7%	—	—
Standard error of regression	—	—	.276	.274
Adjusted R²	—	—	.70	.49
N	1,000	668	668	1,000

Source: October 2010 YouGov survey.

Despite this sustained public support for the president's position, Democratic leaders in Congress were unwilling to bring the issue to a vote. Several moderate members of the Democratic caucus had already come out against letting the tax cuts for top earners expire, and many more were said to be reluctant to cast votes on the issue in the run-up to the election. In light of the popular support for the president's position, was that a political miscalculation? Probably not. For one thing, people in the YouGov survey who said that they expected to vote in the upcoming midterm election were much more evenly divided in their views about the Bush tax cuts, as the results presented in the second column of table 5.6 make clear. The plurality favoring selective cuts going forward shrank from 13 points in the general population to just 2 points among likely voters. Among political independents, projected turnout was more than 30 points higher among those who wanted the top-rate tax cuts renewed than among those who wanted them to expire.

Even more importantly, the sizable minority of people who wanted the tax cuts for affluent taxpayers renewed seem to have attached much more weight to this issue than the slim majority who wanted them to expire. The third column of table 5.6 reports the results of a statistical analysis relating vote intentions in the upcoming 2010 congressional election to views about the Bush tax cuts, taking separate account of prospective voters' broader partisan attachments. The results indicate that people who supported President Obama's position on the tax cuts were only 6% more likely than those who were unsure about the issue to say that they would vote for a Democratic House candidate. Even those who wanted to let all the tax cuts expire were only 9% more likely to vote for a Democrat. By comparison, those who wanted to keep the tax cuts for affluent taxpayers in place were 22% more likely to say that they would vote for a Republican House candidate. For expedient politicians facing reelection, an energized minority trumps a tepid majority every time.

An even more lopsided difference appeared in the impact of tax cut preferences on the president's own approval ratings, shown in the fourth column of table 5.6. People who supported President Obama's position on this issue were only slightly more approving of his overall performance than those who were unsure, while those who wanted to renew all the tax cuts were moved about five times as far toward disapproving. Among political independents, 76% of those who wanted continued tax cuts for the rich said that they strongly disapproved of the president's performance; only 27% of those who supported his proposal for selective extension of the tax cuts were equally disenchanted.

These differences in preference intensity cannot be attributed to simple self-interest. On average, the people who wanted to renew the tax cuts for top earners were somewhat more affluent than the population as a whole, but only 8% said that they had household incomes of $150,000 or more—incomes that might put them within hailing distance of having their own taxes hiked. Half had household incomes of less than $50,000, and almost that many said that they didn't even *know* anyone who earned more than $200,000 per year.

This analysis of the YouGov survey data suggests that candidate Obama's proposal to allow the tax cuts to expire only for the richest 2% of taxpayers turned out to be costly for President Obama and his party in 2010, despite its overall popularity. When Democrats suffered what Obama himself called a "shellacking" in the midterm election, any remaining appetite for acting on the president's proposal was further diminished. A month later, Obama negotiated a deal with "newly empowered Republicans on Capitol Hill" to extend the Bush tax cuts in their entirety for another two years. The agreement also included a temporary cut in payroll taxes, an extension of unemployment benefits, and other elements favored by Democrats. Nonetheless, one press account called Obama's deal "a retreat from his own positions and the principles of many liberals." The top Democratic leaders of the House and Senate were "notably absent" from the ceremony at which the bill was signed into law.[66]

When the Bush tax cuts again came up for reconsideration just after the 2012 election, many observers supposed that a president fresh from reelection would finally achieve his long-standing aim of letting the tax cuts for top income-earners expire. As journalist Jonathan Chait argued, "If there is a single plank in the Democratic platform on which Obama can claim to have won, it is taxing the rich." However, even then the translation of a supposed election mandate into policy turned out to be more complicated than it seemed. This denouement of a policy struggle that had dominated American domestic politics for more than a decade is taken up in chapter 10.[67]

Meanwhile, Obama and Congress also faced the question of what to do about the estate tax, which was similarly enmeshed in the "sunsetting" provisions of the 2001 EGTRRA tax cut. Since it affects only the very wealthiest taxpayers, the estate tax looks on its face like a populist, easy-to-defend form of taxation. Nevertheless, it turns out to be remarkably unpopular. Chapter 6 addresses the fascinating question of why that is—and the even more important question of whether that public opinion really matters.

[66] David M. Herszenhorn and Jackie Calmes, "Tax Deal Suggests New Path for Obama," *New York Times*, December 7, 2010; Lori Montgomery, Shailagh Murray, and William Branigin, "Obama Signs Bill to Extend Bush-Era Tax Cuts for Two More Years," *Washington Post*, December 17, 2010.

[67] Jonathan Chait, "We Just Had a Class War," *New York*, November 11, 2012 (http://nymag.com/news/features/obama-class-war-2012-11/).

CHAPTER 6

The Strange Appeal of Estate Tax Repeal

FOR MANY LIBERALS, the most egregious feature of the Bush tax cuts was the gradual phaseout and temporary repeal of the federal estate tax. The fiscal impact of the estate tax phaseout was relatively modest in the overall scheme of the Bush tax cuts: the Joint Committee on Taxation estimated that it cost the federal government $186 billion through 2011—less than 15% of the total cost of the 2001 EGTRRA legislation alone. Nevertheless, the fight over estate tax repeal seems uniquely symbolic of the skewed class politics of the New Gilded Age. Eliminating what the prominent economist Robert Frank has called "the closest thing to a perfect tax we have" in order to protect the inherited wealth of multimillionaires seems perversely contrary to the interests of the vast majority of American families whose estates will never reach the threshold for taxation.[1] How could a democratic political system arrive at such a policy?

When President Clinton left office, the federal estate tax claimed as much as 55% of estates worth $1 million or more, though even many larger estates were exempted. Under the provisions of the 2001 EGTRRA tax cut, the estate tax exclusion gradually increased to $3.5 million per person ($7 million for a married couple) in 2009, while the tax rate gradually declined. In 2010 the estate tax was totally repealed; however, as with other elements of the 2001 tax cut, it was scheduled to be reinstated in its pre-2002 form in 2011 unless Congress and the president took further action.

New York Times columnist Paul Krugman mocked the apparent illogic of this off-again, on-again scheme: "If your ailing mother passes away on Dec. 30, 2010, you inherit her estate tax-free. But if she makes it to Jan. 1, 2011, half the estate will be taxed away. That creates some interesting incentives. Maybe they should have called it the Throw Momma From the Train Act of 2001."[2] While no wealthy mothers seem to have been dispatched, some fortunate billionaires (including New York Yankees owner

---

[1] Robert H. Frank, "The Estate Tax: Efficient, Fair and Misunderstood," *New York Times*, May 12, 2005.

[2] Paul Krugman, "Bad Heir Day," *New York Times*, May 30, 2001.

George Steinbrenner) did manage to pass away while the estate tax was temporarily repealed.

Between 2001 and 2010, legislation providing for permanent repeal of the estate tax cleared the House of Representatives on more than one occasion, only to fall short of garnering the 60 votes necessary to overcome a Democratic filibuster in the Senate. However, as the end of the strange yearlong estate tax holiday approached, pressure to forestall the reinstatement of the Clinton-era rates escalated. Just two weeks before the deadline, President Obama signed into law the bipartisan 2010 Tax Relief Act, which included an estate tax compromise—a temporary top rate of 35% with a $5 million exclusion, to expire after two years. One financial columnist (apparently writing on behalf of the wealthy) called it "a far better rate and exemption than anyone expected."[3]

The pending expiration of that temporary compromise was one element of the "fiscal cliff" facing the president and Congress at the end of 2012. This time negotiations went past the wire before resulting in a deal, the American Taxpayer Relief Act, which was passed by Congress on January 1, 2013, and signed into law by President Obama on January 2. In addition to making most of the Bush tax cuts permanent, extending the expanded Earned Income Tax Credit and a variety of other tax breaks, and reforming the Alternative Minimum Tax, the deal included a permanent estate tax rate of 40% with a $5 million exclusion indexed for inflation. Thus, fewer estates would be taxed than under the temporary policy, but they would be taxed at a somewhat higher rate. On the other hand, the new tax was considerably lower and much less widespread than it would have been under the scheduled reversion to the Clinton-era policy (a 55% rate with a nominal $1 million exemption); the difference reduced projected federal tax revenue over the subsequent decade by about $375 billion.[4]

As of 2015, only two out of every 1,000 estates owed federal estate tax. The exclusion was $5.43 million per person—almost $11 million for a married couple—and the average effective tax rate on taxable estates was 16.6% (rising from 7.7% on estates in the $5–10 million range to 18.8% on estates over $20 million). That year the House of Representatives voted once again, "largely along party lines," to repeal the estate tax. Republicans called it "an immoral tax and an attack on the American dream," adding,

---

[3] Paul Sullivan, "Estate Tax Will Return Next Year, but Few Will Pay It," *New York Times*, December 17, 2010; Paul Sullivan, "The End of a Decade of Uncertainty over Gift and Estate Taxes," *New York Times*, January 4, 2013.

[4] Jennifer Steinhauer, "Divided House Passes Tax Deal in End to Latest Fiscal Standoff," *New York Times*, January 1, 2013; Sullivan, "The End of a Decade of Uncertainty over Gift and Estate Taxes"; Matthew O'Brien, "The Estate Tax Is a Huge Giveaway in the Fiscal-Cliff Talks," *The Atlantic*, December 31, 2012.

"Why is America punishing success?" The Senate had already voted (54–46) to include repeal in its budget blueprint.[5]

But why was Congress even considering estate tax repeal? In their comprehensive account of the repeal effort, Michael Graetz and Ian Shapiro portrayed the threat to the estate tax as a "political mystery":

> A law that constituted the blandest kind of common sense for most of the twentieth century was transformed, in the space of little more than a decade, into the supposed enemy of hardworking citizens all over this country. How did so many people who were unaffected by the estate tax—the most progressive part of the tax law—and who might ultimately see their own taxes increased to replace the revenues lost if the estate tax disappeared, come to oppose it? Who made this happen?
>
> The answers to these questions reveal a great deal about how American politics actually works in the age of polls, sound bites, think tanks, highly organized membership organizations, and single-issue coalitions.[6]

Graetz and Shapiro assumed as a matter of course that if ordinary people opposed the estate tax, someone—conservative think tanks, interest groups, propagandists—must have "made this happen." In this chapter, I propose another possibility, one that is less conspiratorial but in some ways even more troubling. My account suggests that the estate tax was quite unpopular with the American public long before conservative think tanks, interest groups, and propagandists came along. Indeed, if public sentiment determined public policy, the estate tax would probably have been repealed long ago.

From this perspective, the real "political mystery" of the estate tax is not why the repeal movement has enjoyed so much success in the past two decades, but why such an unpopular tax has lasted as long as it has. The answer to that question reveals a great deal about how American politics has actually worked over the course of the past century. It is not a story of "polls, sound bites, think tanks, highly organized membership organizations, and single-issue coalitions," as Graetz and Shapiro would have it. Rather, it is a story of powerful public officials pursuing their own ideological goals, largely ignorant or heedless of public sentiment. Ironically, in this case the

---

[5] Chye-Ching Huang and Brandon Debot, "Ten Facts You Should Know About the Federal Estate Tax," Center on Budget and Policy Priorities (http://www.cbpp.org/research/ten-facts-you-should-know-about-the-federal-estate-tax, updated March 23, 2015); Peter Baker, "House Votes to Repeal Estate Tax," *New York Times*, April 16, 2015; Jonathan Weisman, "Long Night in Senate, but Real Budget Work Awaits," *New York Times*, March 27, 2015.

[6] Graetz and Shapiro (2005, 3).

powerful public officials happen to have been on the side of ordinary people, while public sentiment has been on the side of the multimillionaires.

Public Support for Estate Tax Repeal

If the extent of public support for the Bush tax cuts documented in chapter 5 is remarkable, the extent of public support for estate tax repeal is even more remarkable. For example, figure 6.1 documents the overwhelming support for estate tax repeal in the 2002 American National Election Studies survey. The survey included two questions focusing on the ongoing controversy about "doing away with the tax on large inheritances": half the respondents were asked about the "estate tax," and the other half were asked about the "death tax." Figure 6.1 shows the distributions of public opinion for both versions.[7]

Since the "death tax" label has been aggressively championed by proponents of repealing the tax, it might be expected to generate more public support for repeal than the "estate tax" wording. It did, but only by a few percentage points. What is more significant is that, regardless of the wording, a substantial majority of survey respondents favored repealing the tax. Combining the results for both versions of the question, 49% of the public "strongly" favored repeal, while another 18% were less strong supporters. Only 27% opposed repeal, and they were slightly more likely to be "not strong" opponents than "strong" opponents. (They were also less likely than supporters of repeal to say that this issue was "very important" to them personally.)

These results are broadly consistent with those of other surveys that have asked about repealing the estate tax. For example, the 2003 survey conducted by National Public Radio, the Kaiser Family Foundation, and Harvard's John F. Kennedy School of Government found 54% of the public in favor of repealing the "federal estate tax" and 16% opposed (with 29% saying that they "don't know enough to say"); 60% favored repealing the tax when the phrase "death tax" was mentioned in the question (with 15% opposed and 26% saying that they "don't know enough to say").[8]

---

[7] "There has been a lot of talk recently about doing away with the tax on large inheritances, the so-called [estate tax/death tax]. Do you FAVOR or OPPOSE doing away with the [estate tax/death tax]? Do you [favor/oppose] doing away with the [estate tax/death tax] STRONGLY or NOT STRONGLY?"

[8] National Public Radio, Kaiser Family Foundation, and John F. Kennedy School of Government, "National Survey of Americans' Views on Taxes," April 2003 (http://www.npr.org/news/specials/polls/taxes2003/20030415_taxes_survey.pdf). As in the 2002 ANES survey, the two questions were asked of random half-samples. "There is a federal estate tax—that is, a tax on the money people leave when they die. Do you favor or oppose eliminating this tax, or don't

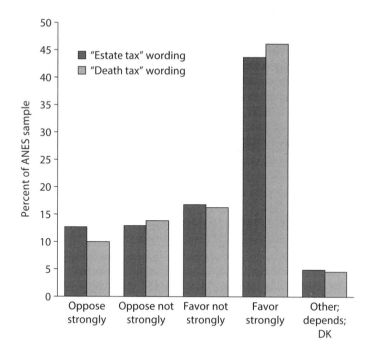

FIGURE 6.1 Public Support for Repealing the Estate Tax

A March 2005 *New York Times* poll found 76% opposing the estate tax, while 18% favored it. A separate question in the same poll found 23% favoring an estate tax with a $1 million threshold and an additional 20% favoring an estate tax with a $3.5 million threshold (while 50% said that the federal tax on all inheritances should be permanently eliminated).[9] In a June 2006 NBC News/*Wall Street Journal* poll, 48% of respondents said that

you know enough to say?" Favor, 54%; oppose, 16%; don't know enough to say, 29%. "There is a federal estate tax that some people call the death tax. This is a tax on the money people leave when they die. Do you favor or oppose eliminating this tax, or don't you know enough to say?" Favor, 60%; oppose, 15%; don't know enough to say, 26%.

[9] *New York Times*, "New York Times Poll: Class Project," March 9–14, 2005 (http://www .nytimes.com/packages/pdf/politics/class-poll.pdf). "Currently the federal government taxes the assets—that is, the property and money—someone leaves when they die if the assets are worth more than a certain amount of money. Do you favor or oppose placing this tax on assets when someone dies?" Favor, 18%; oppose, 76%; don't know/no answer, 7%. "Under the current law, the federal tax on estates will be phased out between now and 2010, when there will be no tax on estates at all. Unless Congress acts, the tax cut will then expire and the tax will again be collected on estates worth more than $1 million. Which comes closest to your opinion? 1. The federal government should tax estates worth more than $1 million, OR 2. It should only tax estates worth more than $3.5 million, OR 3. The federal tax on all inheritances

they would be more likely to vote for a congressional candidate who favored repealing the estate tax, while only 18% said that they would be less likely to vote for such a candidate; the 30-point margin was greater than for any of the other nine issues included in the survey.[10] And a March 2008 CBS News/ *New York Times* poll found 44% of the public favoring no tax on any estate, while another 47% said that "the estate tax should be eliminated for most people, but kept in place for the very largest estates."[11]

Some analysts have cast doubt on the depth of public support for repealing the estate tax implied by survey results like these. For example, the NPR/Kaiser Family Foundation/Kennedy School survey included a series of additional questions proposing various exemption levels for the estate tax; a total of 52% of the sample favored keeping the current tax (15%) or raising the exemption level to $1 million (26%) or to $5 million (11%), while only 26% continued to support repeal even if the tax was "collected only on estates worth $25 million or more."[12] Similarly, a 2001 survey conducted by Mark Penn for the Democratic Leadership Council found substantial support for continuing to apply the estate tax to very large estates; when Penn offered respondents the choice of eliminating the estate tax, leaving it as is, or "exempting small family farms and small businesses from the estate tax, but not multimillionaires," 56% chose the third option, while fewer than one in four continued to favor eliminating the tax.[13] Findings like these

---

should be permanently eliminated." Tax estates worth more than $1 million, 23%; tax estates worth more than $3.5 million, 20%; eliminate all estate tax, 50%; don't know/no answer, 7%.

[10] NBC News/*Wall Street Journal* poll, June 2006 (http://online.wsj.com/public/resources /documents/poll20060615.pdf). "I'm going to read you some positions that someone running for Congress could take. For each one, please tell me whether you would be more likely to vote for a candidate for Congress who takes this position, less likely to vote for this candidate, or would it not make a difference to you either way? . . . Favors repealing the estate tax." More likely, 48%; less likely, 18%; no difference either way, 27%; not sure, 7%.

[11] CBS News, "CBS Poll: 81% Say U.S. on Wrong Track," April 3, 2008 (http://www .cbsnews.com/news/cbs-poll-81-say-us-on-wrong-track/). "Currently the federal government taxes the estates—that is, the property and money—people leave when they die. In a few years, the tax will only apply to estates worth more than $3.5 million, and by 2010 there would be no tax on any estate, no matter what it is worth. Which comes closer to your view? There should be no tax on any estate, or the estate tax should be eliminated for most people, but kept in place for the very largest estates." No tax on any estate, 44%; tax only on large estates, 47%; neither/tax all estates (volunteered), 4%; don't know/no answer, 5%.

[12] "Would you (still) favor eliminating the federal estate tax if it were collected only on estates worth $1 million or more? . . . $5 million or more? . . . $25 million or more?" Keep estate tax, 15%; keep tax but only on estates of $1 million or more, 26%; keep tax but only on estates of $5 million or more, 11%; keep tax but only on estates of $25 million or more, 7%; eliminate tax even on estates of $25 million or more, 26%; don't know/refused, 15%.

[13] Mark J. Penn, "What Americans Really Think About Bush's Tax Cut," March 2001 (http://www.unz.org/Pub/Blueprint-2001q2-00048). "A key feature of President Bush's tax cut proposal is the elimination of the estate tax. The estate tax is now levied against estates of more than $600,000. That exemption will soon rise to $1 million. Only the top 2 percent of estates

TABLE 6.1

Obtuse Support for Repealing the Estate Tax

"There has been a lot of talk recently about doing away with the tax on large inheritances, the so-called [estate tax/death tax]. Do you FAVOR or OPPOSE doing away with the [estate tax/death tax]?"

	Favor repeal	Oppose repeal	N
Total sample	67.6%	27.2%	1,346
Among those who . . .			
have family incomes of less than $50,000	62.9%	29.9%	620 (46%)
want more spending on most government programs	66.3%	28.3%	1,232 (92%)
say income gap has increased *and* that is a bad thing	64.9%	31.9%	596 (40%)
say government policy contributes to differences in income	64.6%	30.1%	813 (63%)
say rich people pay less than they should in federal income taxes	65.2%	31.4%	674 (50%)
All of the above	63.4%	32.8%	134 (10%)

Source: 2002 ANES survey.

suggest that a majority of Americans might favor *some* form of continued estate tax. Nevertheless, what is most striking in the survey data is that a great many people with no material stake in repealing the estate tax have seemed remarkably eager to get rid of it.

The depth of public antipathy toward the estate tax is vividly demonstrated in table 6.1, which shows how support for repeal in the 2002 ANES survey varied with seemingly relevant circumstances and political views of the respondents. In the sample as a whole, almost 68% of the respondents favored repeal. Even among people with family incomes of less than $50,000 (about half the sample), 63% favored repeal. Among people who

---

are now subject to the tax. Which is closer to your view?" "We should eliminate the estate tax," 23%; "we should leave it as it is," 16%; "we should exempt small family farms and small businesses from the estate tax, but not multimillionaires," 56%; don't know, 5%.

wanted to spend more money on a variety of federal government programs, 66% favored repeal.[14] Among people who said that the difference in incomes between the rich and the poor had increased in the past 20 years *and* that that was a bad thing, 65% favored repeal. Among those who said that government policy was a "very important" or "somewhat important" cause of economic inequality (almost two-thirds of the sample), 65% favored repeal. Among those who said that the rich were asked to pay too little in federal income taxes (half the sample), 65% favored repeal. Most remarkably, among those with family incomes of less than $50,000 who wanted more spending on government programs *and* said that income inequality had increased *and* said that that was a bad thing *and* said that government policy contributed to income inequality *and* said that rich people paid less than they should in federal income taxes—the 10% of the sample with the strongest conceivable set of reasons to support continuation of the estate tax—63% favored repeal.

The persistence of overwhelming public support for repeal in the face of such a variety of seemingly contrary considerations is quite impressive. As in the case of the Bush tax cuts more generally, this pattern of support leads one to wonder what considerations led so many people to embrace policies that were so clearly contrary to their material interests.

The statistical analyses reported in table 6.2 relate support for estate tax repeal in the 2002 ANES survey to a variety of indicators of respondents' political values and perceived self-interest.[15] Since the primary direct effect of repealing the estate tax would be to reduce the long-run tax burden of the wealthiest sliver of taxpayers, it seems plausible to suppose that people who believed that the rich paid too much in taxes should have been much more likely to favor repealing the estate tax, while those who believed that the rich paid too little in taxes should have been much more likely to oppose repeal. Since repealing the estate tax would have no direct effect on people's own tax

[14] Respondents who were interviewed in both waves of the 2002 ANES survey were asked whether federal spending in each of 17 specific areas should be increased, decreased, or kept about the same. I counted those who favored more increases than decreases as wanting more government spending. The 17 spending items focused on "building and repairing highways," "AIDS research," "welfare programs," "public schools" (or "big-city schools"), "dealing with crime," "child care," "homeland security" (or "the war on terrorism"), "unemployment insurance," "defense," "environmental protection," "aid to poor people" (or "aid to the working poor"), "foreign aid," "Social Security," "tightening border security to prevent illegal immigration," "aid to blacks," "preventing infant mortality," and "pre-school and early education for poor children" (or "pre-school and early education for black children").

[15] As with the parallel analyses presented in table 5.2, the parameter estimates reported in table 6.2 are from instrumental variables regression analyses. Since the question on estate tax repeal appeared in the post-election wave of the 2002 ANES survey, I use perceived tax burdens in the pre-election survey as instruments for the corresponding perceived tax burdens in the post-election survey.

TABLE 6.2

Self-Interest, Political Values, and Support for Estate Tax Repeal

Parameter estimates from instrumental variables regression analyses (with standard errors in parentheses). Support for estate tax repeal ranges from –1 (oppose strongly) to +1 (favor strongly).

	(1)	(2)	(3)
Own tax burden (–1 to +1)	.332 (.093)	.225 (.092)	.226 (.105)
Rich tax burden (–1 to +1)	.150 (.070)	.009 (.074)	–.003 (.076)
Poor tax burden (–1 to +1)	.101 (.107)	.101 (.106)	.104 (.131)
Republican Party identification (–1 to +1)	—	.189 (.092)	.168 (.113)
Conservative ideology (–1 to +1)	—	.379 (.157)	.454 (.173)
Government spending preferences (–1 to +1)	—	—	.024 (.247)
Perceived government waste (0 to 1)	—	—	–.119 (.256)
Family income (0 to 1)	.195 (.079)	.102 (.079)	.104 (.081)
"Death tax" wording	.061 (.041)	.039 (.040)	.030 (.041)
Intercept	.143 (.058)	.166 (.063)	.233 (.216)
Standard error of regression	.740	.716	.724
Adjusted R²	.01	.07	.05
N	1,346	1,346	1,346

Source: 2002 ANES survey.

burdens (for all but the wealthiest handful) or on the tax burden of the poor, opinions about whether these taxes are too high or too low were less obviously relevant. However, if people recognized that repealing the estate tax was likely to lead, eventually, to increases in other, broader-based taxes (in some combination with reductions in government services and larger budget deficits), those who believed that their own taxes (or the taxes paid by the poor) were too high might be inspired to oppose repealing the estate tax.

Attitudes regarding the tax burden borne by the rich did have a modest positive effect on support for repealing the estate tax. The results presented in the first column of table 6.2 suggest that people who thought that the rich paid too much in federal income taxes were somewhat more likely to favor repeal, while those who thought that the rich paid too little were somewhat less likely to favor repeal. So far, so good. However, this effect was dwarfed by the much larger effect of respondents' attitudes about their *own* tax burdens. The latter effect was also positive, meaning that people who thought that *they* were asked to pay too much in federal income taxes were substantially more likely to support repealing the estate tax—despite the fact that the vast majority of them never had been or would be subject to the tax.

Separate analyses by income class indicate that the effect of respondents' own perceived tax burdens were about equally powerful among upper- and middle-income people, but disappeared among people whose incomes put them in the bottom one-third of the income distribution. The latter group's views about estate tax repeal seem to have been strongly related to their own income levels (oddly, since they were all far below the threshold for paying any estate tax), and perhaps also to their views about the tax burdens of poor people (with support for repeal perversely *higher* among low-income respondents who thought the poor were asked to pay too much).[16]

It is possible that the apparent effects of perceived tax burdens in the first column of table 6.2 are really attributable to more general political dispositions that shape people's views both about tax burdens and about the estate tax. In order to test that possibility, the analysis reported in the second column of table 6.2 includes party identification and political ideology as additional explanatory factors.[17] The results of this more elaborate analysis indicate, not surprisingly, that Republicans and (especially) conservatives were a good deal more likely than Democrats and liberals to favor estate tax repeal. Meanwhile, the apparent effect of people's perceptions of the tax burden of the rich—the most obviously relevant consideration in thinking about the merits of estate tax repeal—disappears entirely once partisanship and ideology are taken into account.

---

[16] The parameter estimates for *own tax burden* are .37 (with a standard error of .11) for the 36% of the ANES sample with family incomes over $65,000, .38 (.16) for the 33% of the sample with family incomes between $35,000 and $65,000, and .03 (.33) among the 31% with family incomes under $35,000. The parameter estimates for family income are .41 (.41), .75 (.49), and 1.38 (.51), respectively. The perceived tax burdens of poor people had no perceptible effect among upper- and middle-income respondents, but a parameter estimate of .39 (with a standard error of .34) among low-income respondents.

[17] As in the analyses reported in table 5.2, I employ the difference in "thermometer ratings" assigned to conservatives and liberals as an instrument for *conservative ideology* and the respondents' 2000 presidential vote as an instrument for *Republican Party identification*.

The analysis reported in the third column of table 6.2 adds two more potential explanatory factors: government spending preferences and perceived government waste.[18] The statistical results presented in table 5.2 implied that these factors influenced people's support for the 2001 tax cut, but the results presented in table 6.2 suggest that they had no perceptible impact on support for estate tax repeal. Here, as in the analysis presented in the second column, support for estate tax repeal seems to have been most strongly affected by political ideology, party identification, and people's perceptions of their own tax burdens.

In assessing the political implications of these results, it is important to bear in mind that the distributions of ideology and partisanship in the American public are not sufficiently skewed for their impact in table 6.2 to imply much *net* support for estate tax repeal. Instead, as with the Bush tax cuts more generally, the most important single factor in accounting for the predominance of public support for estate tax repeal was respondents' attitudes about their own tax burdens. People who said that *they* were asked to pay too much in federal income taxes were substantially more likely to support repealing the estate tax—even though almost none of them would ever be subject to the tax. Even after allowing for the effects of family income, partisanship, ideology, government spending preferences, and perceptions of government waste, those who said that they were asked to pay too much were significantly more likely to favor repeal. Since respondents were much more likely to think that they were asked to pay too much in taxes than too little, the impact of these views on the overall distribution of opinion about repealing the estate tax was substantial, accounting for about one-fourth of the *net* public support for repeal.[19]

While support for estate tax repeal was strongly related to people's views about their own tax burdens, their views about whether the rich paid too much or too little in taxes had no apparent effect, despite the fact that the sole direct effect of repealing the estate tax would be to reduce the long-run tax burden of the wealthiest taxpayers. Nor were people who said that the poor were overburdened by the tax system more likely to oppose repeal, notwithstanding the likelihood that repealing the estate tax would lead to increases in other, broader-based taxes, reductions in government services, or larger budget deficits.

---

[18] I employ an index derived from eight government spending items in the pre-election wave of the 2002 ANES survey as an instrument for the corresponding index of *government spending preferences* in the post-election wave of the survey, and perceptions of trust in government (whether government can be trusted to do what is right, whether government is run for the benefit of all, and whether government officials are crooked) as instruments for *perceived government waste*.

[19] The sample mean value for the (−1 to +1) estate tax variable was .387. Multiplying the sample mean value for *own tax burden*, .410, by the parameter estimate in the third column of table 6.2, .226, accounts for 24% of this net support for repealing the estate tax.

Is Public Support for Repeal
a Product of Misinformation?

As with support for tax cuts more generally, support for estate tax repeal seems to be oddly unconnected to some considerations that would seem on their face to be quite relevant (such as whether rich people pay too much in taxes) and misconnected to some considerations that ought logically to be irrelevant, or even to imply opposition rather than support (such as whether people think their own taxes are too high). Peculiarities like these presumably help to account for why so many of Graetz and Shapiro's Washington informants "attributed the unexpected public support for repeal to misinformation and semantics."[20]

Certainly, proponents of estate tax repeal did not hesitate to rely on specious arguments to make their case. One is the notion that the estate tax poses a mortal threat to small businesses and family farms. A 2005 study by the Congressional Budget Office found that fewer than 5% of taxable estates in 2000 belonged to farmers or family-owned businesses, and that the vast majority of these had sufficient liquid assets (stocks, bonds, bank accounts, and insurance) to cover their estate tax liability. The study identified a total of 138 farm estates that may have lacked sufficient liquid assets (not counting trusts) to cover their estate tax liability, but they would have been able to spread their estate tax payments over a period of up to 14 years. And if the $3.5 million exemption scheduled to take effect in 2009 had been in effect in 2000, only 65 farm estates would have owed any tax at all.[21]

Another common argument of supporters of estate tax repeal is that it unfairly taxes assets that were already taxed as income. For example, a television ad aired in North Dakota by the American Family Business Institute paired images of the D-Day invasion with a claim that "the I.R.S. hits this greatest generation with an unjust double tax, the death tax." However, the reality is that much of the wealth subject to estate taxation consists of "unrealized"—and therefore untaxed—capital gains resulting from increases in the value of stock, real estate, and other assets.[22]

The powerful factual misperceptions bolstering support for estate tax repeal show no sign of losing traction. They continue to be retailed by such prominent figures as Connie Mack, the chairman of President George W. Bush's blue-ribbon tax reform panel. In a brief interview published a week

---

[20] Graetz and Shapiro (2005, 253).

[21] Congressional Budget Office, "The Effects of the Federal Estate Tax on Farms and Small Businesses," July 2005.

[22] Edmund L. Andrews, "Death Tax? Double Tax? For Most, It's No Tax," *New York Times*, August 14, 2005; Jacob Freedman, "Rough Accounting Ahead for Inheritors," *CQ Weekly*, June 16, 2006, 1672.

before the panel filed its report (and a few months after the CBO published its report on the effects of the estate tax on farms and small businesses), Mack was asked about the possibility of repealing the estate tax:

> I think there is a likelihood that Congress will deal with that issue before this term comes to an end. I would vote to eliminate, as we refer to it, the death tax. I think it's an unfair tax.

> *(Really? I think it's a perfect tax. The idea behind it was to allow people to postpone paying taxes until they die, at which point they presumably no longer care. Why do you call it unfair?)*

> Well, let's say, if you are in the farming business and you have the desire to pass this farm on to your children. The problem is that when your parents die, you have to come up with cash to pay the estate tax. One thing you don't have is cash. You've got plenty of land. So I just don't believe it's a fair tax.

> *(That strikes me as a red herring. The issue is not really small farms, but zillion-dollar estates made up of stocks and bonds.)*

> I don't know what the percentage breakdown is. I still go back to the same notion that these individuals who have accumulated these resources have paid taxes on them many times in their life, and then to say, when you die, now you pay more taxes on it? There is a limit.[23]

Perhaps the chairman of the president's tax reform panel—a veteran of the Senate Appropriations, Finance, and Joint Economic Committees—really had no idea how many of the people burdened by the estate tax were family farmers, despite the CBO's report on the subject a few months earlier. Perhaps he really believed that their wealth had already been taxed "many times." Perhaps he knew better but did not care.

Of course, the fact that specious arguments circulate in elite political discourse does not necessarily imply that they penetrate the thinking of ordinary citizens, or that they have significant effects on policy preferences. Nevertheless, the brazenness of conservative efforts to impugn the "death tax" reinforces the suspicion in some quarters that public support for estate tax repeal is largely a product of widespread misunderstanding of how the estate tax actually works.

Opinion surveys provide plenty of support for the notion that public misunderstanding of the estate tax is widespread. For example, the 2003 NPR/Kaiser Family Foundation/Kennedy School survey asked people who favored eliminating the estate tax (57% of the sample) about their reasons for doing so. All four of the reasons proposed in the survey were endorsed by

---

[23] Deborah Solomon, "Taxing Issues," *New York Times Magazine*, October 23, 2005, 23.

substantial majorities: "The money was already taxed once and it shouldn't be taxed again" (92%); "It might force the sale of small businesses and family farms" (74%); "It affects too many people" (62%); and "It might affect YOU someday" (69%).[24] These results suggest that a very substantial number of people who supported repealing the estate tax not only accepted specious conservative arguments regarding its unfairness but also believed that their own taxes might be lower if it was repealed.

Another question in the same survey asked respondents whether "most families have to pay the federal estate tax when someone dies or only a few families have to pay it." Almost half the respondents said that most families have to pay, and an additional 18% said that they did not know. Thus, two-thirds of the American public failed to recognize the single most important fact about the estate tax: that it is paid only by a small number of very wealthy people.[25]

Economist Joel Slemrod showed that confusion on this score contributed to public support for estate tax repeal. He estimated that, other things being equal, support for repeal was ten percentage points higher among people who thought most families have to pay than among those who recognized that only a few families pay estate taxes. (People who said that they didn't know were slightly *more* supportive of repeal than those who were misinformed.) Slemrod concluded that "popular misunderstanding . . . contributes to the widespread opposition to the tax, although a majority would oppose it even in the absence of this particular misconception."[26]

Unlike the NPR/Kaiser Family Foundation/Kennedy School survey analyzed by Slemrod, the 2002 ANES survey did not include specific factual questions about the estate tax or its effects. However, it is possible to examine the effects of political information more generally on support for estate tax repeal among the ANES respondents. The analysis in chapter 5 showed that support for the 2001 tax cut was significantly weaker among better-informed people than among those who were less well informed. Is that true as well of the strong support for repealing the estate tax evident in figure 6.1?

[24] "Why do you favor eliminating the estate tax as it is now? Is this a reason or not?" "The money was already taxed once and it shouldn't be taxed again." Yes, a reason, 92%; no, not a reason, 7%; don't know, 2%. "It affects too many people." Yes, 62%; no, 34%; don't know, 3%. "It might affect YOU someday." Yes, 69%; no, 30%; don't know, 1%. "It might force the sale of small businesses and family farms." Yes, 74%; no, 22%; don't know, 4%.

[25] "Do you think that most families have to pay the federal estate tax when someone dies or only a few families have to pay it?" Most families have to pay, 49%; only a few families have to pay, 33%; don't know, 18%.

[26] Slemrod (2006, 69). Yanna Krupnikov and her colleagues (2006) repeated Slemrod's analysis separately for Democrats and Republicans; they found that the effect of misinformation was about twice as large for Democrats as for Republicans.

TABLE 6.3

Partisanship, Political Information, and Support for Estate Tax Repeal

Ordered probit parameter estimates (with standard errors in parentheses) for probability of (strongly or not strongly) favoring estate tax repeal. Additional response thresholds not shown.

	All	*Republicans*	*Independents*	*Democrats*
Political information	.287	.538	.589	−.268
(0 to 1)	(.143)	(.273)	(.241)	(.252)
Family income	.455	.629	.135	.352
(0 to 1)	(.117)	(.217)	(.202)	(.201)
"Death tax" wording	.086	.255	−.015	.063
	(.062)	(.115)	(.105)	(.105)
Intercept	.048	.052	.178	.097
	(.091)	(.188)	(.151)	(.151)
Log likelihood	−1,807.4	−485.9	−631.2	−638.6
Pseudo-R²	.01	.02	.01	.00
N	1,346	434	471	441

Source: 2002 ANES survey.

The answer is no. In the case of estate tax repeal, the statistical results presented in table 6.3 indicate that better-informed people in the 2002 ANES survey were actually slightly *more* likely than those who were less well informed to favor repeal.[27] Separate analyses for Republicans, independents, and Democrats show strong positive effects of political information on support for repeal among both of the first two groups. Among Democrats the estimated effect is negative, but only slightly so.[28]

[27] As in table 5.4, these analyses allow for additional differences in support for estate tax repeal due to differences in family income and question wording ("estate tax" versus "death tax"). Income had a positive effect on support for repeal, especially among Republicans; the "death tax" question wording produced somewhat more support for repeal among Republicans but had no apparent effect on independents or Democrats.

[28] Krupnikov et al. (2006) reported qualitatively similar results from their analysis of the same data using a different statistical procedure, instrumental variables regression, paralleling and elaborating the analysis of Bartels (2004). The magnitudes of their estimated information effects are larger than for those reported here—in part because the instrumental variables procedure mitigates bias due to measurement error in political information, in part because it ignores ceiling effects in support for estate tax repeal, and in part because Krupnikov and her colleagues classified Democratic and Republican "leaners" as partisans, whereas I classify them here as independents. (Oddly, the apparent information effect is about twice as large for Republican "leaners" as for full-fledged Republican identifiers.)

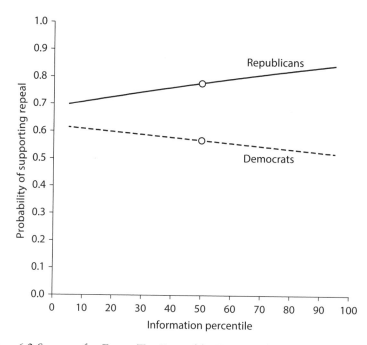

FIGURE 6.2 Support for Estate Tax Repeal by Partisanship and Information Level

The contrasting effects of political information on support for estate tax repeal among Republicans and Democrats are represented graphically in figure 6.2. Among Democrats, support for repeal declined from 62% for the least well informed to 51% for the most well informed. Among Republicans, support for repeal increased from 69% for the least well informed to 85% for the most well informed. Thus, while increasing levels of political information clearly bolstered the relationship between partisanship and views about the estate tax, there is no indication here that a better-informed public would, on balance, have been any less enthusiastic about estate tax repeal.

Table 6.4 provides additional perspective on the interaction between political information and political values in producing support for estate tax repeal. The first and second columns of the table show the impact of political information on support for repeal separately among people who said that rich people paid too little federal income tax and among those who said that the tax burden of rich people was about right or too high. The results suggest that increasing political awareness had a substantial positive effect on support for estate tax repeal in the latter group but no effect at all in the former group. Even very well-informed people who said that the tax burden of rich people was too low were more likely than not to support estate tax

TABLE 6.4
Attitudes About Inequality, Political Information,
and Support for Estate Tax Repeal

Ordered probit parameter estimates (with standard errors in parentheses) for
probability of (strongly or not strongly) favoring estate tax repeal. Additional
response thresholds not shown.

	Rich people pay too little federal income tax	The tax burden of rich people is about right or too high	The income gap is larger and that is a bad thing	The income gap is not larger or the larger gap is not a bad thing
Political information	−.099	.915	−.439	1.011
(0 to 1)	(.184)	(.233)	(.212)	(.204)
Family income	.297	.588	.359	.512
(0 to 1)	(.153)	(.182)	(.171)	(.162)
"Death tax" wording	.033	.189	.103	.083
	(.080)	(.098)	(.092)	(.083)
Intercept	.294	−.290	.394	−.238
	(.121)	(.140)	(.155)	(.117)
Log likelihood	−1,081.6	−702.7	−810.1	−974.5
Pseudo-R²	.00	.03	.01	.03
N	784	562	594	752

Source: 2002 ANES survey.

repeal. Among people who lacked this reason for opposing repeal, however,
uninformed people were about equally divided between support and opposition, but highly informed people were very likely to favor repeal.

The third and fourth columns of table 6.4 present the results of parallel analyses among two more subgroups of ANES respondents. The results
presented in the third column are based on the views of people who said
that the difference in incomes between rich people and poor people in the
United States was larger than it had been 20 years ago *and* that that was
a bad thing; these are the people for whom growing economic inequality
might have provided a reason to oppose repealing the estate tax. (In 2002
these respondents made up slightly more than 40% of the ANES sample.)
The results presented in the fourth column are based on the responses of
people who said that the difference in incomes between rich people and
poor people had not increased (about 25% of the total sample), *or* that the
larger income gap was a good thing (about 5%), *or* that they did not know

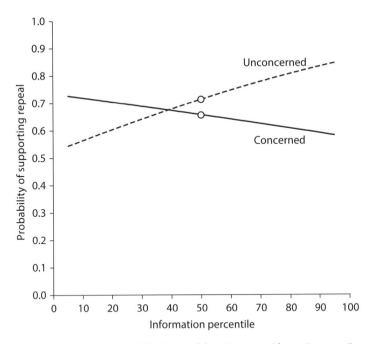

FIGURE 6.3 Support for Estate Tax Repeal by Concern About Income Inequality and Information Level

or had not thought about whether the larger income gap was a good thing or a bad thing (about 28%). What these three groups have in common is that they lacked either a factual basis or a moral basis (or both) for thinking of growing economic inequality as a problem that might be exacerbated by repealing the estate tax.

As figure 6.3 shows, dividing the survey respondents in this way produces dramatically different estimates of the effect of political information on views about estate tax repeal.[29] Among those who had reason to be concerned about growing economic inequality, politically well-informed respondents were significantly more likely than those who were less well informed to oppose estate tax repeal. However, among those who did not

[29] We saw in chapter 4 that better-informed respondents were more likely to recognize that the income gap between rich and poor has grown and more likely to think that that was a bad thing. Thus, it should not be surprising that the average level of political information was higher for the subgroup of respondents analyzed in the third column of table 6.5 than for the subgroup analyzed in the fourth column. Nevertheless, the variation in political information *within* each subgroup is sufficient to estimate the effects of information on policy preferences with tolerable precision.

recognize or did not care about increasing inequality, those who were better-informed were substantially more likely to *favor* repeal.

For people of average political awareness, these results imply very little difference in support for repeal between those who were concerned about inequality and those who were not. For people of less-than-average political awareness, those who were concerned about increasing inequality were actually somewhat *more* likely to favor repeal than those who did not know or did not care that inequality had increased. Only among the best-informed citizens did concern about inequality produce significant resistance to the allure of estate tax repeal—and even the best-informed people who recognized and regretted the fact that inequality had increased were more likely than not to favor repeal.

The pattern of support for estate tax repeal in figure 6.3 highlights the extent to which the political effects of information may hinge on a conjunction between specific bits of policy-relevant knowledge and specific moral interpretations of policy-relevant facts.[30] Among people who happened not to know or care that economic inequality had increased, those who were best informed about politics and public affairs were by far the most likely to *support* repealing the estate tax. Both recognition of the economic trend and a moral judgment that it was "a bad thing" were necessary to make well-informed, politically sophisticated people more likely to *oppose* repeal.

These results highlight the depressing limits of political information as a potential transformative force. In the case of the estate tax, the most powerful effect of greater political awareness was to significantly *bolster* support for repeal among people who did not recognize, or did not care, that income inequality had increased. The countervailing effect among people who *did* recognize and regret the fact that inequality had increased, while significant, was a good deal weaker.

It is important to consider an additional, indirect effect of information on support for estate tax repeal: the evidence presented in table 4.10 suggests that increasing political information tended to produce a substantial overall increase in public recognition of and concern about increasing inequality. In effect, increasing political information would produce not only shifts to the right along the dotted and solid lines in figure 6.3 but also a shift *from* the dotted line *to* the solid line, producing some additional reduction in support for estate tax repeal. However, the overall impact of the direct and indirect effects of increasing political information implied by this analysis remains quite modest.

---

[30] On the significance of specific policy-relevant facts, see Gilens (2001); on moral interpretations, see Stoker (1992).

For people who assume that public support for estate tax repeal must be a product of ignorance or misinformation, these results should be triply disheartening. They suggest, first, that even if every person in America could be made to see that economic inequality has increased *and* made to feel that that is a bad thing, the overall distribution of public opinion about estate tax repeal would change rather little, since declining support for repeal among better-informed people would be largely offset by increasing support for repeal among those who are less well informed. Second, even if the entire public somehow became splendidly well informed about politics and public affairs, there would be little change in the overall distribution of public opinion about the estate tax, since declining support among people concerned about inequality (and an increase in their numbers) would be largely offset by increasing support among people who continued to be unconcerned about inequality. Finally, since even very well-informed citizens who recognize and regret the fact that inequality has increased are more likely to support estate tax repeal than to oppose it, it seems very likely that a majority of the public would persist in favoring repeal even if they were splendidly well informed *and* concerned about inequality. In short, there is no ground here for imagining that the strange appeal of estate tax repeal could be overcome simply by making citizens better informed.

DID INTEREST GROUPS MANUFACTURE PUBLIC ANTIPATHY TO THE ESTATE TAX?

The analysis presented here seems consistent with Slemrod's analysis in indicating that public ignorance and misinformation play a relatively modest role in accounting for the strange appeal of estate tax repeal. Slemrod estimated that eliminating public misconceptions about the reach of the estate tax would decrease public support for repeal only modestly, from 79% to 72%.[31] Similarly, the analysis here suggests that even universal public recognition of increasing economic inequality would decrease public support for repeal from 68% (the overall level of support in the 2002 ANES

---

[31] Slemrod (2006). Slemrod's 79% figure represents support for repeal among people who took a position one way or the other—the 28% of the sample in the 2003 NPR/Kaiser Foundation/Kennedy School survey who said that they "don't know enough to say" are excluded. The estimated 7-point effect of misinformation combines a 10-point decrease in support for estate tax repeal among the 49% of respondents who thought that most families paid estate tax and a 12-point decrease among the 20% who did not know. By comparison, Slemrod estimated that eliminating public misconceptions about the progressivity of the current tax system would decrease public support for a flat-rate tax from 53% to 42% (a decrease of 24 percentage points among the 44% of the public who thought that rich people would pay more under a flat-rate system).

sample) to 57% (reflecting the estimated probability of support among people at the top of the distribution of political awareness who both recognized and regretted increasing economic inequality). As Graetz and Shapiro put it, "folk wisdom in Washington, which attributes the widespread support for repeal to the gap between belief, rhetoric, and reality, misses the real story."[32]

But what is that real story? Graetz and Shapiro's account emphasized the role of conservative political entrepreneurs in framing and selling estate tax repeal as a moral issue rather than an economic issue. These entrepreneurs

> understood that tax debates are not won by giving the public more information. The trick is giving them the right kind of information from your point of view, shaping the lens through which they come to see the issue at hand. . . . The death tax label added moral momentum to the case for repeal, turning the taxman into a pimp for the grim reaper. . . . Jonathan Weisman was not exaggerating when he wrote in *USA Today* . . . that the repeal movement had become "a massive lobbying effort that has swayed public opinion, altered the terms of the debate and proven unstoppable."[33]

In Graetz and Shapiro's account, conservative think tanks played a key role in this propaganda effort: the "growing think tank gap strengthened the hand of the repeal forces considerably. . . . In bringing the conservative tax-cutting agenda from the margins to the mainstream, the new think tanks have . . . transformed the limits of acceptable conduct." In particular, the Heritage Foundation, a "colossus of ideologically focused conservatism, with an annual operating budget in excess of $30 million, would play a major role in moving estate tax repeal into the realm of the politically thinkable." They portrayed estate tax repeal as "an early and intense preoccupation at Heritage," which generated a "flood of activity" on the issue. (Along the way, they found space to describe in loving detail the foundation's headquarters, with its "well-manicured lawn," "dark wood paneling," "gilt mirror," and "gold-etched names of donors.")[34]

Eventually, 240 pages into their account, Graetz and Shapiro mentioned in passing that the Heritage Foundation's total spending on estate tax repeal "from the mid-1990s through 1999" amounted to $250,000. Even with some allowance for the effects of "placing Heritage's considerable resources at the repeal coalition's disposal" in ways that are not reflected in that figure, it strains credibility to imagine that an expenditure of that magnitude—roughly 0.2% of the foundation's total spending during the

---

[32] Graetz and Shapiro (2005, 254).
[33] Ibid., 254, 253, 129–30.
[34] Ibid., 85, 241–42, 89, 94, 98, 92–93.

years in which it pursued the issue of estate tax repeal—could reflect an "intense preoccupation" or produce a "flood of activity," much less play "a major role in moving estate tax repeal into the realm of the politically thinkable."[35]

If the observed political action in this case seems too modest to produce the alleged political reaction, perhaps that is because public opinion did not really need to be "swayed" or "manipulated" into supporting estate tax repeal. The fact of the matter is that Americans have always found the juxtaposition of death and taxes peculiarly unsettling, even before the Heritage Foundation and other conservative groups began to mount a vigorous attack on the supposed iniquities of the "death tax" in the 1990s.

Although major survey organizations seem to have ignored the issue before the mid-1990s, vivid evidence of that antipathy is available from an unlikely source: in-depth interviews with ordinary Americans on the subject of distributive justice.[36] Summarizing the results of these interviews, which she conducted in New Haven in the mid-1970s, Jennifer Hochschild noted that "almost everyone, rich and poor, is incensed that the very wealthy do not pay their fair share of taxes." At the same time, however, she noted that "no one is enthusiastic about, and very few even accept, inheritance taxes. On this point, the sanctity of private property overwhelms the principle of equality in the political domain. Policymakers who seek revenues and support for government expenditures should not publicize inheritance taxes, even for the very wealthy."[37]

The examples that Hochschild provided of her working people's views about inheritance taxes sound uncannily similar to the focus-group-tested rhetoric of the repeal effort described by Graetz and Shapiro 25 years later:

> If I'm working and I'm banking my money, I'm planning for *their* [his children's] future. So hey, if I turn around and pass away, they got every right in the world to get what I worked for.

> It's wrong, taking away money from somebody that has earned it. You pay taxes all your life on the money you earn, and then when you pass away and you leave some money to your relatives, you gotta take *more* money out of it. It seems like tax on top of tax.

> Awful, because it's in the family, and the family has a perfect right to hand it down to their children if they want to.

---

[35] Ibid., 242, 358.
[36] The Roper Center's iPOLL database includes 82 survey questions mentioning the estate tax, death tax, or inheritance tax, but none of those questions was asked before 1996.
[37] Hochschild (1981, 280).

Why should I work all my life and run the risk that three idiots that got jobs out of patronage are going to decide whether my daughter is going to get my money? No way. Before I'll do that, I'll stop working.

Probably shouldn't be one. It's his money, he can do what he wants.[38]

None of these ordinary working people were spurred to indignation by right-wing think tanks, sound bites, or well-organized political activists. They opposed the estate tax because it violated their deeply held views about family, work, and economic opportunity.

Even more surprising evidence of long-standing public antipathy to government interference with inheritance comes from an opinion survey commissioned by *Fortune* magazine in 1935.[39] In the midst of the most cat-astrophic economic depression in American history, *Fortune* asked survey respondents: "How much money do you think any one person should be allowed to inherit?" The results are presented in table 6.5.

Over half of the respondents in the *Fortune* survey said that there should be "no limit" on inheritances; fewer than one-third favored limits of less than $1 million (almost $15 million in current dollars). The editors of *Fortune* characterized these results as "astonishing" and an indication "that the nature of Public Opinion in this country is still all but unknown":

> Despite the various noises made by the Doctors Townsend, Long, and Coughlin, and despite, again, five long years of economic hardship, 44 per cent of the people supported the right of millionaires (constituting probably no more than .004 of 1 per cent of the people) to continue to possess a million invested dollars, subject only to present taxation. It was concluded that this phenomenon was partly due to the fear of a half of the people that any measure destroying the millionaire might come too close to touching their own prospects for attaining what they would consider modest wealth. But there is a difference between self-made wealth, a tradition to which many Americans continue to aspire, and inherited wealth, for which few have well-founded hopes. (In 1933 about 1,300,000 Americans died, of whom only 10,000, or .77 of 1 per cent, left taxable estates—$50,000 or more—with a net average value of $80,000.)[40]

If Hochschild's New Haven working people sound like participants in Heri-tage Foundation focus groups, the editors of *Fortune* here sound like irritated

---

[38] Ibid., 152, 183, 201, 206, 221. The quotations come, respectively, from an unskilled worker, an assembly-line maintenance man, a widowed housewife, a chemical manufacturer, and a 19-year-old living with his parents and working in his father's corner store.

[39] *Fortune*, October 1935, 56–57. I am indebted to Adam Berinsky for calling this survey to my attention.

[40] Ibid., 56.

TABLE 6.5

Views on the Right to Inherit, by Income Class, 1935

"How much money do you think any one person should be allowed to inherit?"

	$100,000 or less[a]	$100,000 to $1,000,000	Over $1,000,000[b]	No limit	Don't know
All	15.1%	15.5%	2.3%	51.7%	15.4%
Prosperous	8.9%	16.1%	2.5%	58.9%	13.6%
Upper middle	13.8%	15.6%	2.8%	51.1%	16.7%
Lower middle	16.0%	16.3%	2.5%	51.2%	14.0%
Poor	17.8%	15.3%	1.9%	47.1%	17.9%
Negro	15.0%	12.0%	1.3%	58.0%	13.7%

Source: *Fortune* quarterly survey, 1935.

[a] Includes "none" responses ranging from 0.4% to 1.0%.

[b] Includes "over $10,000,000" responses ranging from 0 to 0.7%.

21st-century liberals lecturing ordinary Americans about the actual workings of the estate tax and the unreality of their faith in economic opportunity. The lectures have never been very effective. However, it is hard to see any evidence here that the right-wing activism described by Graetz and Shapiro has been particularly effective either. Hochschild recognized 35 years ago that, from the perspective of "policymakers who seek revenues and support for government expenditures," estate tax repeal was a train wreck waiting to happen. At best, the Heritage Foundation helped draw the attention of conservative elites to public antipathy that had gone unrecognized for decades.

ELITE IDEOLOGY AND THE POLITICS OF ESTATE TAX REPEAL

According to Graetz and Shapiro,

> no repeal effort ever got off the ground during the Ronald Reagan and George H. W. Bush administrations largely because most Washington insiders assumed that abolishing the estate tax was politically impossible. According to the orthodox wisdom, the vast majority of Americans would oppose repealing a steeply progressive tax that they would never themselves pay. It was not until the Gephardt-Waxman fiasco in 1992, when their gambit to cut the threshold to $200,000 blew up in Democrats' faces, that conservatives became alert to the possibility that they might have missed something.[41]

[41] Graetz and Shapiro (2005), 118.

My analysis strongly suggests that the "orthodox wisdom" described by Graetz and Shapiro was quite mistaken through much of the twentieth century: far from opposing estate tax repeal, "the vast majority of Americans" would probably have been happy to support it. Thus, for proponents of popular sovereignty, the real "political mystery" is not why the estate tax was temporarily phased out in 2001, but why it lasted as long as it did. The answer to that question has little to do with conservative elites' grasp of public opinion, but much to do with the political leverage of liberal Democratic elites whose own ideological values made them eager to retain "a steeply progressive tax."

This interpretation is indirectly bolstered by Graetz and Shapiro's own account of the last serious attempt to repeal the estate tax, by President Calvin Coolidge and Treasury Secretary Andrew Mellon in the mid-1920s. Mellon—himself one of the wealthiest men in America at the time—proposed abolishing the federal estate tax as part of a $250 million postwar tax cut. As would happen in 2001, estate tax repeal competed with a wide variety of other potentially popular tax cuts. The House of Representatives passed a $336 million tax cut, well in excess of the $250 million envisioned by the administration. However, the chair and ranking minority member of the Ways and Means Committee, William Green (R-IA) and John Nance Garner (D-TX), both strongly opposed estate tax repeal, and they succeeded in keeping it out of the House tax package, though the bill did cut the top estate tax rate in half and substantially increased the credit for state inheritance taxes. According to Graetz and Shapiro, "Green and Garner each faced strong constituent pressures to repeal the tax, but neither budged." In contrast, on the Senate side, Finance Committee chair Reed Smoot supported repeal and managed to win his committee's support for a $362 million tax cut "by trading Republican support for lower income tax rates on middle-income people for Democratic votes for estate tax repeal." A conference committee appointed to reconcile the House and Senate plans ended up producing an even bigger aggregate tax cut than either chamber had originally voted, $381 million. Green succeeded in preventing total repeal of the estate tax; nevertheless, the final bill cut estate tax rates, increased the credit for state estate taxes, and increased the exemption to $100,000.[42]

Nothing in this episode suggests that estate tax repeal was politically unthinkable in the 1920s. Quite to the contrary, it was intensely debated in the context of a broader tax-cutting initiative, it passed in the Senate, and it seems to have fallen by the wayside in conference committee primarily because of the strong opposition of a single strategically placed committee

---

[42] My account of the 1920s repeal effort follows that of Graetz and Shapiro (2005, 221–225).

chair who refused to budge in the face of "strong constituent pressures to repeal the tax."

Having narrowly failed to repeal the estate tax in the 1920s, only a decade after its inception, Republicans would have to wait a long time for another opportunity. The Great Depression, though it could not produce significant public enthusiasm for inheritance taxes, did produce something even more important—durable Democratic majorities in Congress. The House remained in Democratic hands for 60 of the 64 years between 1931 and 1994, and the only instance of unified Republican control for the remainder of the century was a tenuous two-year period at the beginning of the first Eisenhower administration, when the Republicans held a 10-seat margin in the House and a one-seat margin in the Senate.

Republicans won control of the House in 1994 and soon began pushing estate tax repeal. By the late 1990s, predominantly Republican majorities in both houses of Congress favored repeal, but they were far from being able to override a veto by Democratic president Bill Clinton. When the bitterly contested 2000 election left the White House in Republican hands, producing the first unified Republican government in almost half a century, it took less than five months for the estate tax phaseout to be passed and signed into law.

The lesson I draw from this history is that strong public support for estate tax repeal was certainly not sufficient, and probably not necessary, for repeal to happen. When conservative Republicans controlled the levers of power in Washington in the 1920s, they came close to engineering repeal but were stymied by the opposition of a single obstinate committee chair. When Democrats were in control, through much of the rest of the twentieth century, estate tax repeal was the furthest thing from any sensible politician's mind, regardless of what the public thought of the idea. During periods of divided government, including the Reagan and George H. W. Bush administrations, it would have been quite reasonable for "Washington insiders" to continue to assume "that abolishing the estate tax was politically impossible"—not because "the vast majority of Americans would oppose repealing a steeply progressive tax that they would never themselves pay," but because liberal Democratic lawmakers were willing and able to prevent it.

Subsequent attempts to enact a permanent repeal or reduction of the estate tax underscore the importance of both elite partisanship and institutional checks on majoritarian policy-making in the American political system. In 2006, Senate Republican leaders mustered a 53–2 majority for repeal in their own caucus but still fell three votes short of the 60 needed to cut off a Democratic filibuster. According to one press report, Republicans debated "whether to give up on their goal" of repeal "and attack Democrats in the coming midterm elections as obstructionists on a measure that they say has considerable support." Instead, House Republican leaders sought a compromise: a new bill that would retain the estate tax for estates worth more than $5 million ($10 million for couples) while adding a $900 million tax break for the timber industry as a further sweetener for key Democratic moderates in the Senate. The bill duly passed the House, but collapsed in the Senate owing to two-pronged resistance from "Democrats who oppose any big reduction in the estate tax and conservative Republicans who want nothing less than total repeal."[43]

A few weeks later, Republican leaders proposed a "trifecta" combining estate tax reduction and other tax breaks with a long-standing Democratic priority, a $2.10-per-hour increase in the federal minimum wage. This bill, too, passed the House, with 34 Democrats joining 196 Republicans in favor, but in the Senate it again failed to overcome "intense opposition from Democrats and organized labor." Senate Majority Leader Bill Frist "noted that the major provisions of the measure—the wage increase, the estate tax reduction and the package of tax breaks—all enjoyed majority Senate support yet could not clear the procedural hurdles" imposed by the body's filibuster rule.[44]

The fact that Republicans saw potential electoral gains in attacking Democrats as "obstructionists" for opposing estate tax repeal clearly implies that public opinion is not entirely irrelevant in this story. However, it is equally clear that public support for estate tax repeal has been far from sufficient to make it happen. Indeed, Frist's final failed compromise attempt demonstrated that even the combination of public support, majority support in the House, majority support in the Senate, an enthusiastic president, and an attractive package of popular add-ons could not overcome the disciplined resistance of Democratic elites to permanent estate tax repeal.

Although the Bush administration was stymied in its efforts to permanently repeal or substantially reduce the estate tax, it faced fewer hurdles in softening estate tax enforcement, underlining the capacity of those who execute the laws to shape policy through quiet shifts in priorities and procedures. A deputy commissioner of the Internal Revenue Service, Kevin Brown, ordered staff cuts reducing the agency's complement of estate tax lawyers from 345 to 188, saying that "careful analysis showed that the IRS

[43] Edmund L. Andrews, "G.O.P. Fails in Attempt to Repeal Estate Tax," *New York Times*, June 9, 2006; Edmund L. Andrews, "Timber Becomes Tool in Effort to Cut Estate Tax," *New York Times*, June 21, 2006; Rachel Van Dongen, "House Backs Compromise Estate Tax Cut," *CQ Weekly*, June 23, 2006, 1788; Rachel Van Dongen, "Frist Lets Estate Tax Revision Simmer as He Looks for Support," *CQ Weekly*, July 7, 2006, 1876.

[44] David Nather, "Bills Merged in Pre-Recess Flurry," *CQ Weekly*, July 29, 2006, 2110; Carl Hulse, "House Approves Wage Increase Linked to Tax Breaks," *New York Times*, July 30, 2006; David Nather and Rachel Van Dongen, "Frist Loses Estate Tax Showdown," *CQ Weekly*, August 4, 2006, 2176; Carl Hulse, "Wage Bill Dies; Senate Backs Pension Shift," *New York Times*, August 4, 2006.

was auditing enough returns to catch cheats" and that "auditing a greater percentage of gift and estate tax returns would not be worthwhile because 'the next case is not a lucrative case.'" Six of the lawyers whose jobs were likely to be eliminated "said in interviews that the cuts were just the latest moves behind the scenes at the IRS to shield people with political connections and complex tax-avoidance devices from thorough audits," but "Mr. Brown dismissed as preposterous any suggestion that the IRS was soft on rich tax cheats."[45]

When Barack Obama won the White House in 2008, attention turned back to the looming sunset of the Bush tax cuts in 2011. Once again, the power of the status quo cast a long shadow; simply by doing nothing, Democrats could have forced an automatic reinstatement of the Clinton-era estate tax. Instead, as we have seen, they chose not once but twice to barter away this procedural advantage, settling for a much less robust estate tax in exchange for a variety of mostly temporary concessions from congressional Republicans in the lame-duck sessions following the 2010 and 2012 elections. No doubt that strategy was, in part, a concession to the public's strong antipathy to the estate tax. But the concession was a limited one. Notwithstanding the strange public appeal of estate tax repeal, America's wealthiest families were once again made subject to what Robert Frank identified as "the closest thing to a perfect tax we have."[46]

The revived estate tax highlights the limited force of public sentiment when it happens to conflict with the ideological convictions of strategically placed political elites. In the context of the broader politics of inequality, it is ironic that public sentiment in this instance is on the side of multimillionaires, while elite intransigence is centered among liberal Democrats. However, that specific configuration of political forces is neither typical nor essential to the story.

To demonstrate that point, I turn in chapter 7 to a parallel case drawn from the opposite end of the American income spectrum and featuring a very different configuration of political forces—the evolution of the federal minimum wage. In that policy domain, the power of the status quo and the limited force of public sentiment are both even more striking than they are in the case of estate tax repeal, but with very different political ramifications. Whereas liberal Democrats have employed the power of the status quo to frustrate public sentiment opposing a tax on America's wealthiest inheritors, conservative Republicans have used the power of the status quo to frustrate strongly egalitarian public sentiment favoring wage hikes for America's poorest workers.

[45] David Cay Johnston, "IRS Will Cut Tax Lawyers Who Audit the Richest," *New York Times*, July 23, 2006.
[46] Frank, "The Estate Tax: Efficient, Fair and Misunderstood."

CHAPTER 7

The Eroding Minimum Wage

IN MAY 2007, overwhelming majorities in both chambers of Congress passed the Fair Minimum Wage Act of 2007, which increased the federal minimum wage from $5.15 per hour to $7.25 per hour in three annual 70-cent increments. The liberal Economic Policy Institute estimated that 5.3 million workers would be directly affected by the increase, with another 7.2 million indirectly benefiting from "spillover effects." House Speaker Nancy Pelosi hailed the outcome as a victory for "the hardest-working Americans." It was also a victory for Pelosi and the Democratic Party, since they had made a minimum wage increase one of the primary planks in their 2006 midterm campaign platform.[1]

Low-wage workers were, no doubt, very grateful for the raise. However, from a broader historical perspective, the 2007 increase looks less like a

[1] Economic Policy Institute, "EPI Issue Guide: Minimum Wage," April 2007, table 1 (http://epi.3cdn.net/1010456170680f8fc7_lem6b99v9.pdf). Stephen Labaton, "Congress Passes Increase in the Minimum Wage," *New York Times*, May 25, 2007.

major advance in the economic status of the working poor than an isolated break in a long downward trend. Even after the full increase took effect in 2009, the real value of the minimum wage was 26% less than it had been 40 years earlier. (Average real hourly wages for all American workers increased by more than one-third over that period.)[2] Moreover, the real value of the minimum wage began to erode again the moment the new $7.25 wage rate took effect and will continue to do so absent further legislative action.

In this chapter I attempt to account both for the substantial increase in the real value of the minimum wage in the first two decades of the post-war era and for its subsequent decline. From the standpoint of democratic responsiveness, the decline is much more puzzling than the increase, since the public has been broadly and consistently supportive of minimum wage increases throughout this period. How has the real value of the minimum wage fallen by one-third since the late 1960s despite this strong public support? As in the case of estate tax repeal, the politics of the minimum wage seem to be driven much more by partisanship and ideology than by public opinion or, for that matter, economics.

The dramatic rise and fall of the minimum wage over the past 80 years is one of the most remarkable aspects of the political economy of inequality. The original federal minimum wage was one of the major policy innovations of the New Deal era. In 1938, Congress enacted a minimum wage of 25 cents per hour (about $4.23 in 2015 dollars) for "employees engaged in interstate commerce or in the production of goods for interstate commerce"—about 20% of the U.S. labor force. Subsequent legislation gradually expanded coverage to include most workers in large retail and service enterprises, construction, hospitals and nursing homes, hotels and restaurants, farms, and state and local governments, eventually encompassing about 90% of all non-supervisory workers.[3]

While the scope of minimum wage coverage gradually increased, so did the minimum wage rate. By 1950 the minimum was 75 cents per hour, by 1968 it was $1.60 per hour, in 1981 it was $3.35 per hour, and for a decade before the most recent increase it was $5.15 per hour. These periodic increases in the nominal minimum wage rate have of course been eroded by inflation. (Unlike Social Security benefits, which are automatically adjusted to reflect changing price levels, the minimum wage rate has not been indexed to counteract the effects of inflation.) Figure 7.1 shows how the real value of

---

[2] The real value of the minimum wage in 1968 (in 2015 dollars) was $10.96; average hourly pay was $23.23. The corresponding figures in 2009 were $8.06 and $31.22.

[3] U.S. Department of Labor, "History of Federal Minimum Wage Rates Under the Fair Labor Standards Act, 1938–1996" (http://www.dol.gov/whd/minwage/chart.htm); Page and Simmons (2000, 225). Earlier, President Roosevelt established voluntary federal wage standards under the National Industrial Recovery Act, but the act was invalidated by the Supreme Court.

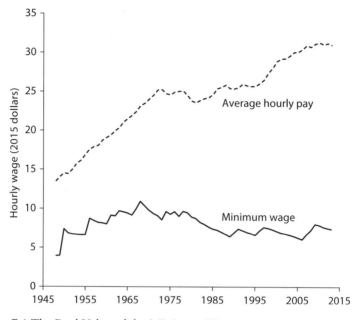

Figure 7.1 The Real Value of the Minimum Wage, 1948–2013

the federal minimum wage has changed over the past 65 years. For purposes of comparison, the figure also shows how the average hourly compensation of American workers has changed over the same period.[4]

The history of minimum wage rates summarized in figure 7.1 can be divided into two distinct periods. During the first two decades of the postwar era, periodic upward adjustments in the nominal minimum wage rate produced substantial increases in its real value, generally keeping pace with real wage gains in the economy as a whole. The average value of the minimum wage in the 1950s was about $7.50 (in 2015 dollars), which was 45% of average hourly pay. The average minimum in the 1960s was equivalent to about $9.60—again, 45% of average hourly pay. The real value of the minimum wage peaked in 1968, at almost $11.00 per hour.

When real wage growth stalled in the economy as a whole in the 1970s, the real value of the minimum wage began to decline, both in absolute terms

---

[4] The minimum wage values in figure 7.1 do not reflect the fact that some states have set higher minimums. Average hourly wage rates are calculated from data provided by the Bureau of Economic Analysis (BEA) dividing "wage and salaries" (table 6.3) by "hours worked by full-time and part-time employees" (table 6.9); BEA, NIPA, "Income and Employment by Industry" (http://www.bea.gov). Both wage series are deflated by the Census Bureau's consumer price index for all urban consumers (CPI-U).

(to $9.38) and in relative terms (to 38% of the average hourly wage). The Reagan era saw a modest increase in average wages but a sharp and steady decline in the real value of the minimum wage, from about $8.80 in 1981 to $6.40 in 1989. (The nominal minimum wage remained unchanged throughout this period, at $3.35.) Modest increases in 1990–1991 and 1996–1997 slowed the downward trend but did not keep pace with wage growth in the broader economy. By 2006, the real value of the minimum wage had declined by 45% from its peak in 1968 (from $10.96 to $6.09 in 2015 dollars), while average hourly pay had increased by more than 30% (from $23.23 to $30.52). In relative terms, whereas minimum wage workers in the 1950s and 1960s earned 45% of the average wage in the economy as a whole, by 2006 the minimum wage was only 20% of the average wage. The 2007 minimum wage hike increased that ratio to 26% in 2009, but by 2013 it had slipped back down to 24%.

In this chapter I examine a variety of possible explanations for the substantial erosion in the real value of the minimum wage over the past 50 years. I consider but reject the possibility that economic evidence has persuaded policy-makers that maintaining the minimum wage is counterproductive. On the contrary, recent economic research suggests that the negative effects of minimum wage laws on employment are much less significant than has often been assumed, while declines in the real value of the minimum wage have contributed substantially to increasing inequality in the bottom half of the income distribution. Similarly, I consider but reject the possibility that public opinion has turned against the minimum wage. In fact, virtually every opinion survey conducted over the past 70 years has found majorities of the public favoring minimum wage increases, usually by margins of two-, three-, or even four-to-one.

The declining political strength of labor unions seems to be a much more important aspect of minimum wage politics. Indeed, the massive decline in union membership since the late 1940s has probably depressed the real value of the minimum wage by almost 40%.[5] Partisan politics has also played a key role. Republican presidents and Republican members of Congress have generally opposed minimum wage increases, and they have utilized the complexities of the legislative process to block or moderate policy changes reflecting majority sentiment on this issue. The result is that the real value of the minimum wage has generally increased when Democrats have had the upper hand in Washington but fallen under Republicans. In response, proponents of minimum wage increases have turned to statehouses and ballot measures to pursue their policy goals, while the federal government has increasingly come to rely on an alternative policy, the Earned Income Tax

---

[5] This estimate is derived from the statistical analyses presented in table 7.1.

Credit (EITC), as a partial substitute for a robust minimum wage in providing income support to low-wage workers.

The Economic Effects of the Minimum Wage

Orthodox economic theory has long held the minimum wage in disrepute, making it (literally) a textbook example of a fruitless attempt to repeal the law of supply and demand. According to the 1992 edition of *The MIT Dictionary of Modern Economics*, for example, "minimum wage legislation has been shown in almost all cases to have had an adverse effect upon employment, particularly that of teenagers. This demonstrates the difficulty of formulating a specific wage that eliminates exploitation without causing unemployment."[6]

A dozen years later, in an election-year editorial blasting the Democratic presidential candidate's proposal to raise the minimum wage to $7 an hour, the editors of the *Wall Street Journal* asked: "How many low-wage workers does John Kerry want to throw out of work?" "Force the price of labor too high," they warned,

> and suddenly businesses hire fewer workers, especially those at the lower rungs of the skill ladder. This is one of the most settled propositions in economics, second only perhaps to free trade. Sure, Mr. Kerry has found a few economists willing to lend their credibility to his proposal, but even they don't deny that some people may lose their jobs—which is why they don't want to raise the minimum *too high*.[7]

Notwithstanding the *Wall Street Journal*'s view, the effect of minimum wage laws on employment seems to be an increasingly *un*settled proposition in economics. A 2000 survey of 308 members of the American Economic Association found only 46% agreeing with the statement, "Minimum wages increase unemployment among young and unskilled workers," while 27% disagreed. (The corresponding figures 10 years earlier had been 62% and 18%.)[8] According to one academic observer, "here's what most labor economists believe: The minimum wage kills very few jobs, and the jobs it kills were lousy jobs anyway. It is almost impossible to maintain the old argument that minimum wages are bad for minimum-wage workers."[9]

---

[6] Pearce (1992, 279).

[7] "The Wages of Politics: How Many Low-Wage Workers Does John Kerry Want to Throw Out of Work?" (editorial), *Wall Street Journal*, June 24, 2004.

[8] Fuller and Geide-Stevenson (2003, 378).

[9] Steven E. Landsburg, "The Sin of Wages: The *Real* Reason to Oppose the Minimum Wage," *Slate*, July 9, 2004. Landsburg argued that the minimum wage concentrates the burden of income maintenance unfairly on low-wage employers, and that an expanded EITC would be fairer and more efficient.

The heretical-sounding view that raising the minimum wage may have no discernible negative effect on employment was bolstered by the research of economists David Card and Alan Krueger in the early 1990s. Card and Krueger exploited a "natural experiment"—an 80-cent increase in the New Jersey minimum wage in 1992—to examine the impact of minimum wage laws on employment and prices. They surveyed 399 fast-food restaurants in New Jersey and neighboring areas of Pennsylvania, where the prevailing minimum wage remained unchanged. Comparing the two sets of restaurants before and after the New Jersey wage increase, they found that employment declined by almost 10% in Pennsylvania but *increased* slightly in New Jersey. Moreover, they found that the increase in employment in New Jersey was concentrated among the restaurants that had previously been paying the lowest wages—those presumably most affected by the minimum wage increase. Restaurants where the starting wage already equaled or exceeded the new minimum experienced declines in employment comparable to those observed in Pennsylvania. A parallel survey of fast-food restaurants in Texas before and after the national minimum wage increase in 1991 showed a similar increase in employment in low-wage restaurants and a similar decrease in employment in restaurants that had already been paying the new minimum wage.[10]

A subsequent study by Arindrajit Dube, T. William Lester, and Michael Reich applied the same approach on a broader scale, examining hundreds of cases in which differences in minimum wage rates in contiguous counties shifted between 1990 and 2006 owing to changes in state laws. Tracking employment and earnings in restaurants and other industries where minimum wage work was prevalent, they found "strong [positive] earnings effects and no employment effects of minimum wage increases" in limited-service restaurants, full-service restaurants, and the accommodations and food services sector.[11]

Card and Krueger were careful to note that their work did *not* imply "that the employment losses from a much higher minimum wage would be small: the evidence at hand is relevant only for a moderate range of minimum wages, such as those that prevailed in the U.S. labor market during the past few decades."[12] No doubt there is *some* minimum wage level so

[10] Card and Krueger (1995, 38, 60). Additional analysis and responses to criticism appear in Card and Krueger (2000).

[11] Dube, Lester, and Reich (2010, 961). In contrast, minimum wage increases had no discernible positive effect on earnings and a small but uncertain negative effect on employment in the retail sector.

[12] Card and Krueger (1995, 393). Dube, Lester, and Reich (2010, 962) registered a similar caveat, noting that "our conclusion is limited by the scope of the actual variation in policy; our results cannot be extrapolated to predict the impact of a minimum wage increase that is much larger than what we have experienced over the period under study."

high that it actually harms minimum-wage workers by reducing their prospects for employment more than it increases their wages. Another economist, Russell Sobel, used a time-series model of labor demand to estimate the value of the minimum wage that would maximize the total transfer of income to minimum wage workers: $5.36 in 1996 dollars, or about $8.15 in 2015 dollars.[13]

The actual value of the federal minimum wage fell below Sobel's estimate of the income-maximizing wage level in the early 1980s and only briefly approached that level again in 2009 before receding once more. Interestingly, the $7 minimum wage rate advocated by John Kerry in the 2004 presidential campaign, and pilloried by the editors of the *Wall Street Journal*, matches Sobel's estimate almost exactly. (A $7 minimum in effect from 2005 to 2009 would have had an average real value, in 2015 dollars, of about $8.10.)

In addition to studying the impact of minimum wage laws on employment, economists have investigated the broader question of how minimum wage laws have affected the overall shape of the income distribution. Card and Krueger used aggregate data on the proportion of workers in each state directly affected by the 1990–1991 minimum wage increase to estimate the impact of that increase on the distribution of earnings. They concluded that "more than 35 percent of the earnings gains generated by the 1990 and 1991 minimum wage hikes were concentrated among families in the bottom 10 percent of the family-earnings distribution," and that raising the minimum wage "rolled back some 30 percent of the previous decade's accumulated increase in wage dispersion."[14]

Card and Krueger noted that their finding regarding the impact on wage dispersion of raising the minimum wage in the early 1990s closely matched an independent estimate of the share of wage dispersion attributable to the decline in the real value of the minimum wage through the 1980s. A subsequent study along similar lines by David Lee produced even more dramatic results, suggesting that "a great majority of the observed growth in inequality in the lower tail of the [income] distribution is attributable to the erosion of the real value of the federal minimum wage rate during the 1980s."[15]

In a presentation summarizing the economic literature and its implications for policy-making, Krueger urged elected officials to focus on political issues of distribution rather than economic issues of efficiency:

I think it is becoming increasingly difficult to support the position that a modest minimum wage hike would have even a noticeable impact

[13] Sobel (1999, 768–75).
[14] Card and Krueger (1995, 308, 297).
[15] DiNardo, Fortin, and Lemieux (1996); Lee (1999).

on employment. . . . The issue, in my view, comes down to questions of fairness: Whether it is fair to workers to allow the value of the minimum wage, after adjusting for inflation, to fall to its lowest level in 50 years; and whether it is fair to impose the costs of meeting a higher minimum wage on business owners and possibly on customers. These are not questions for which economists have any advantage in answering over politicians or the general public.[16]

PUBLIC SUPPORT FOR THE MINIMUM WAGE

Over the past half-century, politicians and the general public have answered Krueger's questions of fairness in very different ways.

The Roper Center's iPOLL archive of opinion surveys includes 125 instances since the late 1940s in which national samples of the public were asked whether they favored or opposed increasing the minimum wage. The surveys were conducted by a wide variety of survey organizations using a wide variety of different question wordings; some asked about specific proposed increases, while others left the amount unspecified. (In recent surveys, the most common form of the question asked respondents whether or not they favored increasing the minimum wage from $7.25 to $10.10 per hour.) The results of these surveys are summarized in figure 7.2, which shows the proportion of each survey sample favoring a minimum wage increase.[17]

Although the survey data are sparse for the first half of this period, there seems to have been a gradual increase in support for raising the minimum wage. By 1987, with the real value of the minimum wage having declined by more than one-third over the preceding two decades, three separate surveys found support for an increase ranging from 75% to 85%. Over the next 20 years, while the real value of the minimum wage declined modestly, public support for increasing the minimum wage was consistent and overwhelming, with most surveys finding 80% or more of the public favoring an increase. Once the increase legislated in 2007 began to take effect, public support for further increases abated somewhat, but most surveys

[16] Alan B. Krueger, "The Economic Effects of New Jersey's Last Minimum Wage Increase," prepared statement before the Labor Committee, New Jersey Senate, January 24, 2005.

[17] The dotted line in the figure is a fourth-order polynomial trend line. This trend line may exaggerate somewhat the consistency of public support for minimum wage increases over the decades covered by the figure, since poll questions focusing on this issue have tended to be most frequent when proposals to raise the minimum wage were politically salient (often at times when the real value of the minimum wage was especially low). Question wording and data for each survey are available from the Roper Center's iPOLL archive.

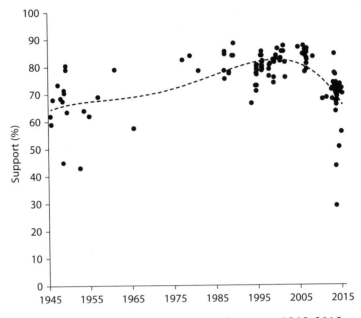

FIGURE 7.2 Public Support for Minimum Wage Increases, 1945–2015

continued to show supporters outnumbering opponents by margins of two- or three-to-one.

Public support for raising the minimum wage is clearly affected by the magnitude of the proposed increase. For example, two of the four recent instances in which fewer than 60% of the public favored a minimum wage increase were cases in which the proposed increase amounted to 70% or more.[18] When a 2013 NBC News/*Wall Street Journal* poll asked about increasing the minimum wage from $7.25 to $15 per hour, only 29% of the respondents favored the idea—a substantially lower level of support than any of the 124 others recorded in figure 7.2. By comparison, 43% of

[18] The other two instances in which minimum wage increases received less than 60% support were polls sponsored by Fox News (September 2014 and April 2015) offering separate options (and arguments) for not raising the minimum wage and for abolishing it entirely. "As you may know, the federal government sets the national minimum wage—the lowest rate in dollars per hour that most workers should be paid—which is now set at seven dollars and twenty-five cents an hour. Which of the following comes closest to your view on how the federal government should handle the minimum wage? The government should raise the minimum wage because it would help lots of people pay their bills, the government should not raise the minimum wage because it would cause businesses to cut jobs, there shouldn't be a minimum wage because government shouldn't tell businesses what to pay their employees." In both polls, about half of the public favored the first option, while about one-fourth favored each of the other two options.

the public favored an increase to $12.50, and 63% favored an increase to $10.10.[19] On the other hand, more modest differences in the magnitude of proposed increases seem to have only modest effects on public support. For example, a survey conducted by the Pew Research Center in March 2006 asked half the respondents whether they favored or opposed raising the minimum wage from $5.15 to $6.45 per hour (a 25% increase) and the other half whether they favored or opposed raising the minimum to $7.15 per hour (a 39% increase). The difference changed the results by just a few percentage points, with respondents favoring the $1.30 increase by an 86–11% margin and the $2.00 increase by an 83–14% margin.[20]

In at least one instance, pairing a minimum wage increase with an automatic cost-of-living adjustment seemed to reduce its popularity—but, again, the effect was fairly modest. A 2013 Gallup poll asked half the respondents whether they would vote for or against raising the minimum wage to $9 an hour; the margin in favor was 76–22%. The other half of the sample was asked about the same raise "with automatic increases tied to the inflation rate"; that proposal produced a 69–28% margin in favor.[21]

Public support for raising the minimum wage also seems to be remarkably firm in the face of counter-argument. For example, a survey conducted by the Service Employees International Union (SEIU) in May 1987 asked a national sample of registered voters whether they supported or opposed raising the minimum wage. Eighty-three percent of the respondents said that they supported an increase (59% "strongly"), while 14% opposed it. Respondents were then asked to agree or disagree with a variety of claims about the minimum wage—for example, "wages should be set by the market and not by the government" (69% agreed) and "raising the minimum wage might result in some job loss" (54% agreed). Then they were asked again whether they supported or opposed an increase. Despite the respondents' apparent willingness to accept strong counter-arguments, their support for a minimum wage increase was virtually unchanged, with 84% supporting

[19] "As you may know, the minimum wage is currently seven dollars and twenty five cents an hour. I'm going to mention a number of different amounts and for each one, please tell me if you strongly favor, somewhat favor, somewhat oppose, or strongly oppose raising the hourly minimum wage to that amount." Eric Morath, "Support for $10.10 Minimum Wage," *Wall Street Journal*, December 11, 2013.

[20] "As I list some programs and proposals that are being discussed in this country today, please tell me whether you strongly favor, favor, oppose, or strongly oppose each. . . . An increase in the minimum wage, from $5.15 an hour to $6.45 [$7.15] an hour." March 2006 News Interest Index poll; $N = 1,405$.

[21] "Next, suppose that on Election Day you could vote on key issues as well as candidates. Would you vote for or against a law that would raise the federal minimum wage to $9 an hour [with automatic increases tied to inflation]?" Andrew Dugan, "Most Americans for Raising Minimum Wage," *Gallup Politics*, November 11, 2013 (http://www.gallup.com/poll/165794/americans-raising-minimum-wage.aspx).

an increase (57% "strongly") and only 13% opposing it. Nor did support for a minimum wage increase seem to vary with knowledge of the current minimum wage rate. Among respondents who knew the current rate, 84% thought that amount was too low and only 3% thought it was too high; when respondents who did not know (most of whom overestimated the current rate) were told the current rate, 85% of them thought it was too low and only 1% thought it was too high.

Finally, public support for minimum wage increases is substantial even in groups that might not be expected to be enthusiastic. While it may not be surprising to find high levels of support among Democrats and poor people, strong majorities of Republicans and affluent people have also generally favored minimum wage increases. Martin Gilens tabulated public support for raising the minimum wage in 13 opinion surveys from the 1990s. His tabulations showed support averaging 88% among Democrats and 86% among people at the 10th percentile of the income distribution. However, 64% of Republicans and 70% of people at the 90th percentile of the income distribution also said that they favored minimum wage increases.[22]

Large-scale surveys mounted by the Cooperative Congressional Election Study (CCES) provide a more recent—and more detailed—picture of the impact of income and partisanship on support for minimum wage increases. During the 2006 and 2008 election campaigns, CCES asked almost 69,000 people whether they favored or opposed increasing the minimum wage.[23] The pattern of public support for an increase is summarized in figure 7.3, which shows how respondents' opinions varied by partisanship and family income level. An overwhelming majority—about 95%—of Democrats at every income level supported raising the minimum wage. Among independents, support ranged from almost 90% among those near the bottom of the income distribution to about 70% among the most affluent. Even most Republicans favored raising the minimum wage, with support ranging from about 75% among those with the lowest incomes down to 45% among those earning more than $150,000 per year. Thus, every group *except* wealthy Republicans favored a minimum wage increase.

[22] I am indebted to Gilens for sharing these unpublished tabulations. The figures for survey respondents at the 10th and 90th percentiles of the income distribution are his imputations based on quadratic regressions of support for minimum wage increases on categorical income data in each opinion survey.

[23] The combined sample included 36,261 respondents interviewed in the fall of 2006 and 32,717 interviewed in the fall of 2008. Respondents in 2006 were asked about "a proposal to increase the federal minimum wage from $5.15 to $6.25 within the next year and a half." In 2008 the specified increase was from $5.15 to $7.25 (as in the legislation passed in 2007). The overall distributions of opinion were similar in both years, favoring a minimum wage increase by margins of 74–21% in 2006 and 76–17% in 2008. Further information about the CCES design and data are available at the project website (http://projects.iq.harvard.edu/cces/home).

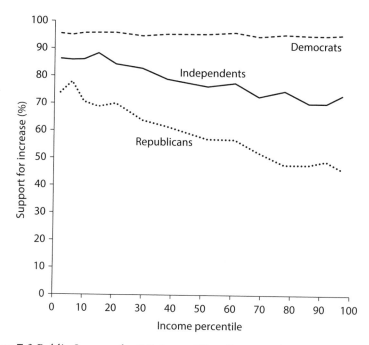

FIGURE 7.3 Public Support for Minimum Wage Increases by Party and Income Level, 2006–2008

THE POLITICS OF CONGRESSIONAL INACTION

The breadth and consistency of public support for raising the minimum wage make it all the more surprising that the real value of the minimum wage has declined so substantially since the 1960s. With even most Republicans favoring minimum wage increases, and with mounting evidence from economists of negligible effects on employment and positive effects on incomes, how and why have elected officials in Washington allowed the minimum wage to erode?

One promising solution to this political puzzle is that setting the minimum wage rate in nominal dollars produces a strong policy bias: without periodic action to increase the minimum wage, inflation produces a steady decline in its real value. Nolan McCarty, Keith Poole, and Howard Rosenthal have stressed the particular significance of this fact in the American legislative context, where institutional checks and balances often make it impossible for a simple majority to produce policy change. "The veto powers of minorities," they wrote, are particularly important when status quo policies are not indexed for inflation. Federal minimum wages are fixed in nominal dollars. A conservative minority has been able to block substantial increases in the minimum, even when the Democrats had unified control of Congress under Jimmy Carter and in the early Clinton administration. Therefore, the real minimum wage has fallen.[24]

This explanation seems compelling as far as it goes. However, it begs the question of *why* minimum wage rates have been set in nominal dollars. After all, many other federal benefits and income thresholds are automatically adjusted to take account of inflation. So are state minimum wages in a dozen states.[25] Meanwhile, Congress has repeatedly considered proposals to index the federal minimum wage rate, but rejected them all.[26]

In discussing the pros and cons of indexing, Card and Krueger pointed out that "a debate over the minimum wage gives politicians a clear opportunity to take a stand on a simple and well-understood issue, and to signal their positions to various constituency groups. Indexation of the minimum wage would eliminate these potentially valuable opportunities."[27] However, the political value of opportunities for position-taking hardly seems sufficient to explain why the minimum wage continues to be set in nominal dollars. Given the breadth and consistency of popular support for raising the minimum wage, position-taking elected officials might be expected to take frequent advantage of opportunities to go on the record in favor of increasing the minimum wage. But that is not what we observe; if it was, the real value of the minimum wage would not have eroded so drastically over the past 50 years. The fact that most elected officials seem remarkably uninterested in championing minimum wage increases brings us back to our basic puzzle: why has overwhelming public support for raising the minimum wage made so little headway against the forces of gridlock in Washington?

Both the significance and the limits of gridlock are illustrated by the sole minimum wage increase of the Reagan-Bush era. In 1989, Democratic congressional leaders engineered passage of a bill that would have increased the minimum wage from $3.35 to $4.55 over a three-year period. President Bush vetoed the bill immediately but used his veto message to reiterate his

---

[24] McCarty, Poole, and Rosenthal (2006, 13–14); see also chap. 6 and Rosenthal (2004). Their analysis builds on Keith Krehbiel's (1998) influential model of "gridlock" in legislative politics.

[25] Arizona, Colorado, Florida, Minnesota, Missouri, Montana, Nevada, Ohio, Oregon, South Dakota, Vermont, and Washington all have existing or scheduled indexing schemes for their state minimum wage rates.

[26] Indexing seems to have come closest to implementation in 1977, when the House defeated an indexing provision by a vote of 223–193.

[27] Card and Krueger (1995, 395).

support for a more modest increase. Given this clear signal—and having already maneuvered the president into exercising a politically unpopular veto—congressional Democrats and labor leaders decided to take what they could get. As the chief lobbyist for the AFL-CIO put it, "It's clear Bush will veto anything over $4.25. . . . At this particular point, we're not interested in playing politics. We want an increase."[28] For their part, "senior members of the Bush administration were growing increasingly concerned that it would be politically difficult and unpopular to again turn back minimum-wage legislation" once the proposed wage increase was scaled back from the bill Bush had vetoed. Bush's chief of staff, John Sununu, and AFL-CIO president Lane Kirkland negotiated what one press account referred to as "a face-saving compromise," which passed by large majorities in both the House (382–37) and Senate (89–8).[29]

In this case, although President Bush used his veto power to moderate the minimum wage increase favored by Congress, his willingness to accept a smaller increase seems to have owed something to a concern that "it would be politically difficult and unpopular" to appear too intransigent on the issue. More often, though, public pressure has been insufficient to overcome legislative gridlock, even in instances where action seemed likely. Another minimum wage hike looked all but certain in the run-up to the 2000 election. One lobbyist called a wage increase "a bullet train coming down the tracks." Four months later, *CQ Weekly* was still reporting that "GOP leaders have resigned themselves to passing a minimum wage increase, an idea many of them dislike but recognize as paramount to some Republicans' political survival." However, when negotiations packaging the minimum wage hike with benefits for small businesses "proved more difficult than expected," the effort collapsed, and with "the minimum wage not emerging as a major campaign issue for Democrats . . . the issue did not come up again in the lame duck session."[30] Public pressure seemed to have evaporated, and what was supposed to be a "perilous issue" for opponents of a minimum wage increase was suddenly easy to ignore.

Additional rounds of congressional inaction in 2005 and 2006 underline the insufficiency of procedural hurdles to account for the continuing erosion

---

[28] "Bush Sends Congress Veto of Minimum-Wage Bill," *CQ Weekly*, June 17, 1989, 1501.

[29] Alyson Pytte, "Ending Minimum Wage Standoff Took Give from Both Sides," *CQ Weekly*, November 4, 1989, 2942; Paul Starobin, "Democrats Rework Strategy on Minimum-Wage Hike," *CQ Weekly*, July 8, 1989, 1692; Alyson Pytte, "Minimum-Wage Bill Cleared, Ending 10-Year Stalemate," *CQ Weekly*, November 11, 1989, 3053.

[30] Gebe Martinez, "House GOP's Pliancy on Minimum Wage Rooted in Election Concerns," *CQ Weekly*, May 8, 1999, 1073; Lori Nitschke, "GOP Hopes Minimum Wage Bill with Tax Benefits Will Lure Votes and Disarm Democrats," *CQ Weekly*, September 25, 1999, 2227; Lori Nitschke, "Minimum Wage Bill Stalls over Issue of Business Offsets," *CQ Weekly*, November 13, 1999, 2711.

of the minimum wage. In 2005, veteran Democratic senator Edward Kennedy proposed a three-stage increase in the minimum wage to $7.25 per hour. As journalist Marilyn Geewax put it,

> Kennedy should have had plenty of support. An estimated 10 million low-income workers would get pay increases if the wage floor were to rise, and polls consistently show four of five Americans want Congress to act. In the midst of the legislative battle, Hurricane Katrina highlighted the problems of low-income families. But the Senator lost.[31]

Kennedy's plan was to offer the minimum wage hike as an amendment to the major bankruptcy reform bill then making its way through Congress. But a newly reelected Republican president and Congress had their own business to do. Intent on preventing the bankruptcy bill from getting "bogged down with amendments" that would make it unacceptable to the House, Senate leaders "set the rules to require a hard-to-reach 60-vote supermajority." In effect, Geewax wrote, Kennedy would be "allowed to engage in a little political theater," but would not have "a realistic chance of slowing the underlying bill." As one lobbyist told her, "The bankruptcy bill is important to a lot of interests."

Despite the overwhelming support for a minimum wage increase expressed in opinion polls, Geewax noted that "relatively few voters ever contacted their elected representatives" about the issue. "In contrast," she wrote, "restaurateurs and small-business owners were organized, energized and informed by top-notch lobbyists who never stopped telling Congress that higher wages would cut profits and limit the ability to create jobs." Given the mismatch in organization and lobbying effort, one public interest advocate told her, "To get something through this Congress that corporate interests don't like would be a Herculean task."[32]

One possible reading of this episode is that it demonstrates the importance of the anti-majoritarian features of the American legislative process: Senate Republican leaders refused to bring a stand-alone bill increasing the minimum wage to a vote, and when Kennedy offered minimum wage amendments to bills that could not be shelved, they used parliamentary tactics to raise the threshold for passage to 60 votes. What that reading overlooks is how modest the underlying support for a minimum wage increase seems to have been, quite aside from the procedural hurdles it faced. In the end, Kennedy's proposal did not attract even a simple majority on the Senate floor.

This outcome is especially significant in light of Card and Krueger's suggestion that elected officials might relish "a clear opportunity to take a stand on a simple and well-understood issue" like the minimum wage. With about

---

[31] Marilyn Geewax, "Minimum Wage Odyssey: A Yearlong View from Capitol Hill and a Small Ohio Town," *Trenton Times*, November 27, 2005.

[32] Ibid.

80% of the public—and almost two-thirds of Republicans—favoring a minimum wage increase, members of Congress might have been expected to leap at the opportunity to signal their support. With procedures in place to ensure that the roll calls would amount to nothing more than "a little political theater," as Geewax put it—and with a Republican majority in the House of Representatives unlikely to act even if the Senate approved a higher minimum wage—senators had a golden opportunity to cast entirely symbolic votes in favor of a minimum wage increase. In each case, however, moderate Republicans and even some Democrats let these putatively valuable position-taking opportunities go unexploited.

During the 2006 campaign, House Democratic leader Nancy Pelosi promised that if her party gained a majority in the election, a minimum wage increase would be on the House floor within 100 hours of the new Congress starting work. However, introducing a bill is not the same thing as passing it. With only a modest majority in the House and an even slimmer majority in the Senate, Democrats recognized that they would need significant Republican cooperation to overcome a Senate filibuster and avoid a presidential veto. In a post-election press conference, President Bush signaled a willingness to compromise, calling a minimum wage increase "an area where I believe we can make some—find common ground." As it turned out, however, that common ground took several months to find, and it was littered with billions of dollars in sweeteners in the form of tax breaks for small businesses.[33]

In the first week of the new Democratic Congress, the House passed a "clean" bill, H.R. 2, raising the minimum wage to $7.25 per hour over a two-year period; 82 Republicans joined all 233 Democrats in supporting passage. Two weeks later, the bill fell six votes short of the 60 needed to forestall a Republican filibuster in the Senate. Democrats responded by adding $8.3 billion in tax cuts for small businesses, and the amended bill cleared the Senate by a 94–3 margin. However, small-business groups led by the National Federation of Independent Business insisted on still more generous tax breaks, while some Republicans continued to oppose any increase in the

---

[33] David Espo, "Pelosi Says She Would Drain GOP 'Swamp,'" *Washington Post*, October 6, 2006 (http://www.washingtonpost.com/wp-dyn/content/article/2006/10/06/AR2006100600056.html); President George W. Bush, press conference, November 8, 2006 (http://www.nytimes.com/2006/11/08/washington/08bush-transcript.html?pagewanted=print&_r=0). Even after the Democrats' midterm victory, many conservatives hoped to extract major policy concessions in exchange for acquiescing in a minimum wage hike. For example, prominent conservative commentator William Safire used his old spot on the *New York Times* opinion page to float the possibility of reviving the minimum-wage-for-estate-tax deal that congressional Democrats had already rejected before the election. Safire suggested that "the window of bipartisan compromise can . . . fit a minimum wage increase tied to inheritance tax reduction," but warned that "the window won't be open long" once liberal congressional committee chairmen got bogged down in partisan "posturing." William Safire, "After the Thumpin'," *New York Times*, November 9, 2006.

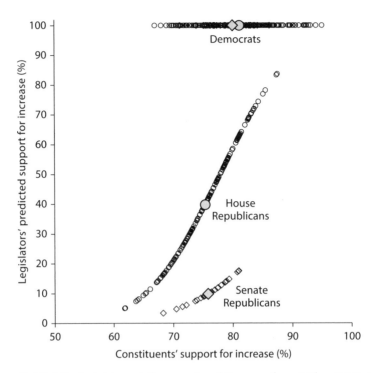

FIGURE 7.4 Public Opinion and Congressional Support for a "Clean" Minimum Wage Increase, 2007

minimum wage. Four months of wrangling were required to produce a compromise, which emerged as part of a larger deal on spending for the war in Iraq, H.R. 2206. The package was approved by substantial margins in both the House (348–73) and Senate (80–14) and signed into law by President Bush. It coupled a three-step increase in the minimum wage—from $5.15 to $5.85 in July 2007, to $6.55 in July 2008, and to $7.25 in July 2009—with almost $5 billion in tax breaks. While Democrats declared the compromise a long-delayed victory for working people, House Minority Leader John Boehner called it "a sneaky way to do business."[34]

In one sense, this policy outcome was clearly responsive to the substantial public sentiment in favor of raising the minimum wage. Moreover, the large majorities in both chambers favoring final passage may suggest that Congress mirrored the public's enthusiasm. However, that interpretation overlooks the fact that most Republicans in both chambers of Congress first

[34] Edmund L. Andrews, "Familiar Problem Stalls Minimum Wage Bill," *New York Times*, February 17, 2007; Stephen Labaton, "Congress Passes Increase in the Minimum Wage," *New York Times*, May 25, 2007.

acted to block an increase despite the fact that *more than 60% of the public in every state and congressional district in the country* probably favored a higher minimum wage.

The 2006 and 2008 CCES surveys, with their very large sample sizes (almost 160 people per congressional district on average), make it possible to examine the relationship between individual representatives' roll call votes on the 2007 minimum wage increase and public opinion in their districts.[35] Figure 7.4, which summarizes that relationship, clearly shows both the sensitivity of elected officials to public opinion and the limits of that sensitivity. The figure depicts a very strong relationship between the roll call votes of House Republicans on the original "clean" minimum wage bill (H.R. 2) and their constituents' support for a minimum wage increase. Roughly 75% of those from the most supportive districts voted in favor, but typical House Republicans, whose constituents favored an increase by a three-to-one margin, were only about 40% likely to go along.

The relationship between constituency opinion and House Republicans' support for H.R. 2 was probably bolstered by the realization that the vote was largely symbolic, since the Senate was highly unlikely to adopt the "clean" bill. Indeed, only five of the 48 Republican senators voted to bring the bill to the Senate floor—despite the fact that their constituents favored a minimum wage increase by margins ranging from two-to-one to four-to-one.[36] Months of further wrangling and billions of dollars in business tax breaks—about $1,000 for every minimum wage recipient—were necessary to translate overwhelming public support for a minimum wage increase into law.

A few days after the first installment of the 2007 minimum wage hike took effect, Senator Kennedy announced that he would introduce further legislation to raise the minimum wage to $9.50 per hour. Presidential candidate John Edwards proposed a similar increase, along with a "national goal" of maintaining a minimum wage equal to half the average wage thereafter.[37] But with additional increases already scheduled for 2008 and 2009, the political momentum for further action had ebbed. By the time the 2007

[35] A parallel analysis relating senators' votes on a 1989 minimum wage increase to the ideology of their constituents produced similar results (Bartels 2008, 244–245). The predicted probabilities of support for Democratic and Republican senators with identical moderate constituencies were 97% and 21%, respectively. By comparison, even extreme constituency opinion had relatively little impact on senators' votes. For example, the predicted probability of a Democratic senator supporting the minimum wage increase was 90% even if he represented the most conservative state in the country (Arkansas), whereas the predicted probability of a Republican senator supporting the minimum wage increase was less than 40% even if he represented the most liberal state (Massachusetts).

[36] Senate vote 23, January 24, 2007. A week later, a further-amended version of the bill cleared the Senate by a vote of 94–3.

[37] John M. Broder, "States Take Lead in Push to Raise Minimum Wages," *New York Times*, January 2, 2006; "Edwards Calls for Minimum Wage Increase as Part of Plan to Build One America," July 5, 2007 (http://www.presidency.ucsb.edu/ws/?pid=93568).

increase was fully implemented, the economy was in the midst of the Great Recession and Washington was in the midst of titanic debates over stimulus spending, health care reform, and financial regulation. According to one member of the Obama administration's economic policy-making team, "I think the feeling was that the economy was too fragile in 2009–2010, and the minimum wage [had] just increased in July 2009. There really wasn't much discussion [of the issue] since the focus was on banks, autos, housing and health care."[38]

With the Republican takeover of the House in 2011, any further federal action to raise the minimum wage was stymied. But that did not dent the political appeal of the issue for Democrats. President Obama called for a minimum wage of $9 per hour in his 2013 State of the Union Address. Several weeks later, Senator Tom Harkin (D-IA) and Representative George Miller (D-CA) raised the bidding to $10.10 per hour. The president endorsed that proposal in his 2014 State of the Union Address. Harkin again raised the bidding, introducing a bill raising the minimum wage to $10.10 over a period of two years and indexing it to the consumer price index thereafter, but the bill died a few weeks later when 41 Republicans refused to bring it to the Senate floor.[39] Senate Democratic leader Harry Reid wasted no time in turning the defeat into a midterm campaign issue. "They're fighting for the billionaires," Reid said of Republicans. "We're fighting for people who are struggling to make a living."[40]

Despite that appeal, Democrats suffered further losses in the 2014 election, losing control of the Senate as well as the House. Still, Reid and his colleagues showed little interest in a possible compromise with moderate Republicans on a more modest minimum wage increase. Instead, they ratcheted their proposals still higher. Shortly after the election, Senator Patty Murray (D-WA) and Representative Robert Scott (D-VA) introduced a bill raising the minimum wage to $12 per hour by 2020. Later that year Democratic presidential candidate Bernie Sanders and other members of the Congressional Progressive Caucus proposed $15 per hour by 2020—more than twice the current minimum. As one press account noted, "A bill that would raise the federal minimum wage to $10.10 per hour has languished in the House for years. The odds are not in favor of legislation calling for an even bigger increase, but the $15 wage proposal gives progressive organizations and their allies in Congress a totem around which to rally."[41]

[38] Personal communication, March 2, 2015.

[39] Only one Republican, Bob Corker (R-TN), voted with Senate Democrats to invoke cloture. In the House, a discharge petition to bring a minimum wage bill to the floor was signed by 195 Democrats but no Republicans.

[40] Susan Davis, "Senate Fails to Advance Minimum-Wage Hike," *USA Today*, April 30, 2014.

[41] Ned Resnikoff, "House, Senate Members Introduce $15 Federal Minimum Wage Bill," *Al Jazeera America*, July 22, 2015.

This bidding war, however symbolic, generated unease among many economists, including some who were generally enthusiastic about raising the minimum wage. For example, Krueger warned that a $15-per-hour minimum "could well be counterproductive" and was "a risk not worth taking," whereas the more modest Murray-Scott proposal for a $12-per-hour minimum phased in over five years "would not have a meaningful negative effect" on employment and would "do more good than harm for low-wage workers."[42]

DEMOCRATS, UNIONS, AND THE ERODING MINIMUM WAGE

Partisan politics has loomed large in every recent effort to raise the minimum wage. The consistent pattern has been for Democrats to support significant increases in the minimum wage while Republicans have gone along infrequently and with apparent reluctance. Thus, it might be tempting to attribute the marked rise and fall of the real value of the minimum wage in figure 7.1 to a parallel rise and fall in the political strength of Democrats in Washington.

A simple tabulation of changes in the real value of the minimum wage provides support for that explanation. In the 29 years between 1949 and 2013 in which Democrats controlled the White House, the real value of the minimum wage increased by $5.10—18 cents per year. In the 36 years in which Republican presidents were in office, the real value of the minimum wage *declined* by $1.64— about 4.5 cents per year.[43]

Statistical analyses of year-to-year fluctuations in the real minimum wage over this period provide more systematic evidence of significant partisan differences. Table 7.1 presents the results of analyses relating fluctuation in the real value of the minimum wage to a variety of potentially relevant political and economic factors, including public support for minimum wage increases, partisan control of the White House and Congress, union membership, and the average wage rate in the broader economy.[44] The analyses differ in whether they allow for the possibility of long-term trends in minimum wage rates independent of these factors (in the second and fourth columns) and in whether they allow for delayed effects of these factors (through the persistence of minimum wage rates from the preceding year in the third and fourth columns).

---

[42] Alan B. Krueger, "The Minimum Wage: How Much Is Too Much?" *New York Times*, October 9, 2015.

[43] Limiting the comparison to the long period of decline in the value of the minimum wage after 1968 produces a smaller but qualitatively similar partisan difference: the real value of the minimum wage fell by 3.5 cents per year under Democratic presidents over this period, but by 10.5 cents per year under Republican presidents.

[44] As in chapter 2, these analyses allow for a one-year lag in the effects of partisan control and other factors on the real value of the minimum wage. However, parallel analyses without the lags produce similar results.

TABLE 7.1
Democrats, Unions, and the Minimum Wage, 1949–2013

Ordinary least squares regression parameter estimates (with standard errors in parentheses) for the real value of the federal minimum wage (in 2015 dollars). Explanatory variables lagged one year.

	(1)	(2)	(3)	(4)
Democratic president	.46	.54	.20	.26
	(.17)	(.17)	(.15)	(.16)
Democratic Congress (%)	.062	.048	.039	.036
	(.015)	(.017)	(.014)	(.015)
Public support (%)	.026	—	−.011	—
	(.028)		(.025)	
Union membership (%)	.339	.315	.124	.127
	(.046)	(.071)	(.060)	(.079)
Average hourly wage ($)	.348	.307	.136	.176
	(.039)	(.090)	(.055)	(.088)
Linear trend	—	3.74	—	−.40
		(3.21)		(3.06)
Quadratic trend	—	−3.15	—	−.46
		(1.24)		(1.31)
Prevailing minimum wage ($)	—	—	.490	.454
			(.102)	(.116)
Intercept	−12.31	−9.10	−3.01	−4.00
	(3.01)	(1.61)	(3.23)	(1.94)
Standard error of regression	.62	.60	.53	.54
Adjusted R^2	.77	.78	.83	.83
N	65	65	65	65

Sources: U.S. Department of Labor; Roper Center iPOLL archive, Mayer (2004); Bureau of Economic Analysis.

In each of these analyses, the real value of the minimum wage was 40 to 55 cents higher under Democratic presidents than under Republican presidents, other things being equal.[45] Democratic strength in Congress had a

[45] Because the analyses presented in the third and fourth columns of table 7.1 include the lagged minimum wage rate among the explanatory factors, the long-run effect of each explanatory factor is magnified by the tendency of minimum wage rates to persist over time. The long-run effects implied by the statistical analyses in the third and fourth columns are 1/(1 − .490) = 1.96 and 1/(1 − .454) = 1.83 times as large as the short-run effects. On the algebra of partial adjustment in dynamic models, see, for example, Gujarati (1995, 599–601) or Kennedy (1998, 156).

substantial additional effect on the minimum wage rate. The most elaborate version of the analysis, presented in the fourth column of table 7.1, implies that the real value of the minimum wage declined by about $1.12, owing to the shift in the partisan composition of Congress from the mid-1960s (when Democrats held 68% of the seats) to 2013 (when Democrats held 51% of the seats).[46] This difference accounts for almost one-third of the observed decline in the real value of the minimum wage since the mid-1960s.

The fate of the minimum wage seems to have hinged even more crucially on the fortunes of the Democratic Party's most important ally in this policy domain, organized labor. The statistical analyses reported in table 7.1 indicate that the real value of the minimum wage has been strongly related to the political strength of labor unions, as measured by the percentage of workers who are union members. Thus, the declining unionization of the American workforce from its high point in the mid-1950s (28.3%) to its current low point (10%) seems to have contributed greatly to the decline in the real value of the minimum wage. The implied cumulative decline in the real value of the minimum wage attributable to declining unionization ranges from $4.25 to $6.20 (in 2015 dollars).[47]

In fact, the real value of the minimum wage has not fallen by as much as these estimated effects—and the historical decline—of Democratic partisanship and unionization imply. The most important reason for that fact is that there is also a consistent, albeit partial, tendency for the minimum wage rate to track changes in wages in the broader economy. The statistical estimates presented in table 7.1 suggest that the minimum wage has increased by about 30 cents for every $1 increase in average pay. Since average hourly pay (in 2015 dollars) increased by almost $18 between the late 1940s and 2013, the apparent responsiveness of minimum wage levels to average wage levels significantly bolstered the real value of the minimum wage, contributing to its increase in the 1950s and 1960s and moderating its decline since then. Over the entire postwar era, the cumulative increase in the real value of the minimum wage attributable to rising average wages

---

[46] The corresponding estimates from the other analyses reported in the table range from 82 cents to $1.30. These estimates are in broad agreement with the findings of a more detailed case study of Senate votes on a 1977 minimum wage increase, which found an estimated difference of 22 cents (87 cents in 2015 dollars) in preferred minimum wage levels between Democratic and Republican senators, even after allowing for differences in union strength and other factors (Krehbiel and Rivers 1988). My measure of congressional partisanship is a simple average of the Democratic percentages of seats in the House and Senate in each year.

[47] The analyses presented in the first two columns of table 7.1 produce estimates at the high end of this range. The analysis presented in the fourth column—which allows for both lagged effects of the prevailing minimum wage and time trends independent of unionization and other explanatory factors—produces the lowest estimate. Data on union membership are from Mayer (2004), supplemented with more recent data from Barry T. Hirsch, David A. Macpherson, and Wayne G. Vroman, "Estimates of Union Density by State," *Monthly Labor Review 124*: 7 (July 2001), updated through 2014 (http://unionstats.gsu.edu/MonthlyLaborReviewArticle.htm).

roughly counterbalanced the cumulative decline attributable to declining unionization.[48]

The statistical analyses presented in the first and third columns of table 7.1 allow for possible shifts in the minimum wage rate in response to public support for minimum wage increases (based on the summary of opinion polls displayed in figure 7.2). Perhaps surprisingly, there is no evidence in either case of any direct responsiveness to public opinion.[49]

The statistical analyses presented in the second and fourth columns of table 7.1 allow for the possibility of trends in the real value of the minimum wage independent of partisanship, unionization, and the overall wage level. However, the cumulative impact of these trends seems to be rather small, and incorporating them in the analyses has very little impact on the magnitudes of the estimated effects of the key explanatory factors.[50] Thus, the combination of Democratic strength in the White House and Congress, union membership, and the average hourly wage rate do a good job of accounting for the pronounced rise and fall of the real value of the minimum wage evident in figure 7.1. Average pay in the economy as a whole increased substantially in the 1950s and 1960s while the political strength of labor unions remained fairly stable; the result was a significant net increase in the minimum wage rate. In the late 1970s and 1980s, however, unionization declined significantly while real wage levels were stagnant, producing substantial downward pressure on the minimum wage rate. Those intersecting trends, together with the rising and falling fortunes of the Democratic Party in Washington, account for the major shifts in the real value of the minimum wage over the postwar period.

The same explanatory factors can be reconfigured to provide an even better account of the ups and downs of the minimum wage in the postwar era. The statistical analysis presented in table 7.2 reflects the notion that

[48] The average wage level (in 2015 dollars) increased from $13.49 in 1948 to $31.18 in 2012. The estimated effects of this increase implied by the four distinct models in table 7.1 range from $4.72 to $6.16.

[49] Indeed, even the simple bivariate relationship between public support for a minimum wage increase in any given year and the following year's change in the real minimum wage rate is slightly negative.

[50] The trend variables are constructed to range from zero in 1948 to one in 2013. Combining the linear and quadratic terms, the estimates in the second column of table 7.1 imply an increase of just 1 cent per year in the real value of the minimum wage, net of other factors, while the estimates in the fourth column imply a decrease of about 2 cents per year. The stability of the estimated effects of average wages and union membership is especially impressive in light of the fact that these factors were both strongly trended over this period; it implies that their apparent importance is not simply an artifact of broader political or economic shifts over the 65 years represented in table 7.1. Since my estimates of public support for raising the minimum wage in each year are derived from the polynomial trend shown in figure 7.2, they are too highly correlated with the trend terms in the second and fourth columns of table 7.1 to include them in the same analyses.

TABLE 7.2
A Partisan Adjustment Model of Minimum Wage Changes, 1950–2013

Non-linear least squares regression parameter estimates (with standard errors in parentheses) for the real value of the federal minimum wage (in 2015 dollars). Explanatory variables lagged one year.

Inflation-adjusted change in real minimum wage = (Equilibrium wage rate – Prevailing minimum wage) × (Partisan convergence rate) + (Delayed adjustment) × Lagged (Equilibrium wage rate – Prevailing minimum wage) × (Partisan convergence rate)

	Equilibrium wage rate ($)	Partisan convergence rate	Delayed adjustment
Public support (%)	.041 (.023)	—	—
Union membership (%)	.468 (.035)	—	—
Average hourly wage ($)	.443 (.034)	—	—
Democratic president	—	1.17 (.27)	—
Democratic Congress (%)	—	.0524 (.0228)	—
Intercept	–13.91 (2.40)	–4.39 (1.26)	—
Delayed adjustment	—	—	.474 (.166)
Standard error of regression	.45		
Adjusted R²	.86		
N	64		

Sources: U.S. Department of Labor; Roper Center iPOLL archive, Mayer (2004); Bureau of Economic Analysis.

the implications for minimum wage policy of public support, union membership, and average hourly wages vary with the political context. When Democrats control the White House and Congress, the real value of the minimum wage may respond significantly to these factors. However, when Republicans are able to block policy action, the real value of the minimum wage is unlikely to change significantly (aside from gradual erosion due to inflation), even when conditions are otherwise ripe for a wage increase. The resulting interactive model includes three separate factors: an equilibrium wage rate determined by public support, union membership, and the average hourly wage rate; a rate of convergence toward that equilibrium determined by partisan control of the White House and Congress; and a delayed adjustment factor reflecting the fact that minimum wage increases are often phased in over more than one year.[51]

In this configuration, public support for raising the minimum wage did have a discernible impact on the equilibrium minimum wage rate. However, that impact was very modest: the estimated difference in the equilibrium wage rate with 64% public support (the observed minimum value in figure 7.2) and with 82% public support (the observed maximum value) amounts to only 74 cents. By comparison, the effects of union membership and average hourly wages were massive, albeit largely offsetting. The decline in union membership from 28.3% (its peak in 1954) to 10% (in 2012) decreased the estimated equilibrium minimum wage rate by about $8.55, while the increase in the average wage in the economy as a whole from $13.49 in 1948 to $31.18 in 2012 increased the estimated equilibrium minimum wage rate by about $7.85.

Figure 7.5 shows how the prevailing minimum wage over the entire postwar period has compared with the equilibrium wage rates implied by these estimates. The estimated equilibrium wage rate has ranged from $6.22 in 1949 to $11.23 in 1973. Since 2000, the estimated equilibrium has fluctuated within a much narrower range, from a high of $8.09 in 2010 to a low of $7.53 in 2013. (The decline in recent years reflects the fact that real wages in the economy as a whole have stagnated since the Great Recession while union membership has continued to decline.) The gap between the equilibrium and actual minimum wage rates has averaged 65 cents (about 8% of the equilibrium rate) but remained over $1 for seven straight years before the 2007 increase took effect.

The results presented in the second column of table 7.2 show that political action to reduce the gap between the actual and equilibrium wage rates has hinged significantly on partisan control of the White House and Congress. For example, a Democratic president with 55% of the seats in Congress would be expected to eliminate the gap between the actual and equilibrium wage rates completely over a two-year period, with about two-thirds of that reduction in the first year and one-third in the second year. On the other hand, a Republican president with 55% of the seats in Congress would be expected to reduce the gap by only about 20% over two years. When the prevailing minimum wage rate falls significantly below the equilibrium rate, action to close the gap is, in large part, a partisan political choice. By capturing this interaction between effective demand for minimum wage increases (primarily reflecting union strength and overall wage growth) and the willingness of

---

[51] This model is closely related to the error correction model described by Engle and Granger (1987) and Beck (1992).

FIGURE 7.5 Political Convergence to the "Equilibrium" Minimum Wage Rate, 1948–2013

elected officials to respond to that demand, the interactive model presented in table 7.2 provides a significantly better statistical account of fluctuations in the real value of the minimum wage than the simpler models employing the same explanatory factors presented in table 7.1.

As in the case of estate tax repeal, it would be an exaggeration to suggest that minimum wage politics is *entirely* a matter of elites pursuing their own ideological convictions. Democrats in the White House and Congress are unlikely to produce substantial increases in the minimum wage when the prevailing wage rate is already close to its equilibrium level, as it has been in recent years. On the other hand, even Republican presidents and legislators may take some modest action when the prevailing wage rate falls far below the equilibrium rate, as it did under Presidents Eisenhower, Nixon, and George W. Bush. In either case, however, strong public support for a higher minimum wage is likely to make little difference to the outcome.

LOCAL ACTION

The estimates of latent demand for minimum wage increases presented in figure 7.5 offer little reason to have expected further federal action on the minimum wage in the wake of the 2007–2009 increases, and especially in the wake of the Republican takeovers of the House (in 2011) and Senate (in 2015). However, President Obama and Democrats in Congress have continued to push for minimum wage increases. When the Senate refused to take up his 2014 proposal to raise the minimum wage, the president charged that Republicans had "said no to helping millions work their way out of poverty." But he added "the good news" that "outside of Washington folks aren't waiting," citing recent actions in four states that had produced minimum wage increases for "over a million workers." Obama urged voters to "get fired up" and offered his support "to every business owner, and mayor, and governor, and county official, and legislator, and organization that's working to give America a raise."[52]

The president's comments were clearly intended to exploit the minimum wage issue in the upcoming midterm congressional campaign. But they also reflected the reality that advocates for increasing the minimum wage have increasingly pursued their goal at the state and local levels, where the political and institutional hurdles to policy change have often seemed less daunting than in Washington. When 71% of voters in Florida—a conservative Republican state with one of the highest levels of economic inequality in the nation—approved a constitutional amendment in 2004 raising the state's minimum wage and indexing it for inflation, grassroots campaigns sprang up to push for minimum wage initiatives in several additional states and localities.[53]

Liberal activists found these efforts appealing not only because they drew directly upon the strong public support for the minimum wage documented in figure 7.2, but also because they seemed likely to "pull progressive voters to the polls," providing an electoral boost for Democratic candidates. As Senator Charles Schumer, the coordinator of the Democratic Party's 2006 Senate campaign strategy, put it, the minimum wage issue "appeals to certain groups of people who don't usually turn out to vote."[54] In 2006 measures to raise state minimum wage rates appeared on the ballot in Arizona,

---

[52] "Remarks by the President on Raising the Minimum Wage," April 30, 2014 (http://www.whitehouse.gov).

[53] The Florida amendment established a minimum wage of $6.15 per hour with automatic annual increases to keep pace with inflation. A year after the measure took effect, one journalist noted that the negative economic consequences predicted by opponents of raising the minimum wage "haven't appeared yet"—the state added 248,000 new jobs, while unemployment fell to a 30-year low. Peter Harkness, "States and Localities: War on Wages Goes Local," *CQ Weekly*, February 6, 2006, 320. By 2015, automatic increases had raised Florida's minimum wage to $8.05, 80 cents higher than the federal minimum.

[54] Dennis Cauchon, "States Say $5.15 an Hour Too Little," *USA Today*, May 31, 2005; Edmund L. Andrews, "Democrats Link Fortunes to Rise in Minimum Wage," *New York Times*, July 13, 2006.

Colorado, Missouri, Montana, Nevada, and Ohio; all six passed, with an average vote margin of almost two-to-one.[55]

By 2015, 30 states including 60% of the country's population had state minimum wage rates that exceeded the federal minimum; weighing each state by population, the average effective minimum in the country as a whole was about $8.00—well above the federal minimum of $7.25.[56] Many, but not all, of the states with higher minimums were relatively wealthy and politically liberal. The first column of table 7.3 summarizes the statistical relationship between public opinion and state minimum wage rates as of early 2015.[57] The effective minimum was clearly higher in states with greater public support for minimum wage increases, but the magnitude of the relationship was fairly modest. The results suggest that states with public support below about 75% (roughly, the median opinion in Republican states and districts in figure 7.4) would be unlikely to adopt state minimum wages exceeding the federal minimum. By comparison, the predicted state minimums in the half-dozen states with the greatest public support for minimum wage increases (83% or more) averaged $8.10 (and the actual minimum rates in those states averaged $8.28).

The statistical analysis reported in the second column of table 7.3 parallels the analysis of federal minimum wage rates in table 7.1. The key explanatory factors are partisan control of state government, union membership, and states' average wage rates.[58] These factors prove to be much more powerful than public opinion in accounting for state minimum wage rates,

[55] John Atlas and Peter Dreier, "Waging Victory," *American Prospect Online*, November 10, 2006. Whether the presence of these measures on the ballot actually worked to "pull progressive voters to the polls" is unclear. However, minimum wage advocates claimed credit for providing Democrats with a crucial edge in Missouri, where proponents spent over $2 million on mobilizing turnout in urban areas and Democratic challenger Claire McCaskill defeated Republican incumbent Jim Talent by a margin of fewer than 50,000 votes, and in Montana, where the minimum wage increase passed by more than 175,000 votes, while Democratic challenger Jon Tester unseated Republican incumbent Conrad Burns by fewer than 3,000 votes.

[56] U.S. Department of Labor, "Minimum Wage Laws in the States—January 1, 2015" (http://www.dol.gov/whd/minwage/america.htm).

[57] The parameter estimates reported in tables 7.3 and 7.4 are from tobit models, which allow for the fact that the federal minimum (currently $7.25) sets a floor on the effective minimum wage rate in each state. The public opinion data are from the 2006 and 2008 CCES surveys (the same data employed in figure 7.4). While public opinion may have changed by 2015, state minimum wage policies presumably reflect public opinion at the time they were adopted, making the earlier data roughly suitable.

[58] National Conference of State Legislatures, "State Partisan Composition" (http://www.ncsl .org/research/about-state-legislatures/partisan-composition.aspx), updated March 16, 2016). I counted each state as Democratic (+1), Republican (−1), or divided (0) in 2010, 2012, and 2014 and averaged the three figures. Hirsch et al., "Estimates of Union Density by State"; Bureau of Labor Statistics, "May 2013 State Occupational Employment and Wage Estimates" (http://www .bls.gov/oes/current/oessrcst.htm).

TABLE 7.3

Democrats, Unions, and State Minimum Wage Rates, 2015

Tobit regression parameter estimates (with standard errors in parentheses) for effective minimum wage rates (in dollars).

	(1)	(2)	(3)
Public support for minimum wage increase, 2006–2008 (%)	.089 (.037)	—	.003 (.030)
Democratic partisan control, 2010–2014 (–1 to +1)	—	.36 (.19)	.35 (.20)
Union membership (%)	—	.067 (.024)	.067 (.024)
Average hourly wage ($)	—	.090 (.037)	.089 (.038)
Intercept	.62 (2.90)	5.03 (.80)	4.83 (2.31)
Standard error of regression	1.02	.69	.69
Pseudo-R²	.05	.29	.29
N	51	51	51

Sources: U.S. Department of Labor; Roper Center iPOLL archive; Mayer (2004); Bureau of Economic Analysis.

improving the statistical fit of the model by about one-third—and when public support is added back into the analysis, in the third column of the table, it has no discernible independent impact.

In light of the prominence of initiative measures in recent efforts to raise state minimum wage rates, the apparent non-effect of public opinion in table 7.3 seems puzzling. Thus, the analyses reported in table 7.4 consider initiative procedures as an additional explanatory factor in accounting for state minimum wage rates. The results presented in the first column indicate that the prevailing minimum wage was about 90 cents per hour higher in states with initiative procedures than in otherwise similar states without initiatives. The separate estimates presented in the second and third columns suggest why. In states without initiative procedures (in the second column), partisan control of state government was the most important factor explaining state-to-state variation in minimum wage rates; the average minimum wage was $2 per hour higher in states run by Democrats than in those run by Republicans. By comparison, partisan control was largely irrelevant in states with initiative procedures (in the third column). In effect, the recourse provided by an initiative procedure sapped the power of Republican elected officials to block minimum wage increases.

TABLE 7.4

The Effect of Initiative Procedures on State Minimum Wage Rates, 2015

Tobit regression parameter estimates (with standard errors in parentheses) for effective minimum wage rates (in dollars).

	All states	Non-initiative states	Initiative states
Initiative procedure	.92 (.22)	No	Yes
Public support for minimum wage increase, 2006–2008 (%)	.050 (.027)	.052 (.061)	.036 (.029)
Democratic partisan control, 2010–2014 (−1 to +1)	.36 (.17)	.98 (.43)	.13 (.19)
Union membership (%)	.062 (.021)	.054 (.032)	.086 (.031)
Average hourly wage ($)	.087 (.032)	.077 (.047)	.055 (.060)
Intercept	.78 (2.13)	.65 (4.32)	3.21 (2.52)
Standard error of regression	.57	.63	.49
Pseudo-R²	.43	.51	.41
N	51	27	24

Sources: U.S. Department of Labor; Roper Center iPOLL archive; Mayer (2004); Bureau of Economic Analysis.

Given a typical configuration of other characteristics, these results imply almost identical wage rates in non-initiative and initiative states under Democratic control ($8.44 versus $8.37), but a substantially lower rate in non-initiative states under Republican control ($6.44—well below the federal baseline of $7.25—versus $8.01). In fact, seven of the 13 Republican states with initiative procedures had state rates ranging from $8.00 to $8.75 per hour, but *none* of the ten Republican states without initiative procedures had minimum wage rates higher than the federal minimum of $7.25. However, states that were mostly controlled by Democrats were very likely to have higher state minimums regardless of whether they had initiative procedures (seven of seven) or not (11 of 13).

The separate results for non-initiative and initiative states also shed interesting light on the role of public opinion and interest groups under "direct democracy." Public support for minimum wage increases was apparently no more consequential in states with initiative procedures than in those without. However, the estimated impact of union membership—and by implication, organized political action—was more than 50% greater in states with initiative procedures than in those where the only path to policy change was through the state legislature.

One advantage of state action is that it can take account of geographical variation in wages and prices rather than imposing the same wage rate across the entire country. Writing in opposition to proposals for a federal $15-per-hour minimum wage, economist Alan Krueger noted that "some high-wage cities and states could probably absorb" that rate "with little or no job loss," but that "it is far from clear that the same could be said for every state, city and town in the United States."[59] Another prominent labor economist, Arindrajit Dube, proposed raising each state's minimum wage to half of the state median wage—a fraction roughly commensurate with the OECD average and with federal policy in the 1960s. Overall, the result would be an average increase of about $2 per hour over the current prevailing rate in each state. However, the resulting state minimums would vary substantially, from about $8.00 (2015 dollars) in Mississippi and Arkansas to $12.50 in Massachusetts.[60] The statistical relationships between actual state minimums and average wage rates in tables 7.3 and 7.4 are a good deal weaker than Dube's proposal would produce, with a $10 difference in average hourly wages (the difference between Mississippi and Massachusetts) producing a difference of only 90 cents in expected minimum wage rates.

In recent years, minimum wage activism has spread from states to cities. Since 2014, Seattle, San Francisco, Los Angeles, Kansas City, and Chicago have all passed laws phasing in significantly higher minimum wage rates than those prevailing in their states. Meanwhile, rallies protesting low wages in the fast-food industry spread from 200 striking workers in New York City in November 2012 to 150 cities in May 2014 and more than 200 cities in April 2015. Labor unions poured tens of millions of dollars into a "Fight for $15" campaign, calculating that they could no longer achieve their aims "without the support of a broader movement of workers," as the president of the SEIU put it.[61]

THE EARNED INCOME TAX CREDIT

While the real value of the minimum wage has eroded substantially over the past 50 years, the federal government has embraced a very different

---

[59] Krueger, "The Minimum Wage: How Much Is Too Much?"

[60] Dube (2014).

[61] Jennifer Medina and Noam Scheiber, "Los Angeles Lifts Its Minimum Wage to $15 per Hour," *New York Times*, May 20, 2015; Noam Scheiber, "In Test for Unions and Politicians, a Nationwide Protest on Pay," *New York Times*, April 16, 2015.

policy to bolster the incomes of low-wage workers: the Earned Income Tax Credit. The EITC was implemented on a modest scale in 1975 and significantly expanded in 1986, 1990, 1993, 2001, and 2009. By 2015, according to an estimate by the Tax Policy Center, the EITC was generating $60 billion in reduced taxes and tax refunds for more than 26 million households.[62] From the perspective of the working poor, the growth of the EITC has by no means fully compensated for the erosion of the minimum wage; whereas the real value of the minimum wage has declined by almost $3.50 per hour since the late 1960s, the average effective wage subsidy provided by the EITC amounts to about $1.15 per hour.[63] Nevertheless, the EITC has rather unobtrusively evolved into "one of the most important federal antipoverty programs," with tax credits and refunds amounting to more than twice the federal contribution to state and local welfare programs and second only to food stamps among federal programs targeted at low-income families.[64]

From the perspective of policy-makers, the EITC has been an admirably flexible program. In the 1970s it provided an appealing alternative to the Nixon administration's proposed "negative income tax"; moreover, "by putting money in the hands of low-income consumers, it complemented President Ford's pledge to stimulate the flagging economy." In the 1980s it "provided the glue that held together" President Reagan's ambitious tax reform package, counterbalancing tax cuts for high-income taxpayers and allowing policy-makers to honor an agreement between the president and congressional leaders to "achieve distributional and revenue neutrality" in the overall package. In the 1990s another significant expansion "eased the transition" from traditional welfare to the more restrictive Temporary Assistance for Needy Families program while fulfilling President Clinton's campaign promise to "make work pay."[65]

The EITC has a variety of significant political advantages. Probably most importantly, tying the income subsidy to wages encourages work and sidesteps the association of traditional welfare programs with the "undeserving poor." This aspect of the program is reinforced by the designation of EITC as a "tax credit," despite the fact that most recipients have little or no income tax liability to offset.[66] Moreover, whereas the minimum wage raises

---

[62] Tax Policy Center, *Briefing Book* (http://www.taxpolicycenter.org/briefing-book/key -elements/family/eitc.cfm).

[63] The subsidy varies substantially with total income and family status—for a full-time minimum wage worker, from about $3.00 per hour (with three or more children) down to $1.65 per hour (with one child) to just 25 cents per hour (with no children).

[64] Slemrod and Bakija (2004, 43); Tax Policy Center, *Briefing Book*.

[65] Ventry (2000, 995, 1015, 1008).

[66] According to Joel Slemrod and Jon Bakija (2004, 43), "In 2000, the total dollar value of the EITC was $32 billion, with $28 billion of that representing the refundable portion" not offset by recipients' tax liability.

the cost of doing business for employers of low-wage workers, the EITC lowers that cost by stimulating low-wage labor supply; by one estimate, every dollar of EITC lowers the pre-tax wages of subsidized workers by 27 cents, providing an annual boon to employers of $15–20 billion.[67]

For all these reasons, conservative economists have generally been much more enthusiastic about the EITC than about the minimum wage. For example, Gregory Mankiw argued that the declining value of the minimum wage was "beside the point" in light of the expansion of EITC, and that "a good case" could be made for repealing the former and relying entirely on the latter. "If, as a nation, we decide we want to do more to supplement the incomes of low-wage workers, that's fine," Mankiw wrote. "But let's do it openly, without artifice, and with broad participation." "Broad participation," for Mankiw, meant that taxpayers rather than employers should bear the cost of subsidizing low-wage work. Business, he wrote, "is already doing more than its share" by providing jobs to unskilled workers. "Asking it to do even more, while letting everyone else off the hook, seems particularly churlish." He didn't mention, or seem to mind, that the EITC actually subsidizes low-wage employers along with their employees.[68]

Despite these significant advantages, the EITC also has two significant disadvantages by comparison with the minimum wage. One is its intricacy; the EITC is "so complex that the IRS publishes more than 50 pages of instructions" for would-be beneficiaries, generating significant implementation problems. On one hand, between 15% and 25% of those who are eligible (and a much higher proportion of those without children) fail to claim the credit. On the other hand, many of the people who receive EITC benefits turn out to be ineligible. Filing procedures were tightened in the wake of a controversial IRS study suggesting that about 30% of EITC benefits claimed in 1999 should not have been paid, and Congress appropriated more than $1 billion for audits of low-income taxpayers. Nonetheless, a subsequent study found that about $17 billion was paid out in error in 2010. In response, House Ways and Means Committee chairman Paul Ryan proposed that any expansion of benefits for childless adults and non-custodial parents should be funded by reducing these EITC overpayments.[69]

[67] Rothstein (2010).

[68] N. Gregory Mankiw, "Help the Working Poor, but Share the Burden," *New York Times*, January 5, 2014.

[69] Dorothy A. Brown, "A Tax Credit or a Handout?" *New York Times*, April 18, 2006; Internal Revenue Service, "Compliance Estimates for Earned Income Tax Credit Claimed on 1999 Returns," February 28, 2002 (https://www.irs.gov/pub/irs-utl/1999_compliance_study _022802.pdf); General Accounting Office, "Earned Income Tax Credit Eligibility and Participation," GAO-02-290R, 2001 (http://www.gao.gov/assets/100/91089.pdf); Scholz (1994); Tax Policy Center, *Briefing Book*; Chuck Marr, "A Double Standard on Tax Compliance," Center on Budget and Policy Priorities, February 13, 2015 (http://www.cbpp.org/blog/a

The second disadvantage of the EITC is that, despite its relative popularity among political elites, it is a good deal less salient—and a good deal less popular—than the minimum wage among ordinary citizens. In the 2003 survey sponsored by National Public Radio, the Kaiser Family Foundation, and Harvard University's Kennedy School of Government, almost 40% of respondents admitted that they had never heard of the Earned Income Tax Credit or that they did not know what it was.[70] In 1995, when Republicans floated the possibility of reducing the EITC, only a bare majority of survey respondents opposed doing so, while 25% said that they favored eliminating it.[71] These survey results leave little doubt that, if policy-makers were guided solely by manifest public enthusiasm for specific government programs, they would not have embraced the EITC in preference to a robust minimum wage.

Near the end of their 400-page study of the effects of minimum wage laws, economists Card and Krueger argued that "the intensity of the political debate surrounding the minimum wage—on both sides of the issue—is out of proportion to its real importance to the economy." They may be right. By 2014, given the increasing prevalence of higher state minimum wage rates, only about 4% of hourly-paid workers—and about 2% of those who worked full-time—were paid at or below the federal minimum rate.[72]

Nevertheless, the symbolic importance of this "modest transfer program," as Card and Krueger called it, is considerable. The substantial erosion of the minimum wage over the past 50 years stands as a dramatic example of the American political system's unresponsiveness to public sentiment. Faced with consistent, overwhelming public support for minimum wage increases—and in a context of accelerating economic inequality—politicians in Washington

---

-double-standard-on-tax-compliance). The "egregious double standard" referred to by Marr is that Congress's concerns about tax compliance seem to be highly selective, "depending on whether low-income working families or small businesses are at issue." The IRS estimated that "a stunning 56 *percent* of business income that individual returns should have reported went unreported in 2006."

[70] "Earned Income Tax Credit . . . Have you heard the term and know what it means, have you heard the term but don't know what it means, or have you not heard the term?" Have heard the term and know what it means, 61%; have heard the term but don't know what it means, 28%; have not heard the term, 11%.

[71] Gallup/CNN/USA Today poll, November 1995: "Based on what you have read or heard, please tell me if you favor or oppose each of the following Republican proposals. . . . Reducing the Earned Income Tax Credit for the working poor"—favor, 39%; oppose, 53%; mixed (volunteered), 2%; don't know/refused, 6%. News Interest Index poll, September 1995: "Some leaders in Washington are talking about getting rid of the Earned Income Tax Credit, which reduces or cancels out income taxes for poor people who work, but make very little money. Would you favor or oppose ending this tax credit?" Favor, 25%; oppose, 68%; don't know, 6%.

[72] Card and Krueger (1995, 395); Bureau of Labor Statistics, "Labor Force Statistics from the Current Population Survey" (http://www.bls.gov/cps/cpsaat44.htm, last modified February 10, 2016).

have mostly procrastinated, obfuscated, impeded, and grandstanded. Republicans in the White House and Congress have generally resisted periodic minimum wage increases despite strong support for those increases among their own rank-and-file voters. Democrats, for their part, have frequently passed up apparent opportunities to compromise on minimum wage increases, seeming to prefer a favorable campaign issue to modest progress.

Still, one may wonder how much light policy-making in this domain sheds on the broader workings of the American political system. Is the erosion of the minimum wage a rare exception to a general pattern of democratic responsiveness, perhaps reflecting the peculiar political dynamics of a policy arena in which the balance of economic power between employers and low-wage workers is so strongly tilted in favor of employers? Or is unresponsiveness endemic in a policy-making process where intense interests have numerous avenues of influence, and where the political ramifications of unequal economic power are pervasive? Those are the questions I explore in chapter 8.

CHAPTER 8

Economic Inequality and
Political Representation

I assume that a key characteristic of a democracy is the
continued responsiveness of the government to the preferences of its citizens, considered as political equals.
—*Robert Dahl, 1971*[1]

THE NOTION THAT governments should be responsive to the preferences of
their citizens is a hallmark of democratic theory. In the past half-century, that
notion has spawned a substantial scholarly literature on political representation describing and assessing the relationship between citizens' preferences
and the policy choices of their political leaders. Armed with more or less
detailed data from opinion surveys measuring citizens' policy preferences,
political scientists have related variation in those preferences across geographical units (such as congressional districts), across issues, or over time to
variation in observed policy choices by elected officials or policy outcomes.[2]

The results of analyses of this sort have been interpreted as providing
"evidence for strong effects of public opinion on government policies" and
even "a sanguine picture of democracy at work."[3] However, that optimistic
interpretation seems questionable in at least two respects. For one thing,
causal attributions of "strong effects" of public opinion on public policies generally overlook many other factors correlated with public opinion
that seem likely to influence policy outcomes. Thus, observed statistical relationships between public opinion and policies may be largely spurious.
As Lawrence Jacobs and Benjamin Page observed in the context of foreign

---

[1] Dahl (1971, 1).

[2] Prominent examples of work in this tradition employing a variety of different research
designs and data include Miller and Stokes (1963), Page and Shapiro (1983), Erikson, Wright,
and McIver (1993), and Stimson, MacKuen, and Erikson (1995). On theories of political representation and their implications for statistical analyses, see Achen (1978).

[3] Shapiro (2011, 1003, 999). Shapiro (2011, 1002–1004) went on to discuss unequal responsiveness as an aspect of "limited democracy," citing a "need for more research on this."

policy-making, public opinion may *seem* to be influential only because it happens to be correlated with the opinion of influential elites, organized interest groups, or the policy-makers themselves.[4]

Second, and relatedly, the fact that policy-makers are responsive to aggregate public opinion (if indeed they are) does not necessarily imply that they are responsive to the preferences of citizens "considered as political equals," as Robert Dahl stipulated. The (usually implicit) assumption underlying these analyses is that elected officials are equally responsive to the views of all their constituents, so that *average* opinion for each district, issue, or time period provides an adequate reflection of mass preferences and an adequate benchmark for assessing responsiveness. However, if policy-makers respond to the opinions of only some constituents—the affluent, well educated, and politically connected—rather than to the public as a whole, an apparently "sanguine picture" of responsiveness may mask a highly undemocratic process in which most citizens' opinions have little or no bearing on policy outcomes.

There are a variety of good reasons to suspect that policy-makers in real political systems do not consider citizens as political equals. For example, wealthier and better-educated citizens are more likely than the poor and less educated to have clearly formulated preferences, more likely to turn out to vote, and significantly more likely to have direct contact with public officials and to contribute money and energy to political campaigns. In light of these realities, it would hardly be surprising to find that actual political systems fall short of the ideal of egalitarian responsiveness. But how far short? And what, if anything, could be done to equalize political influence?

Perhaps surprisingly, political scientists until recently devoted little systematic attention to these questions. However, in the past fifteen years there has been a good deal of progress on this front. Scholars employing a variety of different data and research designs have attempted to assess the extent to which citizens' preferences differentially influence the choices of their elected representatives and the content of public policy at the national and state levels.[5] The implications of that work are far from reassuring. Whether they have focused on individual members of Congress, political parties, state policy, or national policy, political scientists have repeatedly discovered substantial disparities in the apparent political influence of affluent, middle-class, and poor Americans. For example, Elizabeth Rigby and Gerald Wright's analysis showed that "the least fortunate in society have no independent voice in the formulation of party platforms." Patrick Flavin found that "citizens with low incomes receive little or no substantive political representation (compared with more affluent citizens) in the policy

---

[4] Jacobs and Page (2005).

[5] For example, Bartels (2002b; 2008, chap. 9); Gilens (2005; 2012); Bhatti and Erikson (2011); Rigby and Wright (2011; 2013); Flavin (2012, 29); Gilens and Page (2014).

decisions made by their state governments." And Martin Gilens was led to conclude that "the American government does respond to the public's preferences, but that responsiveness is strongly tilted toward the most affluent citizens. Indeed, under most circumstances, the preferences of the vast majority of Americans appear to have essentially no impact on which policies the government does or doesn't adopt."[6]

In this chapter I summarize and extend existing scholarship on disparities in political responsiveness. My primary focus is on national policy-making, including both the roll call votes cast by individual members of Congress and the overall responsiveness of the American political system to the preferences of affluent, middle-class, and poor citizens. In both cases, the available evidence leaves little room to doubt that economic inequality results in immense political inequality. I also provide much more tentative evidence regarding the mechanisms by which economic inequality gets translated into political inequality, and even more tentative evidence regarding the distinctive political preferences of truly wealthy Americans (in contrast to the merely affluent) and the potential implications of those preferences for the course of public policy in the New Gilded Age.

CONGRESSIONAL REPRESENTATION

Systematic empirical research on political representation began with the classic work of Warren Miller and Donald Stokes on "Constituency Influence in Congress." Using survey data from random samples of constituents in a random sample of 116 congressional districts, Miller and Stokes related the attitudes and behavior of incumbent members of Congress to their constituents' views about social welfare, foreign policy, and civil rights. They found strong correlations between constituents' attitudes and their representatives' policy choices in the domain of civil rights, but much weaker relationships for social welfare and foreign policy. A great deal of subsequent work along similar lines has continued to demonstrate that the behavior of elected officials is related—indeed, sometimes strongly related—to the preferences of their constituents. However, those studies have almost invariably treated constituents in an undifferentiated way, using simple averages of opinions in a given district, on a given issue, or at a given time to account for representatives' policy choices. Thus, they shed little or no light on the fundamental issue of political equality.[7]

---

[6] Rigby and Wright (2013, 563); Flavin (2012, 29); Gilens (2012, 1).

[7] Miller and Stokes (1963). Miller and Stokes's American Representation Study is a treasure trove of data on members of Congress and congressional candidates, including information on their backgrounds and careers, activities in Congress, issue preferences, perceptions of district

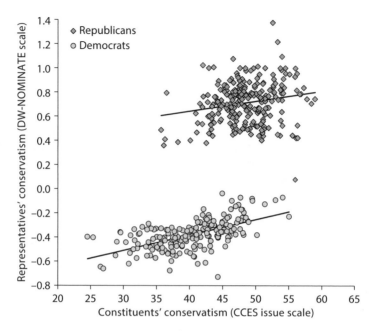

FIGURE 8.1 Constituency Opinion and Representatives' Roll Call Votes, 2011–2013

Figure 8.1 provides an example of this sort of analysis. The figure relates the voting behavior of each member of the House of Representatives in the 112th Congress (2011–2013) to the average policy preference of his or her constituents. My measure of each member's voting behavior is Keith Poole and Howard Rosenthal's DW-NOMINATE score, which provides a convenient summary of all the roll call votes that member cast in the 112th Congress.[8]

opinion, and views about campaigns and elections. Miller and Stokes's projected book-length analysis of these data was never completed, and as a result the data have never been fully utilized. Subsequent studies in the same vein include Achen (1978), Bartels (1991), and Bafumi and Herron (2010), among many others. For additional discussion and historical analysis of variation in patterns of representation in the U.S. Congress from 1875 to 2010, see Bartels, Clinton, and Geer (2016). Douglas Rivers's (n.d.) unpublished analysis of congressional responsiveness to the views of incumbent-party identifiers, opposition-party identifiers, and political independents was a pioneering examination of differential responsiveness, subsequently replicated on a much larger scale by Joshua Clinton (2006).

[8] Poole and Rosenthal summarize the voting behavior of representatives in each chamber using two orthogonal dimensions analogous to the dimensions produced by an exploratory factor analysis. I focus here on their first dimension, which does the lion's share of the work in accounting for members' roll call votes in the contemporary Congress. For extensive discussion and applications of the scaling algorithm, see Poole and Rosenthal (2007). Data and documentation are available from the Voteview website (http://voteview.com/).

The DW-NOMINATE scores are scaled to range, roughly, from –1 for the most liberal member of the House to +1 for the most conservative member.[9]

To measure the policy preferences of each House member's constituents, I employ data from opinion surveys conducted in 2010 and 2012 in all 435 congressional districts as part of the Cooperative Congressional Election Study.[10] Combining data from both surveys produces a total of more than 100,000 responses, an average of almost 240 per congressional district.[11] I construct a summary measure of public opinion by combining responses to a dozen specific questions on topics ranging from the Affordable Care Act to domestic spending, the Iraq War, and abortion. The summary scale ranges from 0 to 100, with lower values reflecting liberal opinion and higher values reflecting conservative opinion. The range of district averages is, of course, much narrower, from 24.5 to 59.0.[12]

Figure 8.1 displays a fairly strong relationship ($r = .69$) between constituency opinion and House roll call votes: more conservative districts tend to have more conservative House members, and more liberal districts tend to have more liberal House members. However, it is important to note that this in itself does not provide much information one way or the other regarding how well any given district is actually being represented. As in most analyses of this kind, citizens' preferences and elite policy choices are measured on incommensurate scales, making it difficult or impossible to assess *congruence* between what citizens in each district wanted and how their member of Congress voted.[13]

---

[9] In order to facilitate meaningful comparisons of representatives' behavior over time, the DW-NOMINATE algorithm constrains the position of each representative on each dimension to follow a simple linear trend over the course of his or her career. As a result, the scores in a given Congress occasionally stray outside the –1 to +1 range. The first-dimension DW-NOMINATE scores for the 112th Congress range from –.729 to +1.376 in the House (with a mean of +.222 and a standard deviation of .565) and from –.732 to +.988 in the Senate (with a mean of +.064 and a standard deviation of .486).

[10] The CCES surveys were conducted by the Internet survey firm YouGov, which employs opt-in recruiting but uses matching and weighting to produce representative samples of adult U.S. citizens (Vavreck and Rivers 2008). Data, codebooks, and a more detailed description of the study design are available at the CCES website (http://projects.iq.harvard.edu/cces/home).

[11] There were a total of 52,464 respondents in 2010 and 51,661 in 2012. The combined sample size in each congressional district ranged from 88 to 515.

[12] My index of CCES respondents' political views is based on a factor analysis of responses to questions on liberal-conservative ideology (with a factor loading of .785), beliefs about climate change (.776), and support for the Affordable Care Act (.751), domestic spending (.734), the Iraq War (.619), gays in the military (.594), gun control (.588), affirmative action (.585), environmental protection (.585), defense spending (.518), a path to citizenship for illegal immigrants (.508), and abortion (.498).

[13] Joseph Bafumi and Michael Herron (2010) provided an unusually careful attempt to assess congruence between members of Congress and their constituents using survey questions designed to mimic actual roll call votes. They concluded that Republican members of Congress

It is also important to note that the overall relationship between constituents' opinions and House members' roll call votes in figure 8.1 is largely due to the fact that more conservative districts were mostly represented by Republicans while more liberal districts were mostly represented by Democrats. The relationships between constituents' opinions and members' roll call votes *within* each party, represented by separate summary lines in figure 8.1, are much more modest. As expected, more conservative districts tended to get more conservative representation, especially among Democrats.[14] However, these differences are dwarfed by the much larger differences in expected voting behavior between Republican and Democratic representatives, even when they represent districts with similar political views. Indeed, the expected difference in roll call profiles between a Republican and a Democrat representing a typical moderate congressional district amounts to about half of the DW-NOMINATE scale, more than twice the largest expected difference attributable to differences in constituency opinion.[15] These findings underscore the extent of partisan polarization in the contemporary Congress and, more generally, the immense significance of elite ideology in the making of American public policy.

Figure 8.2 shows the analogous relationship between constituency opinion and voting records in the U.S. Senate. Here, too, elite partisanship clearly trumped constituency opinion in determining legislators' roll call votes. However, Republican senators seem to have been more than twice as responsive to their constituents' views as Democratic senators were, and also much more responsive than Republicans in the House. This apparent responsiveness is due to somewhat weaker party discipline in the Senate than in the House in this period, and especially to the frequent defections from their party line of three Republican senators representing moderately liberal northeastern states—Susan Collins and Olympia Snowe of Maine and Scott Brown of Massachusetts. However, even setting aside these three outliers, the relationship between constituents' opinions and senators' votes is almost 50% stronger for Republican senators than for Democrats.[16]

---

are generally more conservative than their constituents while Democratic members of Congress are generally more liberal than their constituents.

[14] The regression slopes are .83 (with a standard error of .26) for Republicans and 1.29 (with a standard error of .13) for Democrats. The *t*-statistic for the difference is 1.6.

[15] The expected difference in DW-NOMINATE scores between a Democrat representing the most liberal district in the country and a Democrat representing the most conservative district in the country (extrapolating somewhat beyond the Democratic summary line in figure 8.1) would be .44. The corresponding expected difference between a Democrat and a Republican representing a typical district is more than twice as large, 1.00.

[16] The regression slopes are 3.41 (with a standard error of .78) for Republican senators and 1.64 (with a standard error of .32) for Democratic senators (including Bernie Sanders of Vermont, an independent who caucused with the Democrats). The *t*-statistic for the difference is 2.3.

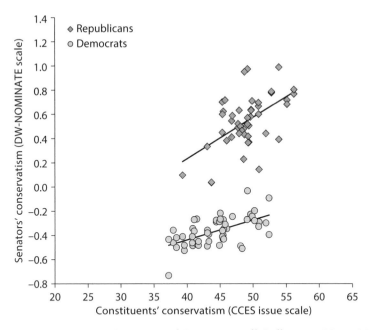

FIGURE 8.2 Constituency Opinion and Senators' Roll Call Votes, 2011–2013

UNEQUAL RESPONSIVENESS

The overall pattern of representation displayed in figures 8.1 and 8.2 has two salient features: a substantial partisan difference in the expected roll call voting behavior of Republican and Democratic members of Congress even when they represent constituents with similar views, and a less substantial positive relationship within each party between the behavior of representatives and the political views of their constituents. The latter relationship may be interpreted as evidence of "rational anticipation" or "incumbent responsiveness" to constituents' opinions (as distinct from "personnel turnover" or "electoral responsiveness").[17] However, as we have seen, even this apparent responsiveness may be illusory if the behavior of elected officials is really influenced by the preferences of a small minority of their constituents rather than by overall opinion in their districts. My aim in this section is to assess the extent to which the apparent responsiveness of representatives to the opinions of their constituents in figures 8.1 and 8.2 reflects *differential* responsiveness to the views of affluent constituents.

[17] Erikson, MacKuen, and Stimson (2002, 287–293); Bartels, Clinton, and Geer (2016, 405–407).

In order to assess the magnitude of class disparities in responsiveness, I classify CCES survey respondents into three income groups: a low-income group with family incomes below $40,000 (40.5% of the weighted sample), a middle-income group with family incomes between $40,000 and $80,000 (38.4%), and a high-income group with family incomes over $80,000 (21.1%).[18] Estimating separately the political preferences of constituents within each of these three groups in each state and congressional district makes it possible to assess whether and how the behavior of elected officials seems to be influenced by each group's distinct preferences.

The statistical model employed here relates each elected official's policy choices (as reflected in roll call votes cast on the floor of the House or Senate) to his or her party affiliation and a weighted measure of constituency opinion in his or her state or district. The weighted measure of constituency opinion combines the opinions of high-, middle-, and low-income constituents with weights chosen to account as well as possible for elected officials' choices. If elected officials respond similarly to the opinions of each income group, the estimated weights will be equal and the model will simply reflect the usual statistical relationship between average district opinion and congressional roll call votes. However, if elected officials respond disproportionately to the opinions of affluent constituents, the estimated relative weights of low- and middle-income opinion will be reduced to reflect that fact.[19]

Table 8.1 presents the results of applying this statistical model to the roll call votes of House members in the 112th Congress.[20] As expected,

---

[18] These thresholds were chosen to make the three income groups as similar as possible in size, given the categorization of family incomes in the CCES surveys. I imputed missing income data for 12% of the survey respondents on the basis of non-missing information about stock ownership, education, occupation, homeownership, marital status, health insurance, race and ethnicity, sex, age, and immigration status. Most of these respondents were classified as middle-income (62%), with 27% low-income and 11% high-income.

[19] Bhatti and Erikson (2011) noted that the model specification used to assess differential responsiveness in the first edition of this book—a linear regression analysis with separate weighted estimates of high-, middle-, and low-income opinion in each state as explanatory variables—could produce misleading results if the opinion measures were not sensibly scaled. They proposed solving this problem by including the proportions of high-, middle-, and low-income constituents in each state as additional explanatory variables. However, that approach is statistically inefficient, since it does not impose constraints on the six separate regression coefficients implied by the fact that the opinions of all three income groups are measured on the same scale. Thus, Bhatti and Erikson produced many statistically "insignificant" parameter estimates and concluded that the evidence for disparate responsiveness was weak. The non-linear model employed here, with one parameter representing the impact of weighted constituency opinion on legislators' roll call votes and two additional parameters representing the weight of low- and middle-income opinions *relative to* high-income opinions within that weighted average, is statistically more efficient but unaffected by affine transformations of the opinion measures.

[20] The Voteview website provides DW-NOMINATE scores for 442 House members and 101 senators in the 112th Congress (including some who served for only part of the relevant

TABLE 8.1

House Responsiveness to Constituency Opinion, 2011–2013

Non-linear least squares regression parameter estimates (with standard errors in parentheses) for the 112th Congress first-dimension DW-NOMINATE scores. (Districts with at least 20 survey respondents in each income group.)

	House	*Republicans*	*Democrats*
Low-income/high-income responsiveness ratio	.49 (.33)	.12 (.27)	1.91 (1.43)
Middle-income/high-income responsiveness ratio	.55 (.37)	.19 (.30)	1.57 (1.30)
Weighted constituency opinion	1.05 (.15)	.81 (.27)	1.30 (.14)
Republican member	1.00 (.02)	Yes	No
Intercept	−.81 (.06)	.31 (.13)	−.90 (.06)
Standard error of regression	.144	.171	.100
Adjusted R²	.93	.04	.33
N	425	238	187

Sources: Voteview.com; 2010 and 2012 CCES surveys.

Republican members were much more conservative than Democrats representing similar constituencies; this difference amounts to a full point on the −1 to +1 roll call scale. Weighted constituency opinion also had a discernible, albeit much smaller, effect on representatives' behavior, with a 34-point difference in constituency opinion—the difference between New York's 15th Congressional District at the liberal end of the scale and Texas's 8th District at the conservative end—corresponding to a shift of about one-third of a point on the roll call scale.

The estimated "responsiveness ratios" reported in the first and second rows of table 8.1 reflect the apparent relative weight of low- and middle-income constituents' views by comparison with high-income constituents' views in this weighted average of constituency opinion. The estimate of .49 in the first row of the first column (based on the observed behavior of representatives from both parties) implies that a typical low-income constituent had only half as much influence on his or her representatives' behavior as a

period). However, my analysis excludes 17 House members from districts in which the CCES surveys did not include at least 20 respondents in each of my three income groups.

TABLE 8.2
Senate Responsiveness to Constituency Opinion, 2011–2013

Non-linear least squares regression parameter estimates (with standard errors clustered by state in parentheses) for 112th Congress first-dimension DW-NOMINATE scores.

	Senate	Republicans	Democrats
Low-income/high-income responsiveness ratio	.01 (.19)	−.09 (.10)	.40 (.23)
Middle-income/high-income responsiveness ratio	.19 (.20)	.27 (.19)	−.05 (.09)
Weighted constituency opinion	1.94 (.41)	3.27 (.52)	1.59 (.26)
Republican member	.79 (.04)	Yes	No
Intercept	−1.25 (.18)	−1.16 (.27)	−1.07 (.11)
Standard error of regression	.146	.170	.095
Adjusted R²	.91	.41	.38
N	101	48	53

Sources: Voteview.com; 2010 and 2012 CCES surveys.

typical high-income constituent did. The estimate of .55 in the second row of the first column implies that a typical middle-income constituent had only a bit more than half as much influence as a typical high-income constituent did. These disparities in apparent influence are estimated with considerable statistical uncertainty, so we cannot rule out the possibility that House members responded equally to the views of low- or middle-income constituents and high-income constituents. On the other hand, we also cannot rule out the possibility that the views of low- or middle-income constituents had no effect at all on the voting behavior of their members of Congress.[21]

Table 8.2 reports the results of parallel analyses relating senators' roll call votes to the opinions of their constituents (differentiated by income group) and to the senators' own party affiliations. Again, as one would expect, Republicans were substantially more conservative than Democrats with

---

[21] The 95% credible interval for the low-income responsiveness ratio ranges from −.16 to 1.14, but the true value probably lies between .27 and .71. The 95% credible interval for the middle-income responsiveness ratio ranges from −.18 to 1.28, but the true value probably lies between .30 and .80.

similar constituencies. This difference amounts to almost half of the total ideological distance between the most conservative senator in the 112th Congress (Mike Lee of Utah) and the most liberal senator (Bernie Sanders of Vermont).

However, constituency opinion seems to have had a rather different impact on the behavior of senators than it had on House members. For one thing, as a comparison of figures 8.1 and 8.2 would suggest, senators seem to have been almost twice as responsive as House members to the political views of their constituents (1.94 versus 1.05). However, this overall difference in responsiveness obscures an even more striking difference in the apparent relative weight of high-, middle-, and low-income constituents. Whereas the views of middle- and low-income constituents seem to have mattered about half as much as those of high-income constituents to House members (55% and 49%, respectively), they seem to have mattered much less or not at all to senators (19% and 1%, respectively). Thus, a difference of 20 points in the opinions of affluent constituents—roughly the difference between Vermont or Hawaii and Idaho or Wyoming—would imply an expected difference of .32 in senators' roll call conservatism, whereas the same difference in the opinions of middle-income constituents would imply an expected difference of only .06, and the same difference in the opinions of low-income constituents would imply virtually no difference at all.[22]

The statistical estimates of relative responsiveness to low- and middle-income constituents are rather more precise for the Senate than for the House. Thus, the null hypothesis of equal responsiveness can be confidently rejected on the basis of these results. Indeed, in the case of low-income constituents, it is highly implausible to suppose that their views had even half as much effect on senators' voting behavior as those of high-income constituents. The statistical results strongly suggest that their opinions were of little or no consequence.[23]

The patterns of differential responsiveness reported in tables 8.1 and 8.2 are summarized graphically in figure 8.3, which shows the estimated weights attached to the views of low-, middle-, and high-income constituents in the voting behavior of House members (on the left) and senators

[22] In order to provide an accurate comparison of per capita responsiveness, I calculate these expected differences in roll call voting behavior on the assumption that high-, middle-, and low-income voters each constituted one-third of a state's population. Given the distribution of the income data in the CCES surveys, there are fewer high-income constituents than middle- or low-income constituents in most states, and so their aggregate impact on senators' voting behavior is somewhat smaller than these calculations imply.

[23] The 95% credible interval for the low-income responsiveness ratio ranges from –.36 to .38, but the true value probably lies between –.12 and .14. The 95% credible interval for the middle-income responsiveness ratio ranges from –.20 to .58, but the true value probably lies between .06 and .32.

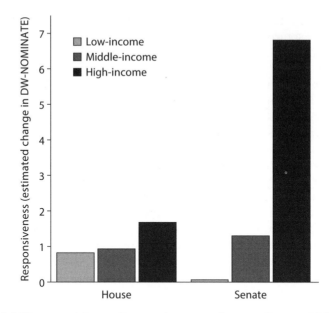

FIGURE 8.3 House and Senate Responsiveness to Income Groups, 2011–2013

(on the right).[24] In the case of House members, the figure shows a rather modest level of responsiveness to the views of high-income constituents and even less responsiveness to the views of middle- and low-income constituents; as the simple graphical presentation in figure 8.1 suggested, the most important factor by far in accounting for the roll call voting records of House members in the 112th Congress was their own partisanship. For senators, there is more evidence of responsiveness in figure 8.3, but also more evidence of dramatic disparities in political influence, with vastly more responsiveness to the views of affluent constituents than of middle-class constituents and no evidence at all of responsiveness to the views of poor constituents.

[24] The non-linear model specification employed here is based on the assumption that the *total* weight of constituency opinion is the same in each state or district regardless of its income distribution. Thus, the weight of each individual constituent's opinion depends on the distribution of income in his or her state or district. In the first column of table 8.1, for example, if all N constituents in a given district had high incomes, their opinions would each receive the same weight, $1.05/N$. However, if half had high incomes and half had low incomes, those with high incomes would each receive more weight—$(1/1.49) \times 2/N = 1.34/N$—while those with low incomes would each receive less weight—$(.49/1.49) \times 2/N = .66/N$. The estimates of responsiveness shown in figure 8.3 are national averages based on the estimated proportions of constituents in each income group in each district and state.

What might account for the apparent difference in responsiveness between the House and Senate in figure 8.3? Perhaps Senate rules offer more scope for individual action, reducing the importance of party-line voting and giving senators more leeway to respond to constituency pressures. (Indeed, while constituency opinion seems to have had more impact on senators than on House members, their own party affiliations seem to have had about 20% less impact on senators than on House members.) In addition, states are generally larger, more heterogeneous, and less politically "safe" than congressional districts. As a result, senators generally need more money to run for reelection than House members do, and they may therefore depend more heavily on affluent constituents for campaign contributions. Whether for this reason or others, the results reported in table 8.2 and illustrated in figure 8.3 suggest that the contemporary U.S. Senate comes a great deal closer to providing equal representation of *wealth* than equal representation of *citizens*.[25]

Of course, one might wonder whether these results from a single Congress in the second half of Barack Obama's first term as president are representative of broader patterns of responsiveness in the American political system. In the first edition of this book, I reported a similar attempt to gauge the responsiveness of U.S. senators in the 101st, 102nd, and 103rd Congresses (1989–1995) using contemporaneous survey data on the political views of their constituents from the American National Election Studies (ANES) Senate Election Study. A reanalysis of those data along the same lines employed here to study the 112th Congress may shed some light on the extent of stability or change in patterns of responsiveness over a period of two decades.[26]

---

[25] The Census Bureau's estimates of median net worth for households in the top, middle, and bottom quintiles of the U.S. income distribution in 2011 were $294,000, $60,000 (20% of the top quintile), and $6,000 (2% of the top quintile), respectively; U.S. Census Bureau, "Wealth and Asset Ownership" (http://www.census.gov/people/wealth/). The estimates in table 8.2 of Senate responsiveness to constituents in the top, middle, and bottom terciles of the income distribution are 1.62, .31 (19% of the top tercile), and .02 (1% of the top tercile), respectively. In the earliest version of my analysis of disparate responsiveness (Bartels 2002b), I included direct measures of average constituency opinion and income-weighted constituency opinion in each state rather than separate measures of opinion among low-, middle-, and high-income constituents. That linear specification of differential responsiveness produced results generally consistent with those reported here.

[26] For details of the original analysis, see Bartels (2008, 254–262). The ANES Senate Election Study surveys were conducted by telephone in the weeks just after the 1988, 1990, and 1992 elections with a combined sample of 9,253 respondents distributed roughly equally across all 50 states. (The state sample sizes ranged from 151 to 223.) I related the roll call votes of senators in each of the three Congresses (and all three combined) to the ideological views of their low-, middle-, and high-income constituents as measured by self-placements on a liberal-conservative scale.

TABLE 8.3

Senate Responsiveness to Constituency Opinion, 1989–1995

Non-linear least squares regression parameter estimates (with standard errors in parentheses) for 101st–103rd Congress first-dimension DW-NOMINATE scores clustered by state.

	Senate	Republicans	Democrats
Low-income/high-income responsiveness ratio	−.09 (.13)	.04 (.18)	−.15 (.19)
Middle-income/high-income responsiveness ratio	.50 (.31)	.27 (.40)	1.08 (.70)
Weighted constituency opinion	1.75 (.34)	2.56 (.79)	1.38 (.34)
Republican member	.62 (.03)	Yes	No
Intercept	−1.32 (.20)	−1.17 (.46)	−1.12 (.19)
Standard error of regression	.133	.175	.081
Adjusted R²	.85	.22	.37
N	304	133	171

Sources: Voteview.com; ANES Senate Election Study surveys.

Table 8.3 reports the results of that reanalysis.[27] They are quite consistent with the more recent results presented in table 8.2 in suggesting that the opinions of constituents in the bottom one-third of the income distribution had no impact at all on the roll call votes cast by their senators. Far from being "considered as political equals," low-income citizens seem to have been entirely *un*considered in the Senate's policy-making process in both eras.[28]

[27] These results differ from those reported by Bartels (2008, tables 9.1, 9.6, and 9.7) for two reasons. First, the non-linear statistical model employed here provides estimates of the impact of overall (weighted) constituency opinion and of *relative* responsiveness to the views of low- and middle-income constituents (by comparison with high-income constituents); the earlier analysis provided separate estimates of the impact of low-, middle-, and high-income opinions, allowing the total estimated impact of constituency opinion to vary in states with different income distributions. Second, in order to provide a more direct comparison with the DW-NOMINATE scores from the 112th Congress, I use updated DW-NOMINATE scores for the 101st, 102nd, and 103rd Congresses. (Owing to the constraints imposed by the DW-NOMINATE algorithm, scores for previous Congresses change each time a new Congress is added to the data set.)

[28] A comparison of the parameter estimates in tables 8.2 and 8.3 suggests that the impact of senators' own partisanship on their roll call votes was more than 25% larger in the 112th Senate than it had been two decades earlier. That difference reflects the increasing partisan

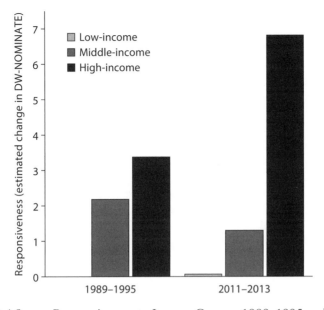

FIGURE 8.4 Senate Responsiveness to Income Groups, 1989–1995 and 2011–2013

On the other hand, the results presented in table 8.3 do suggest some shift in the relative political influence of affluent and middle-class Americans. Although the estimated overall impact of constituents' opinions on senators' votes was roughly similar in magnitude in the two eras, that influence seems to have been rather differently distributed. In the early 1990s, the preferences of middle-income constituents seem to have had about half as much impact on senators' roll call votes as the preferences of high-income constituents. However, by the time of the 112th Congress, the relative influence of middle-income constituents seems to have eroded considerably, from .50 to .19. This difference is displayed graphically in figure 8.4. It would be rash to make too much of the difference, given differences in sample design and measurement.[29] Nonetheless, this evidence suggests that, if anything, disparities in Senate responsiveness have probably increased in recent decades.

---

polarization of Congress highlighted by Thomas Mann and Norman Ornstein (2012) and many other observers.

[29] Most importantly, the ANES Senate Election Study survey lacked the extensive battery of issue questions included in the CCES survey. Thus, in the analysis reported in table 8.3 constituency opinion is measured solely by liberal-conservative ideology rather than by a scale combining responses to a dozen specific issue questions.

Partisan Differences in Responsiveness

My analysis thus far provides considerable evidence that elected officials are more responsive to the opinions of affluent constituents than those of middle-class or poor constituents. In this section I examine whether these patterns of differential responsiveness are similar for Republican and Democratic legislators. Given the distinct class bases of the parties' electoral coalitions, one might expect Republican legislators to be especially sensitive to the opinions of affluent constituents and Democrats to attach more weight to the opinions of less affluent constituents. However, votes, campaign contributions, and the various other political resources associated with higher income are clearly valuable to politicians of both parties. Thus, Democrats as well as Republicans may be especially responsive to the views of resource-rich constituents, notwithstanding the historical association of the Democratic Party with the political interests of the working class and the poor.

I assessed partisan differences in responsiveness by repeating the analyses of differential responsiveness reported in tables 8.1, 8.2, and 8.3 separately for Republican and Democratic legislators. The results of these analyses are summarized in figure 8.5, which shows averages of the three separate estimates of responsiveness for legislators in each party for each income group. For Democrats, these results suggest a modest (and fairly consistent) degree of responsiveness to the views of affluent constituents but rather less responsiveness to the views of middle-class and poor constituents. On average, the views of middle-income constituents received about 85% as much weight as those of high-income constituents, while the views of low-income constituents received about 70% as much weight as those of high-income constituents. However, these estimated disparities in responsiveness varied considerably across the three settings. They suggest that Democratic House members were probably at least as responsive to the views of low- and middle-income constituents as to the views of affluent constituents; but Democratic senators seem to have been much more responsive to affluent constituents than to low- and middle-income constituents.

For Republicans, the results summarized in figure 8.5 imply substantial responsiveness to the preferences of affluent constituents (especially by senators), but much less responsiveness to middle-class constituents and none at all to the poor. The estimates of relative responsiveness to middle-income constituents range from .19 to .27; in each case, they are sufficiently precise to provide very strong evidence of disparate responsiveness. (Indeed, it is impossible on the basis of these results to rule out the possibility that Republican elected officials were utterly unresponsive to the views of middle-class constituents, despite the appearance of responsiveness in figure 8.5.) The estimates of relative responsiveness to low-income constituents range from –.09 to .12 and are sufficiently precise to leave little doubt that their

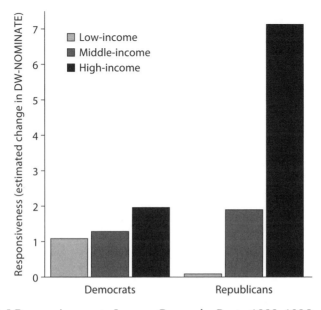

FIGURE 8.5 Responsiveness to Income Groups by Party, 1989–1995 and 2011–2013

views were largely or wholly irrelevant in shaping the roll call votes of Republicans senators and House members.

SYSTEMIC RESPONSIVENESS

So far, I have focused on the responsiveness of individual members of Congress to the preferences of their own constituents. However, a broader and more consequential question is how the political system as a whole responds to the preferences of its citizens. That question is especially pertinent in the context of American government, where a variety of institutional features—perhaps most importantly, the separation of powers among separate legislative, executive, and judicial branches—create substantial obstacles to policy change. If the political system as a whole frustrates the translation of preferences into policy, then the responsiveness of individual members of Congress to their own constituents may be largely beside the point.

Here, too, political scientists until recently focused entirely on the relationship between overall public opinion and policy change. However, the work of Martin Gilens—most notably in his 2012 book *Affluence and Influence*—has provided dramatic evidence of disparate responsiveness by the American political system to the opinions of affluent, middle-class, and poor citizens.[30] Gilens's analysis drew on 1,779 survey questions measuring citizens' preferences regarding a wide variety of national policy issues. For each of these issues, he examined whether a policy change supported or opposed by various segments of the public was subsequently adopted. While he found a strong statistical relationship between the views of affluent citizens and the subsequent course of public policy, the relationship for less affluent citizens was weaker, and when the analysis was limited to issues on which the preferences of different income groups diverged, Gilens found that the well-off were vastly more influential. He concluded that "influence over actual policy outcomes appears to be reserved almost exclusively for those at the top of the income distribution."[31]

Given the limitations of his data, Gilens imputed the preferences of affluent, middle-class, and poor people (at the 90th, 50th, and 10th percentiles of the income distribution, respectively) for each policy on the basis of the statistical relationship between income and responses to the corresponding survey question. For that reason (and perhaps others as well), the three sets of imputed preferences are subject to correlated measurement error, making it even more than usually difficult to disentangle their respective effects on policy outcomes. Thus, most of Gilens's assessments of responsiveness involved separate estimates relating policy outcomes to the preferences of a single income group in isolation rather than more complex analyses incorporating all three groups simultaneously.

Gilens sharpened his comparisons of political influence across income groups and attempted to avoid spurious estimates of influence by focusing on subsets of issues on which the preferences of income groups diverged. For example, the estimated impact of the preferences of middle-income citizens (at the 50th percentile of the income distribution) on policy outcomes for his primary sample of 1,779 issues was .37. The corresponding estimate for affluent citizens, at the 90th percentile of the income distribution, was .49. But when he limited these analyses to 322 issues on which the preferences of the two groups differed by more than 10 percentage points, the estimates of responsiveness were .47 for citizens at the 90th percentile and −.01 for citizens at the 50th percentile. The latter estimates led Gilens to conclude that "for Americans below the top of the income distribution, any association between preferences and policy outcomes is likely to reflect the extent to which their preferences coincide with those of the affluent."[32]

---

[30] Gilens (2012); Gilens (2005); Gilens and Page (2014).

[31] Gilens (2005, 794).

[32] Gilens (2012, 75–83). A more complex multivariate analysis allowing explicitly for correlated measurement error in the measured preferences of all three income groups produced qualitatively similar results, with responsiveness estimates of .51 for citizens at the 90th percentile, .08 for citizens at the 50th percentile, and −.10 for citizens at the 10th percentile (Gilens 2012, 85–87, 253–258).

TABLE 8.4

Policy Outcomes and the Policy Preferences of Average
Citizens, Economic Elites, and Interest Groups

Errors-in-variables regression parameter estimates (with standard errors in
parentheses) for policy outcomes (coded 1 if the proposed policy change took place
within four years of the survey date and 0 if it did not).

	Model 1	Model 4
Preferences of average citizens	.64	.03
	(.08)	(.08)
Preferences of economic elites	—	.76
		(.08)
Alignment of interest groups	—	.56
		(.09)
R^2	.031	.074
N	1,779	1,779

Source: Gilens and Page (2014).

Gilens and Benjamin Page used the same data to assess alternative broad
theories of American politics attributing political power to ordinary citizens,
economic elites, or interest groups. They related Gilens's 1,779 policy outcomes simultaneously to the preferences of "average citizens" (at the 50th
percentile of the income distribution), "economic elites" (at the 90th percentile of the income distribution), and prominent interest groups. Their key
results are reproduced in table 8.4.

Gilens and Page's results provide a dramatic illustration of the disjuncture between simple correlation and real political influence. The results for
their model 1, presented in the first column of table 8.4, suggest a strong
positive relationship between the preferences of average citizens and policy
outcomes. If this was the whole story, it would represent a strong vindica-
tion of the political system's responsiveness to ordinary citizens. However,
the results presented in the second column of the table—from Gilens and
Page's model 4, incorporating the preferences of affluent citizens and interest groups as additional explanatory factors—demonstrate that the strong
positive relationship in the first column is almost entirely spurious, reflecting
the fact that average citizens tend to get their way when their preferences
happen to align with those of affluent citizens and interest groups. Once
the preferences of those more influential actors are taken into account, the
apparent impact of average citizens' preferences on policy outcomes is almost precisely zero. Thus, Gilens and Page's results were quite consistent

with the results from separate subgroup analyses presented in Gilens's book. The authors interpreted these results as providing "substantial support for theories of Economic-Elite Domination and for theories of Biased Pluralism, but not for theories of Majoritarian Electoral Democracy or Majoritarian Pluralism."[33]

One possible objection to these results is that assessing whether the policy change proposed in a brief survey question did or did not occur can sometimes be a delicate matter of judgment. Gilens reported that different research assistants working separately agreed on these assessments 90% of the time, a rather high level of inter-coder reliability. Nonetheless, a closer look at a few of Gilens's most significant examples of "responsiveness" underscores some important limitations of his analysis, while also raising some deeper questions about responsiveness as a normative benchmark.[34]

George W. Bush's presidency is a notable bright spot in Gilens's generally pessimistic account, with unusually strong responsiveness to the preferences of affluent, middle-class, and poor Americans alike. However, the most consequential of Bush's "responsive" policies, by Gilens's assessment, would be hard to characterize as triumphs of the will of the people. For example, as we saw in chapter 5, the 2001 tax cuts had strong public support—but only if we set aside the 40% of the public who said that they "hadn't thought about" whether they favored or opposed the tax cuts, and only if we ignore considerable evidence suggesting that most Americans would have preferred smaller and broader-based tax cuts to the massive, upwardly skewed package adopted by Congress.

The historic expansion of Medicare to provide prescription drugs to seniors was another instance of ambiguous responsiveness. While the basic idea was broadly popular, the Bush administration produced a massive giveaway to insurers by requiring beneficiaries to sign up for private insurance plans and to drug companies by prohibiting the government from negotiating drug prices.[35]

---

[33] Gilens and Page (2014, 564).

[34] Gilens (2012, 224–232). See Larry Bartels, "The Muddled Majority," *Boston Review*, July 1, 2012 (http://www.bostonreview.net/forum/lead-essay-under-influence/muddled-majority-larry-bartels).

[35] A congressional report found that administrative costs, sales expenses, and profits in the new program were six times higher than in traditional Medicare; U.S. House of Representatives, Committee on Oversight and Government Reform Majority Staff, "Private Medicare Drug Plans: High Expenses and Low Rebates Increase the Costs of Medicare Drug Coverage," October 2007. Subsequent studies estimated that annual drug costs were $20 billion or more higher than they would have been at the prices negotiated by other federal programs (Gellad et al. 2008; Baker 2013). The adoption of the prescription drug law was also rife with procedural irregularities. The Bush administration illegally suppressed a government report regarding the program's likely cost and threatened to fire Medicare's chief actuary if he disclosed his own cost estimate; Majority Leader Tom DeLay bribed one of his colleagues to support the bill,

The Iraq War likewise counts as an instance of "responsive" policy in Gilens's analysis. However, public support for the war hinged in significant part on two major misconceptions actively promoted by the Bush administration: the plausible but false belief that Iraq possessed weapons of mass destruction, and the much flimsier notion that Saddam Hussein was somehow implicated in the 9/11 terrorist attacks. In this instance, the appearance of "responsiveness" reflected the success of the administration's "campaign to drum up public support for a preventive war," as Gary Jacobson put it, rather than any genuine influence of ordinary citizens on government policy-making.[36]

On the other hand, the liberal policies adopted during Lyndon Johnson's presidency were often adopted in spite of significant public opposition. According to Gilens, "The Great Society and the war on poverty were not responses to an upwelling of public concern for the disadvantaged or a desire to expand the role of government in addressing social needs. . . . Core middle-class domestic programs like Medicare and aid to education were broadly favored (albeit with less enthusiasm from the affluent), while other policies like immigration reform and the war on poverty were opposed by a majority of Americans at all income levels."[37] With substantial Democratic majorities in Congress, Johnson's policy agenda reflected partisan ideological convictions of the same sort reflected in the gaps in roll call voting between Republican and Democratic legislators in figures 8.1 and 8.2.

Examples like these suggest that classifying policies as "responsive" or "unresponsive" to public preferences may be less straightforward than it appears—especially in cases where public opinion is shallow, confused, or misinformed. As Gilens observed in the case of Lyndon Johnson, "left to their own devices, political parties pursue the policies that their core activists and policy-demanding groups desire."[38] However, he might have added that political elites have considerable leeway to craft the actual content of policy to their own ends even when they seem to be responding to public preferences.

Notwithstanding these limitations, Gilens's work provides the best evidence we have regarding the responsiveness of the American political system to the preferences of its citizens. On the whole, that evidence is

---

earning a reprimand from the House Ethics Committee; and the primary architect of the plan, Representative Billy Tauzin (R-LA), retired from Congress shortly after it passed to head a drug industry lobbying group at a reported salary of $2 million per year. None of these facts figures in Gilens's analysis, but they certainly seem relevant to assessing the *quality* of democratic responsiveness in this instance.

[36] Jacobson (2007, 105).

[37] Gilens (2012, 221–224). Katherine Newman and Elisabeth Jacobs (2010) provided a more detailed account of public ambivalence toward government activism in the New Deal, Great Society, and Reagan eras.

[38] Gilens (2012, 233).

quite consistent with the results of my own analyses relating the choices of individual members of Congress to the preferences of their constituents. In both cases, it seems clear that elected officials were responsive to the preferences of affluent citizens, but largely or even wholly *un*responsive to the preferences of the poor. As Gilens put it, the observed patterns of responsiveness "often corresponded more closely to a plutocracy than to a democracy."[39]

PLUTOCRACY?

One of the most important unanswered questions raised by recent research on unequal responsiveness is whether the opinions that matter politically are really those of a fairly broad stratum of affluent citizens (say, the top one-third or one-fifth of income-earners, as in my analyses or Gilens's) or those of a much loftier stratum of top wealth-holders invisible in typical opinion surveys. Just as the *apparent* influence of the general public in much research on political representation turns out to reflect, in significant part, the unmeasured influence of affluent citizens, the *apparent* influence of the merely affluent may reflect the unmeasured influence of a much smaller set of top wealth-holders.

Unfortunately, detailed evidence regarding the political preferences and behavior of truly wealthy people is extremely scarce. The most careful effort so far to elicit evidence of this sort was a 2011 pilot study, the Survey of Economically Successful Americans (SESA), led by Benjamin Page. Page's team (of which I was a part) managed to obtain interviews with a representative sample of 83 wealthy people in the Chicago area. The respondents' average income was just over $1 million per year—several times the threshold for "affluence" in conventional studies of disparate responsiveness—and their average *wealth* was $14 million. (Almost three-fourths reported wealth of $5 million or more.)[40]

Table 8.5 summarizes some of the striking differences in policy preferences between the wealthy SESA respondents and the American public as a whole. In several major policy areas, including education, health care, income maintenance, and taxation, substantial majorities of the wealthy opposed the broader public's views. Unlike the general public, these wealthy Americans viewed budget deficits as the most important problem facing the

---

[39] Ibid., 234.
[40] Page, Bartels, and Seawright (2013). For additional information on the design and implementation of the study, see Page, Bartels, and Seawright (2011).

TABLE 8.5
Policy Preferences of Wealthy Americans

Policy preferences of wealthy Americans from the 2011 Survey of Economically Successful Americans; policy preferences of the general public from contemporaneous public surveys.

	Wealthy support	General public support
The federal government should spend whatever is necessary to ensure that all children have really good public schools they can go to	35%	87%
The federal government should make sure that everyone who wants to go to college can do so	28%	78%
Minimum wage high enough so that no family with a full-time worker falls below the official poverty line	40%	78%
The government in Washington ought to see to it that everyone who wants to work can find a job	19%	68%
Government must see that no one is without food, clothing, or shelter	43%	68%
Favor national health insurance, which would be financed by tax money, paying for most forms of health care	32%	61%
Willing to pay more taxes in order to provide health coverage for everyone	41%	59%
The federal government should invest more in worker retraining and education to help workers adapt to changes in the economy	30%	57%
Our government should redistribute wealth by heavy taxes on the rich	17%	52%
The government should provide a decent standard of living for the unemployed	23%	50%
Willing to pay more taxes in order to reduce federal budget deficits	65%	34%
Favor cuts in spending on domestic programs like Medicare, education, and highways in order to cut federal budget deficits	58%	27%
Differences in income in America are too large	62%	63%

Source: Page, Bartels, and Seawright (2013).

country.[41] Pluralities favored cuts in government spending on Social Security, health care, homeland security, and environmental protection—all areas in which most Americans wanted *more* spending, not less.[42] Many of these differences are so large in magnitude that, even with a very small sample of wealthy people, they effectively demolish the notion that "extensive political power by the wealthy would be of little practical importance anyway because their policy preferences are much the same as everyone else's."[43]

Perhaps ironically, one point on which the views of wealthy Americans were virtually identical to those of the general public was the last item in table 8.5. Substantial majorities of both groups agreed that "differences in income in America are too large." However, juxtaposing these views with others in the table suggests that wealthy people opposed most of the government policies that would seem most likely to reduce differences in income. Perhaps they believed—or simply hoped—that ordinary Americans could close the gap on their own; but the views of ordinary Americans themselves seem rather more realistic in that regard.

Although the SESA sample was too small to shed much light on variations in policy preferences *among* wealthy Americans, the data suggest that the wealthiest of these wealthy respondents were especially unfavorable toward government regulation, government spending (especially for Social Security), and high taxes.[44] Just as the political views of the top 1% differ from those of the merely affluent, the views of the top 0.1% appear to differ from those of the merely wealthy.

Much more research will be necessary to provide a clear picture of the differences in political views between wealthy Americans—especially the wealthiest of the wealthy—and the general public.[45] Moreover, even a

[41] Page, Bartels, and Seawright (2013, 54–56). Eighty-seven percent of the wealthy respondents rated budget deficits as "very important"—a higher proportion than for unemployment, education, or any of eight other issues. Climate change trailed the list, rated as "very important" by 16% of the wealthy respondents.

[42] Ibid., 56. The difference in views between the wealthy and the general public was most stark in the case of Social Security: the wealthy favored cuts over increases by a 33-point margin, while the public favored increases over cuts by a 46-point margin. The wealthy and the general public both strongly supported increases in spending on public infrastructure, aid to education, and scientific research, and both strongly supported cuts in spending on economic aid to other countries.

[43] Page, Bartels, and Seawright (2013, 57, 58, 59, 61, 63, 68).

[44] Ibid., 64–65.

[45] Page's efforts to secure funding for a full-scale national SESA study have so far been unavailing. In the meantime, Page, Seawright, and Matthew Lacombe (2015, 26) have attempted to characterize the views of the wealthiest 100 American billionaires regarding tax and Social Security policy issues by combing the Internet for reports of their public statements and political activities. They have found that "most (71%) of the one hundred billionaires said nothing whatsoever in public about any of these issues," leaving a skewed collection of statements from a small set of publicly engaged (and disproportionally left-leaning) figures, including Michael

detailed picture of the political preferences of wealthy Americans will not in itself answer the fundamental question of how, and to what extent, their preferences actually shape public policy. However, as Page and his colleagues noted, "the apparent consistency between the preferences of the wealthy and the contours of actual policy in certain important areas—especially social welfare policies, and to a lesser extent economic regulation and taxation—is, at least, suggestive of significant influence."[46]

WHY THE POOR ARE UNREPRESENTED

The evidence presented in this chapter documents substantial disparities in the responsiveness of the American political system to the preferences of citizens. Whether we focus on individual members of Congress, the states, or the federal government, policy-makers seem to be responsive to the views of affluent citizens but largely or entirely *un*responsive to those of the poor.[47] In this section I turn to a brief consideration of the bases of this unequal responsiveness.

One aspect of political inequality that has been extensively documented by political scientists is the disparity between rich and poor citizens in political participation.[48] The extent to which scholarly attention has focused on disparities in participation probably reflects, in part, the simple fact that those disparities are relatively easy to measure. As Sidney Verba and Gary Orren put it, "political equality cannot be gauged in the same way as

---

Bloomberg, Warren Buffett, Bill Gates, and George Soros. On the other hand, "quite a few" served on boards or contributed money to political groups active in these policy domains, and "most of these actions (in contrast to the billionaires' limited public rhetoric) were aimed in a conservative direction—overwhelmingly, for example, toward repealing the estate tax, reducing capital gains and personal and corporate income taxes, and opposing carbon taxes."

[46] Page, Bartels, and Seawright (2013, 68).

[47] The most conspicuous apparent exception to this conclusion is an analysis by Eric Brunner, Stephen Ross, and Ebonya Washington (2013) relating roll call votes by California state legislators to the votes of their constituents in referenda on the same issues. Focusing on *congruence* between legislators and constituents rather than responsiveness, they concluded that legislators usually agreed with both rich and poor constituents, but that Republicans agreed slightly more often with rich constituents while Democrats agreed slightly more often with poor constituents. However, their analysis employed aggregated data on referendum votes in high- and low-income *neighborhoods* rather than individual-level data for high- and low-income *constituents*, and they discarded information regarding the size of the plurality favoring or opposing each issue. Thus, it is not at all clear that "agreement with poor constituents" reflected congruence with the views of even a bare plurality of low-income constituents, much less evidence that legislators' votes were *responsive* to the views of their low-income constituents.

[48] Prominent examples include Verba, Nie, and Kim (1978), Wolfinger and Rosenstone (1980), Verba, Schlozman, and Brady (1995), Schlozman, Verba, and Brady (2012), and Leighley and Nagler (2013).

economic inequality. There is no metric such as money, no statistic such as the Gini index, and no body of data comparing countries. There are, however, relevant data on political participation."[49]

The mere availability of relevant data would probably not be sufficient to inspire much interest in participatory inequality if analysts did not believe that participation has important consequences for representation. However, that presumption does seem to be quite common. For example, Verba, Kay Schlozman, and Henry Brady motivated their monumental study of *Voice and Equality* by stipulating that "inequalities in activity are likely to be associated with inequalities in governmental responsiveness." It is striking, though, how little political scientists have done to *test* the presumption that inequalities in participation have political consequences. For the most part, studies of political participation have stopped short of examining the relevance of participation for governmental responsiveness. Voice, and then what?[50]

Faith in the efficacy of democratic participation is, of course, not limited to political scientists. For example, the distinguished British economist Anthony Atkinson devoted the final page of his book-length study of *Inequality: What Can Be Done?* to assuring individual citizens that *they* "will ultimately determine whether the proposals set out here are implemented and whether the ideas are pursued. They will do so indirectly in their capacity as voters, and—perhaps today more importantly—as lobbyists through campaign groups and social media, acting as countervailing power to the paid members of the lobbying profession. Sending that email message to your elected representative makes a difference." While it is pleasant to think so, Atkinson provided no evidence in support of this assertion, nor even any hint that it is a contestable empirical claim.[51]

In the same spirit, a common reaction to evidence of the sort presented in this chapter is: "Of course the poor don't get represented—they don't vote!" This reaction is a natural reflection of the appealing idea that elected

[49] Verba and Orren (1985, 15).

[50] Verba, Schlozman, and Brady (1995, 14). In their similarly monumental sequel, *The Unheavenly Chorus*, Schlozman, Verba, and Brady (2012) included a chapter entitled "Does Unequal Voice Matter?" But while their avowed aim was to "assess whether inequalities of political voice make a difference," only four of the chapter's 30 pages (142–146) directly addressed the impact of participation on public policy.

[51] Atkinson (2015, 307). The most relevant evidence I know is from a field experiment conducted by Daniel Bergan (2009) in which constituents of undecided state legislators in New Hampshire were randomly encouraged to send emails advocating passage of a smoke-free workplace bill. The treatment produced an average of three emails per treated legislator (from districts with an average of 3,089 constituents). The emails apparently increased legislators' opposition to an effort to table the bill and increased their support for final passage. While these differences were not statistically significant by conventional standards, a more elaborate statistical analysis including a variety of other explanatory factors did reveal statistically significant differences in support for the bill between the treatment and control groups.

representatives are disciplined by a desire to get reelected. The flip side of that appealing idea, as V. O. Key Jr. observed, is that "politicians and officials are under no compulsion to pay much heed to classes and groups of citizens that do not vote."[52] While that may be true, it is by no means obvious that politicians *would* pay much heed to the views of the poor if they *did* vote. Figures 8.1 and 8.2 underline the wide latitude of elected officials to deviate from the preferences of their constituents—and the tendency of elected officials to exploit that latitude in the current environment of partisan polarization. It may be naive to put so much faith in the responsiveness of elected representatives to the preferences of voters—and unfair to push the blame for unresponsiveness, at least implicitly, onto poor non-voters.[53]

The relatively modest magnitude of observed disparities in turnout across income groups casts considerable doubt on the idea that politicians' lack of responsiveness to the poor is simply or primarily due to their failure to vote. For example, in the Census Bureau's Current Population Survey, self-reported turnout in the 2012 election ranged from 78% in the top income quintile (with family incomes over $100,000) down to 51% in the bottom quintile (with family incomes under $30,000). Even with considerable allowance for over-reporting of turnout, it is obvious that tens of millions of low-income citizens are showing up at the polls. Nevertheless, the views of low-income citizens as a group seem to be getting little or no weight in the policy-making process, whereas the views of affluent people are getting considerable weight. Income-related disparities in turnout are simply not large enough to provide a plausible explanation for the income-related disparities in responsiveness documented in this chapter.[54]

Of course, poor people are less engaged in the political process in other potentially relevant ways besides voting. Perhaps their views are ignored because they are less knowledgeable about politics; uninformed constituents

[52] Key (1949, 527). For the implications of this logic for disparities in the "voting power" of citizens, see Bartels (1998).

[53] Matthew Cleary (2010) provided a systematic test of the efficacy of electoral competition for producing governmental responsiveness in contemporary Mexico. He found that direct social pressure on local officials—not changes in electoral competition associated with the collapse of the 70-year electoral dominance of the ruling PRI party—accounted for significant improvements in municipal governments' responsiveness to citizens' needs (as measured by municipal provision of water and sanitation).

[54] U.S. Census Bureau, "Voting and Registration in the Election of November 2012," Report Number P20-568, May 2013, table 7 (https://www.census.gov/data/tables/2012/demo/voting -and-registration/p20-568.html). Leighley and Nagler (2013, 29) used data from the Census Bureau's Current Population Survey to assess differences in presidential election turnout by income group from 1972 through 2008. They found that turnout in the top income quintile averaged almost 80%, while turnout in the bottom income quintile averaged about 50%. Although the income gap between the top and bottom quintiles increased substantially over that period, differences in turnout between those groups may actually have narrowed slightly.

TABLE 8.6

Turnout, Political Knowledge, and Contact with Senators by Income Group

Mean (with standard error in parentheses) of turnout, political knowledge, and contact with senators in ANES Senate Election Study, by income group.

	All income groups	High income	Middle income	Low income
Turnout	.704	.823	.682	.620
	(.005)	(.007)	(.008)	(.010)
Political knowledge	.248	.349	.244	.163
	(.004)	(.007)	(.006)	(.006)
Contact with senators	.146	.201	.141	.100
	(.002)	(.005)	(.004)	(.004)
N	9,253	2,805	3,370	2,381

Source: ANES Senate Election Study surveys.

are less likely to have crystallized preferences on specific political issues and are less likely to be able to monitor their representatives' behavior.[55] Perhaps the views of poor people are ignored because they are less likely to communicate those views to elected officials; personal contact with elected officials and their staffs provides potentially important signals regarding both the content and intensity of constituents' political views.[56]

To test these possibilities, I used survey questions in the ANES Senate Election Study to measure inequalities in political knowledge[57] and contacting[58] as well as turnout. Not surprisingly, knowledge and contact with public officials, like turnout, were much more prevalent among affluent people than among poor people. Indeed, income-related differences in knowledge and contact were considerably larger, in proportional terms, than income-related differences in turnout: the average levels of knowledge and contacting among low-income respondents were only half the average levels among high-income respondents. These differences are summarized in table 8.6, which reports average levels of turnout, knowledge, and contact with elected

[55] Converse (1990); Delli Carpini and Keeter (1996).

[56] Verba, Schlozman, and Brady (1995).

[57] I constructed a four-point political knowledge scale measuring respondents' ability to name their senators (or Senate candidates) and identify which party they represented. The scale was recoded to range from zero (for people who recalled neither senator's name) to one (for people who recalled both senators' names and party affiliations).

[58] I measured contact using a six-point scale derived from respondents' reports of having met with senators or members of their staffs. The six-point scale was recoded to range from zero (for no reported contacts) to one (for having met both senators, talked to members of their staffs, and known family or friends who contacted them).

officials for the entire ANES Senate Election Study sample and for high-, middle-, and low-income respondents separately.

I used these measures of individual citizens' turnout, knowledge, and contacting behavior from the ANES Senate Election Study to construct resource-weighted measures of constituency opinion for each state. For example, turnout-weighted constituency opinion in each state reflects the ideological views of survey respondents in that state who reported voting in the most recent election, but ignores the views of those who said that they did not vote. Insofar as the views of voters differ from the views of non-voters, turnout-weighted constituency opinion should be expected to push senators in somewhat different directions than if they were responsive to overall constituency opinion.

These resource-weighted measures of constituency opinion make it possible to explore the bases of the disparities in responsiveness evident in table 8.3. If those disparities are attributable to differences between rich and poor constituents in turnout, information, or contacting, including direct measures of constituency preferences weighted by turnout, information, and contacting in my analyses should capture those effects. For example, if senators were more responsive to the views of affluent constituents because affluent constituents were more likely to vote, taking separate account of turnout-weighted constituency opinion should eliminate the disparities in responsiveness to different income groups. But if significant disparities in responsiveness to rich and poor constituents still appear even after allowing for differences attributable to turnout, the implication is that the effect of income works through mechanisms other than differential turnout—or perhaps that money matters in its own right (for example, through the responsiveness of elected officials to potential campaign contributors).

Table 8.7 presents the results of two parallel statistical analyses accounting for senators' roll call votes. The analysis reported in the first column of the table relates senators' votes to their partisanship and the preferences of low-, middle-, and high-income constituents; the analysis reported in the second column includes separate measures of turnout-weighted, knowledge-weighted, and contact-weighted constituency opinion as additional explanatory factors.[59] As it turns out, the only one of

---

[59] Since it is unclear how to incorporate turnout-weighted, knowledge-weighted, and contact-weighted constituency opinion in the non-linear model employed in tables 8.1, 8.2, and 8.3, the analyses reported in tables 8.7 and 8.8 follow Bhatti and Erikson (2011) in relating senators' votes to the opinions of constituents in each income group (weighted by their share of the population) and each group's population share (to allow for arbitrary offsets of the constituency opinion scale). Thus, the statistical results presented in the first column of table 8.7 parallel those presented in the first column of table 8.3, but with small differences (and somewhat less precision) in the estimated effects of constituency opinion owing to the more rough-and-ready model specification.

TABLE 8.7
Income, Political Resources, and Differential Responsiveness

Ordinary least squares regression coefficients (with standard errors in parentheses) for 101st–103rd Congress first-dimension w-NOMINATE scores clustered by state. Income group population shares included but not shown.

	(1)	(2)
Low-income constituency opinion	.10 (.80)	.10 (1.21)
Middle-income constituency opinion	2.21 (.95)	1.38 (1.37)
High-income constituency opinion	3.69 (1.42)	2.26 (2.23)
Turnout-weighted constituency opinion	—	–.05 (.81)
Knowledge-weighted constituency opinion	—	–.64 (.51)
Contact-weighted constituency opinion	—	1.13 (.36)
Republican senator	.62 (.03)	.63 (.03)
Intercept	Congress-specific intercepts	
Standard error of regression	.135	.131
Adjusted R²	.85	.86
N	304	304
High- vs. low-income responsiveness gap	3.59 (1.66)	2.16 (1.60)

Sources: Voteview.com; ANES Senate Election Study surveys.

these three resources that seems to have generated increased responsiveness from senators is direct contact with the senators or members of their staffs. The magnitude of the estimated effect suggests that each reported contact with a senator or his or her staff increased the weight attached to the contacting constituent's views by about 15% of the original estimated gap between high- and low-income respondents.[60] Neither turnout nor

[60] The average constituent in the ANES Senate Election Study reported about one contact (for an average score of .15 on the 0-to-1 contact scale); most reported none at all.

political knowledge seems to have increased the impact of constituents' views on their senators' roll call votes.[61]

Significant disparities in responsiveness to affluent and poor constituents still appear in the second column of table 8.7, even after allowing for differences attributable to turnout, knowledge, and contacting. Taking direct account of these differences in political resources and participation reduces the apparent gap in political influence between affluent and poor constituents by about 40% (comparing the estimated gaps in the first and second columns), but the remaining gap is still substantial in magnitude.

Table 8.8 reports the results of two additional analyses focusing on specific salient roll call votes rather than overall voting patterns.[62] On these salient votes (on raising the minimum wage, banning discrimination in employment, and transferring money from defense to domestic programs), contact-weighted constituency opinion again had a substantial impact on senators' votes, accounting for about one-third of the gap in influence between high- and low-income constituents. (Turnout and political knowledge again seemed to do nothing to bolster responsiveness to constituents' views.)

Taken together, the analyses presented in tables 8.7 and 8.8 provide some evidence that direct contact with elected officials may significantly bolster citizens' political influence, but surprisingly little evidence that turnout or political knowledge make any difference at all. Moreover, in each case the estimated disparity in responsiveness to affluent and poor constituents remains substantial even with three additional measures of constituency opinion included in the analysis. Thus, these analyses suggest that the biases I have identified in senators' responsiveness to affluent and poor constituents are *not* primarily due to differences between affluent and poor constituents in turnout, political knowledge, or direct contact with elected officials.

Perhaps, then, the disproportional influence of affluent constituents reflects their disproportional propensity to contribute money to political campaigns. Although the ANES Senate Election Study did not include questions

---

[61] The apparent non-effect of turnout-weighted opinion in table 8.7 contrasts with John Griffin and Brian Newman's (2005) finding that voters are better represented than non-voters. However, their analysis did not take account of the income-based disparities in responsiveness considered here or of alternative resource-based explanations for differential responsiveness. Simplifying my analysis to parallel theirs—replacing the separate opinion measures for high-, middle-, and low-income constituents with a single measure of undifferentiated constituency opinion and including turnout-weighted opinion but not contact-weighted opinion or knowledge-weighted opinion measures—generally produces positive and statistically significant coefficients on turnout-weighted opinion. The fact that these apparent effects disappear when we differentiate the views of high-, middle-, and low-income constituents suggests that voters probably get more representation because they are affluent, not because they vote.

[62] For more detailed information regarding these roll call votes and the analysis presented here, see Bartels (2008, 262–267).

TABLE 8.8
Income, Political Resources, and Differential
Responsiveness on Salient Roll Call Votes

Rescaled probit coefficients (with standard errors in parentheses) for conservative positions on minimum wage, civil rights, budget waiver, and budget cloture votes clustered by state. Income group population shares included but not shown.

	(1)	*(2)*
Low-income constituency opinion	–2.44	–1.65
	(3.27)	(3.30)
Middle-income constituency opinion	8.80	6.85
	(3.27)	(3.78)
High-income constituency opinion	11.31	7.53
	(5.70)	(6.13)
Turnout-weighted constituency opinion	—	–.29
		(2.58)
Knowledge-weighted constituency opinion	—	–1.68
		(1.08)
Contact-weighted constituency opinion	—	2.79
		(1.17)
Republican senator	1.00	1.00
	(.15)	(.14)
Intercept	Roll-call specific intercepts	
σ	.342	.332
Log likelihood	–120.8	–116.6
Pseudo-R²	.56	.58
N	396	396
High- versus low-income responsiveness gap	13.75	9.18
	(6.78)	(5.40)

Sources: Senate Legislative Information System; ANES Senate Election Study surveys.

on political giving, a contemporaneous survey focusing in detail on various forms of political participation provides the data necessary for a very rough test of that hypothesis. Verba, Schlozman, and Brady noted that almost three-fourths of the total value of campaign contributions reported in their survey came from people in the top quartile of the income distribution (with 1989 family incomes exceeding $50,000). People in the broad middle of the income distribution (with family incomes between $15,000 and $50,000) accounted for almost all of the rest; people in the bottom quintile (with family incomes below $15,000) accounted for only 2% of total campaign contributions.[63]

These figures suggest that if elected officials *only* responded to campaign contributions, they would attach about six times as much importance to the views of a typical affluent constituent as to the views of a typical middle-income constituent—and virtually no importance to the views of low-income constituents. The disparities in responsiveness documented in this chapter are generally consistent with the latter implication: averaging the results presented in tables 8.1, 8.2, and 8.3 suggests that senators, at least, attached little or no weight to the preferences of low-income constituents. However, middle-income constituents seem to have garnered almost half as much responsiveness as affluent constituents (more from Democrats, less from Republicans)—a good deal more than could be accounted for on the basis of their share of campaign contributions. Thus, while campaign contributions almost certainly account for part of the differential responsiveness documented here, they are probably not the primary source of political inequality in the American political system.

It is important to reiterate here that I have been using the term *responsiveness* loosely to refer to the statistical association between constituents' opinions and their legislators' behavior. Whether legislators behave the way they do *because* their constituents have the opinions they do is impossible to ascertain definitively using the data and research design employed here. It is certainly plausible to suppose that legislators consciously and intentionally strive to represent the views of (especially) affluent constituents, whether for electoral or other reasons. It is equally plausible to suppose that the consistent correlation between affluent opinion and the choices of policy-makers arises in significant part from unconscious affinity reflecting shared backgrounds, worldviews, and social networks. The fact that most policy-makers are themselves affluent, and in many cases extremely wealthy, hardly seems irrelevant for understanding the strong empirical connection between their choices and the preferences of affluent citizens.[64]

As Nicholas Carnes has noted, "Whether our political process listens to one voice or another depends not just on who's doing the talking or how loud they are; it also depends on who's doing the *listening*." In particular,

---

[63] Verba, Schlozman, and Brady (1995, 194, 565).

[64] The Senate's financial disclosure forms do not allow for precise estimates of senators' overall financial status, much less their economic backgrounds. However, CNN reported on the basis of 2003 disclosure forms that "at least 40" members of that year's Senate were millionaires. Sean Loughlin and Robert Yoon, "Millionaires Populate U.S. Senate," CNN, June 13, 2003 (http://www.cnn.com/2003/ALLPOLITICS/06/13/senators.finances). A subsequent tabulation by the Center for Responsive Politics found that 44% of the members of Congress (Senate and House) in 2008 were millionaires. Brian Montopoli, "237 Millionaires in Congress," CBS News, November 6, 2009 (http://www.cbsnews.com/news/237-millionaires-in-congress/).

Carnes demonstrated that working-class people are virtually absent from the corridors of political power in America, and that their absence is highly consequential for economic policy-making. In 2000, 54% of the American workforce was in blue-collar jobs, but only 2% of members of Congress (and no Supreme Court justices or postwar presidents, and few members of state legislatures) came to politics from blue-collar jobs. Of the 783 members of Congress who served from 1999 to 2008, only 46 (6%) spent any time at all in blue-collar jobs, and only 13 (less than 2%) spent as much as one-fourth of their pre-political working lives in blue-collar jobs. Nor is this disparity new. According to Carnes, "working-class Americans—who have made up more than 50 percent of the labor force for at least the last hundred years—have never made up more than 2 percent of Congress."[65]

Carnes found that "lawmakers from different classes tend to think, vote, and advocate differently on economic issues." Thus, the numerical under-representation of the working class in Congress "skews economic policy making toward outcomes more in line with what more privileged Americans want." Members from working-class backgrounds focused more of their legislative effort on bills dealing with labor, employment, and economics. They sponsored more progressive economic legislation (as gauged by the partisan composition of voting coalitions). They were much more likely to think about lower-class constituents—and less likely to think about business interests—when casting their votes. And they were more likely to support progressive economic and social welfare legislation.[66]

"Even when high-stakes economic legislation is on the line," Carnes observed, "lawmakers from different classes think and vote differently." For example, the 2001 Bush tax cuts almost certainly owed their passage to class bias in the makeup of Congress; even after controlling statistically for a plethora of individual and district characteristics, Carnes estimated that simply reweighting Congress to reflect the proportion of working-class people in the population would have reduced congressional support for Bush's tax bill from 62% to just 28%. Overall, six of the 15 most important economic acts of Congress in the period Carnes studied—including the 2008 Wall Street bailout, two separate packages of corporate tax breaks, a bill limiting business liability for computer malfunctions, and a bill opening millions of acres in the Gulf of Mexico for oil and gas drilling—probably hinged on the over-representation of white-collar professionals in Congress.[67]

There is clearly a great deal more to be learned about the mechanisms by which economic inequality gets reproduced in the political realm. In the

---

[65] Carnes (2013, 10, 20, 7).

[66] Ibid., 3, 74–75, 72, 101, 94.

[67] Ibid., 118–119. Ironically, the effects of class bias on these and other bills were often quite uncertain because there were too few working-class people in Congress to reliably discern how their backgrounds influenced their votes, net of other factors.

meantime, however, my analyses provide remarkably little support for the simple assumption that the rich are more influential than the poor because they are more likely to vote. The notion that they are more influential because they are better informed about politics and government fares equally poorly. There is some significant (though not entirely consistent) evidence suggesting that part of the apparent influence of affluent citizens is attributable to direct contact with government officials, but that is far from being the whole story. The even simpler assumption that affluent people are more influential than the poor because they provide the lion's share of the money fueling contemporary campaigns and lobbying activities is roughly consistent with much of the evidence presented in this chapter, but political scientists have provided little direct evidence connecting political giving and political clout, and in any case, campaign contributions also seem to be far from the whole story.[68]

Whatever their basis, the disparities in responsiveness documented here are impressive in their magnitude and consistency. The fact that scores of millions of poor Americans have *no* apparent influence on the roll call votes cast by U.S. senators or, more broadly, on the fate of proposed policy changes must be profoundly troubling to anyone who accepts Dahl's stipulation that "a key characteristic of a democracy is the continued responsiveness of the government to the preferences of its citizens, considered as political equals."[69]

Some scholars have argued that these disparities in responsiveness may be of little practical consequence because affluent, middle-class, and poor people agree on many political issues. However, that argument misses the fact that unequal responsiveness is likely to produce significant skews in policy outcomes in a variety of important areas where the preferences of affluent, middle-class, and poor people do diverge markedly. For example, Gilens found substantial disagreements between affluent and poor people on issues ranging from increasing unemployment benefits to cutting public works spending to stem cell research to building the MX missile. The disagreements between wealthy people and ordinary Americans documented in table 8.5 are even more ubiquitous and larger in magnitude. In any case, settling for what Gilens and Page referred to as "democracy by coincidence"— ordinary citizens getting their way "only when they happen to agree with elites or interest groups that are really calling the shots"—seems profoundly troubling from the standpoint of the egalitarian procedural values emphasized by Dahl and many other democratic theorists.[70]

<hr />

[68] Hall and Wayman (1990); Ansolabehere, de Figueiredo, and Snyder (2003).

[69] Dahl (1971, 1).

[70] Soroka and Wlezien (2008); Gilens (2009); Gilens (2012, chap. 4); Gilens and Page (2014, 573).

Do these results imply that it is fruitless for poor people to participate in the political process? Not necessarily. Although the evidence presented in this chapter suggests that their views do not have much *direct* impact on the behavior of their elected officials, whether or not they participate, it also underscores the powerful *indirect* effect of public opinion through the electoral process. In every analysis presented here, the differences in voting behavior between Democratic and Republican legislators representing similar constituents were substantial, consistently dwarfing the differences among Democrats (or Republicans) representing constituents with very different political views. Thus, whenever the votes of those poor people who do turn out to vote make the difference between electing a Democratic senator or a Republican, they will clearly be enormously consequential for the course of public policy, despite the fact that their views seem to have rather little *direct* effect on the behavior of Democratic or (especially) Republican officials after they get elected.

On the other hand, affluent citizens can significantly influence the behavior of elected officials both directly and indirectly. While their choices at the polls affect partisan control of the White House and Congress, their political views also seem to have a considerable direct impact on the day-to-day policy choices of their representatives. That impact is a testament to the ubiquitous sway of economic inequality in the American political system.

CHAPTER 9

Stress Test

The Political Economy of the Great Recession

THE WALL STREET meltdown of 2008 and the Great Recession that followed constituted the gravest global economic calamity since the Great Depression. In a best-selling memoir, former treasury secretary Timothy Geithner aptly described the financial crisis as "a stress test of the American political system, an extreme real-time challenge of a democracy's ability to lead the world when the world needed creative, decisive, politically unpalatable action."[1]

What did this "stress test" reveal about the characteristics of the American political system? For both better and worse, much of what happened was surprisingly consistent with the patterns of politics and policy-making described in the preceding chapters of this book and in the broader political science literature. Politicians continued to be driven in significant part by their own ideological convictions; the distinctive views of affluent citizens and powerful economic interests continued to seep into the policy-making process in ways that the policy-makers themselves may not have fully grasped; and ordinary citizens responded with cautious pragmatism and a single-minded focus on their own concrete well-being.

As one might expect based on my analysis of partisan differences in policy aims and priorities in chapters 2, 5, 6, and 7, Democratic and Republican elites took sharply divergent stands on most of the specific policy issues raised by the crisis, including the magnitude and composition of an economic stimulus package, extensions of food stamps, unemployment insurance, and other safety net programs, the use of government funds to bail out struggling auto companies, the possibility of a payroll tax cut, and the question of what (if anything) to do about an escalating federal budget deficit. The partisan conflict extended to many other areas less obviously related to the crisis, such as health care reform, energy policy, and immigration. In

---

[1] Geithner (2014, 19). The literature describing, explaining, and assessing the Great Recession is enormous. See, for example, Scheiber (2011), Blinder (2013a), Irwin (2013), and Eichengreen (2015).

all these cases, Democrats generally supported and Republicans consistently opposed policies that were likely to shore up the incomes and economic security of middle-class and poor people.

The partisan political dynamic was nicely encapsulated in a pair of impolitic comments made by two of the most powerful figures in Washington. The first came less than a week after the 2008 election, when President Obama's incoming chief of staff, Rahm Emanuel, went on a Sunday morning television talk show to lay out the president-elect's ambitious agenda. "Rule one," Emanuel pronounced: "Never allow a crisis to go to waste. They are opportunities to do big things."[2] Conservatives fastened on Emanuel's remark as evidence that the new administration would exploit the crisis to pursue what the *Wall Street Journal* editorial page referred to as a "40-year wish list" of liberal policy proposals.[3]

The mirror image of Emanuel's rather-too-transparent eagerness to leverage the economic crisis to "do big things" came a few weeks before the 2010 midterm election, when Senate Minority Leader Mitch McConnell told an interviewer that "the single most important thing we [Republicans] want to achieve is for President Obama to be a one-term president." As with Emanuel's policy aspiration, McConnell's electoral aspiration was hardly shocking. (One journalist sarcastically referred to it as "Fall-off-your-chair political surprise No. 1," and the White House's indignant response as "Fall-off-your-chair political surprise No. 2.") Nonetheless, Democrats seized the opportunity "to portray Mr. McConnell's remark as the latest example of a Republican Party more committed to obstructing the president's agenda" than to "governing the country."[4]

The fact of the matter is that Emanuel's boss did "do big things," including some that were only tangentially related to the economic crisis. On the other hand, while McConnell and his Republican allies did not succeed in making Obama a one-term president, they did have considerable success in "obstructing the president's agenda," significantly limiting the scope of his policy accomplishments. In both respects, the politics of the Great Recession clearly reflects the partisan ideologies—and the considerable freedom to pursue those ideologies—evident throughout this book.

Where was the public in this ideological clash? In the wake of the 2008 Wall Street meltdown, pundits from across the ideological spectrum seemed to be in considerable agreement regarding the likely political ramifications

---

[2] Jeff Zeleny, "Obama Weighs Quick Undoing of Bush Policy," *New York Times*, November 9, 2008.

[3] "A 40-Year Wish List: You Won't Believe What's in That Stimulus Bill," *Wall Street Journal*, January 28, 2009.

[4] David M. Herszenhorn, "Hold On to Your Seat: McConnell Wants Obama Out," *New York Times*, October 26, 2010.

of the economic crisis. On the right, a *Wall Street Journal* editorial just a month after the collapse of Lehman Brothers worried that "the current financial panic" might provide a "pretext" for "a period of unchecked left-wing ascendancy" comparable to past "heydays of welfare-state liberalism." On the left, Robert Kuttner had already published a book premised on the notion that the economic crisis offered Barack Obama an opportunity to be "a transformative progressive president." Obama's subsequent election impelled John Judis to posit that "liberal views have re-emerged . . . with a vengeance, and can be expected to shift further leftward—especially on economic questions—in the face of coming recession."[5]

Of course, nothing of the sort actually happened. Public opinion moved—insofar as it moved at all—to the right, not to the left.[6] The public's reaction to the crisis and to the Obama administration's response was one of skeptical pragmatism. On one hand, the slow pace of recovery created significant public resistance to the president's policy initiatives; the counterfactual argument that these policies were preventing a much worse economic slump seemed to have little political traction. On the other hand, the perception that Obama and Democrats in Congress were pushing to "do big things" in a remarkable variety of policy domains provoked a reaction familiar to scholars of public opinion: slow down! The primary manifestation of mass political mobilization in response to the recession, the Tea Party movement, harnessed right-wing populism in opposition to big government, bailouts, high taxes, and public debt. The 2010 midterm election proved to be an electoral debacle, decimating Obama's Democratic base in Congress and further constraining attempts to legislate an end to the Great Recession.

Should any or all of this have been surprising? Certainly there were mixed signals before the crisis regarding the likely response of the American public to aggressive policy action. A 2006 survey of views about the "Role of Government" found substantial public support on the eve of the Great Recession for two key "things the government might do for the economy."[7] On one hand, the respondents favored "cuts in government spending" by

---

[5] "A Liberal Supermajority," *Wall Street Journal*, October 17, 2008; Kuttner (2008, 1); John B. Judis, "America the Liberal," *The New Republic*, November 19, 2008.

[6] An accumulation of dozens of Gallup polls showed conservatives outnumbering liberals in the U.S. public by 19 points in 2009, up from 15 points in 2008—and that margin remained undiminished through 2010 and 2011; Lydia Saad, "Conservatives Remain the Largest Ideological Group in U.S.," *Gallup Politics*, January 12, 2012 (http://www.gallup.com/poll/152021/conservatives-remain-largest-ideological-group.aspx). Alternative measures of public opinion considered later in this chapter likewise registered a conservative shift over the course of Obama's first term.

[7] The 2006 Role of Government survey (the fourth in a series dating back to the mid-1980s) was conducted in more than 20 countries as part of the International Social Survey Programme (http://www.issp.org/). In the United States, the questions were asked as part of the General Social Survey, a long-running national study of social attitudes.

an overwhelming margin of 63% to 13%.[8] On the other hand, the same people favored "government financing of projects to create new jobs" by an even more overwhelming margin of 85% to 7%.[9]

To economists and policy-makers, "government financing of projects to create new jobs" and "cuts in government spending" may seem like very different—even contradictory—approaches to macroeconomic policy-making, but these ordinary citizens happily (and simultaneously) embraced both stimulus spending and austerity. This apparent contradiction is compounded by responses to another battery of questions in the same survey, which asked about spending on a variety of specific government programs. The same people who overwhelmingly favored "cuts in government spending" also, just a few minutes later, overwhelmingly favored increases in spending on the big-ticket social programs that account for most of the federal government's budget, including health (by a margin of 80% to 6%), education (84% to 4%), and retirement (65% to 7%).[10]

To complicate the picture still further, overwhelming public support for social spending coexisted with rather limited support for direct government action in the realm of economic redistribution. Additional questions in the same survey asked whether it should be the government's responsibility "to reduce income differences between the rich and the poor" and "to provide a job for everyone who wants one."[11] These propositions referring specifically to "the government's responsibility" generated much less support than the social spending questions, with the public as a whole favoring income redistribution by a razor-thin margin of 51% to 49% and opposing government provision of jobs by a margin of 60% to 40%.

---

[8] "Cuts in government spending." Strongly favor, 26.9%; favor, 35.8%; neither in favor nor against, 23.9%; against, 9.3%; strongly against, 4.0%.

[9] "Government financing of projects to create new jobs." Strongly favor, 40.4%; favor, 44.9%; neither in favor nor against, 8.0%; against, 4.6%; strongly against, 2.1%.

[10] "Listed below are various areas of government spending. Please show whether you would like to see more or less government spending in each area. Remember that if you say 'much more,' it might require a tax increase to pay for it." Health: Spend much more, 36.1%; spend more, 44.4%; spend the same as now, 13.6%; spend less, 4.6%; spend much less, 1.3%. Education: Spend much more, 41.2%; spend more, 42.4%; spend the same as now, 12.6%; spend less, 3.0%; spend much less, 0.8%. Retirement: Spend much more, 24.2%; spend more, 41.0%; spend the same as now, 27.6%; spend less, 5.6%; spend much less, 1.7%. Unemployment benefits: Spend much more, 10.5%; spend more, 25.1%; spend the same as now, 49.6%; spend less, 12.8%; spend much less, 2.1%.

[11] "On the whole, do you think it should be or should not be the government's responsibility to reduce income differences between the rich and poor?" Definitely should be, 27.2%; probably should be, 23.8%; probably should not be, 25.8%; definitely should not be, 23.2%. "On the whole, do you think it should be or should not be the government's responsibility to provide a job for everyone who wants one?" Definitely should be, 16.0%; probably should be, 23.7%; probably should not be, 34.1%; definitely should not be, 26.2%.

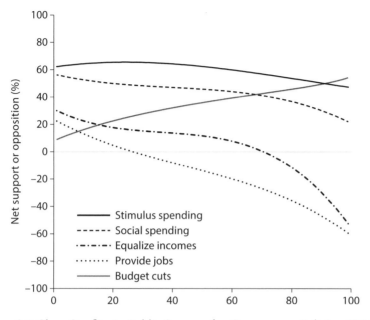

FIGURE 9.1 Class Conflict in Public Support for Government Policies, 2006

How would a government in the midst of a major economic crisis respond to these complex and apparently contradictory public impulses? The
analyses presented thus far in this book suggest that it wouldn't respond
much at all—that politicians would mostly be guided by their own ideological convictions rather than by what the public *said* it wanted. However, to
the extent that public opinion did matter, the evidence presented in chapter
8 suggests that the opinions of affluent people would matter much more
than the opinions of middle-class and poor people. From that perspective,
proponents of doing big things ought to have been chastened by the fact
that, on every one of these questions, the views of affluent people differed
significantly from those of middle-class and poor people. These differences
appear in figure 9.1, which summarizes the views of Americans across the
income distribution regarding each of these policies.[12]

Public support for government spending on "projects to create new jobs"
and on major social programs was high across the board, but tempered
significantly at the top of the income distribution. Meanwhile, net support
for "cuts in government spending" was very modest among poor people
but overwhelming among affluent people. Thus, in a confrontation between

[12] In the case of social spending, I constructed a scale reflecting the average level of net
support for four specific programs: health, education, retirement, and unemployment benefits.

fiscal stimulus and austerity—precisely the policy confrontation that dominated American politics in the wake of the Great Recession—political responsiveness to affluent citizens would tilt the balance substantially away from the preferences of the public as a whole. The views of affluent Americans were even more distinctive regarding the government's responsibility to provide jobs and equalize incomes. Whereas poor people were moderately supportive of government action in these areas and middle-class people were roughly evenly divided, the most affluent Americans were about as strongly *opposed* to government efforts to provide jobs and equalize incomes as they were *supportive* of government budget cuts.

Perhaps surprisingly, these class conflicts in views about government and the welfare state were a good deal more intense in the United States than in other affluent democracies on the eve of the Great Recession. In the case of views about budget-cutting, the U.S. income gradient in figure 9.1 spanned 46 points on the –100 to +100 scale (from +8 at the bottom of the income distribution to +54 at the top), while the income gradient in other affluent democracies was essentially flat (ranging from +29 at the bottom of the income distribution to just +32 at the top). The income gradient in net support for social spending spanned 36 points in the United States but only 14 points in other affluent democracies. Support for welfare state effort (equalizing incomes and providing jobs) varied by a remarkable 86 points in the United States, compared to 57 points in other affluent democracies. Thus, as governments around the world faced the momentous choice between spending and austerity in the wake of the Great Recession, the disparate responsiveness of policy-makers to the views of affluent and poor citizens documented in chapter 8 would have much greater substantive policy consequences in the United States than in other affluent democracies.[13]

The 2008 Election and "the New New Deal"

The 2008 election was conducted in the lengthening shadow of the Great Recession. According to economists charged with dating business cycle expansions and contractions, the downturn began in December 2007.[14] Eco-

---

[13] For related discussions, see Bartels, "U.S. Is a World Leader in Class Conflict over Government Spending," *The Monkey Cage*, April 21, 2014. The collection of "other affluent democracies" in this comparison includes the 16 countries in the ISSP's fourth (mid-2000s) Role of Government module with per capita incomes of $30,000 or more—Australia, Canada, Denmark, Finland, France, Germany, Great Britain, Ireland, Israel, Japan, the Netherlands, New Zealand, Norway, Spain, Sweden, and Switzerland.

[14] According to the National Bureau of Economic Research (NBER) Business Cycle Dating Committee, "U.S. Business Cycle Expansions and Contractions" (http://www.nber.org/cycles .html), "a recession is a significant decline in economic activity spread across the economy,

nomic conditions continued to deteriorate over the course of the election year; real GDP per capita fell by 3.7% between the fourth quarter of 2007 and the fourth quarter of 2008.

The collapse of the venerable investment bank Lehman Brothers in the early weeks of the general election campaign marked the beginning of a new, even more virulent phase of the accelerating economic crisis. However, it was probably neither necessary nor sufficient to account for the 2008 election outcome. As political scientist Alan Abramowitz observed, "support for the Republican ticket [in daily tracking polls] began to decline within a few days after the conclusion of the Republican Convention and well before the onset of the financial crisis in mid-September. . . . For ordinary Americans, the Wall Street meltdown was not a turning point, but rather one more sign of the dire condition of the economy and the failure of the Bush Administration's policies."[15]

Perhaps voters were unmoved by the financial meltdown because, even after the collapse of Lehman Brothers, they still did not seem to grasp the likelihood of a prolonged recession, much less the possibility of a full-scale global depression. The American National Election Studies survey conducted between Labor Day and Election Day found 90% of the public saying that the national economy had gotten worse over the past year—but only 30% predicting that it would get worse over the coming year, while 27% expected it to get better.[16]

In any event, the outcome of the election was, in most respects, quite consistent with familiar American electoral patterns. Some prominent liberal pundits viewed Obama's victory as the dawning of a "New Liberal Order" and "the culmination of a Democratic realignment that began in the 1990s."[17] However, sober analysts immediately pointed out that the pundits' talk of realignment was "much-overblown." As we saw in chapter 3, Obama did about as well as might have been expected given economic and political conditions at the time of the election. The aggregate national vote swing from 2004 to 2008 was no larger than has been typical in presidential

---

lasting more than a few months, normally visible in real GDP, real income, employment, industrial production, and wholesale-retail sales."

[15] Alan I. Abramowitz, "Did the Wall Street Meltdown Change the Election?" *Sabato's Crystal Ball*, February 5, 2009. Larry Bartels, "Obama Toes the Line," *The Monkey Cage*, January 8, 2013.

[16] Expectations were virtually identical among the subset of respondents interviewed in the last 30 days of the campaign, two to six weeks after the collapse of Lehman Brothers: 28% expected the economy to get worse over the next year, while 27% expected it to get better. Author's tabulations based on data from the ANES 2008 Time Series Study (http://www.electionstudies.org/).

[17] Peter Beinart, "The New Liberal Order," *Time*, November 13, 2008; John B. Judis, "America the Liberal," *The New Republic*, November 19, 2008.

elections over the past 30 years—and only about one-third as large as the electoral tide that swept Franklin Roosevelt into the White House in 1932. Nor was there a greater-than-usual amount of "realigning" of specific states or regions or a greater-than-usual erosion of previous partisan voting patterns. While the *social* significance of Obama's victory was obvious, from an *electoral* standpoint the outcome was not at all remarkable.[18]

Nevertheless, Obama's historic election in the midst of an economic crisis suggested irresistible parallels with the dramatic accession of Roosevelt in the midst of the Great Depression. The cover of *Time* magazine pictured Obama as FDR, complete with iconic fedora, cigarette holder, and an evocative title: "The *New* New Deal." A cover story by Peter Beinart argued that if Obama "can do what FDR did—make American capitalism stabler and less savage—he will establish a Democratic majority that dominates U.S. politics for a generation. And despite the daunting problems he inherits, he's got an excellent chance."[19]

Notwithstanding the ubiquity of this historical parallel, the comparison between Obama and FDR was always highly fanciful. For one thing, as political scientist Theda Skocpol noted, "Roosevelt took office several years into the Great Depression, when the U.S. economy was at a nadir," whereas "Obama took office amid a sudden financial seizure that was just beginning to push the national economy into a downturn of as-yet-undetermined proportions." The timing of the unfolding crisis was politically inauspicious for the new administration because, no matter the policy response, ordinary Americans would still be absorbing the pain of the downturn through much of Obama's first term. As some of his aides put it, "The tidal wave was in motion, but it hadn't hit the shore." Indeed, while Obama's economic advisers recognized that the economy "was hurtling toward a depression," it turned out that even they greatly underestimated the actual magnitude of the economic shock.[20]

For another thing, Roosevelt's 1932 landslide swept into office substantial Democratic majorities in the House and Senate, whereas Obama began his first term with just 58 Democratic senators. And even before Obama was inaugurated, Senate Minority Leader Mitch McConnell rallied his caucus around a plan to "deny Democrats any Republican support on big legislation." In an era of pronounced partisan polarization, and with the filibuster having evolved "from an extraordinary expression into a routine

---

[18] John Sides, "Truths and Myths About the 2008 Election," *The Monkey Cage*, November 5–6, 2008; Larry M. Bartels, "Election Debriefing," *CSDP Election 2008 Blog*, November 6, 2008.

[19] Beinart, "The New Liberal Order."

[20] Skocpol (2012, 15); Grunwald (2012, 105, 113). On the depth and duration of previous economic downturns stemming from financial crises, see Reinhart and Rogoff (2009).

obstructive tactic," a disciplined Republican opposition would be able to defeat or dilute any bill the president was likely to propose.[21]

In light of these political realities, the problems that Obama inherited were indeed daunting. According to economist Alan Blinder,

> The new president had to lead the economy out of the deepest recession since the 1930s—presumably with a big fiscal stimulus package. . . . He also had to, first, apply multiple tourniquets to the bleeding financial system, and then nurse it back to health—using whatever was left of the hated TARP [Troubled Asset Relief Program], among other things. While doing so, he had to combat the coming tsunami of home mortgage foreclosures, which would otherwise throw millions of American families out of their homes. Then he almost certainly had to develop and propose sweeping reforms of the financial regulatory system, which had failed the nation badly, with horrific consequences. And he needed a plan for either bailing out the Big Three automakers or limiting the fallout from their demise.[22]

Obama's administration moved swiftly on most of these fronts. Only a few weeks after his inauguration, Congress passed a massive $787 billion stimulus bill, the American Recovery and Reinvestment Act, providing new federal spending on infrastructure and other programs, tax cuts, and grants to state governments. As journalist Michael Grunwald put it, the Recovery Act "was a real-time test of a new administration's ability to spend tax dollars quickly, honestly, and effectively—and to reshape the country in the process." Grunwald called it "the biggest and most transformative energy bill in U.S. history," "the biggest and most transformative education reform bill since the Great Society," "America's biggest foray into industrial policy since FDR, biggest expansion of antipoverty initiatives since Lyndon Johnson, biggest middle-class tax cut since Ronald Reagan, and biggest infusion of research money ever." He quoted one adviser to Obama and Bill Clinton saying, "We probably did more in that one bill than the Clinton administration did in eight years."[23]

Meanwhile, the existing Troubled Asset Relief Program was deployed to recapitalize banks through a Capital Purchase Program, subsidize private

---

[21] Carl Hulse and Adam Nagourney, "Senate G.O.P. Leader Finds Weapon in Unity," *New York Times*, March 16, 2010; Skocpol (2012), 26. Arlen Specter (R-PA) joined the Democratic caucus in late April, and Al Franken (D-MN) was seated in early July when a court finally upheld his disputed razor-thin election margin. Those additions gave Obama a short-lived "filibuster-proof" majority (including independents Joseph Lieberman and Bernie Sanders, who caucused with the Democrats) until Republican Scott Brown was elected to replace the deceased Edward Kennedy (D-MA) the following February.

[22] Blinder (2013a, 218).

[23] Grunwald (2012, 18, 10–11).

investment in the "toxic assets" of financial institutions, fund bailouts of General Motors and Chrysler, and provide grants to reduce the rate of home mortgage foreclosures. The Treasury Department also devised a series of "stress tests" to certify the financial health of major banks, and work began on a major overhaul of financial regulations—an effort that would lead, a year later, to the passage of the Dodd-Frank Wall Street Reform and Consumer Protection Act.

These major policy initiatives seemed to quell the economic turmoil. The rate of job losses began to ease up in March 2009, though the unemployment rate would continue to increase for several more months. After plummeting by almost 5% in the preceding three quarters, real GDP leveled off in the spring and began to increase in the summer. Nonetheless, the public was ambivalent, at best, about the policies themselves. A BBC World Service poll conducted in the summer of 2009 measured public support for three of the most salient policy responses to the economic crisis: "giving financial support to banks in trouble," "increasing government regulation and oversight of the national economy," and "significantly increasing government spending to stimulate the economy." As the results presented in the first column of table 9.1 make clear, none of these programs enjoyed strong public support. The balance of public opinion was slightly negative in the cases of increasing government regulation and stimulus spending, and strongly negative in the case of support for troubled banks. Of the five other affluent democracies included in the BBC survey—Australia, Canada, France, Germany, and the United Kingdom—only Germany showed a similar lack of public enthusiasm for all three of these policy options. These results underline the political pitfalls facing the Obama administration as it grappled with the Great Recession, especially in the period following the first months of acute economic crisis.[24]

As the severity of the crisis seemed to ebb, the administration began to turn its attention to other issues, including health care, energy, education, and financial reform. But as journalist John Harwood observed, the new president was "racing to capitalize" on his high popularity and initial legislative success "for good reason. Political history, and some early signs this spring, suggest that time is not on his side." A majority of the public, Harwood noted, had already begun to think that "Obama had taken on 'too many other issues' besides the economy."[25]

Much of the next year would be consumed by a sustained push for substantial reform of the U.S. health care system and the legislative wrangling

---

[24] BBC World Service poll, "Global Poll Shows Support for Increased Government Spending and Regulation," September 13, 2009 (http://www.globescan.com/news_archives/bbc2009 _globalPoll-04/).

[25] John Harwood, "Link to Economic Crisis Is Vital to Obama Agenda," *New York Times*, May 3, 2009.

TABLE 9.1

Public Support for Government Actions, 2009 and 2010

"In our current economic conditions, do you favor or oppose the [COUNTRY] government doing each of the following?" Net support ranges from +100 ("strongly favor") to –100 ("strongly oppose").

	United States		Other affluent democracies	
	2009	*2010*	*2009*	*2010*
Giving financial support to banks in trouble	–31	–42	–19	–38
Increasing government regulation and oversight of the national economy	–1	–18	+17	+19
Significantly increasing government spending to stimulate the economy	–6	–22	+10	–5
Taking steps to reduce the government's budget deficit and debt by cutting some spending or increasing some taxes	—	+14	—	+9

Source: BBC World Service poll, conducted by GlobeScan. The entries for "other affluent democracies" reflect averaged responses from Australia, Canada, France, Germany, and the United Kingdom.

that led to the passage in March 2010 of the landmark Patient Protection and Affordable Care Act—"the most sweeping piece of federal legislation since Medicare was passed in 1965," according to David Leonhardt's front-page story in the *New York Times*. The administration also pursued a far-reaching energy policy, comprehensive immigration reform, and other measures. As Skocpol put it, "Obama's ambitious agenda for policy change progressed quite remarkably—to institute comprehensive health reform, reform higher education loans, tighten regulation of financial institutions, and tweak many other realms of law and regulation. A new New Deal of sorts *was* successfully launched by President Obama and Congressional Democrats in 2009 and 2010."[26]

The partisan nature of this "new New Deal" is underlined by the pattern of congressional support and opposition to the Obama administration's major policy initiatives. The most important roll call votes in the House and

[26] David Leonhardt, "In Health Bill, Obama Attacks Wealth Inequality," *New York Times*, March 24, 2010; Skocpol (2012, 44).

TABLE 9.2
Congressional Support for Major Aspects of the
Obama Legislative Agenda, 2009 and 2010

Independents are grouped with their party caucuses.

	House		Senate	
	Democrats	*Republicans*	*Democrats*	*Republicans*
American Recovery and Reinvestment Act (conference)	246–7 February 13, 2009 (vote no. 70)	0–176	57–0 February 13, 2009 (vote no. 64)	3–38
Patient Protection and Affordable Care Act	219–34 March 21, 2010 (vote no. 165)	0–178	60–0 December 24, 2009 (vote no. 396)	0–39
Wall Street Reform and Consumer Protection Act (conference)	234–19 June 30, 2010 (vote no. 413)	3–173	57–1 July 15, 2010 (vote no. 208)	3–38
Immigration reform (DREAM Act)	208–38 December 8, 2010 (vote no. 625)	8–160	52–5 December 18, 2010 (vote no. 278)	3–36

Source: GovTrack.us.

Senate are summarized in table 9.2. In each case, the administration garnered strong support among Democrats but met with nearly unanimous opposition from Republicans in both chambers. Just three of 217 Republicans voted for the stimulus bill; *none* supported the Affordable Care Act; six voted for the Dodd-Frank financial regulations, and 11 for immigration reform. This opposition was partly strategic—as Senate Republican leader Mitch McConnell said of the health care fight, it was "absolutely critical that everybody be together because if the proponents of the bill were able to say it was bipartisan, it tended to convey to the public that this is O.K., they must have figured it out." But it was also "rooted in a principled belief that Mr. Obama is pushing the nation in the wrong direction," as one press account put it.[27]

Another striking feature of the roll call votes summarized in table 9.2 is how frequently the administration's key policy victories were achieved with a bare minimum of support in the Senate. Given the willingness of the minority to filibuster anything that moved, the simple fact was that a Democratic president could only be as liberal as the 60th-most-liberal senator

[27] Carl Hulse and Adam Nagourney, "Senate G.O.P. Leader Finds Weapon in Unity," *New York Times*, March 16, 2010.

allowed him to be.[28] It was seldom entirely clear in advance how liberal that would be, and in some cases—most notably in the areas of immigration and energy—major policy initiatives with majority support in both chambers of Congress were stymied by a failure to pull together the 60 votes needed to overcome a Senate filibuster. But when the administration and its allies did manage to construct a winning coalition, they did so without a single vote to spare. Obama's most significant legislative achievements—the economic stimulus bill, health care reform, and financial regulation—were each pushed precisely to the filibuster limit, overcoming key hurdles with exactly 60 votes in the Senate.

In each case, pivotal senators extracted significant concessions in exchange for their support. Winning a few Republican votes for the Recovery Act required substantially shrinking the size of the economic stimulus package and including hundreds of billions of dollars in tax cuts. Passing the Affordable Care Act required a completely unified Democratic caucus in the Senate, which in turn required months of haggling and the eventual jettisoning of the "public option" favored by most Democrats. Maine's Republican senators, Olympia Snowe and Susan Collins, who had bucked their party to support the stimulus bill, crossed over once again to support the White House's plan for financial regulation, but when a purist gesture by Democrat Russ Feingold of Wisconsin left the bill still one vote short, additional concessions were necessary to win a third Republican vote from newcomer Scott Brown.[29]

Politicians on both sides of the aisle were well aware that the public's taste for ambitious policy initiatives was limited. While a substantial majority of Democrats in Congress nonetheless supported most or all of Obama's major policy initiatives, the resulting string of significant legislative achievements had a significant political price tag attached—and the bill came due in the 2010 midterm election.

REACTION AND GRIDLOCK

Having punished Republicans for economic distress as the country slid into recession in 2008, American voters were equally willing to punish Democrats in 2010 for a slow economic recovery. In the first quarter of 2010, real disposable income per capita was still lower than it had been when President Obama was inaugurated a year earlier. The unemployment rate had increased by two full points, to 9.8%. At a Tea Party convention in Tennessee in February, conservative celebrity and former Republican vice presidential

---

[28] On the implications of the filibuster for law-making, see Krehbiel (1998).

[29] Grunwald (2012); Jacobs and Skocpol (2010); McCarty (2012); Kaiser (2013).

candidate Sarah Palin mockingly asked, "How's that hopey-changey thing working out for you?"[30]

In the summer of 2010, a follow-up to the BBC World Service poll conducted the preceding summer asked about the same three possible government responses to the crisis. The results are reported in the second column of table 9.1. Strikingly, the American public's support for all three policies was markedly lower in 2010 than it had been a year earlier. Having experienced bailouts, bank stress tests, and a seemingly massive stimulus program—and feeling little improvement in tangible economic conditions as a result—most Americans were in no mood for counterfactual arguments that these policies had "transformed what might have been an utter catastrophe into something that was merely awful."[31]

In a foreshadowing of the postcrisis political agenda, the 2010 BBC World Service poll included an additional policy option: "taking steps to reduce the government's budget deficit and debt, by cutting some spending or increasing some taxes." That option was distinctly more popular than any of the original three, with 52% of Americans favoring steps to reduce government deficit and debt (28% "strongly") and only 32% opposing (19% "strongly"). When asked *which* of two possible approaches to deficit reduction their government should "focus on more," the survey respondents overwhelmingly chose "cutting spending on government services, including ones you use" over "increasing taxes" (64% to 23%, with the rest choosing neither or both or something else).[32]

Forecasts of the 2010 midterm election outcome employing a variety of economic indicators, poll results, and other political considerations suggested that the incumbent party would probably lose 30 to 50 seats in the House.[33]

---

[30] Kate Zernike, "Palin in 2012? She Says Run Is Possible," *New York Times*, February 7, 2010.

[31] BBC World Service poll, "Governments Misspend More Than Half of Our Taxes—Global Poll," September 27, 2010 (http://www.globescan.com/news_archives/bbc2010_economics/); Blinder (2013a, 345). The decline in popular support for the most salient policy responses to the crisis was by no means limited to the United States; support for aiding troubled banks and increasing government spending declined from 2009 to 2010 in every one of the countries included in both surveys. The average decline in net support was 16 points for increasing government spending and 18 points for supporting troubled banks. Changes in support for increasing government regulation were more mixed, with big declines in Australia and the United States, but increases in Germany and France.

[32] It is tempting to interpret this public support for budget-cutting as a reflection of Americans' deep-seated suspicion (at least in the abstract) of big government. However, the public sentiment in favor of austerity seems to have been widely shared throughout the developed world. At least slight pluralities in all five of the other affluent democracies included in the survey favored deficit reduction measures, with cutting services always substantially more popular than increasing taxes.

[33] A roundup of nine different forecasts available several weeks before the 2010 midterm election suggested that Democrats would probably lose 30 to 50 seats; analyses incorporating

In fact, it turned out to be even worse than that: Democrats suffered a net loss of 63 seats, losing control of the chamber. The result was widely interpreted as an electoral repudiation of the policies of the Obama administration. New York's *Daily News* declared it "a stinging rebuke." In his election night victory speech, new Republican Speaker of the House John Boehner argued that the American people had sent an "unmistakable message" to the president to "change course" by cutting spending, reducing the size of government, and "helping small businesses get people back to work."[34]

Obama himself interpreted the election "shellacking" as primarily a reflection of economic frustration: "If right now we had 5 percent unemployment instead of 9.6 percent unemployment, then people would have more confidence in those policy choices." However, even he grudgingly conceded that voters might have perceived his administration's responses to the economic crisis as amounting to "a huge expansion of government." Indeed, by the fall of 2010 ordinary Americans were a good deal more likely to see Democrats and Obama as "very liberal" than they were to see Republicans as "very conservative." Thus, to the consternation of liberal pundits who had expected the Great Recession to shift the nation's politics to the left, voters punished Democrats for having pursued—and in several cases enacted—a liberal policy agenda extending well beyond what seemed relevant and necessary to the task of economic recovery.[35]

Statistical analyses of district-by-district midterm election results provided substantial evidence that public perceptions of ideological overreach contributed to the Democrats' midterm losses. Democratic incumbents who voted for the Recovery Act did two or three points worse than those who didn't. Supporting the Affordable Care Act probably cost a typical Democrat about five or six percentage points, and perhaps even more in swing districts. Some analyses suggested that supporting the abortive cap-and-trade energy bill and the Dodd-Frank financial reform bill may also have cost Democrats votes.[36]

---

poll results were generally more pessimistic than those relying solely on economic indicators and structural political factors such as the number of seats being defended by each party. John Sides, "Midterm Forecast Update," *The Monkey Cage*, September 12, 2010.

[34] Thomas M. DeFrank, "Midterm Election Results Show Voters Unhappy with President Obama's Leadership," *Daily News*, November 3, 2010; Kimberly Schwandt, "Boehner's Election Night Speech," *Fox News Politics*, November 2, 2010.

[35] "Press Conference by the President," November 3, 2010 (https://www.whitehouse.gov/the-press-office/2010/11/03/press-conference-president). A fall 2010 survey found 31% of the respondents rating Republicans as "very conservative"; 41% rated Democrats as "very liberal," and 43% rated Obama as "very liberal." Tabulations based on data from the ANES 2010 Panel Recontact Study (http://www.electionstudies.org/).

[36] Just a week after the election, Eric McGhee estimated that congressional Democrats who voted for the American Recovery and Reinvestment Act (ARRA) lost 2.8% of the vote, other things being equal, while those who voted for the Affordable Care Act (ACA) lost 4.5% and

The electoral rebuke of Democrats who supported the stimulus package was hardly surprising in light of widespread public skepticism about its economic effectiveness. *USA Today* reported that, "in the partisan war over the economy's performance, the word 'stimulus' has became [*sic*] synonymous with 'boondoggle,' making the notion of a repeat any time soon highly unlikely."[37] However, despite the unpopularity of the Recovery Act, the direct political cost to Democrats of supporting the package was almost surely more than offset by the indirect political benefit of more robust economic growth. If we suppose that the stimulus package added 1% to 1.5% to real GDP growth in 2009 and 2% or so in 2010, then economic conditions at the time of the midterm election were distinctly more favorable to the incumbent party as a result of the stimulus than they otherwise would have been. That additional GDP growth probably added two or three percentage points to the aggregate Democratic vote share in 2010.[38] Thus, the net result of direct punishment and indirect benefit was probably close to zero in districts where Democratic incumbents supported the stimulus bill, and a significant gain in districts held by Republicans or by Democrats (disproportionately in competitive seats) who did not support the bill.

If the Recovery Act very likely "paid for itself," even in strictly electoral terms, that was certainly not true of the Affordable Care Act, whose concrete benefits to prospective voters were both distant and uncertain. Simulations based on district-by-district analyses of the midterm vote suggested that if every vulnerable Democrat (those in districts where Obama received less than 60% of the two-party vote in 2008) had refrained from voting for health care reform, the party would have lost about 25 fewer seats in 2010,

---

those who voted for the cap-and-trade energy bill lost 2.1%; Eric McGhee, "Which Roll Call Votes Hurt the Democrats?" *The Monkey Cage*, November 9, 2010. A subsequent analysis by Brendan Nyhan and his colleagues (2012) put the effect of supporting the ARRA at 1.7%, the cost of supporting the ACA at 6.5%, and the cost of supporting cap-and-trade at 1.7%. A study by Gary Jacobson (2011) limited to 44 Democratic incumbents in Republican-leaning districts estimated that a vote in favor of the stimulus package cost them 3.0% of the midterm vote, while a vote in favor of health care reform cost them 4.9% and a vote in favor of the Dodd-Frank bill cost them 3.7%.

[37] A *Washington Post*/ABC News poll conducted a month before the midterm election found 68% of the public saying that the money the federal government spent on the economic stimulus had been "mostly wasted," while only 29% said that the money had been "mostly well spent." "*Washington Post*/ABC News Poll" conducted September 30–October 3, 2010 (http://www.washingtonpost.com/wp-srv/politics/polls/postpoll_10052010.html); David J. Lynch, "Economists Agree: Stimulus Created Nearly 3 Million Jobs," *USA Today*, August 30, 2010.

[38] My estimate of the impact of the stimulus package on real GDP growth is based on a widely circulated report by economists Alan Blinder and Mark Zandi (2010, table 7), discussed later in this chapter. My estimate of the impact of real GDP growth on the election outcome is derived from a cross-national analysis of elections in OECD countries in the Great Recession era (Bartels 2014a); estimates derived from historical analysis of U.S. midterm election outcomes are in the same ballpark.

bringing the election outcome into close agreement with forecasts based on "fundamentals"—and probably preserving a slim Democratic majority.[39]

Sweeping health care reform had been an aspiration of Democrats for six decades, but even with a (fleetingly) "filibuster-proof" majority in the Senate, Obama and his allies lacked sufficient political support to do it quickly, cleanly, and in a way that would deliver substantial immediate benefits to their constituents. In the end, they proved to be sufficiently determined to do it slowly, messily, and in a way that left them vulnerable to substantial public backlash. Sometimes that is how significant policy change occurs.

But with a new Republican majority in the House of Representatives, it was clear that no further landmark progressive legislation would emerge from Congress. In principle, the looming expiration of the Bush tax cuts provided Democrats with significant bargaining leverage in the lame-duck session of the outgoing Congress. But letting the tax cuts expire would be a shock to the fragile economy and, in the minds of many voters, a violation of Obama's long-standing pledge not to raise taxes on middle-class families. Thus, the president assigned Vice President Joe Biden to broker a deal with Senate Minority Leader McConnell. In exchange for a two-year renewal of the Bush tax cuts, Biden won extensions of unemployment benefits, tax credits for children, college tuition, and the working poor, and a one-year cut in the regressive payroll tax. According to one sympathetic observer, "Unemployment was way too high to walk away from a significant stimulus deal out of pique over goodies for the wealthy." Another observer, perhaps less sympathetic, wrote that "Democrats put aside their objections and bowed to the realignment of power brought about by their crushing election losses."[40]

The next two years produced a series of similarly unedifying attempts at bipartisan policy compromise in the shadow of manufactured deadlines. Less than a month after the 2010 election, a bipartisan National Commission on Fiscal Responsibility and Reform created by President Obama and co-chaired by Alan Simpson and Erskine Bowles issued a proposal for government spending cuts and tax increases that would reduce the federal deficit by nearly $4 trillion over the course of a decade. However, seven of the commission's 18 members opposed the plan, leaving it three votes short of the support required to send it to Congress. The president gamely announced that the report "includes a number of specific proposals that I—along with my economic team—will study closely in the coming weeks." However, even some supporters of the plan said that "they would not vote for it as actual legislation given their opposition to various provisions." As one journalist observed, "the outcome at best sent ambiguous signals about

[39] Nyhan et al. (2012, 862).

[40] Grunwald (2012, 404); David M. Herszenhorn, "Congress Sends $801 Billion Tax Cut Bill to Obama," *New York Times*, December 16, 2010.

whether the White House and Congress could reach an agreement, given the political pain behind the tax and spending decisions that are required."[41]

The following year, Republicans in Congress refused to raise the federal government's debt ceiling unless Democrats agreed to substantial cuts in future spending. As the cap on government borrowing approached, Standard & Poor's downgraded the federal government's credit rating for the first time in history and the stock market tanked. Two days before the Treasury Department's deadline for paying its bills, the president and Congress agreed to a deal that would increase the debt limit by $900 billion in exchange for substantial cuts in federal spending over the following decade. A special congressional joint select committee was appointed to hammer out $1.2 trillion in spending cuts, immune from amendment or filibuster, with a fallback provision that if Congress failed to act, automatic across-the-board cuts would be made to both defense and domestic programs beginning in 2013. This "sequester" provision was intended to be so unpalatable to both parties that they would be forced to reach an agreement. Nonetheless, negotiations collapsed as "Democrats and Republicans remained far apart on major budget issues, especially tax increases on the affluent, which Democrats insist must be part of any deficit solution and which Republicans oppose. . . . The stalemate was the latest sign of partisan deadlock in Washington, which members of both parties do not expect to lift until the 2012 election has clarified which party has the upper hand."[42]

THE POLITICAL IMPACT OF THE RECESSION

Social scientists setting out to examine the impact of economic distress on political attitudes and policy preferences have repeatedly been surprised to find much less than they expected. Sociologists Lane Kenworthy and Lindsay Owens titled their review of evidence from four decades of opinion surveys "The Surprisingly Weak Effect of Recessions on Public Opinion." But perhaps they should not have been surprised. The general tenor of their findings was clearly foreshadowed more than three decades earlier in a book-length study of the political impact of unemployment in the 1970s by political scientists Kay Schlozman and Sidney Verba.[43]

Schlozman and Verba found that "the effects of unemployment are severe but narrowly focused, manifest in ways that are proximate to the joblessness

---

[41] Jackie Calmes, "Obama Sets Up Debt Panel," *New York Times*, February 18, 2010; Jackie Calmes, "Obama Offers Hope for Debt Panel's Plan," *New York Times*, December 3, 2010.

[42] Robert Pear and Catherine Rampell, "Lawmakers in Both Parties Fear That New Budget Panel Will Erode Authority," *New York Times*, August 1, 2011; Eric Lipton, "Lawmakers Trade Blame as Deficit Talks Crumble," *New York Times*, November 20, 2011.

[43] Kenworthy and Owens (2011); Schlozman and Verba (1979).

itself. Many of the connections we had originally expected between un-employment and political beliefs and conduct simply were not made." In particular, they found no tendency for unemployment to produce "general disenchantment with American life, wholesale changes in social ideology, or adoption of radical policy positions." Moreover, "the unemployed as a group contributed less significantly to the electoral outcome in 1976 than the common wisdom would have suggested. . . . Political activity is more a function of beliefs about politics than of specific personal experiences; political beliefs, in turn, are more a function of general social beliefs than of personal experiences. Once again, the severe economic strain of job loss has little direct impact on political life."[44]

Kenworthy and Owens's broader survey of opinion data over four de-cades suggested that "recent economic recessions have had real but mostly temporary effects on American attitudes on key economic, political, and social issues." However, they found "no indication of any increase in sup-port for policies that enhance opportunity, support for the poor, or support for redistribution. . . . Economic downturns, including the Great Recession, have had surprisingly little impact on Americans' views of government, even in the short run."[45]

A narrower but more detailed study by Yotam Margalit examined changes in policy preferences using a panel survey in which the same people were interviewed before, during, and after the crisis phase of the Great Reces-sion. Comparing responses from July 2007 and April 2009, he found some decline in public support for "an increase in the funding of government programs for helping the poor and the unemployed with education, train-ing, employment, and social services, even if this might raise your taxes." However, that decline mostly reflected a preponderance of *support* for such spending increases before the onset of the crisis; among both supporters and opponents, 75% maintained their pre-crisis positions in 2009, while 11 or 12% switched sides.[46]

Among people who actually became unemployed during this period, Margalit found a significant increase in support for "funding of government programs for helping the poor and the unemployed with education, training, employment, and social services." Given the explicit mention of "the unem-ployed" in the question, this effect may be seen as echoing Schlozman and Verba's finding that unemployment was associated with support for specific "policies designed to ameliorate the situation," though not for "wholesale changes in social ideology." Moreover, even this narrow effect was of rather modest magnitude: 59% of those who lost their jobs during the course of Margalit's panel study supported increased funding of these programs, as

---

[44] Schlozman and Verba (1979, 351, 349, 330, 332).
[45] Kenworthy and Owens (2011, 198, 216–217, 204).
[46] Margalit (2013); see also Owens and Pedulla (2014).

compared with 47% of those who kept their jobs. Even over the course of a severe recession, the number of people who lost their jobs was much too small for this shift in views to make a substantial dent in the overall distribution of public opinion.

Moreover, Margalit's analysis of people who became *reemployed* over the course of his panel study suggests that the effect of unemployment was quite transitory: only 49% of them supported increased spending on programs for the poor and unemployed—a figure barely higher than among people who remained employed throughout the recession. Republicans were especially likely to become more favorable toward increased spending on programs for the poor and unemployed when they lost their jobs, but also more likely to revert to their former views once they found new jobs.

Perhaps unsurprisingly, some of the same liberal commentators who had badly misread the political implications of the economic crisis and the 2008 election were prominent among those expressing surprise and disappointment at the political trajectory of Obama's first term. John Judis published a much-talked-about analysis of Obama's "Unnecessary Fall." Robert Kuttner, who had expected "a transformative progressive president," now argued that Obama's presidency was "shaping up as one of American history's epic missed moments."[47] But observers who expected the president to rally the public in support of an ambitious progressive policy response to the economic crisis—or of an even broader progressive agenda unrelated to the crisis—drastically overestimated the ability of this (or any other) president to shape public opinion to suit his political taste.

Much of the criticism from the left hinged on the belief that, as Kuttner put it, a "potent combination of insider leadership, mobilization of public opinion, and alliance with social movements on the ground" should have allowed Obama to engineer policy changes comparable in magnitude to those produced by Franklin Roosevelt and Lyndon Johnson. Skocpol attributed the "endless political controversy and electoral blowback" of Obama's first term primarily to the "incomprehension and anxiety of everyday Americans" faced with bewildering policy debates and to "a veritable explosion of political pushback" from "business interests and many wealthy conservatives." Nevertheless, she, too, viewed "Obama's failure to engage more consistently in high-profile public leadership on the economy" as an instance of "democratic political malpractice." Although the president "travelled the country highlighting economic initiatives and progress in selected areas," she argued, "such efforts lacked the galvanizing, agenda-setting effect of

---

[47] John B. Judis, "The Unnecessary Fall: A Counter-History of the Obama Presidency," *The New Republic*, August 12, 2010; Robert Kuttner, "Unequal to the Moment," *The American Prospect*, February 9, 2011.

a major speech or sustained national communications strategy; and their fragmented focus inherently restricted the White House's ability to present a coherent economic plan."[48]

Arguments of this sort put undue stock in the power to sway public opinion of the "bully pulpit"—a mythical power that has mostly failed to withstand systematic scholarly scrutiny.[49] They also fail to account for the fact that the most costly "electoral blowback" against the president's congressional allies in 2010 seems to have come in reaction not to his misunderstood economic plan but to his ambitious health care reform—the very policy domain in which, by Skocpol's account, "Obama gave major speeches and orchestrated theatrically effective issue forums at key intervals during 2009 and early 2010, displaying presidential leadership and offering framings that proved influential beyond as well as within the Beltway."[50] If this was an example of the "bully pulpit" in action, it is hardly surprising that Democrats in Congress were not eager to stake their careers on further exercises of progressive presidential leadership.

Kuttner's notion that Obama might have advanced a more ambitious progressive policy agenda through "alliance with social movements on the ground" seems even more farfetched. The most significant manifestation of grassroots activism in the wake of the Great Recession, the Tea Party movement, mobilized conservative Republicans in opposition to Obama and his policies. By comparison, the progressive Occupy Wall Street movement offered no clear policy agenda and made little dent in the views of the broader public.[51]

The expectation that ordinary Americans would either push or follow their Democratic president to the political left flew in the face of considerable historical evidence suggesting that the public is much more likely to react *against* perceived shifts in policy than to ratify and reinforce them. Figure 9.2 tracks overall trends in American public opinion over the past six decades using James Stimson's measure of "public policy mood"—an aggregation of hundreds of polls gauging public opinion on a wide variety of domestic policy issues.[52] Liberal shifts in opinion appear as upticks in the figure, while conservative shifts appear as downturns.

[48] Kuttner, "Unequal to the Moment"; Skocpol (2012, 44–45, 37–38, 36).

[49] George Edwards's (2003) book on presidents and public opinion is entitled *On Deaf Ears: The Limits of the Bully Pulpit.*

[50] Skocpol (2012, 35).

[51] On the Tea Party movement, see Zernike (2010). Chapter 10 provides a more detailed assessment of the Occupy Wall Street movement and its political impact.

[52] For explications of the statistical analysis underlying this measure and more detailed descriptions of the policy questions it encompasses, see Stimson (1998) and Erikson, MacKuen, and Stimson (2002, chap. 6). Updated data (through 2014, as of this writing) are available from Stimson's website (http://stimson.web.unc.edu/data/).

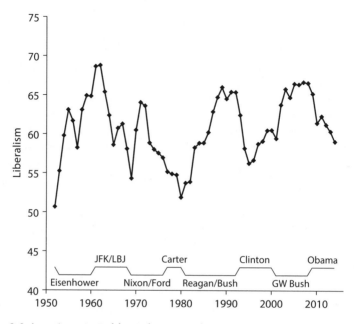

FIGURE 9.2 Americans' "Public Policy Mood," 1952–2014

Matching these movements with shifts in control of the White House reveals a strong counter-cyclical tendency in public opinion. The public grew much more liberal over the eight years of Dwight Eisenhower's presidency, much more conservative while John Kennedy, Lyndon Johnson, and Jimmy Carter were in office, and much more liberal once again under Ronald Reagan. These shifts have tended to be especially pronounced during the first term following a shift in partisan control of the White House. (Under Bill Clinton, the conservative trend bottomed out more quickly than usual, perhaps in response to the advent of Newt Gingrich's Republican House majority in 1995.) The marked downturn in liberalism under Obama, at the very end of the time series, is simply the latest instance of this impressively regular six-decade pattern.

Christopher Wlezien has likened the public to a thermostat, with attentive citizens controlling their elected officials by responding to *increases* in government activism with pressure for *decreases* and to *decreases* in government activism by demanding *increases*.[53] While the metaphor is an appealing one, it seems worth recognizing that *perceived* increases or decreases in government activism may have rather little to do with the actual content of policy; some important policy shifts seem to be largely ignored by the public, while in other cases, modest changes are inflated by political opponents

[53] Wlezien (1995).

into harbingers of socialism or social Darwinism. Nevertheless, insofar as the public does respond to actual shifts in the ideological content of public policy, it seems much more likely to do so as a restraining force than as a propelling force.

The same dynamic appears in attitudes and perceptions regarding the single most important domestic policy issue of Obama's presidency—the appropriate trade-off between government spending and services. Since the early 1980s, respondents in ANES surveys have been asked to place themselves and the two parties' presidential candidates on a scale ranging from wanting government to provide "many more services, even if it means an increase in spending," to wanting government to provide "fewer services, even in areas such as health and education," in order to "reduce spending a lot." Figure 9.3 traces shifts over three decades in the public's views on this issue and their perceptions of the positions of Democratic and Republican presidential candidates.[54]

The average view of citizens has generally fallen near the midpoint of this scale, with demands for more government services balanced by demands for reduced government spending. However, public preferences shifted sharply to the right between 2008 and 2012, by almost nine points on the 100-point scale. This shift seems to reflect much the same sort of negative reaction as in figure 9.2 to the activist government of Obama's "New New Deal." As a result, the net public demand for government spending was lower in 2012 than it had been in at least three decades. Meanwhile, however, the public placed Obama even further to the left on the spending scale than they had in 2008—indeed, significantly to the left of any Democratic presidential candidate since the question has been asked. Thus, whereas Al Gore and John Kerry had been perceived as closer to the public on the issue of government spending than George W. Bush, and Obama in 2008 had been viewed as about equally close to the public as John McCain, Obama in 2012 was placed at a significant disadvantage relative to Mitt Romney—despite the fact that Romney was considered more conservative on this issue than even Ronald Reagan in 1984.[55]

---

[54] "Some people think the government should provide fewer services, even in areas such as health and education, in order to reduce spending. Other people feel that it is important for the government to provide many more services even if it means an increase in spending. Where would you place yourself on this scale, or haven't you thought much about this?" The endpoints of the scale are labeled "reduce spending a lot" and "many more services," respectively. The tabulation of citizens' views presented in figure 9.3 excludes the 14–20% of ANES respondents in each year who said that they didn't know or hadn't thought much about the issue. The tabulations of perceived candidate positions exclude an additional 2–15% who placed themselves but said that they didn't know where the candidates stood.

[55] The ANES surveys also asked about the positions of the Democratic and Republican Parties on the spending scale. Results for the parties are generally similar to those for their presidential candidates. In 2012 the Democratic Party was placed about two points to Obama's right on the 100-point scale, on average, while the Republican Party was placed less than

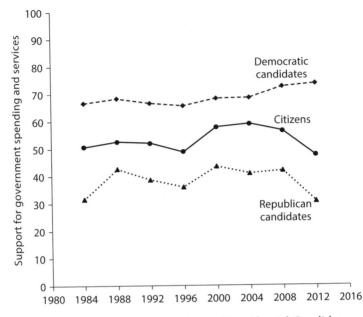

FIGURE 9.3 Citizens' Views and Perceptions of Presidential Candidates on Government Spending and Services, 1984–2012

Meanwhile, public antipathy to the specific policy measures adopted to stem the Great Recession faded somewhat as the economy continued its slow recovery. However, even as Obama stood for reelection in the fall of 2012, the public's verdict on the TARP and stimulus programs remained decidedly mixed. Table 9.3 summarizes these views using data from the Inequality Module of the 2012 Cooperative Campaign Analysis Project (CCAP). When asked about the TARP bailout, a solid majority (57%) of respondents continued to think that it was "the wrong thing for the government to do." When a comparable sample was asked the same question but with a reminder that the program "was approved by Congress in 2008 at the urging of President Bush and his Treasury Secretary," even more (63%) said that it was the wrong thing to do. Associating the program with President Bush still left Republicans opposed by a three-to-one margin. Democrats were a good deal more favorable, with 54% supporting the program even when the question stipulated that it had been adopted at the urging

one point to Romney's right. Using data from the 2012 Cooperative Campaign Analysis Project survey, John Sides and Lynn Vavreck (2013, 203–205) found that Romney had an even greater "proximity" advantage over Obama with respect to positions on a general liberal-to-conservative ideological scale.

TABLE 9.3
The Public's Verdict on the Troubled Asset Relief Program and
the American Recovery and Reinvestment Act, 2012

	Total sample	Democrats	Republicans
The Troubled Asset Relief Program created a $700 billion fund to purchase assets and equity from banks and other financial institutions in order to strengthen the U.S. financial system in the midst of the subprime mortgage crisis. Do you think this was the right thing or the wrong thing for the government to do?			
Right thing	43.4%	67.8%	16.1%
Wrong thing	56.6%	32.2%	83.9%
N	1,444	636	560
The Troubled Asset Relief Program created a $700 billion fund to purchase assets and equity from banks and other financial institutions in order to strengthen the U.S. financial system in the midst of the subprime mortgage crisis. *The program was approved by Congress in 2008 at the urging of President Bush and his treasury secretary.* Do you think this was the right thing or the wrong thing for the government to do?			
Right thing	37.2%	53.6%	24.7%
Wrong thing	62.8%	46.4%	75.3%
N	1,482	663	584
In early 2009, the president and Congress adopted a $787 billion economic stimulus package, the American Recovery and Reinvestment Act. Do you think this was the right thing or the wrong thing for the government to do?			
Right thing	50.2%	82.6%	9.6%
Wrong thing	49.8%	17.4%	90.4%
N	1,450	639	566
In early 2009, the president and Congress adopted a $787 billion economic stimulus package, the American Recovery and Reinvestment Act, *which included new spending on health care, education, aid to low-income workers and the unemployed, energy and infrastructure projects, and $288 billion in tax cuts.* Do you think this was the right thing or the wrong thing for the government to do?			
Right thing	55.3%	90.6%	15.9%
Wrong thing	44.7%	9.4%	84.1%
N	1,489	661	595

Source: 2012 CCAP Inequality Module.

of President Bush and two-thirds expressing support when that reminder was omitted.

The American Recovery and Reinvestment Act was only modestly more popular. In response to a question describing it as "a $787 billion economic stimulus package," the public as a whole was evenly split on whether it was the right thing to do. An alternative version of the question describing the major features of the bill produced a somewhat more favorable 55–45% split. In both cases, the close balance of opinion reflected vastly different views among Democrats and Republicans, with more than 80% of Democrats saying that the stimulus package was the right thing to do and more than 80% of Republicans saying that it was the wrong thing to do.

The massive partisan differences in assessments of TARP and the Recovery Act recorded in table 9.3 testify to the powerful role of partisan loyalties in shaping perceptions of the contemporary political world. This may be another reason why the impact of the Great Recession on public opinion was "surprisingly weak," in Kenworthy and Owens's phrase: the increasing partisan polarization of American politics over the past three decades has probably decreased the scope for substantial shifts in public preferences on issues figuring prominently in partisan political conflict. Given the complexity of public policies and the usual ambiguity of available evidence regarding their effects, controversy among political elites is likely to provide partisans on both sides with arguments and "evidence" bolstering their pre-existing beliefs.

Of course, even in times of crisis, experts sometimes come to considerable agreement about how the world works, but their views may have little sway over people to whom they speak inconvenient truths. For example, a 2012 survey of prominent economists found strong agreement regarding the effectiveness of the 2009 stimulus package.[56] However, as we saw in table 9.3, 85–90% of Republicans still maintained that adopting the stimulus package was "the wrong thing for the government to do."

If partisan loyalties had a big impact on assessments of the policy response to the Great Recession, the reverse does not seem to have been the case. Indeed, the recession and the Obama administration's response to it seem to have had remarkably little effect on the balance of partisan identification in the American public. Whereas Democrats in the New Deal era gained a durable advantage in partisan loyalties (and with it, virtually uninterrupted control of Congress for six decades), the Great Recession produced

[56] The survey was conducted in February 2012 with 41 "distinguished experts with a keen interest in public policy from the major areas of economics" as part of the University of Chicago Business School's IGM Forum. Thirty-three of these experts agreed that the unemployment rate at the end of 2010 was lower than it would have been without the 2009 stimulus package, while only two disagreed; 19 agreed that "the benefits of the stimulus will end up exceeding its costs," while five disagreed. IGM Forum, "Economic Stimulus," February 15, 2012 (http://www.igmchicago.org/igm-economic-experts-panel/poll-results?SurveyID=SV_cw5O9LNJL1oz4Xi).

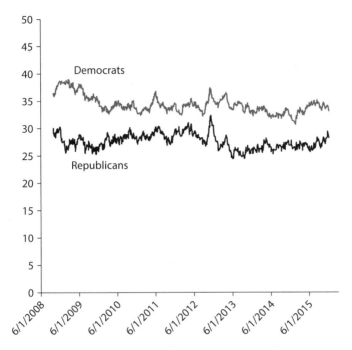

Figure 9.4 Party Identification in the Obama Era, 2008–2015

no comparable partisan legacy. The Democratic plurality in party identification, which had increased fairly steadily through much of George W. Bush's presidency, remained virtually unchanged under Obama. *HuffPost Pollster*'s aggregation of more than 1,000 separate opinion surveys, summarized in figure 9.4, shows a modest decline in identification with *both* parties—and a slight narrowing of the Democratic advantage—during Obama's first year in office, but virtually no net movement over the following six years.[57]

But Did It Work?

In July 2010, in the midst of the Obama administration's public relations campaign touting "recovery summer," prominent economists Alan Blinder

[57] *HuffPost Pollster* compiles findings from several dozen polling organizations. Figure 9.4 summarizes the results of 1,169 separate opinion surveys in a moving average of the 20 most recent poll results at each point in time (through early December 2015). See *HuffPost Pollster*, "Poll Chart: Party Identification" (http://elections.huffingtonpost.com/pollster/party-identification).

and Mark Zandi issued an attention-getting report on "How the Great Recession Was Brought to an End." They used off-the-shelf macroeconomic models to simulate the effects on real GDP and employment of the various policies implemented by the Federal Reserve and the Bush and Obama administrations in response to the economic crisis. They estimated that "without the government's response, GDP in 2010 would be about 11.5% lower, payroll employment would be less by some 8½ million jobs, and the nation would now be experiencing deflation." Most of these effects were attributable to financial policies such as bank bailouts and the Fed's "quantitative easing," but fiscal stimulus alone accounted for an estimated increase of 3.4% in real GDP and 2.7 million additional jobs. Blinder and Zandi concluded that the government's "stunning range of initiatives . . . was highly effective" and "probably averted what could have been called Great Depression 2.0."[58]

Five years later, economist and *New York Times* columnist Paul Krugman provided a roughly consistent assessment, albeit from a glass-half-empty perspective. Comparing the policy responses to the crisis in the United States and Europe, Krugman argued that "Europe has done very badly, while America has done relatively well." He cited the Fed's "willingness to step in and rescue the financial system" and the fact that, unlike the European Central Bank, it subsequently "stood fast in the face of demands that it tighten policy despite high unemployment." Then he turned to the Obama administration:

> Some of us warned from the beginning that the 2009 stimulus was too small and would fade out too fast, a warning vindicated by events. But it was much better than nothing, and was enacted over scorched-earth opposition from Republicans claiming that it would cause soaring interest rates and a fiscal crisis. Again, this is in strong contrast to Europe, which never did much stimulus and turned quickly to savage austerity in debtor nations.
>
> Unfortunately, the U.S. ended up doing a fair bit of austerity too, partly driven by conservative state governments, partly imposed by

[58] Blinder and Zandi (2010, 1–2). Blinder and Zandi's assessment of the economic impact of fiscal stimulus policies is consistent with that of the Congressional Budget Office, which estimated that the Recovery Act increased 2010 real GDP by 1.5–4.2% and created between 1.3 million and 3.4 million additional jobs; CBO, "Estimated Impact of the American Recovery and Reinvestment Act on Employment and Economic Output from January 2010 Through March 2010," May 25, 2010 (https://www.cbo.gov/publication/21492). Later, Blinder (2013a, 345) wrote that "real GDP in 2011 was $1.8 trillion higher than it would have been without all the rescue operations. With that much more output, there were 9.8 million more jobs, and the unemployment rate was 6.5 percentage points lower. These are huge effects that transformed what might have been an utter catastrophe into something that was merely awful."

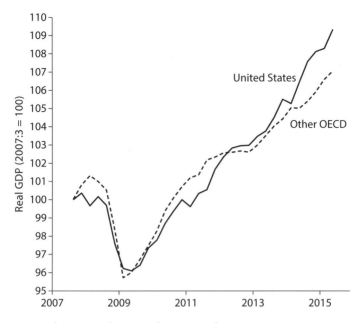

FIGURE 9.5 Real GDP in the United States and OECD, 2007–2015

Republicans in Congress via blackmail over the federal debt ceiling. But the Obama administration at least tried to limit the damage.

The result of these not-so-bad policies is today's not-so-bad economy. It's not a great economy, by any measure: Unemployment is low, but that has a lot to do with a decline in the fraction of the population looking for work, and the weakness of wages ensures that it doesn't feel like prosperity. Still, things could be worse.[59]

Figure 9.5 shows the pattern of economic contraction and recovery in the United States and, for purposes of comparison, in other OECD countries.[60] The steep downturn in GDP in 2008 and recovery in 2009–2010 were essentially similar in the United States and in the rest of the world's affluent economies. However, GDP growth was somewhat faster in the United States than elsewhere from early 2011 through 2015, and by mid-2015 the American economy was more than 9% larger (in real terms) than it had been when

[59] Paul Krugman, "The Not-So-Bad Economy," *New York Times*, December 7, 2015.

[60] OECD Quarterly National Accounts, Historical GDP—expenditure approach, volume estimates, fixed PPPs, seasonally adjusted. Since the United States accounts for about one-third of the total GDP of OECD countries, I subtracted the U.S. figure from the OECD total for purposes of comparison.

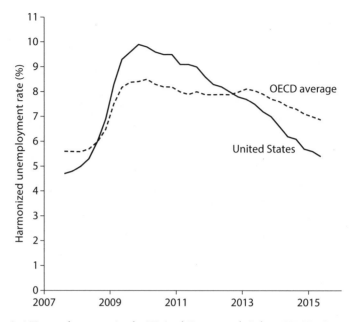

FIGURE 9.6 Unemployment in the United States and Other OECD Countries, 2007–2015

the recession began in 2007; the comparable cumulative growth in other OECD countries was 7%.

Figure 9.6 provides a similar comparison of unemployment rates in the United States and the OECD as a whole over the same period.[61] In the United States, unemployment doubled over the course of 2008 and 2009, from 5% to 9.9%, but declined steadily and substantially after 2009. By comparison, the average unemployment rate in the OECD as a whole increased less during the worst of the recession but also declined much more slowly in its aftermath. Whereas the U.S. unemployment rate declined by 4.5 percentage points between the end of 2009 and the middle of 2015, the OECD unemployment rate declined by just 1.5 percentage points over the same period.

Figure 9.7 shows trends in the real incomes of families in various parts of the income distribution from 2007 through 2014. In 2008, the first full year of the recession, the incomes of middle-class and working poor families fell by about 4%; affluent families fared a bit less badly in proportional terms. However, as the recession continued, the economic fortunes of affluent,

---

[61] OECD Key Short-Term Economic Indicators: Harmonized Unemployment Rate. According to the OECD, U.S. unemployment increased from 5% in the first quarter of 2008 to 9.9% in the fourth quarter of 2009, falling back to 5.4% in the second quarter of 2015. Unlike in figure 9.5, the OECD unemployment rate in figure 9.6 includes the United States.

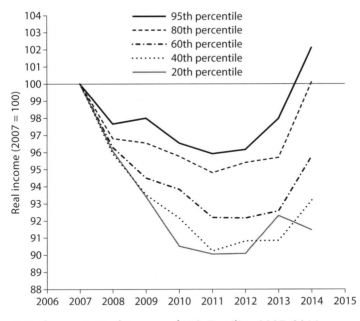

FIGURE 9.7 Changes in Real Income of U.S. Families, 2007–2014

middle-class, and working poor families diverged even more dramatically. In 2011, four years into the recession, the real incomes of middle-class and working poor families were 8 to 10% lower than they had been in 2007, while the real incomes of affluent families had fallen by only half that much. As incomes began to recover, the incomes of affluent families rebounded more strongly than those of middle-class and poor families, further widening the gap. By 2014, the real incomes of affluent families were higher than they had been before the recession (and about 4% higher than they had been in 2009), but the real incomes of middle-class and working poor families were still far below their pre-recession levels.

The disparity of economic fortunes in the wake of the Great Recession was even starker higher up in the income distribution. In 2013 a report by economist Emmanuel Saez documented the extent to which net income growth in the recovery was concentrated among top income-earners. "Top 1% incomes grew by 31.4% while bottom 99% incomes grew only by 0.4% from 2009 to 2012," Saez wrote. "Hence, the top 1% captured 95% of the income gains in the first three years of the recovery." By 2014, incomes had begun to grow for most families (as in figure 9.7), but "top 1% families," Saez calculated, "still capture[d] 58% of total real income growth per family from 2009–2014."[62]

[62] Saez noted that 2012 incomes for the top 1% of income-earners might be artificially high due to income-timing intended to avoid higher top tax rates beginning in 2013. His subsequent

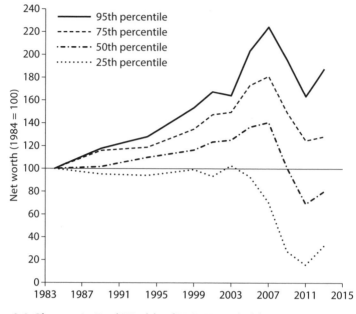

FIGURE 9.8 Changes in Real Wealth of U.S. Households, 1984–2013

While trends in income inequality attracted substantial public attention, the most shocking economic fallout from the Wall Street meltdown and its aftermath was much less discussed—a massive collapse of ordinary Americans' net wealth. Figure 9.8 summarizes Fabian Pfeffer, Sheldon Danziger, and Robert Schoeni's tabulations of changes in real wealth over three decades based on data from the Panel Study of Income Dynamics (PSID). These tabulations show that affluent households (at the 95th percentile of the wealth distribution) were wealthier in 2013 than they had been a decade earlier (though not wealthier than they seemed to be at the peak of the pre-recession housing bubble). In striking contrast, however, the median U.S. household's wealth (financial and real assets minus debts) in 2013 was 36% *lower* in real terms than it had been in 2003, 20% lower than in 2009, and—perhaps most remarkably—20% lower than in 1984. Even more remarkably, households at the 25th percentile of the wealth distribution had *less than half as much* real wealth in 2013 as they had had on the eve of the Great Recession and *less than one-third as much* as they had had three decades earlier.[63]

---

analysis showed that the income share of the top 1% did indeed dip in 2013 before beginning to increase again in 2014 (Saez 2015).

[63] Pfeffer, Danziger, and Schoeni (2014). For the same authors' more detailed analysis of wealth trends through 2011, see Pfeffer, Danziger, and Schoeni (2013).

Edward Wolff's calculations based on data from another source, the Survey of Consumer Finances, are generally quite consistent with those derived from the Panel Study of Income Dynamics. They suggest that median wealth fell by 45% in the wake of the Great Recession—from $115,100 (2013 dollars) in 2007 to $63,800 in 2013—and by 18% from 1983 to 2013. (The corresponding declines represented in figure 9.8 are 43% and 20%.) By comparison, the average net worth of the wealthiest 5% of households increased by 93% over that 30-year span, from $3,408,000 to $6,565,000.[64]

Wolff's decomposition of household wealth into specific asset classes sheds light on what was at stake in the decision to focus government aid in the wake of the Wall Street meltdown on banks and other financial institutions rather than on mortgage-holders. In 2007, at the beginning of the economic crisis, the wealthiest 10% of households owned 82% of the financial assets whose value was most directly bolstered by the Wall Street bailout (including stocks, mutual funds, securities, trusts, pensions, business equity, and investment real estate). The wealthiest 1% of households alone owned most of that 82%. Thus, they were the biggest winners, by far, from the bailout. Middle-class households held only 26% of their wealth in financial assets, including pension accounts, and 65% in their primary residences. Thus, their economic fortunes would rise or—as it turned out—fall with the prices of their homes.[65]

GEITHNER'S WORLD

The catastrophic erosion of middle- and working-class Americans' net wealth following the collapse of the subprime mortgage market was the most calamitous legacy of the Great Recession. To Blinder, "Watching wave after wave of foreclosures sweep across the American landscape was like watching a slow-motion train wreck take a high human toll. But unlike most train wrecks, the government was not a helpless bystander watching an inevitable disaster unfold. It had the power to do something about it—it just didn't. . . . It is hard to resist the conclusion that we just didn't try hard enough."[66]

Why not?

In October 2009, as the worst phase of the financial crisis seemed to be ebbing, the Associated Press published an attention-getting analysis of Treasury Secretary Timothy Geithner's telephone logs. "In the first seven months of Geithner's tenure," the report noted,

---

[64] Wolff (2014, 49, 51).
[65] Ibid., 56, 55.
[66] Blinder (2013a, 321, 342).

his calendars reflect at least 80 contacts with [Goldman Sachs CEO Lloyd] Blankfein, [JPMorgan CEO Jamie] Dimon, Citigroup Chairman Richard Parsons or Citigroup CEO Vikram Pandit. . . . When they call, Geithner answers. He has spoken with them immediately after hanging up with President Barack Obama and before heading up to Capitol Hill, between phone calls with senators and after talking with the Federal Reserve chairman. . . . At the New York Fed and then at Treasury, Geithner helped put together multibillion-dollar bailouts for Wall Street investment firms, including Goldman, JPMorgan, and Citi. Even banks that have repaid the money still enjoy massive subsidies. Their quick returns to record profits and million-dollar bonuses sparked outrage.[67]

A simplistic way to parse these contacts would be to note that Goldman Sachs, JPMorgan, and Citigroup were all among the top ten sources of financial contributions to Obama's 2008 presidential campaign (second, fifth, and seventh, respectively). But then, so were the University of California at Berkeley (first) and Harvard University (third), and no one supposes that *their* contributions bought spots on Geithner's speed dial. In any case, the amounts of money involved were drops in a big bucket: the $1,034,615 that Obama received from contributors associated with Goldman Sachs constituted just 0.14% of his $745 million campaign fund.[68]

Economist Simon Johnson offered a more convincing explanation for the specific contours of Geithner's network:

> The list of phone calls is not the largest banks, because some of the biggest are hardly represented (e.g., Wells Fargo), it's not the most troubled banks (e.g., Bank of America had little contact), and it's not even investment banker-types who were central to the most stressed markets (Morgan Stanley was not in the inner loop). . . . Geithner's phone calls were primarily to and from people he knew well already— who had cultivated a relationship with him over the years, shared nonprofit board memberships, and participated in the same social activities. These are close professional colleagues and in some cases, presumably, friends.[69]

Johnson asked, "How can anyone build an accurate picture of conditions in the entire crisis-ridden financial sector primarily from talking to a few top bankers?"

---

[67] Matt Apuzzo and Daniel Wagner, "Mr. Geithner, Wall Street Is on Line 1 (Again)." *USA Today*, October 8, 2009.

[68] Simon Johnson, "Too Politically Connected to Fail in Any Crisis," *The Baseline Scenario*, October 8, 2009 (http://baselinescenario.com/2009/10/08/too-politically-connected-to-fail-in-any-crisis/).

[69] Center for Responsive Politics, "Barack Obama: Top Contributors, 2008 Cycle" (http://www.opensecrets.org/PRES08/contrib.php?cid=N00009638).

In his memoir, Geithner expressed repeated, understandable frustration with the misperception that he was "a Goldman Sachs alum" or "just another banker at the helm of Treasury, doing the bidding of the banks." When a questioner at a congressional oversight panel referred to him as a lawyer and banker, Geithner interrupted: "I've spent my entire life in public service at the Treasury and the Federal Reserve."[70] But even a dedicated public servant who spends his entire career at the Treasury and the Federal Reserve—and much of his time talking to bankers—may come to see the world through a banker's eyes.

Time and time again, Geithner's account of his judgments and actions seems to reflect a distinctive Wall Street worldview. In the fall of 2008, for example, while Geithner was still at the New York Fed, then-Treasury Secretary Hank Paulson's draft legislation for the Troubled Assets Relief Program proposed giving the treasury secretary sole control over the $700 billion bailout fund, stipulating that his decisions "may not be reviewed by any court of law or any administrative agency." Geithner "liked it," though he "wasn't sure it granted Treasury broad enough powers." Legal subtleties, it seems, could be dispensed with in a financial emergency. On the other hand, a few months later, when insurance giant AIG used TARP money to pay massive bonuses to many of the executives who had generated billions of dollars in losses, Geithner opposed any effort to claw back the bonuses on the grounds that the government "could not force a financial firm to violate a contractual obligation without unleashing a new wave of panic and uncertainty." "The rule of law," he wrote, "was arguably our most important anchor, especially during this limbo period when fears of nationalization and federal interference were pervasive."[71]

Geithner clashed repeatedly with Sheila Bair, the head of the Federal Deposit Insurance Corporation (and a former aide to Republican senator Bob Dole, with varied experience in politics, government, and academia). When Bair allowed the failing Wachovia bank to back out of a pending government-subsidized merger with Citi in order to accept a better deal from Wells Fargo—"seven times Citi's offer, with no government help needed"—Geithner was "livid" that the government was violating its "commitment" to Citi. But several weeks later, when Bank of America CEO Ken Lewis was "threatening to abandon" a pending merger with Merrill Lynch in the face of escalating losses at the brokerage, Geithner "fully supported"

---

[70] Geithner also worked in Henry Kissinger's consulting firm for a few years between government jobs. That connection, too, seems to have left a mark on his social network. Geithner attended a dinner party at Kissinger's New York apartment on the evening before the crucial congressional vote on TARP, reassuring the assembled guests that "we're going to fix this" Geithner (2014, 328, 336, 219).

[71] Geithner (2014), 208–209, 316.

an additional infusion of government aid to Bank of America to ensure that the deal would go through.[72]

Geithner expressed pride in the Obama administration's "focus on getting the policy right first and worrying about the politics later." But some political pressures seem to have been more attention-worthy than others. When it became clear that the Fed and the Treasury "couldn't defuse the crisis until we recapitalized the financial system," Paulson worried that "even mentioning the possibility of direct capital investments would have been bad politics, raising the specter of nationalization. Government ownership stakes in private firms sounded un-American." Thus, policy-makers focused instead on "injecting capital" into failing financial institutions while limiting public ownership. Even "risky and messy deals" were "preferable to government takeovers." Meanwhile, a separate program was constructed to "appease the demand in the financial and political arenas for some kind of government effort to buy illiquid assets." But the "political arena" Geithner had in mind apparently did not include the substantial majority of the American public who, as reported in table 9.1, opposed "giving financial support to banks in trouble."[73]

Geithner's concerns about the problem of "moral hazard"—rewarding reckless behavior by bailing out the perpetrators—were similarly selective. In the case of banks, "Old Testament vengeance appeals to the populist fury of the moment," he wrote, "but the truly moral thing to do during a raging financial inferno is to put it out. The goal should be to protect the innocent, even if some of the arsonists escape their full measure of justice." On the other hand, when it came to mortgage relief, "our goal was not to subsidize borrowers who splurged on over-priced McMansions and vacation homes and investment properties, or took out home equity loans to buy swimming pools and fancy cars. We knew that a few outrageous stories of aid to reckless speculators and scam artists could cripple support for our entire housing program."[74]

Lawrence Summers, the director of the National Economic Council, observed that "debt crises rarely end before governments help reduce excess debt burdens." But Geithner was convinced that "nobody had a feasible proposal for a cost-effective, well-targeted, large-scale debt reduction program for homeowners that could get through Congress." As Blinder put it, both Paulson and Geithner viewed mortgage modifications as "economically difficult, legally problematic, and politically toxic."[75]

In retrospect, Geithner acknowledged that "our housing efforts got off to a rough start, and I set too high a bar for expanding them later on." He admitted making frequent "empathy mistakes" in his meetings with advocates for mortgage relief,

---

[72] Ibid., 222, 255.
[73] Ibid., 266, 224, 324, 255, 285.
[74] Ibid., 9, 301.
[75] Ibid., 302; Blinder (2013a, 323).

pushing them for solutions and inundating them with the constraints we faced instead of listening patiently to their stories and feeling their pain. . . . I once interrupted an advocate early in her passionate description of the human costs of the crisis, saying I knew things were terrible out there. "Let's stipulate that," I said. "Let's talk about what we can do." Afterward, [senior adviser] Sara Aviel walked me back to my office and told me: Don't ever ask them to stipulate the pain and suffering.

Geithner worried that these "empathy mistakes" made him "an ineffective advocate for what we were trying to do." But the problem may have gone beyond salesmanship. Perhaps someone who'd spent his entire life in public service at the Treasury and the Federal Reserve really *was* less attuned than he supposed to "the human costs of the crisis."[76]

Even in retrospect, Geithner's own account of his efforts sometimes calls into question his grasp of "terrible out there." For example, in assessing the overall success of the Obama administration's response to the financial crisis, he noted that "by the end of 2013, our GDP was 6 percent higher than before the crisis; Japan, the U.K., and the eurozone were still below their pre-crisis output levels. After declining by $15 trillion, U.S. household wealth was also higher than the pre-crisis peak. . . . The stabilization of Wall Street and the rest of the financial system saved the Main Street economy from the trauma of another depression."[77]

While there is indeed much to be proud of in this record, Geithner's reassuring picture of rebounding GDP and wealth overlooked both the excruciatingly slow pace of the recovery and, even more tellingly, its remarkable unevenness. If "the Main Street economy" consisted of the top one-tenth of affluent American households, then the recovery from the Great Recession was indeed a considerable success. But for more typical American families, real incomes in 2014 were still not back to their 2009 levels, much less their 2007 levels. Even worse, the Wall Street meltdown and its aftermath had wiped out much of their life savings, leaving the median household's real net worth 20% below where it had been *three decades earlier*. They might be excused for feeling little gratitude.

Not the New New Deal

To Theda Skocpol, Barack Obama's first term was marked by a disjuncture between successful *policies* and unsuccessful *politics*.[78] "A new New Deal of sorts *was* successfully launched by President Obama and Congressional

---

[76] Geithner (2014, 384–385).
[77] Ibid., 494, 496.
[78] For a similar argument, see Blinder (2013b).

Democrats in 2009 and 2010," Skocpol wrote. "But much of what happened was either invisible or ominously incomprehensible to the majority of American citizens." She contrasted this state of affairs with the original New Deal era: "Back in the 1930s, American citizens could see that big, new things were being proposed and debated in Washington DC."[79]

Were the policy changes championed by Franklin Roosevelt really so much more visible and comprehensible—or, for that matter, more popular— than those pursued by Obama? A study by sociologists Katherine Newman and Elisabeth Jacobs of public reactions to government activism from the New Deal era to the present provided a useful reminder that Roosevelt, like Obama, had plenty of disappointed political supporters: "Though we remember Roosevelt today as the man who did more for the poor and dispossessed than any president before, and arguably anyone since, in his own day leftists and labor liberals often complained that Roosevelt's actions were too little, too late, and too tepid." Four years into the New Deal, and a year after Roosevelt's landslide reelection, the editors of *The Economist* offered this frustrated appraisal: "Relief there has been, but little more than enough to keep the population fed, clothed and warmed. Recovery there has been, but only to a point still well below the pre-depression level. The great problems of the country are still hardly touched."[80]

The conventional understanding of the electoral politics of the 1930s is that the Democrats' success in forging a durable new majority hinged crucially on the public's assessment of the measures adopted by Roosevelt to combat the Depression. The eminent political scientist V. O. Key Jr., for example, argued that the Democratic landslide of 1936—the pivotal electoral event in what came to be called the New Deal era—"could only be interpreted as a popular ratification of the broad features of new public policy." In fact, though, Roosevelt's political fate was probably much less dependent on voters' assessments of policies than on their ability to see and feel concrete economic progress. Christopher Achen and I showed that Roosevelt's historic landslide in 1936 was heavily concentrated in states with high income growth rates over the course of the election year—just the sort of myopic economic retrospection that looms so large in contemporary electoral politics. Indeed, our analysis suggested that if the recession of 1938 had happened to occur two years earlier, Roosevelt would probably have been a one-term president, making the New Deal era just as evanescent as the "new Liberal Order" proclaimed by Peter Beinart in 2008.[81]

[79] Skocpol (2012, 44, 42).

[80] Newman and Jacobs (2010, 15); Editors of *The Economist* (1937, 147).

[81] Key (1958, 578–579). Achen and Bartels (2016, chap. 7). As one might expect based on my analysis of voters' myopia in chapter 3, spectacular income growth in 1934 and 1935 seems to have had no discernible effect on Roosevelt's 1936 vote; only income growth in 1936 mattered.

The dramatic recovery of the American economy over the course of Roosevelt's presidency produced a gradual but substantial shift in partisan loyalties. But so, too, did the parallel economic recoveries in many other places around the world, regardless of the ideology or economic policies of whichever party happened to be in office at the time. Thus, it is probably misleading to suppose that the new Democratic majority reflected a considered verdict on the New Deal, as distinct from the economic recovery that happened to coincide with it.

When Roosevelt ran for reelection in 1936, real GDP and disposable income per capita had increased by a stunning 33% in the three years since his inauguration. When Barack Obama ran for reelection in 2012, the corresponding increases amounted to 4%. That would turn out to be enough to get Obama reelected, but it was hardly an epoch-making policy success. The "stunning range of initiatives" improvised by the Federal Reserve, the Treasury Department, and the Obama White House in the six months following the collapse of Lehman Brothers stabilized the financial system and stimulated the economy. According to economists Blinder and Zandi, they boosted real GDP by 4.9% in 2009 and by 6.6% in 2010.[82] Although a long period of painfully slow economic recovery consumed President Obama's entire first term, this was nothing like the "Depression 2.0" that Fed chairman Ben Bernanke and other policy-makers had feared. However, the millions of Americans who had lost their jobs or their homes were unlikely to be cheered by the fact that things could have been much worse.

The Great Recession brought similar political disappointment to progressives in many other affluent democracies. In 2011, prominent political consultant Stanley Greenberg found it "perplexing" that "many voters in the developed world are turning away from Democrats, Socialists, liberals and progressives. . . . When unemployment is high, and the rich are getting richer, you would think that voters of average means would flock to progressives, who are supposed to have their interests in mind—and who historically have delivered for them."[83]

Greenberg's perplexity is understandable if one supposes that voters are animated by the same ideological convictions as politicians, pundits, and political activists. But copious evidence suggests that ordinary citizens are mostly uninterested in ideological manifestos and economic theories, and skeptical of assertions about which parties "historically have delivered for them." They are much more attentive to ends than to means, and they tend to reward or punish incumbent governments based on straightforward assessments of observable success or failure.

---

[82] Blinder and Zandi (2010, table 4).
[83] Stanley B. Greenberg, "Why Voters Tune Out Democrats," *New York Times*, July 30, 2011.

During the Great Recession and its aftermath, dozens of incumbent governments around the world faced their voters under conditions of varying economic distress. The results of these elections show little evidence of any consistent shift in favor of either left-wing or right-wing parties. While left-of-center governments (in Portugal, New Zealand, Britain, and Spain) suffered significant losses, so did right-of-center governments (in Iceland, Japan, and Greece)—and centrist coalitions (in the Netherlands, Austria, Germany, and Finland) fared even worse. The most consistent pattern in these election results is that voters simply, and even simple-mindedly, punished incumbents of every stripe for economic hard times.[84]

In this respect, what may be most striking about the politics of the Great Recession in the United States and elsewhere is how ordinary it looked. In times of crisis, as in good times, ordinary citizens have a stubborn tendency to judge politicians and policies not on the basis of ideology or economic doctrine, but according to perceived success or failure. In the United States, their initial response to the recession produced a (barely) unified Democratic government, while their impatience with the slow recovery produced Republican majorities in Congress and a partisan standoff. In both cases, the result had substantial implications for the course of public policy. Of course, no one may have been entirely satisfied by the outcome. Indeed, for those with a romantic view of American democracy and its capacity for epic moments, it may have been downright disillusioning.

---

[84] On the dominance of retrospection over ideology in electoral responses to the Great Recession in OECD countries, see Bartels (2014a). Nor is there any evidence of consistent ideological shifts outside the context of elections. For example, comparing data from 20 countries in the 2006 and 2010 European Social Surveys (http://www.europeansocialsurvey.org/) reveals an almost imperceptible average shift to the right of 0.04 points on a ten-point ideological scale—and no apparent relationship between the (usually quite modest) shifts observed in specific countries and the severity of their economic downturns.

CHAPTER 10

The Defining Challenge of Our Time?

I believe this is the defining challenge of our time: Making sure our economy works for every working American. It's why I ran for President. It was at the center of last year's campaign. It drives everything I do in this office. And I know I've raised this issue before, and some will ask why I raise the issue again right now. I do it because the outcomes of the debates we're having right now—whether it's health care, or the budget, or reforming our housing and financial systems—all these things will have real, practical implications for every American. And I am convinced that the decisions we make on these issues over the next few years will determine whether or not our children will grow up in an America where opportunity is real.

—*President Barack Obama, 2013*[1]

As POLITICAL SCIENTISTS Jacob Hacker and Paul Pierson noted in their influential study of *Winner-Take-All Politics*, the dramatic escalation of economic inequality in the contemporary United States raises a significant political puzzle: "In a country where public officials must regularly face the judgment of citizens at the polls, how could their efforts come to so persistently favor the very few?" Previous periods of elevated economic inequality in the Gilded Age and the Roaring Twenties were met—eventually—with significant populist backlashes and policy reform efforts. As Kevin Phillips put it, the American public "has distrusted economic elites and periodically used democratic politics to curb their abuses." Why not now?[2]

In the view of some observers, the past several years have brought us significantly closer to that sort of political reckoning. The economic distress

---

[1] "Remarks by the President on Economic Mobility," December 4, 2013 (https://www.whitehouse.gov/the-press-office/2013/12/04/remarks-president-economic-mobility).

[2] Hacker and Pierson (2010, 7); Phillips (2002, 294).

caused by the Great Recession—and the very uneven recovery of economic fortunes in the wake of the recession—stirred concern for the well-being of the middle class and, at least in some quarters, resentment of Wall Street and the wealthy. The Occupy Wall Street movement and its various spin-offs raised the consciousness of "the 99%"—or at least of the highbrow national news media—regarding the issue of inequality. And the 2012 presidential election set the stage for that heightened consciousness to produce a powerful populist backlash against our New Gilded Age.

The incumbent president, who had raised the issue of economic inequality in his 2008 campaign and periodically throughout his term, redoubled his effort to increase its salience with a highly publicized December 2011 speech in Osawatomie, Kansas, on the plight of the middle class. In his 2012 State of the Union Address, he again identified economic inequality and its social ramifications as "the defining issue of our time."[3] And, conveniently for the president, his opponent in the 2012 election, Mitt Romney, was an honest-to-goodness plutocrat with an estimated net worth of $250 million, a controversial career in leveraged buyouts, and attention-getting accoutrements of wealth, including multiple homes, dressage horses, offshore bank accounts, and secret tax returns.

My primary aim in this chapter is to gauge the significance of economic inequality as a political issue in contemporary American politics. Did the Occupy Wall Street movement succeed in bringing the issue of economic inequality to broad public attention? Did increased attention and concern among journalists and scholars significantly increase the political salience of the issue? Did the 2012 election provide a popular mandate for policies that would put a significant dent in inequality? If not, why not?

I examine whether and how prospective voters' views about inequality changed over the years and months leading up to the 2012 election, whether and how those views affected the election outcome, and whether and how they shaped the policy-making environment during President Obama's second term. The results of my analysis suggest that the impact of inequality as a political issue in 2012 had much less to do with concrete policy preferences—or even with broader concerns about inequality—than with the specific, widespread perception that the Republican nominee cared more about wealthy people than about poor (or, for that matter, middle-class) people.

Finally, I assess the Obama administration's success in addressing what the president himself identified as "the defining challenge of our time," as well as some of the political obstacles to successfully addressing that challenge in the years to come.

[3] Alexander Eichler, "State of the Union Address 2012: Obama Calls Income Inequality 'the Defining Issue of Our Time'," *Huffington Post*, January 24, 2012 (http://www.huffingtonpost.com/2012/01/24/state-of-the-union-address-2012_n_1229510.html).

A "National Conversation"?

In December 2011, President Obama traveled to Osawatomie, Kansas, to deliver a major address on economic inequality. More than a century earlier, Theodore Roosevelt had come to Osawatomie to issue a memorable Progressive Era call for "a real democracy" and "an economic system under which each man shall be guaranteed the opportunity to show the best that there is in him." Obama's speech was in much the same spirit. Citing "a raging debate over the best way to restore growth and prosperity, restore balance, [and] restore fairness," the president insisted that

> this is not just another political debate. This is the defining issue of our time. This is a make-or-break moment for the middle class, and for all those who are fighting to get into the middle class. Because what's at stake is whether this will be a country where working people can earn enough to raise a family, build a modest savings, own a home, secure their retirement. . . . This isn't about class warfare. This is about the nation's welfare. It's about making choices that benefit not just the people who've done fantastically well over the last few decades, but that benefits the middle class, and those fighting to get into the middle class, and the economy as a whole.[4]

Journalists interpreted Obama's speech as a reflection of widespread public concern about the issue of inequality inspired by the Occupy Wall Street movement and the fallout from the Great Recession. A. G. Sulzberger of the *New York Times* noted that the speech was infused with "the moralistic language that has emerged in the Occupy protests around the nation." Ezra Klein of the *Washington Post* attributed the president's populist rhetoric "to Occupy Wall Street's success in turning the national conversation towards inequality." Ari Berman of *The Nation* thought it showed "exactly how the Occupy movement has impacted the debate in Washington."[5]

It is always worth bearing in mind, however, that "the debate in Washington" may be a far cry from a "national conversation." Significant shifts in attention within the rather insular community of political activists and commentators may have little traction among ordinary citizens. And even if they do spur significant shifts in public perceptions and concerns, they may

---

[4] "Remarks by the President on the Economy in Osawatomie, Kansas," December 6, 2011 (https://www.whitehouse.gov/the-press-office/2011/12/06/remarks-president-economy -osawatomie-kansas).

[5] A. G. Sulzberger, "Obama Strikes Populist Chord with Speech on G.O.P. Turf," *New York Times*, December 6, 2011; Ezra Klein, "Occupy Wall Street Occupies Obama's 2012 Campaign," *Washington Post, Wonkblog*, December 7, 2011; Ari Berman, "In Osawatomie, Obama Embraces New Populist Moment," *The Nation*, December 6, 2012.

often fail to connect those perceptions and concerns to any concrete issues of public policy.

Indeed, there is remarkably little evidence that the Occupy Wall Street movement—or, for that matter, President Obama's high-profile rhetoric—produced anything like a genuine "national conversation" about economic inequality. As we saw in table 4.6, almost 80% of respondents in the 2012 American National Election Studies survey believed that the difference in incomes between rich people and poor people in the United States had increased over the past 20 years; only about 5% believed that it had gotten smaller. On its face, that sounds like an overwhelming public endorsement of one of the primary factual premises of the Occupy Wall Street movement. But the results of earlier ANES surveys reported in the same table show that public recognition of increasing inequality was actually no greater in 2012 than it had been four years or even eight years earlier—long before the emergence of the Occupy Wall Street movement. Figure 10.1 summarizes these public perceptions of increasing inequality.[6] If one test of a "national conversation" is that it shifts public perceptions of economic or political reality, this one seems to have had no discernible impact.[7]

Nor is there any evidence that widespread discussion of inequality increased public support for egalitarian values. As we saw in chapter 4, Americans have long supported equality in the abstract. For example, almost 90% agree (and more than 60% "agree strongly") that "our society should do whatever is necessary to make sure that everyone has an equal opportunity to succeed." Two-thirds agree that "if people were treated more equally in this country, we would have many fewer problems." However, this sort of symbolic support for equality does not seem to have increased in the wake of the Great Recession and the Occupy Wall Street movement. Figure 10.1 also tracks the average level of support for equality in response to the six items listed in table 4.1, from 1984, when these items were first included in ANES surveys, through 2012. The value for 2012—61.1 on a 100-point scale—is virtually identical to the average value over the whole period and slightly *lower* than in 2004 and 2008.

---

[6] The figure shows the average perception of inequality in each survey from 2002 through 2012, with "much larger" responses coded 100, "somewhat larger" responses coded 75, "about the same" and "don't know" responses coded 50, "somewhat smaller" responses coded 25, and "much smaller" responses coded zero. Simply tabulating the proportion of respondents in each ANES survey who believed that income inequality had increased would produce essentially similar results.

[7] Nor is there any evidence of a longer-term impact. An ANES pilot survey conducted in January 2016 produced a virtually identical picture of perceived inequality, albeit from a sample that is not directly comparable to those in previous ANES surveys (http://www.electionstudies.org/studypages/anes_pilot_2016/anes_pilot_2016.htm).

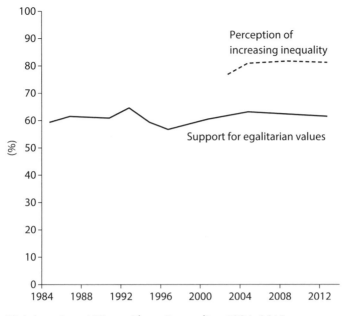

FIGURE 10.1 Americans' Views About Inequality, 1984–2012

Nor is there any evidence that "turning the national conversation towards inequality" produced significant shifts in public views regarding concrete policy issues related to economic inequality and opportunity. Observers have pointed to the absence of any clearly articulated policy agenda as a primary failing of the Occupy Wall Street movement. In Osawatomie, President Obama reiterated previous calls to make the tax system more progressive by extending the 2011 payroll tax cut and letting the Bush tax cuts for high-earners expire. However, data from a series of five YouGov surveys reported in table 10.1 provide remarkably little evidence of any significant shift in public views regarding the Bush tax cuts. In December 2011, in the immediate wake of Obama's speech and at the height of press coverage of the Occupy Wall Street movement, YouGov found 41% of the public favoring the president's long-standing proposal to restore the Clinton-era tax rate for households earning more than $250,000 per year. Another 14% favored letting *all* the Bush tax cuts expire, while only 25% favored making all the tax cuts permanent. The 55–25 margin of public support for reviving the Clinton-era top rate was little changed from 2010 or even 2008, before Obama's election and long before the emergence of Occupy Wall Street.

Two additional YouGov surveys conducted in March and October 2012 suggest that any impact that Obama's rhetoric may have had on views about the Bush tax cuts was quite short-lived. The 30-point margin of

TABLE 10.1

Public Support for the Bush Tax Cuts, 2008–2012

"As you probably know, many of the major tax cuts passed by Congress during the Bush administration are due to expire at the end of [this/next] year. Would you favor . . . ?"	*October 2008*	*October 2010*	*December 2011*	*March 2012*	*October 2012*
Making these tax cuts permanent	30%	28%	25%	28%	31%
Extending the tax cuts for households earning less than $250,000 per year [only]	38%	42%	41%	37%	41%
Letting all the tax cuts expire as scheduled	14%	11%	14%	12%	15%
Don't know	16%	18%	19%	22%	13%
N	1,000	1,000	1,000	1,000	3,000

Source: YouGov surveys.

public support for increasing the top tax rate in the immediate wake of his Osawatomie speech declined to 21 percentage points over the course of the next few months, almost exactly matching the distribution of public opinion in 2008. On the eve of the 2012 election it was back up to 25 percentage points, almost exactly matching the distribution of public opinion in 2010. Thus, there is no evidence of any significant evolution of public views regarding the Bush tax cuts—the most momentous concrete policy issue bearing on the issue of economic inequality—at any point in the first four years of Obama's presidency.[8]

Finally, there is no evidence that the public became increasingly engaged by the debate over the Bush tax cuts during the months in which the Occupy Wall Street movement is supposed to have focused attention on the issue of economic inequality. The proportion of survey respondents who said that they didn't know which option for dealing with the Bush tax cuts they favored was 19% in December 2011, a slightly *higher* proportion than in 2010 or 2008. A few months later it was even higher, 22%, before declining over the course of the 2012 campaign. Again, if there was a "national conversation" about inequality in 2011, it seems to have left little or no mark on the minds of ordinary Americans.

The Class War Gets Personal: Inequality as an Issue in the 2012 Campaign

In the wake of President Obama's speech in Osawatomie, his administration made repeated efforts to keep the issue of inequality on the political front burner. A January speech by Alan Krueger, chairman of the White House Council of Economic Advisers, signaled to one reporter that Obama "is going all in with the 2012 re-election message of stemming the rise in income inequality and reforming a system that's increasingly perceived to be rigged in favor of the rich." In his State of the Union message, the president reiterated his claim that inequality is "the defining issue of our time." In an April 2012 speech, the president argued that "what drags down our entire economy is when there is an ultra-wide chasm between the ultra-wealthy and everyone else." Later the same month the White House staff posted an analysis of "President Obama's Record, Results and Agenda on Income Inequality," an attempt to "refute the baseless claim made by some that income inequality is worse under President Obama than it was under President George W. Bush."[9]

---

[8] Larry Bartels, "Occupy's Impact Beyond the Beltway," *Moyers & Company*, January 18, 2012 (http://billmoyers.com/2012/01/18/has-the-occupy-movement-altered-public-opinion/).

[9] Sahil Kapur, "Krueger's Speech Seals Obama's 2012 Inequality Message," *TalkingPointsMemo*, January 12, 2012 (http://tpmdc.talkingpointsmemo.com/2012/01/kruegers-inequality

The emphasis on inequality was partly a matter of principle and partly a matter of political calculation. The apparent rise of "the 1%" as an object of public apprehension seemed to ensure a fertile political reception for long-standing Democratic policy positions in the areas of taxes, spending, and regulation. "Since Occupy Wall Street and kindred movements highlighted the issue," one journalist noted in March, "the chasm between the rich and ordinary workers has become a crucial talking point in the Democratic Party's arsenal."

The emergence of a wealthy hedge-fund capitalist, Mitt Romney, as the Republican nominee seemed likely both to increase the salience of economic inequality and to heighten Republicans' vulnerability on the issue. Thus, according to another press report, Obama attempted "to shift the focus of the election campaign away from health care and unemployment to a debate about income inequality, betting voters will back his call for tax increases on the rich." The report added that the president's renewed push to raise taxes on the wealthy "complements the Obama campaign's efforts to define Mr. Romney, whose net worth exceeds $250-million, as beholden to billionaire backers and corporate interests."[10]

For his part, Romney seemed to be on the defensive on the issue of inequality throughout the campaign. In a January interview with Matt Lauer on *The Today Show*, Romney was questioned about his characterization of Obama as "a leader who divides us with the bitter politics of envy." Lauer asked, "Are there no fair questions about the distribution of wealth without it being seen as *envy?*" Romney replied, "I think it's fine to talk about those things in quiet rooms and discussions about tax policy and the like. But the president has made it part of his campaign rally. Everywhere he goes we hear him talking about millionaires and billionaires and executives and Wall Street. It's a very envy-oriented, attack-oriented approach and I think it will fail."[11]

At a May fund-raising event secretly videotaped by a bartender and leaked to the press in September, Romney expanded on his view of class politics in the campaign:

> There are 47 percent of the people who will vote for the president no matter what . . . who are dependent upon government, who believe

-speech-seals-obamas-2012-inequality-message.php); Eichler, "State of the Union Address 2012"; Derek Thompson, "Income Inequality Is Killing the Economy, Obama Says—Is He Wrong?" *The Atlantic*, April 3, 2012; Katherine Abraham and Jason Furman, "President Obama's Record, Results and Agenda on Income Inequality," April 13, 2012 (http://www.whitehouse.gov/blog/2012/04/12/president-obama-s-record-results-and-agenda-income-inequality).

[10] Eduardo Porter, "Inequality Undermines Democracy," *New York Times*, March 20, 2012; Konrad Yakabuski, "Obama Finds His Campaign Focus—Inequality," *The Globe and Mail*, July 9, 2012.

[11] Greg Sargent, "Romney: Questions About Wall Street and Inequality Are Driven by 'Envy'," *Washington Post, Opinions*, January 11, 2012.

that they are victims, who believe that government has a responsibility to care for them, who believe that they are entitled to health care, to food, to housing, to you name it. . . . These are people who pay no income tax. . . . So our message of low taxes doesn't connect. And he'll be out there talking about tax cuts for the rich. . . . And so my job is not to worry about those people—I'll never convince them that they should take personal responsibility and care for their lives. What I have to do is convince the 5 to 10 percent in the center that are independents that are thoughtful, that look at voting one way or the other depending upon in some cases emotion, whether they like the guy or not, what it looks like.[12]

Romney's private assessment of how economic populism would shape the campaign seems distinctly less optimistic than his public assertion four months earlier that an "envy-oriented, attack-oriented" appeal on the issue of inequality "will fail." Certainly, opinion polls provided some reason to think that such an appeal might have considerable traction. For example, the YouGov survey conducted a week after the president's speech in Osawatomie revealed a good deal of public support for making the federal tax system more progressive. As we saw in table 10.1, a solid plurality of respondents favored President Obama's long-standing proposal to let the Bush tax cuts on incomes in excess of $250,000 per year expire. More broadly, almost 60% of the respondents favored the idea of increasing taxes on the wealthy, while only 25% opposed that idea. By a roughly similar margin, 52% to 22%, the respondents supported a plan being offered by congressional Democrats at the time to extend the payroll tax cut and offset the cost by imposing a new tax on millionaires. On each of these issues, the public seemed to be considerably closer to the president and his Democratic allies in Congress than to Romney and the Republicans.[13]

Table 10.2 provides additional evidence of public support for taxing the rich from the 2012 American National Election Studies survey conducted during the fall campaign. By a margin of almost seven-to-one, Americans favored increasing income taxes on people making over $1 million per year. Even increasing income taxes on much less wealthy people, those making less than $1 million but over $250,000 per year—the threshold of affluence long favored, though subsequently abandoned, by President Obama in discussions of tax policy—generated overwhelming public support in the

[12] "Full Transcript of the Mitt Romney Secret Video," *Mother Jones*, September 19, 2012 (http://www.motherjones.com/politics/2012/09/full-transcript-mitt-romney-secret-video #47percent).

[13] YouGov survey, "Americans—and Republicans—Would Extend Payroll Tax Cut," December 12, 2011 (https://today.yougov.com/news/2011/12/12/americans-and-republicans-would -extend-payroll-tax/).

TABLE 10.2

Public Support for Taxing the Rich, 2012

"Do you favor, oppose, or neither favor nor oppose increasing income taxes on people making over $1 million per year?"

"Would you favor, oppose, or neither favor nor oppose a plan to reduce the federal budget deficit if it included the following?"

	Increase income taxes on people making over $1 million per year	Increase personal income taxes for those making over $250,000 per year	Increase corporate taxes
Favor	78.8%	70.3%	60.6%
Oppose	11.5%	18.3%	24.5%
Neither	9.0%	10.3%	12.3%
Don't know/refused	0.7%	1.1%	2.5%

Source: 2012 ANES survey. N = 1,929.

context of "a plan to reduce the federal budget deficit." Support for increasing corporate taxes was somewhat less overwhelming, but even here the public strongly favored increasing taxes if doing so would reduce the deficit.

In light of the salience of economic inequality as an issue in the 2012 campaign and the apparent strength of public support for Democratic positions on related policy issues, it is not surprising that Obama's reelection was interpreted in some quarters as a mandate for egalitarian policy change. Less than a week after the election, *New York* columnist Jonathan Chait offered this forceful interpretation of the meaning of the outcome:

> American voters had a chance to lay down their marker on the major social divide of our time: whether government can mitigate the skyrocketing inequality generated by the marketplace. For so many years, conservatives have endeavored to fend off such a debate by screaming "class war" at the faintest wisp of populist rhetoric. Somehow the endless repetition of the scare line inured us to the real thing. Here it was, right before our eyes: a class war, or the closest thing one might find to one in modern American history, as a presidential election. The outcome was plain. The 47 percent turned out to be the 51 percent.[14]

To Chait, the outcome of this "class war" had clear policy implications. "If there is a single plank in the Democratic platform on which Obama

[14] Jonathan Chait, "We Just Had a Class War; and One Side Won," *New York*, November 11, 2012.

can claim to have won," he wrote, "it is taxing the rich." However, that judgment begs the question of whether there *was* a single plank in the Democratic platform on which Obama could claim to have won. Policy "mandates" in elections are often more illusory than real, elite constructions that voters may endorse—or not—in the course of choosing candidates primarily on the basis of group loyalties, retrospective judgments of performance, and other considerations unrelated to party platforms.[15]

A very different, rather less uplifting interpretation of the 2012 outcome was offered the day after the election by Romney campaign adviser Kevin Hassett. "I don't think the Obama victory is a policy victory," he said. "In the end what mattered was that it was about Bain [Bain Capital, Romney's controversial hedge fund] and frightening people that Romney is an evil capitalist."[16] Hassett's interpretation, like Chait's, portrayed inequality as a significant factor in the 2012 election. But it was significant due to an accident of personality—Romney's background as a very wealthy "evil capitalist"— not because the campaign spurred public deliberation and judgment about policies that might address the issue.

As it happens, detailed survey data gathered over the course of the 2012 campaign can shed considerable light on these competing interpretations of Obama's election victory. Those data were gathered as part of the 2012 Cooperative Campaign Analysis Project (CCAP), a large-scale panel study designed by a team of political scientists headed by Lynn Vavreck and implemented by YouGov. The CCAP study included 45,000 "baseline" interviews conducted before the start of the campaign (in December 2011), reinterviews with 1,000 of those respondents each week from early January 2012 through Election Day, and a brief third interview with each respondent following the election.[17]

Figure 10.2 uses the CCAP data to track public support for taxing the wealthy over the course of the 2012 campaign.[18] Because all of the CCAP respondents completed a baseline survey in December 2011, they can be partitioned into three distinct subsets based on their predispositions at the beginning of the 2012 campaign: those who reported supporting Obama

---

[15] See, for example, Lenz (2012) and Achen and Bartels (2016, especially chaps. 2 and 10).

[16] Suzy Khimm, "How Republicans Are Trying to Look on the Bright Side Today," *Washington Post*, *Wonkblog*, November 7, 2012.

[17] YouGov, an Internet survey firm, employs opt-in recruiting of respondents but uses matching and weighting to produce representative samples of the adult population. The content of the second interviews varied from week to week over the course of the campaign season; thus, some of the items employed here were asked of different numbers of respondents at different points in the campaign. John Sides and Lynn Vavreck (2013) provided extensive analysis of the CCAP data.

[18] The dots in figures 10.2 and 10.3 represent weekly CCAP survey results (for weeks in which the relevant questions were asked), while the trend lines are smoothed to better reflect meaningful shifts in opinion.

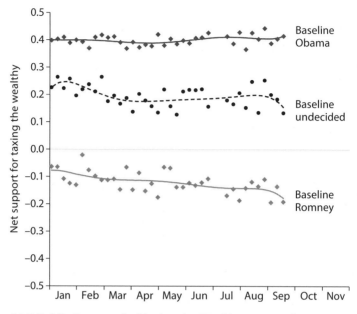

FIGURE 10.2 Public Support for Taxing the Wealthy During the 2012 Presidential Campaign

in the baseline interview (42%), those who reported supporting Romney (38%), and those who either reported being unsure about who they would support or did not answer (20%). Unsurprisingly, the differences among these three groups in tax policy preferences were huge, indicating significant polarization even in the early stages of the election year. As the campaign wore on, however, prospective voters became even more polarized on this issue. While the views of baseline Obama supporters were essentially constant throughout the campaign (at least through early September, when the CCAP surveys stopped asking the question), the views of both baseline Romney supporters and those who began the campaign undecided shifted noticeably, with the latter becoming less favorable toward taxing the wealthy and the former becoming more *un*favorable. Thus, on the whole, the campaign *reduced* public enthusiasm for taxing the wealthy, eroding slightly what had been a significant Democratic advantage.

Similar patterns appear on other survey items tapping public support for more progressive taxation. For example, table 10.1 records that the margin of support for increasing the top tax rate stood at 25 percentage points in October 2012—exactly where it had been two years earlier. Moreover, the proportion of the public favoring a complete extension of the Bush tax cuts, including those for top earners, was six points higher than it had been in the immediate wake of Obama's speech in Osawatomie. Thus, while the 2012 campaign seems to have polarized views about tax policy to some extent, it shows no sign of having generated any net increase in support for more progressive taxation.

The CCAP survey data also make it possible to assess the role of personality in the 2012 election by tracking prospective voters' impressions of Mitt Romney and Barack Obama. One pair of survey questions asked whether each candidate "is personally wealthy"; respondents overwhelmingly said yes for both men, but especially for Romney. Additional items asked whether each candidate "cares" about "people like me," "the poor," "the middle class," and "the wealthy." Obama enjoyed an advantage over Romney in perceived concern for "people like me," "the middle class," and especially "the poor." On the other hand, Romney was much more likely than Obama to be seen as caring about "the wealthy."

The widespread perception that Romney "cares about the wealthy" was presumably attributable in part to the fact that he is a multimillionaire. However, it is worth noting that many respondents also viewed Obama as personally wealthy but did not describe him as caring about the wealthy.[19] Nor does Romney's image in this regard simply reflect a more generic perception that Republicans are the party of the wealthy. When 1,000 CCAP survey respondents in mid-February 2012 were asked about the class sympathies of another contender for the Republican presidential nomination, Rick Santorum, only 31% said that the phrase "cares about the wealthy" described him very well, while 13% said that the phrase "cares about the poor" described him very well—an 18-point disparity. The corresponding percentages for Romney in the same week were 53% and 7%, respectively—a 46-point disparity.

Figure 10.3 traces changing public perceptions of Romney's class sympathies over the course of the 2012 campaign. The figure tracks relative perceptions of Romney's concern for "the wealthy" and "the poor" among baseline Obama supporters, people who did not express a preference for either candidate in the baseline survey, and baseline Romney supporters.[20] Not surprisingly, the differences among these three groups in average perceptions of Romney's relative concern for the wealthy were sizable. Moreover, they increased over the course of the campaign, with baseline Romney supporters

---

[19] At the individual level, the correlation between perceptions of personal wealth and perceptions of concern for the wealthy was only .22 for Obama, but .65 for Romney.

[20] The relative measure ranges from –0.5 (for respondents who said that "cares about the poor" described Romney "very well" while "cares about the wealthy" described him "not well at all") to +0.5 (for respondents who said that "cares about the poor" described Romney "not well at all" and that "cares about the wealthy" described him "very well"). Over the course of the campaign, 30% of the CCAP respondents chose the latter combination of responses, while 0.2%—31 of the 14,000 people who were asked these questions—chose the former combination of responses.

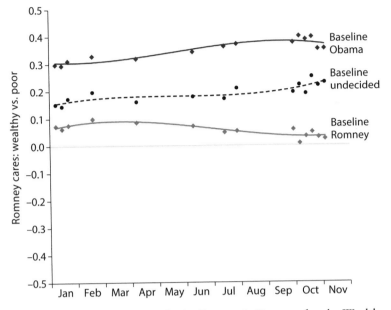

FIGURE 10.3 Public Perceptions of Mitt Romney's Concern for the Wealthy vs. the Poor During the 2012 Presidential Campaign

becoming somewhat less likely to see Romney favoring the wealthy while baseline Obama supporters and undecided voters became somewhat more likely to see Romney favoring the wealthy. However, even near the end of the campaign, even those respondents who began the year predisposed to support Romney were slightly more likely than not to view him as more concerned about the wealthy than about the poor.

Table 10.3 provides a more detailed picture of the bases of public perceptions of Romney's class sympathies at various points in the 2012 campaign. Using the same 14 weekly surveys represented in figure 10.3, it relates respondents' perceptions of Romney's relative concern for the wealthy (on the same −.5 to +.5 scale as in figure 10.3) in the spring, summer, and fall of the election year to a variety of pre-campaign attitudes and demographic characteristics measured in the December 2011 CCAP baseline survey—vote intentions, party identification, ideology, support for taxing the rich, economic perceptions, race, Hispanic origin, sex, education, income, homeownership, church attendance, and residence in a battleground state.[21] The

---

[21] Drawing on published reports of campaign ad expenditures, candidate visits, and other campaign activities, I classify Colorado, Florida, Iowa, Nevada, New Hampshire, North Carolina, Ohio, Virginia, and Wisconsin as battleground states in 2012.

TABLE 10.3

Sources of Romney's Perceived Concern for the Wealthy in the 2012 Campaign

Ordinary least squares regression parameter estimates (with standard errors in parentheses).

	January–April	June–July	September–October
Pre-campaign vote intention (−.5 to +.5)	.150 (.010)	.189 (.012)	.209 (.008)
Pre-campaign party identification (−.5 to +.5)	.047 (.012)	.076 (.015)	.072 (.010)
Pre-campaign liberal ideology (−.5 to +.5)	.078 (.015)	.027 (.019)	.091 (.012)
Pre-campaign support for taxing the wealthy (−.5 to +.5)	.084 (.008)	.108 (.010)	.102 (.006)
Pre-campaign perception of economic trend (−.5 to +.5)	−.003 (.008)	.013 (.011)	.024 (.007)
Black (0/1)	−.005 (.009)	.010 (.012)	−.018 (.007)
Hispanic (0/1)	−.023 (.010)	−.043 (.012)	−.023 (.007)
Female (0/1)	−.048 (.005)	−.032 (.007)	−.031 (.004)
Education (0 to 1)	.054 (.010)	.035 (.012)	.030 (.008)
Income percentile (0 to 1)	.031 (.012)	.029 (.015)	.026 (.009)
Homeownership (0/1)	.019 (.006)	.007 (.008)	.019 (.005)
Church attendance (0 to 1)	−.027 (.009)	−.045 (.011)	−.047 (.007)
Battleground state (0/1)	.010 (.006)	.013 (.008)	.012 (.005)
Intercept	.161 (.009)	.189 (.011)	.203 (.007)
Standard error of regression	.190	.185	.169
Adjusted R²	.27	.38	.50
N	4,998	3,000	6,000

Source: 2012 CCAP panel survey.

results imply that perceptions of Romney were strongly shaped not only by baseline vote intentions (as is evident in figure 10.3) but also by pre-existing partisan loyalties, ideology, and views about taxing the wealthy. Moreover, the apparent impact of these factors on perceptions of Romney tended to increase from spring to summer to fall, just as one would expect if specific perceptions of Romney were manufactured over the course of the campaign, in part, to bolster broader (and in some cases only tenuously related) attitudes and convictions.[22]

Notwithstanding biasing factors of this sort, it is clear from figure 10.3 that most people throughout the campaign were more likely than not to perceive Romney as caring more about wealthy people than about poor people. Insofar as those perceptions inclined voters to support Obama over Romney, they constituted a significant electoral advantage for the incumbent. But to what extent *did* perceptions of Romney's class sympathies incline voters to support Obama? For that matter, to what extent did the broad public support for increasing taxes on the wealthy evident in figure 10.2 contribute to Obama's victory? The CCAP survey data allow us to explore these questions.[23]

The statistical analyses reported in table 10.4 relate vote intentions at various points in the campaign (in the first three columns) and post-election vote reports (in the final column) to these and other factors, including baseline candidate preferences, party identification, ideology, and economic perceptions (all measured in the December 2011 baseline survey), and a battery of demographic characteristics.[24] Thus, the estimated effects reported in the table reflect the extent to which perceptions of Romney's relative concern for the rich and tax policy preferences were associated with *shifts* in vote intentions from the baseline survey that cannot be accounted for on the basis of these political predispositions and social characteristics. As we saw in table 10.3, perceptions of Romney's class sympathies were increasingly

---

[22] For example, the impact of pre-campaign vote intentions increased by about one-third, from .150 in the spring of 2012 to .189 in the summer and .209 in the fall. More broadly, the adjusted R^2 statistic, which measures the fraction of variance in perceptions of Romney's class sympathies accounted for by the full set of explanatory variables, nearly doubled, from .27 in the spring to .38 in the summer to .50 in the fall.

[23] Elsewhere (Bartels 2013a) I have provided more detailed analysis of these data, including separate analyses of battleground states and those that experienced little campaigning, consideration (albeit with a smaller sample of CCAP survey respondents) of the electoral significance of a broader range of specific policy preferences and attitudes related to inequality (employing some of the survey items summarized in tables 10.6 and 10.7, among others), and an experimental study of the role of campaign advertising in altering and priming the electoral relevance of voters' views about inequality.

[24] Each of these analyses includes the battery of demographic factors listed in table 10.3 as well as the attitudes and preferences listed in table 10.4, though the estimated effects of these additional control variables are not reported.

TABLE 10.4

The Impact of Views About Inequality on Support
for Obama in the 2012 Campaign

Ordinary least squares regression parameter estimates (with standard errors in
parentheses). Romney's perceived concern for the wealthy residualized on the basis
of parameter estimates in table 10.3. Demographic control variables are included
in the analysis but not shown.

	January–April vote intention	June–July vote intention	September–October vote intention	Post-election vote report
Romney's perceived concern for the wealthy, January–April	19.94 (1.60)	—	—	16.92 (2.67)
Romney's perceived concern for the wealthy, June–July	—	25.62 (2.10)	—	23.64 (3.39)
Romney's perceived concern for the wealthy, September–October	—	—	25.24 (1.68)	28.50 (2.64)
Pre-campaign support for taxing the wealthy (−.5 to +.5)	10.54 (.87)	9.22 (1.14)	12.49 (.80)	8.46 (.83)
Pre-campaign vote intention (−.5 to +.5)	53.17 (1.10)	46.86 (1.35)	44.69 (1.04)	59.37 (1.07)
Pre-campaign party identification (−.5 to +.5)	17.35 (1.40)	23.18 (1.72)	18.77 (1.29)	24.45 (1.29)
Pre-campaign liberal ideology (−.5 to +.5)	7.18 (1.70)	11.81 (2.15)	11.46 (1.55)	11.35 (1.57)
Pre-campaign perception of economic trend (−.5 to +.5)	6.19 (.94)	8.97 (1.23)	10.22 (.92)	5.00 (.90)
Standard error of regression	21.37	21.32	21.97	25.97
Adjusted R²	.71	.71	.72	.73
N	4,998	3,000	6,000	8,780

Source: 2012 CCAP panel survey.

strongly shaped over the course of the campaign by a variety of political predispositions, including partisan loyalties and pre-campaign vote intentions. Thus, in order to provide a more meaningful assessment of how these sympathies mattered at various points in the campaign, I have adjusted respondents' perceptions of Romney to take account of this gradual coloring of their views.[25] Since perceptions of Romney's class sympathies were measured in only 14 of the 45 weekly surveys conducted over the course of the campaign (and not in the baseline survey), the analyses are limited to the same 13,998 survey respondents as in table 10.3.[26]

A comparison of the separate analyses of vote intentions in the spring, summer, and fall (in the first, second, and third columns of table 10.4, respectively) suggests that perceptions of Romney's concern for the wealthy probably began to matter more in the wake of what one political reporter characterized as "the spring-summer narrative battle . . . to create perceptions that stick with voters through Election Day."[27] These estimates may be exaggerated somewhat if voters who gravitated to Obama for other reasons over the course of the election year then adopted the negative image of Romney proffered by the Obama campaign. However, in order to bias the estimates presented in table 10.4, those other reasons for shifting to Obama would have to be unrelated to the variety of baseline predispositions and characteristics listed in table 10.3. In any case, the apparent effect of Romney's perceived concern for the wealthy seems too large, too early, and too specific to be spurious.[28]

But did these perceptions actually stick with voters through Election Day? The analysis presented in the final column of table 10.4 strongly suggests that they did. For survey respondents whose impressions of Romney were measured in the spring, the apparent impact of those impressions on actual

[25] Specifically, I used the statistical results reported in table 10.3 to estimate how much of each respondent's perception of Romney's class sympathies was grounded in pre-existing attitudes and demographic characteristics measured in the CCAP project's December 2011 baseline survey. Subtracting these predictable reflections of pre-existing attitudes and characteristics left a residual perception for each respondent that was statistically uncorrelated with his or her pre-existing attitudes and characteristics and thus was more plausibly an independent factor in shaping the respondent's voting behavior.

[26] Each respondent appears in one of the first three columns of table 10.4, depending on when the respondent was interviewed between January and October. The final column includes the 63% of respondents who reported in the post-election follow-up survey that they voted for either Obama or Romney.

[27] Richard W. Stevenson, "In Post-Primary Period, Campaigns Race to Define Challenger," New York Times, May 14, 2012.

[28] For example, it does not seem to be the case that prospective voters simply reported favorable impressions of their preferred candidate and unfavorable impressions of his opponent, since perceptions of Obama's relative concern for the wealthy and the poor had little or no apparent effect on vote intentions.

vote choices reported after the election was about 85% as strong as the apparent impact on vote intentions in the spring. For those interviewed in the summer, more than 90% of the apparent impact of Romney's perceived concern for the wealthy persisted until Election Day. For those interviewed in the fall, perceptions of Romney seem to have been even more strongly associated with eventual vote choices than with fall vote intentions. Support for taxing the wealthy, on the other hand, seems to have had rather less impact on eventual vote choices than on vote intentions expressed during the campaign.

While the analyses presented in table 10.4 shed significant light on the determinants of individual vote choices over the course of the 2012 campaign, they do not directly answer the question of how important those factors were in determining the election outcome. The aggregate impact of perceptions regarding Romney's class sympathies depended not only on the magnitude of the individual effects reported in table 10.4 but also on the balance of perceptions in the electorate as a whole. Because voters' perceptions were heavily tilted toward viewing Romney as more concerned about the wealthy than about the poor, the net impact of those perceptions was to bolster Obama's vote share. Multiplying the smallest of the estimated effects in table 10.4, 16.92, by the average perception of Romney among major party voters, .212, produces an estimated impact on Obama's vote share of +3.6%—more than enough to have been decisive in his reelection.[29]

Similarly, multiplying the apparent effect in table 10.4 of support for taxing the wealthy, 8.46, by the net preponderance of support among voters, .138, produces an estimated impact of tax policy preferences on Obama's vote share of +1.2%. That impact is appreciable in the context of a close election; however, it is far too small to warrant the conclusion that public enthusiasm for "taxing the rich" was the key to Obama's victory. Indeed, these estimates suggest that Obama benefited three times as much from the fact that his opponent was viewed as an out-of-touch plutocrat as from any specific public demand for more progressive tax policy.

[29] My calculation of "net impact" parallels Warren Miller and J. Merrill Shanks's (1996, chap. 17) calculations of the "importance" of various explanatory factors in producing aggregate election outcomes. This calculation depends crucially on the choice of a meaningful zero value for each variable (since shifting all of a variable's values up or down by the same arbitrary amount would alter the average opinion without altering the corresponding estimated effect). In the case of Romney's relative concern for wealthy and poor people, the construction of the variable provides a natural zero value (when a prospective voter's responses to the separate "cares about the wealthy" and "cares about the poor" questions are identical). In the case of tax policy preferences, I assign zero values to "not sure" responses, with positive values for those who favor increasing taxes on the wealthy and negative values for those who oppose increasing taxes on the wealthy.

On its face, this evidence is consistent with Kevin Hassett's claim that "what mattered" in the 2012 election was Mitt Romney's image rather than policy preferences related to inequality.[30] However, it does not necessarily follow that this image was a result of the Obama campaign "frightening people" by creating concerns about Romney that would not otherwise have existed, or by increasing the salience of concerns that would otherwise have been less consequential at the polls. As the opinion trends presented in figure 10.3 make clear, the perception that Romney was more concerned about wealthy people than about poor people was well established as early as January, before the Obama campaign began its concerted attempt "to define Mr. Romney . . . as beholden to billionaire backers and corporate interests."[31] Even more tellingly, a comparison between battleground and non-battleground states suggests that months of intensive campaigning in battleground states did nothing at all to shift prospective voters' views about Romney's class sympathies or to increase their impact on voting behavior. Indeed, people in battleground states seem to have attached *less* weight to that consideration than people in non-battleground states—exactly the opposite of what one would expect if the Obama campaign had succeeded in "priming" the issue of inequality, bolstering the weight it received in the voting booth.

Thus, while the issue of inequality seems to have contributed significantly to Barack Obama's reelection in 2012, its contribution seems to have been highly circumstantial. Obama had the good fortune to run against a multimillionaire whose background and rhetoric fueled a widespread public perception that he cared more about wealthy people than about poor and middle-class Americans. Obama's campaign team did its best to exploit that advantage; however, my analysis suggests that those efforts were neither sufficient nor necessary to create the perception and to give it substantial political traction.

While popular accounts of presidential elections frequently turn on the personalities and political skills of the protagonists, scholarly research tends to downplay the significance of personal traits in shaping election outcomes. However, my findings here imply that voters' perceptions of Mitt Romney's class loyalties mattered to an extent that specific, identifiable aspects of a presidential candidate's personal image seldom do.[32]

---

[30] More detailed analysis employing several additional measures of attitudes and policy preferences related to inequality, albeit with a much smaller sample of voters than in table 10.4, reinforces the conclusion that concerns about Romney's class sympathies contributed much more to Obama's victory than tax preferences, views about the tax burdens or political influence of rich and poor people, perceptions of fallout from the recession, and belief in equal opportunity, whether assessed separately or in combination. See Bartels (2013a).

[31] Konrad Yakabuski, "Obama Finds His Campaign Focus—Inequality," *The Globe and Mail*, July 9, 2012.

[32] On the modest role of personality traits in presidential elections, see Bartels (2002c). However, it is worth noting that the trait perception with the strongest and most consistent

OBAMA AND INEQUALITY

From the perspective of democratic theory, it would be nice to think that Obama's reelection signaled a popular mandate for shifting public policy in the direction of "taxing the rich." That interpretation would tend to validate an eminently rational and reassuringly simple notion of how a democratic political system can and should address the challenge of escalating economic inequality: call attention to the issue, propose a logical policy response, invite voters to render their verdict, and assume that that verdict will be translated more or less directly into policy change. Alas, the evidence presented here mostly supports a quite different interpretation of the 2012 election outcome, one that is certainly less tidy and perhaps also less edifying. The "issue" of inequality seems to have mattered a lot, but in a more visceral way—not primarily as a premise in a high-minded debate about good public policy, but as a basis for public concern about Mitt Romney personally as "an evil capitalist," in Kevin Hassett's phrase.

This interpretation casts significant doubt on whether populist concerns about inequality, insofar as they did matter in 2012, could be successfully mobilized in circumstances lacking a convenient personification of wealth, privilege, and the purported "evils" of capitalism. In the meantime, however, this may be a distinction without a difference. Obama's victory may not have reflected a popular mandate for taxing the rich or expanding opportunity, but votes cast due to qualms about Mitt Romney's secret tax returns, offshore bank accounts, and manifest disdain for the "47 percent" counted just as surely as if they had been inspired by an abstract commitment to progressive policy change.

Perhaps the best test of the concrete implications of the 2012 election for the issue of inequality came in the two months after the election, as Democrats and Republicans alike turned their attention to the major policy questions raised by the looming expiration of the Bush tax cuts and the Obama payroll tax cut and by the prospect of significant automatic cuts in defense and domestic spending triggered by the failure of Congress to reach a grand bargain on deficit reduction.

This confluence of deadlines—the "fiscal cliff"—presented President Obama and his Democratic allies with substantial leverage to recast tax and spending policy to their liking. Many observers assumed that Obama's election mandate would further strengthen his hand, ensuring that he would get his way on "taxing the rich"—the issue on which Jonathan Chait and others argued that he could "claim to have won." For Democrats, a clear victory on that issue would have considerable symbolic importance, redeeming the

---

estimated effects on voting behavior is the one most closely analogous to my measure here of Romney's relative concern for wealthy people and poor people—the extent to which each candidate "really cares about people like you" (Bartels 2002c, 61–66).

party's disappointing failure to kill the Bush tax cuts for top earners when they were set to expire in 2010, while Democrats still enjoyed unified control of the White House and Congress.

As it turned out, translating the Democrats' election "mandate" into policy was a good deal harder than it looked. Republicans held firm on their demand that all of the Bush tax cuts should be made permanent, then retreated to a fallback plan in which only incomes in excess of $1 million per year would be subject to higher rates. After weeks of haggling, Congress and the president agreed to a last-minute deal negotiated by Vice President Joe Biden and Senate Majority Leader Mitch McConnell in which the income threshold for permanent tax cuts increased from $200,000 for individuals and $250,000 for families—Obama's long-standing proposal—to $400,000 for individuals and $450,000 for families.

The higher income threshold reduced by more than half the number of income tax filers whose tax rates increased, from just below 2% to about 0.7%. By comparison with Obama's plan, the compromise cost the Treasury about $12 billion in the first year, with about 85% of the benefits going to tax filers in the top 1% of the income distribution, reducing their average tax bill by almost $9,000. Meanwhile, the 2% reduction in payroll tax rates that had begun in 2011—a policy much more consequential for most taxpayers than the fate of the top income tax rate—was allowed to die almost without discussion. According to a summary from CNN, "the deal gives Obama bragging rights for raising income taxes on the wealthiest Americans," but really amounted to "breaking a promise" to significantly increase the progressivity of the overall tax system.[33]

In the run-up to the deal, congressional aides speculated that "Democrats are likely to make concessions on the estate tax to Republicans—who loath high rates on what they've dubbed the 'death tax'—in exchange for keeping the Bush tax cuts at the president's preferred threshold of $250,000."[34] As it turned out, Republicans mostly got their way on the estate tax (a lower rate and higher exemption), the high-income tax cuts (on family incomes between $250,000 and $450,000), *and* the payroll tax.

Within a week after the deal was enacted, some Democrats began to complain that the White House had "made a critical if underappreciated mistake in the final hours of the back and forth: sending Joe Biden to haggle with Senate Republican leader Mitch McConnell once McConnell's talks

---

[33] These figures are based on an analysis by the Tax Policy Center of the "Incremental Effect of Raising 'High-Income' Thresholds to $500,000 for Married Couples" (table T12-0306). Matt Smith, "Obama Signs Bill Warding Off Fiscal Cliff," *CNN Politics*, January 3, 2013 (http://www.cnn.com/2013/01/02/politics/fiscal-cliff).

[34] Suzy Khimm, "The 'Fiscal Cliff's' Estate Tax Fight, Explained," *Washington Post*, *Wonkblog*, December 30, 2012.

with his Democratic counterpart, Harry Reid, had broken down. . . . By involving Biden, Obama undercut Reid and signaled that he wanted a deal so badly he was unwilling to leave anything to chance, even when the odds overwhelmingly favored him."[35] Of course, there is no way to know whether Reid's strategy of "briefly" going over the fiscal cliff would have produced a more favorable policy outcome.

A few weeks after the 2012 election, journalist Zachary Goldfarb had suggested that, for the president,

> the imminent debate over the "fiscal cliff" is not simply a war over taxes, spending, and how to tame the nation's mushrooming debt. As Obama did in legislative fights during his first term he also will be striving to reduce a three-decades-long wave of rising income inequality that has meant that fewer Americans have prospered while more struggle to get by. . . . [B]eneath his tactical maneuvering lies a consistent and unifying principle: to use the powers of his office to shrink the growing gap between the wealthiest Americans and everyone else. If presidents set missions for themselves that are greater than winning the partisan battle of the moment, then this is Obama's.[36]

By that standard, the partisan battle of the "fiscal cliff" must be judged a draw—and the question of whether ordinary Americans can be mobilized for a wider war on skyrocketing inequality remains very much open.

Twenty months later, an exchange between Goldfarb and fellow journalist Timothy Noah illuminated both the successes and the failures of Obama's effort "to shrink the growing gap between the wealthiest Americans and everyone else." Goldfarb argued that Obama had "reduced inequality," while Noah responded that inequality had "gotten worse" under Obama. In fact, both were right.[37]

In part, the apparent disagreement was a matter of focus. Goldfarb concentrated mostly on the impact of Obama's tax policies, while Noah argued that "taxes and transfers don't do all that much" to affect inequality and looked instead at "market" incomes (before taxes and transfers are taken into account). However, the more important source of disagreement

---

[35] Noam Scheiber, "The Inside Story of How Obama Could Have Gotten a Better Tax Deal Without Biden," *The New Republic*, January 9, 2013.

[36] Zachary Goldfarb, "How Fighting Income Inequality Became Obama's Driving Force," *Washington Post*, November 23, 2012.

[37] Zachary A. Goldfarb, "Don't Think Obama Has Reduced Inequality? These Numbers Prove That He Has," *Washington Post*, Wonkblog, July 23, 2014; Timothy Noah, "Has Income Inequality Lessened Under Obama?" MSNBC, July 24, 2014 (http://www.msnbc.com/msnbc/how-inequality-has-changed-under-obama); Larry Bartels, "Obama's Uphill Struggle Against Economic Inequality," *The Monkey Cage*, July 24, 2014.

between Goldfarb and Noah was a matter of perspective. For Goldfarb, "reduced" was a relative term, implying that Obama's policies reduced the level of inequality relative to what it would otherwise have been. Noah conceded that point: "Relative to an imaginary Republican president, Obama has reduced income inequality. That's something to be grateful for." But in absolute terms, inequality still increased.

As we saw in figure 9.7, disparities in real income between affluent, middle-class, and working-poor families grew from 2009 through 2014 (the most recent year for which data are currently available). According to Census Bureau tabulations, the real incomes of affluent families (at the 95th percentile of the income distribution) grew by 4.2% over this period, while the real incomes of working poor families (at the 20th percentile) *fell* by 2.1%; middle-class families' incomes remained unchanged or grew slightly. At the pinnacle of the income distribution, Emmanuel Saez calculated, the real incomes of the top 1% of income-earners grew by 27.1% over this period, while the real incomes of the bottom 99% grew by just 4.3%. The Gini index, a broader measure of inequality, was also higher in 2014 than it had been when Obama was inaugurated.[38]

By these absolute standards, Obama clearly failed to reduce income inequality (at least through 2014). Of course, short-term assessments of this sort can be quite misleading, especially in turbulent times. More broadly, Noah argued that the increase in income inequality was "not really Obama's fault" because "economic forces at work since 1979, hugely exacerbated by decades of conservative government policies," have made inequality "extremely difficult to reverse." The historical analyses of partisan patterns of income growth presented in chapter 2 provide considerable support for that contention.

In the same spirit, *New York Times* columnist Josh Barro observed that the economic fortunes of the poor were "affected greatly" by Obama administration policies during and after the Great Recession, sometimes in ways that did not show up in standard income tabulations:

> Between 2007 and 2012, the share of Americans who would have been poor based on their income before taxes and transfers rose by five percentage points. But after adjusting for taxes and transfers, poverty rose by just a point. Programs like Medicaid and unemployment insurance were highly effective in stopping the sharp rise in unemployment from turning into a sharp rise in poverty. Most of that policy effect was automatic, but a considerable portion was due to specific policy initiatives of the president, such as extending unemployment insurance benefits.[39]

---

[38] Census Bureau, Historical Income Tables; Saez (2015, table 1).

[39] Josh Barro, "What Is 'Middle-Class Economics'?" *New York Times*, February 26, 2015.

In the longer term, as Goldfarb argued, Obama's impact on income inequality may depend as much or more on reshaping taxes and redistribution as on changing patterns of "market" incomes. Most of the "specific policy initiatives" adopted in response to the Great Recession, such as extended unemployment benefits and a reduced payroll tax, turned out to be temporary measures. However, Obama's reelection probably guaranteed that the substantial subsidies for health insurance provided under the Affordable Care Act would survive and expand, substantially boosting the future well-being of poor and middle-class households. Meanwhile, the increased taxes imposed on affluent households to pay for those subsidies would also survive, putting a significant dent in top incomes. As a result, the Affordable Care Act was not only "the most sweeping piece of federal legislation since Medicare was passed in 1965" but also "the federal government's biggest attack on economic inequality" in "more than three decades."[40]

When the Internal Revenue Service released its tabulations of effective federal income tax rates for 2013, they showed that the average income tax rate for taxpayers in the top 1% of the income distribution had risen by four percentage points in a single year, while the average rate for taxpayers in the top .01% had risen by more than six percentage points. According to Paul Krugman,

> what these tables show is that elections really do have consequences. . . .
> [I]f you were expecting Mr. Obama to preside over a complete transformation of America's political and economic scene, what he's actually achieved can seem like a big letdown. . . . [But] while the 2013 tax hike wasn't gigantic, it was significant. Those higher rates on the 1 percent correspond to about $70 billion a year in revenue. This happens to be in the same ballpark as both food stamps and budget office estimates of this year's net outlays on Obamacare. So we're not talking about something trivial. . . . [T]he 2012 election had major consequences. America would look very different today if it had gone the other way.[41]

Of course, these consequences do not imply that "inequality will shrink" in absolute terms anytime soon. As Noah concluded, inequality is "extremely difficult to reverse, even for a president who's made reversing it a top priority." The Sisyphean nature of that challenge was aptly, though perhaps unintentionally, captured in a 2014 remark by Jason Furman, chairman of Obama's Council of Economic Advisers. "Just the tax changes we made in

[40] David Leonhardt, "In Health Bill, Obama Attacks Wealth Inequality," *New York Times*, March 24, 2010.

[41] Paul Krugman, "Soaking the Rich, Slightly," *New York Times*, December 31, 2015; Paul Krugman, "Elections Have Consequences," *New York Times*, January 4, 2016.

this administration undid about half a decade of the increase in inequality," Furman said. "If you add in the Affordable Care Act, it's more than a decade of inequality that was undone."[42] But if a once-in-four-decades policy shift undoes a decade of increasing inequality, it is going to take a very long time to make significant progress in rolling back our New Gilded Age.

The Political Challenge

Having identified equality of opportunity as "the defining challenge of our time" in his 2013 speech to the Center for American Progress, President Obama went on to ask, "Why has Washington consistently failed to act?" His answer hinged in significant part on "the belief that government cannot do anything about reducing inequality." While that answer may attach undue weight to the beliefs and preferences of ordinary citizens in the policy-making process, it underlines the fact that egalitarian sentiment is especially unlikely to have much impact in Washington if it is unconnected to concrete support for things government can actually do to reduce inequality.

A series of surveys from the Pew Research Center nicely documented the disjuncture between the public's apparent concern about inequality and its appetite for plausible policy solutions. As Andrew Kohut of Pew observed, "While the public acknowledges the problem, there is less of a consensus about whether the government should take strong measures to reduce the gap between the wealthy and other Americans. It's a highly partisan and potentially divisive issue." For example, 67% of Democrats but only 19% of Republicans said that reducing income inequality between the rich and poor should be "an absolute priority" for the Obama administration and Congress in 2015.[43]

The 2012 CCAP Inequality Module provides a broader survey of public attitudes, preferences, and perceptions in the realm of inequality. In the final few weeks of the 2012 election campaign, 3,000 people were asked their

[42] Quoted by Goldfarb, "Don't Think Obama Has Reduced Inequality?"

[43] Pew Research Center, "Most See Inequality Growing, but Partisans Differ over Solutions," January 23, 2014 (http://www.people-press.org/2014/01/23/most-see-inequality-growing-but -partisans-differ-over-solutions/); Drew DeSilver, "Americans Agree Inequality Has Grown, but Don't Agree on Why," Pew Research Center, April 28, 2014 (http://www.pewresearch.org /fact-tank/2014/04/28/americans-agree-inequality-has-grown-but-dont-agree-on-why/); Bruce Stokes, "Debate over Inequality Highlights Sharp Partisan Divisions on the Issue," Pew Re- search Center, October 20, 2014 (http://www.pewresearch.org/fact-tank/2014/10/20/debate -over-inequality-highlights-sharp-partisan-divisions-on-the-issue/); Andrew Kohut, "Are Amer- icans Ready for Obama's 'Middle Class' Populism?" Pew Research Center, February 19, 2015 (http://www.pewresearch.org/fact-tank/2015/02/19/are-americans-ready-for-obamas-middle -class-populism/); Janet Hook, "Poll Finds Agenda Gap Between Leaders, American People," *Wall Street Journal, Washington Wire*, January 21, 2015.

views about changing economic conditions, the federal debt, government spending and taxes, the role of labor unions, and equality of opportunity, among other issues. When it came to a direct choice between helping ordinary workers or the wealthy, those views were solidly progressive: 63% (including 40% of Republicans) favored a payroll tax cut extension offset by a new tax on millionaires. However, many more of their responses supplied further evidence of ambivalence about or outright opposition to "strong measures to reduce the gap between the wealthy and other Americans."[44]

For example, responses to several questions in the survey indicate significant public concern about budget deficits and taxes, significantly limiting the political scope for aggressive efforts to stimulate the economy or to seize the opportunity offered by historic low interest rates to invest in human capital or modernize the nation's crumbling physical infrastructure. Only 38% of the public (and 11% of Republicans) agreed that the government should run a budget deficit to stimulate the economy in hard times.[45] Only 45% favored increased federal spending to stimulate economic growth.[46] On the other hand, 65% of the public (and 87% of Republicans) favored cutting taxes on individuals and businesses to stimulate growth.[47] Support for tax-cutting encompassed even highly progressive taxes: 53% favored abolishing the estate tax.[48] These findings are summarized in table 10.5.

The last three rows of table 10.5 report responses to a battery of questions probing the relative importance of government spending, taxes, and the federal budget deficit. Forced to choose between "avoid[ing] raising the taxes paid by middle-class taxpayers" and "maintaining spending on domestic programs like education, food stamps, and highways," 59% of the

[44] I contracted with YouGov to include the Inequality Module in 3,000 CCAP interviews conducted from October 13 through November 2, 2012. For more information on the design and content of the Inequality Module, see Bartels (2013a; 2014b).

[45] "In economic hard times, should the government run a budget deficit to stimulate the economy and create jobs, or should it cut the deficit in order to balance the budget and save money?"

[46] "Some people suggest that the government can help the economy recover from a recession by increasing its spending. Would you favor or oppose increased spending by the federal government to stimulate economic growth?"

[47] "Some people suggest that the government can help the economy recover from a recession by cutting taxes. Would you favor or oppose cutting taxes on individuals and businesses to stimulate economic growth?" Prompting respondents to consider the possibility of tax-cutting (by asking that question first) made them almost six points less supportive of increased government spending than if they were asked about increased government spending first. This difference underlines the contrast in public enthusiasm for tax-cutting and increased government spending to stimulate economic growth.

[48] "Some members of Congress have proposed an extension of last year's payroll tax cut, which has boosted most workers' take-home pay. They want to offset the cost of continuing this tax cut by imposing a new tax on incomes in excess of $1 million. Do you favor or oppose that idea?" "There has been a lot of talk recently about doing away with the 'estate tax' on large inheritances. Do you favor or oppose doing away with the estate tax?"

public preferred to cut spending. In a choice between increasing the federal budget deficit and cutting domestic spending, 56% preferred to cut spending. Clearly, most people's concerns about taxes and deficits trumped their support for (at least these) government programs.[49]

In a choice between increasing middle-class taxes and increasing the budget deficit, 53% of the public preferred to increase the deficit. Democrats were somewhat more concerned about taxes and Republicans were somewhat more concerned about the deficit, but both parties were fairly evenly split on the question. The 17-point partisan difference in responses was by far the smallest in table 10.5; the *average* partisan difference for the other seven items was 48 points, with the biggest differences (in excess of 50 points) on the items involving government spending.

Another battery of questions in the 2012 CCAP Inequality Module pinpointed some of the key political attitudes undergirding Americans' antipathy to policies that might put a serious dent in economic inequality. The responses to these questions are summarized in table 10.6. They indicate that majorities of the public—and overwhelming majorities of Republicans—agreed that "the federal debt is a threat to the American way of life," that "the federal government controls too much of our daily lives," that "poor people have become too dependent on government assistance programs," and that "business people would create more jobs if their profits were taxed at a lower rate."

In each case, these beliefs mitigate against effective policy responses to escalating economic inequality. For example, President Obama repeatedly advocated increased government borrowing to invest in expanding opportunities for the disadvantaged, but that sort of investment is unlikely to gain substantial political support when 65% of the public agrees that "the federal debt is a threat to the American way of life." Expansion of unemployment benefits, health care, and nutrition assistance in the depths of the Great Recession ran up against the same public antipathy to deficit spending, as well as the widespread belief that "poor people have become too dependent on government assistance programs." Regulating banks, insurance companies, and employers is likely to be an uphill struggle when most Americans agree

---

[49] These trade-off questions were asked in two different formats. Half the respondents were asked whether they preferred cutting spending on domestic programs to increasing the taxes paid by middle-class taxpayers, whether they preferred increasing middle-class taxes to increasing the federal budget deficit, and whether they preferred increasing the federal budget deficit to cutting spending on domestic programs. The other half were asked whether it was more important to maintain spending on domestic programs than to avoid raising the taxes paid by middle-class taxpayers, whether it was more important to avoid raising middle-class taxes than to keep the federal budget deficit from growing, and whether it was more important to keep the federal budget deficit from growing than to maintain spending on domestic programs. To a good approximation, the responses to the questions about "cutting" or "increasing" were mirror images of the responses to the questions about "maintaining" or "avoiding"; thus, for the sake of clarity, I combine them here.

TABLE 10.5
Americans' Policy Preferences, 2012

	Total sample	Democrats	Republicans
In economic hard times, government should run a budget deficit to stimulate the economy and create jobs	37.9	63.8	11.2
Favor increased spending by the federal government to stimulate economic growth	35.2	63.1	7.2
Favor cutting taxes on individuals and businesses to stimulate economic growth	65.4	47.2	87.2
Favor payroll tax cut extension offset by new tax on incomes in excess of $1 million	62.8	82.8	39.8
Favor doing away with the "estate tax" on large inheritances	53.0	38.1	74.0
More important to avoid raising middle-class taxes than to maintain spending on domestic programs	58.8	36.7	88.2
More important to keep the federal budget deficit from growing than to maintain spending on domestic programs	55.5	30.8	87.9
More important to avoid raising middle-class taxes than to keep the federal budget deficit from growing	53.1	60.7	43.9
N	3,000	1,325	1,175

Source: 2012 CCAP Inequality Module.

that "the federal government controls too much of our daily lives." On the other hand, tax cuts for the affluent are likely to enjoy significant support from a public confident that "business people would create more jobs if their profits were taxed at a lower rate."

Of course, public antipathy in itself does not make new public investment, an expanded safety net, increased regulation, or tax increases on businesses politically impossible. Indeed, the record of the Obama administration offers

TABLE 10.6
Americans' Political and Social Attitudes, 2012
Agree–disagree (%); remainder chose "neither" or "don't know."

	Total sample	*Democrats*	*Republicans*
The federal debt is a threat to the American way of life	65–15	46–28	90–2
The federal government controls too much of our daily lives	57–23	29–45	88–3
Poor people have become too dependent on government assistance programs	54–27	28–49	89–4
Business people would create more jobs if their profits were taxed at a lower rate	52–26	31–46	81–7
In America, everyone has an equal opportunity to succeed	51–34	35–50	77–15
Labor unions are necessary to protect working people	46–34	73–10	16–68
N	3,000	1,325	1,175

Source: 2012 CCAP Inequality Module.

proof to the contrary. However, policy shifts of this sort are more difficult, more costly in terms of political capital, and thus less likely to occur because the public attitudes summarized in table 10.6 are so uncongenial.

Finally, policy analysts have pointed to the decline of labor unions as an important factor in the politics of inequality. As Jacob Hacker and Paul Pierson put it, "the organizations that traditionally bolstered middle-class democracy have declined. Nowhere is this clearer or more fateful than with regard to American labor. An expanded role for unions would make a big difference." However, they added, "the reinvigoration of unions is unlikely to be the primary catalyst during the early stages of a renewed middle-class politics. Business opposition is too unified and intense; the cross-pressures on many Democrats, too severe."[50] The odds against "an expanded role for unions" are presumably lengthened by the fact that only 46% of Americans agree that "labor unions are necessary to protect working people." Among Republicans, especially, antipathy toward unions is compounded by an

---

[50] Hacker and Pierson (2010, 303, 56–61, 127–132, 139–143). See also, for example, Noah (2012, chap. 8); Stiglitz (2012, chap. 3); Reich (2015, chap. 13).

exaggerated sense of their power: Republicans ranked labor unions second only to the news media in political influence—well ahead of the wealthy, business people, and other groups.[51]

Finally, table 10.7 presents additional results from the CCAP Inequality Module focusing on citizens' beliefs about some objective facts regarding economics and public policy. These results provide two additional grounds for pessimism about the politics of inequality. For one thing, they demonstrate (once again) that the public as a whole is sometimes quite wrong about straightforward and highly relevant facts. For example, only 14% said that their own federal taxes were lower in 2012 than they had been in 2008, despite the fact that federal tax revenues had declined even in nominal dollars. Barely one-third recognized a dramatic increase—from –2.5% to +2.7%—in the rate of economic growth over the same period. And only 35% knew that the growth rate had slowed over the preceding year (from 3.1% to 2.7%).

At the same time, the contrasting beliefs of Democrats and Republicans summarized in table 10.7 demonstrate that the extreme partisan polarization evident in tables 10.5 and 10.6 extended even to the most straightforward objective facts. Republicans overwhelmingly believed that unemployment had increased during President Obama's first term (true) and that the rate of economic growth had declined (false), while most Democrats believed the opposite. Democrats overwhelmingly believed that unemployment had decreased in the past year (true) and that the rate of economic growth had increased (false), while most Republicans believed the opposite. In some cases, these partisan differences in beliefs amounted to 50 percentage points or more. If public consensus about policy issues requires some pre-existing public consensus about the objective state of the world, that consensus is unlikely to be forthcoming in the contemporary political climate.[52]

---

[51] "How much influence do you think each of the following groups has on U.S. politics and public policy?" Respondents rated "the wealthy," "the news media," "business people," "labor unions," "religious groups," "the middle class," and "the poor" on a four-point scale: a great deal (100); a fair amount (66.7); a little (33.3); or none (0). Among Republicans, the groups perceived as most influential were the news media (with an average rating of 85.8), labor unions (83.3), the wealthy (72.2), and business people (62.4).

[52] Larry Bartels, "Our Own Facts," *Model Politics*, March 12, 2012 (http://today.yougov.com/news/2012/03/12/our-own-facts/); Achen and Bartels (2016, chap. 10). Even views about junk food are not immune to partisan biases. In 2011, Herman Cain, the former head of Godfather's Pizza, was a prominent candidate for the Republican presidential nomination. Over the course of the year, a survey tracking public assessments of the company's quality, value, and reputation revealed significant polarization along partisan lines. At the beginning of the year, before Cain's emergence as a partisan figure, Republicans and Democrats had identical, slightly positive views of Godfather's Pizza. In November, shortly before Cain dropped out of the presidential race, Republicans had become substantially more favorable, while Democrats had become distinctly unfavorable. Ted Marzilli, "Cain's Candidacy Splits Pizza Scores," *YouGov BrandIndex*, November 15, 2011 (http://www.brandindex.com/article/cains-candidacy-splits-pizza-scores).

TABLE 10.7
Partisan "Facts" in the 2012 Campaign

	Total sample	Democrats	Republicans
Do you think the *unemployment rate* is higher or lower now than it was a year ago?			
(A little lower or a lot lower)	51.2	72.9	33.0
Do you think the *economic growth rate* is higher or lower now than it was a year ago?			
(A little lower or a lot lower)	34.8	13.2	63.2
Mitt Romney has proposed a major reduction in tax rates financed by the elimination of various tax deductions. Do you think Romney's plan would *increase* or *decrease* the proportion of total income tax paid by middle-class taxpayers?			
(Increase)	40.2	67.6	12.1
Would you say that *the federal budget deficit* is much higher, somewhat higher, unchanged, somewhat lower, or much lower than it was four years ago?			
(Somewhat higher or much higher)	81.4	73.6	95.9
Would you say that *your own federal taxes* are much higher, somewhat higher, unchanged, somewhat lower, or much lower than they were four years ago?			
(Somewhat lower or much lower)	14.4	22.8	6.0
Would you say that *the unemployment rate* is much higher, somewhat higher, unchanged, somewhat lower, or much lower than it was four years ago?			
(Somewhat higher or much higher)	57.2	34.7	85.7
Would you say that *the overall rate of economic growth* is much higher, somewhat higher, unchanged, somewhat lower, or much lower than it was four years ago?			
(Somewhat higher or much higher)	34.4	56.4	12.9
Would you say that *federal spending on domestic programs like education, food stamps, and highways* is much higher, somewhat higher, unchanged, somewhat lower, or much lower than it was four years ago?			
(Much higher or somewhat higher)	59.0	43.8	82.8
N	3,000	1,325	1,175

Source: 2012 CCAP Inequality Module.

Perhaps an eclectic populism of the sort represented by Donald Trump could erode or revise the intense partisan divisions evident in tables 10.5, 10.6, and 10.7. But even if that did happen, it is by no means obvious that the result would be to stimulate broad public support for policies that would reduce economic inequality. The policy preferences and attitudes reported in tables 10.5 and 10.6 that come closest to registering broad support across the political spectrum are mostly consistent with "the belief that government cannot do anything about reducing inequality." A country in which most people agree that the way to stimulate growth is to cut taxes and that the federal debt is a threat to the American way of life is not a country on the verge of a new Progressive Era.[53]

Of course, it is foolhardy when thinking about the political future to rule anything out. Nonetheless, the evidence presented in this chapter seems to cast substantial doubt on the notion that ordinary Americans will rise up anytime soon to recast the politics of inequality in a more progressive mold. If the Great Recession, the Occupy Wall Street movement, and a president who repeatedly declared that inequality is "the defining challenge of our time" had so little apparent impact on public perceptions, values, and policy preferences, why should we expect next year or the year after that to be any different?

Jonathan Chait portrayed Barack Obama's reelection as a populist victory in a "class war" to "mitigate the skyrocketing inequality" of the New Gilded Age. From the standpoint of policy voting and popular mandates, that portrait seems overdrawn; Obama's victory does not seem to have hinged on public support for "taxing the rich" or for progressive policies more generally. However, victories in war are often accidental, stemming from favorable happenstance rather than the orderly application of superior force. If, as I suspect, Americans reelected Obama in significant part because they viewed Mitt Romney as an out-of-touch plutocrat, they reelected him nonetheless. And then, as Paul Krugman put it, "elections really do have consequences." Perhaps that is all we can reasonably hope for.

---

[53] Benjamin Page and Lawrence Jacobs (2009) presented a more optimistic picture of "what Americans really think about economic inequality." However, their focus was on the public's desire to reduce inequality and the popularity of specific progressive programs such as Social Security and education spending, not on the broader range of related attitudes about society and the role of government considered here.

CHAPTER 11

Unequal Democracy

THE IMPACT OF wealth on political life has been a subject of concern at least since the time of Aristotle, who surveyed and critiqued the laws of the various Greek city-states regarding limitations on wealth, inheritance, communal ownership of property, and the extension of citizenship rights to the working class. Indeed, Aristotle made the relationship between wealth and political status the fundamental basis for classifying regimes: "what differentiates oligarchy and democracy is wealth or the lack of it. The essential point is that where the possession of political power is due to the possession of economic power or wealth, whether the number of persons be large or small, that is oligarchy, and when the unpropertied class have power, that is democracy."[1]

In the early modern period, the Italian republics viewed their wealthy citizens as constant threats to political stability and liberty. According to political theorist John McCormick,

> Unless formally restrained, the richest citizens tended to use their privilege to molest fellow citizens with impunity and direct the workings of government toward their own benefit rather than toward that of the general citizenry. . . . If a popular government or republic is not to veer dangerously toward an unaccountable oligarchy, natural or not, institutional affirmative action for common citizens is necessary. In this light, contemporary democracies could do worse than reconsider the extra-electoral practices that earlier republics, their partisans and their theorists often thought were crucial to insure the genuine liberty of citizens.[2]

American history, too, has been marked by periodic popular backlashes against the political effects of concentrated wealth. According to Kevin Phillips, public opinion "has distrusted economic elites and periodically used democratic politics to curb their abuses. Banks, special corporations, railroads, the giant trusts, the 'money power,' Wall Street, and the 'malefactors of great wealth' have all spent decades in the firing zone of angry electorates." The escalating economic inequality and political corruption of the Gilded Age and the Roaring Twenties stimulated the institutional reforms of the Progressive Era and the New Deal. Louis Brandeis, a significant figure in both the Progressive Era and the New Deal, famously wrote that "we can have a democratic society or we can have great concentrated wealth in the hands of a few. We cannot have both."[3]

The economic trends documented in chapter 1 once again raise the question of whether democracy can flourish in the midst of great concentrated wealth. One way of framing this question is to ask, with Sidney Verba and Gary Orren, whether the economic and political "spheres of justice" can be kept "autonomous and their boundaries intact." On that score there seems to me to be little basis for optimism in my examination of the political

---

[1] Aristotle, *Politics*, T. A. Sinclair, trans. (Harmondsworth: Penguin Books, 1962), books II and III, 117.

[2] McCormick (2006, 147, 161). McCormick's suggestions for "institutional affirmative action for common citizens" included a wealth ceiling on eligibility to serve in the House of Representatives, a modified version of California's "recall referendum," and a citizens' assembly selected by lot to monitor and, if necessary, sanction elected officials.

[3] Phillips (2002, 294, 418).

economy of the New Gilded Age. Economic inequality clearly has pervasive, corrosive effects on political representation and policy-making in contemporary America. In light of these effects, the liberal hope for distinct "spheres of justice" with "their boundaries intact" seems naively fastidious and quite probably ineffectual.

Verba and Orren recognized that porous boundaries may allow "transmutation" in both directions: while economic power may be convertible into political power, political power may also be used to alter or mitigate the effects of developments in the economic realm—as it *has* been used more or less effectively in the Progressive Era, the New Deal, and other pivotal moments in American history. Of course, there are substantial risks to justice on that side as well. Still, if economic inequality seriously compromises the values of democracy, it seems worth recalling and assessing the ways and means by which democracy might realistically be employed to constrain economic inequality.[4]

Who Governs?

This book began with the question Robert Dahl asked more than half a century ago: "In a political system where nearly every adult may vote but where knowledge, wealth, social position, access to officials, and other resources are unequally distributed, who actually governs?"[5] I suggested that the answer Dahl provided for New Haven in the 1950s might be obsolete in the vastly more unequal America of the 21st century, where the share of national income controlled by the "economic notables" in the top one-tenth of 1 percent of income-earners is three times as large as it was in the late 1950s.

If Dahl's question is interpreted as asking whose preferences influence policy outcomes, the answer suggested by the evidence presented in chapter 8 is that affluent people have considerable clout while the preferences of middle-class and poor people are much less efficacious. Whether we consider broad patterns of national policy-making, the overall patterns of roll call votes cast by members of Congress, or their votes on specific salient roll call votes, my own analyses and those of other political scientists are remarkably consistent in suggesting severe disparities in political responsiveness stemming from differences in income or wealth. Observers of contemporary American politics may be unsurprised to hear that elected officials attached more weight to the preferences of affluent constituents than of middle- and low-income constituents. However, only the most cynical critic of American democracy could be unsurprised to hear that scores of millions

[4] Verba and Orren (1985, 8).
[5] Dahl (1961, 1).

of ordinary Americans' political views seem to be largely or wholly ignored in the policy-making process.

This pessimistic conclusion seems to me to be of profound importance for our understanding of American democracy. Political leaders do appear to be responding to the policy preferences of millions of affluent citizens. That crucial popular element in the American political system is aptly reflected in a term coined by Dahl: *polyarchy*. However, the pattern of responsiveness portrayed in chapter 8 is a very far cry from approximating Dahl's loftier *democratic* ideal of "continued responsiveness of the government to the preferences of its citizens, considered as political equals." Indeed, as the leading contributor to this vein of research, Martin Gilens, has suggested, "representational biases of this magnitude call into question the very democratic character of our society."[6]

These disparities in representation are especially troubling because they suggest the potential for a debilitating feedback cycle linking the economic and political realms: increasing economic inequality may produce increasing inequality in political responsiveness, which in turn produces public policies that are increasingly detrimental to the interests of poor citizens, which in turn produces even greater economic inequality, and so on. If that is the case, shifts in the income distribution triggered by technological change, demographic shifts, or global economic development may in time become augmented, entrenched, and immutable.

Perhaps future scholarly investigation will demonstrate that these disparities in representation are somehow anomalous or statistical artifacts. So far, however, that does not seem to be the case. Studies focusing on Congress, the states, and other affluent democracies—and employing a variety of different research designs—seem to reinforce the striking and sobering conclusion that effective political equality is unlikely in the face of substantial economic inequality. In Aristotle's terms, our political system seems to be functioning not as a "democracy" but as an "oligarchy." If we insist on flattering ourselves by referring to it as a democracy, we should be clear that it is a starkly *unequal* democracy.

In another sense, the evidence presented in chapter 8 suggests a different answer to Dahl's question. The patterns of responsiveness to constituency opinion documented there were set against a pervasive pattern of divergence in the behavior of Democratic and Republican officials, even when they "represented" the very same constituents. In most cases, even massive differences in the preferences of middle- and upper-income constituents had less effect on senators' policy choices than their own partisan ideologies. Whatever elections may be doing, they are *not* forcing elected officials to cater to the policy preferences of the "median voter." Thus, in a very real

---

[6] Dahl (1971); Gilens (2005, 778).

sense, the answer to the question of "who actually governs" is: whoever makes a successful claim to have won an election. As Joseph Schumpeter noted more than half a century ago, "collectives act almost exclusively by accepting leadership—this is the dominant mechanism of practically any collective action which is more than a reflex. . . . Democracy does not mean and cannot mean that the people actually rule in any obvious sense of the terms 'people' and 'rule.' Democracy means only that the people have the opportunity of accepting or refusing the men who are to rule them."[7]

The scope for independent action by elected leaders may be especially great in cases where public sentiment is divided, unstable, confused, or simply non-existent. In the midst of a generally optimistic survey of the policy preferences of *The Rational Public*, political scientists Benjamin Page and Robert Shapiro portrayed tax policy as "a highly technical realm that is ripe for concealment and mystification." My analysis in chapters 5 and 6 provides ample evidence of confusion, uncertainty, and "unenlightened self-interest" in public opinion about tax policy. Thus, it should perhaps not be surprising to find public officials relying less on citizens' attitudes than on their own ideological convictions for policy direction in this domain. It is tempting to take comfort in the belief that, as Jacob Hacker and Paul Pierson put it, "Not all issues make voters' eyes glaze over in the way that details of tax policy do."[8]

It is important to note, however, that the paucity of elite responsiveness to public opinion extends even to issues on which public opinion seems to be unusually firm and stable. In the case of estate tax repeal, for example, the relevant evidence is extremely fragmentary, but insofar as it exists at all it suggests that the estate tax has been quite unpopular for at least 80 years. For most of that time, the only real obstacle to estate tax repeal was the ideological antipathy of Democratic presidents and members of Congress. Within months of the arrival of a Republican president with Republican majorities in the House and Senate in 2001, an estate tax phaseout was passed and signed into law.

The case of the eroding minimum wage, which I examined in chapter 7, is even more remarkable. There has been abundant evidence of strong, consistent public support for minimum wage increases throughout the past 50 years—a period in which the real value of the federal minimum wage has declined by one-fourth. Here, too, the most important hurdle to the public getting what it says it wants seems to be the conviction of policy-makers—in this case, primarily conservative Republican policy-makers—that a higher minimum wage would have significant adverse consequences unrecognized by the substantial public majority that supports it.

[7] Schumpeter (1950, 270, 284–285).
[8] Page and Shapiro (1992, 166); Hacker and Pierson (2005a, 49).

Partisan Politics and the "Have-nots"

Scholars of political participation and liberal activists often seem to suppose that the cure for political inequality is to educate and mobilize the disadvantaged in support of specific progressive policies. However, the evidence of unresponsiveness to the views of low-income citizens presented in chapter 8 suggests that that strategy is very unlikely to be politically effective. As one energetic critic of the "burgeoning 'democratic inequality studies' field," Robert Weissberg, has argued, political activism "does perform as advertised, but only *sometimes*, and even then usually for those who already enjoy many advantages." Weissberg added that "shouting louder ('voice') is likely to be futile . . . for those mired in poverty."[9]

If raising their "voice" is "likely to be futile" for people on the losing end of economic inequality, is there any hope for progress? My analysis points to two related bright spots in an otherwise gloomy picture. First, the correlation between class positions and political views is not so substantial that support for egalitarian policies is limited to "those mired in poverty." Just as many poor people espouse antipathy to redistribution and the welfare state, many affluent people support egalitarian policies that seem inconsistent with their own narrow material interests. Insofar as the political activism of affluent egalitarians "does perform as advertised," policy-makers may be much more generous toward the poor than the political clout of the poor themselves would seem to warrant.

In any case, my analyses suggest that the specific policy views of citizens, whether rich or poor, have less impact in the policy-making process than the ideological convictions of elected officials. Whether we consider broad patterns of economic distribution (chapter 2), major changes in the tax system (chapters 5 and 6), income support for the poor (chapter 7), votes cast by members of the House and Senate (chapter 8), or responses to a global economic crisis (chapter 9), policy choices seem to depend more on the partisan ideologies of key policy-makers than on the details of public opinion. Thus, even if poor people have negligible *direct* influence on the day-to-day decisions of elected officials, they—and their more affluent ideological allies—may have substantial *indirect* influence by altering the balance of power between Democrats and Republicans in the making of public policy.

The prominent role of political parties in my account of the political economy of inequality calls to mind a famous suggestion by V. O. Key Jr., in his monumental analysis of *Southern Politics in State and Nation*, that "over the long run the have-nots lose in a disorganized politics." Key's assertion was inspired by his close study of the one-party politics of the South in the Jim Crow era, which suggested that the southern states with the most

[9] Weissberg (2004, 36–37).

stable and cohesive factional structures had more genuine competition between "ins" and "outs," a greater "sense of corporate responsibility" among elected officials, less "favoritism and graft" in the conduct of government business, and more "power to discipline wild-eyed men" on the explosive issue of race—all factors contributing, in Key's view, to rational public consideration of the "crucial issues" of "taxation and expenditure."

By comparison, less stable factional structures only sporadically facilitated "the old Populist battle of the poor, white farmer against the plantation regions." States with the most "discontinuous and kaleidoscopic" factional structures were marked by "issueless politics" lacking even "a semblance of factional responsibility," placing "a high premium on demagogic qualities of personality," and providing "great negative power to those with a few dollars to invest in legislative candidates." The implication Key drew from these observations was that stable, organized factional competition—which he thought of as approximating, under the peculiar historical conditions of the one-party South, "the role assigned elsewhere to political parties"—is the most promising "institutionalized mechanism for the expression of lower-bracket viewpoints."[10]

Key's assertion regarding the importance of organized political competition for the fortunes of the economically disadvantaged fits neatly in a broader scholarly literature on party competition and democratic government. The intellectual tradition associated most closely with E. E. Schattschneider—and expressed most famously in the 1950 report of the American Political Science Association's Committee on Political Parties, which he chaired—emphasized the constructive role of political parties and party competition in structuring and adjudicating political conflict. Progressive observers of midcentury American politics bemoaned the obstacles to policy change created by federalism, boss rule, and the institutional separation of powers in Washington. Their favorite prescription for reform was a more "responsible" party system modeled on the British parliamentary system, with voters choosing between cohesive party teams offering distinct platforms and empowered to implement those platforms once elected.[11]

If the analysis and prescription offered by political scientists more than half a century ago were correct, the contemporary American party system would seem to meet the requirements for party government—and, by extension, for progressive policy-making—rather well. In Congress, ideological moderates have largely disappeared, turning the two parties' delegations into increasingly distinct liberal and conservative camps. Party unity and party-line voting increased steadily through the 1970s and 1980s, reaching levels by the 1990s that exceeded those of the 1950s and spurring analyses

[10] Key (1949, 307, 298–310).
[11] Schattschneider (1942); Committee on Political Parties (1950).

of "conditional party government." Meanwhile, the proportion of "strong" party identifiers in the electorate increased substantially beginning in the 1970s, while the proportion of "independents" declined. At the same time, the strength of the relationship between partisanship and voting behavior also increased markedly, with partisan voting in the past four presidential elections reaching levels surpassing those that prevailed in the 1950s. These behavioral manifestations of increasing partisanship have been accompanied by attitudinal manifestations, with citizens increasingly seeing important differences between the parties, recognizing their relative ideological positions, and volunteering more reasons for liking one party and disliking the other.[12]

Schattschneider should have been delighted by these developments. The hitch, of course, is that responsible parties may do little for the "have-nots" if the wrong party wins. Thus, while organized party competition may be a *necessary* condition for progressive policy-making, it is not a *sufficient* condition. Indeed, one recent study of American politics suggests that "the unmatched coordination and cohesion" of the contemporary Republican Party has resulted in "tilting the balance of benefits and protections away from ordinary Americans and toward the well off, the well connected, and the Republican base."[13]

Interestingly, Key himself seems to have abandoned the "have-nots" hypothesis over the course of the 1950s as southern state politics evolved in unexpected ways and his own scholarly focus broadened to include one-party systems in non-southern states. As Key's most distinguished student, David Mayhew, noted that in his book on *American State Politics*, published only seven years after *Southern Politics in State and Nation*, "Key entirely abandoned the 'have-nots' claim. Or at least he carefully refrained from re-stating it." This shift seems to reflect both the "precarious" relationship between dual factionalism and progressive politics in the South—as Mayhew observed, "dual factionalism hardly qualified as a *sufficient* condition for government attention to 'have-nots'"—and the apparent counter-examples of progressive politics in the one-party systems of New England.[14]

Subsequent scholars of state politics have taken Key's hypothesis as an influential starting point. However, most of their analyses have focused not on the *structure* of party competition but on the *closeness* of the electoral division between Democrats and Republicans, as measured by vote shares or seats in state legislatures. Early analyses of this sort found little impact of party competition on state policy outcomes.[15] The results of more recent

---

[12] McCarty, Poole, and Rosenthal (2006); Rohde (1991); Miller (1991); Bartels (2000); Hetherington (2001).

[13] Hacker and Pierson (2005b, 3, 14).

[14] Mayhew (1988, 24, 34); Key (1956).

[15] Lockard (1959); Dye (1966); Winters (1976).

studies are also mixed, but they suggest, if anything, that an even partisan division between Democrats and Republicans may produce policy outcomes generally considered harmful to the political interests of "have-nots." For example, one study found inconsistent but generally negative effects of party competition on the size of state governments, while another found that evenly divided state legislatures produced lower taxes and lower levels of workers' compensation benefits.[16]

Edward Jennings offered a different interpretation of Key's "have-nots" hypothesis, arguing that the *class basis* of party competition rather than the *closeness* of party competition affected the political fortunes of the economically disadvantaged (as measured by the generosity of state welfare benefits). His comparison of social policy in eight states showed that the six states with class-based party systems from the New Deal through the 1960s (Connecticut, Louisiana, Massachusetts, Michigan, Minnesota, and Wisconsin) spent more on welfare than the two that did not (Indiana and Virginia). He also found that the states with class-based party systems spent more on welfare when Democrats controlled state politics than when Republicans were in charge, suggesting that class-based politics is especially good for "have-nots" when their side wins.[17]

Robert Brown's broader analysis of all 50 states failed to support Jennings's assertion that class-based party systems generally produced progressive policy outcomes; on average, states characterized by a class-based "New Deal" cleavage structure provided no more generous welfare benefits than southern or "post–New Deal" states. However, Brown's analysis did confirm that a class-based cleavage structure raised the policy stakes for "have-nots": Democratic control of state governments had a strong positive effect on welfare spending in the "New Deal" states but little or no impact in southern or "post–New Deal" states.[18]

Although there seems to be relatively little empirical support for the proposition that party competition per se produces progressive social policy, Jennings's and Brown's findings are part of a substantial empirical literature establishing the political importance of *which* party controls the reins of government at any given time. Several more recent studies by political scientists and economists have found significant partisan differences in state revenues and expenditures, taxes and spending patterns, and Medicaid spending. They have also demonstrated that welfare benefits tend to be more generous in states with higher absolute or relative turnout rates among low-income voters.[19]

---

[16] Rogers and Rogers (2000); Besley and Case (2003).

[17] Jennings (1979).

[18] Brown (1995).

[19] Rogers and Rogers (2000); Besley and Case (2003); Knight (2000); Grogan (1994); Hill, Leighley, and Hinton-Andersson (1995); Husted and Kenney (1997). Besley and Case (2003) provide a comprehensive review of these and other relevant studies.

These state-level findings are strongly echoed by my findings regarding partisan patterns of policy-making and economic distribution at the national level. In case after case, Democratic officials have provided strong support for policies favoring the "have-nots"—expanding the economy, increasing funding for domestic programs, raising the minimum wage—while Republican officials have pursued policies favoring the "haves"—fighting inflation, cutting taxes, repealing the estate tax. These consistent, long-standing differences in the class interests embodied in the two parties' governing philosophies are revealed most dramatically in the patterns of income growth documented in chapter 2. Over the past sixty-five years, Democratic presidents have generally presided over robust income growth for families across the economic spectrum, while Republican administrations have generally been bad for the economic fortunes of middle-class families and even worse for the economic fortunes of the working poor. The political significance of these stark partisan differences can only be gainsaid by supposing that they are the result of a massive (and highly improbable) historical coincidence.

Large-scale historical analysis of "the macro polity" underscores the impact of political parties on the broad course of American public policy. In the context of a complex analysis relating economic conditions, liberal or conservative shifts in "public mood," partisan loyalties in the electorate, presidential approval, election outcomes, and policy-making in the White House, Congress, and the Supreme Court, Robert Erikson, Michael Mac-Kuen, and James Stimson found that partisan control of government was by far the most important determinant of policy outputs. For example, the estimated effect on White House policy activity of replacing a Republican president with a Democrat was more than three times as large as the estimated direct effect of moving from the most conservative public mood on record (in 1952) to the most liberal public mood on record (in 1961); the estimated effects of partisan control on congressional policy activity were even larger. Although the authors themselves did not stress these findings, it is difficult to read their work without being mightily impressed by how substantially the course of public policy over the past half-century has shifted with changes in partisan control of the reins of national government.[20]

The United States is by no means unique in this regard. Writing in the late 1990s, Carles Boix criticized comparative political economists for "the rather tangential role they have ascribed to electoral politics and the impact of partisanship" in accounting for cross-national differences in economic policies and performance. Summarizing his own research on Europe, Boix asserted that "conservative governments cut taxes, slash public investment programs, sell most public businesses, and revamp the labor market to increase the profitability of capital and to induce the unemployed to actively search for jobs. Socialist cabinets, instead, raise tax rates on high-income

[20] Erikson, MacKuen, and Stimson (2002, 204, 305, 308, 310).

brackets and boost public spending on infrastructure and human capital in order to ease the transition from an unskilled population profile to a well-educated workforce without having to lower the social wage."[21]

What may be surprising, both to Americans and to foreigners, is the extent to which the supposedly tame partisan politics of the postwar United States mimics the contrast Boix portrayed between European socialists and conservatives. Notwithstanding the popular perception that there's "not a dime's worth of difference" between Democrats and Republicans, as George Wallace used to say—and notwithstanding the strong emphasis on the moderating effects of electoral competition in formal theories of majoritarian politics—the fact of the matter is that partisan control of government has been of consistent, substantial importance to the economic fortunes of "have-nots" throughout the postwar era.

The current configuration of the American party system features a highly competitive balance between Republicans and Democrats in the electorate, in Congress, and in the Electoral College. But the parties are not evenly matched because they are indistinguishable; in fact, they are now more ideological, more cohesive, and more distinct in their supporting coalitions than at any time in recent memory. While a large segment of the public remains politically disengaged, attentive citizens have increasingly responded to these developments by choosing up sides and adopting more or less consistent packages of policy positions and partisan loyalties.

The implications of the increasing economic and ideological polarization of the parties and their supporting coalitions appear to depend primarily on the outcome of the partisan struggle for political dominance. Political scientists have found rather little evidence that intense partisan competition per se benefits "have-nots," but considerable evidence that "have-nots" benefit when their party wins. For most of the past century, when Democrats have controlled the reins of government, they have consistently pursued high employment, high taxes, and economic redistribution from the rich to the poor. When Republicans have governed, they have consistently done the opposite. The partisan tenor of the contemporary political environment seems likely, if anything, to reinforce those tendencies, making the stakes for "haves" and "have-nots" alike even higher than in the past—and the political struggle correspondingly more intense.

POLITICAL OBSTACLES TO ECONOMIC EQUALITY

The temptation to suppose that organized political competition must work to the advantage of "have-nots" is grounded in the natural-seeming assumption that "have-nots" will use the power of the ballot to restrain the

---

[21] Boix (1998, 219, 202).

privileges of the less numerous "haves," if not to expropriate their wealth. Certainly that has happened from time to time in the course of American history. Kevin Phillips noted that the American public "has distrusted economic elites and periodically used democratic politics to curb their abuses." Likening the economic circumstances of the current era to the most conspicuous past eras of escalating inequality, the original Gilded Age and the Roaring Twenties, Phillips observed that those periods of concentrated wealth and political corruption ended with the Progressive Era and the New Deal, respectively, and suggested that "a politics in this tradition is unlikely to blink at confronting twenty-first century elites."[22]

So far, however, ordinary Americans have demonstrated little capacity to curb the abuses of the New Gilded Age's "malefactors of great wealth" through the political process. The Wall Street bailouts of late 2008 and 2009 were highly unpopular before, while, and after they occurred, but as we saw in chapter 9, public antipathy was overridden by policy-makers' own judgments of economic necessity. The Occupy Wall Street movement attempted to mobilize public concern about the economic and political clout of "the 1%"; but, as we saw in chapter 10, it had little discernible impact on Americans' perceptions of inequality, egalitarian values, or policy preferences. Public support for increasing taxes on the wealthy had less impact on the outcome of the 2012 presidential election than the fact that one of the candidates, Mitt Romney, was himself a wealthy venture capitalist viewed as unconcerned about ordinary Americans. And two months after the election, despite strong public support for increasing taxes on the wealthy, the president and Congress agreed to a deal providing permanent cuts in income and estate taxes for affluent taxpayers—a draw in the long political battle over the fate of the Bush tax cuts.

In the 2016 election cycle, Bernie Sanders made the issue of income and wealth inequality the centerpiece of his campaign for the Democratic presidential nomination; according to his campaign website, it is "the great moral issue of our time, it is the great economic issue of our time, and it is the great political issue of our time." As of this writing, the impact of Sanders's campaign remains to be seen. But early indications suggest that it, too, will struggle to translate indignation about escalating inequality into significant changes in policy preferences. One early poll found Sanders's supporters somewhat more likely than Hillary Clinton's to say that inequality was increasing, and less optimistic about "opportunity in America today for the average person to get ahead," but also *less* likely to favor raising the minimum wage, increasing government spending on health care, and expanding government services at the cost of higher taxes—all policies that would reduce inequality.[23]

---

[22] Phillips (2002, 294).

[23] "Bernie Sanders on the Issues: Income and Wealth Inequality" (https://berniesanders .com/issues/income-and-wealth-inequality/); Christopher H. Achen and Larry M. Bartels, "Do Sanders Supporters Favor His Policies?" *New York Times*, May 23, 2016.

Perhaps the process of reaction and reform has simply not reached its critical stage. Phillips suggested that "the early twenty-first century should see another struggle" reminiscent of the Progressive and New Deal eras "because corporate aggrandizement in the 1980s and 1990s went beyond that of the Gilded Age—the parallels of political corruption and concentrated wealth—to frame issues of abandoning American workers, communities, and loyalties."[24] Perhaps. However, if the greatest economic crisis in eight decades and the momentous resulting declines in the income and wealth of ordinary Americans cannot animate such a struggle, it is hard to tell what will. In the meantime, while most people favor higher taxes on the wealthy, they also firmly believe that everyone in America has an equal opportunity to succeed, that the federal debt is a threat to our way of life, and that lowering taxes on businesses would create more jobs.

One explanation for these facts is simply that people are confused about what is in their own interest. There is plenty of raw material in this book for an account of contemporary politics emphasizing ordinary Americans' misperceptions, myopia, and missing connections between values and interests, on one hand, and policy preferences and votes, on the other. Perhaps most importantly, my analysis in chapter 3 suggests that Republicans have benefited greatly from voters' peculiar sensitivity to election-year income gains for affluent families. Despite the superior historical performance of Democratic presidents in generating income growth for middle-class and poor families over the past several decades, American voters have shown a strong tendency to punish Democrats and reward Republicans based on the very unrepresentative sliver of economic performance that happens to fall within their narrow focus on "present advantages," as Ostrogorski put it more than a century ago.

There are also significant partisan biases in attributions of responsibility for national economic conditions. For example, several polls conducted over the course of Barack Obama's presidency asked Americans whether Obama or his predecessor, George W. Bush, was "more responsible for the country's current economic problems." As recently as late 2013, a *Washington Post/ ABC News* poll found most people blaming Bush rather than Obama for the state of the economy. However, attributions of blame divided starkly along partisan lines, with 76% of Democrats but only 21% of Republicans (and 48% of independents) continuing to attribute economic responsibility to Bush almost five years after he left office.[25] Whichever side was right, the

[24] Phillips (2002, 413).

[25] "Post-ABC Poll: December Monthly," *Washington Post*, December 17, 2013 (https://www.washingtonpost.com/page/2010-2019/WashingtonPost/2013/12/17/National-Politics/Polling/question_12585.xml?uuid=gU0HumbYEeOZe5ITsX2slw#); "Poll: Nearly Five Years into Obama's Presidency, Most Americans Still Blame Bush for Economic Problems," *Hot Air*, December 19, 2013 (http://hotair.com/archives/2013/12/19/poll-nearly-five-years-into-obamas -presidency-most-americans-still-blame-bush-for-economic-problems/).

strong partisan skew in attributions of responsibility significantly limits the likely effectiveness of political accountability.

Even more fundamentally, the results of public opinion surveys presented in chapters 4, 5, and 10 suggest that the perceptions of economic and social reality that might trigger attributions of political responsibility are themselves strongly colored by political biases. On the eve of the 2012 election, Democrats and Republicans differed sharply on the seemingly straightforward question of whether unemployment was higher or lower than it had been a year earlier. They also differed much more than rich people and poor people did in their perceptions of the extent of economic opportunity in American society. Moreover, greater political engagement and awareness often exacerbates rather than mitigates these biases. For example, conservatives who are generally well informed about politics and public affairs are significantly more likely than less well-informed conservatives to *deny* that differences in incomes between rich people and poor people have increased.

When it comes to thinking specifically about economic inequality as a political issue, Americans may be stymied by our tendency to view economics and politics as "separate arenas." According to Jennifer Hochschild,

> In other Western nations, socialist parties have developed a world view that overcomes this separation; but Americans see class relations, if at all, as only one among many components of public life. . . . When they view redistribution as an economic question, they argue from a principle of differentiation and oppose it. When they view it as a political question, they argue from a principle of equality and sometimes favor it. . . . People who feel torn between two views are unlikely to act forcefully to promote either; therefore by default, they end up "supporting" the status quo.[26]

Reliance on a "principle of differentiation" in moral judgments about inequality is reinforced by a tendency to think of the economic sphere as existing prior to and apart from the political sphere. Thus, a treasury secretary can insist that when "market forces work to provide the greatest rewards to those with the needed skills," the resulting escalation of economic inequality "is simply an economic reality, and it is neither fair nor useful to blame any political party." Here, "market forces" are impersonal but beneficent, "economic reality" is simple and inexorable, and political blame "is neither fair nor useful." The Wall Street meltdown was a temporary embarrassment to the prestige of "market forces," but it does not seem to have prompted much fundamental rethinking of the relationship between economics and politics. As one heterodox economist put it, "Economics

---

[26] Hochschild (1981, 20, 48, 249).

functions in a theological role in our society . . . to justify the ways of the market to men."[27]

Even a cursory examination of trends in other countries provides strong evidence that technological change and globalization do not *have* to produce the glaring disparities in economic fortunes experienced by Americans over the past four decades. Government action can ensure that the economic benefits stemming from these historic developments are widely shared. Studies of income redistribution in affluent democracies suggest that the United States has simply done less than other countries to mitigate the effects of increasingly unequal market incomes. In one such study, 10 of the 11 countries for which data were available (all except the Netherlands) experienced increases in income inequality among working-age households in the 1980s and 1990s. Of these 10 countries, nine engaged in more aggressive redistribution at the end of this period than at the beginning; in general, the increase in redistribution was greatest in countries where the increase in inequality of market incomes was greatest. The glaring exception was the United States, which experienced a larger-than-average increase in income inequality but no corresponding increase in redistribution.[28]

Insofar as Americans have any understanding of the alternative policies pursued by other affluent democracies, they mostly seem to reject those alternatives as inconsistent with America's core cultural values of economic opportunity and self-reliance: European welfare states, they tell themselves, are bloated, ossified, and hidebound. The reality seems to be that European economies have performed about as well as the American economy in generating long-term growth, and that economic mobility is at least as extensive in contemporary Europe as in the United States. However, it seems quite unlikely that most Americans would acknowledge those facts. As Hochschild has observed, the "dominant American world view . . . is complex and flexible, has a long history and deep roots, and has withstood or absorbed great shocks and vehement opposition."[29]

Political pressure for redistribution in the contemporary United States is probably further curtailed by the increasing social isolation of winners and losers in the market economy of the New Gilded Age. As economic inequality increased in the United States after 1970, economic segregation increased as well. Moreover, "as Americans migrated to the suburbs . . . rich and poor have become separated not just by neighborhood but also by municipal

[27] Remarks prepared for delivery by Treasury Secretary Henry H. Paulson at Columbia University, August 1, 2006; Duncan K. Foley, quoted in Peter Steinfels, "Economics: The Invisible Hand of the Market," *New York Times*, November 25, 2006.

[28] Kenworthy and Pontusson (2005). For related evidence, see Kenworthy (2014) and Kerr (2014).

[29] Perotti (1996); Wilensky (2002, chap. 12); Pontusson (2005); Solon (2002); Osberg and Smeeding (2003); Hochschild (1981, 281).

boundaries. With suburbanization, wealth has come to differentiate not just America's citizens but its cities as well."[30]

Perhaps in part for that reason, the Great Recession seemed to create a remarkably stark division between casualties and non-combatants. While victims of the economic crisis in Greece, France, and Britain took to the streets, America's millions of unemployed and foreclosed were largely invisible. A majority of respondents in a 2010 survey said that they *did not know* "anyone who has had their home foreclosed or fallen behind in their mortgage payments in the past year."[31] For many affluent Americans, in particular, a few months of genuine panic fairly quickly faded into the more familiar economic strain of recession and slow recovery.

The remarkable insulation of America's comfortable class from the realities of economic inequality is occasionally underlined by the response of critics and readers to firsthand accounts of poverty. When the writer Barbara Ehrenreich published *Nickel and Dimed*, her colorful account of spending a few months working at a series of low-wage jobs, reviewers called it "illuminating," "jarring," "explosive," "frightening," and "unforgettable." When Linda Tirado—an actual working poor person!—published *Hand to Mouth: Living in Bootstrap America*, it was hailed as "startling," "gripping," "riveting," "deeply unsettling," and "horrifying." Perhaps it had never occurred to these reviewers that waitresses, housecleaners, and sales clerks work hard, endure myriad petty abuses and indignities from employers and customers, and struggle to make ends meet. "I grew up hearing over and over, to the point of tedium, that 'hard work' was the secret of success," Ehrenreich wrote. "No one ever said that you could work hard—harder even than you ever thought possible—and still find yourself sinking ever deeper into poverty and debt." It seems hard to imagine that the parents and grandparents of Ehrenreich's and Tirado's readers would have been so shocked by these glimpses of the practical and moral ramifications of inequality in the everyday lives of the working poor. "There are poor and working-class people everywhere," Tirado informed her readers at one point. "You can just have a conversation with one, like a real human being. Give it a try."[32]

The class divide in contemporary America is no doubt exacerbated by the fact that the people on the losing end of the market economy often have

---

[30] Massey and Denton (1993); Jargowsky (1996); Mayer (2001); Oliver (2001, 69).

[31] "Do you know anyone who has had their home foreclosed or fallen behind in their mortgage payments in the past year?" Yes, 36%; no, 54%; not sure, 9%. YouGov/Polimetrix survey, October 2010.

[32] Ehrenreich (2001, 220); reviews from *New York Times Book Review, Newsweek, New York Times, San Francisco Chronicle*, and *Newsweek*, respectively. Tirado (2014, 206); reviews from *New York Times Book Review, Publishers Weekly, Women's Health, Ms.*, and *Booklist*, respectively.

different skin colors and accents than those that predominate among the affluent and comfortable. Martin Gilens has documented the importance of racial discrimination in accounting for *Why Americans Hate Welfare*. Alberto Alesina and Edward Glaeser have used cross-national data to show that racially and ethnically heterogeneous societies generally have much less generous social policies than those that are more homogeneous. According to one study, even support for the Bush tax cuts stemmed in significant part from Americans' "racial resentments and attachments rooted in the history of slavery and discrimination." Since those resentments and attachments are not going to disappear anytime soon—and since American society will become even more diverse in the coming decades—racial and ethnic divisions will continue to be a major obstacle to greater economic equality.[33]

If social segregation limits public demand for redistribution, it also matters more directly by shaping the attitudes and behavior of political elites. As we saw in chapter 8, Nicholas Carnes found that elected officials are overwhelmingly drawn from the ranks of the affluent and privileged. But the relatively few elected officials who have any personal experience in blue-collar jobs are distinctly more liberal on economic policy issues, even after allowing for differences in party affiliations, constituencies, and other characteristics. That difference seems plausibly attributable to the knowledge and empathy that come with lived experience—experience that the vast, sheltered majority of elected officials lack. According to Carnes,

> as long as policy makers have some discretion and as long as they are drawn overwhelmingly from white-collar America, white-collar Americans will continue to have a disproportionate say in the legislative process, which will in turn tilt economic policy in favor of the interests of white-collar Americans. Even if we somehow equalized routine forms of political participation, even if we somehow stopped organized interests from buying influence, millionaires would still get to set the tax rate for millionaires. White-collar professionals would still get to set the minimum wage for blue-collar workers. People who have always had health insurance would still get to decide whether to help people without it.[34]

THE CITY OF UTMOST NECESSITY

In his book-length examination of *Democratic Faith*, political theorist Patrick Deneen found a compelling basis for political equality in an unlikely source: Plato's *Republic*. Before presenting his famous account of an ideal

---

[33] Gilens (1999); Alesina and Glaeser (2004); Kinder, Burns, and Vieregge (2005, 2).
[34] Carnes (2013, 148).

city ruled by philosopher-kings, Plato described a more rudimentary "city of utmost necessity" in which the farmer, the builder, the weaver, and the cobbler band together to provide for their common needs. Their division of labor reflects the fact that "each of us is naturally not quite like anyone else, but rather differs in his nature; different men are apt for the accomplishment of different work." But if that sounds remarkably like Adam Smith's economic rationale for market capitalism, Plato grounded his account of just collective life in the even more basic fact that "each of us isn't self-sufficient but is in need of much." As Deneen put it, "We are to engage in that form of work for which we have special talent explicitly to avoid *neglect* of our fellow citizens," and out of a fundamental recognition that

> no one of us is capable of creating the good things of life by ourselves alone. . . . Equality's self-evidence is demonstrated every day by the simple existence and permanent persistence of politics. Democracy is not premised upon the eventual perfection of our imperfect city nor the citizens who reside therein but precisely upon the permanent presence of imperfect humans who must, by dint of their equal insufficiency and the permanency of need, inhabit, and govern together, cities of men.[35]

In Plato's account, the "city of utmost necessity," with its just and healthy division of labor, is apt to fall prey to man's appetite for luxuries, resulting in the gradual evolution of a "feverish" city of myrrh and incense and girls and cakes—and a professional army to defend these luxuries from the predations of jealous neighbors. Of course, modern citizens of rich democracies know much more than Plato could possibly have imagined about man's appetite for luxuries. Our cities are so wealthy, complex, and "feverish" that we are very apt to lose sight of their fundamental basis in our common needs. Only in moments of extremity are we likely to see beyond what Deneen referred to as "our apparent difference of position in the shadow of gleaming skyscrapers."[36]

One such moment of extremity occurred in August 2005, when floods triggered by Hurricane Katrina inundated much of the city of New Orleans. Many Americans were shocked and shamed by the televised images of the aftermath of the flooding. Scenes of physical devastation were juxtaposed with even more disturbing scenes of human devastation. Thousands of residents, mostly black and poor, seemed to be trapped in a Hobbesian state of nature, abandoned by government and civilized society. On August 31, as "a major American city all but disintegrated," according to one news account, President Bush flew over New Orleans and the Gulf Coast in Air Force One on his way from Texas to Washington, DC. When he finally arrived on the

---

[35] Deneen (2005, 115–116); Plato, *Republic*, Allan Bloom, trans. (New York: Basic Books, 1968).

[36] Deneen (2005, 116).

ground in New Orleans some two weeks later, he acknowledged in a dramatic televised address from Jackson Square that America had "witnessed the kind of desperation no citizen of this great and generous nation should ever have to know—fellow Americans calling out for food and water, vulnerable people left at the mercy of criminals who had no mercy, and the bodies of the dead lying uncovered and untended in the street."[37]

It would be hard to imagine a starker reminder of the extent to which each of us lives every day in a "city of utmost necessity." Those who escaped the devastation of Katrina may have congratulated themselves on their self-sufficiency, but the truth of the matter is that they differed from those left behind primarily in their access to the collective resources of civilized society. As one reporter wrote, attempting to explain why so many poor people remained in the flooded city, "Evacuation, if you don't have a car, a credit card or a place to go, sounds like trading the deep sea you know for the devil you don't."[38] He might have added, but did not, that having a car would have been of little use without public highways and bridges, that the magical efficacy of credit cards rests on a complex web of legally enforced financial arrangements, and that having "a place to go" was largely a matter of knowing someone with a spare bedroom out of reach of the floodwaters.

According to one press report, "What a shocked world saw exposed in New Orleans . . . wasn't just a broken levee. It was a cleavage of race and class, at once familiar and startlingly new, laid bare in a setting where they suddenly amounted to matters of life and death." Another asserted that "Katrina's whirlwind has laid bare the fault lines of race and class in America. For a lightning moment, the American psyche was singed."[39]

The aftermath of the storm provided an even starker reminder that access to the collective resources of civilized society is vastly unequal, notwithstanding our Platonic equality of need. In his Jackson Square address, President Bush promised "bold action" to "confront" poverty, racial discrimination, and "the legacy of inequality." "These trials," he said, "remind us that we're tied together in this life, in this nation—and that the despair of any touches us all."[40] In a special report on "The Other America," *Newsweek* columnist Jonathan Alter suggested that the shock and shame of Katrina might "strip

---

[37] David Ovalle, Phil Long, and Martin Merzer, "Lawlessness, Floating Bodies as New Orleans Deteriorates," *Seattle Times*, September 1, 2005; "President Discusses Hurricane Relief in Address to the Nation," September 15, 2005 (http://georgewbush-whitehouse.archives.gov /news/releases/2005/09/20050915-8.html).

[38] Jonathan Tilove, "'Our Society Is So Uneven': Katrina Exposes Inequalities of Race, Wealth," *Newhouse News*, September 4, 2005 (http://209.157.64.200/focus/f-bloggers/1477447 /posts).

[39] Jason DeParle, "Broken Levees, Unbroken Barriers: What Happens to a Race Deferred," *New York Times*, September 4, 2005; Tilove, "'Our Society Is So Uneven.'"

[40] "President Discusses Hurricane Relief in Address to the Nation."

away the old evasions, hypocrisies and not-so-benign neglect" surrounding issues of inequality in America. "For the moment, at least, Americans are ready to fix their restless gaze on enduring problems of poverty, race and class that have escaped their attention," and policy-makers in Washington might "think harder about why part of the richest country on earth looks like the Third World."[41]

Alas, the hope for a silver lining proved to be short-lived. Less than a month after the president's stirring speech, amid reports of ideological wrangling over federal and local responsibilities, tax cuts and budget deficits, labor law and housing policy, the lightning moment seemed to have passed.[42] A year after the hurricane, Alter wrote a chagrined admission that the "cynical" critics who called his earlier piece "naïve" were "largely right":

> Not only has the president done much less than he promised on the financing and logistics of Gulf Coast recovery, he has dropped the ball entirely on using the storm and its aftermath as an opportunity to fight poverty. Worker recovery accounts and urban homesteading never got off the ground, and the new enterprise zone is mostly an opportunity for Southern companies owned by GOP campaign contributors to make some money in New Orleans. The mood in Washington continues to be one of not-so-benign neglect of the problems of the poor.

Alter quoted Senator John Kerry's claim that President Bush's Jackson Square speech "ought to stand as one of the all-time monuments to hollow rhetoric and broken promises."[43]

The process of rebuilding in the wake of Katrina continued to expose "fault lines of race and class in America." Eight months after the storm, one reporter contrasted the pace of rebuilding in Eastover, "a gated subdivision that was home to some of this city's wealthiest black residents," and the Lower Ninth Ward, "a predominantly black working-class community where some of New Orleans's poorest people lived." The Eastover Property Owners Association "was so well organized and financed that it recently retained a professional planner to help respond to the city's requirement that devastated neighborhoods devise their own revival blueprints." In contrast, the Lower Ninth Ward—"a community rich in history, home to families whose roots date back generations"—had no neighborhood association until several months after the storm and struggled to find planning assistance when the federal government declined to provide it. As one

---

[41] Jonathan Alter, "The Other America," *Newsweek*, September 19, 2005, 42–48.

[42] Jason DeParle, "Liberal Hopes Ebb in Post-Storm Poverty Debate," *New York Times*, October 11, 2005.

[43] Jonathan Alter, "Still Blind to the Poverty," *Newsweek*, September 4, 2006, 38.

resident said, "People [here] don't have the same training and background and schooling and experience at working the system."[44]

As is often the case, these significant social disadvantages were compounded by significant material disadvantages:

> Even today, nearly eight months after the storm, there are no FEMA trailers in the Lower Ninth Ward because the area is still without gas and drinkable water. . . . Just as disparities between rich and poor were exposed in the days after Hurricane Katrina, class and wealth seem to be playing a significant role as elected officials struggle to determine which neighborhoods will be rebuilt and which should revert to swampland, if not bulldozed and sold en masse to a developer. While Eastover is full of the sound of saws ripping wood and the pneumatic punch of nail guns, the sound of the Lower Ninth Ward is mainly silence.[45]

While class and wealth played a significant role in the disparate fates of New Orleans homeowners, they weighed even more heavily in the fates of people too poor to have owned their own homes. For thousands of them, as a press account almost two years after the original disaster put it, "the shock of evacuation has hardened into the grim limbo of exile." With rebuilding aid targeted to homeowners, "the local and federal governments have done almost nothing to make it possible for low-income renters" to return to New Orleans. As a result, "hardly any of the 77,000 rental units destroyed in New Orleans have been rebuilt," and "there were still more than 30,000 families displaced by Hurricanes Katrina and Rita spread across the country in apartments paid for by the Federal Emergency Management Agency, and another 13,000 families, down from a peak of nearly 18,000, marooned in trailer or mobile home parks, where hunger is so prevalent that lines form when the truck from the food bank appears."[46]

As one resident noted, "It was the people with means who got back to the city first, and they were the ones making the decisions." As a result, "the Lower Ninth seemed last on everyone's list for everything." Some parts of the city experienced a major revival spurred in significant part by federal aid. Eight years after the storm, a real estate developer enthused about "the hidden blessings of New Orleans's near-death experience." So many young professionals were arriving that some called it "Brooklyn on the bayou." But poorer neighborhoods continued to be overlooked. When the Super Bowl

---

[44] Gary Rivlin, "In Rebuilding as in the Disaster, Wealth and Class Help Define New Orleans," *New York Times*, April 25, 2006.

[45] Ibid.

[46] Shaila Dewan, "Road to New Life After Katrina Is Closed to Many," *New York Times*, July 12, 2007.

came to town in 2013, "a group of large homebuilders and the NFL Players Association announced Touchdown for Homes with the idea of building dozens of homes at a barren edge of the Lower Ninth. They paid for three and stopped when they were able to sell only one to a qualified buyer. . . . The adjoining lots were choked with weeds, and there were no stores and no public transportation." Almost a decade after the storm, two-thirds of the Lower Ninth's pre-Katrina mailing addresses had disappeared or remained unoccupied. "At that rate of reoccupation," one observer noted, "it wouldn't be until around 2040 that the area recovered its population."[47]

No doubt it was naive to suppose that a moment of extremity would trigger "bold action" to overcome "the legacy of inequality," as President Bush promised in Jackson Square. Both the legacy of inequality and the present reality of inequality are pervasive and powerful. Pervasive and powerful, yet not entirely immutable. The most important lesson of this book is a very simple one: politics matters. The rising tide of economic inequality in contemporary America has myriad economic and social causes, including technological change, demographic trends, and global competition. Some of these we can influence; others we can only adapt to. But however high the tide of economic forces may rise, we are not condemned to wait behind our levees for disaster to engulf us. Imperfect as they are, the processes and institutions of American democracy provide us with consequential choices. We can reinforce the levees; we can divert some of the fastest-running waters; and we can insist that the most vulnerable among us not be abandoned when the affluent flee to higher ground.

We *can* make these choices. Whether we *will* make them remains to be seen.

[47] Rivlin (2015, 203, 394, 401, 412).

Postscript

November 2015

Dear Professor Bartels,

I am a machinist in New Jersey and a father of two young children. For a long time I have worried about the growing divisions in society and how inequality is shaping the world my children will live in.

You have spoken out on this issue, and so respectfully I reach out to you to let my small voice be heard. If you find anything in my writing that adds to the conversation, I would appreciate your passing it on to others.

All around me, people are being dragged down by the increasing disparity in our country:

- They work more and more hours just to keep a roof over their head and feed their children.
- They juggle multiple part time jobs because corporations do not want to pay benefits.
- And they go to work sick because their company does not provide sick leave for them.

Someone is going to help us at retail stores and restaurants. Someone is going to take care of our elderly parents. Someone is going to stock our grocery store shelves. They successfully complete tasks we all require but are only rewarded with struggle and inequity.

Overall, our society is becoming more and more divided between the haves and the have nots. Resources and educational quality pool into increasingly exclusive and homogenous zip codes, while opportunity and possibility drain from increasingly segregated working class communities.

Where are the better public schools? Where are the best hospitals? Where are the safest neighborhoods? I think we all know the answer to these questions.

What working people need is a larger voice in our Democracy, but they don't have the time. They can't spare the attention. They are struggling to survive. It is almost impossible to see beyond the next month's bills, let alone the next election cycle. They are invisible and there are powerful people who want to keep them that way. I just think they should have a fighting chance.

At the end of the day it is really an issue of basic fairness. That people deserve some dignity for completing the work that society demands, a reasonable quality of life for what they contribute to our common good, and a fundamental understanding that all work has value and deserves respect.

Thank you for your time and understanding.

Sincerely,
Daniel Wasik

References

Aaronson, Daniel, and Bhashkar Mazumder. 2005. "Intergenerational Economic Mobility in the United States: 1940–2000." Working Paper 05-12. Chicago: Federal Reserve Bank of Chicago.

Achen, Christopher H. 1978. "Measuring Representation." *American Journal of Political Science* 22: 475–509.

Achen, Christopher H., and Larry M. Bartels. 2004. "Musical Chairs: Pocketbook Voting and the Limits of Democratic Accountability." Paper presented at the annual meeting of the American Political Science Association.

———. 2016. *Democracy for Realists: Why Elections Do Not Produce Responsive Government*. Princeton, NJ: Princeton University Press.

Alesina, Alberto. 1988. "Macroeconomics and Politics." In Stanley Fischer, ed., *National Bureau of Economic Research Macroeconomics Annual*, vol. 3, 11–55. Cambridge, MA: MIT Press.

Alesina, Alberto, and Edward L. Glaeser. 2004. *Fighting Poverty in the U.S. and Europe: A World of Difference*. Oxford: Oxford University Press.

Alesina, Alberto, John Londregan, and Howard Rosenthal. 1993. "A Model of the Political Economy of the United States." *American Political Science Review* 87: 12–33.

Alesina, Alberto, and Dani Rodrik. 1994. "Distributive Politics and Economic Growth." *Quarterly Journal of Economics* 109: 465–490.

Alesina, Alberto, and Howard Rosenthal. 1989. "Partisan Cycles in Congressional Elections and the Macroeconomy." *American Political Science Review* 83: 373–398.

Alesina, Alberto, and Jeffrey Sachs. 1988. "Political Parties and the Business Cycle in the United States, 1948–1984." *Journal of Money, Credit, and Banking* 20: 63–82.

Alexander, Herbert E. 1980. *Financing Politics*. Washington, DC: Congressional Quarterly Press.

Althaus, Scott L. 1998. "Information Effects in Collective Preferences." *American Political Science Review* 92: 545–558.

Ansolabehere, Stephen, John M. de Figueiredo, and James M. Snyder Jr. 2003. "Why Is There So Little Money in U.S. Politics?" *Journal of Economic Perspectives* 17: 105–130.

Arrow, Kenneth J. 1963. *Social Choice and Individual Values*, 2nd ed. New Haven, CT: Yale University Press.

Atkinson, Anthony B. 1997. "Bringing Income Distribution in from the Cold." *Economic Journal* 107: 297–321.

———. 2015. *Inequality: What Can Be Done?* Cambridge, MA: Harvard University Press.

Bafumi, Joseph, and Michael C. Herron. 2010. "Leapfrog Representation and Extremism: A Study of American Voters and Their Members in Congress." *American Political Science Review* 104: 519–542.

Baker, Dean. 2013. "Reducing Waste with an Efficient Medicare Prescription Drug Benefit." Washington, DC: Center for Economic and Policy Research, January (http://www.cepr.net/documents/publications/medicare-drug-2012-12.pdf).

Bartels, Larry M. 1990. "Public Opinion and Political Interests." Paper presented at the annual meeting of the Midwest Political Science Association.

———. 1991. "Constituency Opinion and Congressional Policy Making: The Reagan Defense Buildup." *American Political Science Review* 85: 457–474.

———. 1996. "Uninformed Votes: Information Effects in Presidential Elections." *American Journal of Political Science* 40: 194–230.

———. 1998. "Where the Ducks Are: Voting Power in a Party System." In John G. Geer, ed., *Politicians and Party Politics*, 43–79. Baltimore: Johns Hopkins University Press.

———. 2000. "Partisanship and Voting Behavior, 1952–1996." *American Journal of Political Science* 44: 35–50.

———. 2002a. "Beyond the Running Tally: Partisan Bias in Political Perceptions." *Political Behavior* 24: 117–150.

———. 2002b. "Economic Inequality and Political Representation." Paper presented at the annual meeting of the American Political Science Association.

———. 2002c. "The Impact of Candidate Traits in American Presidential Elections." In Anthony King, ed., *Leaders' Personalities and the Outcomes of Democratic Elections*, 44–69. New York: Oxford University Press.

———. 2003. "Democracy with Attitudes." In Michael B. MacKuen and George Rabinowitz, eds., *Electoral Democracy*, 48–82. Ann Arbor: University of Michigan Press.

———. 2004. "Unenlightened Self-Interest: The Strange Appeal of Estate Tax Repeal." *The American Prospect* (June): A17–A19.

———. 2005. "Homer Gets a Tax Cut: Inequality and Public Policy in the American Mind." *Perspectives on Politics* 3: 15–31.

———. 2006a. "Is the Water Rising? Reflections on Inequality and American Democracy." *PS: Political Science & Politics* 39: 39–42.

———. 2006b. "What's the Matter with *What's the Matter with Kansas?*" *Quarterly Journal of Political Science* 1: 201–226.

———. 2006c. "A Tale of Two Tax Cuts, a Wage Squeeze, and a Tax Credit." *National Tax Journal* 59: 403–423.

———. 2008. *Unequal Democracy: The Political Economy of the New Gilded Age.* New York and Princeton, NJ: Russell Sage Foundation and Princeton University Press.

———. 2012. "A New Deal Fantasy Meets Old Political Realities." In Theda Skocpol, *Obama and America's Political Future*, 91–110. Cambridge, MA: Harvard University Press.

———. 2013a. "The Class War Gets Personal: Inequality as a Political Issue in the 2012 Election." Paper presented at the annual meeting of the Midwest Political Science Association (https://my.vanderbilt.edu/larrybartels/files/2011/12/Ineq20121.pdf).

———. 2013b. "Political Effects of the Great Recession." *The ANNALS of the American Academy of Political and Social Science 650*: 47–76.

———. 2014a. "Ideology and Retrospection in Electoral Responses to the Great Recession." In Nancy Bermeo and Larry M. Bartels, eds., *Mass Politics in Tough Times: Opinions, Votes and Protest in the Great Recession*, 185–223. New York: Oxford University Press.

———. 2014b. "Remembering to Forget: A Note on the Duration of Campaign Advertising Effects." *Political Communication 31*: 532–544.

Bartels, Larry M., and Henry E. Brady. 2003. "Economic Behavior in Political Context." *American Economic Review 93*: 156–161.

Bartels, Larry M., Joshua D. Clinton, and John G. Geer. 2016. "Representation." In Richard Valelly, Suzanne Mettler, and Robert Lieberman, eds., *The Oxford Handbook of American Political Development*, 399–424. New York: Oxford University Press.

Bartels, Larry M., Hugh Heclo, Rodney E. Hero, and Lawrence R. Jacobs. 2005. "Inequality and American Governance." In Lawrence R. Jacobs and Theda Skocpol, eds., *Inequality and American Democracy: What We Know and What We Need to Learn*, 88–155. New York: Russell Sage Foundation.

Bartels, Larry M., and John Zaller. 2001. "Presidential Vote Models: A Recount." *PS: Political Science & Politics 34*: 9–20.

Beck, Nathaniel. 1982. "Parties, Administrations, and American Macroeconomic Outcomes." *American Political Science Review 76*: 83–93.

———. 1992. "The Methodology of Cointegration." *Political Analysis 4*: 237–247.

Beller, Emily, and Michael Hout. 2006. "Intergenerational Social Mobility: The United States in Comparative Perspective." *The Future of Children 16*: 19–36.

Bénabou, Roland. 1996. "Inequality and Growth." In Ben S. Bernanke and Julio J. Rotemberg, eds., *National Bureau of Economic Research Macroeconomics Annual*, vol. 11, 11–76. Cambridge, MA: MIT Press.

Bergan, Daniel E. 2009. "Does Grassroots Lobbying Work? A Field Experiment Measuring the Effects of an e-Mail Lobbying Campaign on Legislative Behavior." *American Politics Research 37*: 327–352.

Besley, Timothy, and Anne Case. 2003. "Political Institutions and Policy Choices: Evidence from the United States." *Journal of Economic Literature 41*: 7–73.

Bhatti, Yosef Aziz, and Robert S. Erikson. 2011. "How Poorly Are the Poor Represented in the U.S. Senate?" In Peter K. Enns and Christopher Wlezien, eds., *Who Gets Represented?*, 223–246. New York: Russell Sage Foundation.

Biven, W. Carl. 2002. *Jimmy Carter's Economy: Policy in an Age of Limits*. Chapel Hill: University of North Carolina Press.

Blanchard, Oliver J., and Roberto Perotti. 2002. "An Empirical Characterization of the Dynamic Effects of Changes in Government Spending and Taxes on Output." *Quarterly Journal of Economics 117*: 1329–1368.

Blank, Rebecca, and Alan Blinder. 1986. "Macroeconomics, Income Distribution, and Poverty." In Sheldon Danziger and Daniel Weinberg, eds., *Fighting Poverty: What Works and What Doesn't*, 180–208. Cambridge, MA: Harvard University Press.

Blinder, Alan S. 2013a. *After the Music Stopped: The Financial Crisis, the Response, and the Work Ahead*. New York: Penguin Press.

————. 2013b. "The Macroeconomic Policy Paradox: Failing by Succeeding." *Annals of the American Academy of Political and Social Science 650*: 26–46.

Blinder, Alan S., and Mark W. Watson. 2014. "Presidents and the U.S. Economy: An Econometric Exploration." Working Paper 20324. Cambridge, MA: National Bureau of Economic Research.

Blinder, Alan S., and Mark Zandi. 2010. "How the Great Recession Was Brought to an End." Princeton University and Moody's Analytics, July 27 (https://www.economy.com/mark-zandi/documents/End-of-Great-Recession.pdf).

Boix, Carles. 1998. *Political Parties, Growth, and Equality: Conservative and Social Democratic Economic Strategies in the World Economy*. New York: Cambridge University Press.

Bosworth, Barry, Gary Burtless, and Kan Zhang. 2016. *Later Retirement, Inequality in Old Age, and the Growing Gap in Longevity Between Rich and Poor*. Brookings Economic Studies Program (http://www.brookings.edu/research/reports2/2016/02/life-expectancy-gaps-promise-social-security).

Bradbury, Bruce, Miles Corak, Jane Waldfogel, and Elizabeth Washbrook. 2015. *Too Many Children Left Behind: The U.S. Achievement Gap in Comparative Perspective*. New York: Russell Sage Foundation.

Bradbury, Katharine, and Jane Katz. 2002. "Women's Labor Market Involvement and Family Income Mobility When Marriages End." *New England Economic Review Q4*: 41–74.

Brewer, Mike, Alissa Goodman, Robert Joyce, Alastair Muriel, David Phillips, and Luke Sibieta. 2009. "Have the Poor Got Poorer Under Labour?" London: Institute for Fiscal Studies, October 13 (http://www.ifs.org.uk/publications/4637).

Brown, Robert D. 1995. "Party Cleavages and Welfare Effort in the American States." *American Political Science Review 89*: 23–33.

Brunner, Eric, Stephen L. Ross, and Ebonya Washington. 2013. "Does Less Income Mean Less Representation?" *American Economic Journal: Economic Policy 5*: 53–76.

Campbell, Angus, Philip E. Converse, Warren E. Miller, and Donald E. Stokes. 1960. *The American Voter*. New York: John Wiley & Sons.

Campbell, James E. 2011. "The Economic Records of the Presidents: Party Differences and Inherited Economic Conditions." *The Forum 9*: issue 1.

Card, David, and Alan B. Krueger. 1995. *Myth and Measurement: The New Economics of the Minimum Wage*. Princeton, NJ: Princeton University Press.

————. 2000. "Minimum Wages and Employment: A Case Study of the Fast-Food Industry: Reply." *American Economic Review 90*: 1397–1420.

Carnes, Nicholas. 2013. *White-Collar Government: The Hidden Role of Class in Economic Policy Making*. Chicago: University of Chicago Press.

Chetty, Raj, Nathaniel Hendren, Patrick Kline, and Emmanuel Saez. 2014a. "Where Is the Land of Opportunity? The Geography of Intergenerational Mobility in the United States." Working Paper 19843. Cambridge, MA: National Bureau of Economic Research.

Chetty, Raj, Nathaniel Hendren, Patrick Kline, Emmanuel Saez, and Nicholas Turner. 2014b. "Is the United States Still a Land of Opportunity? Recent Trends in Intergenerational Mobility." Working Paper 19844. Cambridge, MA: National Bureau of Economic Research.

Christiano, Lawrence J., Martin Eichenbaum, and Charles L. Evans. 1999. "Monetary Policy Shocks: What Have We Learned and to What End?" In John B. Taylor and Michael Woodford, eds., *Handbook of Macroeconomics*, vol. 1A, 65–148. Amsterdam: North-Holland.

Clark, William Roberts, and Vincent Arel-Bundock. 2013. "Independent But Not Indifferent: Partisan Bias in Monetary Policy at the Fed." *Economics & Politics* 25: 1–26.

Cleary, Matthew R. 2010. *The Sources of Democratic Responsiveness in Mexico*. Notre Dame, IN: University of Notre Dame Press.

Clinton, Joshua D. 2006. "Representation in Congress: Constituents and Roll Calls in the 106th House." *Journal of Politics* 68: 397–409.

Committee on Political Parties. 1950. "Toward a More Responsible Two-Party System." *American Political Science Review* 44 (supplement): v–ix, 1–96.

Conover, Pamela Johnston, Stanley Feldman, and Kathleen Knight. 1987. "The Personal and Political Underpinnings of Economic Forecasts." *American Journal of Political Science* 31: 559–583.

Converse, Philip E. 1964. "The Nature of Belief Systems in Mass Publics." In David E. Apter, ed., *Ideology and Discontent*, 206–261. New York: Free Press.

———. 1990. "Popular Representation and the Distribution of Information." In John A. Ferejohn and James H. Kuklinski, eds., *Information and Democratic Processes*, 369–388. Chicago: University of Illinois Press.

Cutler, David M., and Lawrence F. Katz. 1991. "Macroeconomic Performance and the Disadvantaged." *Brookings Papers on Economic Activity 1*: 1–74.

Dahl, Robert A. 1961. *Who Governs? Democracy and Power in an American City*. New Haven, CT: Yale University Press.

———. 1971. *Polyarchy: Participation and Opposition*. New Haven, CT: Yale University Press.

———. 1982. *Dilemmas of Pluralist Democracy: Autonomy vs. Control*. New Haven, CT: Yale University Press.

———. 2006. *On Political Equality*. New Haven, CT: Yale University Press.

Danziger, Sheldon, and Peter Gottschalk. 1995. *America Unequal*. New York and Cambridge, MA: Russell Sage Foundation and Harvard University Press.

Delli Carpini, Michael X., and Scott Keeter. 1996. *What Americans Know About Politics and Why It Matters*. New Haven, CT: Yale University Press.

Deneen, Patrick J. 2005. *Democratic Faith*. Princeton, NJ: Princeton University Press.

Dew-Becker, Ian, and Robert J. Gordon. 2005. "Where Did the Productivity Growth Go? Inflation Dynamics and the Distribution of Income." Working Paper 11842. Cambridge, MA: National Bureau of Economic Research.

DiNardo, John, Nicole M. Fortin, and Thomas Lemieux. 1996. "Labor Market Institutions and the Distribution of Wages, 1973–1992: A Semi-Parametric Approach." *Econometrica* 64: 1001–1044.

Downs, Anthony. 1957. *An Economic Theory of Democracy*. New York: Harper & Row.

Dube, Arindrajit. 2014. "Designing Thoughtful Minimum Wage Policy at the State and Local Levels," Washington, DC: Brookings Institution, June 19 (http://www .brookings.edu/research/papers/2014/06/19-minimum-wage-policy-state-local -levels-dube).

Dube, Arindrajit, T. William Lester, and Michael Reich. 2010. "Minimum Wage Effects Across State Borders: Estimates Using Contiguous Counties." *Review of Economics and Statistics* 92: 945–964.

Dye, Thomas. 1966. *Politics, Economics, and the Public: Policy Outcomes in the American States*. Chicago: Rand McNally.

The Economist, Editors of. 1937. *The New Deal: An Analysis and Appraisal*. New York: Alfred A. Knopf.

Edin, Kathryn J., and H. Luke Shaefer. 2015. *$2.00 a Day: Living on Almost Nothing in America*. Boston: Houghton Mifflin Harcourt.

Edwards, George C., III. 2003. *On Deaf Ears: The Limits of the Bully Pulpit*. New Haven, CT: Yale University Press.

Ehrenreich, Barbara. 2001. *Nickel and Dimed: On (Not) Getting By in America*. New York: Henry Holt and Company.

Eichengreen, Barry. 2015. *Hall of Mirrors: The Great Depression, the Great Recession, and the Uses—and Misuses—of History*. New York: Oxford University Press.

Engle, Robert F., and C. W. J. Granger. 1987. "Co-integration and Error Correction: Representation, Estimation, and Testing." *Econometrica* 55: 251–276.

Erikson, Robert S. 1989. "Economic Conditions and the Presidential Vote." *American Political Science Review* 83: 567–573.

———. 1990. "Economic Conditions and the Congressional Vote: A Review of the Macrolevel Evidence." *American Journal of Political Science* 34: 373–399.

———. 2004. "Economic Voting: Micro vs. Macro Perspectives." Paper presented at the annual Political Methodology Meeting (http://www.columbia.edu/~rse14/erikson_economic_voting.pdf).

Erikson, Robert S., Joseph Bafumi, and Bret Wilson. 2002. "Was the 2000 Presidential Election Predictable?" *PS: Political Science & Politics* 35: 815–819.

Erikson, Robert S., Michael B. MacKuen, and James A. Stimson. 2002. *The Macro Polity*. Cambridge: Cambridge University Press.

Erikson, Robert S., Gerald C. Wright, and John P. McIver. 1993. *Statehouse Democracy: Public Opinion and Policy in the American States*. Cambridge: Cambridge University Press.

Feldman, Stanley. 1988. "Structure and Consistency in Public Opinion: The Role of Core Beliefs and Values." *American Journal of Political Science* 32: 416–440.

———. 2003. "A Conflicted Public? Equality, Fairness, and Redistribution." Paper presented at the conference "Inequality and American Democracy." Princeton University (https://www.princeton.edu/csdp/events/Inequality2003/feldman.pdf).

Fiorina, Morris P. 1981. *Retrospective Voting in American National Elections*. New Haven, CT: Yale University Press.

Fishkin, James S. 1997. *The Voice of the People: Public Opinion and Democracy*. New Haven, CT: Yale University Press.

Flavin, Patrick. 2012. "Income Inequality and Policy Representation in the American States." *American Politics Research* 40: 29–59.

Fox, Liana, Christopher Wimer, Irwin Garfinkel, Neeraj Kaushal, and Jane Waldfogel. 2015. "Waging War on Poverty: Poverty Trends Using a Historical Supplemental Poverty Measure." *Journal of Policy Analysis and Management* 34: 567–592.

Frank, Thomas. 2004. *What's the Matter with Kansas? How Conservatives Won the Heart of America*. New York: Henry Holt and Company.

Fuller, Dan, and Doris Geide-Stevenson. 2003. "Consensus Among Economists: Revisited." *Journal of Economic Education 34*: 369–387.

Galbraith, James K., Olivier G. Giovannoni, and Ann J. Russo. 2007. "The Fed's *Real* Reaction Function: Monetary Policy, Inflation, Unemployment, Inequality—and Presidential Politics." Levy Institute Working Paper 511. Annandale-on-Hudson, NY: Levy Economics Institute of Bard College.

Geithner, Timothy F. 2014. *Stress Test: Reflections on Financial Crises*. New York: Broadway Books.

Gellad, Walid F., Sebastian Schneeweiss, Phyllis Brawarsky, Stuart Lipsitz, and Jennifer S. Haas. 2008. "What if the Federal Government Negotiated Pharmaceutical Prices for Seniors? An Estimate of National Savings." *Journal of General Internal Medicine 23*: 1435–1440.

Gilens, Martin. 1999. *Why Americans Hate Welfare*. Chicago: University of Chicago Press.

———. 2001. "Political Ignorance and Collective Policy Preferences." *American Political Science Review 95*: 379–396.

———. 2005. "Inequality and Democratic Responsiveness." *Public Opinion Quarterly 69*: 778–796.

———. 2009. "Preference Gaps and Inequality in Representation." *PS: Political Science & Politics 42*: 335–341.

———. 2012. *Affluence and Influence: Economic Inequality and Political Power in America*. New York and Princeton, NJ: Russell Sage Foundation and Princeton University Press.

Gilens, Martin, and Benjamin I. Page. 2014. "Testing Theories of American Politics: Elites, Interest Groups, and Average Citizens." *Perspectives on Politics 12*: 564–581.

Gilligan, James. 2011. *Why Some Politicians Are More Dangerous Than Others*. Malden, MA: Polity Press.

Gitlin, Todd. 2012. *Occupy Nation: The Roots, the Spirit, and the Promise of Occupy Wall Street*. New York: HarperCollins.

Glazer, Nathan. 2003. "On Americans and Inequality." *Daedalus 132*: 111–115.

Graetz, Michael J., and Ian Shapiro. 2005. *Death by a Thousand Cuts: The Fight over Taxing Inherited Wealth*. Princeton, NJ: Princeton University Press.

Griffin, John D., and Brian Newman. 2005. "Are Voters Better Represented?" *Journal of Politics 67*: 1206–1227.

Grogan, Coleen M. 1994. "Political-Economic Factors Influencing State Medicaid Policy." *Political Research Quarterly 47*: 589–623.

Grunwald, Michael. 2012. *The* New *New Deal: The Hidden Story of Change in the Obama Era*. New York: Simon & Schuster.

Gujarati, Damodar N. 1995. *Basic Econometrics*, 3rd ed. New York: McGraw-Hill.

Hacker, Jacob S., and Paul Pierson. 2005a. "Abandoning the Middle: The Bush Tax Cuts and the Limits of Democratic Control." *Perspectives on Politics 3*: 33–53.

———. 2005b. *Off Center: The Republican Revolution and the Erosion of American Democracy*. New Haven, CT: Yale University Press.

———. 2010. *Winner-Take-All Politics*. New York: Simon & Schuster.

Hall, Richard, and Frank Wayman. 1990. "Buying Time: Moneyed Interests and the Mobilization of Bias in Congressional Committees." *American Political Science Review* 84: 797–820.

Harding, David J., Christopher Jencks, Leonard M. Lopoo, and Susan E. Mayer. 2005. "The Changing Effects of Family Background on the Incomes of American Adults." In Samuel Bowles, Herbert Gintis, and Melissa Osborne Groves, eds., *Unequal Chances: Family Background and Economic Success*, 100–144. New York and Princeton, NJ: Russell Sage Foundation and Princeton University Press.

Heckman, James. 1979. "Sample Selection Bias as a Specification Error." *Econometrica* 46: 153–161.

Hetherington, Marc J. 2001. "Resurgent Mass Partisanship: The Role of Elite Polarization." *American Political Science Review* 95: 619–631.

Hibbs, Douglas A., Jr. 1977. "Political Parties and Macroeconomic Policy." *American Political Science Review* 71: 1467–1487.

———. 1987. *The American Political Economy: Macroeconomics and Electoral Politics*. Cambridge, MA: Harvard University Press.

———. 2006. "Voting and the Macroeconomy." In Barry R. Weingast and Donald Wittman, eds., *The Oxford Handbook of Political Economy*, 565–586. Oxford: Oxford University Press.

Hibbs, Douglas A., Jr., and Christopher Dennis. 1988. "Income Distribution in the United States." *American Political Science Review* 82: 467–490.

Hicks, Timothy, Alan M. Jacobs, and J. Scott Matthews. 2015. "Inequality and Electoral Accountability: Class-Biased Economic Voting in Comparative Perspective." Unpublished manuscript, University College London, University of British Columbia, and Memorial University of Newfoundland (http://www.politics.ubc .ca/fileadmin/user_upload/webhome/users/364/CBEVComparative.pdf).

Hill, Kim Quaile, Jan E. Leighley, and Angela Hinton-Andersson. 1995. "Lower-Class Mobilization and Policy Linkage in the United States." *American Journal of Political Science* 39: 75–86.

Hines, James R., Jr., Hilary Hoynes, and Alan B. Krueger. 2001. "Another Look at Whether a Rising Tide Lifts All Boats." Working Paper 454. Princeton, NJ: Princeton University, Industrial Relations Section.

Hochschild, Jennifer L. 1981. *What's Fair? American Beliefs About Distributive Justice*. Cambridge, MA: Harvard University Press.

———. 2001. "Where You Stand Depends on What You See: Connections Among Values, Perceptions of Fact, and Political Prescriptions." In James H. Kuklinski, ed., *Citizens and Politics: Perspectives from Political Psychology*, 313–340. New York: Cambridge University Press.

Hochschild, Jennifer L., and Katherine Levine Einstein. 2015. *Do Facts Matter? Information and Misinformation in American Politics*. Norman: University of Oklahoma Press.

Hout, Michael. 2004. "How Inequality May Affect Intergenerational Mobility." In Kathryn M. Neckerman, ed., *Social Inequality*, 969–987. New York: Russell Sage Foundation.

Huber, Evelyne, and John D. Stephens. 2001. *Development and Crisis of the Welfare State: Parties and Policies in Global Markets*. Chicago: University of Chicago Press.

Husted, Thomas A., and Lawrence W. Kenney. 1997. "The Effect of the Expansion of the Voting Franchise on the Size of Government." *Journal of Political Economy* 105: 54–82.

Irwin, Neil. 2013. *The Alchemists: Three Central Bankers and a World on Fire.* New York: Penguin Press.

Jacobs, Lawrence R., and Benjamin I. Page. 2005. "Who Influences U.S. Foreign Policy?" *American Political Science Review* 99: 107–124.

Jacobs, Lawrence R., and Theda Skocpol. 2005. *Inequality and American Democracy: What We Know and What We Need to Learn.* New York: Russell Sage Foundation.

———. 2010. *Health Care Reform and American Politics: What Everyone Needs to Know.* New York: Oxford University Press.

Jacobson, Gary C. 2007. *A Divider, Not a Uniter: George W. Bush and the American People.* New York: Pearson-Longman.

———. 2011. "The Republican Resurgence in 2010." *Political Science Quarterly* 126: 27–52.

Jargowsky, Paul A. 1996. "Take the Money and Run: Economic Segregation in U.S. Metropolitan Areas." *American Sociological Review* 61: 984–998.

Jennings, Edward T., Jr. 1979. "Competition, Constituencies, and Welfare Policies in American States." *American Political Science Review* 73: 414–429.

Jost, John T., and Mahzarin R. Banaji. 1994. "The Role of Stereotyping in System Justification and the Production of False Consciousness." *British Journal of Social Psychology* 33: 1–27.

Jost, John T., Sally Blount, Jeffrey Pfeffer, and György Hunyady. 2003. "Fair Market Ideology: Its Cognitive-Motivational Underpinnings." *Research in Organizational Behavior* 25: 53–91.

Kaiser, Robert G. 2013. *Act of Congress: How America's Essential Institution Works, and How It Doesn't.* New York: Vintage Books.

Karier, Thomas. 1997. *Great Experiments in American Economic Policy: From Kennedy to Reagan.* Westport, CT: Praeger Publishers.

Keech, William R. 1980. "Elections and Macroeconomic Policy Optimization." *American Journal of Political Science* 24: 345–367.

Kelly, Nathan J. 2009. *The Politics of Income Inequality in the United States.* New York: Cambridge University Press.

Kennedy, Peter. 1998. *A Guide to Econometrics*, 4th ed. Cambridge, MA: MIT Press.

Kenworthy, Lane. 2010. "How Much Do Presidents Influence Income Inequality?" *Challenge* 53: 90–112.

———. 2014. *Social Democratic America.* New York: Oxford University Press.

Kenworthy, Lane, and Lindsay A. Owens. 2011. "The Surprisingly Weak Effect of Recessions on Public Opinion." In David B. Grusky, Bruce Western, and Christopher Wimer, eds., *The Great Recession*, 196–219. New York: Russell Sage Foundation.

Kenworthy, Lane, and Jonas Pontusson. 2005. "Rising Inequality and the Politics of Redistribution in Affluent Countries." *Perspectives on Politics* 3: 449–471.

Kerr, William R. 2014. "Income Inequality and Social Preferences for Redistribution and Compensation Differentials." *Journal of Monetary Economics* 66: 62–78.

Key, V. O., Jr. 1949. *Southern Politics in State and Nation.* New York: Alfred A. Knopf.

————. 1956. *American State Politics: An Introduction.* New York: Alfred A. Knopf.

————. 1958. *Politics, Parties, and Pressure Groups,* 4th ed. New York: Thomas Y. Crowell.

————. 1964. *Politics, Parties, and Pressure Groups,* 5th ed. New York: Thomas Y. Crowell.

————. 1966. *The Responsible Electorate: Rationality in Presidential Voting 1936–1960.* Cambridge, MA: Harvard University Press.

Kinder, Donald R., Nancy Burns, and Dale B. Vieregge. 2005. "Liberalism, Race, and Exceptionalism: Understanding the American Appetite for Tax Reduction." Paper presented at the annual meeting of the American Political Science Association.

Kluegel, James R., and Eliot R. Smith. 1986. *Beliefs about Inequality: Americans' Views of What Is and What Ought to Be.* New York: Aldine de Gruyter.

Knight, Brian. 2000. "Supermajority Voting Requirements for Tax Increases: Evidence from the States." *Journal of Public Economics* 76: 41–67.

Kopczuk, Wojciech, Emmanuel Saez, and Jae Song. 2010. "Earnings Inequality and Mobility in the United States: Evidence from Social Security Data Since 1937." *Quarterly Journal of Economics* 125: 91–128.

Kramer, Gerald H. 1971. "Short-Term Fluctuations in U.S. Voting Behavior, 1896–1964." *American Political Science Review* 65: 131–143.

————. 1983. "The Ecological Fallacy Revisited: Aggregate- Versus Individual-Level Findings on Economics and Elections, and Sociotropic Voting." *American Political Science Review* 77: 92–111.

Krehbiel, Keith. 1998. *Pivotal Politics: A Theory of U.S. Lawmaking.* Chicago: University of Chicago Press.

Krehbiel, Keith, and Douglas Rivers. 1988. "The Analysis of Committee Power: An Application to Senate Voting on the Minimum Wage." *American Journal of Political Science* 32: 1151–1174.

Krugman, Paul. 2007. *The Conscience of a Liberal.* New York: W. W. Norton.

Krupnikov, Yanna, Adam Seth Levine, Markus Prior, and Arthur Lupia. 2006. "Public Ignorance and Estate Tax Repeal: The Effect of Partisan Differences and Survey Incentives." *National Tax Journal* 59: 425–437.

Kuttner, Robert. 2008. *Obama's Challenge: America's Economic Crisis and the Power of a Transformative Presidency.* White River Junction, VT: Chelsea Green.

Lee, David S. 1999. "Wage Inequality in the United States During the 1980s: Rising Dispersion or Falling Minimum Wage?" *Quarterly Journal of Economics* 114: 977–1023.

Leighley, Jan E., and Jonathan Nagler. 2013. *Who Votes Now? Demographics, Issues, Inequality, and Turnout in the United States.* Princeton, NJ: Princeton University Press.

Lenz, Gabriel S. 2012. *Follow the Leader? How Voters Respond to Politicians' Policies and Performance.* Chicago: University of Chicago Press.

Lerner, Melvin J. 1980. *The Belief in a Just World: A Fundamental Delusion.* New York: Plenum Press.

Levy, Frank, and Richard J. Murnane. 1992. "U.S. Earnings Levels and Earnings Inequality: A Review of Recent Trends and Proposed Explanations." *Journal of Economic Literature* 30: 1333–1381.

Levy, Frank, and Peter Temin. 2007. "Inequality and Institutions in 20th Century America." Working Paper 13106. Cambridge, MA: National Bureau of Economic Research.

Light, Paul C. 1999. *The President's Agenda: Domestic Policy Choice from Kennedy to Clinton*, 3rd ed. Baltimore, MD: Johns Hopkins University Press.

Lippmann, Walter. 1922. *Public Opinion*. Reprint, New York: Penguin Books, 1946.

Lockard, Duane. 1959. *New England State Politics*. Chicago: Henry Regnery.

Lowell, A. Lawrence. 1913. *Public Opinion and Popular Government*. New York: Longmans, Green, and Co.

Lupia, Arthur, Adam Seth Levine, Jesse O. Menning, and Gisela Sin. 2007. "Were Bush Tax Cut Supporters 'Simply Ignorant'? A Second Look at Conservatives and Liberals in 'Homer Gets a Tax Cut.'" *Perspectives on Politics* 5: 773–784.

Mann, Thomas E., and Norman J. Ornstein. 2012. *It's Even Worse Than It Looks: How the American Constitutional System Collided with the New Politics of Extremism*. New York: Basic Books.

Margalit, Yotam. 2013. "Explaining Social Policy Preferences: Evidence from the Great Recession." *American Political Science Review* 107: 80–103.

Marmot, Michael. 2015. *The Health Gap: The Challenge of an Unequal World*. New York: Bloomsbury Press.

Massey, Douglas, and Nancy Denton. 1993. *American Apartheid: Segregation and the Making of the Underclass*. Cambridge, MA: Harvard University Press.

Mayer, Gerald. 2004. "Union Membership Trends in the United States." Washington, DC: Congressional Research Service, August 31 (http://digitalcommons.ilr .cornell.edu/cgi/viewcontent.cgi?article=1176&context=key_workplace).

Mayer, Susan E. 2001. "How the Growth in Income Inequality Increased Economic Segregation." Working Paper 230. Chicago: Northwestern University and University of Chicago Joint Center for Poverty Research.

Mayhew, David R. 1988. "Why Did V. O. Key Draw Back from His 'Have-Nots' Claim?" In Milton C. Cummings Jr., ed., *V. O. Key Jr. and the Study of American Politics*, 24–38. Washington, DC: American Political Science Association.

McCall, Leslie. 2005. "Do They Know and Do They Care? Americans' Awareness of Rising Inequality." Paper presented at the Russell Sage Foundation Social Inequality Conference, University of California at Berkeley (May).

———. 2013. *The Undeserving Rich: American Beliefs about Inequality, Opportunity, and Redistribution*. New York: Cambridge University Press.

McCarty, Nolan. 2012. "The Politics of the Pop: The U.S. Response to the Financial Crisis and the Great Recession." In Nancy Bermeo and Jonas Pontusson, eds., *Coping with Crisis: Government Reactions to the Great Recession*. New York: Russell Sage Foundation.

McCarty, Nolan, Keith T. Poole, and Howard Rosenthal. 2006. *Polarized America: The Dance of Ideology and Unequal Riches*. Cambridge, MA: MIT Press.

McClosky, Herbert. 1958. "Conservatism and Personality." *American Political Science Review* 52: 27–45.

McClosky, Herbert, and John Zaller. 1984. *The American Ethos: Public Attitudes Toward Capitalism and Democracy*. Cambridge, MA: Harvard University Press.

McCormick, John P. 2006. "Contain the Wealthy and Patrol the Magistrates: Restoring Elite Accountability to Popular Government." *American Political Science Review 100*: 147–163.

Mead, Lawrence M. 2004. "The Great Passivity." *Perspectives on Politics 2*: 671–675.

Meltzer, Allan H., and Scott F. Richard. 1981. "A Rational Theory of the Size of Government." *Journal of Political Economy 89*: 914–927.

Miller, Warren E. 1991. "Party Identification, Realignment, and Party Voting: Back to the Basics." *American Political Science Review 85*: 557–568.

Miller, Warren E., and J. Merrill Shanks. 1996. *The New American Voter*. Cambridge, MA: Harvard University Press.

Miller, Warren E., and Donald E. Stokes. 1963. "Constituency Influence in Congress." *American Political Science Review 57*: 45–56.

Mishel, Lawrence, Jared Bernstein, and Heather Boushey. 2003. *The State of Working America 2002/2003*. Ithaca, NY: ILR Press.

Mueller, John E. 1973. *War, Presidents and Public Opinion*. New York: John Wiley & Sons.

Neckerman, Kathryn M., ed. 2004. *Social Inequality*. New York: Russell Sage Foundation.

Nelson, Candice J. 2014. "Financing the 2012 Presidential General Election." In David B. Magleby, ed., *Financing the 2012 Election*, 123–142. Washington, DC: Brookings Institution Press.

Nelson, Thomas E., and Donald R. Kinder. 1996. "Issue Frames and Group-Centrism in American Public Opinion." *Journal of Politics 58*: 1055–78.

Newman, Katherine S., and Elisabeth S. Jacobs. 2010. *Who Cares? Public Ambivalence and Government Activism from the New Deal to the Second Gilded Age*. Princeton, NJ: Princeton University Press.

Noah, Timothy. 2012. *The Great Divergence: America's Growing Inequality Crisis and What We Can Do About It*. New York: Bloomsbury Press.

Nyhan, Brendan, Eric McGhee, John Sides, Seth Masket, and Steven Greene. 2012. "One Vote Out of Step? The Effects of Salient Roll Call Votes in the 2010 Election." *American Politics Research 40*: 844–879.

Oliver, J. Eric. 2001. *Democracy in Suburbia*. Princeton, NJ: Princeton University Press.

Osberg, Lars, and Timothy Smeeding. 2003. "An International Comparison of Preferences for Leveling." Unpublished manuscript, version 2.1. Dalhousie University and Syracuse University.

Osberg, Lars, Timothy M. Smeeding, and Jonathan Schwabish. 2004. "Income Distribution and Public Social Expenditure: Theories, Effects, and Evidence." In Kathryn M. Neckerman, ed., *Social Inequality*, 821–859. New York: Russell Sage Foundation.

Ostrogorski, Moiseide. 1902. *Democracy and the Organization of Political Parties*. New York: Macmillan.

Ostry, Jonathan D., Andrew Berg, and Charalambos G. Tsangarides. 2014. "Redistribution, Inequality, and Growth." Staff Discussion Note SDN/14/02. Washington, DC: International Monetary Fund (revised April 2014).

Owens, Lindsay A., and David S. Pedulla. 2014. "Material Welfare and Changing Political Preferences: The Case of Support for Redistributive Social Policies." *Social Forces 92*: 1087–1113.

Page, Benjamin I., Larry M. Bartels, and Jason Seawright. 2011. "Interviewing Wealthy Americans." Paper presented at the annual meeting of the Midwest Political Science Association (https://my.vanderbilt.edu/larrybartels/files/2011/12/MPSA2011InterviewingWealthyAmericansFINAL29March1.pdf).

———. 2013. "Democracy and the Policy Preferences of Wealthy Americans." *Perspectives on Politics* 11: 51–73.

Page, Benjamin I., and Lawrence R. Jacobs. 2009. *Class War? What Americans Really Think about Economic Inequality*. Chicago: University of Chicago Press.

Page, Benjamin I., Jason Seawright, and Matthew J. Lacombe. 2015. "Stealth Politics by U.S. Billionaires." Paper presented at the annual meeting of the American Political Science Association (http://www.demos.org/sites/default/files/imce/ForbesStealthPoliticsAPSA2015August27FINAL_Updated.pdf).

Page, Benjamin I., and Robert Y. Shapiro. 1983. "Effects of Public Opinion on Policy." *American Political Science Review* 77: 175–190.

———. 1992. *The Rational Public: Fifty Years of Trends in Americans' Policy Preferences*. Chicago: University of Chicago Press.

Page, Benjamin I., and James R. Simmons. 2000. *What Government Can Do: Dealing with Poverty and Inequality*. Chicago: University of Chicago Press.

Parker, Jonathan A., Yacine Ait-Sahalia, and Motohiro Yogo. 2004. "Luxury Goods and the Equity Premium." *Journal of Finance* 59: 2959–3004.

Pearce, David W. 1992. *The MIT Dictionary of Modern Economics*, 4th ed. Cambridge, MA: MIT Press.

Perotti, Roberto. 1996. "Growth, Income Distribution, and Democracy: What the Data Say." *Journal of Economic Growth* 1: 149–187.

Persson, Torsten, and Guido Tabellini. 1994. "Is Inequality Harmful for Growth?" *American Economic Review* 84: 600–621.

Pfeffer, Fabian T., Sheldon H. Danziger, and Robert F. Schoeni. 2013. "Wealth Disparities Before and After the Great Recession." *The ANNALS of the American Academy of Political and Social Science* 650: 98–123.

———. 2014. "Wealth Levels, Wealth Inequality, and the Great Recession." New York: Russell Sage Foundation, June (http://inequality.stanford.edu/_media/working_papers/pfeffer-danziger-schoeni_wealth-levels.pdf).

Phillips, Kevin. 1990. *The Politics of Rich and Poor: Wealth and the American Electorate in the Reagan Aftermath*. New York: Random House.

———. 2002. *Wealth and Democracy: A Political History of the American Rich*. New York: Broadway Books.

Piketty, Thomas. 2014. *Capital in the Twenty-First Century*. Cambridge, MA: Harvard University Press.

Piketty, Thomas, and Emmanuel Saez. 2003. "Income Inequality in the United States, 1913–1998." *Quarterly Journal of Economics* 118: 1–39.

Pollin, Robert. 2010. Review of *Unequal Democracy: The Political Economy of the New Gilded Age*. *Journal of Economic Literature* 48: 151–153.

Pontusson, Jonas. 2005. *Inequality and Prosperity: Social Europe vs. Liberal America*. Ithaca, NY: Cornell University Press.

Poole, Keith T., and Howard Rosenthal. 2007. *Ideology and Congress*. New Brunswick, NJ: Transaction Publishers.

Putnam, Robert D. 2015. *Our Kids: The American Dream in Crisis.* New York: Simon & Schuster.

Rawls, John. 1971. *A Theory of Justice.* Cambridge, MA: Belknap Press of Harvard University Press.

Reich, Robert B. 2015. *Saving Capitalism: For the Many, Not the Few.* New York: Alfred A. Knopf.

Reinhart, Carmen M., and Kenneth S. Rogoff. 2009. *This Time Is Different: Eight Centuries of Financial Folly.* Princeton, NJ: Princeton University Press.

Remnick, David, ed. 2000. *The New Gilded Age: The New Yorker Looks at the Culture of Affluence.* New York: Random House.

Rigby, Elizabeth, and Gerald C. Wright. 2011. "Whose Statehouse Democracy? Policy Responsiveness to Poor Versus Rich Constituents in Poor Versus Rich States." In Peter K. Enns and Christopher Wlezien, eds., *Who Gets Represented?*, 189–222. New York: Russell Sage Foundation.

———. 2013. "Political Parties and Representation of the Poor in the American States." *American Journal of Political Science* 57: 552–565.

Riker, William H. 1982. *Liberalism Against Populism: A Confrontation Between the Theory of Democracy and the Theory of Social Choice.* San Francisco: W. H. Freeman and Company.

Rivers, Douglas. N.d. "Partisan Representation in Congress." Unpublished paper. Department of Political Science, University of California, Los Angeles.

Rivlin, Gary. 2015. *Katrina: After the Flood.* New York: Simon & Schuster.

Rodriguez, Francisco R. 1999. "Does Distributional Skewness Lead to Redistribution? Evidence from the United States." *Economics and Politics* 11: 171–199.

———. 2004. "Inequality, Redistribution, and Rent-Seeking." *Economics and Politics* 16: 287–320.

Rodriguez, Javier M., John Bound, and Arline T. Geronimus. 2013. "U.S. Infant Mortality and the President's Party." *International Journal of Epidemiology*, doi: 10.1093/ije/dyt252.

Roemer, John E. 1999. "The Democratic Political Economy of Progressive Income Taxation." *Econometrica* 67: 1–19.

Rogers, Diane Lim, and John H. Rogers. 2000. "Political Competition and State Government Size: Do Tighter Elections Produce Looser Budgets?" *Public Choice* 105: 1–21.

Rohde, David W. 1991. *Parties and Leaders in the Postreform House.* Chicago: University of Chicago Press.

Rosenthal, Howard. 2004. "Politics, Public Policy, and Inequality: A Look Back at the Twentieth Century." In Kathryn M. Neckerman, ed., *Social Inequality*, 861–892. New York: Russell Sage Foundation.

Rothstein, Jesse, 2010. "Is the EITC as Good as an NIT? Conditional Cash Transfers and Tax Incidence." *American Economic Journal: Economic Policy* 2: 177–208.

Saez, Emmanuel. 2015. "Striking It Richer: The Evolution of Top Incomes in the United States (Updated with 2014 Preliminary Estimates)." University of California at Berkeley, June 25 (https://eml.berkeley.edu/~saez/saez-UStopincomes-2014.pdf).

Saez, Emmanuel, and Gabriel Zucman. Forthcoming. "Wealth Inequality in the United States Since 1913: Evidence from Capitalized Income Tax Data." *Quarterly Journal of Economics.*

Schattschneider, E. E. 1942. *Party Government*. New York: Holt, Rinehart, and Winston.

Scheiber, Noam. 2011. *The Escape Artists: How Obama's Team Fumbled the Recovery*. New York: Simon & Schuster.

Schlozman, Kay Lehman, and Sidney Verba. 1979. *Injury to Insult: Unemployment, Class, and Political Response*. Cambridge, MA: Harvard University Press.

Schlozman, Kay Lehman, Sidney Verba, and Henry E. Brady. 2012. *The Unheavenly Chorus: Unequal Political Voice and the Broken Promise of American Democracy*. Princeton, NJ: Princeton University Press.

Scholz, John Karl. 1994. "The Earned Income Tax Credit: Participation, Compliance, and Antipoverty Effectiveness." *National Tax Journal* 47: 63–87.

Schultz, Kenneth A. 1995. "The Politics of the Political Business Cycle." *British Journal of Political Science* 25: 79–99.

Schumpeter, Joseph R. 1950. *Capitalism, Socialism and Democracy*, 3rd ed. New York: Harper Colophon Books.

Shaefer, H. Luke, Kathryn Edin, and Elizabeth Talbert. 2015. "Understanding the Dynamics of $2-a-Day Poverty in the United States." *RSF: The Russell Sage Foundation Journal of the Social Sciences* 1: 120–138.

Shani, Danielle. 2006. "Knowing Your Colors: Can Knowledge Correct for Partisan Bias in Political Perceptions?" Paper presented at the annual meeting of the Midwest Political Science Association.

Shapiro, Robert Y. 2011. "Public Opinion and American Democracy." *Public Opinion Quarterly* 75: 982–1017.

Sides, John, and Lynn Vavreck. 2013. *The Gamble: Choice and Chance in the 2012 Presidential Election*. Princeton, NJ: Princeton University Press.

Skocpol, Theda. 2012. *Obama and America's Political Future*. Cambridge, MA: Harvard University Press.

Slemrod, Joel. 1994. *Tax Progressivity and Income Inequality*. New York: Cambridge University Press.

———. 2006. "The Role of Misconceptions in Support for Regressive Tax Reform." *National Tax Journal* 59: 57–75.

Slemrod, Joel, and Jon Bakija. 2004. *Taxing Ourselves: A Citizen's Guide to the Debate over Taxes*, 3rd ed. Cambridge, MA: MIT Press.

Smith, Hedrick. 2012. *Who Stole the American Dream?* New York: Random House.

Sobel, Russell S. 1999. "Theory and Evidence on the Political Economy of the Minimum Wage." *Journal of Political Economy* 107: 761–785.

Solon, Gary. 2002. "Cross-Country Differences in Intergenerational Earnings Mobility." *Journal of Economic Perspectives* 16: 59–66.

Soroka, Stuart N., and Christopher Wlezien. 2008. "On the Limits to Inequality in Representation." *PS: Political Science & Politics* 41: 319–327.

———. 2014. "Economic Crisis and Support for Redistribution in the United Kingdom." In Nancy Bermeo and Larry M. Bartels, eds., *Mass Politics in Tough Times: Opinions, Votes, and Protest in the Great Recession*, 105–127. New York: Oxford University Press.

Stenner, Karen. 2005. *The Authoritarian Dynamic*. New York: Cambridge University Press.

Stiglitz, Joseph E. 2012. *The Price of Inequality: How Today's Divided Society Endangers Our Future*. New York: W. W. Norton & Company.

———. 2015. *The Great Divide: Unequal Societies and What We Can Do About Them.* New York: W. W. Norton & Company.

Stimson, James A. 1998. *Public Opinion in America: Moods, Cycles, and Swings,* 2nd ed. Boulder, CO: Westview Press.

Stimson, James A., Michael B. MacKuen, and Robert S. Erikson. 1995. "Dynamic Representation." *American Political Science Review* 89: 543–565.

Stoker, Laura. 1992. "Interests and Ethics in Politics." *American Political Science Review* 86: 369–380.

Task Force on Inequality and American Democracy. 2004. "American Democracy in an Age of Rising Inequality." *Perspectives on Politics* 2: 651–666.

Tirado, Linda. 2014. *Hand to Mouth: Living in Bootstrap America.* New York: G. P. Putnam's Sons.

Tobin, James, and Murray Weidenbaum, eds. 1988. *Two Revolutions in Economic Policy: The First Economic Reports of Presidents Kennedy and Reagan.* Cambridge, MA: MIT Press.

Tocqueville, Alexis de. 1835/1840. *"Democracy in America" and "Two Essays on America."* Reprint, London: Penguin Books, 2003.

Tufte, Edward R. 1978. *Political Control of the Economy.* Princeton, NJ: Princeton University Press.

Twain, Mark, and Charles Dudley Warner. 1873. *The Gilded Age: A Tale of Today.* Reprint, New York: Penguin Books, 2001.

Vavreck, Lynn, and Douglas Rivers. 2008. "The 2006 Cooperative Congressional Election Study." *Journal of Elections, Public Opinion, and Parties* 18: 355–366.

Ventry, Dennis J., Jr. 2000. "The Collision of Tax and Welfare Politics: The Political History of the Earned Income Tax Credit, 1969–99." *National Tax Journal 53*: 983–1026.

Verba, Sidney, Norman H. Nie, and Jae-on Kim. 1978. *Participation and Political Equality: A Seven-Nation Comparison.* Cambridge: Cambridge University Press.

Verba, Sidney, and Gary R. Orren. 1985. *Equality in America: The View from the Top.* Cambridge, MA: Harvard University Press.

Verba, Sidney, Kay Lehman Schlozman, and Henry E. Brady. 1995. *Voice and Equality: Civic Voluntarism in American Politics.* Cambridge, MA: Harvard University Press.

Weissberg, Robert. 2004. "Politicized Pseudo Science." *PS: Political Science & Politics 39*: 33–37.

Wilensky, Harold L. 2002. *Rich Democracies: Political Economy, Public Policy, and Performance.* Berkeley: University of California Press.

Wilkinson, Richard, and Kate Pickett. 2009. *The Spirit Level: Why Greater Equality Makes Societies Stronger.* New York: Bloomsbury Press.

Winters, Richard. 1976. "Party Control and Policy Change." *American Journal of Political Science 20*: 597–636.

Wlezien, Christopher. 1995. "The Public as Thermostat: Dynamics of Preferences for Spending." *American Journal of Political Science 39*: 981–1000.

Wolff, Edward N. 2002. *Top Heavy: The Increasing Inequality of Wealth in America and What Can Be Done about It.* New York: The New Press.

———. 2014. "Household Wealth Trends in the United States, 1962–2013: What Happened Over the Great Recession?" Working Paper 20733. Cambridge, MA: National Bureau of Economic Research.

Wolfinger, Raymond E., and Steven J. Rosenstone. 1980. *Who Votes?* New Haven, CT: Yale University Press.

Zaller, John. 1985. "Pre-Testing Information Items on the 1986 NES Pilot Survey." Report to the National Election Study Board of Overseers.

———. 1992. *The Nature and Origins of Mass Opinion.* New York: Cambridge University Press.

Zellner, Arnold. 1962. "An Efficient Method of Estimating Seemingly Unrelated Regressions and Tests for Aggregation Bias." *Journal of the American Statistical Association* 57: 348–368.

Zernike, Kate. 2010. *Boiling Mad: Inside the Tea Party.* New York: Times Books.

Zidar, Owen M. 2015. "Tax Cuts for Whom? Heterogeneous Effects of Income Tax Changes on Growth and Employment." Working Paper 21035. Cambridge, MA: National Bureau of Economic Research.

Index

Aaronson, Daniel, 20n
abortion, 237
Abraham, Katherine, 316n
Abramowitz, Alan, 275
Achen, Christopher, 43n, 77n, 78n, 82n, 106n, 131n, 233n, 236n, 306, 319n, 339n, 353n
affirmative action, 237n
Affleck, Ben, 25
Affluence and Influence (Gilens), 249
Affordable Care Act (Patient Protection and Affordable Care Act; ACA), 65, 237; congressional support, 280–281; impact on inequality of, 279, 333–334; in 2010 election, 283–285
AFL-CIO, 211
after-tax income (CBO), 67
Aid to Families with Dependent Children, 11
AIG insurance company, 303
Alesina, Alberto, 17n, 35n, 39–40, 358
Alexander, Herbert, 94n
Alter, Jonathan, 163–164, 360–361
Alternative Minimum Tax, 165, 171
Althaus, Scott, 156n
Alvaredo, Facundo, 1n
American Economic Association survey, 202
American Family Business Institute, 181
American National Election Studies (ANES) surveys, 88, 93n, 98n, 108, 111, 113–114, 116, 118, 121–122, 125, 127, 132, 145, 146n, 150, 152, 154, 155, 156n, 160–161, 162–163n, 164, 173, 176, 177, 180n, 183, 184, 275, 283n, 291, 312, 317
American National Election Studies (ANES) Senate Election Study, 245, 247n, 260–265
American Representation Study (Miller and Stokes), 235n
American State Politics (Key), 349

American Taxpayer Relief Act, 171
Americans for Tax Reform, 144
Anders, George, 26n
Andrews, Edmund, 143n, 165n, 166n, 181n, 196n, 214n
Ansolabehere, Stephen, 267n
Apuzzo, Matt, 302n
Arel-Bundock, Vincent, 84
Aristotle, 2, 342–343, 345
Arizona minimum wage increase, 224
Arkansas minimum wage, 228
Arrow, Kenneth, 150n
Associated Press (AP), 33, 301
Atkinson, Anthony, 1n, 30–31, 70n, 258
Atlas, John, 225n
attitude polarization: egalitarian values and views about Bush tax cut, 160–162; ideology and views about inequality, 128–134; party identification and views about Bush tax cut, 159–160
Australia, 274n, 278, 282n
Austria, 308
Aviel, Sara, 305
auto industry bailout, 269, 277–278

Bafumi, Joseph, 236n, 237–238n
Bain Capital, 319
Bair, Sheila, 303
Baker, Dean, 252n
Baker, Peter, 172n
Bakija, Jon, 229n
Banaji, Mahzarin, 124n
Bank of America, 302, 303–304
bank bailouts, 266, 296, 353; distributional implications, 301; public opinion, 278–279, 282
Barnes, Lucy, 67n
Barro, Josh, 332

Barshay, Jill, 142n, 144n

Bartels, Larry, 43n, 75n, 76n, 77n, 82n, 88n, 106n, 131n, 152n, 156n, 158n, 184n, 215n, 234n, 236n, 239n, 245n, 246n, 252n, 254, 256n, 257n, 259n, 263n, 274n, 275n, 276n, 284n, 306, 308n, 315n, 319n, 324n, 328–329n, 331n, 335n, 339n, 349n, 351, 353n, 365

Bartlett, Bruce, 165

battleground states in 2012 election, 322n, 328

Baucus, Max, 140

BBC World Service poll, 278–279, 282

Beck, Nathaniel, 35n, 222n

before-tax income (CBO), 66–67

Beinart, Peter, 275n, 276, 306

Beller, Emily, 19n, 20n

Bénabou, Roland, 17n, 31n

Berg, Andrew, 17n

Bergan, Daniel, 258n

Berinsky, Adam, 192n

Berman, Ari, 311

Bernake, Ben, 307

Bernasek, Anna, 17n

Bernstein, Jared, 9n

Besley, Timothy, 350n

Bhatti, Yosef, 234n, 240n, 261n

Biased Pluralism theories, 252

Biden, Joe, 285, 330–331

big business, feeling thermometer, 114–115

Biven, W. Carl, 51n

Blair, Tony, 47, 127

Blanchard, Oliver, 37n

Blank, Rebecca, 30n

Blankfein, Lloyd, 302

Blinder, Alan, 30n, 57, 269n, 277, 284n, 295–296, 301, 304, 305n, 307

Bloom, Allan, 359n

Bloomberg, Michael, 256–257n

Boehner, John, 214, 283

Boix, Carles, 48n, 351–352

Bosworth, Barry, 18n

Bound, John, 73n

Boushey, Heather, 9n

Bowles, Erskine, 285

Bradbury, Bruce, 18n

Bradbury, Katharine, 20n

Brady, Henry, 3n, 257n, 258, 260n, 264, 265n

Brandeis, Louis, 343

Branigan, William, 169n

Breaux, John, 140

Brenner, Lynn, 25n, 26n

Brewer, Mike, 47n

Britain, 19, 274n, 308, 357

Broder, David, 143, 165n

Broder, John, 215n

Brookings Institution, 18

Brooks, David, 21, 27

Brown, Dorothy, 230n

Brown, Kevin, 196–197

Brown, Robert, 350

Brown, Scott, 238, 277n, 281

Brunner, Eric, 257n

Budget Control Act of 2011, 286

budget deficits, 64, 137, 143, 178, 180, 269, 285–286, 329, 361; public opinion about, 149, 254, 279, 282, 318, 335–337, 340

Buffett, Warren, 256–257n

Bureau of Economic Analysis, U.S., 53n, 200n

Bureau of Labor Statistics, U.S., 45n, 53n, 225n, 231n

Burns, Arthur, 82

Burns, Charles Montgomery, 136

Burns, Conrad, 225n

Burns, Nancy, 358n

Burtless, Gary, 18n

Bush, George H. W., 63, 165, 193, 195, 210–211

Bush, George W., 22, 24, 30, 33, 37, 42n, 47, 58, 59, 63, 64, 65, 72, 101, 102, 120, 181, 193, 196–197, 213–214, 223, 252, 275, 291, 292, 295, 296, 315, 354; and Hurricane Katrina, 359–363; tax cuts of (see Bush tax cuts)

Bush tax cuts, 5, 31, 63–64, 135, 252, 266, 358; estate tax repeal, 170–171; passage of, 136–144; public concern about distribution of benefits, 146–147; public opinion about, 144–164, 313–315, 317, 320–321; "sunsetting" of, 139, 164–169, 197, 285, 329–330

business people, feeling thermometer, 114–115

Caine, Herman, 339n

Calmes, Jackie, 169n, 286n

campaign contributions and political influence, 234, 261, 263–265, 267

campaign spending, 76, 93–97; measurement of, 94n; political consequences of, 98–100; sources of incumbent advantage, 94–97

Campbell, James, 42

Canada, 18, 19, 57, 92, 274n, 278

capital gains tax, 257n

Capital in the Twenty-First Century (Piketty), 15

Card, David, 203, 204, 210, 212, 231

Carnahan, Jean, 140

Carnes, Nicholas, 3n, 265–266, 358

Carter, Jimmy, 51–52, 62, 63, 120, 210, 290

Case, Anne, 350n

Cayman Islands, 26

CBS News/*New York Times* poll, 146, 149, 175

Census Bureau, U.S., 7, 8n, 12n, 35, 46, 53n, 62, 78n, 82–83, 245n, 332; and consumer price index (CPI-U), 53n, 200n

Center for American Progress, 334

Center for Responsive Politics, 265n, 302n

Center on Budget and Policy Priorities, 137, 230–231n

Chait, Jonathan, 169, 318–319, 329, 341

Chamber of Commerce, U.S., 142

Cheney, Dick, 127, 143

Chetty, Raj, 19n, 20n

Chicago minimum wage increase, 228

Christiano, Lawrence, 37n

Citigroup, 302, 303

Citizen Participation Study (Verba, Schlozman, and Brady), 93n

Citizens for Tax Justice, 137n, 141

Citizens United v. FEC, 2

Clark, William, 84

class bias in economic voting, 75–76, 87–92; political consequences of, 98–100

class sympathies, 107, 113–115, 136; and social welfare policy preferences, 115–116

Cleary, Matthew, 259n

Cleland, Max, 140

climate change, 237n

Clinton, Bill, 24, 34, 47, 58, 63, 64, 65, 137, 170, 195, 210, 229, 277, 290

Clinton, Hillary, 166n, 353

Clinton, Joshua, 236n, 239n

CNN, 330

Cochran, John, 143n

Collins, Susan, 238, 281

Colorado minimum wage increase, 225

Committee on Political Parties (American Political Science Association), 348

Community Action Program, 50

Comprehensive Employment and Training Act (CETA), 51–52

Congress, partisan control, 37

Congressional Budget Office (CBO), 63–69, 137, 181–182, 296n

Congressional Progressive Caucus, 216

congruence between constituents and representatives, 237, 257n

Conrad, Kent, 141

Conservative Party government, United Kingdom, 47

contact with public officials and political influence, 212, 234, 260–263, 267; measurement, 260n

Converse, Philip, 106n, 113n, 260n

Coolidge, Calvin, 194

Cooperative Campaign Analysis Project (CCAP) survey, 292–294, 319–327, 334–340

Cooperative Congressional Election Study (CCES) surveys, 208, 215, 225n, 237, 240, 241n, 243n, 247n

Corker, Bob, 216n

corporate taxes, 63, 257n, 266, 318

Couglin, Father Charles, 192

Council of Economic Advisers, 17, 49, 315, 333

CQ Weekly, 139, 211

Current Population Survey, 7n, 8n, 46, 259

Cutler, David, 30n

cycles in economic growth, 39

Dahl, Robert, 1–2, 3, 23, 24, 25, 31, 233, 234, 267, 344–345

Danziger, Sheldon, 52n, 300

Daschle, Tom, 140

Dave Leip's Atlas of U.S. Presidential Elections, 74n
Davis, Susan, 216n
de Figueiredo, John, 267n
death tax, 173, 182, 191
Debot, Brandon, 172n
debt, government: debt ceiling, 286, 297; public opinion, 335–336, 338, 341, 354
defense spending, 237n
DeFrank, Thomas, 283n
DeLay, Tom, 252–253n
Delli Carpini, Michael, 156n, 260n
Democratic Faith (Deneen), 358
Democratic Leadership Council, 175
Deneen, Patrick, 358–359
Denmark, 19, 274n
Dennis, Christopher, 35
Denton, Nancy, 357n
DeParle, Jason, 360n, 361n
Department of Labor, U.S., 199n, 225n
DeSilver, Drew, 334n
Dewan, Shaila, 362n
Dew-Becker, Ian, 21–22
Dilemmas of Pluralist Democracy (Dahl), 2n
Dimon, Jamie, 302
DiNardo, John, 204n
disparities in political responsiveness, 6
Dodd-Frank (Wall Street Reform and Consumer Protection Act), 278; congressional support for, 280–281; in 2010 election, 283–285
Dole, Bob, 303
domestic spending, 286, 329, 351; and partisan politics, 351; public opinion about, 148–149, 237, 253, 255, 289, 291, 335–337, 340
Dow Jones & Company, 44n
Downs, Anthony, 31n
Dreier, Peter, 225n
Dube, Arindrajit, 203, 228
Dugan, Andrew, 207n
DW-NOMINATE scores (Poole and Rosenthal), 96n, 236–237, 238, 240–241n, 246n

Earned Income Tax Credit (EITC), 11, 64, 171, 201–202, 202n, 228–231; perceived eligibility for, 151; political advantages of, 229–230
Eastover (New Orleans), 361–362
economic conditions, perceived, 93n; in 2012 election, 322–325
Economic-Elite Domination theories, 252
Economic Growth and Tax Relief Reconciliation Act (EGTRRA), 138–142, 164, 166n, 169, 170
economic inequality, 7–16; assessments of, 121–122; explanations fpr, 122–123; perceptions of, 107–108, 118–120, 124–135, 312–313, 353; and support for estate tax repeal, 186–188
economic mobility, 19–21, 356
Economic Policy Institute, 198
economic voting, 75–82; and class bias, 75–76, 87–92; myopic, 75, 77–82
Economist, 24, 118, 306
Edin, Kathryn, 11
Edwards, George, 289n
Edwards, John, 26, 215
egalitarian values, 7, 32, 107–113, 136, 312–313, 353; and social welfare policy preferences, 111–113; and support for Bush tax cuts, 160–162
Ehrenfreund, Max, 27n
Ehrenreich, Barbara, 357
Eichenbaum, Martin, 37n
Eichengreen, Barry, 269n
Eichler, Alexander, 310n, 316n
80/20 income ratio, 70–71
Einstein, Katherine Levine, 134n
Eisenhower, Dwight, 49, 52, 101, 102, 195, 223, 290
Electoral College, 352
Emanuel, Rahm, 270
energy policy, 269, 278, 279, 281; in 2010 election, 283–285
Engle, Robert, 222n
Enron scandal, 106
environmental protection, 237n, 256
equal opportunity, 19, 32; and public perceptions, 107, 124, 328n, 335, 338, 354; public support for, 109–110, 113, 312
Erikson, Robert, 76n, 105n, 233n, 234n, 239n, 240n, 261n, 289n, 351

error correction model, 222n
errors-in-variables regression, 251
Espo, David, 213n
estate tax repeal, 5, 135, 137, 144, 169,
    170–173, 199, 223, 257n, 330, 346;
    history of, 193–197; interest groups and,
    189–193; and partisan politics, 195–197,
    351; public opinion of, 173–193,
    335–337
European Social Surveys, 308n
Evans, Charles, 37n

factor analysis, 110n, 236n, 237n
Fair Minimum Wage Act of 2007, 198
false consciousness, 75; and support for
    Bush tax cuts, 150–163
Federal Deposit Insurance Corporation, 303
Federal Election Commission, 94n
Federal Emergency Management Agency
    (FEMA), 362
Federal Reserve, 48, 64, 82, 84, 296,
    303–305, 307
Federal Reserve Bank of New York, 302
Federal Reserve Bank of St. Louis, 44n
feeling thermometer, 113–114
Feingold, Russ, 281
Feinstein, Diane, 140
Feldman, Stanley, 106, 109n
"Fight for $15" minimum wage campaign,
    228
filibuster, 139, 196, 213, 276–277, 280–281,
    285
financial regulation, 216, 278, 280–281
Finland, 19, 274n, 308
Fiorina, Morris, 77
Firestone, David, 143n, 144n
fiscal cliff, 171, 329–331
Fishkin, James, 156n
flat tax, 189n
Flavin, Patrick, 234–235
Florida minimum wage increase, 224
Foley, Duncan, 356n
Fontevecchia, Agustino, 19n
food stamps, 7n, 50, 62, 67, 269, 333, 335
Forbes 400 list, 19
Ford, Gerald, 50–51, 120, 229
Fortin, Nicole, 204n

Fortune magazine, 192
Fox, Liana, 11n
Fox News polls, 206n
France, 18, 57, 274n, 278, 282n, 357
Frank, Robert, 17n, 170, 197
Frank, Thomas, 75n
Franken, Al, 277n
Freedman, Jacob, 181n
Friedman, Joel, 137n
Frist, Bill, 196
Fuller, Dan, 202n
Furman, Jason, 316n, 333–334

Galbraith, James, 84
Gale, William, 137n
Gallup poll, 102, 124, 207, 271n
Gallup/CNN/*USA Today* poll, 231n
Garner, John Nance, 194
Gates, Bill, 256–257n
gay men and lesbians: and feeling thermome-
    ter, 114; in the military, 237n
GDP growth, 39, 42; and effect on incomes,
    55–57; in Great Recession, 297–298, 305,
    307; partisan differences about, 53–57
Geer, John, 236n, 239n
Geewax, Marilyn, 212–213
Geide-Stevenson, Doris, 202n
Geithner, Timothy, 6, 269, 301–305
Gellad, Walid, 252n
General Accounting Office, U.S., 230n
General Social Survey, 16n, 271n
Gephardt, Richard, 163, 193
Germany, 19, 57, 123, 274n, 278, 282n, 308
Geronimus, Arline, 73n
Gilded Age, 309, 343, 353, 354
Gilens, Martin, 3n, 156n, 188n, 208, 234n,
    235, 249–254, 267, 345, 358
Gilligan, James, 72
Gingrich, Newt, 290
Gini coefficient, 21n, 47, 66–69, 258, 332
Giovannoni, Olivier, 84
Gitlin, Todd, 14n
Glaeser, Edward, 358
Glazer, Nathan, 106
Godfather's Pizza, 339n
Goldfarb, Zachary, 331–334
Goldman Sachs, 302, 303

Gordon, Robert, 21–22

Gore, Al, 72, 291

Gottschalk, Peter, 52n

government spending, 51, 285; partisan differences over, 57; preferences and support for Bush tax cuts, 152–153, 156; preferences and support for estate tax repeal, 180; public opinion of, 149, 256, 271–274, 278–279, 282, 291–292

government waste, perceived: and support for Bush tax cuts, 152–154; and support for estate tax repeal, 178–180

Graetz, Michael, 172, 181, 190–191, 193–195

Granger, C.W.J., 222n

Grassley, Charles, 140, 142, 143

Great Compression, 29

Great Depression, 52, 269, 276

Great Recession, 6, 12, 26, 72, 103, 135, 215–216, 222, 269–271, 336, 357; policy response to, 277–281, 295–305, 332; political impact of, 286–295, 305–308, 341; timing and, 274–276; and 2008 election, 274–276; and 2010 election, 281–285; and views about inequality, 309–315

Great Society (Johnson), 50, 58, 253, 277

Greece, 308, 357

Green, William, 194

Greenberg, Stanley, 307

Griffin, John, 263n

Grogan, Coleen, 350n

Gross, Daniel, 22n

Grunwald, Michael, 276n, 277, 281n, 285n

Gujarati, Damodar, 69n, 218n

gun control, 237n

Hacker, Jacob, 3n, 31n, 147–149, 309, 338, 346

Hall, Richard, 267n

Hand to Mouth: Living in Bootstrap America (Tirado), 357

Harding, David, 20n

Harkin, Tom, 216

Harris, Benjamin, 137n

Harris poll, 119–120, 146

Harwood, John, 278

Hassett, Kevin, 319, 328, 329

Hastert, Dennis, 127

health care, 62, 336, 353; reform of (*see* health care reform; Affordable Care Act)

health care reform, 216, 269, 278, 280–281, 284–285, 289, 316; Obama (*see* Affordable Care Act

Heckman, James, 152n

Heritage Foundation, 190–191, 192–193

Herron, Michael, 236n, 237–238n

Herszenhorn, David, 169n, 270n, 285n

Hibbs, Douglas, 35, 48, 50n, 51n, 52, 53, 69, 78

Hicks, Timothy, 92

Hill, Kim, 350n

Hines, James, 30n

Hinton-Andersson, Angela, 350n

Hirsch, Barry, 219n, 225n

Historical Income Tables, 8, 35

Hochschild, Jennifer, 106–107, 122, 134, 149n, 191–192, 192–193, 355, 356

homeland security, 256

home mortgage foreclosures, 277–278, 301, 304–305, 357

homicide rate, partisan difference, 72

"honeymoon" period, presidential, 39, 84

Hook, Janet, 334n

House Ethics Committee, 253n

House of Representatives, 6, 37, 127, 141–144, 165, 171, 194–196, 210n, 211–216, 224, 230, 282–283, 285–286, 290, 343n, 346; responsiveness to constituency opinion, 236–238, 240–242, 243–245; support for Obama legislative agenda, 279–281

House Oversight and Government Reform Committee, 252n

House Ways and Means Committee, 141, 194, 230

Hout, Michael, 19n, 20n

Hoynes, Hilary, 30n

Huang, Chye-Ching, 172n

Hubbard, R. Glenn, 142

Huber, Evelyne, 48n

HuffPost Pollster, 295

Hulse, Carl, 196n, 277n, 280n

Hurricane Katrina, 212, 359–363

Hurricane Rita, 362

Hussein, Saddam, 253
Husted, Thomas, 350n

Iceland, 308
IGM Forum survey of economists, 294n
immigrants, illegal, 237n
immigration policy, 269, 279; congressional
    support for, 280–281
income growth: under Democratic and
    Republican presidents, 35–47, 332, 351;
    and electoral cycle, 82–87; in Great
    Recession, 298–299; historical pattern of,
    7–13; and and macroeconomic perfor-
    mance, 54–57
income inequality, 7–15; under Democratic
    and Republican presidents, 58–62; in
    Great Recession, 332
income shares, 13–14
incumbent party tenure and presidential elec-
    tion outcomes, 80
inequality and economic growth, 17
Inequality Module (CCAP survey), 292–294,
    334–340
Inequality: What Can Be Done? (Atkinson),
    258
infant mortality rate, partisan difference, 73
Inflation: effect on incomes, 55–57; and
    electoral cycle, 82; partisan differences
    about, 53–55
inheritance, 192–193
initiative and referendum process, 201,
    226–228
Institute for Fiscal Studies, 47
Institute on Taxation and Economic Policy,
    137
instrumental variables regression analysis,
    97, 152n, 153, 180n
intergenerational mobility, 20
Internal Revenue Service, 11, 12n, 181, 333;
    and Earned Income Tax Credit, 230; estate
    tax auditing, 196–197
International Monetary Fund, 17
International Social Survey Programme
    (ISSP), 16n, 123, 271n, 274n
iPOLL archive, 148n, 191n, 205
Iraq War, 237, 253
Ireland, 274n

Irwin, Neil, 269n
Israel, 274n

Jackson, Andrew, 29
Jackson Square, New Orleans, 360–363
Jacobs, Alan, 92
Jacobs, Elisabeth, 253n, 306
Jacobs, Lawrence, 2n, 3n, 233–234, 281n,
    341n
Jacobson, Gary, 253, 284n
Japan, 274n, 308
Jargowsky, Paul, 357n
Jefferson, Thomas, 29
Jeffords, James, 140, 141
Jennings, Edward, 350
Jim Crow era, 347
Job Corps, 50
Jobs and Growth Tax Relief Reconciliation
    Act (JGTRRA), 142–144, 166n
Job Training Partnership Act (JTPA), 52
Johnson, Lyndon, 49–50, 253, 277, 288,
    290
Johnson, Simon, 302
Johnson, Tim, 140
Johnston, David Cay, 14n, 197n
Joint Committee on Taxation, 138–139,
    142n, 170
Joint Economic Committee, 182
Jordan, Michael, 25
Jost, John, 124n, 125n, 126n
JPMorgan, 302
Judis, John, 271, 275n, 288
"just world" theories, 124

Kaiser, Robert, 281n
Kansas minimum wage increase, 228
Kapur, Sahil, 315
Karier, Thomas, 64n
Katz, Jane, 20n
Katz, Lawrence, 30n
Keech, William, 35n
Keeter, Scott, 156n, 260n
Kelly, Nathan, 62–63, 69n
Kennedy, Edward, 212, 215, 277n
Kennedy, John, 49, 63, 290
Kennedy, Peter, 69n, 218n
Kenney, Lawrence, 350n

Kenworthy, Lane, 58n, 62, 286–287, 294, 356n
Kerr, William, 356n
Kerry, John, 33, 102, 202, 204, 291, 361
Key, V. O., Jr., 77, 103, 259, 306, 347–349
Khimm, Suzy, 319n, 330n
Kim, Jae-on, 257n
Kim, Walter, 23n
Kinder, Donald, 113n, 358n
King, Stephen, 25
Kinsley, Michael, 19, 32
Kirkland, Lane, 211
Kissinger, Henry, 303n
Klein, Ezra, 311
Kluegel, James, 118n
Knight, Brian, 350n
Kohl, Herbert, 140
Kohut, Andrew, 334
Kopczuk, Wojciech, 20n, 21n
Kramer, Gerald, 76n, 77
Krehbiel, Keith, 210n, 219n, 281n
Krueger, Alan, 17, 30n, 203, 204–205, 210, 212, 217, 228, 231,, 315
Krugman, Paul, 15n, 21, 29–30, 70n, 163, 170, 296–297, 333, 341
Krupnikov, Yanna, 183n
Kuttner, Robert, 271, 288–289

Labaton, Stephen, 165n, 198n, 214n
labor force participation, 44–45
labor unions, 2, 4, 5, 29, 107, 196, 338; and minimum wage, 201, 211, 217–223, 228; feeling thermometer, 114–115; public opinion, 335, 338–339
Labour Party government, United Kingdom, 47
Lacombe, Matthew, 256n
Landrieu, Mary, 140
Landsburg, Steven, 202n
Lane, Randall, 19n
Lauer, Matt, 316
Lee, David, 204
Lee, Mike, 243
Lehman Brothers, 271, 275, 307
Leighley, Jan, 257n, 259n, 350n
Lemieux, Thomas, 204n
Lenz, Gabriel, 319n

Leonhardt, David, 19n, 279, 333n
Lerner, Melvin, 124n
Lester, T. William, 203
Levy, Frank, 14, 30n
Lewis, Ken, 303
liberal-conservative ideology, 112n, 237n, 245n, 247n
Lieberman, Joseph, 277n
Lincoln, Blanche, 140
Lippmann, Walter, 118
Lipton, Eric, 286n
Londregan, John, 39n
Long, Huey, 192
Long, Phil, 360n
Los Angeles minimum wage increase, 228
Los Angeles Times poll, 148, 149n
Lott, Trent, 144
Loughlin, Sean, 140n, 265n
Lowell, A. Lawrence, 105n
Lower Ninth Ward (New Orleans), 361–363
Luxembourg Income Study, 18n
life expectancy, 18
Lupia, Arthur, 158
Lynch, David, 284n

Mack, Connie, 181–182
MacKuen, Michael, 105n, 233n, 239n, 289n, 351
Macpherson, David, 219n
Madonna, 25
Major, John, 47
Majoritarian Electoral Democracy theories, 252
Majoritarian Pluralism theories, 252
Mankiw, Gregory, 230
Mann, Thomas, 247n
Margalit, Yotam, 287–288
market income (CBO), 66–67, 331
Marmot, Michael, 18n
Marr, Chuck, 230–231n
Marshall, Ray, 51n
Martinez, Gebe, 211n
Marzilli, Ted, 339n
Massachusetts minimum wage, 228
Massey, Douglas, 357n
Matthews, J. Scott, 92
Mayer, Gerald, 219n

Mayer, Susan, 357n
Mayhew, David, 349
Mazumder, Bhashkar, 20n
McCain, John, 102–103, 140, 141, 166, 291
McCall, Leslie, 17n, 118n, 119
McCarty, Nolan, 31n, 209–210, 281n
McCaskill, Claire, 225n
McClosky, Herbert, 106–107, 125n
McConnell, Mitch, 270, 276, 280, 285, 330–331
McCormick, John, 343
McGhee, Eric, 283–284n
McIver, John, 233n
Mead, Lawrence, 34
median voter, 30, 31n, 345
Medicaid, 50, 332, 350
Medicare, 7n, 50, 67, 139, 146n, 147–148, 149n, 253, 279, 333; Medicare payroll tax, 151; prescription drug benefit of, 252
Medina, Jennifer, 228n
Mellon, Andrew, 194
Meltzer, Allan, 31n
Merrill Lynch, 303
Merzer, Martin, 360n
middle-class people, feeling thermometer, 114–115
Miller, George, 216
Miller, Warren, 233n, 235, 327n
Miller, Zell, 140n
minimum wage, 5, 30, 32, 51, 135, 196, 197, 198–228, 231–232, 346; and average hourly wage, 199–201, 220–223, 225–228, 353, 358; and congressional inaction, 209–217; and congressional representation, 214–215; effects on earnings, 203–204; effects on employment, 201, 203–205; effects on inequality, 204; history of, 199–201; indexing for inflation, 209–210; and labor unions, 217–223, 225–228; local action regarding, 224, 228; partisan control of state governments, 225–228; and partisan politics, 217–223, 351; public opinion of, 199, 201, 205–209, 217–228; state action regarding, 224–228
Mishel, Lawrence, 9n
misinformation and support for estate tax repeal, 181–189

Mississippi minimum wage, 228
Missouri minimum wage increase, 225
MIT Dictionary of Modern Economics, 202
monetary policy, partisan differences, 57, 84
Montana minimum wage increase, 225
Montgomery, Lori, 169n
Montopoli, Brian, 265n
moral hazard, 304
Morath, Eric, 207n
Morgan Stanley, 302
Munk, Nina, 19n
Murdoch, Rupert, 19
Murnane, Richard, 30n
Murray, Patty, 216
Murray, Shailagh, 169n
Muslims, feeling thermometer, 114
MX missile, 267
myopic economic voting, 4, 75, 77–82; political consequences of, 100–101

Nagler, Jonathan, 257n, 259n
Nagourney, Adam, 277n, 280n
Nather, David, 144n, 196n
National Bureau of Economic Research (NBER) Business Cycle Dating Committee, 274n
National Conference of State Legislatures, 225n
National Economic Council, 304
National Federation of Independent Business, 213
National Industrial Recovery Act, 199n
nationalization of banks, 303, 304
National Public Radio/Kaiser Family Foundation/Kennedy School of Government survey, 151, 173, 175, 182–183, 189n, 231
Nature and Origins of Mass Opinion (Zaller), 130
"Nature of Belief Systems in Mass Publics" (Converse), 106n
NBC News/Wall Street Journal poll, 146, 148, 149, 174, 206
Neckerman, Kathryn, 18n
Nelson, Ben, 140
Nelson, Candice, 94n
Nelson, Thomas, 113n

Netherlands, 274n, 308, 356
Nevada minimum wage increase, 225
New Deal era, 58, 253n, 294, 306–307, 343–344, 354
New Economic Policy (Nixon), 50
New Gilded Age, 15, 24, 26, 27, 32, 75, 76, 107, 108, 170, 235, 310, 334, 341, 344, 353, 356
New Haven, CT, 1, 344
New New Deal (Obama), 6, 274, 276, 279, 291, 305–307
New Orleans, 359–363
New York City minimum wage campaign, 228
New York Times, 14, 143
New York Times Magazine, 26–27
New York Times poll, 174
New Zealand, 274n, 308
Newman, Brian, 263n
Newman, Katherine, 253n, 306
News Interest Index poll, 207n
Nickel and Dimed (Ehrenreich), 357
Nie, Norman, 257n
Nitschke, Lori, 140n, 141n, 142n, 211n
Nixon, Richard, 50, 82, 101, 223, 229
Noah, Timothy, 331–334, 338n
non-linear least squares regression, 221
non-linear model of congressional responsiveness, 244n, 246n, 261n
Norquist, Grover, 144
Norway, 19, 123, 274n
Nyhan, Brendan, 284n, 285n

Obama, Barack, 6, 37, 58, 63, 65, 94n, 102–103, 120, 171, 245, 270–271, 290, 306–307, 354; and Bush tax cuts, 165–169, 197; and inequality, 309–315, 329–334; and minimum wage, 224; response to Great Recession, 277–281, 295–297, 303–305; and 2008 election, 275–276; and 2010 election, 282–285; and 2012 election, 315–329
O'Brien, Matthew, 171n
obtuse support for estate tax repeal, 176–177
Occupy Wall Street movement, 6, 14, 289, 353; and views about inequality, 310–316, 341

Ohio minimum wage increase, 225
oil prices, 43–44, 52, 62
oligarchy, 21, 342–343, 345
Oliver, Eric, 357n
On Deaf Ears: The Limits of the Bully Pulpit (Edwards), 289n
On Political Equality (Dahl), 2n
Organization of Petroleum Exporting Countries (OPEC), 50
Ornstein, Norman, 247n
Orren, Gary, 6–7, 28, 113, 257–258, 343–344
Osawatomie, Kansas (Obama speech), 310–315, 321
Osberg, Lars, 18n, 123n, 356n
Ostrogorski, Moiseide, 74, 75, 102, 354
Ostry, Jonathan, 17n
Ota, Alan, 142n, 144n
Ovalle, David, 360n
Owens, Lindsay, 286–287, 294

Page, Benjamin, 3n, 64n, 199n, 233–234, 234n, 250n, 251–252, 254, 256n, 257, 267, 341n, 346
Palin, Sarah, 281–282
Pandit, Vikram, 302
Panel Study of Income Dynamics, 300, 301
Parade magazine, 25–26
Parks Daniel, 139n, 141n, 142n, 165n
partial adjustment in dynamic models, 69n
partisan polarization, 259, 294, 339–341, 353
partisan politics, 4; and homicide, 72; and income growth, 35–47, 58–62, 351; and infant mortality, 73; and macroeconomic performance, 53–57; and minimum wage, 201, 217–223; and national policy, 351; and redistribution, 62–69; and state policy, 350; and suicide, 72
partisan turnover, presidential, 41–43
party competition, 352; and political inequality, 347–352
party identification, 88, 112, 294–295, 351; and support for estate tax repeal, 179–180, 184–185, 349; and support for minimum wage, 208–209; in 2012 election, 322–326; and views about Bush tax

cut, 152–160, 158n; and voting behavior, 349

Paulson, Henry, 22, 33, 70, 303, 304, 356n

payroll tax cut, 169, 269, 285, 313, 317, 329, 330, 333; public opinion of, 335, 337

Pear, Robert, 286n

Pearce, David, 202n

Pedulla, David, 287n

Pelosi, Nancy, 198, 213

Penn, Mark, 175

Perotti, Roberto, 17n, 31n, 37n, 356n

Persson, Torsten, 17n

Peru, 25

Peterson, Peter, 143n

Pethokoukis, James, 166n

Pew Research Center, 207, 334

Pfeffer, Fabian, 300

Phillips, Kevin, 29, 309, 343, 353, 354

Pickett, Kate, 18n

Pierson, Paul, 3n, 31n, 147–149, 309, 338, 346

Piketty, Thomas, 1n, 11–16

Plato, 358–359

pluralism, 1

plutocracy, 254–257

political business cycle, 82–87

political ideology, 107, 112; and electoral responses to the Great Recession, 307–308; and perceptions of inequality, 124–135; and support for estate tax repeal, 179–180; in 2012 election, 322–325; and views about Bush tax cut, 152–155

political information, 107; measurement of, 127, 260n; and partisan biases in perceptions, 131, 355; and political influence, 260–263, 267; and views about Bush tax cut, 155–163; and views about inequality, 127–135

political participation and political influence, 257–263

political parties, macroeconomic policies, 48–52

political representation, 215, 233–268, 344–345; unequal (see responsiveness, unequal)

political salience of economic inequality, 23

Politics, Parties, and Pressure Groups (Key), 103n

Pollin, Robert, 58

polyarchy (Dahl), 345

Pontusson, Jonas, 356n

Poole, Keith, 31n, 209–210, 236

poor people, feeling thermometer, 114–115, 118

Porter, Eduardo, 6n, 11n, 165n, 316n

Portugal, 308

post-tax income, 62, 63n

poverty, 11, 18, 47, 107, 224, 253, 332, 357, 360–361

pre-tax income, 7, 62, 63n

PRI (Mexico), 259n

probit regression model, 88–89n

Progressive Era, 311, 341, 343–344, 353, 354

public policy mood (Stimson), 289–290, 351

public works spending, 267

Putnam, Robert, 18n

Pytte, Alyson, 211n

quantitative easing, 296

Rampell, Catherine, 286n

Rangel, Charles, 141, 144

Rational Public (Page, Shapiro), 346

Rawls, John, 16

Reagan, Ronald, 24, 47, 52, 58, 63, 64, 65, 69, 165, 193, 195, 201, 229, 253n, 277, 290, 291

Recovery Act (American Recovery and Reinvestment Act), 277; congressional support of, 280–281; in 2010 election, 283–285; public opinion about, 292–294, 296n

redistribution of income, 17, 31, 62–69, 136, 333, 352, 356; public support for, 121–122, 272, 287, 347, 355–356, 358

Rehnquist, William, 127

Reich, Michael, 203

Reich, Robert, 338n

Reid, Harry, 216, 331

Reinhart, Carmen, 276n

Remnick, David, 15n

Republic (Plato), 358–359

Republican success in presidential elections, 74–76; due to biases in economic accountability, 101–104; and impact on inequality, 69–73

Resnikoff, Ned, 216n
Responsible Electorate (Key), 103n
responsiveness, unequal, 239–247, 345, 347; and political resources, 257–265; and partisan differences, 248–249; systemic, 249–254
retrospective voting, 76–77, 103
rich people, feeling thermometer, 114–115
Richard, Scott, 31n
Rigby, Elizabeth, 234
Riker, William, 150n
Rivers, Douglas, 219n, 236n, 237n
Rivlin, Gary, 362n, 363n
Roaring Twenties, 309, 343, 353
Rodriguez, Francisco, 31n
Rodriguez, Javier, 73n
Rodrik, Dani, 17n
Roemer, John, 31n
Rogers, Diane, 350n
Rogers, John, 350n
Rogoff, Kenneth, 276n
Role of Government survey, 271–273
Romney, Mitt, 291, 310, 316–329, 353; class sympathies of, 321–327, 341
Roosevelt, Franklin Delano, 29, 199n, 276, 277, 288, 306–307
Roosevelt, Theodore, 311
Roper Center, 148n, 191n, 205
Rosenbaum, David, 143n
Rosenstone, Steven, 257n
Rosenthal, Howard, 31n, 39n, 209–210, 236
Ross, Stephen, 257n
Rothstein, Jesse, 230n
Ruffing, Kathy, 137n
Russo, Ann, 84
Ryan, Paul, 230

Saad, Lydia, 271n
Sachs, Jeffrey, 35n
Saez, Emmanuel, 1n, 2n, 11–16, 20n, 21n, 299, 300n, 332
Safire, William, 213n
Sahadi, Jeanne, 65n
Samuelson, Paul, 49
Samuelson, Robert, 106
San Francisco minimum wage increase, 228
Sanders, Bernie, 216, 238n, 243, 277n, 353

Santorum, Rick, 321
Sargent, Greg, 316n
Schattschneider, E. E., 150, 348–349
Scheiber, Noam, 228n, 269n, 331n
Schlozman, Kay, 3n, 257n, 258, 260n, 264, 265n, 286–287
Schoeni, Robert, 300
Schumer, Charles, 224
Schumpeter, Joseph, 346
Schwab, Charles, 142
Schwabish, Jonathan, 18n
Schwandt, Kimberly, 283n
Scott, Janny, 19n
Scott, Robert, 216
Seattle minimum wage increase, 228
Seawright, Jason, 3n, 254n, 256n, 257n
seemingly unrelated regression (SUR) estimator, 43n
Senate, 6, 37n, 127, 139–144, 149, 165, 171, 172, 182, 194–196, 211–216, 224, 346; responsiveness to constituency opinion, 237–239, 242–247; support for Obama legislative agenda in, 279–281
Senate Appropriations Committee, 182
Senate Budget Committee, 141
Senate Finance Committee, 140, 182, 194
separation of powers, 249
sequester provision (of Budget Control Act of 2011), 286
Service Employees International Union (SEIU), 207, 228
Shaefer, Luke, 11
Shani, Danielle, 131n
Shanks, J. Merrill, 327n
Shapiro, Ian, 172, 181, 190–191, 193–195
Shapiro, Robert, 233n, 346
Shea, Christopher, 23n
Sides, John, 276n, 282–283n, 292n, 319n
Simmons, James, 64n, 199n
Simpson, Alan, 285
Simpson-Bowles Commission (National Commission on Fiscal Responsibility and Reform), 285
Simpson, Homer, 136
Sinclair, T. A., 343n
Skocpol, Theda, 2n, 276, 277n, 279, 281n, 288–289, 305–306

Slemrod, Joel, 62n, 183, 189, 229n
Sloan, Allan, 143n
Smeeding, Timothy, 18n, 123n, 356n
Smith, Adam, 359
Smith, Eliot, 118n
Smith, Matt, 330n
Smoot, Reed, 194
Snow, John, 22
Snowe, Olympia, 140, 238, 281
Snyder, James, 267n
Sobel, Russell, 204
Social Security, 7n, 62, 67, 78n, 139, 146n, 147–148, 199, 256, 341n; Social Security payroll tax, 151
Social Security Administration, 18
Solomon, Deborah, 182n
Solon, Gary, 20n, 356n
Solow, Robert, 49
Song, Jae, 20n, 21n
Soroka, Stuart, 47, 267n
Soros, George, 19, 256–257n
Southern Politics in State and Nation (Key), 347–349
Spain, 123, 274n, 308
Specter, Arlen, 277n
spheres of justice, 28, 106, 343–344, 355
SpongeBob Squarepants, 25
"stagflation," 52
Standard & Poor's, 286
Starobin, Paul, 211n
Stein, Ben, 33–34, 70
Steinbrenner, George, 171
Steinfels, Peter, 356n
Steinhauer, Jennifer, 171n
stem cell research, 267
Stenner, Karen, 125n
Stephens, John, 48n
Stevenson, Richard, 326n
Stiglitz, Joseph, 17, 70, 338n
Stimson, James, 105n, 233n, 239n, 289–290, 351
stimulus spending, 51, 216, 269, 277, 280–281; public opinion about, 272–273, 282–285, 292–294, 296
Stoker, Laura, 188n
Stokes, Bruce, 334n
Stokes, Donald, 233n, 235

suicide rate, partisan difference, 72
Sullivan, Paul, 171n
Sulzberger, A. G., 311
Summers, Lawrence, 304
"sunsetting" of Bush tax cuts, 139, 164–169, 197
Sununu, John, 211
super PACS, 2
Supreme Court, 199n
Survey of Consumer Finances, 16n, 301
Survey of Economically Successful Americans (SESA), 254–256
Survey Research Center, University of Michigan, 88n
Sweden, 19, 92, 123, 274n
Swindell, Bill, 141n, 142n, 165n
Switzerland, 274n
system justification theories, 124

Tabellini, Guido, 17n
Talbert, Elizabeth, 11n
Talent, Jim, 225n
Task Force on Inequality and American Democracy (American Political Science Association), 2–3, 34
Tauzin, Billy, 253n
Tavernise, Sabrina, 18n
tax burdens, perceived, 116–118, 136, 138, 339–340; and support for estate tax repeal, 177–180; and views about Bush tax cut, 152–155, 166
tax cuts, 51, 63–65, 194–195, 277, 281, 361; Bush administration (*see* Bush tax cuts); estate tax (*see* estate tax repeal); public opinion about, 254–257, 279, 282, 335–338, 341
Tax Policy Center, 137, 229, 230n, 330n
tax rates, 62, 65–66; partisan differences, 57
Tax Relief Act (2010), 171
taxing the rich, 6, 316–327, 353, 354
Taylor, Andrew, 139n, 140n
Tea Party movement, 271, 281–282, 289
Temin, Peter, 14, 30n
Temporary Assistance for Needy Families, 11, 229
Tester, Jon, 225n
Thatcher, Margaret, 47

Thomas, Bill, 142
Thompson, Derek, 316n
Throw Momma From the Train Act of 2001 (estate tax repeal), 170
Tilove, Jonathan, 360n
Time magazine, 276
Tirado, Linda, 357
Tobias, Andrew, 25
Tobin, James, 49, 64n
tobit regression analysis, 225n, 226, 227
Tocqueville, Alexis de, 28
Torricelli, Robert, 140
Townsend, Francis, 192
transfer payments, electoral cycle, 82
Treasury Department, 48, 278, 286, 301–305, 307
"trickle-down" income growth, 46
Troubled Asset Relief Program (TARP), 277–278, 303; public opinion about, 292–294
Trump, Donald, 19, 25, 341
Tsangarides, Charalambos, 17n
Tufte, Edward, 48, 49, 73, 76n, 82, 83
turnout and political influence, 234, 258–263, 267
Twain, Mark, 28–29
2000 presidential election, effect on inequality, 72
2008 presidential election, 274–276
2010 midterm election, 271, 281, 282–285
2012 presidential election, 286, 310, 353; effect on inequality, 333, 341

Uchitelle, Louis, 15n
Uganda, 25
unemployment, 316, 332, 339; and effect on incomes, 55–57; and electoral cycle, 82; in Great Recession, 298; partisan differences about, 53–55; and perceptions, 355
unemployment benefits, 62, 69, 78n, 169, 267, 269, 285, 332, 333, 336
unenlightened self-interest, 150–155, 346
Unheavenly Chorus, The (Schlozman, Verba, Brady), 258n
United Kingdom, 47, 57, 92, 123, 278
USA Today, 284

Van Dongen, Rachel, 196n
Vavreck, Lynn, 237n, 292n, 319
Ventry, Dennis, 229n
Verba, Sidney, 3n, 6–7, 28, 113, 257–258, 260n, 264, 265n, 286–287, 343–344
Vieregge, Dale, 358n
Voice and Equality (Verba, Schlozman, Brady), 258
Vroman, Wayne, 219n

Wachovia bank, 303
Wagner, Daniel, 302n
Wall Street Journal, 202, 204, 270, 271
Wall Street meltdown of 2008, 6, 135, 269m 270–271, 275, 300–301, 355
Wallace, George, 48, 352
Warner, Charles, 28–29
Washington, Ebonya, 257n
Washington Post/ABC News poll, 284n, 354
Wasik, Daniel, 366
Watson, Mark, 53
Waxman, Henry, 193
Wayman, Frank, 267n
Wealth and Democracy: A Political History of the American Rich (Phillips), 29
wealth inequality, 15–16; in Great Recession, 300–301, 305
Weidenbaum, Murray, 49n, 64n
Weisman, Jonathan, 172n, 190
Weisman, Steven, 165n
Weissberg, Robert, 347
welfare benefits, 350
welfare recipients, feeling thermometer, 118
Wells Fargo, 33, 302, 303
Why Americans Hate Welfare (Gilens), 358
Wilensky, Harold, 356n
Wilkinson, Richard, 18n
Will, George, 142n
Winfrey, Oprah, 19
Winner-Take-All Politics (Hacker, Pierson), 309
Wlezien, Christopher, 47, 267n, 290
Wolff, Edward, 15n, 301
Wolfinger, Raymond, 257n
working-class people: feeling thermometer, 114–115; political representation, 266, 358

World Bank, 11n
World Top Incomes Database, 1n, 12n, 13n
World War II, 29
Wright, Gerald, 233n, 234

Yakabuski, Konrad, 316n, 328n
Yakovenko, Victor, 23
Yoon, Robert, 140n, 265n
YouGov surveys, 166–169, 237n, 313–315, 317, 319, 335n, 357n

Zaller, John, 76n, 106–107, 127n, 130–131, 149n
Zandi, Mark, 284n, 295–296, 307
Zeleny, Jeff, 270n
Zellner, Arnold, 43n
Zernike, Kate, 282n, 289n
Zhang, Kan, 18n
Zidar, Owen, 64n
Zucman, Gabriel, 2n, 15–16